TRAVEL
LEGEND AND LORE

AN ENCYCLOPEDIA

TRAVEL
LEGEND AND LORE

AN ENCYCLOPEDIA

RONALD H. FRITZE

ABC-CLIO

Santa Barbara, California
Denver, Colorado
Oxford, England

Library of Congress Cataloging-in-Publication Data

Fritze, Ronald H.
    Travel legend and lore : an encyclopedia / Ronald H. Fritze.
        p.   cm.
    Includes bibliographical references and index.
        1. Travel—Encyclopedias.   2. Travel—Folklore—Encyclopedias.
    I. Title
    G151.F75   1998   910.4—dc21   98-45613

ISBN 0-87436-759-X (hc) 1-57607-127-8 (pb)

04 03 02 01 00 99 98   10 9 8 7 6 5 4 3 2 1 (cloth)

ABC-CLIO, Inc.
130 Cremona Drive, P.O. Box 1911
Santa Barbara, California 93116-1911

This book is printed on acid-free paper ∞.
Manufactured in the United States of America

... the distant Ethiopians, the furthest outposts of mankind, half of whom live where the Sun goes down, and half where he rises.
Homer, *The Odyssey*, ch. 1

Out in the dark blue sea there lies a land called Crete, a rich and lovely land, washed by the waves on every side, densely peopled and boasting ninety cities.
Homer, *The Odyssey*, ch. 19

And the Lord said unto Satan, Whence comest thou? Then Satan answered the Lord, and said, From going to and fro in the earth, and from walking up and down in it.
Job 1:7

Travelling is a portion of punishment.
The prophet Muhammad (ca. 570–632)

A scholar's education is greatly improved by traveling in quest of knowledge and meeting the authoritative teachers (of his time).
Ibn Khaldun (1332–1406), the Muqaddimah

A medal of St. Christopher he wore
Of shining silver on his breast, and bore.
Geoffrey Chaucer (ca. 1343–1400), *The Canterbury Tales*,
"The Prologue," describing the Yeoman

And she had thrice been to Jerusalem,
Seen many strange rivers and passed over them;
She'd been to Rome and also to Boulogne,
St. James of Compostella and Cologne,
And she was skilled in wandering by the way.
Geoffrey Chaucer, *The Canterbury Tales*,
"The Prologue," describing the Wife of Bath

Travel, in the younger sort, is a part of education; in the elder, a part of experience. He that travelleth into a country before he hath some entrance into the language, goeth to school, and not to travel.
　　　Sir Francis Bacon (1561–1626), *Essays,* "Of Travel"

It is a strange thing that, in sea voyages, where there is nothing to be seen but sky and sea, men should make diaries; but in land travel, wherein so much is to be observed, for the most part they omit it, as if chance were fitter to be registered than observation.
　　　Sir Francis Bacon, *Essays,* "Of Travel"

As I walked through the wilderness of this world.
　　　John Bunyan (1628–1688), *The Pilgrim's Progress*

All travel has its advantages. If the passenger visits better countries, he may learn to improve his own, and if fortune carries him to worse, he may learn to enjoy it.
　　　Dr. Samuel Johnson (1709–1784)

I will briefly describe the qualifications which I deem most essential to a traveller. He should be endowed with an active, indefatigable vigour of mind and body, which can seize every mode of conveyance, and support, with a careless smile, every hardship of the road, the weather, or the inn. The benefits of foreign travel will correspond with the degrees of these qualifications.
　　　Edward Gibbon (1737–1794)

Queequeg was a native of Kokovoko, an island far away to the West and South. It is not down in any map, true places never are.
　　　Herman Melville (1819–1891), *Moby Dick* (1851)

The gladdest moment in human life is the departure upon a distant journey into unknown lands.
　　　Sir Richard F. Burton (1821–1890)

Many and powerful as were the attractions which drew us toward the settlements, we looked back even at that moment with an eager longing toward the wilderness of prairies and mountains behind us. For myself I had suffered more that summer from illness than ever before in my life, and yet to this hour I cannot recall those savage scenes and savage men without a strong desire again to visit them.
　　　Francis Parkman (1823–1893), *The Oregon Trail*

For My Lovely Wife,
Twylia,

and

My Two Beautiful Young Women in England,
Victoria and Stephanie

CONTENTS

PREFACE

"Travel is a blessing."
"Every journey is a little bit of Hell."

Almost all of us travel at some time in our lives for one reason or another. As the two Arabic proverbs above show, many cultures display contrasting attitudes toward travel. We look forward to or dread the beginning of a journey and are glad or sad to arrive back home. Many religions and individuals view life itself to be a sort of journey: "As I walked through the wilderness of this world," John Bunyan wrote in *The Pilgrim's Progress.*

Travel is not solely a modern phenomenon. Contrary to popular belief, people of the past were not all that sedentary. Research has demonstrated that many people traveled frequently or even moved their entire homes several times in a lifetime. Travel played an important role in ancient mythologies, as witnessed by the tales of Gilgamesh, Odysseus, and Aeneas. The Bible is full of stories that include travel. Cain journeys into exile to the land of Nod because of his murder of Abel. Abraham leaves Ur to take possession of the promised land of Canaan. Joseph and his brothers travel to Egypt, voluntarily or involuntarily. The Children of Israel leave Egypt in order to return to their promised land. Jesus is born while Mary and Joseph are visiting Bethlehem. The Holy Family later flees to Egypt to escape the wrath of King Herod the Great.

Travel continued through the Middle Ages. William of Rubruck, Marco Polo, and Ibn Battuta are among the best-known travelers of the Middle Ages, but untold others trudged the caravan routes along the Silk Road and across the Sahara or sailed the seas of Asia, Africa, and Europe. The age of European discovery during the fifteenth and sixteenth centuries greatly widened the geographical horizons of travel by Westerners. But it took centuries for Western civilization even to approach a comprehension of the new lands and peoples that had been revealed. By 1900, travelers had reached the empty and unknown places on the map. Meanwhile, mass tourism with its industrial organization was largely supplanting traditional travel. The days of travel as an experience of wonder, surprise, and more than a little danger were drawing to a close.

In the realm of travel, myth can be every bit as significant as fact—and sometimes more significant. The fictional Sir John Mandeville's travel book influenced late-medieval European geographical concepts to a far greater degree than the (probably) real-life account of Marco Polo. Columbus was drawn to sail west across the Atlantic to reach Asia by reports of Far Eastern riches, reports that were infused with myth and legend. The pseudoknowledge of the Marvels of the East affected what Europeans expected to find in India and the Far East for centuries.

This book is concerned largely with the expectations of travelers before the twentieth century. What did they expect to encounter regarding roads, sea travel, accommodations, foreigners, and strange lands? The 284 entries in this encyclopedia concern people, places, things, events, and concepts. Some of the entries are about the factual aspects of travel. What were the Inca roads like? What kind of accommodations did a food and lodging stand along the Natchez Trace provide to travelers? Where did Margery Kempe go on her travels and what did she experience? Other entries deal with the mythical and legendary knowledge associated with travel, such as the wanderings of Odysseus, monstrous races at the edges of the earth, and Chinese isles of immortality. Most entries cite works for further reading; some of the shorter entries that do not instead direct the reader to a related larger entry that does include bibliographical references.

The subject of travel over the course of most of human history is both a big subject and an open-ended one. This book could have been much bigger but the practical economics of publishing impose, and rightly so, certain limitations. This book aims to be an introductory reference work about travelers and their expectations. It does not pretend to be exhaustive, but it does attempt to be fairly comprehensive. The materials available for researching the topic of travel tend to make coverage of many topics a bit Eurocentric, but whenever possible Asian, African, Islamic, and pre-Columbian American topics have been included. It is hoped that no really important topic has been excluded or neglected and that readers of this book will always find the first topic that they try to look up either as an entry or in the index. The reality, however, is that that may not always be true. Nevertheless, it is hoped that most readers will find what they are looking for or at least obtain some guidance as to where else they might look.

Omne meum, nihil meum.

ACKNOWLEDGMENTS

Finishing a book is generally a happy occasion. It is the sedentary equivalent of completing a long and arduous journey. When completed, one has a sense of accomplishment and a sense of relief. That is particularly the case with this book. It took longer to write than I originally anticipated. Three years respectively as secretary, vice-president, and president of the faculty senate of Lamar University took much time away from research and writing. Fortunately for me the people at ABC-CLIO were very understanding and accommodating, particularly Heather Cameron, former president of the company. Alicia Merritt, my acquisitions editor has also been a great source of encouragement. In fact, without her gentle prodding, I would almost certainly still be working on the manuscript. Martha Whitt, my production editor, also deserves the highest praise. The staff of ABC-CLIO is a joy to work with and always make a book better.

I would also like to thank Lamar University for its support of my research. Dr. Robert Moulton, vice-president for research, and the Research Enhancement Council awarded me a research enhancement grant, which helped to get me started. Robert Williams and Leslie Lawhon each worked as my research assistant and they have my gratitude. John Storey and my other colleagues of the history department graciously allowed me some release time from teaching to help me complete this book. The staff of the John Grey Library of Lamar University also provided invaluable support. Of course, my good friend Larry Allen of the Economics Department has been a traveling companion on the road of writing for ABC-CLIO. We have explored many a used bookstore together and have solved the problems of the world numerous times in the course of those expeditions.

Concordia University at River Forest, Illinois has employed me to teach a summer school course for them in 1994, 1996, 1997 and 1998. Besides getting to revisit my alma mater, teaching a summer course there allowed me access to the scholarly resources of Chicago, especially those of the great Newberry Library. I would like to thank George Nielson and Kurt Stadtwald for giving me that welcome opportunity.

On the home front, my faithful feline companion Flacius gave his usual blessing to my writing. Unfortunately he died at the tender age of 15 years on 22 December 1997 and so did not live to see this book completed. He will be missed. Meanwhile my 18-month-old grandson, Mark, has had to live with this book his entire life. Lately when he visits on the weekends, he likes to make his way to grandpa's study and see what I am doing. He actually seems interested but it may be that he is just being simply kind and polite. Either way, Mark I am so glad you are with us. My wife Twylia has had to live with this book for too long. She has consistently been very patient and supportive. Her love, friendship, and company make each day better. Dearest, I love you more than words can say.

A

ABYSSINIA
See Ethiopia.

AENEAS, WANDERINGS OF

According to mythological accounts, the Trojan Aeneas, son of the mortal Anchises and the goddess Aphrodite (Venus), escaped the sack of Troy by the Greeks. He and his fellow refugees wandered for many years, ending up in Italy, where they founded Rome, or at least Lavinium. Aeneas's story is most commonly known through Vergil's (70–19 B.C.) famous poem *The Aeneid,* which became the national epic of the Roman Republic and Empire. However, Vergil did not invent the story of Aeneas; the great Roman historian Livy (59 B.C.–A.D. 17) refers to Aeneas and his wanderings in Book One of his monumental *History of Rome,* and archaeological and literary evidence indicates that versions of the myth predated Vergil and Livy by over four centuries. Thanks to Vergil, the story of Aeneas is a classic of world literature and the archetype of the homeless refugee who manages not simply to survive, but to triumph.

The wanderings of Aeneas and his companions begin on the night that Troy fell. Aeneas manages to escape, along with his aged father, Anchises, his son, Ascanius, and a group of other Trojans. Proceeding to the foot of Mount Ida (about 25 miles southwest of Troy), the group settles in for the winter. The following summer they travel to Thrace and found a town, but fear of continued Greek attacks cause them to move again. The group stops at the island of Delos to consult the oracle of Apollo, who tells them to return to the lands of their ancestors, where they will found a powerful empire. Some of the Trojans originally came from Crete, so they sail to that island to found their new settlement. But ill fortune strikes, and a series of plagues blight humans, crops, and farm animals. In the midst of their suffering, Aeneas receives a vision from the gods informing him that Hesperia (Italy), not Crete, is the Trojan promised land. Troy's founder, Dardanus, came from Italy, so the Trojans once more take to their ships.

Sailing up the western coast of Greece, Aeneas stops his fleet at Strophades, where the Trojans encounter the horrible Harpies, who made the island their home after Jason and the Argonauts defeated them in Asia Minor. Grotesque creatures with the body of a bird and the head of an emaciated woman, the Harpies steal and befoul the refugees' food. The Trojans' efforts to combat them is fruitless; instead, Aeneas garners a curse from Celaeno, the Harpy leader.

The Trojans stop at Actium, where they are surprised to find other Trojan refugees: Andromache and Helenus. The couple warn Aeneas and his party of dangers ahead; many Greeks had colonized southern Italy and posed a potential threat to the refugees. Farther on, they will come to the strait of Messina (between Italy and Sicily), home of the monsters Scylla and Charybdis. Andromache and Helenus advise Aeneas to consult with the Sybil of Cumae, a great prophetess. After departing from Actium, the Trojan fleet sails safely past the Greek outposts and avoids passing between Scylla and Charybdis. They land on the southern coast of Sicily near Mount Etna, a dangerous decision because this is the land of the Cyclopes. Fortunately, they first encounter one of Odysseus's sailors, Achaemenides, who was left behind accidentally during their escape from the cyclops Polyphemus. The terror-stricken Achaemenides warns them of the danger, and the Trojans flee to their ships—not a moment too soon, because the blinded Polyphemus appears. Hearing them escape, he wades into the sea after them and gropes for their ships, but they row beyond his grasp and reach deep waters before other Cyclopes can arrive. Sailing westward along the south coast of Sicily, the Trojans reach Drepanum, where Anchises dies. They try to round the western end of Sicily, but the goddess Hera, a great enemy of the Trojans, sends a great storm to destroy them. They survive the tempest but are blown westward to Carthage, on the coast of North Africa.

Carthage later became Republican Rome's deadliest enemy, and Aeneas's actions help to explain that animosity. When the Trojans arrive, Queen Dido, a beautiful widow, rules Carthage. Dido and Aeneas fall in love, a course of events assisted by Aeneas's mother, Aphrodite, who commands Eros (Cupid) to make Dido fall in love with Aeneas. The Trojans are shown hospitality by the Carthaginians, who hope they will settle. However, Zeus, the king of the gods, sends his messenger Hermes to order the Trojans to continue on to Italy. An obedient Aeneas makes preparations to depart. Because of tears and recriminations from the distraught Dido, Aeneas ultimately sneaks off during the night. The spurned Dido commits suicide, thus leading to the future animosity between Rome and Carthage—or so myth would have it.

Aeneas and his fleet return to Sicily, and after holding funeral games for Anchises, continue on to Cumae in Italy. As instructed by Helenus, Aeneas seeks out the Sybil, who describes the many struggles he must undergo before achieving victory in his new homeland. Aeneas asks the Sybil to take him to Hades, the realm of the dead, so that he can speak with his father. A gate to Hades opens in the earth, and the Sybil and Aeneas venture down to the River Acheron, where the ferryman Charon carries them to the other side. They pass through various parts of the underworld including the sections for dead infants, suicides (where an uncomfortable encounter with Dido takes place), and fallen warriors, as well as Tartarus, the place of punishment for grievous sinners. They reach the Elysian Fields, a blissful land where the pure and holy dead live, and locate Anchises, who gives Aeneas more details of Rome's majestic future. Heartened by this information, Aeneas returns to the land of the living. The Trojans board their ships and continue north. Passing the island of the sorceress Circe, they reach Latium at long last. Years of struggle with hostile natives awaits the Trojans, but Aeneas's wanderings are over.

Unlike the voyages of Odysseus and Jason, Aeneas's was firmly rooted in the known geography of the Mediterranean world. Nevertheless, the legends of Aeneas, particularly Vergil's, contain significant borrowings of mythical monsters and places from the tales of Odysseus and Jason. Vergil made his epic realistic by careful use of geography and, at the same time, emphasized the close relationship between Greek and Roman culture by demonstrating the interconnections between his *Aeneid* and the epics of Jason and Odysseus. The geography described in *The Aeneid* also illustrates the vast increase in geographical knowledge that occurred between the ages of Homer and Vergil.

See also

Carthage; Cyclopes; Elysian Fields; Jason and the Argonauts, Voyage of; Odysseus, Wanderings of; Scylla and Charybdis.

For further reading

G. K. Galinsky, *Aeneas, Sicily, and Rome,* 1969.

AFRICA   Since late antiquity, the word *Africa* has been used to refer to the continent, one of three constituting the known world of Europe and Islam before 1492 (the others are Europe and Asia).

The ancient Greeks called this continent "Libya." They considered it a largely hot, sandy wasteland, which in the south merged into the uninhabitable Torrid Zone, and had little awareness and less knowledge of sub-Saharan Africa. In 146 B.C., the Romans created the province of Africa from the core of the empire of the defeated city-state Carthage in what is now Tunisia. The province expanded to include Cyrenaica and Mauretania, bounding the region now known as North Africa. Under the emperor Diocletian (d. A.D. 313), lands along the southern coast of the Mediterranean Sea were organized into the diocese of Africa, which now corresponded to the ancient Greeks' Libya. As a result, "Africa" superseded "Libya" as the name for the entire continent. Awareness of the sub-Saharan regions increased slowly; by the late nineteenth and early twentieth centuries, a complete geographical outline emerged, although badly marred by racist stereotyping and prejudices. Africa had become the Dark Continent of Western civilization's imperial imagination.

See also

Carthage; Dark Continent; Libya; Mediterranean Sea.

ALAMUT   Headquarters and chief castle of the religious sect of the Assassins, Alamut was located in the Daylam region of Persia (present-day Iran), near the southern end of the Caspian Sea. Marco Polo made the place famous in the West when he described it in his *Travels*, along with the activities of its fearsome ruler, the Old Man of the Mountain.

Alamut, meaning "the eagle's teaching" in the language of the Daylami, was an inaccessible castle erected in the mountains of Daylam in 1090. Hasan-i-Sabbah, leader of the revolutionary branch of the Ismaili sect of Islam, seized the stronghold of Alamut from a vassal of the sultan of the Seljuk Turks. From this secure base, Hasan and succeeding Ismaili leaders—all known by the title "Old Man of the Mountain"—sent out both missionaries and the notorious Assassins.

Hasan and his followers irrigated the arid valley that lay below the castle, transforming it into fertile farmland capable of feeding their community. This irrigation project probably gave rise to the story, which Marco Polo repeated, about how the Old Man of the Mountain had created a lush pleasure garden to imitate the Islamic concept of Paradise in order to dupe his followers into believing that he controlled their entry into heaven. Crusader historians who wrote about the Assassins generally had contact with only the Syrian branch of the sect, and therefore knew little or nothing about the main body of the sect in Persia. In 1256 the Assassins surrendered Alamut to the Mongol general Hülegü, who razed it.

See also

Assassins; Old Man of the Mountain; Polo, Marco.

ALEXANDER THE GREAT, ROMANCES OF   A complex of narrative works about Alexander the Great in the form of prose or poetry that flourished in various languages of Europe and the Middle East for almost 2,000 years from the Hellenistic era through the Middle Ages. These romances related both the historical and fictional exploits of Alexander the Great and included considerable fantastic, geographical lore.

The Macedonian conqueror Alexander the Great (356–323 B.C.) spread Greek culture throughout the Middle East. His accomplishments transformed him into a towering figure in the minds of people living in the Mediterranean basin and central Asia for centuries after his death. It is not surprising that Alexander became a popular subject among writers of histories and epic poetry soon after his death. Some writers took a sober, factual approach and produced accurate histories of his career. Others romanticized and exaggerated Alexander's achievements and mingled fiction with fact. From these fantastic adventure narratives and hero-tales, the romances of Alexander evolved. None of the earliest romances survive, but modern scholars believe they contained a minimal amount of fantastic material. The original authors are unknown, although Alexander's companion and chronicler Callisthenes is credited by some.

However, the romances describe events in Alexander's life that took place after Callisthenes's death; hence, the unknown author of the early Romances is referred to as Pseudo-Callisthenes.

Alexander the Great's military conquests meant that he and his soldiers were among the most widely traveled people of their day. Their journeys took them from one end of the Persian Empire to the other and into northern India. Stops along the way included the sacred Oasis of Ammon in the western Egyptian desert, the wilds of central Asia, and the great city of Babylon. The authors

Coin with a bust of Alexander the Great imprinted on it.

of the romances and their subsequent redactors spiced up the narrative by bringing Alexander into contact with myths and legends of travel and geography that were widely believed in antiquity and the Middle Ages. The Romances of Alexander became a catalog of the wonders and marvels that people expected to encounter in Asia and along the edges of the earth.

Many manuscripts survive, in many different languages: Syriac, Arabic, Ethiopic, Armenian, Greek, Latin, and various western European languages. Three basic traditions, or recensions, of the text differ significantly in their contents, but the basic story is as follows. Alexander is portrayed as the son of Nectanebo, the refugee pharaoh-wizard of Egypt, rather than the son of Philip of Macedon. Alexander shows himself to be an extraordinary person, as when he tames the fierce horse Bucephalus. At the death of Philip, Alexander leads the Macedonians against Greece and Persia. The sequence of events is badly garbled in the Romances. Alexander is credited with the conquests of Rome and Carthage, which never took place. Numerous other inaccuracies appear in the text, such as the statement that Alexander's wife, Roxane, was the daughter of the Persian king Darius.

Mingled with the basic factual narrative of Alexander's conquests are various fantastic adventures. At one point, he travels with some of his soldiers to the edge of the world. Along the way, he encounters strange plants and animals, including sirens, centaurs, Cynocephali (dog-headed men), Pygmies, and other monstrous races. When he and his companions attempt to reach the Land of the Blessed, they instead become lost in the fearsome Land of Darkness. Coming across the Water of Life (Fountain of Youth), Alexander fails to drink, and so loses his chance to become immortal. He also attempts a descent into the sea using a glass diving bell and an ascent into heaven using a basket carried by eagles. Both endeavors fail. Later, Alexander encounters the Bragmanni, or Brahmans, and the Amazons. He also defeats the unclean nations of Gog and Magog, allies of King Porus. He encloses them behind an iron gate in a narrow, steep mountain pass to keep them separate from the civilized peoples of the earth. At the end of the romances, Alexander the Great dies young at the height of his success.

The Romances of Alexander the Great incorporated much of the lore of travel associated with the Marvels of the East and the monstrous races. Because these romances were so popular during the medieval eras of both Christendom and Islam, much erroneous geographic and ethnographic information was perpetuated. The later legends about Prester John include considerable material from the Romances of Alexander the Great. Expectations and perceptions of medieval travelers were profoundly influenced by these romances for centuries.

See also

Amazons; Bragmanni; Cynocephali; Fountain of Youth; Gog and Magog; Marvels of the East; Monstrous Races; Oasis; Prester John and His Kingdom.

For further reading

George David Cary, *The Medieval Alexander,* 1956; D. J. A. Ross, *Alexander Historiatus,* 1963; Richard Stoneman, ed. and trans., *The Greek Alexander Romance,* 1991.

ALEXANDRIA   One of the greatest cities of the ancient and medieval Mediterranean world. Alexander the Great founded Alexandria in 331 B.C. Ptolemy I Soter (d. 283/282 B.C.), the first Greek king of Egypt, made it his capital, and it became the premier cultural center of the Hellenistic world. Alexandria, located in the Nile delta, was home to the great lighthouse known as the Pharos, one of the Seven Wonders of the Ancient World, and to the legendary Library of Alexandria, the greatest collection of books in the ancient world. Alexandria also served as an important port of trade, particularly for supplying wheat to hungry Rome. Roman rule began in 30 B.C., but by the end of the fifth century A.D., control shifted to the Byzantine Greeks. Alexandria was not only an important Christian center, but a patriarchal city (that is, home to one of the five patriarchs of the early Church), along with Jerusalem, Antioch, Constantinople, and Rome.

Arab armies conquered the city in 642 and permanently established their rule in 646. Under Arab rule, Alexandria ceased to be the capital of Egypt but continued to enjoy special privileges. During the Middle Ages, Alexandria assumed an important position in the network of trade routes that carried Asian luxury goods to western Europe. Venetian merchants began trading in Alexandria in 828, and European merchants from Genoa, Pisa, and other commercial ports soon joined them. Unlike the situation at Cairo, Christians were allowed to trade in Alexandria and lived in their own *funduqs,* or trading posts. During the Crusades, Alexandria suffered attacks in 1167 and 1365. The latter raid left the city badly damaged.

Ancient Alexandria was a true metropolis. Estimates of its population at the time of the Arab conquest of 642 are between 200,000 and 600,000 inhabitants. By the thirteenth century, the city's population declined to the 60,000s. Domenico Trevisan, the Venetian ambassador to the Mamluk sultan of Egypt, reported in 1512 that 90 percent of Alexandria was in a state of ruins. The Portuguese diversion of the spice trade to the new all-sea route around Africa undercut the city's role as a port of trade. Still, Alexandria survived, and today is one of Egypt's great cities, serving as a spice market.

See also

Alexandrian Library and Museum; Constantinople; Jerusalem; Pharos (or Lighthouse) of Alexandria; Rome; Seven Wonders of the Ancient World.

For further reading

Alfred J. Butler, *The Arab Conquest of Egypt*, 1978; Peter Marshall Fraser, *Ptolemaic Alexandria*, 1972.

ALEXANDRIAN LIBRARY AND MUSEUM
This library, located in Alexandria, Egypt, was the greatest repository of books in the ancient world. Although it was not included among the Seven Wonders of the Ancient World, its reputation has passed from history into legend.

Popular history merges the separate but related institutions of the Alexandrian Library and Museum into one entity. In fact, the older of the two was the Museum (*Mouseion*), which is the Greek word for a temple dedicated to the Muses, the nine goddesses of the musical and literary arts. Ptolemy I Soter (d. 283/282 B.C.), on the advice of Demetrius of Phaleron (fl. late fourth and early third century B.C.), founded and handsomely endowed the Museum.

Most Greek museums, particularly the Alexandrian, possessed far wider scholarly interests than merely the subjects patronized by the Muses. Scientific investigations figured prominently in the work of scholars of the Alexandrian Museum, which was more a Hellenistic-style research institute or think tank than a temple. During the third century B.C., the Museum was the center of the flowering of Hellenistic science and attracted visiting scholars from all over the Greek world. Although the Museum declined in the second century B.C., it remained a significant institution of learning well into the era of imperial Rome.

The Library of Alexandria was a sister institution to the Museum. King Ptolemy II Philadelphus of Egypt (r. 283–246 B.C.) generally receives credit for its foundation, but it seems likely that his father, Ptolemy I Soter, and his adviser Demetrius may have begun the work that the son finished. Legend has it that Ptolemy II founded the library to serve as a repository for a copy of every book in Greek literature and for Greek translations of books in other languages. The Ptolemies maintained a strong interest in collecting foreign writings. Again, the sources give conflicting details, but either Ptolemy I Soter or Ptolemy II Philadelphus sponsored the translation of the Hebrew sacred scriptures into Greek, known as the Septuagint. Such collecting, translating, classifying, and editing projects were consistent with the philosophy of the Aristotelian or Peripatetic school of learning, which emphasized an encyclopedic approach.

It is not clear that the early Ptolemies literally intended to create a universal library, but they certainly wanted it to be the biggest and the best. They were also not too particular about how they achieved that goal. Ptolemy III Euergetes (r. 246–222/1 B.C.) ordered that all ships entering the port of Alexandria with books in their cargo were to turn them over for copying by the staff of the Alexandrian Library. On another occasion, the same king borrowed the official Athenian copy of the works of the three great tragedians, Aeschylus, Euripides, and Sophocles. After copying them, the king returned the new copy and kept the original for his own library. The Ptolemies jealously resented any competition to their great library. When King Eumenes II of Pergamum (r. 197–159 B.C.) began a collection of books that rivaled the Alexandrian Library, Ptolemy V Epiphanes (r. 204–180 B.C.) forbade the export of Egyptian papyrus, which was used instead of paper by the ancient peoples of the Mediterranean world. Such competition drove up the demand for books and quickly resulted in the appearance of many forgeries and pseudoepigraphic works (that is, works falsely attributed to famous authors).

The Library, located within the precincts of the royal palace, remained one of Alexandria's important tourist attractions for centuries. Its scholars studied and ate their meals there, but whether it also contained their living quarters is unclear. Little is known about the physical aspects of the Alexandrian Library, but most sources agree that from early on there were two libraries—one in the palace and a smaller one outside the palace. The best modern scholarship places the palace library inside the Museum, although many argue for a separate building that was destroyed by Julius Caesar during the Alexandrine War of 48 B.C. According to the twelfth-century Byzantine scholar John Tzetzes, as early as the time of Callimachus (fl. 270 B.C.) it contained 400,000 *symmigeis* scrolls (a scroll that is part of a multiscroll work) and 90,000 *amigeis* scrolls (a scroll that contains one entire work). The other library was located in the Serapeum, or temple of Serapis (the Greek name for Osiris, the Egyptian god of resurrection). Ptolemy III Euergetes built that temple, and its library contained some 40,000 scrolls. In addition, the Alexandrian Library apparently maintained a warehouse for collecting, copying, and cataloging new acquisitions in the city's harbor district.

Throughout their existence, the Library and Museum of Alexandria attracted visitors from all over the Hellenistic and later the Roman world. That international flavor was reflected in the origins of the first six librarians: Zenodotus of Epheseus, Apollonius of Rhodes (who was born in Alexandria), Erastophenes of Cyrene, Aristophanes of Byzantium, Apollonius the Eidograph (also probably from Alexandria), and Aristarchus of Samothrace. Several of these scholars—Zenodotus, Apollonius of Rhodes, and Aristarchus—also served as tutors to the royal children.

The fate of the Alexandrian Library is one of the great mysteries of antiquity, at least according to popular history. Three different persons and occasions receive the blame for its destruction. Julius Caesar supposedly burned the library inadvertently during the Alexandrine War of 48 B.C. In fact, if he burned anything it was the library's warehouse in the harbor district. Next, a bigoted Christian mob led by Theophilus, the corrupt patriarch of Alexandria (385–412), supposedly destroyed the library in 391. Actually, the mob stopped pagan worship at the Serapeum and converted it into a church, leaving the library unscathed. In 646, the Muslim conquerors of Alexandria allegedly burned the books of the Alexandrian Library to heat the water of the city's bathhouses. According to a romantic tradition, the scholar John Philobonus pleaded for the survival of the library with the sympathetic Arab commander Amrou Ibn el-Ass. Unfortunately, Amrou wrote to the caliph Omar for instructions. Because that narrow-minded fanatic considered the Koran to be the only book worth preserving, he ordered the destruction of the library. Many scholars from Edward Gibbon on dispute whether this Arab burning of the Alexandrian Library actually occurred. Other scholars argue that at least some destruction took place. This episode is certainly the best documented of the three, and that documentation includes several Islamic historians, including Ibn al-Kifti.

By the time of the Arab conquest, the Alexandrian Library was probably a shadow of its former self. The venerable institution had existed for almost a thousand years with ever-diminishing resources to maintain the deteriorating collection. It is most likely that no dramatic conflagration extinguished this beacon of ancient learning. Rather, the bulk of the Alexandrian Library's collection died the slow death of most books—they simply wore out. Furthermore, most classical bibliographers believe that the foremost works of Greek and Roman literature survive, and that no great trove of profound philosophy, literary masterpieces, or ancient superscience was lost with the Alexandrian Library. What Alexandria did lose was a library that provided a great magnet for traveling scholars.

See also
 Alexandria; Seven Wonders of the Ancient World.
For further reading
 Luciano Canfora, *The Vanished Library*, 1990; Peter Marshall Fraser, *Ptolemaic Alexandria*, 1972; Edward Alexander Parsons, *The Alexandrian Library*, 1952.

AMAZON RIVER   This great river of South America is named after the women warriors of classical mythology. The Amazon River and its vast surrounding rain forest are the home of mysterious peoples, animals, and plants. Its wonders, both real and mythic, have attracted explorers and travelers for centuries.

In terms of volume of water, the Amazon River and its tributaries form the largest river in the world. At its mouth, it is 100 miles wide, including the intervening islands. The Amazon discharges so much fresh water into the Atlantic Ocean that the waters remain fresh up to 100 miles out to sea, and it can be detected up to 200 miles out. The Amazon is 4,000 miles long if the Marañón River is included, making it the world's second longest river after the Nile.

Native Americans lived along the Amazon during pre-Columbian times. Spanish explorers reported the riverbanks to be thick with native settlements, many of considerable size. Only the coming of European settlements caused the Native Americans to withdraw deep into the rain forest.

The first European to see the Amazon River was the Spaniard Vicente Yáñez Pínzón in 1500. Four decades later, Francisco de Orellana (1511–1546) led two brigantines of conquistadors down the Amazon after he became separated on 26 December 1541 from the ill-fated Spanish expedition of Gonzalo Pizarro. Cruising down the Napo River, Orellana and his men entered the Amazon River on 11 February 1542. Hostile natives frequently attacked the Spanish, but without much effect. Near the Rio Negro, the Spanish entered the territories of the powerful Omaguas, which Orellana believed was the land of the Amazons. On 24 June, while fighting Omaguas, the Spanish encountered fierce Amazons leading the Omagua males into battle. This incident gave birth to the great river's eventual name and also the belief that persisted for over 200 years that the Amazons of classical mythology lived along the Amazon River. On 26 August 1542, Orellana and his men reached the sea.

The mouth of the Amazon River and its lower reaches lay in the Portuguese territory of Brazil. Both Spain and Portugal's efforts to secure their far-flung colonial empires were so thinly spread, the inhospitable rain forest and grasslands of the Amazon basin were ignored, except by a few deluded conquistadors seeking the nonexistent land of El Dorado and by the Portuguese establishing a fort at Belém at the mouth of the Amazon in 1616. In 1637–1639, a Portuguese soldier traveled up the Amazon to Quito in Spanish territory and back. Thirty years later, in 1669, the Portuguese established the outpost of Barra far up the Amazon. Barra was renamed Manaus in 1850 during the early stages of the Brazilian rubber boom.

The first scientific account of the Amazon appeared in 1745, the work of the Frenchman Charles Marie de La Condamine. After making some measurements of the earth's size at the equator, La Condamine traveled down the Amazon in 1743. Along the way, he gathered folklore about the Amazons and did not reject the possibility of their literal existence. Other scientific travelers followed. The lands around the Amazon were a treasure trove of unknown flora and fauna. From 1799 to 1800, the great Alexander von Humboldt (1769–1859) and Aimé Bonpland traveled the Orinoco and Amazon Rivers, proving that they were connected by a tributary, the Casiquiarre River. The bloodthirsty conquistador Lope de Aguirre stumbled across the connection in 1560, but it remained uncharted for almost 250 years. Humboldt also cast serious doubt on the existence of Amazons. Other scientific Amazon travelers included the evolutionary theorist Alfred Russel Wallace (1823–1913) and his coworker Henry Walter Bates in 1848. Even former U.S. president Theodore Roosevelt (1858–1919) traveled the Amazon for scientific purposes in 1913–1914. Thanks to these travelers, Amazonia and its wonders were at last known objectively.

The Amazon rubber boom accelerated after 1850. Steamboats first appeared on the Amazon in 1853. Wealth from rubber caused Manaus to grow quickly into one of the richest and most sophisticated cities in the Western Hemisphere.

The rubber boom reached its height in 1910, and by 1915 collapsed because of competition from the East Indies. Today, the Amazon lands are threatened by a gold rush in the Guiana Highlands and slash-and-burn agriculture, which gravely depletes the rain forest. Nevertheless, for travelers and tourists, the Amazon basin continues to be a land of mystery and adventure.

See also
    Amazons; El Dorado.
For further reading
    Alain Gheerbrant, *The Amazon*, 1992; Anthony Smith, *Explorers of the Amazon*, 1990.

AMAZONS   This ancient travelers' legend refers to any society in which women lived and fought as warriors without the presence of men or, more rarely, were warriors and rulers over their men. Legends about Amazons serve as speculations about the possibility of the reversal of traditional male dominance or as warnings against the dire effects of female rule. Ancient and medieval writers classified Amazons as one of the monstrous races.

Amazon stories are common throughout the cultures of the world, indicating that the very concept of women dominating men possesses a strong fascination. No true Amazon society has ever been discovered by historical, archaeological, or anthropological research. Various scholars speculate about the historical background and origin of these myths. One theory suggests that, on initial contact with a bow-wielding tribe of short, beardless Asiatic nomads, the inhabitants of the eastern Mediterranean region mistook them for women. Other theories identify the Amazons with the ancient Hittites of Asia Minor or as fighting priestesses of the great mother goddess or the moon goddess. One plausible explanation is that tales of Amazons arose from encounters by patriarchal cultures with societies practicing matriarchal customs. Recent archaeological discoveries in the steppes of Russia supply evidence that women warriors may have existed among the horse-riding tribes of ancient Scythia.

The oldest, most elaborate, and most persistent of the Amazon myths derives from the ancient Greeks. Some authorities claim that the name *Amazon* derives from the Greek *a mazos*, meaning "no breast." Others assert that its origin is an Armenian word meaning "moon-women." Amazons supposedly cauterized or cut off their right breast so that it would not impede their javelin throwing or bow firing. Another story states that Amazons simply did not breast-feed. Greek legends and art describe the Amazons as fierce mounted warriors armed with bows and arrows. Some even credit the Amazons with being the first to use cavalry.

When the Amazons were not fighting, they were hunting. They lived without men, although at certain times they would get together with neighboring males for procreation. From the babies born of these liaisons, the Amazons would raise the females to be warriors, while the males were given away, killed, or disabled. By the Middle Ages, scholars of the monstrous races evolved the

11

story that Amazons periodically mated with the Cynocephali, or dog-headed men. The females born of such unions were normal females who were raised as Amazons. The male children, however, were dog-headed and grew up among their Cynocephalic fathers.

Ares, the god of war, and Artemis, the goddess of the hunt, were the chief deities of the Amazons. Greek myth identifies the original Amazons as the children of Ares and the naiad Harmonia. At first, they settled on the Tanais (Don) River but moved south to the Thermodon River on the northeast coast of Asia Minor, where they built three cities, including Themiscyra. Their warlike nature caused them to build a great empire encompassing most of Asia Minor and part of Syria. Eventually, it fell, and they returned to their lands on the Thermodon. Another group lived in western Libya and assisted the god Dionysus in his war with the Titans in Egypt. After Dionysus's adventures in India, these same Amazons opposed him, so he killed many and scattered the survivors. Some stories claim that the temple of Artemis at Ephesus was founded by refugee Amazons. In the course of performing his tenth labor, acquiring the cattle of Geryon, Hercules passed through Libya. Already a prodigious chastiser of Amazons, he obliterated the last Amazons remaining there.

The Amazons of Asia Minor had a more extensive history. Hercules's ninth labor involved an expedition to obtain the girdle of Queen Hippolyta of Themiscyra. The fierce Hippolyta found the muscular Hercules attractive and planned to give him her girdle after an appropriate amount of passion. Hercules's enemy, the goddess Hera, ruined the couple's amorous accord by spreading a rumor throughout Themiscyra that Hercules planned to abduct Hippolyta. The enraged women warriors attacked Hercules and his companions, but to no avail. Hercules killed Hippolyta, took her girdle, and slaughtered large numbers of

Amazons after a hunt. Lithograph; nineteenth-century tobacco label.

Amazons. He took others captive, but these women managed to kill their guards and flee across the Black Sea to Scythia. At first, they fought with the local tribesmen, but later the refugees mated with them. The result of these unions, according to the historian Herodotus, was the Sauromatian people living on the Tanais River, the original Amazon homeland.

Jason and the Argonauts passed by the Amazons of the Thermodon River without incident on their way to Colchis. Theseus, the Athenian hero, sailed specifically to Amazonia, where he met the Amazon queen Antiope. According to some versions of the legend, he abducted her, but in others the couple fell in love and she voluntarily returned to Athens with him. Either way, the loss of Antiope prompted an Amazon invasion of Athens led by Oreithyia, Antiope's outraged sister. Led by Theseus, the Athenians defeated the fearsome invaders. The Greater Eleusinian Mysteries supposedly commemorate this defeat of the Amazons. Amazons also fought on the side of the Trojans, and the great Achilles killed their formidable queen Penthesileia in battle.

Amazon stories do not simply feature figures from mythology. Several ancient writers, including Plutarch, tell the story of Alexander the Great's encounter with the Amazon queen Thalestris. Hearing of his glorious accomplishments, the Amazon queen approaches Alexander's conquering army while it is in Bactria. She states that she desires to bear a child by Alexander. The accommodating Macedonian king agrees to her request, and the couple spend a lusty 13 days together.

From the Greeks, the Amazon legend was passed on to medieval Christian scholars, who made them part of the pantheon of monstrous races encountered at the edges of the known world. Arab geographers of the tenth century continued to locate the Amazons in Scythia. The historian/geographer Adam of Bremen (ca. 1040–1081) placed the Amazons in the Rhipaean Mountains, which lay north of Scandinavia and were home to many of the monstrous races.

The Amazons were not physically monstrous. They were strange because they stood traditional patriarchy on its head with their military matriarchy. They fought as warriors, which women were not supposed to do, and they refused to marry, which was the prime duty of women. However, most ancient and medieval writers treated the Amazons with the respect due brave warriors. The Amazons normally appeared in myths as chaste and abstemious; Thalestris's encounter with Alexander the Great was a rare account of an Amazon exhibiting lust. On those occasions when Amazons, such as Hippolyta and Antiope, were not chaste, they ultimately suffered death.

Medieval writers and illustrators portrayed most monstrous races as club-wielding, naked primitives, but not the Amazons. Amazons carried the same weapons as civilized peoples; hence, medieval illustrators depicted them as armed like medieval knights and men-at-arms. Amazons also appeared fully and richly clothed rather than naked, as was typical for most monstrous races. Low-budget film depictions of lusty and bikini-clad Amazons are a twentieth-century affectation. Like the Gymnosophists and Bragmanni, Amazons were treated sympathetically and viewed as wise by medieval writers. One Talmudic tradition described how Alexander the Great encountered some Amazons in

Libya and asked them for bread. When they gave him a loaf of gold, the great conqueror saw in their gesture an implicit commentary on the vanity of wealth. As he left the land of the Amazons, he commented that he had been a fool until instructed by women.

All these myths and tales led ancient and medieval travelers to expect to meet Amazons in the course of their travels. Christopher Columbus thought that Amazons lived close to the islands he claimed for Spain. The Spanish conquistador Francisco de Orellana (1511–1546) claimed to have fought with the Amazons in the course of his journey down the Amazon River. He even named that great river after the fierce women warriors he encountered. It appears that those Amazons were simply the women of a jungle tribe who fought bravely alongside their men. Nineteenth-century travelers observed that the kings of Dahomey in West Africa employed a regiment of Amazon warriors in their army. Women warriors existed at various times and places, but not a true Amazon society. Still, travelers looked for the Amazons until the last unknown sections of the earth were explored. Nowadays, science-fiction literature and film program people to expect Amazons somewhere out in space.

See also

Alexander the Great, Romances of; Bragmanni; Cynocephali; Gymnosophists; Herodotus; India; Jason and the Argonauts, Voyage of; Libya; Scythia.

For further reading

Josine H. Blok, *The Early Amazons*, 1995; Jeannine Davis-Kimball, "Warrior Women of the Eurasian Steppes," *Archaeology* 50 (Jan./Feb. 1997): 44–48; John Block Friedman, *The Monstrous Races in Medieval Art and Thought*, 1981; Robert Graves, *The Greek Myths*, 1955; Abby Wettan Kleinbaum, *The War against the Amazons*, 1983; Guy Cadogan Rothery, *The Amazons*, 1910; William Blake Tyrell, *Amazons*, 1984.

ANIAN, STRAIT OF   Name for the hypothetical strait that divided the unexplored northwest part of North America from Asia. Early-modern European cartographers used the name "Anian" on their maps from the sixteenth century until 1728, when Vitus Bering proved the strait existed; it was subsequently named in his honor.

The name Anian derived from a land of Ania, mentioned by Marco Polo as located in the extreme northeastern part of Asia. Jacopo Gastaldi published a pamphlet in 1562 containing the first mention of the Strait of Anian. He cited a lost map of the contemporary Venetian geographer Mateo Pagano as his source. A few years later, Bolognino Zaltieri drew the earliest surviving map to show the Strait of Anian, which remained a common feature on maps of the world until Vitus Bering's explorations in 1728.

The geographical concept of a Strait of Anian was significant to sixteenth- and seventeenth-century Europeans. Unless such a strait existed and divided Asia from North America, neither a northwest nor a northeast passage could exist to provide a much-desired sea route from Europe to China or Japan.

See also
   Northeast Passage; Northwest Passage; Polo, Marco.
For further reading
   Raymond H. Ramsay, *No Longer on the Map*, 1972.

ANTHROPHAGI
See Cannibals.

ANTICHTHONES   Meaning "opposite world" or "antiearth," it first referred to a concept of the Pythagorean philosophers who postulated that an unknown planet orbited the sun in opposition to the earth, and so was hidden from humans. Later writers adopted the term "antichthones" to refer to the landmass located in the southern half of the earth's sphere. Used in this sense, it was interchangeable with the word "antipodes."

There is some confusion about the usage of "antichthones" in the terminology of the Cratesian theory of the four quarters of the earth. Crates (fl. 150 B.C.) and his commentators Cicero (106–43 B.C.) and Macrobius (fl. fourth and early fifth century A.D.) did not use the word, but Martianus Capella (fl. late fifth century A.D.) called the quarter of the earth corresponding to what is now North America by the name "antichthones." An earlier Cratesian scholar, Cleomedes (fl. second century A.D.), gave the same quarter the name "periocci." Some twentieth-century writers mistakenly applied "antichthones" to the quarter of the earth now containing South America and in turn applied "antipodes" to the quarter containing North America. This confusion is partially attributable to the Pythagorean-derived usage of "antichthones" to refer to the entire southern half of the globe.

See also
   Antipodes; Crates of Mallos.
For further reading
   Lloyd B. Brown, *The Story of Maps*, 1949; Gabriella Moretti, "The Other World and the 'Antipodes'," in *The Classical Tradition and the Americas*, vol. 1, 1994; James S. Romm, *The Edges of the Earth in Ancient Thought*, 1992.

ANTILLIA   Legendary island of the western Atlantic widely believed by fifteenth-century Europeans to be a real place. It was sometimes thought to be the island of the legendary Seven Cities.

The name *Antillia* probably derives from a combination of the Latin words meaning "opposite island." Martin Behaim's globe of 1492 contained an annotation next to Antillia stating that a Spanish ship had sighted it in 1414. Antillia's earliest datable appearance on a map occurs in the nautical chart of Zuane Pizzigano of Venice from 1424. It is shown as a rectangular island with a north-south orientation, located directly west of Portugal and of approximately the same size. Zuane Pizzigano's map also located the legendary Seven Cities on Antillia, a detail often omitted in later maps.

Antillia appeared frequently on maps during the rest of the fifteenth century, often as the largest of a group of islands, but other important mapmakers, such as Fra Mauro, ignored its existence. Nevertheless, it was widely assumed that Antillia existed and that the Portuguese had visited it. Around 1481, Paolo del Pozzo Toscanelli recommended it to Columbus as a potential stopover during transatlantic voyages to Asia. Columbus took that advice and included it in his itinerary. After the European discovery of the New World, the West Indies were assumed to be related to Antillia, and therefore were called the Antilles by the Dutch and French. Meanwhile, the failure to find the Seven Cities caused some people to shift Antillia's location to the mainland of South America.

Today, scholars speculate that the appearance of the legendary Antillia on fifteenth-century maps vaguely reflects a visit by European seamen to Cuba. Whether or not Antillia was based on some forgotten voyage, belief in its existence provided encouragement to those searching the Atlantic for unknown islands or contemplating a transatlantic voyage.

See also
Seven Cities, Legend of.
For further reading
William H. Babcock, *Legendary Islands of the Atlantic,* 1922; Donald S. Johnson, *Phantom Islands of the Atlantic,* 1994; Kenneth Nebenzahl, *Atlas of Columbus and the Great Discoveries,* 1990.

ANTIPODES Geographical concept in classical and medieval Europe that postulated the existence of unknown, possibly inhabited regions in other quarters of the spherical earth. This theory encouraged European belief in the possibility of traveling to unknown lands lying west and south in the Atlantic Ocean. By the late eighteenth century, the term "antipodes" referred to the newly discovered lands of Australia and New Zealand, and is still used in that sense in the twentieth century.

Thanks to the teachings of the Pythagorean philosophers, by the fifth century B.C. belief in the sphericity of the earth was common among educated Greeks. The Greeks called the known, inhabited world the "oikoumene," but they recognized that the oikoumene was only a portion of the whole globe. The zonal theory of climate claimed five zones. Uninhabitable frigid zones lay at both poles, while an uninhabitable Torrid Zone corresponded to the equator. Northern and southern temperate zones lay on either side of the Torrid Zone and were capable of sustaining human life. Another common belief of the Greeks and other ancient peoples was that the known world was surrounded by an encircling ocean, which also ran along the equator.

Plato (ca. 429–347 B.C.) was the first Greek scholar to refer to the southern temperate zone as the antipodes, or land of the opposite-footed men, in his dialogue *Timaeus*. A new level of sophistication was added with the concept of a second meridional river-ocean dividing the planet from pole to pole. One ocean girded the earth running north and south, while the other divided the earth running east and west, splitting the earth into four quarters. Some modern scholars credit the Greek philosopher Eudoxus of Cnidos (408–355 B.C.) with the idea of two river-oceans. In his poem *Hermes*, Erastothenes (b. 280 B.C.), the great

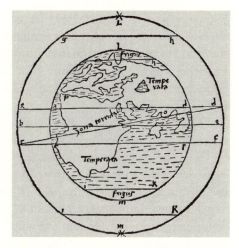

Sixteenth-century Italian map showing the location of the antipodes.

scholar and librarian of Alexandria, used "antipodes" as his term for the quarter of the southern temperate zone that had both opposite days and nights and opposite seasons from the oikoumene, making him the first to use "antipodes" in the sense it retains today.

During the second century B.C., Crates of Mallos formalized this theory that the earth consisted of four quarters. Besides the known oikoumene, he identified three other regions. Later Latin scholars, such as Cicero, Macrobius, and Martianus Capella, elaborated on Crates's ideas and gave names to the other three quarters. Directly south of the oikoumene lay the "antoikoi," or "opposite men" (southern Africa). In that land, the seasons were reversed from those of the oikoumene. Directly opposite the oikoumene was the "antichthones," or "opposite land," or "antiearth," also called the "periocci." It corresponded to the quarter of the globe North America occupies, and its night and day were the reverse of the oikoumene. Finally, south of the antichthones lay the "antipodes," or "land of opposite-footed men." South America is located where the antipodes were thought to be. In that land, both day and night and the seasons were the reverse of the oikoumene. Crates's theory created the possibility that three other inhabitable regions existed on the earth besides the oikoumene. Classical and medieval usage of the names for these quarters was often imprecise. "Antoikoi" and "antichthones" were not commonly used. Sometimes "antichthones" appeared as the name for the entire Southern Hemisphere. Much more commonly, the term "antipodes" referred to all three of the "opposite" quarters, not just the southern one.

Crates's theory of the opposite quarters, or antipodes, suggested two important questions: Were they inhabited? Could they be reached from the oikoumene? The ancient Greeks thought that the Torrid Zone along the equator could not be crossed because of its deadly heat. By the time of the great geographer Claudius Ptolemy (fl. A.D. 127–148), however, sufficient evidence had accumulated to show that the tropics were inhabited and so could be crossed safely. Little was known about the antipodal regions, which led some writers to use the antipodes as a motif of satire. Serving as places where things were very different from the world of the oikoumene, the antipodes could be used to compare and contrast the actions and customs of the inhabitants of the oikoumene. Lucian of Samothrace (fl. second century A.D.) used the antipodes in that way in his satirical *True History*.

The decline of the Roman Empire after the time of Ptolemy and Lucian also led to a decrease in the store of human knowledge, including geography. Older discredited ideas crept back into acceptance and challenged belief in the existence of the antipodal regions. The Christian apologist Lactantius (ca. 250–ca. 325) was a determined believer in the flat-earth theory. He based his arguments against the existence of the antipodes on the contention that everything would fall off the bottom half of the earth if it were a sphere. About the same time, the idea that the Torrid Zone was uninhabitable and uncrossable also regained general acceptance in medieval Europe. The late-fourth-century grammarian Servius claimed that the antipodes were the land of the afterlife. Nevertheless, Crates's theory of the four quarters also survived, thanks to the support of two scholars from the fourth century: Ambrosius Theodosius Macrobius and Martianus Capella. Both men's writings were popular among the scholars of the early Middle Ages.

The loss of so much geographical knowledge from the classical era left Crates's theory vulnerable to challenges and modifications during the Middle Ages. Aristotle (384–322 B.C.), a Greek philosopher whose writings were considered authoritative by the scholars of medieval Europe, never accepted the existence of the northern antipodes. Instead, he concluded that between the west coast of Europe and the east coast of Asia was merely a relatively narrow Atlantic Ocean. As a result, most medieval geographical thinking, including that of Christopher Columbus, did not speculate about the existence of northern antipodes. Furthermore, Aristotle lived in a time before it was proven that the Torrid Zone was inhabited. In his writings, he stated that the Torrid Zone was too hot to be crossed, a belief that persisted to the sixteenth century despite much evidence to the contrary.

Aristotle's belief about the uninhabitability of the Torrid Zone also caused conceptual problems for many Christian writers because it meant that the southern antipodes were completely cut off from contact with the oikoumene, the known world. Although others speculated that the temperate zone of the antipodes was inhabited, such a belief was theologically unacceptable to the early fathers of the Christian church, particularly St. Augustine of Hippo (354–430). St. Augustine asked two questions. If there was only one creation, where did antipodeans come from? If the antipodes were inaccessible, how could the gospel of Christ be preached throughout the world as the Bible said it was? The possibility of multiple creations (polygenesis) or multiple incarnations of Christ was considered heretical by the church. Therefore, belief in the existence of antipodeans was unbiblical, and many churchmen considered it to contain the seeds of potential heresy. During the eighth century, Bishop Virgil of Salzburg received condemnation from Pope Zachary for just that belief. Still, the church never officially declared belief in the regions of the antipodes to be a heresy. St. Augustine and others who followed him—Cosmas in the sixth century, Isidore of Seville (ca. 560–636), and the Venerable Bede (ca. 673–735)—accepted the existence of the antipodes as a logical consequence of the sphericity of the earth. However, they denied belief in the existence of antipodeans because of its theological unacceptability.

Despite the potential danger from the church hierarchy, medieval scholars speculated about the antipodes and even antipodeans. Lambert of St. Omer wrote his *Liber Floridus* about 1130, vaguely describing the earth as a sphere divided into five climatic zones and split by the great equatorial ocean. He included antipodes, but they were uninhabited and inaccessible because of the deadly heat of the Torrid Zone over the equatorial ocean. This view was theologically correct, but not everyone agreed. In the next century, both Albertus Magnus (1206–1280) and Roger Bacon, in his *Opus Maius* of around 1266, argued that the antipodes were inhabited, but their ideas failed to achieve general acceptance. Some medieval writers made the antipodes the home of the Garden of Eden or Terrestrial Paradise because both the antipodes and the Garden of Eden were supposed to be inaccessible to humans. Dante Alighieri (1265–1321) placed the purgatory of his *Divine Comedy* in the unreachable antipodes. Even at the beginning of the fifteenth century, Cardinal Pierre D'Ailly in his influential *Imago Mundi* of 1410 and his *Compendium Cosmographiae* of about 1414 adhered to the belief that the high temperatures of the Torrid Zone prevented humans from living there or traveling through it. Belief in the antipodes frequently became mixed up with another prevalent geographical idea: the existence of a great southern continent known as Terra Australis. Still, belief in the antipodes provided considerable encouragement for speculation about the existence and accessibility of unknown lands up to and during the great age of discovery in the fifteenth and sixteenth centuries. In his *Book of Prophecies,* Christopher Columbus pondered the possibility that his explorations had opened the way to the antipodes. Later sixteenth-, seventeenth-, and eighteenth-century explorations of the vast Pacific Ocean ultimately revealed the literal antipodes of Australia, New Zealand, and the other lands of Oceania.

See also
Antichthones; Antoikoi; Crates of Mallos; Paradise, Terrestrial.
For further reading
Gabriella Morreti, "The Other World and the 'Antipodes'," in *The Classical Tradition and the Americas,* vol. 1, 1994; W. G. L. Randles, "Classical Models of World Geography and Their Transformation Following the Discovery of America," in Vol. I: *The Classical Tradition and the Americas,* 1994; James S. Romm, *The Edges of the Earth in Ancient Thought,* 1992; John Kirtland Wright, *The Geographical Lore of the Time of the Crusades,* 1925.

ANTOIKOI   Meaning "opposite-men land," according to Crates of Mallos (fl. 150 B.C.), the name was given to the landmass located in the quarter of the earth lying directly south of the oikoumene, or that portion of the world known to the ancient Greeks and Romans. The antoikoi was separated from the oikoumene by the deadly Torrid Zone and the equatorial river-ocean. Fifteenth-century Portuguese explorations down the west coast of Africa proved that the continent extended well past the equator, and that no equatorial river-ocean existed. The Portuguese rounding of the Cape of Good Hope in 1487 also showed that there was no landmass of antoikoi.

See also
Crates of Mallos.

For further reading
W. G. L. Randles, "Classical Models of World Geography and Their Transformation Following the Discovery of America," in *The Classical Tradition and the Americas*, vol. 1, 1994.

ARCADIA   Many travelers have used the term "Arcadia" to describe a land of bucolic bliss. Historically, Arcadia was the region of Greece located in the middle of the Peloponnesian peninsula, and visitors commented on the beauty of its mountains. The valleys of Arcadia were reasonably fertile, and most of its inhabitants made their living as shepherds. A herding economy meant that Arcadians tended to live in small villages, and thus the region had no important city-state. Manpower was Arcadia's only important resource, and Arcadian mercenaries achieved a favorable reputation during the wars of the fifth century B.C. Arcadians also had a reputation for being fine musicians. Because of its geographic isolation, many quaint customs and religious practices continued to exist in Arcadia. The god Pan supposedly lived there.

The Roman poet Vergil (70–19 B.C.) idealized Arcadia as a land of happy shepherds leading simple, happy lives. In 1590, Sir Philip Sidney transformed Arcadia into a blissful fairyland in his massive poem *Arcadia*. From then on, Arcadia became the generic word for any simple and happy rural land.

ARSU   Guardian god worshiped at ancient Palmyra, a trading town located in a desert oasis between Syria and Babylonia. It flourished from ca. 100 B.C. until A.D. 273, when the Roman emperor Aurelian destroyed it. The Palmyrans and other northern Arabs thought that the evening star personified the god Arsu. The Palmyrans associated Arsu with horses, and particularly with camels; in some instances, Arsu was portrayed as a camel. This practice indicates the centrality of the carrying trade in Palmyra's economic life and the importance of the camel to it.

See also
Camel; Horse.

ASIA   The largest and most populous of the continents, Asia has been a realm of mystery and splendor in the minds of Westerners for millennia.

Asia was one of three continents in the known world of Greco-Roman and Judeo-Christian traditions (the other two were Europe and Africa). Asia was associated by Jews, Christians, and Muslims with Noah's son Shem. It took centuries for Westerners to appreciate the true vastness of Asia; the ancient Romans had only the dimmest awareness of the great empire of China. Not until the journey of John of Plano Carpini in 1245–1247 did Europeans have a reasonably accurate concept of China and the Far East. Once aware of Asia's true size, Westerners began to exaggerate it. Classical geographers, such as Claudius Ptolemy, extended Asia's length eastward considerably farther than it actually went. Columbus adopted the error and used it in the formulation of his plan to sail west to get to Asia.

Columbus's hopes to sail to Asia were part of a general European desire to reach the Far East and the Spice Islands to buy their many luxury goods: silks, spices, gems, and perfumes. That same desire motivated Portuguese explorers, including Vasco da Gama, Magellan, and various seekers of northwest or northeast passages. Contact with Asia played a tremendous role in altering European culture during the sixteenth, seventeenth, and eighteenth centuries. Superior military technology temporarily allowed the Europeans to dominate first the Asian seas and later the Asian lands between 1500 and 1945. Throughout the centuries, Asia has beckoned to the imaginations of Westerners, accurately or not, as a land of exoticism and mystery. Whether it is Marco Polo's golden-roofed palaces of Japan, the serene lamas of Tibet, the magnificence of the Forbidden City of China, or the Arabian Nights splendor of the Taj Mahal, Asia exercises an undeniable fascination for Westerners.

See also

Africa; Europe.

For further reading

Donald F. Lach, *Asia in the Making of Europe,* 1965–1994; J. R. S. Phillips, *The Medieval Expansion of Europe,* 1988; Edward W. Said, *Orientalism,* 1979.

ASSASSINS   A sect of Shia Islam that became famous among the Crusaders and other medieval European travelers in the Middle East for both the intense devotion and the murderousness of its adherents.

The Assassins were a branch of Ismailism. During the last quarter of the eleventh century, the Ismaili movement split during a dispute over the succession of the Fatimid caliphate in Egypt. One branch unsuccessfully supported Nizar, a son of the caliph al-Mustansir. When the crisis reached its climax with the death of al-Mustansir in 1094, Nizar launched a revolt in which he was ultimately defeated and killed. In 1090, one of his followers, Hasan-i-Sabbah, seized the castle of Alamut in Persia. From this remote citadel, Hasan sent out missionaries, who gained converts in the mountainous regions of Quhistan,

Kurdistand, and Syria. More castles were given to or seized by the followers of Hasan.

The Assassins derived their name from the Arabic word *hashish*, meaning grass in general and the intoxicant hemp in particular. Traditionally, the Assassin leaders were thought to use the drug hashish to secure the obedience of their followers. If that were the case, the name "Assassin" would be a corruption of the Arabic word *hashshish*, meaning a hashish smoker. But the word used in the contemporary Arabic accounts is *hashishi* or *hashishiyyin*, meaning "dry grass" or "fodder." Thus, the name derives not from any supposed practice of drug use but rather was a term of abuse, referring to the bizarre behavior of the Assassins. Furthermore, only in the Syrian region were members of the sect called Assassins. In their Persian homeland, they were called *Muliech* or *Mulihet*, meaning "deviator," a reference to their heretical variance from orthodox Islam.

Assassins are most famous for their daring and ruthless murders of opposition leaders, so much so that "assassin" has become a common Western word for a professional killer of any type. The sect used terrorism as a means to destroy the dominant Sunni denomination of Islam and those secular rulers, such as the officials of the Seljuk Empire, who supported Sunnism. Fanatical followers of the Assassin sect called *fidais* performed most of the murders. Their obedience became legendary, and numerous stories described how the leader of the Assassins, known as the Old Man of the Mountain, would command his *fidais* to hurl themselves off cliffs or towers as an ultimate demonstration of their devotion. In the West, the Assassins were initially more famous for devotion to their cause than for murderousness.

The Assassins killed many high-ranking leaders, both religious and secular, among the Sunni majority in the regions of present-day Syria, Iraq, and Iran, including a grand vizier of the Seljuks and two caliphs. Even the great Islamic leader Saladin (1138–1193) suffered two attempts on his life by the Assassins. Non-Muslims had little to fear from them, although some Crusader leaders died at their hands, most notably Conrad of Montferrat, the king of Jerusalem in 1192. The Mongols feared that *fidais* of the Assassins had even infiltrated their distant capital of Karakorum seeking to kill the Great Khan. Assassins also threatened the life of the saintly Louis IX of France during his Crusades. A body of myth and rumor grew up around the Assassins as their record of murders accumulated. In 1175, an envoy of the German emperor Frederick Barbarossa told how the sect of the Assassins lived in remote castles on mountaintops. The leader raised young boys to give him absolute obedience, and in return he claimed to possess the power to admit them into Paradise when they died. Besides obedience, the boys were trained in many languages, such as Arabic, Greek, and Latin. When needed, the leader gave them golden daggers and commanded them to kill an enemy of their faith. If they died in obedience to their leader, the youths were assured of entering Paradise. William of Tyre gave a similar description of the Assassins in his chronicle, and Arnold of Lübeck's chronicle added the detail of the Assassin leader—the Old Man of the Mountain—commanding his *fidais* to leap to their deaths as a demonstration of their unquestioning loyalty. The best-known account of the Assassins came from the pen of Marco Polo. In 1273, he passed through Persia, where he heard tales of the fearsome Assassins. The stories tell how the Old Man of the Mountain created an earthly paradise in a remote mountain valley guarded by an impregnable castle. Young men were drugged and transported to his paradisial valley, where they lived in the lap of luxury and were served by beautiful women in every way. It was the very picture of the Muslim Paradise, which is where the young men believed they were. When the Old Man needed the services of one

Gustave Doré woodcut of Edward I struggling with an Assassin sent to kill him in his sleep.

of them, he would have the young man drugged and brought into his presence. Angry and bewildered at being wrenched from Paradise, the young man would do anything to get back. The Old Man promised to do just that if the youth would kill a specified enemy for the sake of the Assassin faith. His young dupes almost never refused him because they believed he had the power to admit them or deny them entry into Paradise.

The Assassins focused their murderous activities on their Sunni opponents, but they collected tribute or protection money from many Crusader leaders. Only the military orders of the Templars and the Hospitalers refused to pay; in fact, the military orders even made themselves overlords of the Syrian branch of the Assassins. The various Old Men of the Mountain also gained a reputation for hiring out their *fidais* as professional killers. Some rumors claimed that Richard the Lionhearted of England hired the Assassins to kill Conrad of Montferrat and King Philip Augustus of France, and that the Muslim leader Gümüshtigin of Aleppo supposedly persuaded the Old Man to make an attempt on the life of Saladin. As a result, fear of the Assassins rose to fantastic heights. *Fidais* of the Assassins were supposedly traveling to Europe to carry out hired killings. During the siege of Milan in 1158, it was rumored that Emperor Frederick Barbarossa captured an Assassin in his own camp. At Chinon in 1195, Richard the Lionhearted rounded up 14 Assassins hired by the king of France to kill him. Such stories are false, but as late as 1332, long after the Mongol destruction of Alamut, a German priest named Brocardus warned Philip VI of France to beware of Assassins if he went on a Crusade to the Holy Land. Brocardus recommended that the king isolate himself from anyone who had not personally accompanied him from his homeland because the Assassins were masters of disguise and deception.

Greatly feared by the Crusaders and other Western travelers, the Assassins actually posed little threat to them. Rather, their Islamic opponents—the adherents of the Sunni faith—suffered from the knives of the Assassins. Such notorious and murderous activities secured the survival of their name in the consciousness of popular history.

For further reading
Bernard Lewis, *The Assassins*, 1967; Charles E. Nowell, "The Old Man of the Mountain," *Speculum* 22 (Oct. 1947): 497–519.

ATLANTIC OCEAN
This body of water separates Europe and Africa from North and South America. It covers an area of 41 million square miles and is an extremely important component of maritime commerce.

Of the three major oceans, the Atlantic has been the most important to the course of Western civilization. The early Hebrews had little idea of its existence beyond the Strait of Gibraltar. Homeric and later Greeks thought it was part of the world-encircling River Ocean. Medieval Arabs of Islamic Spain and North Africa called it the Green Sea of Darkness and generally feared to sail on it. By the time of Christopher Columbus in the late fifteenth century, Europeans called it by local variations of the grand name of Ocean Sea. They thought that fabled Cathay, the Golden Chersonese, and the Spice Islands lay at its western limits.

Two wind patterns—the trade winds and the westerlies—dominate the Atlantic Ocean. Trade winds blow from northeast to southwest between 30°N latitude and the equator in the Northern Hemisphere, and from southeast to northwest between 30°S latitude and the equator in the Southern Hemisphere. A band of still air called the "doldrums" separates the northeast trade winds from the southeast trade winds. Westerly winds flourish between 30°N to 60°N latitude and from 30°S to 60°S latitude. They blow from southwest to northeast and from northwest to southeast, respectively. In the Southern Hemisphere, they form part of the "Roaring Forties."

This pattern of winds combines with the heating and cooling of the ocean's waters at the different latitudes to produce regular, circulating currents of water. The north and south equatorial currents flow from east to west and are creations of the trade winds. Turning north, the north equatorial current is joined by part of the south equatorial current, which is diverted northward by Cape São Roque. Together, they flow through the Caribbean Sea and Gulf of Mexico to form the current known as the Gulf Stream. This famous current carries warm water across the Atlantic and splits at the British Isles. The portion continuing northward is called the North Atlantic Drift, while the water moving south becomes the relatively cool Canaries current.

In the Southern Hemisphere, the remaining part of the south equatorial current heads south at Cape São Roque to become the Brazil current. Below 30°S latitude, it merges with the west-to-east current of cold water created by the Roaring Forties, known as the Cape Horn current near South America and becoming the West Wind Drift by the time it reaches midocean. At the Cape of Good Hope, the current splits; some of it proceeds into the Indian Ocean, and the rest turns north along the southwestern coast of Africa to become the Benguela current. The Atlantic Ocean contains two great circular patterns of water currents, which flow in a clockwise fashion in the Northern Hemisphere and counterclockwise in the Southern Hemisphere.

The Atlantic Ocean experiences greater differences in air and water temperatures than do the other two great oceans. Surrounded by large landmasses and more open to climatic influences from the Arctic and Antarctic regions, the seas of the Atlantic are rougher and produce more stormy weather. As a result, experienced sailors consider the Atlantic Ocean to be the most challenging.

Prehistoric sailors along the coast of western Europe were the first to travel on the turbulent waters of the Atlantic Ocean. Intrepid Phoenician seamen ventured from the Mediterranean Sea into the Atlantic well before 490 B.C., when the expeditions of Hanno and Himilco explored the Atlantic coasts of Africa and Europe. It appears that Phoenician ships reached the Madeira and Azores Islands. The Greek Pytheas of Massilia circumnavigated the British Isles sometime between 325 and 300 B.C. Roman ships sailed along the coast of Europe, but the Romans were not nearly as adventurous as the Carthaginians.

One problem that Mediterranean sailors faced upon entering the Atlantic Ocean was that their galleys were not suited for its rough waters.

After the Western Roman Empire fell in A.D. 476, knowledge of the Atlantic temporarily regressed. Irish monks traveled to Iceland well before 795. Soon after, daring Norse or Viking sailors from Scandinavia burst upon the Atlantic world. The first Viking raid occurred in 793. Soon, the Norse ventured far into the Mediterranean Sea and deep into the interior of Russia, eventually making their way across the Atlantic to North America. The first Norse accidentally reached Iceland in 860, and permanent settlement began during the 870s. Other Norse ships sighted Greenland sometime between 900 and 930, although the first colony did not appear until 986. In that same year, while on his way to join the first settlers on Greenland, Bjarni Herjolfsson was blown to North America. Declining to go ashore, he made his way to Greenland as quickly as he could, but his discovery prompted Leif Ericsson to attempt a permanent settlement on "Vinland" (present-day Greenland) in 1001 or shortly thereafter. Leif's effort failed, as did several other Norse attempts to colonize North America. The Norse settlements scattered across the Atlantic slowly contracted as the climate turned cooler. Between 1450 and 1500, the last Norse settler on Greenland died.

Other Europeans developed the ability to sail on the high seas of the Atlantic. During the fifteenth century, fishermen of both England and the Hanseatic League of Germany vied for control of the Icelandic fishing grounds. Some scholars speculate that Bristol fishermen may have reached the Grand Banks of Newfoundland in the 1480s, several years before Columbus's historic first voyage of 1492. Farther south, the Portuguese expanded down the coast of Africa and into the Atlantic. Beginning in 1415, Portuguese expeditions sailed down the coast in search of trade, their efforts culminating in the discovery of the Cape of Good Hope and a sea route to India in 1487–1488. Portuguese sailors also reached the Madeira Islands in 1419 and the eastern Azores in 1427; Corvo and Flores, the westernmost islands of the Azores, were not discovered until 1452. Other voyagers attempted to penetrate farther into the western Atlantic but failed to make much progress because of the contrary westerly winds. During his 1497 voyage in the South Atlantic, Vasco da Gama used the prevailing winds and currents to develop the efficient sailing route of the Volta do Brasil, which involved sailing far out into the western Atlantic before catching the westerlies and turning east. Pedro Cabral accidentally discovered Brazil in 1500 when he sailed too far west while following the Volta do Brasil.

Fifteenth-century Europeans thought that the Atlantic Ocean separated Europe from Asia; they had no idea that the Americas existed. German geographer Martin Behaim's (ca. 1436–1507) world globe of 1492 reflected that belief. In 1474, the Florentine Paolo Toscanelli dal Pozzo (1397–1482) suggested to the king of Portugal the possibility of sailing west to reach Asia. Christopher Columbus (1451–1506) spent years trying to gain support for a similar project from the king of Portugal and then from Ferdinand and Isabella of Spain. When the Spanish monarchs finally granted him support, he sailed in 1492, only to find the islands of the Bahamas, Cuba, and Hispaniola rather than fabled Cathay and Chipangu. Europeans first thought Columbus had reached some outlying islands of Asia, and Columbus himself died believing that was what he had found.

By 1500, Europeans recognized that another great continent existed (now known as South America), but knowledge of the existence of North America took a bit longer. Martin Waldseemuller's world map of 1513 demonstrated a groping awareness of North America, and Juan Vespucci's world map of 1526 clearly showed a solid wall of land in the temperate and tropical latitudes blocking European ships from reaching Asia. Ferdinand Magellan, by his discovery of the Straits of Magellan in 1520, showed one way of getting from the Atlantic to the Pacific Ocean. Others vainly looked for usable northwest and northeast passages in Arctic waters during the rest of the sixteenth century. By this time, the Atlantic Ocean and its sea lanes were reasonably well known to Europeans. The maritime trade on the Atlantic quickly grew, and the center of European economy shifted from the Mediterranean Sea in the fifteenth century to the Atlantic Ocean by the seventeenth and has remained so ever since. Until the appearance of reasonably priced passenger flights in the early 1960s, a sea voyage was the only way across the Atlantic. For Western culture, it remains "the ocean."

See also

Carthage; Cathay; Chipangu; Golden Chersonese; Good Hope, Cape of; Greenland; Hanno, Voyage of; Himilco, Voyage of; Iceland; Phoenicians; Pytheas of Massilia, Voyage of; Roaring Forties; Trade Winds.

For further reading

Vincent H. Cassidy, *The Sea around Them,* 1968; Kenneth Nebenzahl, *Atlas of Columbus and the Great Discoveries,* 1990; Leonard Outhwaite, *The Atlantic,* 1957.

ATLANTIS   The most famous of all the legendary lost continents, Atlantis was first mentioned by the Greek philosopher Plato (ca. 429–347 B.C.), who located it in the Atlantic Ocean, where it sank with great loss of life and total destruction about 12,000 years ago. Many considered Atlantis the original home of humanity and the source of civilization. The higher civilizations of ancient times, both in the Eastern Hemisphere and the Americas, were credited to the Atlanteans. Periodically, some explorer or traveler tried to locate Atlantis, remnants of the lost continent, or some lost colony of Atlantean survivors.

The first written reference to Atlantis occurred in Plato's *Timaeus,* followed by more information in his unfinished *Critias.* Written toward the end of Plato's life, the two dialogues tell of a great island civilization that dominated the ancient world of about 9500 B.C. until it was destroyed by earthquakes and floods and sank beneath the ocean. That end, however, marked the beginning of centuries-long debate over the historicity of the Atlantis story. Atlantis became the goal of explorers and travelers from the sixteenth century onward.

Greek and Roman writers seldom discussed Atlantis. Strabo's *Geography,* which appeared 300 years after Plato, makes the next surviving reference to

Atlantis. It quotes Aristotle as stating, "Its inventor [Plato] caused it [Atlantis] to disappear," which indicates that Aristotle thought Atlantis was a fictional place. Other ancient writers, such as Poseidonius and Lysius Proklus, disagreed. Archaeological evidence clearly shows that the great city of Athens that supposedly fought the Atlanteans to a standstill never existed, nor has any archaeological evidence of Atlantis ever been found. Scholars of classical literature point out that internal evidence from Plato's dialogues gives further credence to the position that Atlantis was a fictional creation, like those described in Sir Thomas More's *Utopia* and Samuel Butler's *Erewhon*. In *Timaeus*, Plato mentions that the Atlantean story was told as part of a storytelling festival in Athens, a clue to its fictional origins. Later, in *Critias*, the description of Atlantis conforms so closely to Socrates's earlier description of what an ideal state should be like that even characters in the dialogue comment on the similarity. This little episode strikes most scholars as a case of Plato joking with his readers over the fictionality of his story. Although some ancient writers claimed it was a true history, Plato's Atlantis story was not widely discussed, and during the Middle Ages it almost disappeared from the writings of scholars.

Columbus's revelation of the existence of the Americas quickly reopened discussion about Atlantis, which continues unabated. Prompting the renewed interest in Atlantis was the question of the origin of Native Americans. Where had they come from? The first to suggest an Atlantean origin was the Spaniard Francisco López de Gómara in 1552. Others followed his lead, but by the early eighteenth century the theory had receded into obscurity. Yet fascination with Atlantis continued, despite skepticism and scientific evidence to the contrary.

Modern theories about Atlantis begin with Ignatius Donnelly (1831–1901), a Populist congressman from Minnesota and the best-known scholar of the lost continent. Donnelly was a reader of wide interests and inexhaustible energy, and out of his reading and research emerged his classic of 1882, *Atlantis: The Antediluvian World*. He argued the existence of a real Atlantis as the source of all succeeding civilizations, in both the Eastern and Western Hemispheres. As in Plato's account more than 2,000 years earlier, Donnelly's Atlantis was overwhelmed by earthquake and flood. According to the author, the flood myths of peoples all over the globe are a memory of the tragic sinking of Atlantis. He believed that the existence of these myths, along with other supposedly shared cultural traits, proved that Atlantis existed.

Advances in science render Donnelly's theory of Atlantis untenable. *Atlantis: The Antediluvian World*, however, was initially considered a work of serious scholarship. In his day, Donnelly's theories were quite believable, even though he was credulous in his use of sources and evidence. He worked inductively from the assumption that Atlantis existed and gleaned his evidence so as to prove it. Still, compared with the many books about Atlantis that claim spiritual communications as their main source of information, Donnelly's "scholarship" remains far and away the best.

Donnelly's efforts were only the beginning of modern Atlantis scholarship. Rosicrucians, Theosophists, and Anthroposophists incorporated Atlantis and other lost continents into their religious beliefs. During the 1920s, the mythologist Lewis Spence made a series of Donnelly-like attempts to prove the existence of Atlantis in a scholarly manner. His efforts began with *The Problem of Atlantis* (1924), followed by *Atlantis in America* (1925) and *The History of Atlantis* (1926). Several more books followed, including one on the lost continent of Lemuria in 1933. Other writers followed suit. By 1954, the popular writer and expert on lost-continent literature L. Sprague de Camp estimated that some 2,000 books had been written about Atlantis. Since that date, hundreds more have been written. These writings inspire many people to look for Atlantis and give credence to other legends of lost cities and lands.

Scholars agree that the Atlantis of Plato and Donnelly never existed. Atlantean colonists or refugees did not create the ancient civilizations in the Americas or the Old World. Nevertheless, many serious scholars suggest that some ancient catastrophe may have inspired the Atlantis legend, and cite the gigantic volcanic explosion that destroyed the Greek island of Thera about 1500 B.C. as a possible candidate.

See also
Atlantic Ocean.
For further reading
L. Sprague de Camp, *Lost Continents*, 1954; Ignatius Donnelly, *Atlantis*, 1882; Kenneth L. Feder, *Frauds, Myths, and Mysteries*, 1990.

AVALON   In Arthurian legend, Avalon was the western island located in the Atlantic Ocean, similar to the Fortunate Isles of classical antiquity.

The medieval chronicler and mythographer Geoffrey of Monmouth (d. ca. 1155) talked about Avalon in his *History of the Kings of Britain* and *Life of Merlin*. According to his Latin account, Avalon, or the *Insula Avallonis*, was an island in the western ocean where the sword Excalibur was forged and where the gravely wounded King Arthur went after his last great battle with Modred. The great seaman Barinthus supposedly transported Arthur to Avalon. Geoffrey of Monmouth claimed that the Welsh name for Avalon was *Ynys Avallach*, which meant "isle of apples." Hence, he referred to it in Latin as *Insula Pomorum*. He also called Avalon "the Fortunate Isle," thus linking it with the Greco-Roman traditions of the Fortunate Isles. Apparently, the Avalon of Celtic mythology and the Arthurian romances was an analog of the Isles of the Hesperides. Both islands were associated with apples, and both were the paradisial homes of nine maidens. Early versions of the Arthurian legends named a benevolent Morgan-le-Fay as the leader of the nine maidens. The Avalon of Geoffrey of Monmouth and the later Arthurian romances apparently evolved from much older Celtic depictions of the island as the far-western dwelling place of the dead.

Avalon has also been identified with Glastonbury and its monastery. Glastonbury is located on high ground that at one time was surrounded by swamps, so during wet weather it would literally be an island. Other people speculate, less plausibly, that Avalon might reflect some vague contact be-tween the ancient Celts and North America. Although no traveler ever visited Avalon, belief in its existence may have inspired people to sail west during the Middle Ages.

See also
 Atlantic Ocean; Fortunate Isles.

For further reading
 Geoffrey Ashe, *Avalonian Quest*, 1982; Geoffrey Ashe, ed., *The Quest for Arthur's Britain*, 1960; Geoffrey of Monmouth, *The History of the Kings of Britain*, 1966.

B

BAEDEKER   A famous publisher of tourist guidebooks whose name has become synonymous with guidebooks since the early nineteenth century.

Dietrich Baedeker (1680–1716) began the family publishing business in the early eighteenth century at Bielefeld in Germany. In 1789, the company moved to Essen. In 1829, Karl Baedeker (1801–1859) published the firm's first guidebook, for the city of Koblenz. More successful was the guidebook to the Rhine River from Mainz to Cologne in 1832. Baedeker began publishing its guidebooks in other languages in 1846.

By making tourist guidebooks a mass-consumption product, Baedeker filled an important need. The success of the Baedeker guides is attributable to their high quality, but it is also evidence of the concurrent growth of commercial tourism in European society. Guidebooks had been around for millennia; travelers have always needed reliable directions and informed descriptions of the lands they visit. The earliest guidebook, *On the Cities in Greece,* dates from the third century B.C. and was written by Heraclides Criticus. Pausanias of Magnesia's (fl. ca. A.D. 150) *Description of Greece,* with monuments as its primary interest, is the only complete guidebook of antiquity to survive. Pilgrimage sites—the Holy Land, Rome, Santiago de Compostela—each had its pilgrims' guides from the early Middle Ages. The writing of guidebooks continued through the Renaissance and the Enlightenment, during which they were needed by participants in the Grand Tour. Baedeker took the existing genre of the guidebook and basically industrialized it for the mass market. The company's example has been followed by Michelin, Fodor, and many others.

See also

Grand Tour; Holy Land; Rome; Santiago de Compostela.

BARBARY COAST   From the Middle Ages to the nineteenth century, Europeans applied this name, or simply "Barbary," to the coast of North Africa from Morocco to Egypt, including Algeria, Tunisia, and Libya.

The term "Barbary" is related to the modern word "Berber," which refers to the Hamitic peoples who inhabited the coastlines of North Africa prior to the

Phoenician and Greek colonizations and the Roman and Arabic conquests. Their language is closely related to ancient Egyptian. Berber tribes of the Sanhaja and the Tuareg also spread into the Sahara and the savannah of the Sudan that lay to the south.

The modern word "Berber" evolved from the Arabic *barbar* (noisy and confused talking). Some authorities assert that the Arabic *barbar* derived from the similar Greek *barbarous* and the Latin *barbarus,* meaning "foreigner." Others maintain that the Arabic word bears no relation to either. Early Arab geographers called North Africa by the name of "Barbary," and medieval Europeans adopted the name for the country, although they continued to call the inhabitants "Moors." This usage lasted until the nineteenth century, when Europeans began to use "Berber" for the non-Arab inhabitants of North Africa. The very name "Barbary Coast" thus had connotations of strangeness and exoticism that held great appeal for writers and their readers during the romantic and Victorian eras. A good example of this is the wild area of old San Francisco known as the "Barbary Coast."

For further reading
Edward William Bovill, *The Golden Trade of the Moors,* 1968; Michael Brett, "Berbers," in *Dictionary of the Middle Ages,* 1982–1989.

BARBARY PIRATES   Also known as the Barbary Corsairs, these Muslim sea raiders operated out of the states of Algiers, Tunis, and Tripoli (the area known as the Barbary Coast) from the early sixteenth century through the early nineteenth century.

At the beginning of the sixteenth century, the Muslim states of North Africa faced a threat of conquest by the Christian rulers of Spain and Portugal. The Portuguese had already captured Ceuta in 1415, and by 1511 Spain had taken Oran, Algiers, and Tripoli. The Ottoman Empire was advancing into the western Mediterranean Sea from the east. A naval struggle ensued between Spain and the Ottoman Turks. The Turks employed "captains of corsairs," sea raiders legally commissioned to attack enemy shipping. Among them were the famous Kheireddin Barbarosa and Turgut Reis (Dragut). Thanks to their exploits and those of other captains, the Ottomans drove the Spanish forces out of North Africa by 1580. However, hostilities did not end. Barbary corsairs attacked Spanish and Portuguese shipping until the late eighteenth century and expanded their depredations to the ships of other Christian nations, including the United States.

Piracy became a way of life and a permanent government institution in the Barbary states. The various local governors, nominally subject to the Ottoman sultan, licensed the corsairs and regulated their activities. The Barbary corsairs' raids against Christians were considered a legitimate form of religious warfare; they warred primarily on Christian vessels and did not attack those of fellow Muslims. They practiced their seaborne pillaging in a businesslike

Undated painting of a fleet of the Barbary Coast pirates during the Tripolitan War.

manner. Corsairs belonged to a guild called the Taife Reisi, which regulated and administered all aspects of piratical activity, from recruitment of new members to licensing of ship's captains to divisions of booty. The members of the Taife Reisi elected an official called the Captain of the Sea, who served as chair of the council of sea captains directing the guild.

During the early seventeenth century, Christian renegades taught the Barbary corsairs how to construct ships capable of sailing in the Atlantic's rough waters. This era of geographically expanded operations marked the zenith of the Barbary pirates' power. The various wars in western Europe, associated with the expansionism of Louis XIV of France in the late seventeenth century, created intense European competition to build larger warships and muster bigger fleets. The Barbary states fell behind in naval technology, and rather than pose a serious military threat the Barbary pirates became merely a nuisance to European shipping. Many countries, such as the Dutch, found it simpler and cheaper to pay off the pirates with protection money or tribute rather than respond with military force. Even the young United States of America paid tribute to the Barbary states, although the greed of local rulers resulted in wars with Tripoli in 1801–1805 and with Algiers in 1812–1815. Other European powers, such as Britain, France, and the Netherlands, became more willing to send punitive expeditions against the Barbary states when their piratical activities grew to be too irritating. The age of the Barbary pirates came to an end when France occupied Algiers and the Ottomans asserted closer control over Tunis and Tripoli.

For three centuries, Christian sailors and travelers faced the threat of robbery, death, or enslavement by the Barbary pirates. Although Christian pirates—the Knights Hospitaler of Malta and the Uskoks—posed equal if not deadlier threats to Mediterranean travelers, whether Christian or Muslim, during the early-modern era, the Barbary pirates achieved the greatest notoriety, and memory of them survives in the consciousness of popular culture.

See also

Barbary Coast; Pirates.

For further reading

Sir Godfrey Fisher, *Barbary Legend*, 1957; Stanley Lane-Poole, *The Barbary Corsairs*, 1901.

Bath　Provincial town in the county of Somerset in southwestern England that was famous for its hot springs. During the eighteenth century, it blossomed into a popular resort and tourist attraction.

The hot springs of Bath were supposedly discovered by the legendary King Bladud. During their occupation of Britain, the Romans built a spa called Aquae Sulis at the site of Bath sometime during the first and second centuries A.D. The medieval town of Bath was a cloth-making center and is probably best known as the home of Chaucer's Wife of Bath. In 1597, the King's Bath was built; it provided medicinal therapy during the seventeenth century. Operating purely as a health resort, Bath experienced only modest growth in its population and economy. By 1700, the population stood at 2,000 to 3,000 people.

During the first two decades of the eighteenth century the town's orientation and fortunes changed significantly. Writing during 1724–1726, Daniel Defoe described the transformation of Bath:

> In former times this was a resort hither for cripples. . . . But now we may say it is the resort of the sound, rather than the sick; the bathing is made more a sport and diversion, than a physical prescription for health; and the town is taken up in raffling, gaming, visiting, and in a word, all sorts of gallantry and levity.

Several people figured prominently in bringing about this change. Richard "Beau" Nash (1674–1761) was the first; he established the pattern of social life at Bath and popularized it with both the aristocratic and middle-class patrons. Ralph Allen (1694–1764) was Bath's promoter. He encouraged investment and expansion yet maintained a sedate public image of morality and wholesomeness for Bath's amusements. All the while, Allen shrewdly enriched himself by judicious investment in the pleasure industry and its facilities at Bath. A father-and-son duo of architects, both named John Wood (father: ca. 1704–1754; son: d. 1782), beautified Bath during their careers. Queen's Square, the Circus, and the Royal Crescent were renovated or rebuilt, along with various other buildings and streets. The Woods' labors transformed Bath into one of the loveliest of the Georgian towns.

Bath's popularity as a tourist resort caused its permanent population to soar to almost 35,000 by 1800, and only London had a larger number of tourists. In 1750, some 12,000 people visited Bath during the spa season. Although top aristocrats visited Bath, the true foundation of the town's prosperity was formed by middle-class tourists. In 1765 and 1766, an estimated £10,000 a week (an astronomical sum at that time) was spent by tourists in Bath. Taking the waters at Bath, along with its other diversions, was a powerful symbol of status in Georgian England. With such success, Bath found itself imitated by other resorts springing up at Malvern Wells, Freestone, and Cheltenham.

Not everyone found the pleasures of Bath to be either enjoyable or wholesome. Elizabeth Montagu (1720–1800), a perceptive member of the famous Bluestocking Circle of learned women, found the social regimen at Bath to be too rigid and tedious for her tastes. On the other hand, the evangelical minister Charles Wesley (1707–1788) regarded Bath as not dull enough, and considered it to be "the headquarters of Satan." Despite such criticisms, Bath remained popular into the early nineteenth century, until changing tastes and competition from a wider variety of popular recreations and tourist attractions caused it to decline. Bath was probably one of the first recognizable tourist attractions (in the modern sense) in England.

For further reading
R. S. Neale, *Bath*, 1981.

BETHLEHEM

Meaning "house of bread" in Hebrew, this famous biblical town is located about five miles south of Jerusalem. Because it was the birthplace of Jesus Christ, it has been an important destination for pilgrimages for almost 2,000 years.

Bethlehem's site has been inhabited since the lower Pleistocene era over 10,000 years ago. After the Hebrew conquest of Canaan (ca. 1300–1100 B.C.), members of the tribe of Ephraim eventually occupied it, and later it was associated with King David and his family. Bethlehem played an insignificant part in biblical history until the birth of Christ. Only the Gospels of Matthew and Luke

"The Nativity," a woodcut by Albrecht Dürer illustrating The Small Passion, *1511.*

mention Bethlehem as the birthplace of Jesus, but they are also the only two gospels to provide detailed birth narratives.

At first, Bethlehem was unimportant to the early Christians. In A.D. 135, it was occupied by a Roman garrison during the final phase of the Bar Kochba rebellion. Early Christian tradition placed the birth of Jesus in a cave: Justin Martyr (ca. 100–ca. 165) was the first to write about a cave as the site of the Nativity. By the early fourth century, the Nativity became associated with a specific cave located in Bethlehem, and Emperor Constantine built the famous Church of the Nativity over it in 330. Although heavily damaged during the Samaritan revolt of 529, Emperor Justinian repaired it to its original form. It is one of the oldest Christian churches in the world, and the present-day structure includes much of the original building. Meanwhile, in 386, the great biblical scholar St. Jerome (ca. 342–420) settled in Bethlehem and established a monastery. He was joined in his efforts by St. Paula (347–404) and her daughter St. Eustochium (370–ca. 419). All three saints' tombs were located in the caves below the Church of the Nativity along with the tomb of Joseph of Arimathaea. During the Crusades, Bethlehem contained a hospice for pilgrims.

Bethlehem has been a popular destination for Christian pilgrimages for centuries. Both St. Cyril and St. Jerome included it prominently on their lists of places for pilgrims to visit in the Holy Land. In 1177, the German monk Theodorich devoted a chapter to Bethlehem in his popular *Guide to the Holy Land*. Besides the tombs of saints, he described how pilgrims could kiss the manger of Jesus as a form of devotion. Even today, Bethlehem is a powerful magnet to Christians, particularly during the Christmas season.

See also

Holy Land; Jerusalem; Pilgrimage.

For further reading

C. Kopp, *The Holy Place of the Gospels*, 1963; Theodorich, *Guide to the Holy Land*, 1986; Robert L. Wilken, *The Land Called Holy*, 1992.

BLACK SEA   Also known as the Euxine Sea by the ancient Greeks and the Pontus by the Romans, the Black Sea played an important role in European history and travel from ancient times through the modern era.

The ancient Greeks called the Black Sea by the name Euxine, meaning "hospitable." In fact, compared to the balmy Mediterranean Sea, its waters are colder, and frequent storms sweep over it. The straits of the Dardanelles and the Bosporus are full of tricky and dangerous currents that made it difficult for small sailing ships to travel from the Aegean Sea to the Black Sea. Many ancient writers predicted that the Black Sea and the Sea of Marmora would eventually silt up, a forecast that has never been fulfilled because the Black Sea's swift, strong currents erode alluvial deposits.

The early Greeks initially viewed the waters and the littoral of the Black Sea as a terra incognita. Only epic heroes like Jason and his Argonauts or the demigod Hercules could travel across it to mysterious places like Colchis. Some lands along the Black Sea were thought to be home to abnormal people such as the fierce Amazons of the Thermodon River. Nevertheless, Greek voyaging into the Black Sea began well before 700 B.C. During the sixth century B.C., Greeks, mostly from Miletus, established colonies around the Black Sea. An extensive trade crisscrossed the Black Sea during the classical era of roughly 500 B.C.–A.D. 500, carrying goods into the Aegean and Mediterranean Seas. The historian Polybius (ca. 200–118 B.C.) described the lands around the Black Sea as rich in cattle, slaves, and dried fish as well as luxury items like honey and wax. Inhabitants of the Black Sea region were equally eager to buy such Mediterranean products as wine and olive oil. Such a busy, valuable trade would make any city strategically located at the straits of the Bosporus or the Dardanelles very rich, and legendary Troy, followed by historic Byzantium and Constantinople, became wealthy from this bustling trade.

Constantinople and the Eastern Roman Empire survived and throve long after Rome's fall and the final days of the Western Empire in A.D. 476. As the Silk Road developed and matured for trade with the Far East, the Black Sea's importance as a trade route only increased. Jewels, silks, and spices traveled along it from the Far East to the Mediterranean world, and the final stage of the Silk Road passed over the Black Sea. During the Middle Ages, the Black Sea trade was dominated in turn by the Byzantines, the Crusaders, and the Genoese. Founded by the Genoese in 1266, the trading city of Kaffa (Caffa) on the Crimea grew to the size of Seville, with a population of about 50,000. It was joined by Tana and Trebizond.

The rise of the Ottoman Turks during the fifteenth century destroyed the Genoese trading network in the Black Sea. Constantinople fell to the Turks in 1453, followed by Trebizond in 1461 and Kaffa in 1475. However, Turkish control did not diminish the importance of the Black Sea trade. The Turks were as anxious to grow rich from that trade as the previous proprietors. Only after 1498, the year of Vasco da Gama's successful return from India, did the Black Sea gradually decline in importance. The oceanic trade routes eventually became the most important links between Europe and Asia.

The Black Sea's importance became linked to the rise of Russia as a great power. Russia's Black Sea coastline contained its only warm-water connections to the West. Russia's problem was that it did not control Constantinople and the strategic Dardanelles and Bosporus. Many nineteenth-century diplomatic incidents, as well as the Crimean War and other minor wars, originated from Russia's desire to control the Black Sea's access to the Mediterranean. Tsarist Russia's fall in World War I (1914–1918) was closely connected to its failure to open a supply route through Constantinople. The Black Sea remains important in the twentieth century, although it no longer maintains the paramount importance as a trade route that it did during antiquity and the Middle Ages.

See also

Amazons; Bosporus; Constantinople; Dardanelles; Jason and the Argonauts, Voyage of; Mediterranean Sea.

For further reading

E. H. Bunbury, *A History of Ancient Geography,* 1883; M. Cary and E. H. Warmington, *The Ancient Explorers,* 1963; Boies Penrose, *Travel and Discovery in the Early Renaissance,* 1955; J. R. S. Phillips, *The Medieval Expansion of Europe,* 1988.

BLESSED, ISLES OF THE   The early-medieval Irish Christians believed that an earthly paradise was located in the western Atlantic Ocean. St. Brendan the Navigator sought and found this wonderful land during his legendary voyage. Some scholars suggest that such reports about the Isles of the Blessed are really murky reflections of medieval contact with North America. A more plausible explanation is that the Irish Isles of the Blessed are a Christianized fusion of Celtic legends of a western paradise and Greco-Roman concepts of the Fortunate Isles and the Elysian Fields. The Islands of the Blessed was also an alternate name for the Elysian Fields in some classical traditions.

See also

Atlantic Ocean; Elysian Fields; Fortunate Isles; St. Brendan the Navigator, Voyage of.

For further reading

Vincent H. Cassidy, "Other Fortunate Islands and Some That Were Lost," *Terrae Incognitae* 1 (1969): 35–40; Raymond H. Ramsay, *No Longer on the Map,* 1972.

BOJADOR, CAPE   Dangerous section of the Atlantic coast of North Africa that discouraged European seamen from sailing farther southward. Gil Eanes, while in the service of Prince Henry the Navigator, successfully sailed beyond Cape Bojador in 1434, thus opening the way to further exploration down the coast of Africa.

Cape Bojador was long regarded by late-medieval sailors as the southernmost feasible point of navigation along the Atlantic coast of Africa. They had various reasons to avoid sailing past Cape Bojador. The tropical seas were thought to become boiling hot as one sailed farther into the Torrid Zone. In that region, the sun shone so intensely that people's skins turned black—or so Aristotle and sailor's tales said. Real dangers also faced seafarers who approached Cape Bojador. Between Cape Nun and Cape Juby, the ocean's current was squeezed between the Canary Islands and the African mainland, gaining speed and force. Wind and swells combined with the strong current to create a very heavy surf. Ships sailing along such a coastline would have a difficult time moving farther out to sea. However, sailing ships needed to stay about five miles out to sea to safely clear Cape Juby, a spit of sand extending into the sea for several miles. No promontory warned sailors that they were approaching the cape; instead, mists from the heavy surf and the fine windblown sands of the desert combined to create a haze that often obscured Cape Juby until it was too late. Many unwary ships came to grief there.

After Cape Juby, the current slowed, but the coastline was still pounded by heavy surf. The only serious navigational hazard was a reef that projected over a mile into the sea just north of Cape Bojador, but Cape Bojador is marked by a 70-foot-high red cliff, and sailing ships had plenty of warning before they reached the reef. Compared to Cape Juby, Cape Bojador was easy to sail past. Some scholars suggest that the Cape Bojador of fifteenth-century seamen was more dangerous than modern Cape Juby because the physical hazards ascribed to Cape Bojador by fifteenth-century chroniclers far more accurately describe Cape Juby. Other scholars maintain that the medieval Cape Bojador and the modern one are identical, and that the barriers that kept sailors from passing Cape Bojador were largely psychological.

Other difficulties also discouraged people from venturing past Cape Bojador. Beyond Cape Nun the coastline became desolate and uninhabited. Fifteenth-century chroniclers reported that some sailors saw little point in cruising down a bleak coastline when rich trade opportunities existed farther north and in the Canary Islands. Others worried about how a ship sailing past Cape Bojador would be able to return home. Both winds and currents readily carried a ship south, but how could a ship powered only by sails return home against such strong winds and currents? The early explorers sailed in light barques that the crews could row against the current, but merchant vessels could not, owing to their greater weight and size. Only later was the technique discovered of taking to the high seas on the so-called *volta do mar* as the most efficient way of sailing back to Europe from West Africa.

Both psychological and physical barriers blocked medieval Portuguese sailors from voyaging beyond Cape Bojador. Prince Henry the Navigator was determined to break down the barrier of Cape Bojador as the first major step in his encouragement of African exploration. According to the Portuguese chronicler Gomes Eanes de Zurara, between 1415 and 1433, 15 Portuguese expeditions scouted the African coastline leading up to Cape Bojador. One of these voyages, led by Gonçalo Velho, a member of Prince Henry's household, reached an unidentified place called "Terra Alta" just short of Cape Bojador in 1426. In 1433, another member of the prince's household, Gil Eanes, tried but failed to go beyond the intimidating cape. When Eanes returned home, Prince Henry promised him rewards far greater than any dangers that he might face if he would try again and succeed. Thus properly motivated, Eanes and his crew managed to sail past Cape Bojador in 1434, and an important psychological barrier was broken. By 1448, 51 Portuguese ships had voyaged south of Cape Bojador engaging in trade, including the infamous slave trade, and further exploration. Thanks to Prince Henry the Navigator and Gil Eanes, Portuguese efforts culminated in Bartolomeu Dias's discovery of the Cape of Good Hope in 1487/ 1488 and Vasco da Gama's voyage to India in 1497.

See also

Africa; Canary Islands; Good Hope, Cape of.

For further reading

Bailey W. Diffie and George D. Winius, *Foundations of the Portuguese Empire, 1415–1580*, 1977; J. H. Parry, *The Discovery of the Sea*, 1981.

BOSPORUS   A narrow strait that, along with the Dardanelles, connects the Black Sea with the Aegean Sea and thus separates Europe from Asia. The waters of the Black Sea flow through the Bosporus and ultimately into the Aegean Sea with a strong current. The Bosporus, however, was readily navigable by ancient sailing ships and boats. Furthermore, its waters and those of the neighboring Black Sea and Sea of Marmara (or Propontis) were particularly rich for fishing, and much trade passed through the Bosporus in ancient and medieval times. In A.D. 324, the emperor Constantine built the city of Constantinople on the site of the earlier town of Byzantium along the shores of the Bosporus to take advantage of this strategically and commercially important location. The site possessed a natural harbor, the Golden Horn, and quickly superseded Rome as the center of the Western world. Constantinople and the Bosporus served as the western terminus of the fabled Silk Road into the sixteenth century. The Bosporus and the associated straits of the Dardanelles retained strategic significance into the nineteenth and twentieth centuries.

See also

Black Sea; Constantinople; Dardanelles; Golden Horn.

For further reading

Ellen Churchill Semple, *The Geography of the Mediterranean Region*, 1931.

BOZEMAN TRAIL   John M. Bozeman developed his Bozeman Trail between 1863 and 1865 as a route to take settlers and miners from Fort Sedgewick, Colorado, to the goldfields around Virginia City, Montana. The prospect of large numbers of whites moving across their territories was extremely unwelcome to the local tribes of Native Americans. Such heavy human traffic disrupted hunting and crucially affected their ability to feed themselves. The Teton Sioux, Arapaho, and Cheyenne began attacking parties of whites traveling along the Bozeman Trail in 1865. Their wrath was further aroused when the U.S. Army established Forts Reno, Phil Kearny, and C. F. Smith along the route to provide better protection to the miners and settlers.

From 1866 to 1867, Chief Red Cloud and his warriors successfully made war on the United States. Traffic along the road halted because of the grave danger from attack by hostile tribes, and the garrisons of the three forts came under siege. Most dramatically, on 21 October 1866, the Native Americans destroyed an entire cavalry unit of 80 troopers, called the Fetterman Massacre.

At the same time, American public opinion increasingly favored the Native Americans and opposed the needless expense and human losses caused by the war. In 1868, the United States made peace with Red Cloud, agreeing to abandon the Bozeman Trail and the forts so hated by the Native Americans. After the final defeat of the Sioux in 1877, the Bozeman Trail reopened as an important route for cattle drives.

For further reading
Grace Raymond Hebard and Earl Alonzo Brininstool, *The Bozeman Trail*, 1922.

BRAGMANNI   A group of naked, cave-dwelling wise men who formed one of the many monstrous races thought by ancient and medieval peoples to exist on the fringes of the known world. Their name was obviously derived from that of the Hindu caste of the Brahmans, but some medieval writers clearly differentiated between the Brahmans of India and the imagined Bragmanni. Although they were frequently lumped together with the physically deformed monstrous races, the Bragmanni were normal in appearance. Like the cannibals and the Amazons, the Bragmanni differed from other humans because of their unique lifestyle. Unlike the cannibals and the Amazons, the behavior of the Bragmanni was extraordinarily good, rather than evil or perverted. Medieval Europeans considered the Bragmanni a survival of the lost Golden Age of Humanity or some sort of natural or ur-Christians. The earliest writers located the Bragmanni in India proper, but over time medieval scholars moved them farther east into a land of their own located close to the Terrestrial Paradise. According to *The Travels of Sir John Mandeville*, the land of Bragman housed a utopian society. Alexander the Great threatened to conquer it, but the Bragmanni dissuaded him by pointing out that their only wealth was the peace that prevailed in their land. Given their character as a Golden Age race with an exotic lifestyle, the Bragmanni were frequently merged or confused with a similar group of wise men known as the Gymnosophists.

See also
Alexander the Great, Romances of; Amazons; Cannibals; Gymnosophists; India; Monstrous Races; Paradise, Terrestrial.

BRAZIL
See Hy-Brazil.

BRENDAN'S ISLAND   Also known as the Isle of St. Brendan, European sailors commonly believed that this mythical island was the Land of Promise of the Saints visited by Saint Brendan during his famous voyage. The belief flourished in the Middle Ages and lasted as late as 1759.

Medieval people believed that St. Brendan literally made an Atlantic voyage and that the lovely Land of the Blessed Saints he visited was a real island. It first appeared on a map of the world in Hereford Cathedral made around 1275. Brendan's Island appears as part of the Canary Islands, which were known in classical antiquity. In the 1339 map of Angelino Dulcert of Majorca, the location of Brendan's Island moved to the site of the present-day Madeira Islands, which Europeans had discovered (or rediscovered) during the fourteenth century. About 30 years later, a map by the Pizigani Brothers of Venice (dated 1367) also identified Brendan's Island with the Madeiras. Brendan's Island moved to an area of the Azores after their discovery in 1427. The Venetian mapmaker Andrea Biancho labeled the largest of the islands in the Azores as St. Brendan's on his map of 1448. By 1492, Martin Behaim's globe showed Brendan's Island as a large island located to the west of the Cape Verde Islands, where no such island exists. Later, an English map from 1544 placed Brendan's Island in the middle of the Atlantic at about the same latitude as northern Newfoundland. Gerard Mercator, the great cartographer, adopted this location for Brendan's Island in 1567, and Abraham Ortelius followed him in 1571. There the peripatetic island remained until the middle of the seventeenth century, when it gradually disappeared from maps of the Atlantic. Some people, however, continued to believe that Brendan's Island was a little-known island in the Canaries until at least 1759.

The belief in the existence of Brendan's Island was part of a general late-medieval notion that the Atlantic Ocean was sprinkled with islands such as Antillia and Hy-Brazil. Many were thought to be large and pleasant places that could be visited, without much danger, by the ships of that era. Such beliefs encouraged explorations of the Atlantic by the Portuguese and sailors of other nations.

See also
Atlantic Ocean; Canary Islands; St. Brendan the Navigator, Voyage of.
For further reading
William H. Babcock, *Legendary Islands of the Atlantic,* 1922; Raymond H. Ramsay, *No Longer on the Map,* 1972.

C

CALIFORNIA TRAIL   At different times in North American history, various roads to California have been called the California Trail. The oldest California Trails were the routes up the Baja Peninsula or overland from Sonora. When the Old Spanish Trail from Sante Fe to California opened up in 1776, it was referred to as the California Trail, as were other paths across the Southwest. After 1840, the portion of the Oregon Trail that led to California was sometimes called the California Trail.

See also
   Old Spanish Trail; Oregon Trail.
For further reading
   George R. Stewart, *The California Trail*, 1962.

A Peril of the Plains: The First Emigrant Train to California. *Woodcut after a painting by Frederick Remington.* Century Magazine, *November 1890.*

CAMEL   It is well known that camels are considered "ships of the desert," a metaphor used even by the Koran (ch. XXIII:22). Just as ships made journeys across the sea possible, camels made travel across the deserts of North Africa, Arabia, and central Asia possible throughout most of human history.

Two types of camels exist in the Eastern Hemisphere. Those having only one hump are called Dromedaries *(Camelus dromedarius)*, and two-humped camels are called Bactrians *(Camelus bactrianus)*. Both types are similar in size and skeletal pattern, the basic difference being the number of humps, which represent adaptations to specific environments. Dromedaries, natives of the Syrian and Arabian Deserts, are best adapted to hot, extremely arid conditions. Their one large hump consists of fatty tissue, which is used to sustain the camel during long periods without water and food. Hairier than Dromedaries, Bactrian camels are better adapted to colder, relatively moist climates such as exist in their natural habitat, the mountains and plateaus of central Asia. They also store life-sustaining fat in their two humps, but cannot go without water and food for nearly as long as Dromedaries. Otherwise, the two species are quite similar, sharing a stubborn and ill-tempered nature that is well adapted to life in an extremely harsh environment.

Dromedaries no longer exist in their original wild form. Any wild Dromedaries are the feral descendants of domesticated camels. A few wild Bactrian camels have been discovered in the Altai Mountains of Mongolia, but all other Bactrians are domesticated or feral. Prehistoric peoples first exploited camels by hunting them for meat and hides. Then, some desert or mountain tribes began to keep tame camels in herds until their meat, milk, and hides were needed. Archaeological evidence indicates that Dromedaries were probably first domesticated in southern Arabia between 3000 and 2500 B.C. Domesticated Bactrian camels first made their appearance around 2500 B.C. in the area of northeastern Iran and western Turkmenistan.

The Dromedary has long been the more important as a provider of transportation. Prehistoric peoples living in southern Arabia began to use Dromedaries as riding and pack animals. The Arabic word for a riding camel is *mehari* or *mehri* (may-ah-reé), and pack camels are called *djemel* (jay'-mell). Slowly but surely these practices spread northward to the Syrian Desert as various Arab tribes used the camel to create a nomadic lifestyle in the heretofore uninhabitable desert. Meanwhile, a lucrative trade developed to take southern Arabian incense to the eastern Mediterranean and Mesopotamia, and the nomadic tribes and their camels became the primary providers of transportation for this trade. The producers and merchants of the incense grew rich, but the nomadic Arabs remained poor.

The early camel-using tribes largely remained weak because they lacked effective riding and pack saddles for their ungainly animals. Creating the first serviceable harnesses and saddles for draft, pack, or riding animals was never a simple task, and camels presented a unique and difficult challenge. A saddle for horses and donkeys would not work on a camel because of its hump, so special saddles had to be created. The first adaptation of a camel saddle was the South Arabian saddle, which was placed behind the hump. Unfortunately, the rider's control over his mount was diminished, and as a pack saddle it was inefficient. Another early saddle was the cushion saddle, which placed the rider on top of the hump. The problem was that it provided no support, and riders easily lost their balance and fell off during combat or when the camel galloped.

The nomadic Arabs revolutionized their military and economic position when they developed the North Arabian saddle sometime between 500 and 100 B.C. This saddle was a wooden frame that sat over the hump of the Dromedary, supported by the beast's shoulders, haunches, and rib cage. The rider was firmly supported, and could fight with a lance and sword without undue fear of falling off his mount. In fact, warriors mounted on top of their camels' humps now gained the advantage of height over their adversaries. The North Arabian saddle allowed the nomadic Arabs to become the masters of the caravan trade in incense, and their pack camels could carry much heavier loads. Even before the rise of Islam, great Arabian trading cities appeared at Petra (ca. 300 B.C.–A.D. 100), Palmyra (ca. 50 B.C.–A.D. 273), and Mecca (ca. A.D. 500), and Dromedaries spread from the Arabian Desert to the Sahara in Africa. Nabataean Arabs from Petra apparently first brought Dromedaries to Africa during the last two centuries B.C. for use in the caravan trade between the Nile Valley and the Red Sea. Camel-breeding tribes arose in the deserts east of the Nile River and later spread westward across the Sudan and the Sahara. The caravan trade of the Sahara was largely created by the Dromedary, which also made possible the lifestyle of those ferocious desert tribesmen, the Tuaregs.

The Dromedaries with their efficient North Arabian pack saddles also spread into the highlands of the Middle East in Iran and Afghanistan. Many areas abandoned their traditional Bactrian camels in favor of their single-humped cousins. Dromedaries also became an important part of the transportation network associated with the legendary Silk Road, a route by which caravans traveled to and from China. However, environmental limits to the range of the Dromedary meant that Bactrian camels remained the best suited for traveling in the cold, moister climates of the Asian mountains and high plateaus. A combination of both types of camel was needed to traverse the Silk Road most expeditiously.

Historian Richard Bulliet points out that for many centuries, Dromedaries were more efficient carriers of goods than other draft animals pulling carts and wagons. Horses and donkeys could not pull heavy loads because of inefficient early harnesses that either choked them or failed to fully utilize their pulling power. Because pack camels possessed such an economic advantage, wheeled transportation largely disappeared in those areas of the Middle East and North Africa where camels could flourish. The disappearance of wheeled vehicles also caused existing roads to decline and new ones never to be built. This lack of roads in the Middle East was not a sign of underdevelopment. Instead, Middle Eastern rulers put their resources into building caravanserai at regular intervals, as well as needed bridges. Middle Eastern cities also acquired their characteristic narrow, winding streets. Loaded pack camels could easily negotiate them, and cumbersome carts requiring wider streets were no longer used. Not until the late nineteenth and the twentieth centuries did the pressures of westernization and modernization bring a return of wheeled transport and the accompanying roads. These developments have brought a decline of the pack camel as an important source of transportation after millennia of faithful service.

See also
Caravanserai; Mecca; Sahara; Silk Road; Tuareg.
For further reading
Richard W. Bulliet, *The Camel and the Wheel*, 1975; Juliet Clutton-Brock, *A Natural History of Domesticated Mammals*, 1987; Frederick E. Zeuner, *A History of Domesticated Animals*, 1963.

CAMELOT   The principal residence and castle of King Arthur, it was a relatively late addition to the corpus of the Arthurian legends. Camelot first appeared in the late-twelfth-century writings of Chrétien de Troyes. As time went by, embellishers of the Arthurian legends transformed Camelot into an idealized land consisting of fertile farms, delightful woodlands, a lovely town, and a beautiful castle. By the mid-twentieth century, it had become a place where it never rained (except at night), among other good attributes. Camelot also became a literary allusion for any place where things were perfect, or at least seemed to be.

For further reading
Norris J. Lacy, ed., *The New Arthurian Encyclopedia*, 1996.

CANALS   Artificial inland waterways constructed to link rivers, lakes, and seas to facilitate water transportation. Canals are also used for irrigation, flood control, and sanitation.

Canals used for travel or transportation consisted of two basic types. Lateral canals were simply channels cut between two waterways of equal elevation separated by relatively flat ground. Summit-level canals connected bodies of water separated by terrain of greater elevation, and employed systems of locks to raise or lower canal boats by filling the locks with water. Some summit-level canals used an inclined plane to haul up canal boats or lower them. The inclined-plane system limited the canal boat to a size that could be readily winched up or down.

Most canals consisted largely of artificially created channels. The tremendous amounts of earth that needed moving was done by the muscle power of men and beasts throughout most of human history. Expensive to build, canals also required ongoing maintenance to keep locks in repair, and channels had to be dredged to prevent silting up and keep canal walls from collapsing. Because canals were constructed as level waterways, except at locks, they had little or no water current. Towpaths were constructed to allow men or animals to pull the canal boats along.

1907 picture of a fisherman in the Grand Canal, Peking, China.

The idea of building a canal is very ancient. Anytime someone looked at two bodies of water and wished they were connected, they built a canal in their minds. The ancient Egyptians built or attempted to build a canal between the Nile River and the Gulf of Suez several times. Various Roman emperors or Muslim caliphs periodically reopened the canal before the modern Suez Canal was built in the mid-nineteenth century. China's famous Grand Canal linking Peking to Hangchow took 2,000 years to construct, and it periodically fell into disrepair. The great Julius Caesar (100–44 B.C.) contemplated building a canal across the Isthmus of Corinth, but his assassination ended that project.

Europeans began to build canals systematically in the seventeenth century, with the French leading the way. Leonardo da Vinci (1452–1519) toyed with the engineering problems associated with canal building, but not for another century was the political and economic atmosphere right for implementing some of his ideas. In 1642, the French constructed the 34-mile-long Canal de Briare, which connected the Loire and Seine Rivers using 41 locks, based on da Vinci's designs. Even more impressive was the Canal du Midi, connecting the Bay of Biscay on the Atlantic coast of France with the Mediterranean Sea. It cut across the hitherto isolated province of Languedoc, greatly increasing its economic prosperity. Built between 1660 and 1681, it was 140 miles in length and used 103 locks. This marvel of construction later inspired various Americans, including Thomas Jefferson, to build such canals in the new and underdeveloped United States.

England entered the canal age in 1755 with the Sankey Brook Canal for carrying coal to Liverpool. Even more impressive was the canal built by the duke of Bridgewater between 1759 and 1761 to carry coal to Manchester. Thereafter, enthusiasm and competition over canal building quickly grew into a craze, which reached its height between 1768 and 1776. The Grand Trunk, or Trent and Mersey Canal, linked the east and west coasts of northern England by connecting the Trent and Mersey Rivers with 94 miles of canal. Commencing in 1766 and completed in 1777, the Grand Trunk Canal soon had various tributary canals attaching themselves to it, and internal transportation and travel were greatly facilitated. By 1790, the total length of English canals reached 2,223 miles, primarily for carrying coal and agricultural products, although some used them for travel.

The canal craze came late to the United States because of the country's lack of capital and engineering expertise. Improved transportation and communication between the eastern seaboard and the undeveloped but rich lands of the Ohio and upper Mississippi River valley were greatly needed, but

American canal builders faced the problem of crossing the Appalachian Mountains. Schemes to link the Potomac and Susquehanna Rivers with the Ohio River proved to be prohibitively expensive engineering nightmares.

One promising area was the Mohawk River valley of upstate New York, which became the site of the famous Erie Canal linking the Hudson River and New York City with the Great Lakes. Constructed between 1817 and 1825, it was 363 miles long with 83 locks. All sorts of goods traveled up and down the Erie Canal, promoting economic growth in New York and the United States. Elegant passenger boats soon appeared on the canal, carrying people in great comfort at a leisurely pace. The Erie Canal was a tremendous success that generated respectable profits from the very start and catapulted New York City into the position of being the most populous and prosperous of American cities.

Others tried to emulate the Erie Canal's success, but neither the Chesapeake and Ohio Canal nor the Pennsylvania Main Line Canal were able to match even a small fraction of the Erie's success. Farther west, the states of Ohio, Indiana, and Michigan built canal systems that attached to the Erie. The state of Ohio's Ohio and Erie Canal connected the Great Lakes with the Ohio River in 1845. This and other Ohio canals were generally successful. Illinois also had good results from constructing canals linking the Mississippi River with Lake Michigan, greatly enhancing Chicago's prosperity. Indiana did not fare so well. Its Wabash and Erie Canal was started in 1836 and completed in 1853. At a length of 450 miles, it was the longest canal in the United States, but it put the state some $13 million in debt.

All-American canal project—the Imperial Dam, California and Arizona. View upstream along channels 23 and 24. Photograph by Benjamin D. Glaha, 22 February 1939.

The rise of railroads undermined the profitability of all canals to some extent after 1860. Even earlier, financial interests had begun to shift from constructing canals to building railroads. Railroads were faster and less subject to the elements, but even more expensive to build than canals. Competition from railroads halted the canal boom in Ohio by the 1850s, and closed down the luckless Wabash and Erie by 1872.

Strong canals like the Erie held their own much longer, although transporting bulk goods increasingly became their source of revenue. The canals' elegant passenger service was phased out because of competition from the much faster passenger trains. The same process occurred among the industrial nations of Europe.

The canal-building boom ended in the 1850s, although existing canals carried goods for many years afterward. Today, goods travel by canal in only a few areas. In their day, the canals helped to bind the young United States together as a nation and foster economic development of this country as well as European nations. Vestiges of canals are scattered across the landscape in the northeastern and lower midwestern United States and in many parts of Europe.

See also
Erie Canal; Grand Canal; Mississippi River; Nile River.
For further reading
Russell Bourne, *Floating West*, 1992; E. R. C. Hadfield, *British Canals*, 1979; Alvin F. Harlow, *Old Towpaths*, 1926; Ronald E. Shaw, *Canals for a Nation*, 1990.

CANARY ISLANDS   Pleasant archipelago located approximately 60 miles off the coast of Morocco and extending another 400 miles westward. Juba II, the king of Mauretania (25 B.C.–A.D. 23) sent an expedition to the islands and gave them the name of Canary because of the race of large dogs (Latin, *canis*) that inhabited the island of Gran Carnaria. The ancients also considered the islands to be the fabled Fortunate Isles.

The Canaries consist of seven large islands and six small islands of volcanic origin. Proceeding from east to west, the large islands are: Lanzarota, Fuerteventura, Gran Canaria, Tenerife, Gomera, La Palma, and Hierro. Lanzarota and Fuerteventura in the east are rather arid due to their lack of mountains high enough to create rain. The five western islands are quite mountainous (Mount Tiede, a dormant volcano on Tenerife, rises to an elevation of 12,152 feet) and so are well watered and verdant. Of the several island groups in the Atlantic, only the Canaries were inhabited prior to the arrival of Europeans in the fourteenth century. The aboriginal Canarians were collectively known as the Guanches, although some writers claim that the term referred only to the warlike natives of Tenerife. The first Guanches arrived in the islands no earlier than the second millennium B.C. European sources describe them as white, although some appeared more swarthy, and they were generally tall and agile.

Guanches were obviously emigrants from the pre-Arabic Berber population of North Africa, but how they got to the Canaries is a mystery. The waters between the Canaries and the mainland of Africa are tricky to navigate but are by no means impossible for light craft. Once the Guanches arrived on the Canaries, they apparently lost all knowledge of seafaring, so that eventually even interisland communication no longer existed. By the time medieval Europeans came to the Canaries in the fourteenth century, the Guanche population was 80,000–100,000, with La Palma, Tenerife, and Gran Canaria the most heavily populated.

The ancient Carthaginians, who sailed the west coast of Africa, undoubtedly knew about the Canaries, but they were highly reticent about their geographical knowledge. As a result, the ancient Greeks had only a vague awareness of these islands. During the Roman Empire era, the Canaries briefly entered the orbit of the Mediterranean world when King Juba II's expedition returned from the Canaries with a detailed description. Later, the geographer Claudius Ptolemy (fl. second century A.D.) used the islands as the prime meridian of his grid system of mathematical cartography. Classical maps, however, indicated only two islands, not seven. The collapse of the Roman Empire resulted in medieval Europeans losing their knowledge of the Canaries.

During the early Middle Ages, Muslim cartographers continued to use the Canaries as the prime meridian on their grid maps, but direct contact was largely lost. The medieval Arab seafarers known as the Maghrurín, or Wanderers of Lisbon, came across an inhabited but unidentified island during their voyage on the Atlantic that may have been one of the Canaries. It is probable that the Vivaldi brothers stopped off at the Canaries during their ill-fated voyage of no return in 1291.

European contact with the Canaries was restored when the Genoese Lanzarotto Malocello and Nicoloso de Recco visited the islands in 1336 and 1341. These voyages in the service of Portugal marked the beginning of European attempts to conquer the islands. Several unsuccessful efforts were made to settle the islands, and Malocello died at the hands of the natives when he tried to create a permanent settlement. A Portuguese settlement existed on Lanzarota from 1370 until 1385, when a native uprising destroyed it. Meanwhile, Castilian adventurers reconnoitered the Canaries. Permanent conquest began in 1402 when Norman knights loosely associated with Castille arrived under the command of Jean de Béthencourt. They conquered Lanzarota, Fuerteventura, and Hierro; Gomera was conquered soon after. The Portuguese kept trying to conquer the Canaries for themselves between 1416 and 1466, but to no avail. They also tried to dislodge the Normans and Castilians from their conquests, and occasionally even aided the Guanches in their struggle against Castilian conquest. The Treaty of Alcaçovas in 1479 between Castille and Portugal resulted in the latter power giving up all claim to the Canaries in exchange for a recognition of its monopoly over European trade with Guinea in West Africa. This agreement eased the way for the completion of the Castilian conquest of the islands. Gran Canaria fell in 1483, followed by La Palma in 1493 and Tenerife in 1496, even though the Guanches mounted a heroic and determined resistance. European settlement quickly resulted in the extinction of the Guanches as a distinct ethnic group. Diseases introduced from the mainland drastically reduced the native population, as did the European practice of selling the Guanches into slavery and shipping them off. The survivors were absorbed into the growing population of Castilian immigrants.

The Canaries were conveniently located to serve as a waystation for Spanish ships sailing to the Americas, thanks to the pattern of winds and currents in that part of the Atlantic Ocean. Columbus stopped off at Gomera during his first voyage of 1492 and again during his second voyage in 1493. Thousands of other Spanish ships followed suit over the centuries. Many residents of the Canaries participated in the Spanish settlement of the Americas, developing reputations as great travelers willing to go far away for long periods of time to make their fortunes in Latin America. As the twentieth century progresses, tourism is increasingly important to the Canaries. Their beauty and springlike climate make them a favored site for Europeans seeking a restful vacation.

See also
Carthage; Fortunate Isles.
For further reading
Alfred W. Crosby, *Ecological Imperialism*, 1986; John Mercer, *The Canary Islands*, 1973; Henry Myhill, "Canary Islands," in *The Sea*, vol. 3, 1974; Charles Verlinden, "Canary Islands and Béthencourt," in *Dictionary of the Middle Ages*, 1982–1989.

CANNIBALS
Man-eating peoples almost universally thought to inhabit the peripheries of the known world along with other monstrous races of humans. Cannibals terrorized and consumed their hapless neighbors and innocent travelers, according to numerous tales and legends through the centuries and into the present. Until the sixteenth century, cannibals were known by their Greek name of anthrophagi (man-eaters). Christopher Columbus coined the name cannibal, and it quickly became the word for man-eating humans in the various languages of Europe. The idea that such humans exist was almost universal among the many cultures of the world. Explorers, travelers, missionaries, geographers, and ethnographers frequently heard tales of cannibals in distant and ill-defined locations. Some suggest that accusations of cannibalism are simply a means to dehumanize an enemy, whether internal (witches) or external (cannibal tribes). Supposedly, such accusations are unfounded, and cannibalism has quite literally never existed in any human society. Other scholars reject these contentions and assert that certain peoples have indubitably practiced cannibalism, such as the Aztecs and some tribes of highland New Guinea.

Cannibals form part of that group of peoples known as the monstrous races. From ancient times to well into the sixteenth century, the monstrous races were thought to live at or beyond the edges of the known world. Generally, cannibals are normal humans who engage in the repellent custom of eating their fellow humans. Some are said to eat the dead of their own families, known as endocannibalism. It is usually practiced by eating or drinking some ash from

New Guinea tribesmen, feared by Westerners as cannibals. Stereoscopic image by Keystone, 1919.

the cremated bodies of dead family members, and is often merely symbolic. Other cannibals, however, ate strangers or neighboring enemies, known as exocannibalism. All forms of cannibalism are practiced in a highly ritualistic manner with much accompanying symbolism, because gaining mere nourishment has little to do with it. Instead, cannibalism is the magical acquisition of power, strength, courage, and wisdom from a dead and devoured enemy. Needless to say, any people practicing exocannibalism were particularly feared by their neighbors and posed a hideous threat to travelers and visitors.

Not all cannibals were normal humans in their physical appearance. Some of Odysseus's men fell victim to the man-eating Cyclops Polyphemus, and the rest barely escaped his hunger. Other Cyclopes also practiced cannibalism, as did the savage giants known as the Lystraegonians. Giants were commonly thought to be cannibals, as clearly illustrated by the fairy tale of "Jack and the Beanstalk," in which Jack narrowly evades becoming the main course in the giant's supper. Several Christian saints avoided being eaten by menacing cynocephali by converting them to Christianity. Christian cynocephali always eschewed cannibalism, and sometimes took on the appearance of normal humans after becoming Christian. Medieval scholars frequently associated cannibalism with descent from the accursed Cain, the first murderer, or Ham, the execrable disrespecter of his father Noah. The connection of Ham with cannibalism also served to connect his supposed descendants, the inhabitants of Africa, with cannibalism in the minds of many medieval Christians.

Cannibals could be found anywhere that was not properly civilized in the minds of the people making the accusation. Herodotus located cannibals or anthrophagi to the north of Scythia. Pliny the Elder followed Herodotus and located cannibals in the same general place. Medieval German geographers and historians Ragewin, in his *Gesta Friderici* (after 1156), and Gunther of Pairis, in his *Ligurinus* (1186), claimed that the ferocious peoples of Scandinavia and farther north were cannibals. The harsh climate of those lands supposedly precluded any significant agriculture, thereby forcing the inhabitants to engage in the predatory activities of piracy and cannibalism. These northern cannibals did not even scruple at killing and eating family members. Several centuries later, in 1448, the German Benedictine cartographer Andreas Walsperger of Constance again placed cannibals in the far north of his *mappamundi*. The *mappamundi* in the Hereford Cathedral located its cannibals in northeast Asia. Other medieval writers also located cannibals in the Far East, while some writers placed them in Africa.

Since cannibals and other monstrous races were always located at the edges of the known world, it is not surprising that Columbus thought he had found cannibals in the fierce Carib tribes. Columbus's original conception was that he would sail west until he reached Asia. When he got to the outlying islands of the Americas, he thought they were islands off the eastern coast of Asia. According to medieval traditions, those lands were the abode of monstrous races, including cannibals. When the friendly Tainos, or Arawaks, told Columbus that the Caribs were man-eaters, Columbus was programmed by the lore of medieval European geography to believe such reports. His greatest confusion was his failure to sight any other monstrous races.

Thanks to Columbus and the Taino/Arawaks, the Caribs became the archetypal cannibals, and their very name became the source for the word *cannibal*. Taino had several dialects, and in one the Caribs were known as *canibas* or *canibalés*. From these Taino words came the new word *cannibal*, meaning man-eating human. Variations of the word quickly entered the major languages of Europe and supplanted the older word *anthrophagi*. Ironically, considerable acrimonious debate continues among modern scholars about whether or not the Caribs were truly cannibals. The Taino/Arawaks had their own reasons for wanting to blacken the reputations of the Caribs, and in turn, the Spaniards were eager to believe them since it was lawful to make war on cannibals and enslave them. The number of man-eating tribes encountered by the Spanish multiplied and became suspiciously high as their need for forced labor increased. At the same time, recent research bears out the truth of claims by early-sixteenth-century travelers that the Tupinamba Indians of Brazil practiced cannibalism. Their cannibalism formed part of an elaborate ritual of vengeance that focused on enemy captives.

During the eighteenth and nineteenth centuries, cannibalism was considered to be a common threat to explorers, travelers, and missionaries traveling in Africa, South America, and the Pacific islands. The practice of cannibalism, however, was far less common than once thought. The image of white hunters, missionaries, or other travelers being placed in a large pot for consumption by a waiting cannibal tribe is largely, if not entirely, a fantasy.

See also
Cyclopes; Cynocephali; Herodotus; Mappamundi; Monstrous Races; Odysseus, Wanderings of; Pliny the Elder; Scythia.

For further reading
William Arens, *The Man-Eating Myth*, 1979; Hans Askenasy, *Cannibalism*, 1994; D. W. Forsyth, "The Beginning of Brazilian Anthropology," *Journal of Anthropological Research* 39 (1983): 147–178; John Block Friedman, *The Monstrous Races in Medieval Art and Thought*, 1981; Peggy Reeves Sanday, *Divine Hunger*, 1986.

CANTERBURY
Cathedral city for the archbishop of Canterbury and the most important pilgrimage site in England, it was settled by the prehistoric Britons before 200 B.C. St. Augustine of Canterbury made it his cathedral city shortly after A.D. 597. During the early Middle Ages, Canterbury served as an important cultural and educational center. Its true fame dates to 29 December 1170, when knights of King Henry II murdered Archbishop Thomas à Becket in his own cathedral. Miracles soon followed Becket's martyrdom, and the church canonized him in 1173. His tomb was initially located in the crypt, but in 1228 was moved behind the altar of the cathedral. Thousands of pilgrims, often bringing rich gifts, gravitated to the shrine during the later Middle Ages. Geoffrey Chaucer immortalized the institution of taking a pilgrimage to Canterbury in his *Canterbury Tales* (ca. 1388), and housing and feeding pilgrims became an important aspect of Canterbury's economy. Henry VIII and his minister Thomas Cromwell suppressed the shrine of St. Thomas à Becket at Canterbury in 1538, ending a centuries-old tradition of pilgrimage. Nevertheless, travelers never stopped visiting lovely Canterbury.

See also
Pilgrimage.

For further reading
John Butler, *The Quest for Becket's Bones*, 1995.

CARAVANS
A group of merchants or pilgrims who band together in an organized group for mutual protection and assistance during the course of their journey. Caravans were used extensively along the Silk Road across central Asia and the trade routes across the Arabian and Sahara Deserts.

Traveling as a caravan involved organization and rules. Saharan caravans organized themselves by appointing a leader known as a *khabir*. The *khabir* had authority over the whole caravan, but he was also responsible for any losses of life or property that occurred as a result of his negligence or incompetence. Merchants selected men to be *khabirs* who knew the desert routes, the locations of water holes and oases, navigation by night, methods of healing sickness and injuries, and the art of negotiating with towns and tribes along the way. *Khabirs* were installed by a formal ceremony involving readings from the Koran.

In Arabia and the Sahara, all members of the caravan would be Muslims. As a group of believers, they formed a religious congregation, and they appointed a muezzin to call them to prayer and an *imam* to lead them in prayer. Each caravan also included a scribe to keep records of transactions, especially any buying and selling, that occurred between members. If a member of the caravan died en route, the scribe sold off his goods and turned over the proceeds to the *khabir* for safekeeping until they could be given to the heirs. Sometimes caravans employed special guides called *takshifs* to help them get through particularly tricky or dangerous parts of the desert.

Caravans were generally all-male societies, and the members frequently swore oaths of chastity. While on the move, caravans traveled to music and readings of the Koran. Various tribes preyed on caravans when they had the opportunity, and Tuaregs were the great menace to travelers across the Sahara. In Arabia, Shiite tribes of the high desert raided caravans, particularly those of Sunni Muslims, whenever and wherever political and military control was weak. The long Silk Road suffered from depredations by numerous isolated tribes and brigands, but a well-organized and well-armed caravan was generally able to protect itself. Sometimes treachery threatened a caravan's survival.

Camel caravan in India, ca. 1924.

Occasionally a dishonest *khabir* sold out the caravan he was leading to the Tuaregs. Sandstorms and thirst were great dangers to caravans, as were the cold and snows of the central Asian mountains. Western Saharan caravans occasionally ran out of water, with disastrous results, and entire parties of over a thousand people were known to have perished miserably. If traveling in a caravan was hazardous, traveling alone or in groups too small was almost suicidal.

For thousands of years, caravans were the safest and surest way to travel the inhospitable wastelands of central Asia and the deserts of North Africa and Arabia. Today, the great caravans of the Silk Road and the Sahara are no more. Technology in the form of motorized vehicles has rendered them obsolete and unneeded.

See also
Sahara; Sandstorm; Silk Road; Tuareg.
For further reading
Roland Oliver, ed., *The Cambridge History of Africa*, vol. 3, 1981.

CARAVANSERAI
Waystations or hostelries built at periodic intervals along the trade routes of the Islamic world to provide shelter, supplies, and protection to travelers and caravans. In Turkish areas such as Anatolia, caravanserai are called *han*. Caravanserai located in cities are called *khans* in the eastern Islamic world and *funduqs* (also funduks or fonduks) along the coast of North Africa.

Caravanserai, khans, and funduqs have been described as the Islamic equivalent of American motels with their provision of shelter, food, water, and a stable all-in-one establishment. The origins of caravanserai are pre-Islamic. Herodotus, the ancient Greek historian, described how the Achaemenid Persian king Cyrus the Great built waystations along his system of royal roads. Christian churches in the medieval Byzantine Empire provided accommodations to needy strangers in buildings called *pandocheion*, from which the word *funduq* derives. Establishments like caravanserai and funduqs filled an obvious need. Ancient and medieval trade routes were well used, and at the same time traversed miles of inhospitable territory. Caravanserai provided several needed services: shelter, food, water, and protection.

Almost all caravanserai share a common architectural plan: they are large square buildings of at least two stories, with a large, open courtyard in the center. Generally, only one gate, big enough for a fully loaded camel to pass through, provided entry into the caravanserai and its courtyard. The bottom floor of the building was used for stables and bulk storage, while guests and their more valuable goods occupied rooms in the upper floors. All caravanserai contained a water supply. Larger establishments included a bathhouse, special rooms for very important guests, a resident staff, and special shops such as bakeries and tea rooms. The architecture of the caravanserai may have evolved from fortress architecture. Roman frontier forts and a type of Islamic monastery-fortress called a *ribat* appear to have inspired the floor plans of caravanserai. The urban khans and funduqs were almost identical to caravanserai in their floor plans, which

Caravansary of Mayer. Lithograph by Eugene Flandin from Voyage en Perse, *1840–1841.*

consisted of an enclosed courtyard with one entry gate. Khans and funduqs devoted more space to shops and warehouses, and less to stables. They also served as secure quarters for merchants, including foreign merchants. Various Italian merchants occupied funduqs in major North African ports, the earliest being the Pisan funduq at Tangier. Khans and funduqs allowed merchants to close their gates and secure their persons, goods, and shops against the dangers of urban rioting. The Turkish han represents an exception to the basic architectural plan of the caravanserai by having some or all of its courtyard covered and transformed into a great hall. The gates of hans also tended to be highly ornate.

Few examples of caravanserai, khans, and funduqs survive. The modernization of Islamic cities and the decline of the caravan routes caused them to be abandoned or torn down to make way for other buildings. In their day, caravanserai and khans were an integral and ubiquitous part of travel in the Islamic world, as the testimony of travelers like Ibn Battuta make clear.

See also
Caravans; Roads, Persian; Silk Road.
For further reading
Eleanor Sims, "Markets and Caravanserai," in *Architecture of the Islamic World*, 1978.

CARTHAGE   Ancient city-state located on the coastline of what is now Tunisia, Carthage was famous for its skilled sailors and merchants and its monumental conflicts with Rome in the three Punic Wars.

The Phoenician city of Tyre founded Carthage between 800 and 750 B.C. Blessed with a fine harbor and fertile hinterlands, the city blossomed into the most successful of the Phoenician settlements, achieving independence by the sixth century B.C. Carthaginian influence spread through the western Mediterranean. It has been said that, of all the ancient states, trade was most crucial to the well-being of Carthage. Territorial and trading rivalries brought the Carthaginians into conflict with the Greek colonies in the western Mediterranean. Although the Carthaginians were able to maintain fairly tight control over the Strait of Gibraltar and the Spanish coastline, they fought a series of seesaw wars with the Greeks of Sicily, which ultimately brought the Carthaginians into a series of disastrous wars with Rome. Rome won a marginal victory in the first Punic War (264–242 B.C.). The brutal and monumental second Punic War (218–201 B.C.) resulted in Carthage's definitive defeat. For the most part, the final destruction of Carthage in the third Punic War (149–146 B.C.) was a botched mopping-up operation.

At their height, the Carthaginians ruled the waves in the western Mediterranean and eastern Atlantic coasts of Europe and Africa. They maintained an effective monopoly over seaborne trade and jealously guarded the Strait of Gibraltar from incursions by interlopers. Not content just to keep their trade routes and discoveries a close secret, they also spread geographical disinformation in the form of terrifying tales about sea monsters, huge storms, and curdled seas. It is difficult to separate the impressive achievements of the Carthaginians from those of the Phoenicians in general. The famous voyages of Hanno and Himilco, however, were definitely Carthaginian. Although it is doubtful they reached the Americas (some fringe scholars maintain they did), the Carthaginians rank among the boldest voyagers of the ancient world. They certainly put their Roman conquerors to shame when it came to achievements in travel and discovery.

See also

Atlantic Ocean; Hanno, Voyage of; Himilco, Voyage of; Mediterranean Sea.

For further reading

S. Lancel, *Carthage*, 1995; B. H. Warmington, *Carthage*, 1960.

CASTAWAYS AND MAROONS

Seamen and passengers who were shipwrecked or abandoned on desolate and isolated coasts and islands, often for years at a time. The danger of sea travelers becoming castaways or maroons was significant into the early twentieth century.

These terms are frequently used interchangeably; however, *castaway* most accurately refers to people shipwrecked on an unfamiliar shore. The familiar fictional characters in *Robinson Crusoe* and *Swiss Family Robinson* are good examples of castaways. On the other hand, *maroons* are people deliberately abandoned by their fellow crewmen on some remote shore. Some maroonings were involuntary. In 1568, Sir John Hawkins was forced to maroon some of his men on the Gulf Coast of Mexico after fighting his way out of the harbor of San Juan de Ulloa. His own ship was too overloaded with men from other ships in his fleet to risk sailing on the high seas, so excess passengers needed to be put ashore. Spanish authorities captured most of these English maroons, but a small party, including David Ingram, incredibly made its way across North America to Newfoundland and rescue. Other maroons were victims of pirates, who abandoned unwanted prisoners on some remote coastline. Pirates and other seamen frequently used marooning as a punishment for a serious infraction of the rules of the sea. A maroon was given the choice of death or abandonment. Death was often the first choice. One famous voluntary maroon was Alexander Selkirk (1676–1721). Serving as the master of the warship *Cinque Ports*, Selkirk quarreled incessantly with the ship's captain. Finally, in exasperation he asked to be put ashore on Juan Fernandez Island off the coast of Chile in October 1704. Expecting to be alone for only a few months, Selkirk lived as a maroon for four years before he was rescued. His story became the inspiration for Daniel Defoe's *Robinson Crusoe* (1719).

The condition of being a castaway is as ancient as sea travel. The fictional Odysseus and Sindbad both suffered being castaways numerous times. St. Paul was shipwrecked and a castaway on Malta. Sometimes castaways received caring treatment from the people on shore. Other times, they were most inhospitably enslaved or murdered. In 1707 a squadron of the royal navy blundered into the Scilly Islands in the fog, causing several ships to wreck with great loss of life. When the flagship *Association* went down, all but two people drowned. One of the two fortunates who managed to crawl onto the beach was the admiral Sir Clowdisley Shovell. Back on land, his luck ran out—a Cornish woman murdered him for his emerald ring—so much for charity toward those who went down to the sea in ships.

Alvar Núñez Cabeza de Vaca (1490–1556) is one of the best-known castaways. Shipwrecked on Galveston Island, Texas, in November 1528, Cabeza de Vaca was initially enslaved by his Native American hosts. Later, he developed a reputation as a healer and traveled around Texas as a peddler. By the spring of 1536, his wanderings took him farther into the southwestern part of the present-day United States and northern Mexico, where he encountered the Spanish expedition that rescued him.

Another horrific episode of castaways involved the survivors of the whaling ship *Essex*. Hunting whales in the central Pacific Ocean between the Hawaiian Islands and the Galápagos Islands, an enraged whale rammed and sank the *Essex* on 20 November 1820. Only three whaleboats remained, filled with the surviving crew. After three months at sea with a one-week stop at Henderson Island in the Pitcairn group, only eight crew members remained alive. Thirst and starvation had claimed the others, and those still living were forced to engage in cannibalism of the dead. The true story of the *Essex* inspired Herman Melville to write his classic novel *Moby-Dick* (1851) with its eponymous avenging white whale.

Tales of castaways and maroons provided perennially popular reading for armchair travelers. Enduring years of privation and isolation, surviving castaways and maroons exemplify self-reliance and perseverance of the highest levels. They also illustrate the very precarious nature of sea travel throughout most of human history.

See also
Odysseus, Wanderings of; Pirates; St. Paul, Missionary Journeys of; Sindbad, The Seven Voyages of.

For further reading
Edward E. Leslie, *Desperate Journeys, Abandoned Souls,* 1988.

CATHAY   Name for China commonly used during the Middle Ages by Europeans, particularly Marco Polo. Cathay was a land of fabulous wealth, exotic customs, and strange plants and animals. The name derived from the Khitan, a nomadic tribe from Manchuria. Beginning in 907, they invaded China and conquered considerable territory in the north, where they established themselves as the Liao dynasty. In 1114, the Khitan Empire in China was attacked by an alliance of a new nomadic tribe called the Jurchen and the Sung dynasty of southern China, and by 1124 the Khitan kingdom in China was no more. A remnant of the once-great empire fled into central Asia, where they established the Kara-Khitai Empire. In China, all that remained of the Khitans was their name. Europeans referred to China as Cathay well into the sixteenth century. Only after the expansion of their geographical knowledge did Europeans realize that the China of the sixteenth-century Ming dynasty was the same land as Marco Polo's thirteenth-century Cathay.

For further reading
Boies Penrose, *Travel and Discovery in the Early Renaissance,* 1955; Robert Silverberg, *The Realm of Prester John,* 1972.

CENTAURS   A mythological race having the head and torso of a man and the body of a horse. The ancient Greeks commonly associated centaurs with remote Thessaly. Because of their hybrid nature, centaurs were regarded by the Greeks as violent, lustful, and undisciplined creatures prone to rape, drunkenness, and unprovoked attack.

Many scholars believe that tales about centaurs or centaurlike creatures are the result of horse-riding peoples coming into contact with non-horse-riding peoples. Throughout history, non-horse-riding peoples at first viewed horse and rider as one creature; certainly, that is how the pre-Conquest Mexicans viewed Hernán Cortés and his cavalry in 1518. Because the first people to domesticate horses were the nomadic barbarian tribes of the steppe regions of Russia, it is not surprising that centaurs and uncivilized behavior became associated with each other in the minds of the more sedentary Greeks. Out of such encounters grew the legends of the centaurs that titillated Greeks traveling beyond what they considered the civilized world.

See also
Horse.

CHENG HO (OR ZHENG HO), VOYAGES OF (1405–1433)   The

early Ming emperors of China sponsored this series of seven voyages under the command of the grand eunuch Cheng Ho. The Ming fleet sailed from Nanking for the Indian Ocean and reached as far as Mecca in Arabia and Mogadishu and Malindi in East Africa.

The Ming Dynasty established itself in China in 1368 by ousting the hated Mongol conquerors. Under Ming rule, China experienced one of its greatest eras of power and prosperity. The early Ming emperors manifested their great power by sending military expeditions to demand tribute from distant princelings and potentates. Cheng Ho's expeditions provide the most dramatic example of such Ming diplomatic activity.

Cheng Ho (ca. 1371–ca. 1433/1436) was born as Ma San-po in Yunnan Province. His family was possibly Turkish or Mongol, and may have formed part of the local Mongol garrison. They were Muslims, as is indicated by their surname Ma, which is Chinese for Muhammad. Both Cheng Ho's father and grandfather also claimed the title of Haji, which shows that they had made the pilgrimage to Mecca. In 1381, Cheng Ho was recruited for service in the emperor's palace and became a eunuch at the age of ten. The operation apparently did not stunt Cheng Ho's growth; family tradition credited him with being seven feet tall and having a waist of five feet around. He was assigned to the service of Prince Chéng Tsu (or Chu ti, who later became the emperor Yung-lo, or Yongle), where he performed great deeds as a warrior during the campaigns against the Mongols and Chéng Tsu's successful revolt against his brother in 1402. After taking on the new name of Yung-lo, the new emperor renamed his faithful eunuch Cheng and gave him the title of Grand Eunuch and the office of Superintendent of the Office of Eunuchs.

On 11 July 1405, Yung-lo commanded Cheng Ho to make the first of his seven great maritime expeditions. The destination was the Indian Ocean, or Western Ocean, as the Chinese called it. The reason for the expedition is not clear. Some sources claim that its purpose was to search for the deposed emperor Chien-wen (Jianwen), who may have escaped the burning of his palace by rebel forces. The search must not have been too important, because little time was spent looking for the fugitive during the expedition. A more plausible and substantial reason for this and the following expeditions was the emperor's desire to demonstrate his power unquestionably to various foreign states and so enhance his prestige, both at home and abroad. For a Chinese emperor, Yung-lo had an unconventionally strong interest in foreign affairs and expansion, which was probably encouraged by Cheng Ho and his associates.

Cheng Ho's first expedition, like those that followed, was fitted out at Nanking, and consisted of 317 vessels and 27,870 crew and soldiers. Sixty-two of the ships were the so-called treasure ships, which were reported to be 452 feet long and 183 feet wide and carried crews of 600 men. Such vessels were far larger than the biggest ships in the fleets of Columbus and Vasco da Gama. After leaving Nanking, this fleet and those that followed sailed to the mouth of the Min River in Fukien Province to await favorable monsoon winds in January and February to carry the fleet to the coast of Indochina. On this first expedition, Cheng Ho's vast armada visited Champa, Java, Ceylon, and finally Calicut on the Indian subcontinent. Calicut, an important depot in the pepper trade, was the principal destination of the voyage. Along the way, the Chinese picked up exotic products and treasures, and arranged for foreign embassies to visit the Ming capital at Nanking. During the return voyage, Cheng Ho's force stopped at Palembang, where it defeated and captured the renegade Chinese pirate Chèn Tsu'i and killed 5,000 of his men. Such an action affirmed the preponderance of Ming military might to the local rulers and simultaneously freed the seas of a dangerous predator. On 2 October 1407, the fleet arrived back at Nanking, where the emperor ordered the execution of the hapless Chèn Tsu'i.

Yung-lo was apparently pleased with the results of Cheng Ho's expedition, because he ordered a second one almost immediately, in late 1407. Cheng Ho did not accompany this fleet of 249 ships, which probably departed Nanking in January 1408. Its mission was simply to attend the installation of Mana Vikrama as the new king of Calicut. Little else was accomplished, and the fleet returned to China during the late summer of 1409. Meanwhile, yet a third expedition had been ordered during late January or early February 1409, and Cheng Ho assumed personal command of this fleet of 48 ships and some 30,000 crewmen. The flotilla left the Nanking area during October or early November 1409 and caught the monsoons at Fukien in January 1410. It visited Champa, Java, Malacca, Ceylon, Cochin, and Calicut, but its outstanding accomplishment was the defeat and capture of the Sinhalese king Alagakkonara on Ceylon. Cheng Ho carried him back to Nanking on 6 July 1411, where the emperor ordered his release—but not before a new king was put into place. Once again, the strength of the Chinese military clearly manifested itself, this time to the states of the Indian subcontinent.

On 18 December 1412, the emperor ordered a fourth expedition to be prepared with 63 ships and 28,560 crew. It left Nanking in the fall of 1413 and caught the monsoon at Fukien in January 1414. Besides stopping at the usual ports of call, the expedition also visited the Maldives Islands and Hormuz in the Persian Gulf. This action marked the first time that the Chinese ventured beyond India. A subsidiary expedition also traveled to Bengal. On its way home, the expedition descended on Sumatra, where it carried out imperial orders and defeated the usurper Sekander of Semudera and restored Sultan Zain Al-Abidin as the rightful ruler. On 12 August 1415, the fleet returned home, where the emperor ordered the execution of the captive Sekander. For a second time, Chinese military superiority was manifestly demonstrated in Southeast Asia, and the Chinese naval presence expanded even farther into the Indian Ocean.

Ming naval expansion continued with the ordering of a fifth maritime expedition on 28 December 1416. The fleet departed in the fall of 1417 with the ostensible purpose of escorting ambassadors from 19 kingdoms to their homelands. The expedition also opened up new territory by visiting La'sa and Aden on the Arabian peninsula and Mogadishu and Malindi on the East African coast, the first Ming contacts with Africa. These new contacts were not altogether peaceful; violent confrontations occurred at La'sa and Mogadishu. Still, when the expedition returned to Nanking on 8 August 1419, it carried new foreign ambassadors to honor the Ming emperor. This success necessitated a sixth expedition, because the new foreign ambassadors had to return home eventually. The emperor ordered that voyage on 3 March 1421, with a fleet of 41 vessels. Cheng Ho apparently did not accompany the fleet on its entire journey, because he was definitely back in China by late 1422.

The death of Yung-lo in 1424 resulted in the cancellation of preparations for a seventh expedition by his successor Hongxi (r. 1424). Expansionism under Yung-lo had caused a strain on China's resources, and antiexpansionist sentiment resurfaced among the Confucian bureaucrats. The next emperor, Xuande (r. 1424–1435), at first continued Hongxi's antiexpansionist policy, but in 1430 he relented, ordering Cheng Ho to assemble a new fleet of 100 ships. It sailed from Fukien on 12 January 1432, with the main fleet traveling to Hormuz. Two subsidiary expeditions reached Mogadishu in East Africa and Jidda and Mecca in the Red Sea. Some accounts claim that Cheng Ho died at Calicut during this expedition, which returned to the new Ming capital of Peking on 22 July 1433. True or not, the maritime venture was the last for both Cheng Ho and the Ming dynasty. Xuande's death left China with an eight-year-old emperor and the antiexpansionist Confucian bureaucrats firmly in charge of the government.

Scholars continue to debate over why the Ming dynasty ordered these massive expeditions and why it then abandoned them so completely. The first expedition may have been partially motivated by a search for the deposed emperor Jianwen. It might have been an attempt to outflank the marauding armies of Tamerlane that were threatening China's central Asian borders. The Strait of Malacca needed to be cleared of pirates, and Cheng Ho certainly managed to do that. The large-scale naval expeditions also displayed the might of the Chinese Empire, thereby promoting obedience at home and abroad. They also allowed the Ming emperor to expand the traditional tribute system of Chinese diplomacy deep into the lands of the Indian Ocean. Commercial contacts naturally followed the expansion of political contacts, and so benefited certain areas of the Chinese economy. The great fleets also sought treasure to bring home for the delight of the emperor, whether in the form of spices, gold, exotic animals such as giraffes, or harem girls. Finally, these massive maritime ventures were a clear-cut demonstration of Chinese cultural superiority, a theme dear to the hearts of the Chinese elite.

Cheng Ho's naval adventures were not universally popular. The Confucian bureaucrats opposed them for a number of reasons. At a basic political level, Confucian bureaucrats despised eunuchs in the government, and Cheng Ho and the other supporters of overseas expansion were eunuchs. At a practical level, the Confucian bureaucrats considered the great fleets tremendously expensive, producing little benefit to China, and they opposed such egregious wastes of the nation's resources. As traditionalists, they also opposed the expansionist policy on principle; it was militaristic, and they were antimilitarists. The expeditions promoted commercial expansion, while they desired economic self-sufficiency for China, and increased China's foreign contacts, while the Confucians advocated isolationism. The Confucian bureaucrats won the struggle by winning over succeeding emperors to their point of view. China withdrew from the rest of the world, and a little over 60 years later, Vasco da Gama reached India by sea from Europe. In one of history's ironic twists of fate, it was Vasco da Gama's tattered little fleet of a few vessels and his small, dirty crew that truly changed the course of history, not Cheng Ho's magnificent armada with its crew in the tens of thousands. Ming China did not become a nation of world travelers—the Western world came to them.

See also

Hajj; Indian Ocean; Mecca; Pirates.

For further reading

Jan Julius Lodewijk Duyvendak, *China's Discovery of Africa,* 1949; Robert Finley, "The Treasure-Ships of Zheng He: Chinese Maritime Imperialism in the Age of Discovery," *Terrae Incognitae* 23 (1991): 1–12; Louise Levathes, *When China Ruled the Seas,* 1994; J. V. G. Mills, "Introduction," in Ma Huan, *Ying-Yai Sheng-Lan,* 1970; William Willetts, "The Maritime Adventures of Grand Eunuch Ho," *Journal of South-East Asian History* 2 (1964): 25–42.

CHILDREN OF ISRAEL, WANDERINGS IN THE WILDERNESS OF

Refers to the 40 years of travel by the Children of Israel that occurred between their receiving the Ten Commandments at Mount Sinai and the beginning of the conquest of Canaan as described in the Bible.

The Children of Israel spent one year in the vicinity of Mount Sinai after God's giving of the Ten Commandments. They then traveled through the Wildernesses of Paran and Zin for approximately 150 miles to the springs at Kadesh-barnea and Wadi Quderiat in the Negeb region. Along the way, God provided them with quail for food and other necessities of life. Moses sent 12 spies, including the future leader Joshua, into southern Canaan around Hebron. Returning after 40 days, the spies brought good news and bad news. They reported that Canaan was a land of milk and honey, and brought back a gigantic cluster of grapes to prove its bounty. Canaan was also densely populated, and not just by Canaanites. Hittites, Jebusites, and the fearsome giants known as the Anakites also lived there. Its cities were so heavily fortified that they seemed to be "walled up to heaven." The spies' report frightened the Children of Israel, and they were reluctant to begin the invasion. Once more, God was enraged by their lack of faith in his plan. He ordered that no one above the age of 20 at that time would ever enter the land of Canaan, except for the families of Joshua and Caleb. Even Moses was barred from entering Canaan. The Children of Israel were condemned to roam the desert for 40 years as a punishment before they would be allowed to successfully invade Canaan. Remorseful but still disobedient, the Israelites tried to invade Canaan despite God's command to the contrary. Defeat at the hands of the Amalekites and Canaanites quickly followed.

Little is known about those 40 years of wandering. The Children of Israel obviously lived the life of seminomadic herders, and like other desert tribes grew tough and more capable of conquering Canaan. Some biblical accounts characterize the 40 years in the wilderness as a time of aimless roaming. It is more likely, however, that their movements were dictated by the demands of an arid environment on a herding people. Their range of pasturage was most likely the Negeb, which is more a dry steppe of grass than a parched land of sand dunes or rocks.

At the end of the 40 years, the Israelites again planned their invasion at Kadesh-barnea. This time, they decided to invade from the east rather than the south, and they asked the Edomites if they could pass through their land on the ancient King's Highway. They were refused, so the Israelites slipped through between the kingdoms of Edom and Moab. Arriving in the lands east of the Jordan, the Israelites quickly conquered the Amorites and the people of Bashan, and slaughtered the hostile Midianites. These successes left them nicely placed to cross the Jordan and attack Canaan proper. At long last, the Children of Israel were about to acquire a homeland. God told Moses to climb Mount Nebo and go to the adjacent top of Pisgah to view the land of Canaan. Moses then died at the age of 120 years. God buried him close to Beth-peor in the land of Moab, "but no man knoweth of his sepulchre unto this day." The wanderings of the Children of Israel, one of the best-known journeys in the history of Western civilization, were about to come to an end.

See also
Exodus.
For further reading
Yohanan Aharoni and Michael Avi-Yonah, *The Macmillan Bible Atlas*, 1968; G. I. Davies, "Wilderness Wanderings," in *The Anchor Bible Dictionary*, 1992; Werner Keller, *The Bible as History*, 1964.

CHINA
See Cathay.

CHIPANGU   Also known as Zipangu, the name for Japan by late medieval and early-modern Europeans. It derived from the Chinese word *Jih-pên-kwé*, meaning "land of the rising sun." Marco Polo (1254?–1324) first introduced Europeans to Chipangu, or Japan, in his famous *Travels*. Although he never visited Chipangu, Polo left a vivid and tempting description of that land. Chipangu was a large island inhabited by a white race of idol-worshipers. Especially intriguing to Europeans was Polo's comment, "I can tell you the quantity of gold they have is endless." Chipangu's wealth in gold was so great that its ruler had a palace roofed in gold in the same manner that Europeans roofed their buildings with lead, and even the palace's floors and pavements were gold. Beautiful pearls were also common in Japan. Polo told of Kublai Khan's unsuccessful attempts to conquer Japan in 1274 and 1281.

Polo was the first European to leave a written account of Japan before the sixteenth century. His description of Chipangu supplied part of Columbus's motivation for sailing west in 1492 to reach the fantastic riches of Asia, including gold-roofed Japan. Columbus initially thought that Cuba was Japan, but later changed his mind and identified Hispaniola as the island of Chipangu. Given Polo's fabulous description of Chipangu, it is understandable that Columbus's wish to find that fabled land was the father to his several

Statue of Buddha photographed in Kamakura, Japan, in 1877.

misidentifications. Nor did Polo exaggerate in his account of Chipangu. Because of its remote location and few opportunities for trade, medieval Japan was rich in gold. The medieval Arab geographer al-Idrisi called Japan by the name Sila; he had heard that gold was so common that it was used to fashion dog collars. Various Chinese sources mention the gold-roofed palaces of the ruler of Chipangu and the wonderful pearls. Polo's *Travels* ultimately helped to inspire Europe's great age of discovery and expansion in the fifteenth and sixteenth centuries.

See also
Cathay; Polo, Marco.
For further reading
Valerie I. J. Flint, *The Imaginative Landscape of Christopher Columbus*, 1992; Henry Yule and Henri Cordier, eds., *The Travels of Marco Polo*, 1929.

CIRCUIT RIDERS   A system of traveling ministers of religion created by English evangelist John Wesley and largely associated with Methodism, although it was occasionally imitated by other denominations.

John Wesley (1703–1791) conceived of the system as the most efficient way to bring preaching and the Christian gospel to large numbers of people. Basically, the preaching minister traveled an itinerary, or circuit, of preaching stations. This system was a rejection of the standard practice of Protestant denominations, in which a highly educated clergyman served a single parish or congregation for his entire career.

Although Wesley first developed the idea in England, Robert Strawbridge introduced it to North America in 1764. Circuit riding was well adapted to the needs of the largely rural American society and its rapidly expanding but thinly populated frontier. By 1783, approximately 100 circuit riders operated in the new nation, and American Methodism experienced a dramatic growth in membership. From less than 1,000 members in 1770, Methodism grew to over 250,000 members in 1820 and to 1 million by 1840, at which time there were some 7,000 itinerant preachers. Circuit riding also resulted in spreading Methodism quite evenly across the country.

During the early nineteenth century, the typical preaching circuit was quite large—200 to 500 miles in circumference, with 25 to 30 preaching stations located along a single circuit. The traveling ministers were expected to complete their itineraries every two to six weeks, with four weeks considered the norm. Circuit riders traveled in all seasons and every kind of weather, which spawned a proverb for describing miserable weather conditions as so foul that "there is nothing out today but crows and Methodist preachers." Most circuits had two traveling preachers, so a congregation could expect to hear a sermon every two weeks. Besides preaching, circuit riders' duties included teaching religion classes and making home visits. At some stations, local lay preachers prepared for the arrival of the circuit riders and assisted them in their duties.

Francis Asbury (1745–1816), the early leader of American Methodism, originally followed a policy of moving itinerant ministers from one circuit to another every six months. In 1804, the general conference of the Methodist Church adopted a policy of two-year assignments, and after 1865 increased tenure to three years in the North and four years in the South. In this way, the Methodist ministry sought to avoid popular disrespect and too-close identification with wealthy members. The system was also designed to maintain the religious enthusiasm of the clergy and promote a national viewpoint for the church.

Circuit riders initially received a salary of $64 a year, which was raised to $100 in 1800 (compared to the $400 annual salary of Congregational ministers). However, Methodist ministers could earn a little extra money by selling Bibles and hymnals to the people of their circuit. Early Methodist ministers were not highly educated; their equipment consisted of a horse, a Bible, the Book of Discipline, and a hymnal. Circuit riding was a hard life, and itinerant Methodist ministers had to be tough. They frequently faced drunken hecklers in their audiences and occasionally were threatened with violence or death. Circuit riders were discouraged from marrying, and over half died before the age of 33 from the rigors of the road. Others thrived on the life: Peter Cartwright served a prodigious 71 years as a circuit rider. The great Francis Asbury traveled over 250,000 miles on horseback and preached 17,000 sermons during his long career. As American society changed—cities grew, rural America declined, and the frontier came to an end—circuit riding gradually died out, to be replaced by a more settled congregation-based ministry, characteristic of modern Methodism.

For further reading

Hunter Dickinson Farish, *The Circuit Rider Dismounts*, 1938; John H. Wigger, "Holy 'Knock-em-Down' Preachers," *Christian History* 14 (no. 1, 1995): 22–25.

CIRCUMNAVIGATIONS OF AFRICA, EARLY

From the time of Homer to the voyage of Vasco da Gama in 1497, Europeans and Middle Easterners speculated about the possibility of sailing around Africa. A number of people attempted the voyage; some may even have completed it.

The peoples of the ancient Mediterranean world believed that the world consisted of the three continents of Africa (Libya), Asia, and Europe, which were surrounded by the circular River Ocean. This worldview led them to assume that Africa was a long but thin landmass much smaller than it actually was. According to this erroneous image, a voyage around the southern coast of Africa would not be significantly longer than a voyage along the North Africa coast.

Pharaoh Necho (r. 609–593 B.C.) of Egypt first conceived of sailing around Africa after his fruitless attempts to link the Nile River with the Gulf of Suez by means of a canal. He wanted to find an all-water route between the Red Sea and the Mediterranean Sea, so he hired Phoenician seamen to make the voyage around Africa. From the Red Sea, they sailed down the eastern coast of Africa. Three years later they arrived back in Egypt, having sailed the 16,000 miles of African coastline. Along the way, they stopped twice to grow crops for their food supply. They also reported that for a time the sun was on their right as they sailed west (they were deep into the Southern Hemisphere). Necho's Phoenicians sailed clockwise around Africa, the easiest route for a sailing ship. Unfortunately, such a long voyage was not commercially viable, and neither the Egyptians nor the Phoenicians followed up on this accomplishment.

The ancient Persians made the next attempt to circumnavigate Africa. A prince named Sataspes committed a rape and faced execution for it. When he requested mercy, King Xerxes (r. 485–465 B.C.) of Persia sentenced Sataspes to circumnavigate Africa. Sataspes arranged for a ship in Egypt and sailed west through the Strait of Gibraltar. Proceeding south for months, the expedition observed a race of Pygmies. At that point the ship could no longer make southward progress because of contrary winds and currents. The Persians apparently reached the vicinity of the Gulf of Guinea before being forced to turn back. On his return, Sataspes was executed.

About the same time (490 B.C.), the Carthaginian Hanno made his way down the west coast of Africa. His ships may have traveled as far south as present-day Liberia, but apparently he never planned on circumnavigating Africa. His mission was to investigate the commercial possibilities along West Africa, and he established thriving trading colonies possibly as far south as the Senegal River. Later, a Greek named Euthymenes of Massalia also sailed as far south as the Senegal River, which he incorrectly assumed was a branch of the Nile. Euthymenes may have been a contemporary of the famous voyager Pytheas of Massalia (ca. 240–238 B.C.). Neither Hanno nor Euthymenes came close to equaling the accomplishment of the Phoenicians of Necho in sailing all the way around Africa.

Early in the second century B.C., rumors circulated about mysterious ships of Gades (Cadiz), a Phoenician colony in Spain, that were supposedly circumnavigating Africa and carrying Asian trade goods to the Atlantic coast of Europe and the lands of the western Mediterranean. Such rumors intrigued Eudoxus of Cyznicus (fl. ca. 125–100 B.C.). He had made two sea voyages to India, but on his return, the Ptolemaic rulers of Egypt had confiscated his profits. Hoping to bypass them, Eudoxus made two attempts to sail around Africa in a counterclockwise direction. He abandoned the first attempt and never returned from the second. The great historian Polybius (ca. 200–after 118 B.C.) also sailed down the West African coast as far as the Senegal River and then turned back. Significantly, neither Eudoxus nor Polybius encountered any ships of Gades. Nevertheless, the rumors persisted until about 27 B.C., the beginning of the reign of Emperor Augustus. They prompted the young Gaius Caesar to contemplate a clockwise circumnavigation of Africa about 1 B.C., but the project never got out of the planning stages. With that stillborn effort, the ancient world's interest in circumnavigating Africa subsided. The absence of lucrative trade caused sailors to lose interest in making such an arduous voyage.

The decline of the Roman Empire caused trade to decline and resources to constrict. In addition, early-medieval geographical concepts about the uninhabitability of the Torrid Zone did not encourage thoughts of circumnavigating

Africa. By the twelfth and thirteenth centuries, European civilization had recovered; the Crusades and the increase of trade with Mongol China along the fabled Silk Road created a taste and demand for Asian luxury goods. A thriving trade developed by the end of the thirteenth century, only to be threatened by the resurgence of Islam. The fall of Acre, the last Crusader outpost, to the Mamluks of Egypt forced Genoese merchants to consider developing alternate routes to Asia. Pope Nicholas IV also ordered an embargo on trade with Muslim Egypt. Seeking to find a new route to India, the brothers Ugolino and Vadino Vivaldi sailed through the Strait of Gibraltar in two galleys in 1291. Reaching the vicinity of the Canary Islands, they sailed on and were never seen again. Some scholars suggest that they were trying to reach Asia by sailing west across the Atlantic Ocean. Most of their contemporaries and most modern scholars, however, feel that they intended to sail around Africa to reach India. Although the reliability of these reports is questionable, later fourteenth- and fifteenth-century reports of supposed Vivaldi survivors and descendants encountered in both West and East Africa bolster the African circumnavigation hypothesis.

Interest in circumnavigating Africa picked up once again during the fifteenth century with the Portuguese voyages down the coast of Africa. Prince Henry the Navigator (1394–1460) is traditionally credited with developing the plan to circumnavigate Africa to reach India, but it is untrue; his horizons were pretty well limited to exploring West Africa. After the death of Prince Henry, Portuguese exploration of Africa stagnated until King João II (r. 1481–1495) came to the throne. The new king was definitely interested in reaching India by sea, and in 1482 he instructed Diogo Cao to explore the African coast as far as the Congo River. Cao made a second voyage in 1485 that reached as far south as Walvis Bay or Angra Pequena. What happened to Cao on his second voyage is unclear. It seems most probable that he was lost at sea, but some historians speculate that João II secretly executed him for failing to round Africa. Bartolomeu Dias's expedition followed in 1487–1488, and passed the southern tip of Africa to enter the Indian Ocean, but his fearful crew forced him to return home. However, the way was now clear for the circumnavigation of Africa to trade with India, something that had not been done for 1,500 to 2,000 years, if at all. Vasco da Gama finally accomplished a round-trip from Portugal to India in 1497–1499 using the route around Africa. Unlike the Phoenician voyage sponsored by Pharaoh Necho and the mysterious ships of Gades, the Portuguese succeeded in opening a trade route that was not only viable, but highly profitable. Despite some initial uncertainty, the sea road around Africa to reach Asia has been used ever since. The ancient dream of circumnavigating Africa became a common though still dangerous activity during the sixteenth century and afterward.

See also
    Africa; Atlantic Ocean; Hanno, Voyage of; Phoenicians.

For further reading
    Rhys Carpenter, *Beyond the Pillars of Heracles*, 1966; M. Cary and E. H. Warmington, *The Ancient Explorers*, 1963; Bailey W. Diffie and George D.

Winius, *Foundations of the Portuguese Empire, 1415–1580*, 1977; Sanjay Subrahmanyan, *The Career and Legend of Vasco da Gama*, 1997.

CIRCUMNAVIGATIONS OF THE EARTH, EARLY

Although it had been known for over 2,000 years that the earth was a sphere, the first voyage of circumnavigation, organized and led by Ferdinand Magellan (1480?–1521), did not take place until 1519. Sir Francis Drake's (1540/1542–1596) voyage of 1577–1580 was the next, and from then on, the number and frequency of circumnavigations increased until they were fairly routine by the late eighteenth century.

Contrary to popular opinion, knowledge of earth's sphericity dates back to the ancient Greeks and was widespread. Sailors observed the curvature of the earth every time they saw a ship gradually appear or disappear on the horizon. Pythagorean philosophers in ancient Greece first argued that the earth was a sphere on philosophical grounds, not scientific. Later Greek scholars such as Crates of Mallos advanced more scientific reasons for their belief in a round earth. Although it was accepted that the earth was round, no one attempted to circumnavigate it or even contemplated such a voyage.

The Genoese brothers Ugolino and Vadino Vivaldi may have been the first to attempt a circumnavigation of the earth. Sailing through the Strait of Gibraltar in 1291, they announced that their goal was a sea voyage to India. It is unclear whether they meant to get to India by sailing west across the Atlantic Ocean or south down the coast of Africa. The first route argued for a circumnavigation of the earth, the second for a circumnavigation of Africa. Because the Vivaldis disappeared after passing the Canary Islands, their intention must remain a mystery.

The *Travels of Sir John Mandeville,* written about 1356/1366, describes a fictional circumnavigation of the earth. By the late fifteenth century, the idea of sailing the Atlantic to reach Asia was discussed seriously. Obviously, Christopher Columbus (1451–1506) supported it, but he was not alone. In 1474, the Florentine armchair geographer Paolo Toscanelli (1397–1482) advocated a western voyage across the Atlantic to the king of Portugal. John Cabot (ca. 1450–ca. 1499), the Venetian seaman, developed an idea for a western voyage to Asia independently of Columbus. Joining the service of Henry VII of England, he made a western voyage in 1497, but found North America, not China.

The Americas not only blocked access to Asian luxury goods, they blocked a potential circumnavigation, leading to a frantic search for a way around or through them, or north around Eurasia. The searchers for a northwest or northeast passage were manifestations of the quest to find another sea route to Asia. Some seamen speculated that a passage to Asia existed somewhere far to the south along the coast of South America, and various expeditions searched many river mouths in the vain hope that they were straits opening into the Pacific Ocean.

Ferdinand Magellan, a Portuguese seaman familiar with the seas around the Spice Islands, joined the service of Spain in 1517. He lobbied for a royal grant to command a fleet with the mission of locating a western sea route to Asia by finding the elusive South American strait. In 1519, he was given command of five ships and 250 men, and assigned to find a passage through South America and cruise across the Pacific to the Spice Islands. Setting sail on 20 September 1519, Magellan located and entered the strait named after him on 21 October 1520. On 27 November, he reached the Pacific Ocean, and then made a horrendous voyage of over 90 days, crossing the equator on 13 February 1521. By the time the Spanish reached Guam on 6 March, scurvy and starvation had killed many crewmen and left the others gravely weakened. After fresh food restored them to health, Magellan moved on, reaching the Philippines on 16 March and claiming them for Spain. Unfortunately, he became embroiled in local conflicts and died in battle on Mactan Island on 26 April 1521. The surviving members of the expedition continued on under the leadership of Sebastian de El-Cano. On 8 September 1522, the one remaining ship with its ragged crew of 18 reached Spain. The first circumnavigation had been completed in 12 days less than three years. The participants paid such a fearsome price in terms of death and suffering that no one tried another circumnavigation for over 50 years.

England's Sir Francis Drake made the second circumnavigation of the earth. His original plan was to pass through the Strait of Magellan, plunder the Pacific coast of Spanish America, and make his way home to England through the Strait of Anian and the Northwest Passage. If he had carried out this plan, he would have been the first to circumnavigate the Americas. Departing Plymouth on 13 December 1577 with five ships and 166 men, Drake masked his true intentions by claiming to be making a voyage to Alexandria in Egypt. Sailing past the Strait of Gibraltar, he reached the Strait of Magellan on 21 August 1578. Incredibly, his passage through the tricky strait took only 16 days, but only his flagship, the *Golden Hind,* made it through. After successfully raiding Spanish shipping, Drake sailed north a bit past San Francisco Bay, where he decided that using the Strait of Anian was not feasible. Turning west and crossing the Pacific, Drake eventually returned to England on 21 September 1580 after a voyage of two years, ten months, and four days, becoming the first Englishman to lead a circumnavigation of the earth.

Drake's success tempted others to imitate him. Anxious to raid Spanish treasure ships, Sir Thomas Cavendish (1560–1592) followed in Drake's wake a few years later. Leaving Plymouth on 21 July 1586, Cavendish sailed to South America. His voyage proved to be rather mediocre in its accomplishments, capturing relatively little treasure from the now-alert Spanish. However, Cavendish completed his voyage fairly quickly—two years and 50 days—and he had the honor of being the third person and the second Englishman to circumnavigate the world.

After Cavendish, English interest in circumnavigation faded with the decline of easily acquiring Spanish loot. Instead, the intrepid Dutch began their attempts. Eager, even desperate, to trade with the Spice Islands, the Dutch sought sea routes that would bypass the hostile Portuguese. Some considered the Strait of Magellan a viable alternative to the Cape of Good Hope. One attempt by Jacques Mahu and Simon de Cordes left Rotterdam on 27 June

1598, but never made it home. A second fleet under Olivier van Noort left Rotterdam on 13 September 1598. They suffered a difficult passage through the Strait of Magellan, which they entered on 4 November 1599. Not until 29 February 1600 did van Noort's ships enter the Pacific Ocean, and once there, he found the opportunities slim for raiding Spanish spice and treasure ships. Finally, on 26 August 1601, he returned to the Netherlands with little profit to show for his efforts. Van Noort gained the distinction of being the first Dutch person to circumnavigate the globe, although his attributes as a sea captain hardly qualified him to be considered among the Netherlands' greatest sailors.

Despite van Noort's lack of success, the Dutch remained interested in the South American route to the Spice Islands. On 8 August 1614, Joris van Spilbergen began another expedition through the Strait of Magellan. Picking up spices in the Moluccas, van Spilbergen returned to Zealand on 1 July 1617 after a voyage of two years and 328 days. While in the East Indies, he picked up as passengers Willem Schouten (1567?–1625) and Jacob LeMaire (d. 1616), who had been making their own voyage of circumnavigation.

At that time, the Dutch East India Company held a monopoly on the use of routes to the Spice Islands using the Cape of Good Hope and the Strait of Magellan, so envious Dutch merchants sought alternate routes. Departing the Netherlands on 14 June 1615, Schouten and LeMaire sailed past the Strait of Magellan. They sought and soon found what became known as Cape Horn on 25 January 1616. By avoiding the Strait of Magellan to reach the Pacific Ocean, they had legally circumvented the Dutch East India Company's monopoly. Unfortunately, Jan Pieterzoon Coen, an irascible officer of the company at Djarkarta in the East Indies, refused to believe their story and had them arrested. Van Spilbergen was taking them home as prisoners when LeMaire died en route. Schouten, however, arrived safely. His circumnavigation, partly by courtesy of van Spilbergen, only took two years and 17 days.

From then on, circumnavigations became more common and generally less hazardous, and few crews suffered the intense privations of Magellan's pioneering seamen. In the mid-eighteenth century, Captain James Cook led a circumnavigation in which not a single sailor died of scurvy. Charles Darwin's voyage around the world in the HMS *Beagle* during 1832–1836 was not particularly remarkable except for the revolutionary theory that Darwin developed as a result of his scientific observations. By the late nineteenth century, speed records became important in circumnavigations, as illustrated by the popularity of Jules Verne's novel *Around the World in Eighty Days* (1873). Circumnavigation was on its way to becoming a curiosity of modern mass tourism.

See also

Anian, Strait of; Atlantic Ocean; Crates of Mallos; Good Hope, Cape of; Horn, Cape; Magellan, Strait of; *Mandeville, Travels of Sir John*; Northeast Passage; Northwest Passage; Pacific Ocean; Spice Islands.

For further reading

Robert Silverberg, *The Longest Voyage*, 1972; Derek Wilson, *The Circumnavigators*, 1989.

CLASHING ROCKS

CLASHING ROCKS   In Greek, these navigational hazards are called *Symplegades*. Sometimes referred to as the Crashing Rocks, they are distinct from the similar Wandering Rocks *(Planctae)*. Both sets of rocks guarded narrow passages in the sea and crashed together whenever an unwary ship or creature attempted to pass between them. Some authorities consider the Clashing Rocks and the Wandering Rocks to have been a single hazard in the earliest versions of the Greek myths.

The Clashing Rocks were located in the Bosporus, which was the eastern entrance to the Mediterranean Sea from the Black Sea. On their way to Colchis, Jason and the Argonauts barely managed to pass between them in safety. As a result of their success, the rocks became fixed in place and no longer menaced shipping. On their way back from Colchis, Jason and the Argonauts faced danger from the Wandering Rocks, which supposedly guarded the western entrance of the Mediterranean. This time, the goddess Hera sent the Nereids, a group of friendly sea nymphs, to help them quickly pass between the lethal rocks. The Wandering Rocks, however, did not become fixed in place because of Jason's success. A generation later, Odysseus was forced to bypass them by going through the hazardous strait of Scylla and Charybdis. Both the Clashing Rocks and the Wandering Rocks represent the type of dangers that early seafarers faced when they passed through a narrow strait in a sailed or oared vessel. Waves and tides could make it appear that the rocks moved. Some suggest that such moving rocks may represent a dim awareness of icebergs. Another variation of this theory speculates that the Clashing Rocks were ice floes that entered the Black Sea from the various Russian rivers during the spring thaw. The early Greeks knew that the Mediterranean was an inland sea, and placed the Clashing Rocks at the eastern entrance and the Wandering Rocks at the western entrance. The Wandering Rocks should not be confused with the Pillars of Hercules, which were not a part of Homeric geographical knowledge. If anywhere, the early Greeks located the Wandering Rocks in close proximity to the Strait of Messina, traditionally believed to be the home of the monsters Scylla and Charybdis. Of course, the Wandering Rocks are purely mythological and therefore have no literal geographic location. Instead, they are part of the misty geographical worldview of the Homeric Age that later and more skeptical ancient authors such as Diodorus Siculus rejected as superstition.

See also
> Black Sea; Bosporus; Homer; Jason and the Argonauts, Voyage of; Mediterranean Sea; Pillars of Hercules; Scylla and Charybdis.

For further reading
> Janet Ruth Bacon, *The Voyage of the Argonauts*, 1925; Robert Graves, *The Greek Myths*, 1955.

CLIPPER SHIPS   These fabled American sailing ships, which flourished during the first half of the nineteenth century, could outsail any other sailing ship.

Lithograph of a clipper ship by N. Currier, 1856.

Clipper ships were designed to attain maximum speeds. Designers built them with narrow hulls that cut through the water like knives. Their masts were up to 200 feet in height and were crowded with large amounts of sail that could catch the slightest breeze. These features allowed the clipper ships to sail at dramatically higher rates of speed than other sailing vessels. Such speeds also allowed clipper ships to evade pirates and blockades, and beat their competition when time was important. Their narrow hulls limited the amount of cargo they could carry, so they specialized in valuable freight, like tea, silk, and opium, or passengers who were in a hurry and willing to pay a premium for passage. They rarely carried cannons for protection, relying instead on speed.

These early two-masted or Baltimore clippers first appeared before the American Revolution (1775–1783), and by 1845 evolved into larger and faster ships. Initially, clipper ships were used to fetch the luxury goods of China but the California gold rush of 1849 put them into the business of hauling passengers from the east coast of the United States around Cape Horn to the gold-fields of the West. Journeys of less than 90 days to cover the 16,000 sea miles between the eastern seaboard and California were commonplace. The clipper *James Baines* sailed around the world via Australia in a mere 132 days, setting an average speed record of 21 nautical miles per hour.

By 1853, some 270 clipper ships had been built, and built well; clipper ships generally had long lives of profitable service to their owners. The competition of steam-powered ships did not immediately affect the clippers, but by 1860 steamships had developed more efficient engines and larger cargo capacities. Steamships now had speed equal to the clippers, with an economical expenditure of energy, and they could carry more cargo.

Clipper ships represented the ultimate in efficient design for a sailing ship. These vessels were things of beauty that closed out the age of sailing ships as the principal means of travel on the high seas.

See also
Horn, Cape.
For further reading
Arthur H. Clark, *The Clipper Ship Era*, 1910; John Jennings, *Clipper Ship Days*, 1952.

COCKAIGNE, LAND OF Also spelled Cokayne, in German it was known as *Schlauraffenland*. In the popular culture of the late Middle Ages and the sixteenth century, Cockaigne was a fantasyland where normal values and conditions of life were turned upside down. It is doubtful that very many people believed in the literal existence of Cockaigne.

Getting to Cockaigne was difficult. Some said it was west of Spain (an area of trackless ocean in the minds of most medieval Europeans), and others that it lay three miles west of Christmas, to the left of Paradise. The route to the Land of Cockaigne was often extremely disgusting, because it involved wading through pig excrement or snot for seven miles or seven years. Once travelers arrived in the Land of Cockaigne, they found a paradise of materialism from the point of view of average people during the late Middle Ages. Virtually everything in the Land of Cockaigne was not only edible but delectable. Rivers flowed with milk or wine, and it rained honey and snowed sugar. Cooked chickens, geese, or ducks literally flew into people's mouths to be consumed. Even houses were constructed of delicious food. Clothing grew on trees or dropped from heaven, and women were always available and willing to have sexual relations. In this inverted land, laziness was the virtue and hard work was the vice; lies were rewarded and telling the truth was punished. The Land of Cockaigne was a permanent Mardi Gras.

The earliest complete literary description of the Land of Cockaigne appeared in the French work *Li pais a non Coqaigne* (ca. 1250). An English work, *Land of Cokayne*, dates from the early fourteenth century and describes a fleshly paradise for monks. In Italian literature, the Land of Cockaigne first appeared in some of the tales of the *Decameron*. It also figured in late-medieval German and Spanish stories. Tales of the Land of Cockaigne were basically a form of escapist literature in which the main point was that Cockaigne was a land that stood in contrast to the real world.

For further reading
Louise O. Vasvari, "The Geography of Escape and the Topsy-Turvy Literary Genres," in *Discovering New Worlds*, 1991.

COLOSSUS OF RHODES One of the Seven Wonders of the Ancient World, this gigantic bronze statue, measuring 110 feet tall, was the principal landmark of the rich port of ancient Rhodes.

Rhodes is a large island located off the southwest coast of Asia Minor (the present-day Republic of Turkey). Its inhabitants benefited from the land's rich soils and its favorable location along the shipping lanes of the eastern Mediterranean Sea. In 408 B.C., the Rhodians agreed to consolidate the entire island under one common government, with its new capital called Rhodes. From 355 to 333 B.C., the Rhodians submitted to Persian rule. They regained their independence in 323 B.C. during the breakup of Alexander the Great's empire.

During the wars of the Diadochi (successors) of Alexander the Great, a general named Antigonus sent his son Demetrius to besiege Rhodes for not becoming an ally in his war with Ptolemy I of Egypt. The siege began in 305 B.C. and lasted for a year, during which the latest and grandest military technology was employed. Nevertheless, the indefatigable Rhodians refused to surrender, and eventually Demetrius lifted the siege and abandoned his equipment. Such a great deliverance demanded a commemoration, so the Rhodians used the proceeds from selling off Demetrius's abandoned siege engines to commission the sculptor Chares of Lindos to create a great bronze statue of Helios, the patron god of Rhodes. Chares and his men worked on the 110-foot statue between 294 and 282 B.C.

The Colossus of Rhodes is one of the most obscure of the Seven Wonders of the Ancient World. It stood intact for the shortest length of time of any of the Seven Wonders because an earthquake caused its knees to buckle in 226 B.C. The ruins remained on view for another 900 years, until plundering Arabs hauled them away in A.D. 654. Most scholars think that the Colossus was posed in the same fashion as the modern Statue of Liberty, but no reliable picture exists to confirm that opinion. Its location in Rhodes is also uncertain. Many older illustrations show the Colossus standing astride one of the harbor entrances, but the mouth of the smaller harbor is 1,300 feet wide. Another common but incorrect belief is that the Colossus functioned as a lighthouse. More likely, the Colossus was erected in the midst of the city near the temple of Helios. While it neither graced the harbor entrance nor served as a lighthouse as the Statue of Liberty does today, it was still a famous tourist attraction of the ancient world.

See also

Seven Wonders of the Ancient World.

For further reading

Peter Clayton and Martin Price, eds., *The Seven Wonders of the Ancient World*, 1988.

CONESTOGA WAGON
Famous freight wagon developed by the Pennsylvania Dutch of the Conestoga Valley during the middle of the eighteenth century. These large, sturdy wagons were designed to haul freight and settlers' possessions across the passes of the Allegheny and Appalachian Mountains and were pulled by teams of four to six draft horses. Their wide wheels were well suited for traveling over rough dirt roads, and the bed was constructed higher at both ends to prevent cargo from falling out when the wagon went up and

down hills and mountains. Characteristically, a Conestoga wagon was painted blue on its bottom half and red on top. The makers supplied them with canvas covers, an innovation used in the design of the prairie schooners in which settlers traveled the overland trails to California and Oregon.

See also
    Prairie Schooner.
For further reading
    Seymour Dunbar, *History of Travel in America*, 1915.

CONSTANTINOPLE   Also called Byzantium, it was located at the crossroads of trade between Asia and Europe. During the early Middle Ages, Constantinople was the great political and commercial capital of Christendom. Over the centuries, countless travelers have visited its beautiful monuments, magnificent buildings, and impressive harbors. The Ottoman Turks conquered the city in 1453, but its name was not changed to Istanbul until 1930.

Some sort of settlement existed on this site from the beginning of the second millennium B.C. Its strategic location at the junction of several trade routes meant that it was an important city under the Greeks and the Romans. Emperor Constantine's founding of Constantinople by consecration in 324 and dedication in 330 was a renaming of Byzantium, a preexisting city of 20,000. The new city was to be a "Second Rome" and serve as a dual capital of the entire Roman Empire or the sole capital of the Eastern Roman or Byzantine Empire. With the consecration of Constantinople, a massive imperial building program began, and so did an impressive growth of the city's population: by 539, the city had grown to 500,000. The reign of Emperor Justinian (527–565) was a golden age for Constantinople, but that era was followed by a series of terrible invasions from 626 to 860 that devastated the empire and greatly reduced its size. Persians, Avars, Slavs, Arabs, and Russians all threatened the survival of Constantinople. The fortunes of the empire revived under the Macedonian dynasty from 867 to 1056. Another period of instability set in from 1056 to 1081 when various competing generals and nobles jostled for the Byzantine imperium until the Comneni dynasty (1081–1185) was victorious. This internal turmoil was accompanied by external threats from the Cumans and Petchenegs of the northern steppes and the Seljuk Turks, who badly defeated a Byzantine army at the battle of Manzikert

The Crusaders enter Constantinople. Woodcut in Boyd, The Crusades.

in 1017. As a result of this defeat, Asia Minor came under the domination of Islam and caused the Byzantine emperors to seek Western aid, an effort that helped to bring on the Crusades.

The Comneni emperors were more interested in promoting the Byzantine Empire's military might than its commercial power, and they allowed foreigners, especially Venetians and Genoese, to take over the Asian luxury trade. Antiforeign feeling grew, and the Westerners reciprocated. The low point came when the soldiers of the Fourth Crusade captured and sacked Constantinople in 1203 and 1204. The Latin Empire ruled the city from 1204 to 1261, when the Paleologi family reconquered it from the Greeks. The restored Byzantine Empire and Constantinople were a shadow of their former greatness, and the city's population had fallen to between 50,000 and 70,000. By 1394, the Ottoman Turkish threat was so obvious that the city's fall to Sultan Mohammed II in 1453 was rather anticlimactic. The Ottomans made it their new capital, and it remained the Turkish capital until 1923, when the modern Republic of Turkey was founded. Constantinople retained its strategic and commercial importance because of its location on the Bosporus and its proximity to the Dardanelles, but its relative commercial importance gradually declined after the opening of a sea route to Asia by Vasco da Gama in 1497. Despite strenuous military efforts by the Ottomans, much of the Asian luxury trade came under Portuguese control.

The city of Constantinople was a cornucopia of architectural wonders that had been built by the early emperors. The Great or Sacred Palace, the Hippodrome, the Hagia Sophia of Justinian, the forum of Constantine, and the Theodosian Walls are just some of the more important wonders. The port facilities of the Golden Horn could still awe visitors during the mid-sixteenth century. Constantinople was the most important city in Christendom through most of the Middle Ages, and travelers' accounts acknowledged that fact.

See also
Bosporus; Dardanelles; Genoa; Silk Road; Venice.
For further reading
Glanville Downey, *Constantinople in the Age of Justinian*, 1960; Pierre Gilles, *The Antiquities of Constantinople* [1561], 1988; Dean Miller, *Imperial Constantinople*, 1969; David Talbot Rice, *Constantinople from Byzantium to Istanbul*, 1965.

COTTON KINGDOM
Name for the antebellum Southern states of the United States, particularly the Deep South states from South Carolina to Texas.

The antebellum Southern states formed a distinctive region of the United States because of the widespread practice of slavery and the plantation system of agriculture. The predominant cash crop of the region was cotton, which provided about two-thirds of the value of all U.S. exports during the 1850s. Prior to 1861, the American South supplied about 80 percent of the world's raw cotton. All the other Southern cash crops—rice, sugar, and indigo—taken together represented only a fraction of cotton's importance. It was said that cotton was king in the South, and hence the South was the Cotton Kingdom.

The institutions of slavery and plantation agriculture helped form a distinctive Southern culture very different from the industrialized Northern states. From this socioeconomic difference arose the plantation myth—from the Southern point of view, the South was a genteel land of aristocratic planters, sturdy yeoman farmers, and contented slaves. Everyone had a place and a role in that society, and knew what they were. Honor, chivalry, and hospitality were distinctive virtues. Work and making money were a means to an end, not an end in themselves. Southern society thought it re-created the best of the characteristics of feudal Europe and the cavaliers of seventeenth-century England. Many Northerners bought into the Southern version of the plantation myth, partly because it satisfied a craving for nostalgia and exoticism. The tune and text of "Dixie" were the creation of Daniel D. Emmett of Ohio in 1859, and exemplified the positive Northern image of the Cotton Kingdom.

Other Northerners held a considerably more negative view of the Cotton Kingdom. Abolitionists demanded an end to the corrupting institution of slavery. Egalitarian Northerners resented the aristocratic powers and pretensions of the Southern planters. To them, the Cotton Kingdom was a backward, savage land where mindless defenses of personal honor led to deadly duels or grisly rough-and-tumble fights. Slavery permitted free rein to sadism and sexual exploitation. Harriet Beecher Stowe's classic novel *Uncle Tom's Cabin* (1852) epitomized the negative image of the Cotton Kingdom.

Many Northerners traveled in the Antebellum South, and although their impressions varied, a number had a rather negative view of the Cotton Kingdom. The accounts of their Southern travels found a ready audience among the North's reading public. The greatest and most objective of these Northern travelers was Frederick Law Olmsted (1822–1903). He took two long trips through the South from 1852 to early 1854, and his initial impressions appeared as a series of newspaper articles in the *New York Daily Times*. The articles were later gathered and published as three books—*A Journey in the Seaboard of the Slave States* (1856), *A Journey through Texas* (1857), and *A Journey in the Back Country* (1860). Olmsted condensed and combined the three books into the two-volume *Journeys and Explorations in the Cotton Kingdom* (1861). Although he came to oppose slavery and shared the common Northern assumption of Southern backwardness, Olmsted's account revealed the complexity and diversity of the South with great clarity. Historians are able to use his writings as accurate descriptions of the land known as the Cotton Kingdom at its height in the early 1850s. The myth of the Cotton Kingdom, however, endures in the products of popular culture and history.

For further reading
William E. Dodd, *The Cotton Kingdom*, 1919; Raimondo Luraghi, *The Plantation South*, 1975; Elizabeth Stevenson, *Park Maker*, 1977.

CRATES OF MALLOS (FL. CA. 150 B.C.)

Also spelled Krates, this Greek scholar speculated that the earth was divided into four landmasses, each located in a quarter of the globe. His ideas were very influential during the early Middle Ages and the Age of Discovery of the late fifteenth and sixteenth centuries.

Crates studied in the great Library of Pergamum at the invitation of its founder, Eumenes II (r. 197–159 B.C.). He later served as a diplomat to Rome for Attalus II (r. 159–138 B.C.), supposedly kindling Roman interest in serious scholarship as a result of his lectures. He is best known as the chief exponent of the Stoic school of anomaly in grammatical studies. Historians of geographical thought know him for his theory that the earth was divided into four quarters by the two equatorial and meridional river-oceans. Each quarter contained a landmass of approximately equal size that Crates termed a *maculae*. The landmass that formed the world known to Crates and the peoples of the Greco-Roman culture was called the oikoumene. Directly south of the oikoumene and across the equatorial river-ocean was the antoikoi. The antichthones, or periocci, was the landmass in the Northern Hemisphere, separated from the oikoumene by the meridional river-ocean. South of the antichthones and across the equatorial river-ocean lay the antipodes. Some accounts credit Crates with constructing a globe with the four landmasses to illustrate his theory. However, in 1937, the German classicist F. Gisinger claimed that the true originator of the Cratesian theory of four landmasses was the much earlier Greek scholar Eudoxus of Cnidos (408–355 B.C.).

The Cratesian theory was one of several Greek cosmographical or geographical worldviews. Since no one ventured out of the oikoumene, the existence of the other three landmasses was pure speculation. Crates's ideas found favor with some later scholars. Cicero (106–43 B.C.) discussed them in his *Dream of Scipio*, which was preserved and expounded upon in a commentary by Macrobius (early fifth century A.D.). Martianus Capella (late fifth century A.D.) added further details to the theory. Since both Macrobius and Martianus Capella were widely read by scholars of the early Middle Ages, the Cratesian theory of the four quarters was also well known.

The Cratesian theory's influence declined during the thirteenth and fourteenth centuries as Aristotle's ideas were rediscovered. Aristotle denied the existence of other landmasses besides the oikoumene, and his ideas pushed aside those of Crates. During the fifteenth century, the pace of European exploration quickened, reviving interest in Crates's ideas. His theory provided Europeans with both a way to understand new geographic discoveries and a means by which they could anticipate—rightly or wrongly—what further exploration might reveal. The long and ultimately fruitless search for the southern continent of Terra Australis originated from Crates's ideas, and the geographical term *antipodes* is a relic of Cratesian geography.

See also

Antichthones; Antipodes; Antoikoi; Pergamum, Library of; Terra Australis.

For further reading

Boies Penrose, *Travel and Discovery in the Early Renaissance,* 1955; W. G. L. Randles, "Classical Models of World Geography and Their Transformation Following the Discovery of America," in *The Classical Tradition and the Americas,* vol. 1, 1994.

CRETANS

Also known as the Minoans, this Bronze Age civilization flourished on the island of Crete from about 2500 to 1100 B.C. They were part of a movement of people settling the various Aegean islands about 7000 B.C. Archaeological evidence indicates that by 2500 B.C., the Cretans were heavily involved in the eastern Mediterranean network of trade. By 2000 B.C., the great palaces of Knossus and other sites began to appear. The Cretans also developed writing in the form of Cretan hieroglyphics and the script Linear A. Trading and seafaring increased, but after 1470 B.C., the Mycenaeans of mainland Greece conquered the Cretans, and evidence of decline appears. A fresh wave of barbarian invaders finished off the Cretans in the years after 1250 B.C. The Cretans developed the first significant maritime and trading civilization of the Mediterranean world.

See also

Mediterranean Sea.

For further reading

W. V. Davies and C. Schofield, eds. *Egypt, the Aegean, and the Levant,* 1995; R. Hägg and N. Marinates, eds., *The Minoan Thalassocracy,* 1984.

CROSSING-THE-LINE CEREMONIES

Elaborate initiation rituals held by the crew whenever a ship crosses the equator or the longitude 180°. All crew members who have never before crossed those lines of latitude or longitude are initiated.

The ceremonies originated in very ancient rituals to appease the gods of the sea. Ancient peoples believed that gods or large sea monsters were responsible for certain dangerous areas of navigation such as whirlpools or fierce currents, thought to be the vortex of the monster Charybdis. Rituals and sacrifices were developed to appease such gods and monsters whenever a ship passed a tricky cape or dangerous strait. Over time, these pagan rituals became Christianized among Western sailors. Eventually, advances in Western science and general knowledge undermined belief in sea monsters. The rituals, however, continued.

The most well known and best-documented ceremony of crossing the line is that of crossing the equator. First documented in 1529, the next reference to the ceremony occurred in 1557, and both speak of the ritual as long-standing. However, because the first recorded Atlantic crossing of the equator by a European vessel was Diogo Cao in 1482 or 1485, such a ceremony could not have occurred before then. Only after 1497, the year of Vasco da Gama's voyage to India, did Europeans cross the equator regularly and in large numbers.

The initial crossing ceremony was religious in nature, involving prayers and throwing silver coins into the sea as an offering. Before the end of the sixteenth century, the ceremony evolved into a more secular, mock-pagan ritual. The classic crossing-the-line ceremony centered on an experienced crew member dressed as King Neptune. All the crew, including officers, who had never crossed the equator would be gathered before King Neptune. The initiated were called "pollywogs" in some versions of the ritual. In earlier rituals, King Neptune demanded a payment in silver. Those who could pay were left alone, while those unable to pay were shaved and doused in salt water, either by having containers of water thrown on them or by being dunked into the sea. As time went by, people were no longer permitted to buy their way out of the initiation, and the rituals became more elaborate. Rather than just one sailor costumed as King Neptune, others dressed up as Mercury or as Tritons to form an elaborate court. Neophytes, or pollywogs, were tarred and then shaved. In addition to being soaked in seawater, they were forced to run a gauntlet, in which veteran sailors spanked them with oars. At the end of the ceremony, the initiates would promise to do the same thing to future neophytes whenever the situation arose. With that, the initiates became "Sons of Neptune," along with the rest of their fellows. A similar ceremony took place on ships crossing longitude 180° in the Pacific Ocean, although its participants were initiated into the Order of the Dragon. Over the years, rituals similar to crossing-the-line ceremonies were carried out on ships rounding either Cape Horn or the Cape of Good Hope, entering the Baltic Sea, or sailing to the whaling waters of the Arctic.

For further reading
Horace Beck, *Folklore and the Sea*, 1973.

CUMBERLAND GAP   Famous pass in the Appalachian Mountains near the junction of the borders of Kentucky, Tennessee, and Virginia. Native Americans and buffalo used the pass, the most convenient route to cross through the mountains, for millennia before the arrival of European settlers. Dr. Thomas Walker and his exploring party went through the pass in 1750 and gave it its present name.

The Cumberland Gap played a significant role in the settlement of Kentucky and Tennessee. Frontiersman Daniel Boone and his associates used it frequently, and they cut the Wilderness Road through it in 1775. Brisk commercial freight-wagon traffic quickly developed. During much of the late eighteenth and nineteenth centuries, Kentuckians used the Cumberland Gap to drive their stock to markets on the East Coast. Mail delivery through the pass began in 1792, and both Kentucky and Virginia improved the road that led into it from either direction. To help pay for its road improvements, Kentucky

Daniel Boone escorting pioneers through the Cumberland Gap. Nineteenth-century colored print by Artext Prints after the painting by George Caleb Bingham.

established a tollgate slightly north of the gap in 1797, but this idea was not well received by people using the Cumberland Gap. The Southern was the first railroad to reach the pass at the rather late date of 1889, and it was quickly joined by the Louisville and Nashville in 1890. A modern highway now makes its way through the Cumberland Gap, where a museum commemorates the important role played by the pass in settlement and travel.

See also
　　Wilderness Road.
For further reading
　　Mary Verhoeff, *The Kentucky Mountains*, 1911.

CUMBERLAND ROAD
　　See National Road.

CYCLONES
　　See Hurricane.

CYCLOPES
In classical mythology, a race of one-eyed giants who threatened travelers. The three original Cyclopes were the sons of Uranus (the heavens) and Gaia

(the earth), and worked as assistants to Hephaestus, the god of metalsmithing. They were also prodigious builders of walled cities. Their descendants lived as simple, solitary herdsmen in a distant western land frequently identified as part of Sicily. Odysseus encountered these Cyclopes during his wanderings and was taken prisoner by Polyphemus the Cyclops, who claimed the sea god Poseidon as his father. Using his wiles, Odysseus blinded Polyphemus and escaped with most of his men. A few years later, Aeneas and his Trojans visited the land of the Cyclopes on Sicily and narrowly escaped capture and death.

Travelers throughout the ages have populated distant lands with monstrous races, of which the Cyclopes are an early example. Some authorities claim that the single eye of a Cyclops is a symbol for sun worship. Others suggest that the Cyclopes were simply a distant tribe of humans who tattooed an eye or a similar symbol on the middle of their foreheads. Early Greek travelers brought home reports of such tribes, ultimately embellished into a savage race of one-eyed giants.

See also
Aeneas, Wanderings of; Monstrous Races; Odysseus, Wanderings of.
For further reading
Robert Graves, *The Greek Myths*, 1955.

CYNOCEPHALI   The Cynocephali, or dog-headed men, were among the most perennially popular of the various monstrous races thought by ancient and medieval travelers and writers from the West to inhabit India or other places on the periphery of the world.

The Cynocephali were one of many monstrous races to play an important part in the complex of geographical tales known as the Marvels of the East. During the fourth and third centuries B.C., the Greek writers Ctesias and Megasthenes reported dog-headed humans living in India. Pliny the Elder (23/24–79 A.D.) repeated their accounts in his very influential *Natural History*, saying, "On many mountains [in India] there are men with dogs' heads who are covered with wild beasts' skins, they bark instead of speaking and live by hunting and fowling, for which they use their nails. He [Megasthenes] says they were more than 120,000 in number when he published his work."

Pliny's description attributes many of the standard traits of a monstrous race to the Cynocephali. Besides the obvious physical deformity of having dogs' heads, the Cynocephali are not fully human or civilized in other ways. They wear animal skins instead of clothing, lack speech, and obtain their food by hunting rather than farming. Later writers described the Cynocephali as quite warlike, and credited them with being man-eaters. As such, they presented a serious hazard to ancient travelers. Cynocephalic warriors battled Alexander the Great in the medieval romances dealing with his career, and the Cynocephali were one of the savage nations he enclosed behind the Iron Gates of the Caucasus, along with the fearsome Gog and Magog.

Despite such unpromising characteristics, the Cynocephali were not totally savage, and could be converted to Christianity. St. Andrew and St.

Bartholomew converted a Cynocephalic giant named Abominable, thus saving his soul (and themselves from being eaten). St. Mercurius used Cynocephali as helpers and bodyguards. The most famous Cynocephalic convert to Christianity was St. Christopher. According to one version of his legend, St. Christopher was originally a dog-headed giant named Reprobus. Conversion to Christianity and baptism transformed him into a physically powerful human, and he took the name Christopher, or Christ-bearer.

Both the *Letter of Prester John* and the *Travels of Sir John Mandeville* describe the Cynocephali as inhabitants or neighbors of the mysterious realm of Prester John. Neither source describes the dog-headed people as Christian, but Mandeville, at least, considered them civilized. Some accounts of the Cynocephali talk about both male and female members of that monstrous race. Other versions claim that the Cynocephali and the Amazons associated with one another for procreation. Cynocephali and Amazons periodically mated, with the odd result that all male babies were born Cynocephali and all females born human. In this way, both groups of outsiders perpetuated themselves without recourse to civilized human society.

Originally, the Cynocephali were associated with India, but as European geographical interests expanded, Cynocephali appeared in Africa and the far northern regions. Interestingly, the Cynocephali are the only monstrous race of humans to have an animal's head as its deformity; there are no cat-headed, bear-headed, or horse-headed races. This phenomenon indicates the long and close connections between humans and dogs. Some scholars attribute the inspiration for a Cynocephalic race to a dog-faced species of baboons in Ethiopia, believing that early travelers may have mistaken them for monstrous humans. The scholar of religious studies David Gordon White points out that Western, Indian, and Chinese civilizations all have legends about a dog-headed race of monstrous humans. Westerners placed the Cynocephali in India and classified them as part of the Marvels of the East, the Chinese located them in the West, and Indians thought the dog-headed people lived in the far north. White speculates that various nomadic peoples of central Asia provided the inspiration for the Cynocephali. Many of these tribes attributed the creation of their ethnic group to some sort of mating between a human and a dog or wolf, or to the rearing of a human child by dogs or wolves in the same manner as in the legend of Romulus and Remus. The civilized peoples of the West, China, and India picked up on these distant legends and transformed the threatening nomads of central Asia into Cynocephali. No ancient or medieval traveler ever encountered a true Cynocephali, but for thousands of years people believed that they existed somewhere in the margins of the known world.

See also

Alexander the Great, Romances of; Amazons; Cannibals; Gog and Magog; *Mandeville, Travels of Sir John*; Marvels of the East; Monstrous Races; Pliny the Elder; Prester John and His Kingdom; St. Christopher.

For further reading

David Gordon White, *Myths of the Dog-Man*, 1991.

D

DARDANELLES   Also known as the Hellespont, it was one of two narrow straits (the other is the Bosporus) leading from the Black Sea to the Aegean Sea. For the ancient Greeks, the Dardanelles divided Europe from Asia. Navigation through them was tricky and dangerous for sailing ships because of the strong current that flowed from the Black Sea into the Aegean. Cities located along the Dardanelles were generally prosperous due to the rich fishing in that area and the strategic location at the intersection of various trade routes between Europe and Asia. Fabled Troy was located on the Asian shore of the Dardanelles. The width of the Dardanelles was narrow enough that in 480 B.C., the Persian king Xerxes ordered the construction of a bridge of boats between Sestos and Abydos, allowing his army to cross by foot from Asia to Europe during his ill-fated invasion of Greece. Alexander the Great and his army crossed the Dardanelles in the opposite direction in 334 www.porndolls.com on their way to conquer the Persian Empire. Control of the straits has been an important strategic consideration throughout most of history, and great competition for control took place in the nineteenth century. During World War I, the Allies unsuccessfully attempted to capture them from the Turks in 1915.

No great city has grown up on the Dardanelles because of the lack of an adequate harbor. Still, for millennia the Dardanelles have been a familiar landmark for travelers between Europe and Asia.

See also
    Black Sea; Bosporus; Constantinople.
For further reading
    Alan Moorehead, *Gallipoli*, 1956; Ellen Churchill Semple, *The Geography of the Mediterranean Region*, 1931.

DARK CONTINENT   Stereotypical expression used by Westerners during the nineteenth and early twentieth centuries to describe Africa. The phrase "Darkest Africa" is a corollary and described those regions where white control was tenuous or nonexistent. Both expressions emphasized the backwardness and benightedness of African societies and the blackness of their skins.

The image of Africa as a Dark Continent was applied exclusively to sub-Saharan Africa. Europeans first viewed Africa as strange and mysterious when the Portuguese slowly made their way down the coast of West Africa during the fifteenth century. Western traders seeking gold, ivory, and slaves during the sixteenth, seventeenth, and eighteenth centuries confined their activities to a few coastal forts and factories. The African interior remained forbidding and largely unexplored, but compared with the interiors of North and South America and large parts of Asia, Africa was no more unknown or dangerous than any other continent. In fact, around the 1780s and 1790s, European knowledge of Africa was generally more detailed and accurate than for other parts of the world.

During the first half of the nineteenth century, the European image of Africa as the Dark Continent took shape. Opposition to the slave trade grew during the final decades of the eighteenth century, culminating in Great Britain outlawing it in 1807. Other nations followed suit, and the British navy patrolled the West African coast to prevent the illegal smuggling of slaves. Nevertheless, opponents of the slave trade recognized that Africans needed an alternative form of economic activity. In the eyes of the British and other Europeans, these efforts to diversify the African economy were their way of bringing European enlightenment to a benighted land.

As the heartland of the Atlantic slave trade, West Africa provided the initial focus for Dark Continent imagery. Unfortunately, as Europeans tried to uplift the Africans, often they also looked down on them with a culturally arrogant contempt. Adopting the image of Africa as the Dark Continent reinforced these Western prejudices. Geographical ignorance also contributed to the Dark Continent image, as maps of Africa contained large areas of unexplored territory during much of the nineteenth century. By the 1850s, the image of Africa as the Dark Continent had become a stereotype of Western geographical thinking, and the image persisted into the twentieth century, long after Africa was fully explored, mapped, and almost everywhere under some sort of Western colonial control.

Those who are familiar with Africa see it as a continent of continual change and endless variation. The Dark Continent stereotype transforms its varied landscape into a homogeneous and static place full of hostile tribes and dangerous beasts in an untamable jungle, where only the bravest white hunter on safari would venture, or so the explorers of the late nineteenth century portrayed it. The famous, or perhaps notorious, Henry M. Stanley helped

The death struggle between Tarzan (Frank Merrill) and one of the apes in a Jack Nelson play, "Tarzan the Mighty," from the 1920s.

fix the stereotype in the popular reading public's mind with his memoirs, *Through the Dark Continent, or, The Sources of the Nile* (1878) and *In Darkest Africa, or, The Quest, Rescue and Retreat of Emin, Governor of Equatoria* (1890). Myriads of similar "true" accounts of exploration and adventure reinforced this image, as did novelists such as H. Rider Haggard and G. A. Henty.

The Dark Continent of Africa was also viewed as a place of both great antiquity and primitivism. It was supposedly at the bottom of the evolutionary scale, which in turn explained why the natives were allegedly so backward.

The Dark Continent was also a mysterious place in which lay hidden a decadent antiquity of lost cities and civilizations. Haggard's *She* dwelt in Africa, and he located King Solomon's mines in southern Africa in his novel of the same name. Later writers continued to pepper Africa with lost cities. During the 1920s through the 1940s, Edgar Rice Burroughs's many Tarzan novels created so many lost cities that they threatened to jostle each other off the edge of Africa. Burroughs knew little about Africa. For example, in his original Tarzan manuscript, Lord Greystoke beat up both lions and tigers, but an alert and zoologically more informed editor made Burroughs excise the strictly Asiatic tigers from his Dark Continent. His Tarzan novels are a typical example of how Dark Continent imagery persisted into the twentieth century. Cartoons, movies, television, and novels such as Michael Crichton's *Congo* continue to present the stereotype today.

European colonialism and imperialism did not end the stereotype, although for a brief period in the late nineteenth and early twentieth centuries, Europeans thought that the African colonies could be transformed into an idyllic New Zion. This view put only the smallest dent in the prevailing Dark Continent imagery. World War I came and went, leaving Europeans much more pessimistic, and Europeans in Africa came to view the Dark Continent as impermeable to European efforts to civilize and enlighten it. Many felt that Joseph Conrad had gotten it right in his "Heart of Darkness" (1902): Europeans did not conquer Africa, Darkest Africa conquered them. Such ideas continue to influence Western thinking about Africa despite massive historical and contemporary evidence to the contrary.

See also

Africa; Safari; White Man's Grave.

For further reading

Philip D. Curtin, *The Image of Africa*, 1964; Dorothy Hammond and Alta Jablow, *The Myth of Africa*, 1977; Jan Nederveen Pieterse, *White on Black*, 1992.

DELPHI   City in central Greece located on the southern slope of Mount Parnassus near the northern shore of the Gulf of Corinth. Delphi was a sanctuary for the cult of Apollo, including the famous Delphic Oracle, and it hosted the Pythian games, which were second only to the Olympic games in prestige. The ancient Greeks considered Delphi the geographic center (or navel) of the world.

People lived on the site of Delphi in Mycenaean times. Evidence for activity associated with the cult of Apollo began around 800 B.C., with the first temple built shortly before 700 B.C. Some traditions claim that Apollo founded his sanctuary with the help of the Cretans, but others give credit to the Hyperboreans. Various temples stood in the sanctuary over the centuries. War and natural disasters caused some destruction, but sometimes a new temple appeared—simply because a new, larger, and more magnificent structure was desired.

Visitors came to Delphi from all over Greece to worship at the sanctuary of Apollo, but that was not its only attraction for pilgrims. Beginning in 591/590 or 586/585 B.C., the Pythian games were held every eight years, and consisted of a contest to sing hymns in praise of Apollo. More musical and athletic competitions were added, and the games took place every four years, during the third year of each Olympiad.

The highly respected Oracle of Delphi provided the sanctuary's most famous draw for travelers. Its origins date to shortly before 800 B.C., and it developed into the most important oracle in all of Greece. Both cities and individuals consulted with the oracle about politics, colonies, laws, and various religious and cult-related questions. Visitors paid a consultation fee before the rituals of prophecy even began. A series of sacrifices was conducted, after which the visitor was brought into the presence of the oracle, or *Pythia*, by interpreters called the *prophetai*. In the innermost sanctum of the temple (the room containing the *omphalos*, or navel of the earth), the *Pythia* sat on a tripod chair. Going into a trance, the *Pythia* would utter pronouncements, which were further interpreted by the *prophetai*. The end products of this process were rather vague prophecies that the recipients could interpret in any number of ways. The most famous prophecy by the oracle at Delphi occurred as the invading army of Xerxes of Persia threatened Greek independence. The Athenians sought the advice of the oracle, who told them to put their faith in the wooden wall. Some took the prophecy to mean the wooden palisade surrounding the Acropolis, so they barricaded themselves inside, and the invading Persians massacred them. Others thought the prophecy referred to the fleet of Athens. They evacuated Athens, and were later vindicated by the Greek fleet's defeat of the Persians at Salamis in 480 B.C. The oracle mainly supplied advice and guidance, rather than functioning as some ancient psychic hot line. The ancient Greeks took such pronouncements very seriously, and people traveled long distances and expended much time and money to consult the oracle. They remained well satisfied over the centuries, making Delphi one of the leading tourist attractions of ancient Greece.

See also

Hyperborea; Pilgimage.

For further reading

J. Fontenrose, *The Delphic Oracle*, 1978; N. Marinatos and R. Hägg, eds., *Greek Sanctuaries*, 1993.

Dog-Headed Race
See Cynocephali.

Donkey
Also called ass or burro, the donkey is a member of the genus *Equus* and is closely related to the horse. Unlike the horse, most human societies throughout history looked down on the humble donkey. Donkeys are notoriously stubborn and generally do not exhibit individual personalities like horses do. However, donkeys can perform a great deal of labor on very poor fodder. As a result, they have become the beast of burden of the poor in many cultures, and their status in the human hierarchy of animals is correspondingly low. For thousands of years, one of the most important functions of male donkeys in human societies has been to breed with female horses to produce the very useful mule.

Donkeys are natives of Africa and are classified as *Equus africanus* in their wild state, while domesticated donkeys are *Equus asinus*. It seems probable that the ancient Egyptians domesticated the donkey as early as the fourth millennium B.C., and definitely by the Fifth dynasty (ca. 2500 B.C.), because tomb paintings of domesticated donkeys appeared then. From Egypt the domesticated donkey expanded into Palestine, a region closely associated with Egypt. Further spread slowed, although it reached Mesopotamia about 1800 B.C., and Asia Minor during the Hittite era (1600–1200 B.C.). Although a native of the desert, the donkey proved to be very adaptable to wetter and cooler climates such as Ireland. This trait allowed the donkey to spread throughout the world; poor farmers needed a strong, easily maintained beast of burden even if it was rather unglamorous.

The donkey was not always an object of contempt. Ancient Egyptians greatly prized their donkeys, as did the Romans, who associated the animal with Vesta, the goddess of hearth and home. Although both the Egyptians and Romans rode donkeys, the ancient Hebrews and Nubians most regularly used donkeys as riding animals. Of course, the most famous donkey ride in history is Christ's entry into Jerusalem on the first Palm Sunday. People use donkeys for riding, but not for galloping, because the donkey's gait is too bouncy for comfort. More commonly, the hardy donkey is used as a pack animal by people traveling in arid or mountainous regions. The grizzled prospector with his reliable donkey is a stock character in many Western movies and television shows. On the other hand, donkeys were never commonly used as draft or plow animals. Still, for thousands of years donkeys have assisted travelers, particularly the poorer segments of human society.

See also
Horse; Jerusalem; Mule.

For further reading
Juliet Clutton-Brock, *Horse Power*, 1992; A. Dent, *Donkey*, 1972; Frederick E. Zeuner, *A History of Domesticated Animals*, 1963.

DONNER PARTY

DONNER PARTY   This tragic wagon train party was forced to engage in cannibalism when it was trapped by winter storms in the Sierra Nevada Mountains on its way to California.

The Donner party consisted of 87 people, mostly from Sangamon County, Illinois. Although called the Donner party, the group was initially led by James Reed, a well-to-do family man. Conflicts and jealousies broke out along the trail, which resulted in Reed being banished. Reaching the vicinity of Salt Lake City, the wagon train decided to take the advice of Lansford Hastings's guidebook and try a shortcut. Unfortunately for them, the course they took proved to be longer than the regular route and extremely rugged. Their progress was so delayed that winter storms trapped them in the Sierra Nevada Moountains during Novemer 1846. Starvation set in. Some of the emigrants darkly contemplated killing two friendly Indians who had been guiding the party. The canny Indians managed to slip away before their potential murderers had steeled themselves to commit the gruesome act. Soon the weak began to die, and the living, desperate to survive, began to eat them.

Meanwhile, rescue parties from California tried to reach the trapped wagon train. Eventually they got through and brought the remaining members of the Donner party to safety. Only 47 people survived, while 40 had died. The Donner party disaster did little to stem the flood of wagon trains rolling toward California and Oregon. It was also an exceptional event. Although there were a few similar tragedies, most wagon trains made it through safely. Popular culture has tended to exaggerate the perils of overland emigration to the West Coast. It was difficult, but it was not all that deadly. The Donner party was just more unlucky than most.

See also

Oregon Trail; Wagon Trains.

For further reading

George R. Stewart, *Ordeal by Hunger,* 1960; John D. Unruh, *The Plains Across, 1840–1860,* 1979.

DRAGONS

DRAGONS   Giant winged reptiles who often breathed fire, they frequently guarded the stolen treasures or captive maidens lying at the end of many heroes' quests.

The existence of dragons is almost universal in the mythologies of cultures throughout the world. Dragons are frequently associated with myths of creation, order, and chaos, and are usually portrayed as intelligent creatures with the power of speech. In Western culture, dragons are generally considered to be dangerous, hostile, or outright evil. Oriental culture, however, views dragons as generally benevolent creatures who bring rain and promote order. Wicked dragons were believed to inhabit remote wilderness areas far from civilization, although they made occasional forays to harass their hapless human neighbors. In the legend of St. George, a dragon ravaged the region of Cappadocia in Asia

Knight in armor slaying a dragon. From Raoul Lefèvre, Le receuil des histoires de Troyes, *Haarlem 1485.*

Minor. The residents appeased him by giving him young men and women to eat. The sacrificial victims were chosen by lot, and one day, the daughter of the king drew the fateful lot. After much delay, she presented herself to the hungry dragon, but the heroic St. George intervened. In some versions, he killed the dragon, and in others he overcame and tamed it. Either way, the king's daughter was saved. Similar stories occur in Norse and Teutonic mythology, and in modern times in J. R. R. Tolkein's *The Hobbit* (1937). Belief in dragons was common in the early Middle Ages, and it gave nervous travelers something to think about as they passed through the barren wildernesses favored by dragons.

E

EDEN, GARDEN OF
See Paradise, Terrestrial.

EGERIA
Also known by the names Etheria, Eutheria, Aetheria, and Silvia, this nun of the late fourth or early fifth century left the first Christian account of a journey to the Holy Land. That account is the beginning of travel literature describing Christian pilgrimages.

The *Peregrinatio* of Egeria survives in a partial manuscript from the eleventh century, discovered in 1884, in the form of a letter from Egeria to her fellow nuns in a Spanish monastery. Beginning at Mount Sinai, Egeria's journey follows the route of the Exodus, and describes the various stops along the way to Jerusalem in terms of their Old Testament connections. Upon reaching Jerusalem, the narrator shifts to descriptions of various churches and their services. Egeria also visited the tomb of St. Thomas at Edessa and stopped at Constantinople during the return journey.

Little is known about Egeria. Most scholars identify her as a nun or abbess from a Spanish monastery, possibly located in Galicia. Her manuscript was initially credited to St. Sylvia, but the discovery of a seventh-century reference to the *Peregrinatio* in a library catalog identified the author as Egeria. Some authorities claim that she lived in Italy or France, and some date her pilgrimage as late as the sixth century. Sometimes she is referred to as young and uneducated, while others claim she was an older, well-educated woman. Egeria was a pioneer of pilgrimages and travel accounts of them, but her long-term influence on the form and practice of pilgrimages to the Holy Land was slight.

See also
Constantinople; Exodus; Holy Land; Jerusalem; Pilgimage.

For further reading
Mary B. Campbell, *The Witness and the Other World*, 1988; George E. Gingras, ed., *Egeria*, 1970; John Wilkinson, trans., *Egeria's Travels in the Holy Land*, 1981.

EL DORADO   Geographical myth that tempted European explorers to
search for a golden king or a golden land in the inaccessible mountains and
jungles of northern South America during the sixteenth and early seventeenth centuries.

The origin of the legends of El Dorado was a genuine ritual of a Native
American tribe living in what is now Colombia by Lake Guatavita on the Bogatá
plateau, or Cundinamarca. Once a year the tribe reconsecrated their king by
covering his body with sticky turpentine and having him roll in gold dust. Clothed
in this magnificent way, the king led a procession to the shores of the lake,
where he boarded a canoe and was paddled to the middle. After throwing offer-
ings of gold and precious stones into the waters, the king dove in to wash off the
gold dust. He then returned to shore and participated in further festivities.
Such a ritual was extremely impressive, and word of it spread among the neighboring tribes and kingdoms. Although the Chibcha overlords of Cundinamarca
suppressed the ritual around the beginning of the sixteenth century, the legend
of El Dorado persisted. As Spaniards settled the Isthmus of Panama and the
northern coast of South America up to 1530, they heard rumors of the legend
from various tribes. Out in the unexplored regions lay the golden man, *el hombre
dorado,* and his wealthy realm. Such a kingdom certainly sounded plausible to
the Spanish.

From 1519 to 1521, Hernán Cortés conquered the splendid empire of the
Aztecs in Mexico. Tales of other rich but undiscovered lands proliferated. Francisco Pizarro had been trying to reach fabled Peru since 1524. He finally succeeded in 1531, and by 1533 the fantastically rich Inca Empire had fallen to
him and his fellow conquistadors. In this feverish atmosphere of gold hunger
and get-rich-quick conquests, the search for El Dorado began.

In 1527, Emperor Charles V of Spain and Germany granted the region of
Venezuela to the Welser bankers of Augsburg as partial payment for some of his
debts. Welser agents arriving in Venezuela quickly learned about the existence
of El Dorado, the golden king. Hopes and dreams of treasure soon transformed
the king's yearly bath of gold into a daily occurrence, and his kingdom's wealth
was said to rival or exceed that of the Aztecs. In 1529, Welser agent Ambrosius
Ehinger (or Alfinger, d. 1533) led the first expedition to find El Dorado. Starting at the port of Coro, he made his way into the mountains of Colombia, reaching the site of modern Pamplona. His route brought him close to Cundinamarca,
but the rigors of wilderness travel caused him to return home rather than press
forward. Ehinger failed to find El Dorado, but his example triggered a stampede
of searchers that was most intense during the 1530s and continued fairly steadily
into the early seventeenth century. At certain times in the 1530s, up to three
simultaneous expeditions careened through the jungles, llanos, and mountains
of Venezuela and Colombia vainly seeking El Dorado.

In 1530, another Welser employee, Nicholas Federmann (d. 1542), led an
expedition in search of El Dorado. Leaving from Coro, he and his party worked
their way through the jungle at the bottom of the eastern cordillera of the Andes
with no success. Ehinger himself made a second attempt from 1531 to 1533 and
plunged into the mountains of northern Colombia. Rugged terrain, an inhospi-

table climate, and hostile natives took their toll. Ehinger died after being hit by a poisoned arrow.

A Spaniard named Diego de Ordaz also become inflamed by the rumors of El Dorado. He tried to find the elusive golden king in 1531 by entering the mouth of the great Orinoco River and traveling upstream. Contrary river currents and the steamy jungle environment hampered the search for the nonexistent realm, but native informants told the Spaniards that El Dorado lived up the Meta River, a large tributary of the Orinoco in western Venezuela. Apparently, the natives had discovered that the fastest and easiest way to get the unwelcome Spanish visitors to move on was to tell them that El Dorado lay ahead somewhere. At that time, however, Spanish credulity remained at a high level, so in 1533 another fruitless expedition led by Alonso de Herrera made its way up the Orinoco and the Meta. All Herrera found for his troubles was more stories of El Dorado. The difficulty of traveling up the flood-swollen Orinoco caused another conquistador, Jeronimo de Ortal (d. ca. 1545), to reach the river and El Dorado by traveling cross-country. Thick jungles hampered Ortal, and on his first journey in 1536, he failed to reach the Orinoco. His exasperated men abandoned him in the jungle. Trying again in 1540, he succeeded in reaching the Orinoco, but it proved to be of no avail in the quest for El Dorado.

Despite so many failures, the riches of the gold king beckoned with their fascinating but deadly promises. Georg Hohermuth von Speyer (d. 1540) set out for the Meta region, traveling down the eastern cordillera, during 1535–1537. The savage terrain devastated his party. Although he heard rumors of a wealthy kingdom on the other side of the mountains, he could find no pass to cross them. Worn down, he returned to Coro with only one-quarter of his original 400 men.

The man who finally reached Cundinamarca was the Spaniard Gonzalo Jiménez de Quesada (1509–1579). Traveling up the Magdalena River in 1536, Quesada and his men reached the Bogatá plateau and conquered the Chibcha Empire occupying the highland region. While they were doing so, two more parties of frantic seekers joined them in 1539. A party led by Nicholaus Federmann had made its way through the jungles and found a pass through the eastern cordillera. Another party under the leadership of Sebastian de Belalcazar traveled from Quito through the Andes. The wealth of the Chibchas, while substantial, paled when compared to that of the Aztecs and the Incas. Because they had no sources of gold, they had to trade for it with other tribes. Thus, once the conquistadors plundered them, the Chibchas stayed plundered. The Chibcha Empire also contained Lake Guatavita, source of the legend of the fabled golden king. Unfortunately, its reality fell short of the legend's magnificence. The Spanish conquistadors concluded that the Chibchas were not nearly rich enough to be the kingdom of El Dorado—it must lie somewhere else. The real El Dorado having been rejected, the supposed location of the legendary El Dorado began a steady eastward movement into the trackless rain forests of the Amazon and Orinoco river basins, and eventually reached the Guiana Highlands.

In 1541, two widely separated expeditions set out to find El Dorado. Gonzalo Pizarro (1512–1548), a younger brother of Francisco, led a band across the Andes to the Napo River, a tributary of the Amazon. Heat, humidity, and dwindling supplies chipped away at the thoroughly disoriented expedition. A desperate Pizarro sent his friend Francisco de Orellana (1511–1546) downriver in a brig constructed by the Spaniards to look for food, but the river's swift, strong current precluded his return. Orellana's Spaniards had no alternative, so they proceeded downriver, encountering numerous hostile natives (including some supposed Amazons). They also heard more rumors of El Dorado as they passed through the territory of the Omaguas near the Rio Negro. By August 1542, they managed the incredible feat of reaching the Atlantic Ocean by traveling the length of the mighty Amazon River.

Meanwhile, the last of the German conquistadors, Philipp von Hutten (1511–1546), traveled from the Venezuelan coast deep into the interior during 1541–1546. Like previous travelers in the rain forest, von Hutten and his men experienced horrendous living conditions and trials. As they advanced south, they heard stories from the natives about a rich city of the Omaguas. Marching toward it in late 1542 with his much depleted force, von Hutten hoped that he had finally located the long-sought-after El Dorado. Instead, he found an impressive and populous settlement of decidedly hostile Omaguas. Only his cavalry saved von Hutten and his party from annihilation. Since it was obviously hopeless to enter the dangerous country of the Omaguas, von Hutten began the arduous return trip to Coro. He arrived in the midst of deadly and treasonous in-fighting among the Spaniards, which resulted in his own grisly death. Philipp von Hutten was the last of the ill-fated Welser agents to operate in Venezuela. As a result of von Hutten's account of his adventures, the term *El Dorado* shifted from referring to the golden king to the wealthy city or kingdom of the golden king. From then on, El Dorado meant a place, not a person.

After the failures of Gonzalo Pizarro and Philipp von Hutten, the fevered seeking of El Dorado stopped for a few years. In 1559, interest revived. A party of Brazilian Indians led by a chief named Viraratu fled up the Amazon to escape brutal warfare in their native land. Reaching Peru, the refugees spoke of a large lake surrounded by mountains and inhabited by brave warriors commanded by a golden king. When the Spanish heard this story, they immediately thought of the El Dorado of the Omaguas. The newly arrived viceroy of Peru, the marquis of Onate, immediately organized an expedition headed by the noble Pedro de Ursua. Unfortunately for Ursua, flocking to his banner were the dregs of Spanish Peru, including the homicidal megalomaniac Lope de Aguirre. As the Spanish force plunged farther into the quagmire of the rain forest searching for El Dorado, Ursua's authority disintegrated. A mutiny instigated by Aguirre resulted in Ursua's death, and the remaining conquistadors concocted a fantastic scheme to take over Peru from the Spanish crown. With this goal in mind, Aguirre wanted to avoid the distraction of El Dorado. Heading north away from the Amazon basin and the land of the Omaguas, he followed the complex network of tributaries to the Orinoco River. Reaching the Atlantic Ocean, Aguirre died fighting the local Spanish authorities in 1561. The Ursua/

Aguirre journey began with a search for El Dorado, but ended with an audacious act of treason.

Despite the repeated failures to locate El Dorado, others continued the quest. The venerable Gonzalo de Quesada made another attempt from 1569 to 1572 to find El Dorado in the jungles and llanos east of the Andes in what is now Venezuela. Exploration of the llanos and rain forests of the lowlands made it clear that El Dorado was not located there. Europeans were unwilling to give up on El Dorado, so they simply "moved it" to the unexplored and mysterious Guiana Highlands.

Antonio de Berrio (ca. 1520–1598) sought El Dorado in the Guiana Highlands that lay south of the Orinoco. Between 1581 and 1591, he led five expeditions into the upper reaches of the Orinoco and later into the Guiana Highlands. In 1593, he sent a sixth expedition under Domingo de Vera to investigate the Caroni River, a tributary of the Orinoco. The Caroni supposedly provided a good route for reaching El Dorado and its great city of Manoa. But no El Dorado was found. Instead, in 1595, the Englishman Sir Walter Raleigh appeared with a small fleet at the mouth of the Orinoco. After capturing Berrio, Raleigh and a party of his men proceeded upriver. Apart from establishing cordial relations with the natives, the English did not explore any territory that the Spanish had not already visited many times. However, Raleigh gathered some dubious intelligence about the location of El Dorado. Native informants told him of a rich, warlike people who lived in the Guiana Highlands. The capital of this particular El Dorado was the fabled city of Manoa. These El Doradans were reputed to be related to the Incas of Peru. An early version of the Incan/El Doradan connection claimed that the El Doradans were Incan refugees who fled the Spanish conquest and tyranny in Peru. A later variation reversed the movement of people and identified the El Dorado of the Guiana Highlands as the original Inca homeland. Raleigh left the Orinoco, taking these stories back to England and Europe. He spread the legend of El Dorado though his book *The Discoverie of the Large, Rich, and Bewtiful Empyre of Guiana, with a Relation of the Great and Golden Citie of Mano (which the Spaniards call El Dorado)* (1596). Raleigh hoped to return to the Orinoco quickly, but events conspired against him. In 1603, James I became the king of England, and soon after, Raleigh found himself imprisoned (1603–1616) for allegedly participating in a plot to overthrow the new king. On 12 June 1617, Raleigh's second expedition to the Orinoco sailed at last. He was under strict orders not to engage in hostilities with the Spanish, but armed conflict broke out soon after the English arrived. Raleigh's son Wat died at the hands of Spaniards. Almost equally tragic for the desperate Raleigh, the expedition failed to locate either El Dorado or gold. The miserable results of Raleigh's second expedition gave James I an excuse to have him executed. Raleigh's failure to find El Dorado may have killed him, but it did not kill the legend.

Raleigh was the last important seeker of El Dorado, although a few minor expeditions were launched in the following years. By the eighteenth century, El Dorado had become a fantasyland. In Voltaire's novel *Candide* (1759), his protagonists visited El Dorado, but it is obvious that Voltaire did not take its existence seriously. El Dorado became the name of various mining towns during the gold rushes of the nineteenth century. Spaniards, Germans, and English sought the elusive El Dorado for a hundred years, and its legend lives on today.

See also
Amazon River.
For further reading
Robert Silverberg, *The Golden Dream*, 1996; John Hemming, *The Search for El Dorado*, 1978; Charles Nicholl, *The Creature in the Map*, 1995; Victor Wolfgang von Hagen, *The Golden Man*, 1974.

ELEPHANT   Throughout history, elephants have inspired awe and wonder because of their great size and strength. That very size has also prevented elephants from playing more than a limited role as a means of transportation or as a beast of burden—they need too much food and tire too easily.

At the beginning of human civilization, elephants survived in two distinct species—the African and the Indian. African elephants (*Loxodonta africana*) are the larger of the two, with bigger ears and two fingerlike appendages at the tips of their trunks. However, a smaller subspecies of the African elephant, *Loxodonta africana cyclotis*, existed in North Africa during the Roman Empire. It may be the main source for most tame African elephants used in the Mediterranean world, and is probably responsible for the frequent comments by classical authors that African elephants are smaller than Indian elephants.

Indian elephants are not as large, have smaller ears, and their trunks have only one fingerlike appendage. All elephants are highly intelligent, and in captivity readily submit to training. Indian elephants are considered more docile and trainable than African elephants.

The first domestication of elephants occurred in the civilization of Mohenjo-Daro, located in the Indus Valley and flourishing from 2500 to 1500 B.C. Tame elephants were confined to the Indian subcontinent until 326 B.C., when Alexander the Great defeated the elephant-equipped army of King Porus of the Punjab. The use of the elephant as a weapon of war quickly spread across the Middle East and the Mediterranean. The Carthaginians of North Africa used them no later than 262 B.C.

Elephants are generally not bred and raised in captivity because they are too expensive to keep. Females cannot work during their long pregnancy of 22 months. Elephants are famous for being long-lived creatures who frequently reach the age of 70 and more. They also go through a lengthy childhood and adolescence, during which they are capable of little work. Wild adult elephants, on the other hand, can be captured with relative ease and readily respond to training. Nevertheless, because they consume prodigious amounts of fodder, the use of domesticated elephants is largely confined to areas of lush forests such as India, where elephants can browse for their meals at little expense to their owners. Generally, elephants perform tasks of heavy lifting or hauling under the guidance of a human called a *mahout*. *Mahouts* perform their duties either by leading their elephants or by riding on their necks and directing them with a prod. Other passengers can ride on an elephant's back in a *howdah*, a platform with seats that is attached to the elephant's back like a saddle. Riding on an elephant has always been a relatively rare mode of transportation, but various potentates liked to ride on elephants in processions to impress their subjects. The use of elephants for long-distance travel was confined to India, and even there, it was a rarity. In Jules Verne's *Around the World in Eighty Days* (1872), when their railroad trip was unexpectedly interrupted, the fictional Phileas Fogg and his traveling companions undertook an elephant journey only as a last resort.

The basic reason for the spread of tamed elephants outside the Indian sub-continent was war. Elephants served as an ancient version of the tank, and they could double as a pack animal. Alexander the Great's successors—the Seleucids of Syria, the Antigonids of Macedonia, and the Ptolemys of Egypt—all deployed large numbers of elephants in their armies. The Carthaginians of western North

The procession of the elephants, Delhi, India. Stereo photo by Underwood and Underwood, 1903.

Africa adopted the practice no later than 262 B.C. When Hannibal begin his invasion of Italy in 218 B.C., his army contained 37 elephants, one of which was an Indian elephant named Surus (the Syrian). Surus was the only elephant able to survive the rigors of the army's march from Spain to Italy, which included arduous crossings of the Pyrenees and the Alps.

Despite being an impressive weapon, elephants were unreliable, and they were by no means invulnerable. Eleazar Maccabee managed to kill a Seleucid elephant in battle by getting underneath it and stabbing it in the unprotected belly, but the dying animal in turn crushed him (1 Maccabees 6:46). The elephants' intelligence made them readily aware of the dangers they faced on a battlefield, and they naturally fled when frightened or in too much pain. The annals of ancient warfare are full of battles in which elephants greatly disrupted their army's lines by fleeing when they should have charged. For example, Ptolemy IV Philopator's elephants refused to fight at the battle of Raphia in 217 B.C.; fortunately, he still won the battle. At the battle of Zama in 202 B.C., the Carthaginians' elephants panicked, and their masters lost the fight. Once the Romans conquered the Mediterranean basin, they abandoned the elephant as a weapon of war and never adapted it to serve as a beast of burden or transportation. Instead, the elephant became a rare curiosity and an object of fascination for medieval Westerners. Even today, the elephant is one of the best-loved animals in zoos.

See also

Carthage.

For further reading

Juliet Clutton-Brock, *A Natural History of Domesticated Mammals*, 1987; H. H. Scullard, *The Elephant in the Greek and Roman World*, 1974; Frederick E. Zeuner, *A History of Domesticated Animals*, 1963.

ELYSIAN FIELDS

Or Elysium, the counterpart of Paradise or Heaven in Greco-Roman mythology. For the peoples of the Mediterranean world during the classical era, the landscape of Paradise was a meadow in springtime with a bubbling brook passing through it and a grove of trees at the side. Such a scene described the Elysian Fields in the land of the dead. The Elysian Fields were the part of Tartarus, or Hades, where those people judged to be good went to live for eternity. Its happy inhabitants enjoyed an inexhaustible supply of high-quality food and drink along with continual good health.

The Homeric Greeks placed Tartarus far to the west on the other side of the world-surrounding River Ocean. Later traditions transformed Tartarus into an underworld, literally located below the surface world of the living. The Roman poet Virgil's hero Aeneas visited the Elysian Fields during his journey to the underworld. The historian Plutarch also believed that the Elysian Fields, along with the rest of Tartarus, were located inside the earth. Unlike the rest of Tartarus, however, the bucolic Elysian Fields were never completely and permanently banished underground. Perhaps the incongruity of locating a lovely land of eternal spring underground contributed to keeping the Elysian Fields somewhere on the surface of the earth. According to some authors, the island of Leuce, near the mouth of the Danube River in the Black Sea, was the site of the Elysian Fields. For many ancient writers, the Elysian Fields were a paradisial island or islands located somewhere in the vast western ocean. Some people thought that the Fortunate Isles (the classical name for the Canary Islands) were the Elysian Fields. The cosmologies of many ancient mythologies located an idyllic land of the dead or an earthly paradise in the western ocean or in lands on the other side of it. Out of such traditions came the various stories of the Fortunate Isles, the Isle of the Blessed, and Avalon.

See also

Aeneas, Wanderings of; Fortunate Isles; Paradise, Terrestrial; Tartarus.

For further reading

Lempriere's Classical Dictionary, 1788.

ERIE CANAL   Also known as "Clinton's Ditch" because of DeWitt Clinton's crucial role in getting it built across western New York between 1817 and 1825, it was the best-known and most economically important canal built inside the United States.

Europeans had been building canals with great success since the middle of the seventeenth century, and in the 1780s, various Americans began talking about and building canals to improve the internal transportation system of the young United States. A number of people saw the obvious utility of building a canal from the Hudson River down the Mohawk Valley, taking advantage of existing rivers and lakes to reach Lake Ontario and Lake Erie.

After considerable debate, the New York legislators provided funding for the canal, and work began in 1817. Builders divided the canal's construction into three segments: from Rome, New York, to the Hudson River; Rome to the Seneca River; and Buffalo to the Seneca River. The eastern sections were completed first, and their toll revenues provided the money needed to finish the rest of the canal. Completion took eight years, and the entire canal opened on 26 October 1825. The canal was 363 miles long and 40 feet wide, with towpaths on both sides. In 1862, it was improved and widened to 70 feet. Eighty-three locks were built along the canal to raise and lower canal boats over steep elevations. The most famous were the set of five double-locks at Lockport, New York. This magnificent canal cost over $7 million to build.

The Erie Canal proved to be a huge success. Immense numbers of canal boats passed up and down its waters, and both New York State and New York City were greatly enriched by it. Freight boats traveled an average of 55 miles per 24-hour day, although an express passenger boat could travel 100 miles in 24 hours. Passenger boats were equipped with sleeping berths and dining facilities. Despite competition from the railroads, the Erie Canal made good profits until 1882, when its tolls were abolished. The canal proved to be an excellent and cost-effective way to move people and goods between the East Coast and the Midwest in the days before the railroads matured as a means of transportation and travel.

See also
    Canals; Railroads.
For further reading
    Russell Bourne, *Floating West*, 1992.

ETHIOPIA   Also known as Abyssinia, this ancient kingdom was located near the Horn of Africa. Ethiopia adopted Christianity during late antiquity, but the rise of Islam in the late seventh and early eighth centuries cut off the kingdom from the rest of Christendom. When it reemerged into European consciousness in the thirteenth and fourteenth centuries, Ethiopia made a very good candidate for being the mysterious Christian kingdom of Prester John.

Ethiopia derives from the Greek and means "land of the burnt-faced people," and like the names Guinea and Sudan, refers to the lands and black skins of sub-Saharan Africans. The ancient state of Axum (or Aksum), which flourished during the first millennium B.C., was the ancestor of Ethiopia. When the ancient Greeks first visited Ethiopia in 665 B.C., they apparently had a great deal of respect for the natives. In the beginning of the *Odyssey*, Homer states that Poseidon had gone to accept a great sacrifice of cattle and sheep from the Ethiopians and participate in a festival held in his honor.

The ancient Greeks considered Ethiopia the land of the Negroes, or blacks. It was, from early on, closely linked with India. In the *Odyssey*, Homer spoke of eastern (Indian) and western (African) Ethiopians. Homer's distinction between the two types received confirmation in Herodotus's *History* (bk. 7, ch. 70), in which he describes the various nations comprising the massive army Xerxes mustered to invade Greece. Herodotus wrote, "The eastern Ethiopians . . . differed in nothing from other Ethiopians, save in their language and the character of their hair. For the eastern Ethiopians have straight hair while they of Libya [Africa] are more woolly-haired than any other people in the world." Apparently, Herodotus and his fellow Greeks lumped the dark-skinned peoples of India and the Negroes of sub-Saharan Africa into one group called Ethiopians.

The conflation of Ethiopia and India continued into the Middle Ages. Some medieval geographers mistakenly believed that India and Ethiopia were located very close to each other, with only a small section of sea separating them. Others maintained that land physically connected the two countries in a manner reminiscent of the landlocked Indian Ocean described in Claudius Ptolemy's *Geography*. Ptolemy believed that the Indian Ocean was an inland sea surrounded by land; if it had been true, India and Ethiopia would literally be linked. Vague memories of Ptolemy's geographical concepts may have influenced

Gervase of Tilbury (fl. 1211) to classify India as part of Ethiopia in his *Otia Imperialia,* while the anonymous author of *De Imagine Mundi* (ca. 1100) considered the land of Sheba also to be part of Ethiopia. The persistence of such ideas illustrates the degree to which the rise of the Islamic Empire had isolated Ethiopia from Europe.

During the era of the European Crusades in Palestine (1095–1291), Ethiopian power revived under the Zagwe (1137–1270) and Solomonid (1270–1525) dynasties. The knowledge of the existence of Ethiopia, a large and powerful Christian kingdom in Africa, reemerged among Europeans. By the fourteenth century, this knowledge prompted various ideas about establishing alliances between Europeans and Ethiopians against the Muslims. It also caused some to identify Ethiopia as the realm of Prester John, a powerful and mysterious Christian kingdom originally thought to be located in central Asia.

European interest in Ethiopia continued through the late fifteenth and early sixteenth centuries. The Portuguese king João II sent Pedro da Covilha to scout out the lands of the Indian Ocean and Ethiopia. Covilha ended up staying in Ethiopia permanently, and married a native woman supplied by the Ethiopian king. This episode, however, marked the zenith of European interest and contact with Ethiopia until the nineteenth century. Poor and primitive transportation facilities, rugged terrain, and a cruel climate combined to keep Ethiopia an isolated land of mystery until the visit of the Scotsman James Bruce in 1769–1773. In 1896, the country became the target of unsuccessful Italian imperialistic expansion during the European scramble for Africa. The Italians returned in 1936 to conquer Ethiopia, one of a series of fascist aggressions that led up to World War II. Modern Ethiopia is no longer a land of mystery; it is instead a land pathetically and chronically vexed by poverty and famine.

See also

Guinea; Herodotus; India; Prester John and His Kingdom.

For further reading

E. H. Bunbury, *A History of Ancient Geography,* 1883; J. R. S. Phillips, *The Medieval Expansion of Europe,* 1988; John Kirtland Wright, *The Geographical Lore of the Time of the Crusades,* 1925.

EUPHEMUS OF CARIA (FL. BEFORE 150 A.D.), VOYAGE OF

Blown through the Strait of Gibraltar, this Greek mariner was carried far into the Atlantic Ocean until he reached an unknown land, a lovely island inhabited by people with red skins and horses' tails. The natives proved to be hostile, and Euphemus returned home. His story raises a number of questions. Did his voyage actually take place? and where did he make landfall? Pausanias (fl. second century A.D.) tells the story of Euphemus in his *Guide to Greece* in the context of discussing satyrs, hence the red-skinned people with horses' tails. Otherwise, he is quite vague about when Euphemus sailed and how long his voyage lasted. Pausanias may have simply made up the story of Euphemus, but some suggest that Euphemus reached the West Indies, and that his red-skinned people were Caribbean islanders. It is also possible that Euphemus was blown in a more southerly direction and reached the Canary Islands. The aboriginal Guanches of the Canaries could be described as red-skinned. Whether real or not, Euphemus's voyage had little impact on Western geographical thought other than to add one more vague report of a western land, or Terra Occidentalis, across the Atlantic Ocean.

See also

Atlantic Ocean; Canary Islands; Terra Occidentalis.

For further reading

M. Cary and E. H. Warmington, *The Ancient Explorers*, 1963.

EUROPE   The smallest of the continents of the world, Europe was the seat of Western civilization and Christendom during the Middle Ages, and the foremost region practicing imperialism and colonialism from the late fifteenth to the early twentieth centuries.

Europe was one of the three continents of the known world of the Greco-Roman and Judeo-Christian traditions (the other two are Africa and Asia). Europe was associated with Noah's son Japheth. During the pre-Christian eras, Western civilization centered on Egypt, the Middle East, and the Aegean Sea region, and the size and shape of Europe were no better known than those of Asia or Africa. Some ancient scholars postulated that Europe was bounded on the north and west by the encircling River Ocean, but the ancient historian Herodotus (484–420 B.C.) disputed that contention. Others extended Europe's eastern boundaries to include the dimly perceived area now known as Siberia, which made Europe the largest of the three known continents. It also accounts for why some northern Asiatic peoples were biblically classified as Japhethites. The bounds of Europe shrank as the voyages of the Carthaginian Himilco and the Greek Pytheas proved the existence of Europe's Atlantic Ocean and North Sea boundaries. Traditional geographies also set Europe's eastern boundary at the Ural Mountains and the Don River, giving vast Siberia to Asia.

Meanwhile, the Roman Empire brought much of Europe under its sway, including modern England, France, Belgium, Switzerland, Spain, Portugal, a substantial part of Germany, and most of the Balkan Peninsula. After the collapse of the Western Roman Empire by A.D. 476, medieval Christendom replaced the Romans and brought the rest of present-day Europe into the fold during the course of centuries of missionary work. Superior naval and military technology allowed the Europeans to embark on successful colonial ventures that brought much of the earth under their control for varying periods of time between the sixteenth and twentieth centuries. Europe perceived itself as an area of the highest civilization and cultural sophistication, and much of the world shared that view at the beginning of the twentieth century. That is certainly what travelers visiting Europe came to expect in the nineteenth and early twentieth centuries. The devastations and dislocations of the two world wars did much to gradually erode that image.

See also

Africa; Asia; Himilco, Voyage of; Pytheas of Massilia, Voyage of; Siberia.

EXILES People who have been forced to leave their homeland and live some-place else for a period of time.

People go into exile, voluntary or involuntary, for all sorts of reasons. Some are escaping religious persecution. Islam officially began in 622 with the prophet Muhammad's flight from Mecca into exile at Medina. Sixteenth-century England had its Protestant exiles during the reign of Mary Tudor (1553–1558) and its Roman Catholic exiles during the reign of Elizabeth I (1558–1603). In Russia, Old Believers fled into the wilderness of Siberia, and Doukobhors fled to Canada to escape persecution by the Orthodox Church and the Tsarist government. Parsis from Iran made their way to India in 937 to avoid forced conversion by the Islamic conquerors of Sassanid Persia. Numerous other examples of religious exiles abound.

Political persecution motivated other groups to leave their homelands. Karl Marx ended up living in London because no other country in nineteenth-century Europe would allow him to stay. Even the relatively tolerant English contemplated deporting him to the United States. Lenin and his fellow Russian Bolsheviks formed an exile community in Zurich in the years before and during World War I. Although lonely and alienated, they avoided the considerably less pleasant prospect of becoming internal exiles in harsh, distant Siberia, which the Tsarist government inflicted on hundreds of thousands of Russians. French novelist Victor Hugo lived on the island of Guernsey from 1851 to 1870 because Emperor Napoléon III banished him from France.

Some exiles were fallen rulers and politicians. The Athenian general and politician Alcabiades (ca. 450–404 B.C.) fled into exile twice during his career because of political intrigues and military defeats; during the second exile, his enemies murdered him. Hannibal (247–183 B.C.), the great Carthaginian general, had to go into exile in the Seleucid Empire of Syria because of the vindictiveness of the victorious Romans. Their continued hounding forced him to move on to Bythnia, where in despair he finally committed suicide. The great Napoléon I (1769–1821) experienced two exiles as a result of military defeats—first on the Isle of Elba for a period of a few months in 1814–1815, and then on St. Helena's Island from 1815 to 1821 after his defeat at Waterloo. Scores of other rulers, politicians, and generals have faced exile when their luck ran out, although the physical conditions of these exiles varied from luxurious to the torturous.

Exiles were frequently used as a punishment for committing crimes, engaging in unpopular behavior, or the act of rebellion. The ancient Athenians held votes of ostracism to decide about banishing some popular person. In an important episode in the diaspora of the Jews, after the Romans captured rebellious

Mounted Tsarist Cossacks follow a wagon carrying Old Believers along a snow covered road to Siberia.

Jerusalem in A.D. 70, they sent the survivors into exile. By the seventeenth century, various European countries sent criminals into exile as involuntary settlers in faraway colonies, where they lived under meager conditions. In 1685, the infamous Judge George Jeffries (1645–1689) sent many of the Monmouth Rebels into exile and slavery on the Caribbean islands. Daniel Defoe's (1660–1731) fictional heroine Moll Flanders was transported to the Virginia colony for her crimes, an experience she shared with many real American colonists. This punishment, called "transportation," was just another name for involuntary exile or banishment. The colony at Botany Bay in Australia was originally settled largely by English convicts sentenced to transportation. Sometimes convicted felons were given a choice between hanging or transportation to Australia. Surprisingly, many chose hanging.

Some people have gone into exile voluntarily as a result of political or military defeat or disgrace. When the American Revolution (1775–1783) ended, thousands of Loyalist Americans voluntarily—or feeling compelled by persecution from their neighbors—left their homes for Canada or the West Indies, never to return. Aaron Burr (1756–1836) went into self-exile from 1808 to 1812 as a result of the scandal associated with his alleged conspiracy to create a new secessionist country out of the Old Southwest of the United States.

Exile is generally a sad sort of travel even when its physical conditions are comfortable or even luxurious. No matter how pleasant exile might be, the exiled cannot return home. Most journeys are completed when the traveler arrives back home, but the exile often never experiences home again.

See also
Siberia.
For further reading
John Simpson, ed., *The Oxford Book of Exile*, 1995.

EXODUS   Latinized version of the Greek word *exodos*, meaning "exit" or "going out." It is the title of the second book of the Old Testament in the Bible and refers to one of the most famous departures in human history—the Children of Israel, or the Israelites, leaving Egypt to return to the Land of Canaan.

Most biblical scholars in the mid-twentieth century believed that the Exodus was a historical event, not simply a mythic epic of the ancient Hebrews, although some modern biblical scholars dispute this. Assuming the Exodus was a real event, biblical, extrabiblical historical evidence, and archaeological evidence place its approximate date between 1279 and 1209 B.C., possibly within the even narrower time frame of 1260–1220 B.C. The number of people involved may be as high as 72,000. On the days that they marched, the Children of Israel probably traveled about 15 miles.

The Exodus began after God sent the ten plagues against the Egyptians. After stubbornly enduring nine plagues and refusing to let the Israelites depart from their bondage in Egypt, the pharaoh succumbed to the tenth plague, the slaying of the firstborn. Encouraged by the fearful Egyptians, the Israelites hurriedly left their home at Rameses/Goshen and traveled to Succoth on the frontier of Egypt. The shortest and easiest way from Egypt to Canaan was the coastal highway that passed through the land of the warlike Philistines. Such a route was too dangerous, and instead God directed the Israelites past Etham into the wilderness by the Red Sea. By day a pillar of cloud led the Children of Israel, and at night, a pillar of fire, allowing them to travel both night and day.

God decided to send one more tribulation against the pharaoh of Egypt as a demonstration of his divine power. He caused the pharaoh to retract his decision to release the Israelites and send his army to capture them. Meanwhile, God led the Children of Israel to encamp at Baalzephon, a location that seemingly trapped them between the chariots of the pursuing Egyptians and the sea. When word of the pursuing Egyptians reached the Israelite camp, panic ensued, but God protected his chosen people. First he placed a pillar of cloud between them and their pursuers, which confused and delayed the Egyptians. Next, he instructed Moses to hold out his hand. A strong east wind arose, and the waters of the sea parted. This miracle allowed the Israelites to cross in safety, but when the Egyptian chariots tried to follow, they were engulfed in the returning waters and destroyed.

Traditionally, this episode is known as the crossing of the Red Sea and has been located at the Gulf of Suez. The identification is incorrect, however, because the Hebrew words used in the Book of Exodus should be translated as the

Sea of Reeds, not as Red Sea. Biblical scholars variously identify this Sea of Reeds as the Bitter Lakes, the southernmost inlet of Lake Menzaleh, or Lake Sirbonis. The miraculous parting of the waters has also been given naturalistic explanations. Waters in the shallow lakes in that part of Egypt are known to be affected by strong winds. Tides, and even a combination of earthquake and tidal wave, are considered plausible explanations. Some detractors object that the destruction of the Egyptian army is not in their records—to which other experts respond that the records of Egypt and other ancient monarchies never mention defeats and failures.

After thanking God for their deliverance, Moses and his people entered the Wilderness of Shur on the Sinai peninsula. At Marah they encountered bitter water, but God allowed Moses to sweeten it miraculously by throwing a certain tree into it. From Marah they traveled to the 12 springs of Elim, and entered the Wilderness of Sin. By now, they had been traveling about 45 days and missed the comfort of assured meals in Egypt, so God sent them manna in the mornings and quail in the evenings. Later, the Israelites began to run out of water, and complained to Moses. God responded by having Moses strike the rock at Horeb with his staff. Water poured out. Nearby at Rephidim, the Amalekites attacked the Children of Israel, but were defeated in the famous battle in which, at God's command, Moses had to hold his staff in the air to ensure an Israelite victory.

The Israelites entered the Wilderness of Sinai about 90 days after they left Egypt. They encamped before Mount Sinai or Mount Horeb, and God's presence descended to the summit of Mount Sinai in the form of a thick cloud with thunder and lightning. After several days, Moses ascended Mount Sinai to receive the laws from God. The process of God giving the Ten Commandments and other laws to Moses was lengthy, and he was away from the Israelite camp for 40 days. During the long wait, the Children of Israel became restless and asked Aaron, Moses's brother, to make them gods. Aaron fashioned an idol in the form of a golden calf. God observed this apostasy and contemplated destroying the Israelites, but Moses successfully pleaded for mercy. Moses returned to the camp, where he broke the tablets of the Ten Commandments and destroyed the golden calf. The sons of Levi joined Moses and they slaughtered 3,000 idolaters while God sent a plague into the camp. After repentance had occurred, God replaced the broken tablets of the Ten Commandments and gave instructions for building both the Ark of the Covenant to carry the tablets and the tabernacle to house it. The ark would also be accompanied by the pillar of cloud to guide the Children of Israel during their subsequent journey through the wilderness to Canaan.

See also
Children of Israel, Wanderings in the Wilderness of.

For further reading
T. W. Ferris, *The Date of Exodus*, 1990; K. A. Kitchen, "The Exodus," in *The Anchor Bible Dictionary*, 1992; Alfred Lucas, *The Route of the Exodus*, 1938; Nathan M. Sarna, *Exploring Exodus*, 1986.

F

FINK, MIKE (CA. 1780–CA. 1823)   Legendary keelboatman of the American frontier rivers, he spelled his name Miche Phinck.

Born near Pittsburgh, during his teens Fink served as an army scout in the Indian wars. Like many of his fellow frontiersmen, he engaged in prodigious bragging, but not all of it was exaggeration. He was an extremely efficient keelboat captain, physically very strong and agile, a crack shot, and a copious consumer of hard liquor. Fink may have epitomized the harsh values of frontier manhood, but its dark side included bullying and terrorizing his string of mistresses, black slaves, lawmen, and unsatisfactory members of his hapless crews. The folklore of the western rivers transformed him from an obnoxious man into a legendary figure akin to Paul Bunyan, but Fink was definitely mortal. In 1823, he engaged in a marksmanship contest that led to the shooting of a friend. When the drunken Fink mentioned that he might have killed the man on purpose, another enraged companion shot him to death. Mike Fink's life and death exemplified the raw life of the keelboatmen of the Ohio, Mississippi, and Missouri Rivers from the late eighteenth through the mid-nineteenth centuries.

See also
  Flatboats; Keelboats; Mississippi River; Missouri River.
For further reading
  Walter Blair and J. Meine Franklin, *Half Horse, Half Alligator*, 1933.

FLATBOATS   Simple raftlike craft, they appeared on the rivers of North America about 1750, and were used extensively for carrying bulk goods down rivers. Using the river's current for propulsion, flatboats could be steered with a rudder and poled or rowed in still waters. Their journeys were almost exclusively one way. Farmers of the Ohio River valley annually constructed flatboats to carry their crops to market, particularly to New Orleans. Once the flatboats reached their destination and their cargo was unloaded, they were broken up and sold for lumber. The flatboatmen made their way home up the Natchez Trace by horse or foot, or later by steamboat. Settlers also used flatboats to transport their families and possessions downstream to potential new homes.

The virtues of flatboats lay in their low cost and simplicity. If one was not in a hurry, they were a very economical way to get goods to market. As a result, they survived the competition of keelboats and, later, the steamboats for decades. Animosity between the mostly amateur flatboatmen and the professional keelboatmen was legendary. The young Abraham Lincoln participated in a trip to New Orleans by flatboat. Huckleberry Finn and Jim traveled on a raft or flatboat during the course of most of Mark Twain's famous novel. Flatboats formed an important mode of transportation and travel in the greater Mississippi River valley during the nineteenth century.

See also

Keelboats; Mississippi River; Missouri River; Natchez Trace.

For further reading

Leland D. Baldwin, *The Keelboat Age on Western Waters*, 1941; Frank Donovan, *River Boats of America*, 1966.

FLIGHT TO EGYPT   This famous episode in the Gospel of St. Matthew (2:13–15) tells how Mary and Joseph took the baby Jesus and fled to Egypt to escape the cruel King Herod's efforts to eliminate potential rivals for his throne. It is the only journey by Jesus outside of Palestine mentioned in the Bible.

The biblical account of the flight to Egypt supplies few details beyond the fact that it took place and that Jesus and his family did not return to Judaea until after the death of Herod the Great (r. 37–4 B.C.). Other sources supply additional details. One story tells how the family fled, with Herod's soldiers in hot pursuit. As the fugitives crossed a newly sown wheat field, Mary asked the farmer to tell their pursuers that he had seen them pass right after planting his seed. By the time Herod's men arrived, only a short time later, the wheat had miraculously grown to maturity and was ready to harvest. Seeing the advanced development of the wheat, the soldiers concluded that the three travelers mentioned by the farmer could not possibly be the wanted Jesus, Mary, and Joseph they sought because too much time would have passed. The soldiers abandoned their pursuit.

Another tradition has the family taking refuge at the village of Mataria, six miles north of Cairo in Egypt. Mataria was the home of a colony of Jewish gardeners who had been brought there a few years before the birth of Christ by Queen Cleopatra to cultivate the aromatic and valuable balsam bush. Inside a small garden stands an ancient, hollow fig tree, and according to local legend, the Holy Family hid inside the fig tree's trunk, and a spider miraculously spun a thick web across the opening to hide them. As a result, the fugitives escaped discovery. Mataria has become a popular Christian pilgrimage site and houses the Church of the Holy Family, built by French Jesuits.

For further reading

Gaston Duchet-Suchaux and Michel Pastoureau, *The Bible and the Saints*, 1994; Werner Keller, *The Bible as History*, 1964.

"Flight into Egypt" from the Book of Hours of the Duc de Berry, *Paris ca. 1410, ms. 11060-61 f. 106. Bibliothèque Royale Albert 1, Brussels.*

FLYAWAY ISLANDS

FLYAWAY ISLANDS   Sailors' nickname for islands that appear to seafarers but later disappear when someone comes looking for them a second time. Such islands are also known as moving islands or floating islands. Phantom islands are the product of people at sea mistaking a cloud bank or some other natural phenomenon for land, a common optical illusion similar to a mirage on land.

In the past, people believed that such illusions were real islands that floated because they were not fixed to the ocean floor, or they moved because of magic. Hy-Brazil is a good example of an island that appeared and disappeared by magical means. Other islands rose above and sank below the waves at different times. Volcanic or seismic activity may explain most of these instances. Other islands floated about aimlessly, propelled by the winds and currents. Old sea charts frequently recorded the locations of such islands, or at least their last known locations.

The folklore of many countries contain accounts of flyaway islands. In Norse, the word for a flyaway island is Flajgland, which means "flying or floating land." They also referred to such islands as Villuland, or mirage land. Sightings of flyaway islands were common in Scandinavian waters for centuries or even millennia. The ancient Greeks believed that the island of Delos floated about the seas for a long time before it became fixed in its permanent location. Medieval Europeans thought that the lovely, mystical island of Perdita (Lost) lay out in the Atlantic. Seafarers occasionally stumbled across it, but anyone who set out purposefully to find it could never locate it. Some authorities located it close to the Fortunate Isles, and others believed that it was one of the islands visited by St. Brendan the Navigator. Reports of lost islands beyond the Canaries occurred frequently up to and around the time of Christopher Columbus's voyage of 1492. Tales circulated about devilish flyaway islands that lured sailors to destruction in the English Channel. Flyaway or disappearing islands also appeared in the legends of the Iroquois tribe and the ancient Chinese. Such phantom islands formed an important aspect of the folklore of sea travel through the ages.

See also

Hy-Brazil; St. Brendan the Navigator, Voyage of.

For further reading

Samuel Eliot Morison, *The European Discovery of America,* 1971; Fridtjof Nansen, *In Northern Mists,* 1911.

FLYING DUTCHMAN

FLYING DUTCHMAN   Also known as *Der Fliegende Holländer* or the *Voltigeur.* According to legend, God condemned this accursed sea captain to roam forever in the seas around the Cape of Good Hope, terrorizing other ships and sometimes leading them to destruction.

Many seafaring societies have tales about ghost ships that are doomed to wander for all eternity across the face of the deep because of some arrogance or malefaction on the part of the captain and/or the crew. The legend of the Flying Dutchman is the most famous example of such stories.

The Dutch are one of Europe's greatest seafaring peoples. Their sailors first honed their skills on the treacherous waters of the North Sea and the English Channel. By the seventeenth century, intrepid Dutch seamen sailed to the Spice Islands of Asia to interlope on the very lucrative Portuguese spice monopoly. By ruthlessly deploying their superior naval power, the Dutch quickly made that monopoly their own. Soon, Dutch shipping regularly plowed the waters between the Netherlands and the Spice Islands—a long, tedious, and perilous voyage. Besides the dangers posed by enemy warships and pirates, the route itself was perilous. The waters around the Cape of Good Hope (originally and more accurately named the Cape of Storms) were particularly hazardous due to their proximity to the Roaring Forties. Many ships were lost.

According to the legend of the Flying Dutchman, a proud, irascible sea captain named Vanderdecken was taking his ship to Asia. Vanderdecken considered himself a sort of ultimate rugged individualist. He rejected the existence of saints and did not believe in God. As his ship rounded the Cape of Good Hope, a fearsome tempest blew up. Both crew and passengers implored Vanderdecken to seek the shelter of a port. The fearless captain refused to listen; instead, he mocked his fearful companions and blasphemed against God. A giant, misty figure descended from the sky onto the ship's deck, causing even greater panic among the crew and the passengers. Stopping before the captain, the mysterious presence told him that he was mad. The imperturbable Dutchman remained unmoved. He ordered the supernatural being to leave his deck immediately or he would shoot it. He took one of his pistols, cocked the hammer, and fired at his spectral visitor. Instead of hitting the misty figure, he shot himself in the hand. Further maddened by his wound, the reckless captain tried to strike his unwelcome visitor a blow with his hand. Instead, his arm became paralyzed. At that point, the supernatural being—thought by many to be God in person—pronounced a terrible curse on Vanderdecken: from then on, the haughty captain would have to sail the sea until the end of time without ever being able to land. His only drink would be gall, and his chewing tobacco would be red-hot iron. If he tried to sleep, a sword would painfully stab him every time he closed his eyes. Strong winds and clouds would follow the accursed captain throughout his eternal voyage. Other ships sighting the Flying Dutchman would experience terror and bad luck. Many sightings were reported over the years, and credulous sailors claimed they encountered the Flying Dutchman as late as 1881. The Flying Dutchman also inspired works of fiction. Captain Marryat wrote the novel *The Phantom Ship* (1839), in which the son of the Flying Dutchman searched for his father. More famous was Richard Wagner's depiction of the accursed Vanderdecken in his opera *Der Fliegende Holländer* (1843). Tales of phantom vessels such as the Flying Dutchman reflect the hazards and terrors facing seafarers in the age of sailing ships.

See also

Good Hope, Cape of; Roaring Forties; Spice Islands.

For further reading

Angelo S. Rappoport, *Superstitions of Sailors*, 1928.

FORTUNATE ISLES   Also known as the *Insulae Fortunatae*, Isles of the Blest, and Blessed Islands, these names refer to the paradisial islands believed to exist somewhere in the Atlantic Ocean by peoples of the Mediterranean world during the classical era.

The early Greeks of the Homeric Age had only a limited knowledge of geography. In their worldview, a great River Ocean encircled the known world, and somewhere on its far western shores lay the misty, amorphous land of the dead. Later traditions divided the land of the dead into a place of torment for the wicked and a pleasant place of reward for the good. The land inhabited by the spirits of the good became known as the Elysian Fields, which in some traditions of Greek mythology became an island or two islands somewhere in the Great or Atlantic Ocean. These island paradises became known variously as the Blessed Islands, the Isles of the Blest, or the Fortunate Islands.

The Atlantic Ocean contains several groups of real islands, and as people began to sail its waters, some were identified as the Fortunate Isles. One unique tradition from Ptolemaic Egypt, however, identified the island of Socotra near the mouth of the Red Sea in the Indian Ocean as the Fortunate Island. More commonly, sailors identified the Azores, the Madeiras, and the Canaries of the Atlantic Ocean as the Fortunate Isles, with the Canaries being the most widespread and persistent identification (the ancient world had only the vaguest knowledge of the Madeira and Azores Islands, if in fact they knew about them at all). The Phoenicians or the Carthaginians were the first people from the ancient Mediterranean cultures to sail extensively on the Atlantic Ocean. Their ships ranged north to Britain and south to places on the west coast of Africa. Some accounts claim that Phoenician sailors circumnavigated Africa, so it seems likely that they knew about the Canaries even though documentary evidence is lacking. No ancient Greeks or Romans dared to sail through the exclusively Carthaginian waters around the Strait of Gibraltar to reach the Canaries. Rumors about paradisial islands in the Atlantic, however, continued to circulate. Even the fall of Carthage in 146 B.C. did not immediately open the Canaries or Fortunate Isles to the Greco-Roman world. The great Roman general Sertorius (d. 86 B.C.) knew of the Fortunate Isles and expressed a desire to visit them, but never made the journey. That task fell to Juba II (r. 2 B.C.–A.D. 23), the cultured and scholarly king of Numidia and Mauretania. He led an expedition to the Canaries, finding traces of previous human habitation but no current native population. His account described six of the seven islands in the most pleasant and attractive terms. Roman colonists, however, were not tempted to settle on these Fortunate Isles, and they were left for later settlement by the Guanches from the African mainland. Early in the first century after Christ, the Roman geographer Pomponius Mela also described the Canaries or Fortunate Isles as pleasant and fertile. He added the intriguing description of two fountains that supposedly existed on the islands. Anyone drinking from one of them would start laughing and continue to laugh until they died. The water of the second fountain, however, could cure any illness or injury. The Roman geographer Claudius Ptolemy (fl. second century A.D.) used the Canaries or Fortunate Isles as the prime meridian or longitude line in his world map grid system. His contemporary, the geographer Solinus, added the claim that at least one of the Canaries or Fortunate Isles had no snakes. Even at that late date, the belief persisted that the Fortunate Isles were a sort of Elysian Fields. In his famous *True History*, the protagonists of satirical poet Lucian of Samothrace (fl. second century A.D.) visited the Fortunate Isles and their famous dead inhabitants.

The fall of the Roman Empire caused the Canaries to lapse into legendary status once more. Early-medieval scholars relied on the work of classical geographers such as Ptolemy, Strabo, and Pliny for information about the Fortunate Isles. The fifth-century Christian historian Paulus Orosius knew of the Fortunate Isles off the coast of Africa, as did his approximate contemporary, Martianus Capella. Isidore of Seville (ca. 560–636) ventured the opinion that the Fortunate Isles were not the true Paradise. He speculated that their great fertility caused visitors to think they were Paradise. Later writers such as the Irishman Dicuil (fl. ca. 825) and Vincent of Beauvais (ca. 1190–1264) agreed with Isidore's opinion. Not surprisingly, the widespread knowledge of the Fortunate Isles from classical antiquity merged with preexisting Celtic legends of a western land of the blessed dead to create the legend of King Arthur's Avalon. Otherwise, Christian Europe lost direct contact with the Fortunate Isles or Canaries for centuries.

The Arabs of Islamic Spain did little seafaring on the Atlantic, but since the world of Islam extended far down the coast of West Africa and across the Sahara to Timbuktu, they had knowledge of the Canaries. The voyage of the *Maghrunín* of Lisbon took place before 1147 and included a visit to islands that sound suspiciously like the Canaries. The Vivaldi brothers of Genoa stopped at the Canaries during their mysterious voyage of 1291 (assuming they got that far or even went in that direction). Lanzarotto Malocello of Genoa permanently reestablished European contact with the Canaries about 1336. During the fifteenth century, the Guanches of the Canaries were conquered, enslaved, and ultimately exterminated by European settlers while the Spanish and Portuguese jostled for control of that lovely group of islands. Such events ended the Canaries' career as the legendary Fortunate Isles. Although a few early-modern geographers speculated that the Fortunate Isles were located in some unexplored region of the Atlantic Ocean, the legend quickly faded altogether from the lore of travel.

See also

Atlantic Ocean; Avalon; Blessed, Isles of the; Canary Islands; Elysian Fields; Ptolemy, Claudius.

For further reading

M. Cary and E. H. Warmington, *The Ancient Explorers*, 1963; Vincent H. Cassidy, *The Sea around Them*, 1968; J. R. S. Phillips, *The Medieval Expansion of Europe*, 1988.

FOUNTAIN OF YOUTH   Name for a magical spring whose waters are capable of transforming an old person into a healthy 30-year-old. Spanish explorer Juan Ponce de León (ca. 1460–1521) looked for this fabulous fountain during the course of his explorations of the Bahamas and Florida in 1513.

Legends of a Fountain of Youth are very ancient and widespread. Some scholars thought the idea was an indigenous legend of the Native American tribes of the Bahamas and Florida, and others believed that the natives simply made up the story to get the unwelcome Spanish exploring parties to move on. Both ideas are wrong; belief in a Fountain of Youth is a geographical legend of the Old World that migrated to the Americas during the first years of contact in the early sixteenth century.

The legend of magical waters capable of restoring youth and health originated in East Asia and spread to Europe during the Middle Ages. It was first mentioned in 1165 in the forged document known as the *Letter of Prester John.* The fountain or spring of magical restorative waters was also placed in close proximity to the Terrestrial Paradise, supposedly located on Ceylon (Sri Lanka). Originally, it was associated with other fountains that supplied waters capable of resuscitating the dead and bestowing immortality. By the time of Marco Polo's travels to China in 1271–1295, the Fountain of Youth's location had moved east to the fabulous island that supposedly lay beyond Japan. Medieval romances (ca. 1170) describing the adventures of Alexander the Great in Asia included tales of his encounters with the Fountain of Youth. Later, Sir John Mandeville, the widely read and believed (although fictional) traveler, visited and drank from the Fountain of Youth when he visited Ceylon during his Asian journeys, set in 1322–1356. By the fourteenth and fifteenth centuries, the belief in a Fountain of Youth became part of a complex of geographical legends known as the "Marvels of the East."

The first Spaniards to settle on Hispaniola and Cuba believed they had reached the fantastic islands thought to lie east of Japan. They did not comprehend that they had blundered into hitherto unsuspected islands and continents. Columbus, the man who led them there, went to his death in 1506 believing that he had found a western sea route to Asia. The existence of South America was vaguely recognized, but that of North America was unimagined. Instead, the early Spanish explorers and settlers were programmed, through reading medieval romances and Sir John Mandeville, to expect monstrous races and other wonders. They had supposedly found their man-eating anthrophagi in the Caribs. Could the other Marvels of the East be far off? At various times, Columbus believed he was close to the Terrestrial Paradise or the island of the Amazons. Therefore, Ponce de León's search for a Fountain of Youth was a logical by-product of the faulty geographical concepts prevailing among early-sixteenth-century Europeans. Of course, the main purposes of Ponce's expeditions were to locate gold and make new conquests; locating a Fountain of Youth was never the primary goal of his expeditions.

See also

Alexander the Great, Romances of; *Mandeville, Travels of Sir John;* Marvels of the East; Paradise, Terrestrial; Prester John and His Kingdom.

For further reading

Leonardo Olschki, "Ponce de León's Fountain of Youth," *Hispanic American Historical Review* 22 (Aug. 1941): 361–385.

FOUR CORNERS OF THE EARTH

Or simply corners of the earth, this expression appears seven times in the Bible, and refers to the edges or outermost boundaries of the world, or to any distant land or place. This biblical concept remained part of the geographical consciousness of medieval Europe and is still a common expression for referring to distant lands. Corners of the earth and ends of the earth were used interchangeably by the ancient Hebrews.

Ancient Hebrews believed that the universe had three levels: the heavens, the earth, and Sheol, which lay below the primeval waters. The earth was a finite circular disk with Jerusalem at the center. Like other ancient peoples, the Hebrews developed a concept of four cardinal directions. One system of directions was based on the observer facing east. The east was called "front," with the north being "left," the south "right," and the west "behind." A second system was based on the sun, so that "east" was the word roughly meaning sunrise, while "west" meant sundown. The derivation of the words for north and south is uncertain.

The metaphor of the four corners of the earth developed out of the four cardinal directions. Because the ancient Hebrews believed that the earth was circular, the four corners had no literal existence; they simply provided a convenient figurative expression for the outermost boundaries. Isaiah 11:12 says, "he [God] will assemble the scattered people of Judah from the four corners of the earth," meaning distant lands. Ezekiel 7:2 reads, "the end has come upon the four corners of the land," meaning the whole of Israel. Revelation 7:1 expands the references to mean the whole earth with the words, "I saw four angels standing at the four corners of the earth, holding back the four winds of the earth." Later, in Revelation 20:7–8, it describes how "when the thousand years are over, Satan will be released from his prison and will go out to deceive the nations of the four corners of the earth—Gog and Magog—to gather them to battle." While the author of Revelation, John of Patmos, meant these things allegorically, Christians and Muslims came to believe in a literal Gog and Magog who were imprisoned at the edges or the corners of the earth.

In most ancient cultures, including the Hebrews, the number four expresses a powerful symbolism for completeness. Medieval Christians also accepted that symbolism. Besides the four cardinal directions, there were four elements, four humors, four winds, four seasons, and four gospels. Medieval mappaemundi frequently depicted many of these combinations of four. Although medieval scholars, with few exceptions, believed the earth was a sphere, it did not stop them from indicating the existence of the four corners of the earth on their mappaemundi. Sometimes the four corners are shown as a square enclosing the circle of the earth, each corner corresponding with one of the four directions. Other mappaemundi place the square of the corners of the earth inside the circle. In no case, however, is the literal existence of the corners of the earth indicated. The general phrase "the four corners of the earth" has for centuries continued in use as a reference to distant lands.

See also
Gog and Magog; Jerusalem; Mappamundi.

For further reading

Philip S. Alexander, "Earth, Jewish Geography," in David Noel Freeman, ed., "Geography and the Bible (Early Jewish)," in *The Anchor Bible Dictionary*, 1992; David Woodward, "Medieval Mappaemundi," in *The History of Cartography*, vol. 1: *Cartography in Prehistoric, Ancient, and Medieval Europe and the Mediterranean*, 1987.

FUSANG   Name given by the ancient Chinese to a land located to the east of Asia in the Pacific Ocean. It was visited by the Buddhist missionary Hoei-Shin in A.D. 499. The name Fusang refers to a plant growing in this eastern land that resembles a tree the Chinese called Fusang. In 1761, the early French sinologist Joseph De Guignes first identified the country of Fusang as California or Mexico. Modern sinologists, however, reject the identification of Fusang as North America, pointing out that the name Fusang had a long career in Chinese cosmography as the name for a fictional eastern land. The usage first appeared in the late Chou and early Han periods (ca. 400 B.C.–A.D. 9) as a reference to a marvelous eastern otherworld. Later the name was used as a poetical reference to Japan. Other stories involving Fusang could refer to the islands of the Ainu, Sakhalin, Kamchatka, or simply some fantasyland in the eastern Pacific. Fusang was obviously not a specific place.

For further reading

Joseph Needham, *Science and Civilization in China*, vol. 4, pt. 3, 1971.

G

GANESHA God of wisdom and good fortune, he was one of the most popular deities in the Hindu pantheon. Ganesha was the son of Shiva and Parvati. Shiva decapitated him, but his mother Parvati had him brought back to life with the head of an elephant. In his later adventurers, Ganesha always exhibited mischievousness and shrewdness. Hindus commonly begin any enterprise, particularly travel, by invoking Ganesha.

GANGES RIVER Sacred river located in northern India, it originates in the Himalayas and flows for over 1,500 miles, forming a vast delta over 200 miles wide before entering the Bay of Bengal. The Ganges is traditionally thought to be one of the four rivers of Paradise, but its primary religious significance is connected to Hinduism.

In the Hindu religion, the Ganges River is an important *tirtha*, or site, for the performance of sacred rituals. Bathing in the Ganges or leaving hair, nail clippings, or some part of the body on the left bank of the river supposedly allowed faithful Hindus to enter *Svarga*, or Heaven. A particularly popular site is the holy city of Benares (also spelled Banaras or Varanasi). Benares is sacred to the god Shiva and is supposed to have existed since creation. Besides containing many magnificent temples, the banks of the Ganges in Benares are provided with over 70 *ghats* (steps or platforms) for entering the waters of the Ganges to engage in ritual bathing. Hindus believe that anyone who dies in Benares and utters the "crossing over" mantra will gain liberation from *karma*. The Ganges is obviously a river to travel *to* rather than a river to travel *on*.

See also
Paradise, Four Rivers of; Pilgrimage.
For further reading
Simon Coleman and John Elsner, *Pilgrimage*, 1995; Diana L. Eck, *Banares, City of Light*, 1982.

GENIES Also known as Jinn, in Islamic cosmology these were the names for the various inhabitants of the immaterial world, or *alam al-malakut*. The immaterial

A statue of the elephant god, Ganesha, in an East Indian temple.

world consisted of ether (it possessed form but not substance), and its inhabitants were spiritual beings. Some genies were without reason, and therefore approximated the animals of the material world, but others possessed intellect and consciousness. These intelligent genies had the ability to believe in Allah or some other form of religion. They were also capable of visiting the material world and becoming involved in human affairs. Many genies possessed magic powers, as did the genie in the familiar tale of Aladdin and the magic lamp. Islamic tradition credits King Solomon with the ability to command genies. He supposedly ordered them to build his great temple and perform other stupendous feats. Muhammad the Prophet was said to have preached to a group of genies, converting them to Islam. Genies could be beautiful or they could be ugly. Ifrits and ghuls (or ghouls) were particularly frightful. Some genies were well disposed toward humans, while others were hostile. The emptiness and loneliness of the desert was congenial to them. Marauding genies of the Ifrit or ghul orders roamed at night terrorizing travelers, or so it was believed in the Islamic world.

For further reading

Cyril Glassé, *The Concise Encyclopedia of Islam*, 1989.

GENOA   Italian city located in Liguria along the extreme northwest coast of Italy. It was one of the great trading cities in the last half of the Middle Ages. Merchants from Genoa were particularly active in the Black Sea region, the western Mediterranean, and the Atlantic islands.

During the Roman Empire era, Genoa was a minor port. With the fall of Rome in the fifth century A.D. and the accompanying decline of maritime trade and roads, the city was virtually reduced to a village. Muslim raids between 930 and 935 forced the local community to unite and focus their energies on mutual protection. Their efforts brought about a remarkable improvement in Genoa's fortunes. Not only were Muslim forces beaten off, the Genoese took the offensive after 1000, vigorously and successfully entering into the trading networks of the Mediterranean Sea. From 1015 to 1016, Genoese and Pisan forces reconquered Sardinia from the Muslims. In 1088, they captured Al-Madhiya, the capital of present-day Tunis, which enabled them to coerce trading rights from the local ruler. Genoese merchants were soon trading all over the Mediterranean world as well as north of the Alps.

From approximately 1100 to 1350, Genoese power and prosperity were at their height, and Genoa was second only to Venice as a naval power in the Mediterranean. Its merchants established trading posts, or funduqs, in most of the significant ports from Ceuta to Constantinople. With the fall of Acre, the last of the Crusader states, in 1291, the Genoese lost some of their more lucrative outposts, but they compensated by expanding their trading activities into the lands around the Black Sea, England, the Canary Islands, and Morocco. This geographic shift was the context for the ill-fated voyage of the Vivaldi brothers into the Atlantic Ocean in 1291.

By 1350, Genoa faced increasingly serious problems over which the city had no control. The Black Death reduced the city's population from 100,000 to 50,000. This, along with the Hundred Years War, threw the entire European economy into turmoil, to the detriment of Genoese interests. The disintegration of the Mongol Empire and its replacement by the Ming dynasty as the rulers of China, plus the expansion of the Ottoman Turks, undermined Genoa's ability to make a profit in the international trade of Asian luxury goods. The Genoese turned to new economic enterprises: stepped-up banking activity, manufacture of silk cloth, and investments in foreign alum mines. They also invested in the Iberian Peninsula.

By the late fifteenth century, Genoa's greatest days were in the past. Still, in 1500, the city was still important, and its bankers, merchants, and seamen were respected throughout Europe. The great age of Genoese explorers and travelers was hardly over, as the careers of Christopher Columbus and John Cabot, both sons of Genoa, so amply attest.

See also

Atlantic Ocean; Black Sea; Mediterranean Sea; Venice.

For further reading

Gerald W. Day, *Genoa's Response to Byzantium, 1155–1204*, 1988; Steven Epstein, *Genoa and the Genoese, 958–1528*, 1996; Benjamin Z. Kedar, *Merchants in Crisis*, 1976.

GIANTS   The belief in the existence of a race of extraordinarily large humans is virtually universal among the various cultures of the world. Ancient discoveries of the outsized bones of prehistoric animals reinforced the belief, and travelers therefore expected to find lands inhabited by giants, and told tales about alleged encounters with them.

The idea of a giant race, as well as a Pygmy race, is one of the simplest and most common variations on the theme of monstrous races. Usually, giants were larger than normal humans, but otherwise exhibited no physical deformities. The Cyclopes, who possessed only one eye, were an exception, as was a giant race that was part-human and part-horse, and St. Christopher, who in some legends was said to be a giant Cynocephali. Ancient Greeks told of the race of Titans, or giants, who were the sons of Uranus and Gaia, the earth. The Titans warred against the Olympian gods, but were defeated and buried under mountains, which became volcanoes. The most ancient Hebrew traditions speak of the Nephilim, "There were giants in the earth in those days; and after that, when the sons of God came unto the daughters of men, and the bare children to them, the same became mighty men which were of old, men of renown." (Genesis 6:4) Much later, on the eve of the invasion of Canaan, the scouts of the Children of Israel reported that, "there we saw the giants, the sons of Anak, which come of the giants; and we were in our own sight as grasshoppers, and so we were in their sight." (Numbers 13:33) Norse mythology also contains a race of fierce giants. The Sumerian hero Gilgamesh fought with the wild giant Enkidu and domesticated him, and the Anglo-Saxon hero Beowulf defeated and killed the monstrous giant Grendel. That long-suffering traveler Odysseus not only encountered the man-eating Cyclops Polyphemus, his fleet was destroyed by the savage and equally cannibalistic race of giant Laestrygonians. According to the Romances of Alexander the Great, he defeated a race of giants in India. In the minds of ancient people, giants were everywhere and presented a frequently mortal hazard to travelers.

Medieval Europeans tended to Christianize the stories about giants, and they placed the land of the giants in the Far East near the Terrestrial Paradise, where they were able to survive the great Deluge of Noah. Some traditions followed Genesis 6:4 and called the giants the sons of angels and human women. Other traditions said that marriages between the sons of Seth and the daughters of Cain produced giants as offspring. This sinful union is sometimes cited as God's main reason for sending the universal flood. The Anglo-Saxon epic *Beowulf* also credits Cain with being the father of a race of giants. A medieval Irish account, however, places the giants among the monstrous children of Ham, the cursed son of Noah, as does a variant French version of the late-medieval *Travels of Sir John Mandeville*. The sixteenth-century French satirist François Rabelais claimed that giants and other monstrous races appeared at the same time as the confusion of the languages of the human race at the Tower of Babel.

Giants could be either civil or savage. Some possessed smooth skins; others were hairy like beasts. Often they were club-wielding wildmen of the wilderness. Such savage giants were frequently deadly man-eaters, a sure sign of their barbaric nature. In some accounts, the barbarian kings Gog and Magog are called giants. Other giants were civilized and lived in harmony with their normal-sized neighbors. Certain medieval accounts treated giants in a moralizing manner. In other cases, giants were depicted in a manner showing the vanity of relying on mere human power and might, no matter how great.

Giants were one monstrous race that may have a naturalistic explanation. Exaggerated reports of the very tall African tribe of the Watusi may have kept the belief in giants alive among travelers through most of recorded history.

See also
Alexander the Great, Romances of; Cyclopes; Cynocephali; Gilgamesh; Gog and Magog; Monstrous Races; Paradise, Terrestrial; Pygmies; St. Christopher.

For further reading
John Block Friedman, *The Monstrous Races in Medieval Art and Thought,* 1981.

GIBRALTAR, STRAIT OF
See Pillars of Hercules.

GILGAMESH

GILGAMESH   Epic hero of Sumerian and Babylonian mythology whose character is loosely based on a real King Gilgamesh of Uruk who ruled during the early third millennium.

The strong, handsome Gilgamesh goes on several quests or journeys in his lifetime. In one, Gilgamesh and his equally powerful companion Enkidu travel to a sacred forest to cut down a cedar. A fire-breathing dragon named Humbaba guards the forest, and attacks them. With divine assistance, the two heroes kill the dragon and bring back the sacred log. Other gods, angered by the death of Humbaba, send the Bull of Heaven to punish Gilgamesh and his people. A tremendous struggle ensues, but Gilgamesh and Enkidu succeed in destroying the Bull of Heaven. Now the gods are even more angry. They inflict an illness on Enkidu that kills him and leaves Gilgamesh devastated by grief. Fearful about his own death, Gilgamesh undertakes a long journey to visit Utnapishtim, the Mesopotamian Noah, who has been granted immortality by the gods. The traveler experiences many adventures on his way to the shores of the ocean of death. Once there, he persuades the ferryman Urshanabi to carry him over the water to the paradise where Utnapishtim lives with his wife. Gilgamesh asks Utnapishtim how he gained eternal life, and Utnapishtim answers by telling him the tale of the great deluge that destroyed the earth. He survived by building a boat to hold his family and some animals. In the end, the gods rewarded him and his wife with immortality. Divine favor, he points out to Gilgamesh, is the only way to gain immortality. As the disappointed Gilgamesh is ready to depart, Utnapishtim takes pity on him and tells him about a sea plant that can restore his youth. On his return voyage to the land of mortals, Gilgamesh dives into the sea and picks the precious plant. Unfortunately, once he goes ashore, a snake steals the plant and ends Gilgamesh's hope of recovering his youth. Besides the literal journeys that Gilgamesh makes, his entire life serves as an allegory for humanity's vain quest for fame and immortality. The epic of Gilgamesh is probably the oldest archetype for the hero-quest of myth and legend.

For further reading

Stephanie Dalley, *Myths from Mesopotamia, the Flood, Gilgamesh, and Others*, 1989; Penelope Lively and Rosalind Kerven, *The Mythic Quest*, 1996; N. K. Sandars, *The Epic of Gilgamesh*, 1972.

GINNUNGAGAP   Norse word meaning "yawning gap" or "gaping chaos." According to Norse mythology, the ginnungagap was the greatest of all abysses, the primordial chaos. When Odin and the other gods defeated and killed the great giant Ymir, they placed his body in the ginnungagap and thus created the world. Ymir's blood was the water, and his flesh and bones the dry land. Beyond these lay what remained of the ginnungagap.

By the year 1000, the medieval Norse conceived of the earth as a world circle. The three continents of Europe, Asia, and Africa and their various inland seas formed the shape of a platter. Around that world circle surged the

Ocean Sea, and beyond it lay the fearsome ginnungagap. In this geographical conception, the Atlantic Ocean was an inland sea largely surrounded by land, although sailors could reach the Ocean Sea by sailing through the passages or strait between Helluland, Markland, and Vinland. By the later Middle Ages and the early-modern era, the concept of a spherical earth replaced the platterlike world circle, but belief in the existence of the ginnungagap persisted. Some accounts located it in the little-known waters between Greenland and Vinland, while others placed it in the Hudson Strait or the St. Lawrence Estuary. By this time, however, the ginnungagap had shrunk from being a primordial, world-encompassing chaos to merely a giant whirlpool. Needless to say, either version of the ginnungagap represented a terrifying hazard to those who dared sail the icy waters of the North Atlantic.

See also

Atlantic Ocean; Helluland; Markland; Vinland.

For further reading

Gwyn Jones, *The Norse Atlantic Saga*, 1986.

GOG AND MAGOG   Both medieval Christians and Muslims believed that these two savage tribes lived somewhere in the hinterlands of Asia. Alexander the Great supposedly enclosed Gog and Magog behind a range of rugged mountains and blocked the only pass with a great iron gate. When the Mongols invaded Europe in the early thirteenth century, many people apocalyptically identified them as Gog and Magog freed from captivity.

The legends of Gog and Magog originated in the Bible. Genesis 10:2 refers to Magog as a son of Japheth, the son of Noah. Later Hebrew tradition identified Magog as the ancestor of the Scythians. Gog and Magog next appeared in the prophecy found in Ezekiel 38 and 39. Gog was a prince of Meshech and Tubal from the land of Magog. He would lead a great army out of the far north against Israel, but God would plague his endeavors with defeats and natural disasters, and he would die and be buried in Israel. Revelation 20:7–8 describes Gog and Magog as nations living in the four corners of the earth who are tricked by Satan into joining his cause. God then destroys Satan in the final battle. These vague, contradictory references formed the various medieval geographical legends about Gog and Magog.

Gog and Magog became linked with Alexander the Great by various Jewish legends around A.D. 395 or later. According to the mature form of the legend, Alexander the Great fought with the savage tribes known as Gog and Magog. After defeating them, he drove them through a pass in the Caucasus Mountains, after which he built a great iron gate across the pass to keep them away from civilized humanity. There they would remain until they were released to join in the last battle between good and evil at the end of the world.

Several Jewish legends melded together to form the story of Alexander the Great's imprisonment of Gog and Magog. Jews of the Hellenistic and Imperial

Roman eras, such as the historian Josephus, regarded Alexander the Great as a national hero. One legend credited him with building a gate in a pass of the Caucasus Mountains to exclude the barbarian tribes of the north, who were generically known as Scythians. By the time of Josephus, people equated Gog and Magog with the Scythians. It took several centuries, but by 395 the legend evolved into Alexander the Great defeating the biblical tribes of Gog and Magog and secluding them beyond the Caucasus.

Christian writers were quick to adopt the legend as their own, turning Alexander the Great into a Christian hero. The Syrian *Christian Legend Concerning Alexander* told how he imprisoned the Huns, including their kings Gog and Magog, behind a great gate in the Caucasus Mountains, where they would stay until the last days of the world. The Byzantine historian Procopius (d. 562) repeated the same story in his *De Bellico Persica*. Muslims were also the heirs of Jewish traditions, and they too believed in the legend of Gog and Magog. According to the Koran of the prophet Muhammad, Alexander the Great (under the name of Dulcarnain) defeated the barbarous tribes of Yajuj and Majuj (Gog and Magog) and enclosed them behind a great range of mountains, where they will stay until the Last Judgment. The unknown author of the prophecies known as *Pseudo-Methodius* about A.D. 640 included the story of Alexander's imprisonment of Gog and Magog, and the prediction that they would break out at the end of the world to join in the last battle between good and evil. *Pseudo-Methodius* was widely read and copied during the Middle Ages, so this version of the legend became well known and highly influential. Thanks to the influence of *Pseudo-Methodius*, Europeans identified the Mongols as Gog and Magog, and therefore viewed the Mongol invasions as a harbinger of the Apocalypse. The twelfth-century writer Lambert li Tors added the detail that Gog and Magog were vassal-kings of the historical Indian king Porus and supplied 400,000 men for his army. After Alexander defeated Porus, he chased Gog and Magog into the mountains and enclosed them behind a great wall. Alexander's successor, Antigonus, was assigned the task of keeping watch over Gog and Magog. In his chronicle, Otto of Freising (d. 1158) supplied a further variation on the legend of Gog and Magog, which he derived from some earlier writers. Supposedly, the Byzantine emperor Heraclius sought revenge against the invading Saracens by releasing the savage tribes whom Alexander the Great had imprisoned. However, God considered Heraclius's action as sacrilege, and killed 52,000 of his soldiers with lightning, a divine punishment that also killed Heraclius. For medieval people, Alexander's gate was a real place, and Gog and Magog were real people or tribes who could be released from their imprisonment—although only at the risk of divine wrath. Ultimately, the release of Gog and Magog was a sign that the end of the world was at hand.

If Alexander's Gate was a real place, what was it and where was it located? Alexander's Gate was built of a metal that could not be destroyed or broken by steel or fire. Additional defenses prevented Gog and Magog from going under, over, or around it. A dense thicket of brambles grew in front of the gate and prevented anyone from approaching it. Alexander's craftsmen built mechanical iron men who pounded hammers against the metal wall to give the impression that improvements and strengthenings of the defenses were constantly under way. An Arabian legend adds the detail that a magic stone eagle stood atop the gate and let out a warning screech any time Gog and Magog came near. Another told how Alexander set up trumpets that were automatically blown by the action of the wind. This continuous noise convinced the tribesmen of Gog and Magog that a large garrison permanently manned Alexander's Gate.

Some early legends identified the Dariel Pass in the Caucasus Mountains as Alexander's Gate. Others claimed it was the pass known as the Iron Gate of Derbend between the Caucasus and the Caspian Sea, although its proximity to the sea is not consistent with any of the legends. In truth, the historical Alexander the Great never visited the Caucasus, but then he never defeated Gog and Magog, either. Such details had no impact on the survival and elaboration of the legend of Gog and Magog. When the Caucasus region became better known, Alexander's Gate moved to more remote regions in northern Europe or Asia. Medieval Muslim scholars believed that Alexander the Great visited China after his conquest of Porus of India, and that he encountered and defeated Gog and Magog in the Far East, enclosing them until the end of time. Some medieval Christian writers copying from Islamic sources repeated this version of the legend, causing some people to equate the Great Wall of China with Alexander's Gate. Islamic and Russian sources identified the Ural Mountains with the mountainous prison of Gog and Magog. God supposedly raised up the Urals around the evil Gog and Magog, and Alexander simply finished the job by building his gate. Other Christian and Islamic sources placed Gog and Magog in the far north of Europe or Asia on the edge of the northern ocean. The Hereford and Ebstorf mappaemundi put Alexander's Gate in northeastern Europe, while the Arab geographer al-Idrisi located it in northeastern Asia. By the thirteenth century, the reports of William of Rubruck, Marco Polo, and other travelers showed the Caspian to be an inland sea, and no evidence of Gog and Magog in the Caucasus Mountains could be found. People continued to consider the pass of Derbend to be Alexander's Gate, but the land of Gog and Magog moved to the remote and unknown far north, where it slowly faded from being considered a real place at all.

The belief that Alexander the Great enclosed the tribes of Gog and Magog behind his metal gate prompted speculation among actual nomadic tribes as to their identity. Later versions of the Romance of Alexander elaborated further. The Syrian *Christian Legend Concerning Alexander* was the first book to specify that 24 nations or tribes were enclosed, including Gog and Magog. *Pseudo-Methodius, Pseudo-Callisthenes,* and Aethicus Ister later lowered the number to 22. Sources for the names of the 22 or 24 excluded nations included those from the genealogical listings in Genesis 10; various barbarian invaders of Europe such as the Huns, Alans, and Sarmatians; and monstrous races such as the Cynocephali. *Pseudo-Callisthenes* added the telling detail that the peoples of Gog and Magog were cannibals, a sure sign of their evil, depraved natures.

The Jewish historian Josephus equated Gog and Magog with the Scythians, a loose Greco-Roman term for any northern barbarian tribe on the steppes.

Other Christian writers of the first century A.D., such as Eusebius, thought the Celts were Gog and Magog. St. Ambrose and Isidore of Seville credited the Goth tribes invading the Roman Empire with being Gog and Magog, or—as they slightly adjusted the terminology—Goth and Magoth. One chronicler claimed that the Aquitainians were descended from Gog and Magog. Writing about A.D. 650, the early-medieval geographer Aethicus Ister identified the Turks as Gog and Magog. *The Revelations of Pseudo-Methodius*, written about the same time, discussed Gog and Magog and the invading Arab adherents of Islam at the same place in the text. Later medieval writers erroneously began stating that *Pseudo-Methodius* identified the Arabs as Gog and Magog, making it part of the common currency of apocalyptic prophecy. The later medieval chronicler Rudolf of Ems, shortly before 1250, wrote about Alexander the Great's defeat of Gog and Magog, who he thought corresponded to the biblical Midianites. Other ancient and medieval writers linked Gog and Magog to the Khazars and the Parthians. Of course, the fury of the Mongol invasions in the early thirteenth century caused many apocalyptically minded Europeans to see in those events signs of the imminent approach of the end of the world. The Mongols were Gog and Magog on the loose.

During the twelfth and thirteenth centuries, various Christian scholars considered Gog and Magog the descendants of the Ten Lost Tribes of Israel. According to First Chronicles 5:26, the Assyrians carried off the Ten Tribes to live in exile at the cities of Halah, Habor, and Hara along the headwaters of the Euphrates River in the northwestern part of present-day Iraq. Other accounts moved them farther away. In the Apocrypha, the book of 2 Esdras 13:40–50 describes how the Ten Lost Tribes fled from Assyrian control and traveled for a year and a half to reach the uninhabited land of Arzareth. There they would live in accordance with Jewish law until God summoned them forth during the Last Days. Some sources placed the Ten Lost Tribes in the land of Hyrcania by the Caspian Sea, and others had them dwelling north of the Caucasus Mountains and the Caspian Sea. During late antiquity and the Middle Ages, some prophets of the Apocalypse, such as Otto of Freising, had the Ten Lost Tribes joining forces with the Antichrist and Gog and Magog during the final battle between good and evil. Inevitably, the Ten Lost Tribes and Gog and Magog fused into one entity. Godfrey of Viterbo, in the mid-twelfth century, stated that Alexander the Great enclosed Gog and Magog, who were the Lost Tribes of the Jews, in the mountain prison of the Caucasus. A century later, Matthew Paris considered the Tartars, Gog and Magog, and the Ten Lost Tribes the same group of tribes or nations. In this way, two of the out-groups of medieval Christendom—the foreign barbarian and the Jew—were merged.

From shortly after Alexander the Great's death in 323 B.C. until well into the age of European expansion during the sixteenth and seventeenth centuries, the Romances of Alexander were thought to be authentic history. Therefore, Gog and Magog and Alexander's Gate were also considered to be real, although they were also symbols. Gog and Magog were the ultimate barbarians who threatened the very existence of civilization, particularly Christian civilization. Alexander the Great became a Christianized hero who saved civilization from barbarian destruction, and Alexander's Gate was a bastion that would protect Christendom until the end of the world. Ultimately, European explorations failed to find Alexander's Gate and the land of Gog and Magog. No traveler ever stumbled across the great gate or encountered Gog and Magog. The Alexander Romance and its details graduated from history to legend.

See also

Alexander the Great, Romances of; Cynocephali; Four Corners of the Earth; Polo, Marco; Scythia; Tartary.

For further reading

Andrew Runni Anderson, *Alexander's Gate, Gog and Magog, and the Inclosed Nations,* 1932; John Kirtland Wright, *The Geographical Lore of the Time of the Crusades,* 1925.

GOLDEN CHERSONESE
Name used on Ptolemaic maps to refer to the Malay Peninsula. Medieval and Renaissance geographers considered the fabled Golden Chersonese to be one of the easternmost parts of the world. As stories of Christopher Columbus's second voyage of 1494 filtered back to Europe, it was assumed that he had reached the Golden Chersonese. In Amerigo Vespucci's first voyage of 1499, he tried to sail around the landmass of South America to reach the Golden Chersonese. In 1520, Ferdinand Magellan hoped that once he cleared the western opening of the South American strait named in his honor that he would be close to the Golden Chersonese. Obviously, Europeans had not yet grasped how large the earth really was. Magellan and his crew would learn at great cost the true vastness of the Pacific Ocean, but meanwhile the enticingly named Golden Chersonese beckoned to European travelers and merchants with its promise of the riches of Asia.

See also

Cathay; Chipangu; Spice Islands.

For further reading

J. H. Parry, *The Discovery of the Sea,* 1981.

GOLDEN HORN
Also called the Bay of Ceras, for centuries this famous body of water formed part of the bustling port of Constantinople. The Golden Horn was aptly named. Its nickname of "golden" came from the rich fishing found in its waters. Later, those same deep but calm waters made it an ideal harbor for commercial vessels. For over a thousand years, Constantinople was one of the richest cities in the world. The city's wealth was based on its very strategic location along the trade routes of the Mediterranean and Black Seas. In 1544, Pierre Gilles described how the Turkish sultan could look from his palace, the Seraglio, and see "vessels sailing up and down the Bay of Ceras,

where there is also an abundance of ferries and small boats always rowing from side to side." The volume of trade had been even greater before the Turkish conquest of Constantinople in 1453. The Golden Horn with its teeming quays was an object of awe and envy among the trading nations of Europe and the Mediterranean.

See also

Constantinople; Genoa; Venice.

For further reading

Pierre Gilles, *The Antiquities of Constantinople* [1561], 1988; David Talbot Rice, *Constantinople from Byzantium to Istanbul*, 1965; Ellen Churchill Semple, *The Geography of the Mediterranean Region*, 1931.

GOOD HOPE, CAPE OF   Well-known landmark at the southern tip of Africa for those sailing between the Atlantic and Indian Oceans. Seafarers can see its promontory from many miles away. It is not the southernmost point of Africa, however; that distinction belongs to the visually less impressive Cape Agulhas, located 100 miles to the east-southeast.

The fifteenth-century Portuguese speculated that it was possible to sail around Africa to reach Asia, although no one had done so since the ancient Phoenicians. Many Portuguese expeditions methodically explored the west coast of Africa, but the honor of first to enter the Indian Ocean from the Atlantic fell to Bartolomeu Dias. In 1487, Dias sailed farther down the African coast than previous Portuguese sailors. On 23 December 1487, he left the coast at Hottentot Bay and spent over 13 days on the high seas, heading south and then north. Land was sighted at 23°E 35°S around Mossel Bay on the east coast of Africa. Traveling eastward along the coast for several days, Dias passed beyond the Great Fish River, but the fears of his crew finally forced him to turn back. Sailing westward, Dias reached False Bay and the promontory of the Cape of Good Hope on 16 May 1488; he returned to Lisbon in December. According to the Portuguese chronicler João de Barros, Dias named the promontory *Cabo Tormentoso*, or Cape of Storms. Later, the public relations–conscious King João II changed the name to Cape of Good Hope. Duarte Pacheco, who sailed with Dias during part of his return voyage to Portugal, credited Dias with giving the Cape of Good Hope its name.

Experience would later show that Dias was fortunate to round the Cape of Good Hope by swinging far out to sea and traveling from west to east. During the winter, winds and currents along that section of coastline are particularly treacherous for sailing vessels. Thus, Dias fortuitously followed the best route for rounding the Cape of Good Hope, where—despite the cheery name—the seas are very dangerous. Because of its proximity to the Roaring Forties, its waters are uncommonly stormy. Sadly, Dias fell victim to the tempest-prone seas around the Cape of Good Hope when his ship foundered in a storm on its way to India with the fleet of Pedro Cabral in 1500.

The Cape of Good Hope became an important way station along the sea route between Europe and Asia. Its strategic location caused the Dutch to colonize it in 1652, and in turn, the British to conquer the Dutch colony in 1795. It remained part of the British Empire until South Africa became an independent republic in 1960.

See also

Atlantic Ocean; Circumnavigations of Africa, Early; Indian Ocean; Phoenicians.

For further reading

Bailey W. Diffie and George D. Winius, *Foundations of the Portuguese Empire, 1415–1580*, 1977; J. H. Parry, *The Discovery of the Sea*, 1981.

GOOD SAMARITAN

Well-known parable of Jesus that answered the question "Who is my neighbor?" It also illustrated the perils of travel in New Testament Palestine.

Jericho was an ancient city located approximately 30 miles northeast of Jerusalem. The account in Luke 10:30–37 tells how "a certain man went down from Jerusalem to Jericho," a statement that accurately describes the relatively steep descent from the heights of Jerusalem into the depths of the valley of the Jordan River and the Dead Sea, which are part of the Great Rift. Along the way, thieves beat and robbed the nameless traveler and left him for dead. The

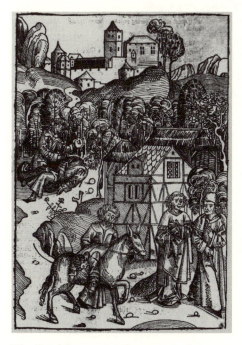

The Good Samaritan. German woodcut, 1491. Staatsbibliothek, Munich.

road was not deserted, however, and other travelers passed the injured man. Seeing him bleeding on the side of the road, the first two—a priest and a Levite, eminently respectable members of Jewish society—passed on the other side of the road to avoid him.

A third traveler, from Samaria, stopped and provided assistance to the injured man. After tending to his wounds, the Samaritan placed the victim on his own animal (probably a donkey) and took him to a nearby inn. The next day, the Samaritan had to continue his own journey, but he left two denarii, the equivalent of two days' wages for a laborer, to cover the wounded man's expenses. He also instructed the innkeeper: "Take care of him; and whatsoever thou spendest more, when I come again, I will repay thee."

Jesus used this story of the Good Samaritan to illustrate the proposition that

Christians have a duty to treat all people as their neighbors. In the parable, it is a Samaritan—a member of a group that Jews looked down upon—who behaves properly, in contrast to the supposedly respectable priest and Levite. The parable also tells much about the conditions of travel during that era. Even with steady traffic along the route between Jerusalem and Jericho, robbers were a very real danger. Inns existed along the route to serve the needs of travelers. Some travelers routinely used that highway, hence the Samaritan's "when I come again" comment to the innkeeper. A certain amount of credit and trust also existed, because the innkeeper trusted the Good Samaritan to repay him. In the ages before car phones, checkbooks, and credit cards, hospitable behavior like the Good Samaritan's rendered the highways and seaways less fearsome than might otherwise have been the case.

See also
Hospitality.
For further reading
Gaston Duchet-Suchaux and Michel Pastoureau, *The Bible and the Saints*, 1994.

GRAND CANAL

In China it is known as Yün-Ho (Transport River) or Yu-Ho (Imperial River). This massive system of canals connecting Peking to Hangchow is about 1,000 miles long and has been in operation for several thousand years.

The Grand Canal took 2,000 years to complete, beginning in the sixth century B.C. Along the present route of the Grand Canal, the Chinese dug various canals. Over time, they linked them into larger systems of canals. Emperor Yang Ti of the Sui dynasty completed the biggest component of the system in A.D. 610 From the tenth to the thirteenth centuries, the canal suffered from neglect. Kublai Khan repaired the Grand Canal from 1282 to 1292, and extended it from Tientsin to Peking. As Marco Polo described the renovated canal:

> The Emperor hath caused a water-communication to be made from this city [Hangchow] to Cambulac [Peking], in the shape of a wide and deep channel dug between stream and stream, between lake and lake, forming a great river on which large vessels can ply.

The Ming dynasty (1348–1644) made additional improvements to the Grand Canal, and Western visitors considered it a remarkable piece of collective engineering. It remains in use today, although railroads and modern highways carry much of its former traffic.

See also
Canals; Polo, Marco.
For further reading
Joseph Needham, *Science and Civilization in China*, vol. 4: *Physics and Physical Technology, part 3, Civil Engineering and Nautics*, 1971.

GRAND TOUR   Name for extended educational travel through Europe, particularly Italy, commonly undertaken by young English aristocrats, especially during the eighteenth century.

The Grand Tour originated in the late sixteenth century. Young Elizabethan aristocrats took many extended European journeys to broaden their cultural and educational horizons and gather intelligence for the state. Sir Philip Sidney spent three years traveling through Europe from 1572 to 1575 as part of his training before entering the Elizabethan diplomatic corps. The normally parsimonious Queen Elizabeth considered such travel beneficial enough to national interests that she sometimes provided subsidies for the young travelers. The practice grew in popularity during the seventeenth century despite the unsettled conditions on the Continent created by the Thirty Years War (1618–1648). In 1670, Richard Lessels, in his book *Voyage of Italy*, gave this form of educational travel its formal name of "Grand Tour."

Most of the aristocrats who went on the Grand Tour were age 18 to 20. Their parents sent them on the Grand Tour to sharpen their language skills, develop their cultural tastes, and improve their manners. To achieve those goals, an older tutor or "bear-leader" accompanied the youth, guiding his studies and protecting his morals. Society generally viewed most tutors as ineffectual and worthless, and many tutors were unable to maintain control over their high-spirited charges. However, some ranked among the great scholars and literary men of their time: Adam Smith, Thomas Hobbes, Joseph Addison, and John Horne Tooke all spent time as tutors on the Grand Tour.

Participants in the Grand Tour needed guidebooks, and in response to the demand, many were written. Practically everyone embarking on the Grand Tour acquired one or more of these guidebooks to direct their travels. The Grand Tour had no fixed itinerary, but most people left England from Dover and sailed to Calais in France. From there they made their way across France to Paris, where they would spend some time. Moving on through France to Switzerland, they made stops at Geneva, Lausanne, and Basel.

After traveling over the Alps, participants in the Grand Tour finally arrived in Italy, the heart of the entire tour enterprise. The point of focusing on Italy was to allow the young people to visit the many antiquities of that land and experience its gracious living. Genoa, Florence, Milan, Naples, and Venice were all important places to visit. Visiting Rome, however, was the pinnacle.

From Italy the Grand Tour's route headed north into Austria and Germany. The attractions of those countries included their great universities, excellent spas, and famous cities such as Vienna, Munich, and Frankfort. After Germany the Grand Tour moved on to the Low Countries (present-day Belgium and the Netherlands). The participants experienced the fabled cleanliness of the Dutch and their fine roads and comfortable inns. All of this traveling took two to four years.

Although it was generally cheaper to live on the Continent than in England, most Grand Tour participants spent lavishly. In the seventeenth century, John Evelyn spent the rather large amount of £300 a year. Most young men, however, found it quite possible to spend much less and still live in considerable style and comfort.

Living conditions along the Grand Tour were mixed. Many inns, particularly in France and Italy, were dirty and unpleasant. Travelers ran the risk of catching various diseases. Local authorities required bribes and gratuities. Thieves pilfered travelers' luggage. On the road, brigands and bandits frequently robbed and murdered lone travelers or those in groups too small to defend themselves.

The Grand Tour was supposed to be an educational experience, not a recreational one. Participants were to study and practice their foreign languages, investigate architecture, examine local customs, and view the general topography. They were urged to take copious notes of what they heard and make sketches of what they saw. Of course, the young Grand Tourist often neglected such serious tasks and instead engaged in heavy drinking, prodigious gambling, and insatiable wenching. From William Cecil Lord Burghley in the sixteenth century, to John Locke in the seventeenth, and Adam Smith and Samuel Johnson in the eighteenth century, numerous doubts were expressed about the efficacy of the Grand Tour as an educational experience. Critics charged—in some cases quite accurately—that young aristocrats returning to England had been transformed into foppish debauchees. Some thought the participants ought to be older and more mature, at least in their early twenties, so they would get more out of their travels.

The Grand Tour produced some good results. English tastes in architecture and art were uplifted substantially. A host of travel memoirs based on experiences from the Grand Tour appeared. Some of them became celebrated works of English literature, such as those by Joseph Addison, Tobias Smollett, Laurence Sterne, and Horace Walpole. The coming of the French Revolutionary Wars in the 1790s interrupted Grand Tours. When the fighting ended in 1815, the coming of the railroads in the 1820s and 1830s quickly changed the character of traveling, ending the Grand Tour as an English institution.

For further reading
Jeremy Black, *The British Abroad*, 1992; Christopher Hibbert, *The Grand Tour*, 1969.

GRAND TRUNK ROAD   Great road in northern India that stretches some 1,400 miles between Calcutta and Peshawar.

The Grand Trunk Road is a famous highway for travel and commerce, linking the length of the Ganges River from the Bay of Bengal over to Punjab and the Indus River valley. Some accounts credit the Mogul emperor Sher Shah (1540–1545) with its construction. Other accounts claim that the officials of the British East India Company began work on the road in 1839.

By 1846 or 1847, the Grand Trunk Road extended about 700 miles from Calcutta. Although heavily used, its surface was described as being as smooth as a bowling green. The road reached Peshawar in the turbulent Punjab by 1857, and was instrumental in the pacification of that region. The early success of the Grand Trunk Road led to the start of other trunk roads between Bombay and Agra and Bombay and Calcutta in 1840. The Grand Trunk Road and its imitators greatly improved internal commerce within the Indian subcontinent.

For further reading
Percival Griffiths, *The British Impact on India*, 1953.

GREAT IRELAND   Also known as Irland-ed-Mikla, Hvítramannaland, White Man's Land, and Albania Superior, Great Ireland is the name for the legendary settlement established by Irish monks during the early Middle Ages when they fled from the Norse invaders of Iceland. It supposedly lay somewhere in the western Atlantic Ocean, which was widely believed to be sprinkled generously with habitable islands. Mentions of Great Ireland appear in the Norse sagas of the *Landnamabok*, *Erik the Red's Saga*, and *The Eyrbyggia Saga*. Belief in its existence was widespread enough that the great Islamic geographer Idrisi (1099–1180) talked about *Irlandah-al-Kabirah* (Great Ireland) in his famous description of the world commonly known as the *Book of Roger*. Possibly Great Ireland was simply one more mythological place that medieval people came to believe was real. The number of references to the existence of Great Ireland in medieval documents convinced certain scholars that such a place actually existed, and its location was set in North America in locations as far north as the Gulf of St. Lawrence and as far south as the Carolinas. However, no convincing archaeological evidence exists to support this speculation. Other scholars suggest that Great Ireland and Greenland may have been one and the same. Different groups of travelers simply gave different names to the same land.

See also
Hvítramannaland; Iceland.
For further reading
Geoffrey Ashe, *Land to the West*, 1962.

"GREAT SEA OF DARKNESS"   Translation of the Arabic name for the Atlantic Ocean or Western Ocean. According to the geographer Abu al-Hasan 'Ali al-Masudi (d. 956; the common Western form of his name is al-Massoudy), it was not possible to sail past the Strait of Gibraltar. As he described the Atlantic, "no vessel sails on that sea; it is without cultivation or inhabitant, and its end, like its depth, is unknown." That belief persisted through the time of Abu 'Abd Allah Muhammad al-Idrisi (1099–1180; the common Western form of his name is Edrisi). In his great geographical treatise *The Book of Roger*, Edrisi described how a permanent darkness hung over the Atlantic, whose waters were thick and black. Frequent storms and high winds swept over this unpleasant sea, making it impossible to navigate. Al-Dimashqi

(1256–1327), a later Arab geographer from Syria, echoed Edrisi's account when he wrote this description:

> The ocean encompasses all sides of the earth. The western part of it, in the north, is called the Sea of Darkness and the Black Northern Sea. It is called "black" and "dark" because the fogs which ascend from it are not dissolved by the sun because it does not rise on it, so its water thickens, its mists become dense and sight cannot determine the quality of its water. Because of the magnitude of its waves, the denseness of its darkness, the blowing of its winds, and the multitudes of its terrors, nobody knows more than a part of its coasts and such of its islands as are close to inhabited land.

Medieval Arabs obviously feared the Atlantic Ocean. Apart from the legendary Adventurers *(Maghrurin)* of Lisbon, who supposedly sailed the Great Sea of Darkness and possibly reached the Canary Islands sometime before 1147, little evidence exists of high-seas voyaging in the Atlantic by Islamic peoples of the Maghrib or western North Africa and the Iberian Peninsula. This ignorance of the techniques and technologies needed to sail safely on the Atlantic persisted among the North African Arabs into the early seventeenth century. In 1586, an Albanian called Murat Reis (1534–1638) led the first expedition of the Barbary pirates into the Atlantic to raid the Canary Islands. The Dutchman Simon Simonson (d. 1616) taught the Barbary pirates how to build and navigate the round-ships that were best able to survive the rough Atlantic waters. However, the Arabs of North Africa never developed into skillful and daring sailors like the Arab seamen of the Indian Ocean who followed in the bold wake of Sindbad the Sailor.

See also
Atlantic Ocean.

For further reading
Charles Raymond Beazley, *The Dawn of Modern Geography*, 3 vols. [1897–1906], reprint, 1942; N. Levtzion and J. F. P. Hopkins, eds., *Corpus of Early Arabic Sources for West African History*, 1981; A. J. Wensinck, *The Ocean in the Literature of the Western Semites*, 1918.

GREENLAND   Large island in the Arctic waters of the North Atlantic that was the westernmost permanent Norse settlement from 986 until its demise in 1450–1500. Greenland marked the far western limit of European geographical knowledge and travel until the expansion of the late fifteenth and sixteenth centuries.

Gunnbjorn Ulfsson first sighted the coast of Greenland sometime between 900 and 930 when a storm drove him too far west while traveling from Norway to Iceland. Because he had sailed to Greenland's desolate, heavily glaciated eastern coast, Gunnbjorn made no attempt to land or return later to his discovery. In 982, another Norse named Eric the Red sailed west from Iceland in search of Gunnbjorn's discovery. After reaching Greenland, Eric

"The Discovery of Greenland." Harper's Weekly, *1875.*

headed south and rounded Cape Farewell, where he saw meadowlands capable of sustaining a Norse community. Eric liked what he saw, and returned to Iceland in 986 singing the new land's praises. To make it even more attractive to settlers, he called it Greenland. The ploy worked, and that same year Eric sailed from overcrowded Iceland with 25 ships carrying several hundred people. Only 14 of them reached Greenland; the rest either perished in the stormy seas or turned back to Iceland. Still, enough people arrived to give the new colony a good start.

The Norse quickly formed two main settlements. The largest was called the Eastern Settlement, and was located just west of Cape Farewell. At its height it may have had 5,000 inhabitants. The Western Settlement lay 300 miles farther up Greenland's west coast. It was considerably smaller than the Eastern Settlement, numbering no more than 1,500 people at its high point. Between the two settlements was a minor Middle Settlement with several hundred residents, but it probably regarded itself as an outlying part of the Eastern Settlement rather than a separate colony.

Although the Norse found an empty land, they came upon abandoned stone buildings and skin boats left by earlier inhabitants. Some attribute these remains to refugee Irish monks fleeing from the Viking raids on Ireland, but archaeological evidence indicates that the remains belonged to Eskimos of the Dorset culture, who abandoned the area as the climate warmed. A warming climate during the eleventh and twelfth centuries made the Norse settlement of Greenland possible. It calmed the seas, making sailing there easier, and the warmer weather permitted the Norse to graze their cattle and sheep successfully. Hunting of harp seals, walruses, and caribou was also aided by the milder climate. The Norse apparently traded for furs, walrus ivory, and wood with the various Native American groups inhabiting Greenland and Labrador. The Norse of Greenland were able to live as well as the Icelanders, but they had insufficient resources to extend their colonization westward, as shown by the failures of Thorvald Ericsson and Thorfinn Karlsefni to establish settlements in Vinland.

Greenland was very much a part of the wider world of the medieval Norse. When Iceland adopted Christianity in the year 1000, Greenland soon followed suit, although Eric the Red remained incorrigibly pagan. In 1124, the pope consecrated an Arnald as the first bishop for Greenland; his cathedral was located at Gardar. In 1261, the Greenlanders decided to give up their republic and accept the sovereignty and protection of the king of Norway, as did Iceland a few years later. This decision, however, could do nothing to protect the Greenlanders from the doom that would eventually befall the isolated colony.

The climate began to cool in the late thirteenth century, and things got worse in the fourteenth and fifteenth centuries. Norse grazing and hunting became less productive, and communication with Europe became more difficult. The better-adapted Eskimos of the Thule culture began moving south with the cold. Relations between the Norse and the Eskimos had long been a mixture of cautious trading and sporadic hostility. Although some writers suggest that Eskimo raiders wiped out the dying Norse settlements in Greenland, it is far more likely that a declining economy and food supply led to malnutrition among the Norse, followed by disease, depopulation, and extinction. In 1448, Pope Nicholas V mentioned a heathen fleet attacking the Norse in Greenland, but the archaeological evidence shows that the Norse settlement just faded away. Eskimos occupied the Western Settlement by 1341 and the Middle Settlement by 1380. The Eastern Settlement seems to have expired sometime between 1450 and 1500. Eskimo folktales tell of the hunting and killing of Olaf, the last survivor of the Eastern Settlement. The best judgment on the extinction of the Norse settlements in Greenland blames it on their failure to adopt an Eskimo-style economy in the face of a deteriorating climate, rather than on their failure to defeat the Eskimos in battle.

See also
    Iceland; Vinland.

For further reading
    Gwyn Jones, *The Norse Atlantic Saga,* 1986; Thomas H. McGovern, "The Economics of Extinction in Norse Greenland," in *Climate and History,* 1981; Thomas H. McGovern, "The Lost Norse Colony of Greenland," in *Vikings in the West,* 1982.

GRIFFINS   Also spelled Griffons or Gryphons, they were monstrous creatures with the head and wings of eagles, the bodies of lions, and, in some accounts, the tails of serpents. In classical mythology they pulled the chariots of Zeus,

Apollo, and Nemesis. Some travelers' accounts claimed that in Scythia the Griffins and the monstrous race of one-eyed people known as the Arimaspians engaged in perpetual warfare reminiscent of the battles between the Pygmies and the cranes. In India, Griffins fought with giants. Griffins also guarded deposits of gold, silver, or precious gems in Scythia and on the islands of the Indian Ocean. The Jewish traveler Benjamin of Tudela (d. ca. 1173) described an incident in which some ships blundered into the deadly Sea of Nikpa off the coast of China. Some of the sailors escaped by sewing themselves into the skins of cattle and throwing themselves into the water. Hungry Griffins swooped down and snatched them from the water, thinking they were real cows. Carrying their prey to eyries on the mainland, the Griffins instead found themselves killed by the knives of the resourceful sailors, who then walked to safety. This story is very similar to that of how the Roc carried Sindbad to safety during one of his voyages. Marco Polo, in his description of Madagascar, heard local stories about the Roc, and incorrectly assumed the natives were talking about Griffins. Medieval medical lore held that a cup made from a Griffin's claw would change color if filled with a drink containing poison, and such cups were considered valuable possessions by those fearful of being poisoned by their enemies. Belief in the existence of Griffins was widespread in the ancient and medieval world even though they were purely mythical creatures. Travelers expected that they might encounter a Griffin, who although fearsome was the possessor of valuable claws and a harbinger of nearby treasure.

See also
Monstrous Races; Roc; Scythia; Sindbad, The Seven Voyages of.
For further reading
John Kirtland Wright, *The Geographical Lore of the Time of the Crusades*, 1925.

GUIDES AND INTERPRETERS   Throughout the ages, travelers in an unfamiliar land where they did not speak the local language depended on the services of guides and interpreters; a guide was often the difference between life and death. The mythical Trojan hero Aeneas used the Cumaean Sibyl as a guide during his trip to Hades to visit his dead father, and returned unscathed to the land of the living. Not all guides were reliable, however. William of Rubruck employed a guide and interpreter during his mission to the Mongol khan at Karakorum. The guide proved to be a chronic drunkard and a poor translator. After William learned the Mongol language for himself, he discovered just how inaccurate his guide's translations were. He survived his incompetent guide, but undoubtedly many hapless travelers died as the result of poor or treacherous guides.

Good guides were essential to the success of many expeditions. Both Doña Marina (ca. 1500–1526) for the expedition of Hernán Cortés into Mexico in 1518–1521 and Sacajawea (ca. 1790–1812 or 1884) for the Lewis and Clark expedition to the Pacific coast saved their employers from destruction on a number of occasions. The African Sidi "Bombay" Mubarak greatly contributed to the success of Sir Richard Burton and John Hanning Speke's travels in East Africa during the mid-nineteenth century.

Guides and interpreters have been characterized as living between two worlds, and so belonging fully to neither their homeland nor the world of the visitors. Often, certain families specialized in working as guides and interpreters. The family of Sarah Winnemucca (1844–1891) served white Americans, the U.S. Army, and the Bureau of Indian Affairs as guides for several generations. Relations between guides and their employers sometimes became quite intimate. Doña Marina became Cortés's mistress, although he ultimately cast her off to marry a Spanish woman. The Goldi guide Dersu Usala (1850–1908) became extremely good friends with the Russian army officer who employed him as a guide.

The role of guide and interpreter survives into the present because the need continues. Although guidebooks and foreign phrase books eliminate the need in much of the industrial West, tour groups still employ them today. The heroic age of personal guides and interpreters has disappeared with the growth of mass tourism throughout the world.

For further reading

Frances Karttunen, *Between Worlds*, 1994.

GUINEA   Geographical term used by Europeans to refer to sub-Saharan West Africa, especially during the fifteenth through the nineteenth centuries. Occasionally the fifteenth-century Portuguese applied the term Guinea to all of the African continent.

Guinea traditionally encompassed the west coast of Africa from the Gambia River to the Niger River's delta. Some writers claim that the name Guinea comes from a Portuguese corruption of Ghana, the name of an early-medieval Sudanese trading empire. That derivation is impossible, however, because the first use of Guinea as a place-name occurred on a map of Giovanni de Carignano dated 1320, long before the Portuguese exploration of West Africa had begun. The author of the fourteenth-century *Book of the Knowledge of All the . . . World* also used the name Guinea to refer to West Africa. Leo Africanus, the sixteenth-century Arab geographer, hinted that Guinea might be a distortion of Jenne, an important trading city closely associated with Timbuktu.

The best etymology for Guinea links it to the Berber word *aguinaou,* which means Negro, or land of the Negroes. A twelfth-century gate in Marrakesh was named the Bab Aguinaou, or Gate of the Negro. The geographical term "Guinea," along with Ethiopia (land of burnt-faced people) and Sudan (from *Beled es-Sudan,* meaning "land of the blacks"), comes from references to sub-Saharan Africa as a land of black people. In 1461, King João II of Portugal obtained papal permission to style himself as "Lord of Guinea." In 1662, an English gold coin was called a guinea because West African gold was used to mint it. Geographically, the name survives in the West African nations Guinea (a former French colony, independent 1958) and Guinea-Bissau (a former Portuguese colony, independent 1973).

See also

Africa.

For further reading

Edward William Bovill, *The Golden Trade of the Moors*, 1968; J. R. S. Phillips, *The Medieval Expansion of Europe*, 1988; UNESCO *General History of Africa*, vol. 4: *Africa from the Twelfth to the Sixteenth Century*, 1981.

GYMNOSOPHISTS   A legendary group of wise men living in India who went about naked, stood first on one foot and then on the other while staring at the sun, and practiced an ascetic lifestyle. From ancient times through the Middle Ages, they were considered one of the Marvels of the East.

Ancient Greek and medieval European accounts of the Gymnosophists grouped them with the various monstrous races, but, like the similar Bragmanni and the fierce Amazons, Gymnosophists were not physically deformed. Rather, they practiced a way of life that seemed strange or alien to Westerners. Their character evoked a positive response from medieval Christian writers who admired their otherworldly and ascetic mode of living. Gymnosophists and Bragmanni were frequently regarded as primitive Christians who led Christian lives even without the benefit of exposure to the preaching of the Gospel or as leftovers of the mythic Golden Age of humanity. Various medieval writers, including the author of the *Travels of Sir John Mandeville,* told how Alexander the Great visited the Gymnosophists and was so impressed by their goodness that he declined to conquer them. Medieval travelers' accounts of the Gymnosophists provided their readers with uplifting moral lessons that contrasted most favorably with the warlike and corrupt aspects of European society. Although the Gymnosophists did not literally exist, it is highly likely that the Western travelers' encounters with sun-worshipping Parsees or Zoroastrians inspired the tales of the Gymnosophists.

See also

Bragmanni; Monstrous Races.

For further reading

John Block Friedman, *The Monstrous Races in Medieval Art and Thought,* 1981.

H

HAJJ Arabic name for the pilgrimage to Mecca required of all Muslim men. Both the Koran and the teachings of the Five Pillars of Islam require that every free, able-bodied Muslim make a pilgrimage, or hajj, to Mecca if he can afford one. Simply visiting Mecca does not constitute a proper hajj. Any true pilgrimage is directed toward visiting the Kaaba, the small but ancient temple known as the House of Allah. A simple pilgrimage to the Kaaba is called an *'umra*, and does not equal a hajj. An *'umra* can be made at any time of the year and involves a set of rituals performed at the Kaaba.

The hajj is a much more complex act of piety, and can be performed only during *Dhul-Hijja*, the last month of the Muslim calendar. When male pilgrims reach the boundary of the *haram*, or holy territory, around Mecca, they change into a two-piece white garment and sandals. Until they complete the hajj, the pilgrims cannot wear other clothing or shoes, cut their hair or nails, engage in sexual intercourse, argue, fight, or hunt. They enter a ritual state called *ihram*.

Once in Mecca, pilgrims go to the great mosque Masjid al-Haram, which houses the Kaaba, and walk around the Kaaba in a ceremony called *tawaf*. Next, they perform the running ceremony called *sa'y*, which recalls both Satan's temptation of Abraham and the relief of Hagar and Ishmael by the appearance of the sacred well of Zamzam. If possible, pilgrims kiss the sacred Black Stone embedded in the eastern corner of the Kaaba. These rituals take place during the first few days of *Dhul-Hijja*, and if they are all that a pilgrim does, they constitute the lesser pilgrimage of *'umra*.

On the seventh day of *Dhul-Hijja*, the true hajj begins. Pilgrims hear a sermon. The next day they walk about five and one-half miles across a plain east of Mecca to Arafat, the place where Adam and Eve met after their expulsion from the Garden of Eden. The pilgrims stand and pray from noon until sunset of the ninth day in a ceremony called *wuquf*, which symbolizes the Day of Judgment. During the tenth day of the hajj, pilgrims travel to Mina and throw seven stones at the rock called Jamrat al'Aqaba, a ceremony that figuratively drives out the devil. They also perform *'Id al'Adha*, the ritual sacrifice of an animal, which re-creates the sacrifice of Abraham when God spared Isaac. Pilgrims then return to Mecca and perform another *tawaf* at the Kaaba. Now they can have their heads shaved or their hair cut, and their state of *ihram* is finished. For the next three days, the pilgrims can visit holy places around

Mecca; many choose Muhammad's tomb in Medina. Periodically, they are supposed to continue throwing stones at the sacred rocks at Mina.

Once Muslims complete the hajj, they are entitled to use the highly respected title of hajji; many Muslims make multiple hajjs. The hajj is an international phenomenon. Ibn Battuta and Ibn Jubayr traveled from Morocco and Spain to Mecca. Others came from the Far East of China and Indonesia. The great Chinese admiral Cheng Ho's father was a hajji.

Making the hajj has always taken a great deal of time, money, and effort during most of Islam's history. It was not always safe, either. The Crusader Renald de Châtillon attacked caravans of pilgrims going on the hajj as they passed through Palestine. Vasco da Gama brutally massacred the hajjis on the pilgrimage ship *Mîrî* as it sailed for home across the Indian Ocean in 1502. Non-Muslims, however, were not the only people to prey upon pilgrims. Shiite bedouin tribes had few scruples about attacking caravans of devout Sunni Muslims. Nevertheless, the hajj helped form and preserve an Islamic ideal of universal brotherhood and community that transcended nationality, tribe, or race. In the late twentieth century, the hajj remains a fundamental part of Islam.

See also
Mecca; Pilgrimage.
For further reading
F. E. Peters, *The Hajj*, 1994.

HANNO, VOYAGE OF (CA. 490 B.C.)   Ancient Carthaginian explorer and colonizer of West Africa, widely believed during the sixteenth century to have visited America.

Around 500 B.C., the Carthaginian government decided to promote exploration and the systematic establishment of trading posts beyond the Strait of Gibraltar. Large expeditions were sent out both north and south along the Atlantic coastline, led by the brothers Himilco and Hanno, governors of the Carthaginian settlers in Andalusia. Himilco commanded the northern expedition, which may have reached Britain, marking the beginning of the Carthaginian takeover of the ancient Atlantic tin trade.

Hanno's expedition sailed south along the West African coastline. Its most important accomplishment was the foundation of the colony of Cerne (probably Herne Island at the mouth of the Rio de Oro), which served as a trading post for the trans-Saharan gold trade. Some of the expedition continued to sail south for three weeks, encountering dense forests and mysterious natives. Supplies began to run short, however, and they were forced to turn back. In the vicinity of the Senegal River, the Carthaginians encountered hippopotami and crocodiles. Sailing along various sections of the coast, they witnessed tremendous grass fires. Most scholars think that Hanno reached as far south as Sherbo Sound near the western border of present-day Liberia. He and his crew encountered gorillas or some other form of great ape there, and being unfamiliar with such creatures, the Carthaginians mistook them for some sort of savage, hairy humans. Given that ancient and medieval travelers roamed the earth with a strong expectation of encountering members of the monstrous races, it was not a particularly surprising mistake.

Knowledge of Hanno's African voyage is preserved in a Greek translation of the original Punic document, which provided a heavily censored account of the event. The Carthaginians were very secretive about their commercial activities, which makes any assessment of the significance of Hanno's voyage difficult. The Mediterranean world's contact with the coast of West Africa apparently declined after Rome's defeat of Carthage in 201 B.C., and not until the Portuguese voyages down the West African coast in the fifteenth century were the achievements of Hanno and the Carthaginians equaled or surpassed.

After Columbus's voyage to America in 1492, some scholars seriously suggested that Hanno had also visited the New World during his great expedition to Africa. The source for these speculations appears to be Hanno's reference to an inhabited island of forests far out in the western Atlantic. However, it probably refers to a forgotten Carthaginian discovery of the Azores rather than America.

See also

Carthage; Circumnavigations of Africa, Early.

For further reading

M. Cary and E. H. Warmington, *The Ancient Explorers*, 1963; C. Kaeppel, *Off the Beaten Track in the Classics*, 1936; J. V. Luce, "Ancient Explorers," in *The Quest for America*, 1971.

HECATAEUS OF MILETUS (CA. 550–490 B.C.)

Early geographer and historian, thought to be the first Greek to write in prose rather than poetry. Much of the meager amount known about his life comes from the historian Herodotus. Hecataeus participated in the Ionian revolt against Persian rule from 500 to 494 B.C. Forced into exile, he engaged in scholarship. His writings do not survive as complete works; the fragments remaining are often mere citations. A man with a practical and critical mind, Hecataeus's goal was to separate the truth about geography and history from the fabulous fictions that commonly circulated among the Greeks of his day. His geographical work, titled *Periegesis*, presents a systematic survey of the lands around the Mediterranean and Black Seas, along with Scythia and Persia, and he is considered the father of the study of geography. It is not known how much of his work was based on firsthand observation and how much was gleaned from the testimony of other travelers. Herodotus used Hecataeus's *Periegesis*, although to what degree is not known. *Genealogies*, or *Histories*, was the title of Hecataeus's other book, the surviving fragments of which indicate that he analyzed myths in a rational manner by trying to uncover their historical basis. The appearance of a thinker and writer like Hecataeus demonstrates the growing importance of trade and travel among the Greeks of the classical era.

See also
Herodotus.
For further reading
Robert Drews, *The Greek Accounts of Eastern History,* 1973; Lionel Pearson, *Early Ionian Historians,* 1939.

HELLULAND   Meaning flat-stone land or slab land in Norse, this name was given by the Norse explorers of North America to the heavily glaciated land of stone they first sighted after leaving Greenland. The Vinland Sagas describe it as lying either two or four days' sail west of Greenland. Scholars generally agree that Helluland was Baffin Island, but the nineteenth-century Danish scholar Carl Rafn and his followers, such as Hjalmar Holland, thought that Newfoundland was Helluland. According to the *Greenlanders' Saga,* it was the third and last land sighted by Bjarni Herjolfsson, although he did not land on it or name it. Later, Leif Ericsson landed there and named it Helluland. The Norse considered it a worthless country. *Eirik's Saga* credits Thorfinn Karlsefni with naming this stony country Helluland. It is described as being full of stone slabs (hence the name) and foxes. Given the nature of Helluland, the Norse made no attempt to settle, but they apparently traded with Dorset and Thule culture Eskimos who lived on Baffin Island and the surrounding areas. Because of its barren nature, Helluland exercised a minimal influence on the geographical imagination of the medieval Norse, and little or none on the rest of Europe.

See also
Greenland; Markland; Vinland.

HERODOTUS (484–420 B.C.)   Historian, geographer, and traveler, he wrote *The Histories,* the first surviving prose work of history and a compendium of ancient history, geography, and ethnography that has fascinated and informed its readers for over two millennia.

Herodotus was born at Halicarnassus on the southwest coast of Asia Minor. His family belonged to the local elite, which meant that Herodotus became involved in politics. The Persians had conquered Halicarnassus and made it part of their vast empire, and Herodotus joined the opposition to Cygdamis, the Persian-supported tyrant of Halicarnassus. When his allies were defeated, Herodotus was forced to go into exile, beginning extensive travels throughout the known world: the Black Sea coastlands, the steppes along the Dnieper River valley, Babylon, Tyre, and Egypt as far up the Nile River as Elephantine. He was also acquainted with European Greece and Asia Minor, especially Delos and Delphi, and resided for considerable periods of time at Athens, Samos, and Thurii, a largely Athenian colony in southern Italy. Wherever he went, Herodotus questioned the locals or his fellow travelers about history, geography, and local customs, information he used in his monumental *Histories*.

Herodotus wanted to tell the story of the great conflict between the Greeks and the Persians (490–479 B.C.). To accomplish that goal, he divided his larger work into nine books. In book one, the causes of the conflict are discussed. Books two through five describe Persian expansion into Egypt, Scythia, and northern Greece along with the abortive Ionian Revolt. Book six tells the story of the Persian king Darius's attack on Athens and his defeat at the battle of Marathon, and books seven through nine narrate the events of the next Persian king's

Statue of Herodotus by Daniel C. French, nineteenth century.

(Xerxes) massive invasion of Greece and its ultimate failure. Throughout his larger history, Herodotus tells numerous peripheral stories relating to his major theme. Book two represents Herodotus's reconstruction of Egypt's history and culture, and tells how the Persians conquered that ancient land. In other places he describes the alien customs of the various nomadic tribes of Scythia. At one point he tells the story of the Phoenician circumnavigation of Africa, and his account of the Royal Road of the Persians provides another fascinating interlude. These excursuses make Herodotus's *Histories* a treasure trove of the history, geography, folklore, and anthropology of the ancient world.

Almost all of Herodotus's information was derived from interviews. Some of it is completely fantastic, but much is reliable. Herodotus never claimed to stand by everything that he included in his *Histories;* instead, he was careful to qualify the reliability of his sources. At the same time, Herodotus was limited by the overall Greek knowledge of geography and cosmography. A follower of the Pythagorean school of philosophy, he believed the earth was flat, along with other erroneous geographical concepts. He also thought that the earth's geographical features were organized in a symmetrical manner (e.g., the Nile and the Danube Rivers were supposedly mirror images of each other). Unaware of the Nile's division into the White and Blue branches, he thought that the waters of the Nile turned westward and that its source lay in West Africa. He may have been conflating the Nile with the Niger River. Unlike some ancient writers, he correctly depicted the Caspian Sea as an inland sea rather than an inlet of the northern River Ocean.

Herodotus was the first Greek prose writer whose works survived intact. A number of writers known as logographers preceded him, but their works are lost except for scattered excerpts extracted or quoted by later ancient writers. The most famous of these logographers was Hecataeus of Miletus, who wrote extensively on historical and geographical subjects. It is clear that Hecataeus influenced Herodotus, but the extent of that influence cannot be determined because of the loss of Hecataeus's writings.

Herodotus's *Histories* have been popular since the time of their completion. They tell a dramatic story and are filled with engaging details and anecdotes. During much of the Middle Ages, European knowledge of Herodotus faded. Most medieval scholars got their information from Herodotus indirectly through the epitomes of Isidore of Seville and Solinus. By the fourteenth and fifteenth centuries, European scholars read Herodotus directly and derived some of their historical and geographical knowledge from him. Herodotus's *Histories* had a big impact on the geographical lore of travelers from ancient times to the early eighteenth century. He was a great traveler himself, and a great asker of questions. It is no wonder that his book endures.

See also

Black Sea; Hecataeus of Miletus; Nile River.

For further reading

M. Cary and E. H. Warmington, *The Ancient Explorers,* 1963; J. A. S. Evans, *Herodotus,* 1982; Margaret T. Hodgen, *Early Anthropology in the Sixteenth and Seventeenth Centuries,* 1964; James S. Romm, *The Edges of the Earth in Ancient Thought,* 1992; H. F. Tozer, *A History of Ancient Geography,* 1897.

HIGHWAYMEN
See Robbers.

HIMILCO, VOYAGE OF (CA. 490 B.C.)

Himilco was a Carthaginian admiral who led an expedition to explore the coast of Europe; he probably reached the tin-producing lands of Brittany and Cornwall.

Little is known about his voyage, but it is thought to have taken place at the same time as the voyage of Hanno; in fact, the two men were supposed to be brothers. Unlike Hanno's, the only surviving information about Himilco's voyage is a brief mention in Pliny's (A.D. 23/24–79) *Natural History* and a garbled passage in the poet Avienus's (fl. mid-fourth century A.D.) work *Ora Maritima.* According to Avienus, Himilco's voyage lasted four months. The Carthaginians experienced slow progress because of vexing calms and seaweed-clogged waters. All the while, menacing sea monsters cavorted around their ships in waters so shallow that the bottom could be seen. Despite these difficulties, Himilco reached the Oestrymnid Islands, where tin was traded.

Modern scholars find the accounts of Himilco to be perplexing. Both Pliny and Avienus lived centuries after the Carthaginian voyage, and no other corroborating documents have come to light. The confused nature of Avienus's account leads some writers to suggest that Himilco sailed south along the African coast like Hanno, visiting the Canary Islands and perhaps the Cape Verde Islands. This scenario, however, flatly contradicts the words of Pliny and Avienus, and therefore is almost certainly wrong. Other writers speculate that Himilco sailed out into the Atlantic Ocean and reached the Azores Islands. Along the way he would have encountered seasonal doldrums and the Sargasso Sea, but no shallow seas lay in that direction. It seems most likely that Himilco simply sailed north and reached Brittany and Cornwall. Allowing for a certain amount of exaggeration, Himilco could have encountered shallows, calms, floating seaweed, and pods of whales in those waters. The Carthaginians jealously guarded the secrets of their trade, and they had a strong interest in emphasizing the terrors of any Atlantic sea voyage to potential interlopers. Not surprisingly, Carthaginian accounts of voyages such as Himilco's were vague and full of dangers and horrors.

See also
> Atlantic Ocean; Carthage; Hanno, Voyage of; Pliny the Elder.

For further reading
> Rhys Carpenter, *Beyond the Pillars of Heracles*, 1966; M. Cary and E. H. Warmington, *The Ancient Explorers*, 1963.

HOLY LAND   Also known as Palestine and the land of Israel, common name for the region located in the southeastern corner of the Mediterranean Sea. Christians and Jews consider this land special because it is the setting for much of the activity described in the Old and New Testaments of the Bible.

The Book of Genesis tells how God gave Palestine, or the Land of Canaan, to the patriarch Abraham and his descendants. Seven years of famine caused his great-grandchildren to move to Egypt, where they worked as slaves for generations. Finally, God raised up Moses as the leader of the Hebrews, or Children of Israel. Moses secured their release from Egyptian slavery and led them into the wilderness. After 40 years of wandering, under the leadership of Joshua the Children of Israel invaded the Land of Canaan and conquered it over several generations. They established a monarchy, with Saul as their first king, followed by the great David (ca. 1010–ca. 970 B.C.) and his son Solomon (ca. 970–ca. 930 B.C.). From that high point, the Israelite kingdom split into bickering northern and southern kingdoms. Meanwhile, the great Middle Eastern empires loomed ominously over the Hebrews. By 722 B.C., the northern kingdom fell to the Assyrians, and the Babylonians conquered Jerusalem, the capital of the southern kingdom, in 597 and 586 B.C. The conquerors exiled the leading citizens of Jerusalem to Babylon until 538 B.C., when the newly dominant Persians allowed them to return home and rebuild Jerusalem.

Gustave Doré illustration of European pilgrims worshiping at the Church of the Holy Sepulchre in Jerusalem.

During this time of exile, nostalgia for and veneration of Palestine as their Holy Land began. The writings of the prophets Ezekiel (fl. 593–571 B.C.) and Zechariah (fl. 520–518 B.C.) exemplify the growth of the concept of the Jewish Holy Land. This idea has pervaded Judaism ever since, and is an important source for Zionism, the idea of the scattered Jews returning to their original homeland of Israel (Palestine).

At first, early Christians did not emphasize the physical land of Palestine as a holy land; rather, their concept was spiritual and otherworldly. Heaven was the Holy Land for such early church fathers as Origen (ca. A.D. 185–254). This situation changed during the reign of Emperor Constantine the Great (306–337). Beginning in 312, Constantine gave Christianity official recognition and favor, and a magnificent program of church building commenced. In Palestine, churches were constructed over various sites of biblical significance (e.g., Bethlehem as the birthplace of Jesus, and Jerusalem as the site of his trial, death, and resurrection). Excavations at Jerusalem uncovered the tomb or Holy Sepulchre of Christ and the True Cross of the crucifixion. Legend attributed these finds to Empress Helena (d. 330), Constantine's mother, who made a pilgrimage to Palestine in 326. Christian pilgrims visited Palestine during the third century, but from the time of Constantine onward, Christian pilgrimage became very popular. Palestine had become a land populated by a Christian majority, and all Christians venerated it as a holy land. Pilgrims' accounts of and guidebooks to the Holy Land appeared, such as that of Egeria in 381–384, the earliest pilgrimage narrative to survive intact. The prestige of the Holy Land with its capital of Jerusalem grew so great that it appeared to be on the verge of eclipsing Rome and Constantinople.

Beginning in 614, Christianity lost political control of the Holy Land. In that year it fell temporarily into the hands of the Sassanid Persians. Although Emperor Heraclius recaptured Jerusalem and Palestine after years of hard fighting, his efforts were for naught. Sweeping out of the desert, the armies of the newly arisen Islam took control of Jerusalem in 637 and kept control until the Crusader conquest in 1099.

The Muslim conquest of the Holy Land did not end Christian pilgrimage. Muslim rulers tolerated Christians as "people of the Book" (the Bible) and welcomed the revenues pilgrims generated. However, under the mad caliph Hakim in 1010, Christian pilgrims suffered persecution, and Christian shrines were destroyed. In western European Christendom, the fascination with and longing for the Holy Land grew, contributing to the rise of the crusading movement in the eleventh century.

The soldiers of the First Crusade restored Jerusalem and most of Palestine to Christian control in 1099. The Latin Kingdom of Jerusalem lasted until 1187, when the great Muslim leader Saladin vanquished its armies and recaptured its capital. During the Crusaders' years of control, they rebuilt or restored ancient Christian shrines and churches. New institutions for pilgrims such as the Hospital of St. John of Jerusalem appeared, along with the military orders of the Hospitalers, Templars, and Teutonic Knights, whose mission was to protect Christian pilgrims and interests in the Holy Land. New pilgrims' guides appeared, such as Theodorich's *Guide to the Holy Land* (1171). Christian rulers regained temporary control of Jerusalem through diplomatic means in 1229–1239 and 1243–1244, but the resurgence of Islamic political and military power in the Middle East under the Mamluks of Egypt doomed the Crusader outposts to extinction.

The Christian view of Palestine as the Holy Land has never been extinguished. Pious and curious Christians continued to make pilgrimages in droves. These pilgrims ranged from the obsessive Margery Kempe in 1413 to St. Ignatius Loyola, founder of the Society of Jesus, in 1523 to the Americans John Lloyd

Stephens in 1836 and Samuel Clemens (Mark Twain) in 1867. Pilgrimage and tourism to the Holy Land continues unabated, except in wartime, throughout the twentieth century.

See also

Bethlehem; Children of Israel, Wanderings in the Wilderness of; Egeria; Exodus; Hospitalers, Knights; Jerusalem; Pilgimage; Templars, Knights; Teutonic Knights.

For further reading

Jonathan Riley-Smith, *The Atlas of the Crusades,* 1991; Theodorich, *Guide to the Holy Land,* 1986; Robert L. Wilken, *The Land Called Holy,* 1992.

HOMER (BEFORE 700 B.C.)

Epic poet and author of *The Odyssey,* the archetypal travel adventure of the ancient world.

Homer has been renowned for thousands of years as the author of the classic epic poems *The Iliad* and *The Odyssey.* Little is known for certain about his life, variously dated from the time of the Trojan War (ca. 1200 B.C.) to 675 B.C. (a later date is more consistent with internal evidence from the poems). His home is commonly thought to be the island of Chios or Smyrna. Again, evidence from the poems make it most probable that he came from somewhere in the region of Ionia. As long-standing traditions maintain, he probably was blind. Some scholars contend that Homer did not exist, that *The Iliad* and *The Odyssey* were simply compilations of various oral traditions. Close study of the texts of the two epics belie this theory, because both works exhibit a high level of thematic unity that can only be the result of a single author. However, because *The Iliad* and *The Odyssey* are different stylistically, other scholars suggest that two separate authors created the individual works. Most scholars today believe that a single author wrote both *The Iliad* and *The Odyssey,* with *The Iliad* being the earlier work.

Homer is significant in the study of the lore of travel for two reasons. First, *The Odyssey* is a valuable source of information about early Greek geographical concepts. Second, *The Odyssey* provided the archetype for the travel adventure narrative, which was widely imitated through the centuries.

See also

Odysseus, Wanderings of.

For further reading

M. I. Finley, *The World of Odysseus,* 1977.

HORN, CAPE

Southernmost point of land in South America, ships sailed around Cape Horn to pass from the Atlantic to the Pacific Ocean rather than go through the difficult Strait of Magellan.

Cape Horn is located on an island at approximately 56°S and 67°W, and is marked by a rugged peak at its south end. The seas around Cape Horn are stormy, and the whole area is almost constantly buffeted by the winds of the Roaring Forties. Europeans did not discover the sailing route around Cape Horn until 1616, even though Ferdinand Magellan first navigated the strait named in his honor in 1520. Geographical knowledge was haunted by the theory that a southern continent named Terra Australis existed in the southern latitudes. Magellan assumed that the large island of Terra del Fuego was part of Terra Australis, and therefore made no attempt to go around it. In 1578, Sir Francis Drake passed through the Strait of Magellan. When he cleared the western end of the strait, fierce storms blew his ships south and east until he reached present-day Henderson Island, located about two miles south of latitude 55°30'S. Open seas to the east and south convinced Drake that Terra del Fuego was an island and not part of some southern continent. Drake did not attempt to round Terra del Fuego from the south, however, and English, Spanish, and Dutch ships that followed him continued to use the Strait of Magellan as their route to the Pacific.

In 1602 the Dutch Republic established the United East India Company to take over the Portuguese spice trade in Asia. Not all Dutch merchants were members of the company, and nonmembers were prohibited from sailing around the Cape of Good Hope or through the Strait of Magellan. These prohibitions were intended to prevent interlopers from trespassing on the East India Company's valuable spice supplies. Not all Dutch merchants were willing to respect the company's monopoly over the Asian spice trade, and they sought ways to circumvent it. Isaak La Maire of Amsterdam and Willem Cornelison Schouten of Hoorn speculated that an unknown cape lay south of the Strait of Magellan. Sailing around it was not prohibited by the monopoly of the Dutch East India Company.

On 14 June 1615, La Maire and Schouten sailed from the Netherlands with two ships—the *Unitie* and the *Hoorne*—looking for a new route from the Atlantic to the Pacific. Sailing past the eastern entrance to the Strait of Magellan on 24 January 1616, they spotted a passage they named the Strait of La Maire. Proceeding through the opening, on 29 January they passed a high prominence, which they named Cape Hoorn (Horn) after Schouten's hometown and the ship *Hoorne*, which had been lost because of a fire on board. By 12 February, Schouten had sailed far enough west to feel secure that he was in the Pacific Ocean, so he brought out wine to celebrate with his crew. He sailed to the Spice Islands, where overzealous officials of the Dutch East India Company seized his vessel, but he successfully sued the company for damages. Far more significant than the commercial success of his voyage was the fact that Schouten demonstrated the existence of a feasible sea route around Cape Horn for future seafarers.

Sailing around Cape Horn is not a particularly pleasant or easy experience for a sailing ship because of the storminess of the seas at that latitude. Many ships were lost trying to make the trip, but sailors remained undeterred; it was a superior route compared to navigating the treacherous Strait of Magellan. During the California Gold Rush of 1849, those with sufficient funds preferred sailing around Cape Horn to get to the gold fields rather than traveling overland with the wagon trains. Sailing around Cape Horn remained common until 1914, when the opening of the Panama Canal provided a shortcut.

See also

Circumnavigations of the Earth, Early; Magellan, Strait of; Roaring Forties; Spice Islands; Terra Australis.

For further reading

Samuel Eliot Morison, *The European Discovery of America,* 1974; Jose Phillips, "The Uttermost Cape," in *The Sea,* vol. 3, 1977.

HORSE

Throughout history the horse has been the most widely used and best loved of the domesticated animals that provide transportation for humans. Horses and donkeys belong to the genus *Equus.* All species of equids evolved from a small browsing mammal called Eohippus, which flourished in North America about 65 million years ago. By the Pleistocene era (2 million–10,000 years ago), various species of the genus *Equus* had evolved and spread into South America, Asia, Europe, and Africa. The equid species of North and South America, however, suffered extinction about 8000 B.C. because of overhunting by the Paleo-Indians. Meanwhile, wild horses (*Equus ferus*) throve on the steppes of Europe and Asia, where they served as the occasional prey of Neolithic hunters. Although humans began domesticating goats and sheep, and then cattle and pigs, by about 7000 B.C., the first domesticated horses (*Equus caballus*) appeared in the Ukraine only about 4000 B.C.

Early domesticated horses were used largely as pack or draft animals, although riding most likely occurred from the beginning of domestication. Mounted herdsmen were the only effective way to move large numbers of horses. Scholars of folklore and mythology commonly believe that the legends of the centaurs—half-horse and half-human—arose among the early Greeks when they encountered the unfamiliar phenomenon of mounted peoples from Thessaly. Since the Native Americans of Mexico made the same mistake when they first encountered the mounted troops of Hernán Cortés, the theory is probably correct.

Horses soon became the mainstay for the wandering lifestyle of the nomadic peoples of Eurasia, from the ancient Scythians to the Mongols of Genghiz Khan. Thanks to their horses, nomads could travel swiftly and then concentrate their military might to crush their more sedentary opponents in a piecemeal fashion. As a result, nomads periodically conquered numerically superior civilizations and remained a potent threat until the industrial revolution gave the sedentary powers an overwhelming technological advantage.

Meanwhile, the sedentary civilizations adopted the domesticated horse very slowly. About 2300 B.C., tame horses appeared in northern Mesopotamia and Anatolia, where they were mainly used to pull war chariots. From Mesopotamia, the Hyksos brought horses into Egypt when they conquered that land about 1800 B.C. During the following centuries, horses spread along the coast of North Africa, into the Arabian peninsula, and through the mountainous region of Persia. Domesticated horses may have entered China as early as 2400–1850 B.C., and had definitely appeared by the early Shang dynasty (1850/1766–1500 B.C.). In China, as in the Middle East, the horse's primary function was to pull war chariots. The civilization of Mohenjo-Daro in the Indus Valley may have used horses by 2000 B.C., and the Aryan invaders of India in 1500 B.C. used war chariots pulled by horses.

The use of cavalry became more common in ancient civilizations about 1000 B.C., and by 700 B.C. cavalry supplanted the war chariot among the ferocious Assyrians. A similar evolution occurred in Greek society; the historian Xenophon lovingly compiled information on the care and riding of horses in his *Art of Horsemanship*. Alexander the Great of Macedonia used cavalry to the best effect. When he invaded and conquered the Persian Empire from 334 to 329 B.C., the Macedonian cavalry gave his army an extraordinary degree of mobility. The Romans adopted the horse as an instrument of war, following the example of the Greeks and the Numidian cavalry of the Carthaginians. Unlike the Greeks, the Romans were not great lovers of horses, but they expanded the functions of horses by using them as pack animals, for pulling carts and carriages, and for the carrying of the post and couriers. Of course, horses were also used in the ubiquitous games celebrated by Roman society, particularly the chariot races made famous by the novel and movie *Ben Hur*.

For riding, the Romans preferred geldings, while the Greeks favored stallions. Cavalry did not form the core of the Roman army, but they engaged in warfare with several mounted opponents. From 69 to 20 B.C., the Romans were intermittently at war with the Parthians, a Middle Eastern military power that relied heavily on mounted archers. Later barbarian groups pressing against the declining Roman Empire also practiced mounted warfare, especially the fearsome Huns, who terrorized Europe under their king, Attila, from 450 to 455. In fact, as Roman power weakened, the importance of cavalry rose in European society. Mounted knights dominated medieval Europe until archers armed with long bows, massed pikemen, and gunpowder supplanted them in the fourteenth century. Cavalry remained an important branch of the army until the early twentieth century, but it never again dominated warfare except in very limited circumstances.

Modern riders of horses may not be aware of how long it took to develop the proper equipment for riding. Obviously, the first riders rode bareback (horse blankets did not appear until 900 B.C.). The first riding saddles appeared in Asia among the Sarmatian nomads and the Chinese, probably adapted from existing pack saddles. The Romans did not use saddles until the fourth century A.D. Stirrups probably developed first as leather loops to aid in mounting a horse, and early riders soon used the loops to maintain their balance and stay mounted. The Scythians first developed stirrups during the fourth century B.C., and the idea spread from the Black Sea region to India and China by the fifth century A.D. The Chinese made improvements by inventing a metal stirrup sometime between the second and fifth centuries A.D. By the late seventh century, the stirrup arrived in eastern Europe, and spread through western Europe during the eighth and ninth centuries. Stirrups and saddles enabled the existence of lance-wielding, heavily armored knights of feudal Europe.

Riding and carriage transportation are the animal's most important role in the history and lore of travel. Although horses can be used as pack animals, the mule and donkey are superior. For riding, however, horses are far preferable. Donkeys and mules have a very jarring gait and are uncomfortable to ride at any pace faster than a walk. In comparison, horses can be ridden faster in relative comfort, which is not to say that a lengthy horse ride will not produce a sore posterior. Horses are also capable of pulling buggies, carriages, and coaches at a swifter pace than mules or donkeys. For those who could afford it, riding a horse or riding in a horse-drawn carriage was the common and preferred means of travel for centuries. Transportation by horses held its own against the railroads in the industrialized world until finally displaced by the bicycle and the automobile and other motorized vehicles.

See also

Centaurs; Donkey; Scythia.

For further reading

Harold B. Barclay, *The Role of the Horse in Man's Culture*, 1980; Juliet Clutton-Brock, *Horse Power*, 1992; A. Dent, *The Horse through Fifty Centuries of Civilization*, 1974.

HOSPICES AND HOSPITALS　　In the Middle Ages, from about A.D. 800–1500, these two terms referred interchangeably to religious institutions providing lodging for travelers, strangers, and pilgrims.

During the time of the Roman Empire, religious institutions providing accommodations for travelers were called *xenodochia*. As the Roman Empire became increasingly Christianized in the third, fourth, and fifth centuries, Christians established their own *xenodochia* near their churches, and these institutions assisted the local poor and sick as well as travelers. Scottish pilgrims traveling to Rome founded the first hospitals or hospices in that city for pilgrims from their own country. Bishops, monastic orders, rulers, and wealthy nobles and merchants endowed the operations of hospitals and hospices with land and money. The Augustinian Order of monks took a particularly strong interest in creating and maintaining hospices for pilgrims. Among the better known were those serving the pilgrim road to Santiago de Compostela and in the Great and Little St. Bernard passes in the Alps. Merchants from Amalfi founded the famous Hospital of St. John of Jerusalem in 1070 to accommodate pilgrims visiting Jerusalem. The caretakers of the institution evolved into the military/religious order of the Knights Hospitalers.

Visitors to hospices and hospitals always received lodging and a meal. The quantity and quality of the meal varied with the economic circumstances of the individual hospice or hospital. A bowl of soup was the minimum, but if the institution was well supplied, the meal could be large and varied. High demand for accommodation often forced hospices to limit travelers' stays to three days. Sleeping quarters for men and women were separate.

Hospices were often located in remote or inhospitable places where no alternate accommodations were available. Such institutions frequently saved the lives of weary, disoriented travelers caught in inclement, dangerous weather. Only in the eighteenth century did hospitals become exclusively associated with the care and the housing of the sick.

See also

> Hospitalers, Knights; Jerusalem; Pilgimage; Rome; St. Bernard Passes; Santiago de Compostela.

For further reading

Norbert Ohler, *The Medieval Traveler*, 1989.

HOSPITALERS, KNIGHTS

Also known as the Order of the Hospital and the Knights of St. John of Jerusalem, after 1310 they were referred to as the Knights of Rhodes, and after 1530 were commonly called the Knights of Malta. This famous military religious order originated shortly after the First Crusade's conquest of Jerusalem in 1099 and provided accommodations to pilgrims, along with general almsgiving and medical care. By about 1123, the Hospitalers added the task of providing military protection for pilgrims.

Jerusalem has been an important pilgrimage site for Christians from the very beginnings of the church, and this led to the establishment and maintenance of hostels or hospitals for pilgrims from the earliest times, an example of which was the great hospital of the Knights Hospitalers. According to one Hospitaler tradition, their hostel was founded during the era of Judas Macabees (d. 161 B.C.), and Mary and St. John the Evangelist stayed there at the time of the crucifixion of Jesus. Another Hospitaler tradition credited Pope Gregory the Great and his agent Abbot Probus of Jerusalem with founding the hostel in about 600. Modern scholars believe that the hostel was founded by merchants of Amalfi about 1070 and was under the authority of the nearby Benedictine monastery of St. Maria Latina, another Amalfitan establishment.

The Crusaders' conquest of Jerusalem in 1099 stimulated the foundation of the order of the Hospitalers. Gerard, the rector of the hospital at that time, was largely responsible for the emergence of the new order. Arriving in Palestine as a pilgrim from either Provence or the village of Scala near Amalfi, Gerard decided to stay, so he took employment at the hospital. His knowledge of local conditions made him a valuable asset to the Crusaders, and he in turn used their high regard to secure the hospital as an independent, well-endowed religious institution. On 13 February 1113, Pope Paschal II issued a papal bull officially recognizing the new order and making it independent of all ecclesiastical authorities except the papacy. At that time, the Hospitalers' activities were completely focused on running their hospital or hostel, giving alms to the poor, and providing medical care for the needy. They retained that focus until after the death of Brother Gerard, who served as the first Grand Master of the order, in 1120.

The next Grand Master was the Frenchman Raymond Du Puy, who held the office from 1120 until his death in 1160. Sometime between 1145 and 1153, he placed the order under Augustinian rule, and under his leadership the Hospitalers added their military functions. Two local developments stimulated this shift in purpose. One was the formation in 1118 of the Knights Templar as a religious order to provide military protection for pilgrims. Another was the increase in Muslim counterattacks against the Crusader states in the early 1120s. Both Templars and Hospitalers aided pilgrims, and the need for protecting them was never-ending. Therefore, the Hospitalers expanded their purpose to include the military protection of the pilgrims and the Crusader states. The exact date for this militarization is not known, but it took place as early as 1123 and no later than 1126, when the Hospitaler records first refer to the existence in their order of the military official known as a constable. Their famous battle dress of a red tunic with a white eight-pointed cross, now commonly known as a Maltese Cross, was not adopted until 1259.

In the chivalrous atmosphere of Europe in the High Middle Ages, military service in a religious order proved popular. The Hospitalers and Templars attracted numerous recruits and rich endowments. Both orders progressed from simply providing escorts to pilgrims to guarding the frontiers against Muslim raiders. In 1137, King Fulk of Jerusalem gave the Hospitalers the castle of Beth Gibelin, which guarded the road between Gaza and Hebron and stood as a deterrent to Muslim raiders from Egypt. Possession of other castles followed, including Belvoir, the supposedly impregnable Marqad (Margat), and the famous Krak des Chevaliers.

The military activities of the Hospitalers and the Templars made them the object of fierce Muslim hatred. Even the normally magnanimous Muslim leader Saladin executed all captured Hospitalers and Templars after the battle of Hattin in 1187.

Unlike the Templars, who focused almost exclusively on military activities, the Hospitalers never forgot their origins as providers of accommodations for pilgrims, alms for the poor, and medical care for the sick. As early as 1113, the Hospitalers established other rest houses or hospitals for pilgrims at St. Gilles, Asti, Pisa, Bari, Messina, and Otranto. During the Grand Mastership of Raymond Du Puy, the Hospitalers rebuilt their convent and the hospital. The project was done on a grand scale, with accommodations for 1,000 pilgrims. In fact, the entire establishment was so magnificent that it aroused the wrath of Patriarch Fulcher of Jerusalem by outdoing his rebuilding of the Church of the Holy Sepulchre. The Hospitalers needed such a huge establishment because the Crusader conquest of the Holy Land had greatly stimulated pilgrimages. Those 1,000 beds were regularly full of grateful pilgrims. Hospitalers were also widely respected for their generous almsgiving, which amazed visitors and far surpassed that of the Templars. The order also established a true hospital for the needy sick, which operated even after the Muslim reconquest of Jerusalem in 1187.

The Hospitalers and Templars provided the bulk of the standing army protecting the Crusader states. Unfortunately, the two orders quickly became bitter rivals who often worked at cross-purposes, and both groups were thoroughly disliked by the ecclesiastical authorities of Palestine because of their independence and great wealth. Patriarch Fulcher resented the magnificence of the new hospital, especially when the sound of its bells drowned out his sermons at the chapel on the neighboring Hill of Calvary. Neither the Templars nor the Hospitalers always put the welfare of the Crusader states as their first priority, although the Hospitalers were far more altruistic than the Templars.

Closeup showing ornate details of a Knights of Malta uniform.

The disunity of the Christian forces boded ill for the survival of the Crusader states, especially as the various Muslim states began to regain their own unity. In 1250, the Mamluk Turks took over Egypt and decisively defeated the Mongols at Ain Jalut in 1260. The Mamluk sultan Baibars (1260–1277) began the conquest of the remaining Crusader outposts, capturing the formidable Krak des Chevaliers in 1271. His successor, Kala'un (1277–1290), captured the supposedly invulnerable Hospitaler castle of Marqab in 1285 and Tripoli in 1289. Kala'un's son Khalil Malik al-Ashraf completed the process by capturing the last Crusader outpost at Acre in 1291.

Throughout this process of Mamluk conquest, the Hospitalers and other Christian refugees fled to the island of Cyprus, where a new Crusade against the Mamluks was planned. The expedition never materialized, but the Hospitalers joined in the conquest of a number of islands off the shore of Asia Minor. Operations against Rhodes began in 1306, and by 1309 or 1310 the island was under the Hospitalers' control and the site of their new headquarters. They began a new career as naval Crusaders resisting Muslim forces in the eastern Mediterranean. Although they were quite successful and had transformed Rhodes into the most strongly fortified place on earth, by the latter part of the fifteenth century the growing power of the Ottoman Turks threatened their survival. In 1480, the Hospitalers successfully defended Rhodes against an Ottoman assault ordered by the great sultan Mohammed II. This defeat deterred the Turks for four decades while their empire went through a temporary period of weak leadership, but peace did not last forever. At the time of his death in 1520, the Ottoman sultan Selim the Grim was planning an attack on

Rhodes. It was carried out by his son Suleiman the Magnificent in 1522. A fiercely contested siege followed from 28 July until 1 January 1523, when Suleiman agreed to let the surviving Hospitaler garrison and inhabitants surrender and withdraw with all the honors of war.

The Hospitalers were without a home for seven years. In 1530, the Holy Roman Emperor Charles V granted them the island of Malta (hence the tribute of a golden falcon that serves as the plot focus of the classic film *The Maltese Falcon*). From this base they defended Christian shipping in the Mediterranean from the Ottoman navy and Barbary corsairs. Under the leadership of their Grand Master, Jean de la Valette, they heroically withstood another siege by the forces of their old enemy Suleiman the Magnificent in 1565. A few years later (1571), they participated in the great Christian naval victory over the Ottoman fleet at Lepanto. During the seventeenth and eighteenth centuries, the order declined in discipline and morals. Its nadir came with the treacherous surrender of Malta to Napoléon in 1798. From then on, the Knights Hospitalers concentrated on charitable activities, particularly the support of hospitals, successfully returning to their roots. Still, for many centuries the swords, ships, and castles of the Knights Hospitalers gave a genuine sense of security to Christian travelers on the sea lanes of the Mediterranean and the dusty roads of the Levant.

See also

Holy Land; Hospices and Hospitals; Jerusalem; Pilgimage; Templars, Knights; Teutonic Knights.

For further reading

E. J. King, *The Knights Hospitallers in the Holy Land,* 1931; Hans Eberhard Mayer, *The Crusades,* 1988; Jonathan Riley-Smith, *The Knights of St. John in Jerusalem and Cyprus c. 1050–1310,* 1967.

HOSPITALITY   From ancient times, various codes of conduct determine how hosts properly and civilly receive traveling guests and strangers into their homes and establishments. Hospitality is the act of providing strangers and guests with food and shelter, not necessarily done as a way to make a living.

People traveled for commercial or religious purposes even in prehistoric times. Often, inns or hostels providing travelers with room and board did not exist, so travelers sought accommodations in private homes or dwellings. Without private hospitality, travel would have been virtually impossible in the primitive conditions of the ancient world. Private individuals had a number of motivations for providing such hospitality. First, if one provided hospitality to a stranger, that action would later be reciprocated if the need arose. Second, travelers often brought trade goods and news of the outside world, both desirable commodities. Third, most ancient religions taught that God or the gods traveled among mortals in the guise of strangers. To render them aid was to secure a blessing; to refuse was to incur their wrath and dire punishments.

Hospitality imposed obligations on both host and guest. Hosts provided food and lodging, perhaps even some entertainment, and were obligated to protect guests from harm. Guests were expected to behave with good manners while in a host's home. Gluttony, rudeness, stealing, raping, and, most importantly, not overstaying their welcome were to be avoided by the polite guest.

The Bible contains many stories illustrating hospitality. Abraham provided three strangers with a meal, and they announced to him that he and his wife Sarah would be having a baby (Genesis 18). Lot provided shelter to two angels visiting him in Sodom. Hearing that Lot had visitors, the men of Sodom surrounded Lot's house and demanded that he turn them over to the mob to be raped. Lot steadfastly protected his guests saying,

> Behold now, I have two daughters which have not known man; let me, I
> pray you, bring them out unto you, and do ye to them as is good in your
> eyes: only unto these men [the guests] do nothing; for therefore came they
> under the shadow of my roof. (Genesis 19:8)

In Homer's *Odyssey*, the hero Odysseus experiences much hospitality in the course of his travels, particularly from the Phaeacians and Circe. On the other hand, back in Ithaca, Penelope's suitors are the archetypal bad guests, overstaying their welcome and abusing the host's generosity.

During the Middle Ages, people of the Christian, Jewish, and Islamic faiths frequently served as hosts to traveling coreligionists. Providing hospitality to people of the same faith, especially traveling scholars, was a religious obligation. For example, Ibn Battuta traveled throughout the world of Islam and almost always received a ready, even bountiful welcome. Religious institutions for accommodating travelers developed among Jews, Christians, and Muslims in the form of monasteries with guest houses, hospitals, and colleges. The monastaries located in the St. Bernard passes and the great Hospital of St. John of Jerusalem are famous examples.

As societies developed more complex, specialized economies, commercial institutions appeared to provide hospitality to travelers. Inns and taverns were followed by hotels and restaurants, and private hospitality became less relevant for most travelers. Some places retained or gained reputations for being particularly hospitable, such as the American South, especially in the antebellum period. Other places developed reputations for rudeness and inhospitable behavior to strangers, like Paris or New York City. Reputations frequently were exaggerated: southern hospitality was far more selective than the legends imply, and visitors to Paris were not forced to run gauntlets of rude waiters and gendarmes. Hospitality is simply the traveling equivalent of the basic premise that civil behavior helps keep human society functioning smoothly.

See also

Good Samaritan; Ibn Battuta, Abu 'Abd Allah Muhammad; Inns and Taverns.

For further reading

John Koenig, *New Testament Hospitality,* 1985; Norbert Ohler, *The Medieval Traveler,* 1989; Joe Gray Taylor, *Eating, Drinking, and Visiting in the South,* 1982.

HURRICANE   Name for gigantic, tropical cyclonic storms at sea whose winds circulate in a counterclockwise direction in the Northern Hemisphere and clockwise in the Southern Hemisphere. Hurricanes are known as typhoons in the western part of the North Pacific. In the Bay of Bengal and the northern Indian Ocean, they are called cyclones. Everywhere else they are called hurricanes, although such storms never form in the South Atlantic.

Hurricanes begin as tropical depressions or areas of low air pressure and strengthen into tropical storms with wind speeds of 39–73 miles per hour. When wind speeds reach 74 miles per hour, the tropical storm becomes a hurricane. From that point, the winds of a hurricane can accelerate up to dangerously destructive levels of well over 100 miles per hour. It is estimated that the hurricane that devastated the Florida Keys in 1935 contained winds of up to 250 miles per hour.

The word *hurricane* derives from the Maya word *huraken,* the name for the god of storms. Variant forms of the word such as *aracan, arican,* and *huiranvucan* were used by other Native American groups throughout the Caribbean Sea and the Gulf of Mexico. Besides referring to hurricanes, these words also meant "evil spirit" and "big wind." When the Spanish arrived in the Americas, they adopted the word and transformed it into *furicane.* French seamen called it *ouragan,* while the English variously used *hyrricane, haurachana, uracan,* or *herocano* to refer to the great storms, finally settling on hurricane.

It took many years for seamen to understand the true nature of hurricanes as great cyclonic storms. The great English voyager William Dampier, in 1687, was the first to recognize that hurricanes and typhoons were identical types of storms. He experienced and survived both in American and Asian waters. In 1831, the British engineer William Reid used data from past storms to prove conclusively that hurricanes' winds had a counterclockwise circulation.

Hurricanes and typhoons have menaced sailors and coastal dwellers in the tropics through the ages. Cyclones in the Bay of Bengal and typhoons on the coast of China have been known to kill hundreds of thousands of people. These great storms sometimes change history. Kublai Khan, the Mongol ruler of China, sent two invasion fleets against Japan in 1274 and 1281, but both were destroyed by chance typhoons just as the Mongol armies were establishing beachheads. The Japanese honored their stormy saviors with the name *kamikaze,* or "divine wind." European sailors had no experience with hurricanes until Columbus's voyages to the Americas. Columbus encountered hurricanes in 1494, 1495, and 1502. Because he possessed extraordinary abilities as a sailor and observer of the sea, Columbus quickly recognized the signs of an approaching hurricane. In 1502, he tried to warn Governor Nicolás de Ovando of an approaching hurricane. Arrogantly ignoring Columbus, Ovando sent a treasure fleet into the Mona Passage; the hurricane caught it, sinking most of the ships and killing many of the passengers and crew.

Hurricanes caused many shipwrecks. A conquistador named Valdivia and 20 of his men encountered a hurricane that left them castaways on the coast of the Yucatán peninsula. Maya Indians took them prisoner, enslaving some and sacrificing others, including Valdivia. Hurricanes destroyed the earliest Spanish attempts to colonize Florida in 1559 and disrupted a French attempt to conquer Florida in 1562. Damage resulting from a hurricane in 1568 forced John Hawkins and his fleet to put in for repairs at the Spanish port of San Juan de Ulloa on the Gulf of Mexico. The forces of the Spanish viceroy attacked the English, killing many and capturing others, and the incident raised the level of animosity between England and Spain to an unreconcilable level. In 1609, hurricane damage diverted colonists bound for Jamestown colony in Virginia to Bermuda, where they decided to establish a permanent settlement. Over the years, hurricanes plagued Spanish treasure fleets and ships of all nations in the Gulf of Mexico, the Caribbean Sea, and especially the Florida Straits. A particularly powerful hurricane plowed through the Caribbean and Gulf regions in 1780. Typhoons and cyclones have similarly menaced shipping and travelers in the Far Eastern waters and the Indian Ocean. Hurricanes, typhoons, and cyclones comprise one of the most destructive forces in nature, although an experienced sea captain can easily avoid them if proper attention is paid to weather signs and wind directions.

For further reading

Gordon E. Dunn and Banner I. Miller, *Atlantic Hurricanes*, 1964; David E. Fisher, *The Scariest Place on Earth*, 1994; Ivan Ray Tannehill, *Hurricanes*, 1952.

HVÍTRAMANNALAND   From the Norse words *hvítir*, meaning "white," and *manna*, meaning "man's." Hvítramannaland is the Norse name for Great Ireland, a legendary settlement of early-medieval Irish monks located somewhere in the western Atlantic close to Vinland. It is referred to in the *Landnamabok* and the *Eyrbyggia Saga*. Some later scholars place Hvítramannaland in various parts of the eastern seaboard of North America, but no convincing archaeological evidence exists to support that speculation. The medieval Norse's belief in Hvítramannaland is simply one aspect of the widespread geographical belief that the Atlantic Ocean was full of islands.

See also

Great Ireland.

For further reading

Geoffrey Ashe, *Land to the West*, 1962; Samuel Eliot Morison, *The European Discovery of America*, 1971.

Hy-Brazil

Also known as O'Brazil, Brazil, Breasil, and Bersil, it was a mystical island thought to be located off the west coast of Ireland.

The name Hy-Brazil is a combination of two Gaelic words—*breas* and *ail*—which are superlatives that can be translated respectively as "great" and "wonderful." The prefix *hy* is Gaelic for "ancestor of." Hy-Brazil may be equated with the Islands of the Blest or the Fortunate Isles. Hy-Brazil first appeared in 1325 on the nautical chart of Angelino Dulcert. The map placed it about 100 miles off the west coast of Ireland and depicted it as a circular island with a channel or a strait through its middle, making Hy-Brazil two half-moon-shaped pieces of land. According to long-standing Irish legends, Hy-Brazil materialized off the coast of Ireland every seven years and appeared to be inhabited. If curious persons attempted to land on it, the island disappeared. Throwing fire on the island before setting foot on it was said to break the spell that caused it to disappear.

Some maps continued to show Hy-Brazil to the west of Ireland, but others placed it elsewhere or changed its shape. A Catalan map of 1375 kept Hy-Brazil off Ireland's western coast, but showed it as a circular atoll with nine islands inside the lagoon. Another Catalan map from 1480 moved a circular Hy-Brazil much farther to the west and placed it in close proximity to an Insula Verde, which was probably Greenland. Other maps added a second island of Brazil, which appears to be the island of Terceira in the Azores group.

The various legends and rumors of Hy-Brazil or Brazil inspired many attempts to reach the elusive island. In 1452, Diogo de Teive sailed in search of Hy-Brazil at the command of Prince Henry the Navigator. Working his way against contrary winds into the waters of the North Atlantic, Teive failed to find anything, but along the way he discovered the two westernmost islands of the Azores: Corvo and Flores. John Lloyd, a seafarer from Bristol, England, set out in 1480 to look for Brazil to the west of Ireland, but found only stormy seas in nine weeks of sailing. Bristol merchants made other attempts to locate Hy-Brazil for some years, forming part of the context that led up to John Cabot's famous voyage of discovery to North America in 1497.

Hy-Brazil, or Brazil, was an Irish variation on the legends of the Fortunate Isles or the Islands of the Blest. As such, it served as an elusive destination for adventurous seamen for many years.

See also
Blessed, Isles of the; Fortunate Isles.

For further reading
William H. Babcock, *Legendary Islands of the Atlantic*, 1922; Samuel Eliot Morison, *The European Discovery of America*, 1971; Raymond H. Ramsay, *No Longer on the Map*, 1972.

Hyperborea

Meaning "beyond the North Wind," this land of Greek mythology was supposed to be a northern paradise rather than the expected frigid wasteland.

The ancient Greeks conceived of Hyperborea and the Hyperboreans as a paradisial land inhabited by exemplary people who were in every way superior to the Greeks. Hyperborea was located in the far north beyond the place where the north wind, Boreas, originated. It also lay on the other side of the Rhipaean Mountains, which shielded it from the cold and snow produced by the north wind and so gave it a mild climate. The Hyperboreans were closely associated with the god Apollo and could be considered his chosen people. Legend had it that in the distant past the Hyperboreans founded the centers for Apollo's worship at Delphi and Delos in Greece, which gave the Greeks a closer connection to the superior Hyperboreans than any other nation or people. Apollo liked to visit the Hyperboreans, whose life was a continual festive banquet. Considered to be the most blessed of mankind, the Hyperboreans were a peaceful people unaffected by sickness or old age; they lived to be a thousand years old. While other mortals might wish to visit Hyperborea, its northerly isolation and the rugged terrain of its borders made it almost impossible. Only the greatest of heroes, such as Hercules and Perseus, could overcome the tremendous obstacles in traveling to Hyperborea. The ancient Greeks took seriously the literal existence of the Hyperboreans even though they never met one. Herodotus (ca. 484–ca. 425 B.C.) discussed the Hyperboreans as real people in his *Histories*. Ultimately, the Hyperboreans are just one manifestation of the persistent fictional motif that the Arctic fastness conceals a lost utopian civilization. The Hyperboreans themselves have become a sort of literary allusion for any people dwelling in the far north.

See also

Herodotus.

For further reading

James S. Romm, *The Edges of the Earth in Ancient Thought*, 1992.

I

IBN BATTUTA, ABU 'ABD ALLAH MUHAMMAD (1304–1369)

Also spelled Battutah, this Moroccan legal scholar and traveler is frequently and rightly compared with the European Marco Polo. Western authors variously call him the "Arab Marco Polo," "the Marco Polo of the Muslim world," or "the Marco Polo of the Tropics." In fact, Ibn Battuta deserves to be recognized as the greatest traveler of the ancient and medieval worlds. After spending 24 years traveling in the Middle and Far East, Ibn Battuta returned to Morocco—only to make two more journeys into Muslim Spain and the sub-Saharan empire of Mali. He traversed over 75,000 miles, far exceeding Marco Polo's achievement.

Ibn Battuta was born at Tangier in the Marinid sultanate of Morocco in 1304. His family made their living as scholars and judges of the Islamic legal system. The young Ibn Battuta followed the family tradition and received a good education as befitted a well-to-do Islamic gentleman of the fourteenth century. At the age of 21, Ibn Battuta embarked on his travels. Like all faithful Muslims, he wanted to make the obligatory pilgrimage to Mecca. Furthermore, traveling east would take him to the heartlands of Islam, where he could study with the finest scholars.

Leaving Tangier on 13 June 1325, the young Ibn Battuta traveled eastward across the Maghrib, the Arabic name for the western part of North Africa (the present-day countries of Morocco, Algeria, and Tunisia). He was excited at first, but hardships, loneliness, and homesickness soon lowered his mood. After eight to nine months of travel, he reached the great port of Alexandria in 1326 and saw the remains of the fabled lighthouse of Pharos. He had entered the Mamluk Empire of Egypt, the greatest Islamic power of its day. Ibn Battuta began his decades-long habit of sightseeing excursions, so instead of pushing on to Mecca with the pilgrim's caravan from Cairo, he explored the Nile delta. Sailing down that great river past Luxor to Idfu, he traveled across the desert to the climatically dreadful port of 'Aydhab on the Red Sea. Unable to make a crossing to Jidda, he went back up the Nile to Cairo, and from there went to Damascus, the Syrian capital of the Mamluks, on 9 August 1326. He visited with legal scholars until 1 September 1326, when he joined a pilgrimage caravan bound for Medina and Mecca.

During the first 15 months of his travels, Ibn Battuta learned that traveling gentlemen-scholars like himself were the frequent objects of almsgiving by pious, prosperous Muslim merchants. He also found that his glib, entertaining manner and his quickly developing sycophantic ways endeared him to his betters and secured their hospitality. As a scholar, Ibn Battuta was a welcome guest at the many *madrasas*, or colleges, dedicated to the study of Islam and its laws that liberally dotted the landscape of Muslim countries. Through his strong interest in Sufism, the mystical branch of Islam, Ibn Battuta also received a ready welcome and hospitality from the Sufi lodges located in most Islamic towns of any size or importance. Thanks to this network of benefactors and colleagues, Ibn Battuta could travel with the expectation of generous hospitality and gifts throughout the lands of Islam.

Ibn Battuta reached Mecca in mid-October 1326, visting Medina and the tomb of the prophet Muhammad along the way. He participated in the rites of the great pilgrimage, or hajj, for the first time. After completing that complicated religious observance, Ibn Battuta set out to the north for Baghdad in November 1326. The territory he entered had been badly devastated by the invading Mongols. He traveled for a year in the khanate of the Ilkhans of Persia and visited such cities as Mosul, Tabriz, Basra, and Isfahan. Returning across the Arabian Desert, Ibn Battuta went back to Mecca, which he reached in the fall of 1327. After making a second hajj, he remained in Mecca for at least one year, possibly three. Between either 1328 and 1330 or 1330 and 1332, Ibn Battuta visited various cities and ports on the Red Sea, the coast of East Africa, and the southern coast of Arabia, including the Gulf of Oman and the Persian Gulf. His stops included Aden, Mogadishu, Kilwa, Muscat, and Oman. He returned to Mecca in the winter of 1330 (or 1332) for his third pilgrimage by crossing the Arabian Desert.

Ibn Battuta did not stay long in Mecca. News circulated through the Islamic world that Muhammad Tughluq, the sultan of Delhi, was hiring foreign Islamic scholars to help him run his kingdom. The ambitious Ibn Battuta decided to seek employment in India. Always the eager sightseer, he took the very circuitous and unlikely route of traveling through Anatolia, the steppe lands north of the Black Sea, and the region of the Caspian to get there. Traveling through Palestine and Syria toward the end of 1330 (1332), he made his way to the port of Latakia, where he embarked on a voyage to Alanya on the southern coast of Asia Minor. From there he made his way overland through Izmir, Bursa, and other cities to the port of Sinope on the southern coast of the Black Sea, from which he sailed to the Crimea in early 1332 (1334). During his stay in the Crimea, Ibn Battuta made a side trip to the great city of Constantinople in the early fall of 1332 (1334). After returning to the Crimea, he made his way into the domains of the Kipchak khanate, visiting Astrakhan and the capital of the Kipchaks at New Saray in late November 1332 (1334). He then traveled through the region of the Caspian Sea and beyond, visiting such cities as Bukhara, Samarkand, and Kabul. Crossing the Khawak pass in the Hindu Kush Mountains in May 1332 (1335), he reached the Indus River on 12 September 1332 (1335). In the spring of 1334 (1336), Ibn Battuta arrived at last in

Delhi. He met with Sultan Muhammad Tughluq, who (as was rumored) generously appointed Ibn Battuta to be a qadi, or judge. He served in that post until 1341.

Under the ineffectual Muhammad Tughluq, the sultanate of Delhi was a disintegrating state. The sultan focused on providing a proper Islamic atmosphere at his court, neglecting the day-to-day business of his empire. Overly high taxes crushed his predominantly Hindu subjects, corruption was rampant, military conspiracies abounded, and peasant uprisings were endemic. Ibn Battuta soon realized that he was in a dangerous situation that gave every indication of getting worse. Unfortunately, Muhammad Tughluq did not take kindly to foreign scholars leaving his service. Meanwhile, envoys arrived from China, and Muhammad Tughluq wanted to return the favor and send back an embassy of his own. In 1341, he asked the well-traveled Ibn Battuta to be his envoy and carry expensive gifts back to the emperor of China. Ibn Battuta readily agreed, and departed from Delhi on 2 August 1341, planning to take a ship from the western or Malabar coast of India and sail all the way to China.

It was a disastrous mission. Hindu brigands and rebels plagued the diplomatic party and killed several of Ibn Battuta's traveling companions. Ibn Battuta himself experienced several brushes with death. Still, after months of struggle he reached the coastline in February 1342. He arranged passage to China on a ship leaving from the port of Calicut. He even managed to secure a private cabin with enough room for him and his accompanying slave girls to frolic. Ibn Battuta then piously visited a mosque to pray for a successful journey. Allah ignored his supplications. That night a storm struck the harbor and destroyed the ship containing Sultan Tughluq's rich gifts for the emperor of China. The ship carrying Ibn Battuta's personal goods and his slave girls managed to clear the harbor, but it disappeared. Ibn Battuta's diplomatic mission lay in utter ruin. Unwilling to presume on Muhammad Tughluq's very limited good nature, the indefatigable Ibn Battuta decided to continue on to China as a private person rather than risk painful execution for failure in Delhi.

Meandering around the Malabar coast of India for about two years, Ibn Battuta reached the Maldives Islands off the southwest coast of India in December 1343. He found it to be a tropical paradise that had converted to Islam, an event that did not halt the native women's traditional practice of going topless. The Maldivians needed a qadi, and Ibn Battuta needed a job. He served in that position until August 1344, at which time he became deeply involved in local political intrigues that ultimately forced his departure.

Resuming his journey to China, Ibn Battuta stopped at the fabled island of Ceylon. He climbed the mountain known as Adam's Peak because it supposedly had an imprint of the first man's foot at its top. Ibn Battuta left Ceylon in October 1334 and sailed into the Bay of Bengal. By the time he passed through the Strait of Malacca in April 1336, he had stopped at the port of Chittagong and the island of Sumatra. Following the monsoons, he reached the south coast of China in the summer of 1346, and visited Canton and Chuanchou. Although he claimed to have reached Peking, many scholars are skeptical because his departure for India in the fall of 1346 did not give him enough time. In December 1346 or January 1347, Ibn Battuta returned to Quilon on the Malabar coast of India. Now he began the long journey that would ultimately take him back to Tangier in Morocco.

When Ibn Battuta journeyed into the central lands of Islam, that vast region was being hit by a great outbreak of bubonic plague known as the Black Death. He was most fortunate not to contract it, because it killed about one-third of the population wherever it struck. Leaving India, Ibn Battuta reached Zafar on the south coast of Arabia on 13 April 1347. Sailing up the Arabian Sea, he stopped at Hormuz, then continued up the Persian Gulf, reaching Baghdad in January 1348. Crossing over the desert to Damascus during the late-winter season of 1348, he stayed in the plague-ravaged city until July 1348. By the fall of 1348, he was in Cairo. From there he made his fourth and final pilgrimage to Mecca, performing the *tawaf*, the ritual walk around the Ka'ba on 16 November 1348. After completing the rituals, he returned to Cairo and departed from Egypt on a ship sailing along the coast of North Africa. On 31 May 1349 he reached Kabis in Ifriqiya. Arriving at his home in Tangier, he learned that his mother had died mere weeks before his arrival. He went on to Fez, the capital of Marinid Morocco, arriving on 8 November 1349. He had traveled for 24 years in Asia and Africa.

The ever-adventurous Ibn Battuta was still not finished. Warfare between the Muslims and Christians of Spain prompted him to join a military expedition seeking to relieve beleaguered Gibraltar about March or April 1350. A peace was arranged before he arrived, providing him with the leisure to tour the realm of Granada, Islam's last possession in Spain. By the end of 1350, he returned to Ceuta in Morocco and again reached Fez by the early fall of 1351.

Ibn Battuta decided to make one last great journey: a visit to the empire of Mali, a Muslim state on the other side of the fearsome Sahara and the only major Islamic land he had not visited. Leaving Fez in late 1351, he made his way to Sijilmasa, an oasis that formed the last Moroccan outpost before travelers entered the high desert. He joined a caravan that departed Sijilmasa in February 1352, and began the very dangerous journey across the desert. Passing through the grim salt-mining settlement of Taghaza, the caravan reached the ancient trading city of Walata in late April. Ibn Battuta found his trip across the Sahara a particularly unpleasant experience. By 28 July 1352, he reached the capital of the empire of Mali (the capital was probably the town of Niani, but scholars are not certain). Ibn Battuta hoped to meet Sulyaman, the Malian king, or musa. Unfortunately, he failed to obtain a royal audience, and Mali proved to be a great disappointment for Ibn Battuta. Although he spent eight months in the capital, he found the local customs strange and off-putting. Leaving the Malian capital on 27 February 1353, he traveled along the Niger River to visit the important cities of Timbuktu and Gao. From Gao he went east to the oasis of Takedda, from which he began his journey back to Morocco on 11 September 1353. This caravan route was much less daunting, and took him through the Air and Tuat regions before returning to Sijilmasa. By early 1354, he was back in Fez.

The trip to Mali marked the end of Ibn Battuta's prodigious journeys. He was age 50, and ready to settle down to a sedentary career as a Muslim jurist. However, Sultan Abu 'Inan had something in mind for him first. At that time in the Maghrib, a genre of travel literature called the *rihla* was flourishing. A *rihla* focused on the aspects of travel associated with a religious pilgrimage, and since Ibn Battuta had made the pilgrimage to Mecca four times, his journeys were a fit subject for presentation as a *rihla*. Furthermore, during the course of his travels, Ibn Battuta visited many important *madrasas* (colleges) of Islamic studies, many pious Sufis, and important Islamic holy places such as Caliph Ali's burial place at Najaf in Iraq and Adam's Peak on Ceylon. After Ibn Battuta's return to Morocco, Sultan Abu 'Inan ordered him to produce a *rihla* based on his travels in collaboration with an accomplished young Andalusian scholar named Ibn Juzayy. The two worked on the manuscript between 1354 and 1355. Ibn Juzayy apparently put the finishing touches on the book, and Ibn Battuta probably did not read—let alone correct—the final version. Ibn Juzayy then died prematurely in 1356 or 1357. The *rihla*, titled *Tuhfat an-nuzzar fi ghara'ib al-amsar wa-'aja'ib al-asfar*, was not greatly appreciated in its day. The great Moroccan historian Ibn Khaldun, who would have been a youth when Ibn Battuta's *rihla* appeared, commented that many people at the Moroccan court found the great traveler to be a mediocre scholar with a tendency to exaggeration and puffery. It was not a universal judgment, but Ibn Battuta's *rihla* quickly became a forgotten classic of Arabic literature. It survived only in fragments until the mid-nineteenth century, when two complete manuscripts were discovered in Algeria. Ibn Battuta owes the revival of his reputation as the greatest traveler of the premodern era to Western scholars, a circumstance that would probably come as a great surprise to a man who spent his last years in obscurity as a minor qadi in a Moroccan town, dying in 1369.

See also

Hajj; Mecca; Polo, Marco.

For further reading

Charles F. Beckingham, ed., *The Travels of Ibn Battuta*, vol. 4, 1994; Ross E. Dunn, *The Adventures of Ibn Battuta*, 1986; H. A. R. Gibb, ed., *The Travels of Ibn Battuta*, vols. 1–3, 1958–1971.

ICEBERGS   Large pieces of the polar ice shelf that break off into the sea and become floating mountains of ice, icebergs can present a serious hazard to shipping. They occur in both Arctic and Antarctic waters, but present a problem to shipping only in the seas off Newfoundland during the months of April through June. It is estimated that the glaciers of the west coast of Greenland produce some 5,400 icebergs annually. Many are carried south by the Labrador current to 48°N latitude, where they can collide with passing ships. Other polar areas

Icebergs in Glacier Bay, southeast Alaska, 24 July 1919.

also produce icebergs, but Antarctic icebergs and icebergs from the east coast of Greenland usually melt before they reach shipping lanes. The *Navigatio Sancti Brendani* described how St. Brendan and his companions encountered a crystal mountain on the high seas, an obvious sighting of an iceberg, which also shows how unfamiliar icebergs were to people in the early-medieval period. Norse sailors traveling to Iceland, Greenland, or North America were probably the only Europeans to regularly encounter icebergs before the fifteenth century. Icebergs were not much of a hazard to sailors until the sixteenth century, when substantial sea traffic developed between Europe and North America.

Thanks to an iceberg sinking the supposedly unsinkable *Titanic* in 1912 with the consequent loss of 1,500 lives, people commonly think that icebergs are nothing but a danger to ships. However, in the age of sail, seamen mined icebergs for the freshwater locked in their ice. Icebergs also could provide shelter for a sailing ship during a fierce storm by breaking the wind and waves. These great mountains of floating ice could be awe-inspiring and were definitely dangerous, but they also had beneficial aspects.

See also

St. Brendan the Navigator, Voyage of.

For further reading

David Limbert, "Ice and Icebergs," in *The Sea*, vol. 5, 1974.

ICELAND   This large island located in the eastern North Atlantic Ocean was first settled by Irish monks and later by Norse farmers during the early Middle Ages. It is well documented that the Norse or Viking settlers eventually went from Iceland to Greenland and from there to Vinland in North America.

Iceland has sometimes been identified as the Thule or Ultima Thule of ancient Greek and Roman geography, but that is almost certainly incorrect, especially considering that Greek and Roman ships were not suited for survival in the dangerous northern waters around Iceland. The curragh used by the Irish, however, made high-seas voyaging to the Faeroe Islands and Iceland quite possible. It is not known when the Irish first reached Iceland, but archaeological evidence indicates that they were Iceland's first inhabitants. Iceland appeared in the Irish sea-voyage stories known as *immrama*, beginning with the famous voyage of the mythological Irish hero Mael Dúin, which dates at least as far back as the eighth century. Dicuil (fl. 825), an Irish geographer living in the court of the Frankish emperor Charlemagne, mentioned that a group of Irish churchmen visited Iceland in 795. This reference is the earliest date for an Irish presence in Iceland, but Dicuil does not call it a voyage of discovery or consider it out of the ordinary. The implication is that the Irish were well aware of Iceland by the time Dicuil wrote. Iceland provided an ideal place to settle for anchorite monks seeking seclusion, which they did throughout the first two-thirds of the ninth century.

The blessed solitude of the Irish in Iceland was rudely interrupted after 860 by the unwelcome arrival of Norse settlers. Contrary winds blew a Norse vessel bound for the Faeroes to Iceland instead. Some sources give credit to Gardar Svavarsson, a Swede, while others point to Naddod the Viking or some unnamed merchants. Permanent settlers arrived under the leadership of Ingólf during the 870s, according to the sage *Landnámabok* of Ari the Learned (Fródi). The arrival of the Norse immediately caused the Irish to abandon Iceland.

Iceland quickly developed a substantial Norse population of 30,000–35,000 by 930. The unification of Norway by King Harold I Fairhair (ca. 860–ca. 930) caused many people opposed to him to emigrate to Iceland. A general land shortage in Scandinavia also motivated many of Iceland's early settlers. The island remained an independent republic until its union with Norway under King Hakon IV during the years 1262–1264. Iceland also continued to attract Norse settlers. When he was 16, the family of Eric the Red (father of Leif Ericsson) left Norway to settle in Iceland because of a blood feud. A similar blood feud forced the adult Eric the Red to leave Iceland and led to his discovery of Greenland in 982. Thus, Iceland provided an important starting point for Norse explorations of the western North Atlantic and their discovery of North America. It also formed part of a vague collection of real and imagined Atlantic islands that fascinated western Europeans during the Middle Ages and the early-modern era.

See also
Atlantic Ocean; Greenland; *Immrama*; Thule; Vinland.
For further reading
Bruce E. Gelsinger, "Iceland," in *Dictionary of the Middle Ages*, 1982–1989; G. J. Marcus, *The Conquest of the North Atlantic*, 1981.

IMMRAMA   Genre of early-medieval Irish literature consisting of tales about sea voyages to strange or mythical islands.

The development of the highly seaworthy curraghs by the early Christian Irish opened up the Atlantic Ocean for voyages of both fact and imagination. Curraghs were particularly popular among the Irish monks, who engaged in many daring, long-distance sea pilgrimages. St. Brendan's voyage and the tales of Great Ireland were merely extreme examples, and probably fictional. Furthermore, pre-Christian Celtic mythology was filled with heroes seeking the otherworld across the seas. These two monkish and pre-Christian elements came together to form the *immrama*, a genre of literature based on narratives of fictional voyages. The *Voyage of Bran*, written about A.D. 700, is the oldest surviving *immrama*. It tells how the god-hero Bran sailed to the two wonderful islands of Joy and Women in the Western Ocean. When Bran and his companion returned to Ireland, they discovered that centuries had elapsed in their absence. A more fully developed *immrama* is the *Voyage of Mael Duin*, which dates as early as the eighth century and no later than 920. Mael Duin, the son of a warrior of Aran and an Irish nun whom he raped, is a sort of Irish Odysseus. When he reached adulthood, Mael Duin learned that sea raiders had killed his father. Swearing vengeance, he went to sea with 60 companions. During their voyage, the seafarers visited many strange islands. Giant ants inhabited one, while another was the home of beautiful birds. Other islands contained boiling rivers, talking birds, hermits, weeping black people, and a Fountain of Youth. Eventually, Mael Duin located his father's killers, but when they asked to make peace, rather than slaughter them, he agreed. If the earlier dating of the *Voyage of Mael Duin* is correct, the *Voyage of Mael Duin* is older than the *Navigatio Sancti Brendani Abbatis*, which dates from 900 to 920. Many scholars think that the *Voyage of Mael Duin* provided a model for the composition of the *Navigatio*. Other surviving *immrama* were composed later; over the years, many have been lost.

Some scholars consider the *Navigatio Sancti Brendani Abbatis* to be a Christianized *immrama*. Others argue from the chronology of events that actual voyages of various Irish monks, including St. Brendan, inspired the writers of the *immrama*. They point out the greater authenticity of the narrative elements of St. Brendan's voyage and other stories of sea pilgrimages by Irish monks. These tales pay far more attention to details such as the direction of sailing and the length of time involved in a voyage than the secular *immrama*. Almost no scholar claims that the account of St. Brendan's voyage literally describes a particular journey, but many argue that the story reflects knowledge of historical Atlantic travels made by Irish monks. Certainly, the *immrama* and related tales of the monks' voyages show that the early Irish traveled far more often and extensively on the Atlantic Ocean than is generally recognized.

See also

Atlantic Ocean; Great Ireland; St. Brendan the Navigator, Voyage of.

For further reading

Geoffrey Ashe, *Land to the West*, 1962; Geoffrey Ashe, *Mythology of the British Isles*, 1990; Thomas Wentworth Higginson, *Tales of the Enchanted Isles*, 1898.

INDIA For travelers and geographers of the late-classical and medieval eras, the term *India* represented a vague concept that frequently encompassed more than the Indian subcontinent.

Greeks of the classical and Hellenistic eras became increasingly aware of India, particularly because Alexander the Great's (356–323 B.C.) armies briefly and victoriously campaigned there. The geographical writings of Ctesias (fl. early fourth century B.C.) and Megasthenes (ca. 350–290 B.C.) describe India as a land of fantastic gems, monstrous races, strange plants, gold-bearing rivers, and impossibly high mountains, among other so-called Marvels of the East. Roman merchants of the Imperial era visited India regularly, using the monsoonal sea routes of the Indian Ocean. General geographical knowledge, however, was weak; Pliny the Elder's (23–79) great *Natural History* based its descriptions of India on the inaccurate and sensationalistic accounts of Ctesias and Megasthenes rather than the readily available firsthand descriptions of Roman merchants. For both Greeks and Romans, India was the easternmost part of Asia, although some vague knowledge of China or the land of Sires occasionally manifested itself.

As the Roman Empire declined, the geographical concept of India became more complicated and confused. A distinction was made between India Major and India Minor no later than the fourth century. India Major, or Greater India, referred to the southern part of the Indian subcontinent and was also known as Further India. India Minor, or Lesser India, referred to the northern part of the Indian subcontinent and was called Nearer India. Some medieval geographical works included Persia as part of India Minor. Meanwhile, by the early Middle Ages, all awareness of the existence of China was lost, exemplified by a report from the patriarch John of India to the pope in Rome in 1122 that referred to India as being at the eastern end of the world.

From the twelfth century on, the scholars of the Christian West talked of three Indias. A Middle India was added, and oddly referred to the geographically distant Ethiopia or some land that bordered on it. This conflation of India and Ethiopia goes back as far as the Homeric Greeks, and reflects the persistent belief that the Indian Ocean was an inland sea, and therefore India and Ethiopia were physically connected by the southern shore. In consequence, Europeans considered lands ranging from eastern Africa to the Far East to be part of the three Indias. Many medieval mappaemundi depicted the three Indias. Ordericus Vitalis (1075–1142?) mentioned three Indias in his *Historia Ecclesiastica,* while the fraudulent *Letter of Prester John* claimed that this great Christian monarch ruled over the three Indias. As a result, European travelers expected to find Prester John in the real India and central Asia, and even in far-removed Ethiopia. In the early thirteenth century, Gervase of Tilbury wrote of the apostles who evangelized the three parts of India as St. Bartholomew in India Superior (southern India), St. Thomas in India Inferior (northern India, Parthia, and Persia), and St. Matthew in India Meridiana (Ethiopia). Marco Polo (1254?–1324) also thought of India as having three parts. This belief in a threefold India persisted into the late fifteenth and sixteenth centuries, and contributed to Columbus's reference to the islands of Cuba, Hispaniola, and the Antilles as the Indies. According to the geographical concepts with which he was familiar, these islands were the easternmost part of Asia (India Major, or Further India). The idea of three geographically indistinct Indias caused much confusion for travelers and explorers of the later Middle Ages and the early-modern era.

See also

Alexander the Great, Romances of; Ethiopia; Marvels of the East; Pliny the Elder; Prester John and His Kingdom; St. Thomas, Legend of.

For further reading

J. R. S. Phillips, *The Medieval Expansion of Europe*, 1988; John Kirtland Wright, *The Geographical Lore of the Time of the Crusades*, 1925.

INDIAN OCEAN   Great ocean bounded by Africa on the west, the Middle East and south Asia on the north, Australia on the east, and Antarctica and its waters to the south.

The Indian Ocean covers an area of 28,350,000 square miles. Compared to the Atlantic and Pacific Oceans, the Indian Ocean has very weak currents. The south equatorial current flowing from the East Indies to the coast of East Africa is the only current of any significance in the Indian Ocean. It carried Indonesian natives to the great island of Madagascar prior to European contact in the late fifteenth century. Flowing between Madagascar and East Africa, it creates the tricky Mozambique current. Relative to the Pacific Ocean, the Indian Ocean contains few islands.

The wind patterns of the Indian Ocean are unique. South of the equator, the southeast trade winds blow normally. Unimpeded by any significant landmasses, the southern westerlies of the Indian Ocean form part of the harsh winds of the Roaring Forties of the Atlantic and Pacific. In the northern Indian Ocean, the wind patterns become quite different. Seasonal monsoons prevail; in the winter they blow from north to south, and in the summer they blow from south to north. They are a product of the seasonal heating and cooling of the Asian landmass in comparison to the temperature of the waters of the Indian Ocean.

People first sailed on the Indian Ocean before the first civilizations were established in the Middle East. Some archaeologists believe that the ancestors of the ancient Sumerians of Mesopotamia came from what is now Oman on the southeastern coast of the Arabian peninsula. They left their original homeland, Dilmun, and sailed up the Gulf of Oman and the Persian Gulf to Mesopotamia. During the reign of Queen Hatshepsut, ancient Egyptian merchants visited the mysterious land of Punt in their trading vessels. Scholars variously locate Punt at modern Aden, Somalia, Tanzania, or Mozambique. The latter three locations would have necessitated sailing on the Indian Ocean. By the sixth century B.C., maritime trade existed between the cities of the Indus Valley and Babylonia. Merchants from the early civilization of the Indus at Harappa and Mohenjo-Daro may have sailed the coastal waters of the Arabian Sea (which forms part of the Indian Ocean) about 2600 B.C. The Phoenicians sailed the Indian Ocean to trade with enigmatic Ophir during the reign of King Solomon (973–933 B.C.) of Israel. Some scholars believe that Ophir and Punt are different names for the same land. Others place Ophir in India, Sri Lanka, or Malaysia. Most of these locations would require the Phoenicians to leave the Red Sea and enter the Indian Ocean proper, which was definitely the case with the purported Phoenician circumnavigation of Africa in 600 B.C.

The first Greek to sail the Indian Ocean was Scylax in 510 B.C. Carrying out the orders of Persian king Darius I, Scylax sailed from the Indus River across the Arabian Sea and up the Red Sea to the Gulf of Suez. The voyage took a leisurely two and a half years. About 200 years later, another Greek named Nearchus led a large fleet down the Indus River, westward along the coast of the Indian Ocean, and up the Persian Gulf (between 326 and 325 B.C.). Nearchus performed this feat for his king, Alexander the Great. Alexander's successors, the Seleucids of Syria and Mesopotamia and the Ptolemies of Egypt, both did some oceanic trading with India. The most famous voyage was that of Eudoxus of Cyzicus, who reopened Scylax's sea route to India. Unlike Scylax, his achievement was widely imitated.

Oceanic trade with India, particularly for its exotic spices, grew in importance during the Romans' domination of the Mediterranean world. The Romans inherited the Ptolemies' network of trade with India when they added Egypt to their empire in 30 B.C. Under Emperor Augustus (r. 27 B.C.–A.D. 14), some 120 ships a year sailed from Egyptian ports on the Red Sea to trade with northeast Africa and India. A Greek named Hippalus unraveled the seasonal pattern of the monsoons during the reign of Emperor Tiberius (A.D. 14–37).

The Greeks and Romans called the northern Indian Ocean the Erythraean Sea (meaning "red"). Collectively, the name referred to the modern Red Sea, the Persian Gulf, and the Arabian Sea. During the first century A.D., an unknown navigator wrote the *Periplus of the Erythraean Sea*, describing its waters and coasts. The waters of the Indian Ocean south of the Erythraean Sea were known as the Mare Prasodum, or the Mare Obscurum ("unknown sea"). By the second century A.D., the great geographer Claudius Ptolemy concluded that the Indian Ocean was landlocked, like the Mediterranean Sea, and that India and Africa were connected by the great southern continent of Terra Australis. Off and on, this belief remained common among medieval and early-modern Europeans even after Vasco da Gama's voyage to India in 1497–1499 proved it manifestly false.

During the years 500–1500, Persian, Arab, and Gujarati merchants dominated the waters of the Indian Ocean. These sailors knew the secrets of successfully navigating the Indian Ocean, and were the models for the legendary Sindbad the Sailor. Their various sailing ships—dhows, baggalas, and kotias—plied the waters of the Indian Ocean and South China Sea from far south along the coast of East Africa to the ports of China. From 1405 to 1433, the Ming Chinese, led by the great admiral Cheng Ho, temporarily entered the Indian Ocean. They lacked staying power, and the rich spice trade of the Indian Ocean remained a Muslim monopoly until the arrival of the Portuguese in 1497.

Vasco da Gama's voyage to India during 1497–1499 opened up direct European contact with Asia, a connection that has never been severed. The Portuguese succeeded in taking over the Indian Ocean spice trade, but in turn were displaced by the Dutch and English in the early seventeenth century. Dutch ships quickly learned to use the current of the West Wind Drift and the winds of the Roaring Forties to carry them across the southern Indian Ocean to the East Indies. In 1605, they encountered Australia by using this route. Meanwhile, the Indiamen of the Europeans (armed ships carrying Asian luxury goods) sailed across the Indian Ocean and around Africa in increasing numbers during the sixteenth through the mid-nineteenth centuries. Then, the building of the Suez Canal created a shortcut that diverted much of the Asian trade up the Red Sea.

From 1497 to 1945, the guns of European warships dominated the waters of the Indian Ocean. Some Asian historians call this period the Vasco da Gama era. Europeans controlled the external trade of the Asian nations because they controlled the Indian Ocean. The Indian Ocean has been an important highway of maritime commerce for well over 2,000 years, something that cannot be said of either the Atlantic or Pacific Oceans.

See also

Atlantic Ocean; Cheng Ho, Voyages of; Monsoons; Ophir; Pacific Ocean; Scylax, Voyage of; Sindbad, The Seven Voyages of; Spice Islands; Terra Australis.

For further reading

George Fadlo Hourani, *Arab Seafaring in the Indian Ocean in Ancient and Early Medieval Times*, 1995; Auguste Toussaint, *History of the Indian Ocean*, 1966.

INDIES, EAST

See Spice Islands.

INNS AND TAVERNS
Names for the business establishments where travelers could stop for food and lodging. They were the hotels or motels for most of human history.

Inns have existed almost since human travel began. Compared with modern accommodations, early inns were extremely modest, even spartan. They ranged from a household that rented out one or two extra rooms and served a meal to travelers to large inns with specialized buildings that catered to large numbers of guests. Inns and taverns existed throughout the ancient Near East and Greece, and in Indian and Chinese civilizations as well. Greek inns, which generally did not serve food, spread through much of the Near East after the conquests of Alexander the Great during the era of the Hellenistic kingdoms. Under the Roman Empire, the provision of inns became more sophisticated, and more historical evidence survives. After Augustus became emperor in 27 B.C., the Romans established the *Cursus Publicus*, or the imperial post system, to move the emperor's mail and officials speedily around the empire. Scattered along the Roman roads were various inns that provided officials with food, lodging, and a change of horses. The Latin word for these inns was *tabera,* from which is derived the modern word tavern.

Two basic types of inns comprised the *Cursus Publicus.* The *mansio* was the most elaborate, and provided fancier facilities. The lesser *mutatio* was a simple hostel that provided only food, lodging, and a change of animals, hence the name. *Mansiones* were located about 25–35 miles apart, or a day's journey. Between the *mansiones, mutatios* were located at intervals of 10–12 miles. In settled areas, the imperial government drafted existing inns into the *Cursus Publicus,* and the government built *mansiones* or *mutatios* in remote areas. These inns served the general public as well as government officials, although the latter had priority and received free services upon presentation of an official pass.

In heavily populated areas, many private inns operated outside the *Cursus Publicus.* Country inns provided the expected food, lodging, and change of animals. At the edges of towns and cities, inns called *stabularum* specialized in taking care of travelers' animals. Inns within the city proper lacked room for large stables, but they provided various qualities of food and lodging. They also acted as local restaurants, bars, and entertainment centers for their neighborhoods. The most respectable inns were called *hospitum* or *deversorium,* and lower-class establishments were called *caupona.* Some inns provided private or semiprivate rooms, while others offered barracks-style sleeping in a large room that doubled as the dining hall. Lavatory facilities were outdoor latrines or chamber pots in the guests' rooms. Generally, travelers visited the local public baths to clean up, although the largest and most elaborate inns had their own bathhouses. Inns frequently had connections with brothels, and chambermaids often doubled as prostitutes. These basic features of a Roman inn remained constant in the succeeding inns of the medieval and early-modern eras, with the exception that the cleanliness standards of medieval people were lower.

A 1776 pen-and-ink drawing of the host of the Blue Anchor Inn in Philadelphia serving food.

Archaeological evidence from the Middle East indicates that the khans or caravanserai from Islamic times were the direct descendants of Hellenistic or Roman *mansiones*. Medieval and Renaissance descriptions of inns are also strikingly
similar to Roman inns.

Medieval and early-modern inns could be as simple as a house that provided wayfarers with a bed. In such minimal establishments, travelers supplied
and cooked their own food. Other inns were elaborate complexes of buildings
with stables, guest houses, kitchens, and brew houses. By 1400, English accommodations for travelers were variously classified as inns, which provided lodging and possibly food; taverns, which served wines; and alehouses, which served
beer. Other regions of Europe classified their inns in roughly the same way, with
the qualification that drinking wine tended to be more common in southern
Europe, while drinking beer was more common in northern Europe. Drunkenness was common among travelers, especially the well-to-do; to be drunk was
considered a status symbol. Meals varied from the extremely basic to the elaborate, depending on the quality of the inns and the amount of money the traveler was willing to pay. Travelers universally complained about bad food, but
such criticisms often stemmed from a provincial reaction to an unfamiliar cui-
sine. Immigrants often ran inns, catering to travelers from their homeland; for
example, Germans traveling in Poland generally stayed at an inn run by a fellow
German.

Privacy and cleanliness were lacking in medieval and early-modern inns,
unless the travelers paid significantly more for the accommodation. Of course,
people from those eras did not have our modern expectation of privacy. Rooms,
and the beds in them, were shared with strangers. The Great Bed of Ware on
display at the Victoria and Albert Museum in London was famous both for its
size and the number of people who could be crowded onto it. Bedclothes were
not changed with any regularity, and fleas and other vermin commonly plagued
guests. Public bathhouses were rarely available, and frequently were nonexistent. Bathing was not a common practice in either the medieval or early-
modern eras. However, some inns were so bad that they offended even those
with generous sensibilities.

The quality of inns varied with the region. English inns generally received
higher marks for their food and accommodations, probably reflecting a higher
standard of living than on most of the Continent. Of course, many of the commentators supplying these judgments were English. In contrast, the inns of London had a reputation for poor quality and high prices, as might be expected in a
big city with many visitors and limited accommodations. Dutch inns acquired a
good reputation for quality, and especially cleanliness. French inns exhibited
extremes of grandeur and vileness, while German inns were noted for generally
good food and surly staff. Spanish inns, with a few notable exceptions, were
apparently of poor quality. For the most part, Italian inns were considered quite
satisfactory. Switzerland boasted one of the most elegant inns in all Europe—
the Crown at Uri. Inns in colonial America and the early-nineteenth-century
United States tended to be of good quality, except those in frontier regions. As
a general rule, the inns in the more peripheral regions were the most modest,

and sometimes the nastiest. In mainstream and core regions, the average quality of inns was usually better.

As the hosts of their establishments, innkeepers were expected to play the part with conviviality and honesty. Needless to say, some were more congenial than others. Various laws regulated them through the ages because travelers were particularly vulnerable to dishonest innkeepers. Roman law held innkeepers liable if a guest suffered a theft under their roof, thus making them responsible for the honesty of their servants. Reasonable limits were placed on their liability, and they could protect themselves by providing strongboxes for storing travelers' valuables. Some innkeepers were themselves dishonest, and served as scouts for bandits and highwaymen. A few even took to the road as highwaymen when a tempting opportunity arose. Overall, most innkeepers were relatively honest, or travel would quickly have ground to a halt.

Travelers sometimes encountered the problem of the available inns being full or even nonexistent. Such unfortunates had to sleep in the streets or out in the open. The baby Jesus, along with Mary and Joseph, are the most famous victims of "no room at the inn." Travelers in early-modern Poland chronically experienced this problem, and their journals and diaries frequently contain references to sleeping outdoors because of inns being full. Still, from the earliest civilizations to well into the nineteenth century, inns provided travelers with needed accommodations.

See also
> Hospices and Hospitals; Hospitality.

For further reading
> Lionel Casson, *Travel in the Ancient World*, 1974; M. H. Dunlop, *Sixty Miles from Contentment*, 1995; Antoni Maczak, *Travel in Early Modern Europe*, 1995; Norbert Ohler, *The Medieval Traveler*, 1989; Joan Parkes, *Travel in England in the Seventeenth Century*, 1925.

INVENTIO FORTUNATA (CA. 1365)

Lost geographical book of the Middle Ages that supposedly described the Arctic region, including parts of North America. Various fifteenth- and sixteenth-century students of geography, including Columbus, mentioned its existence.

The *Inventio Fortunata* is one of the Middle Ages' lost books, although some claim that a fragment survives. In 1589, Richard Hakluyt asserted that Nicholas of Lynn, an English Carmelite of the late fourteenth century, wrote it, but Hakluyt seems to have no basis for his attribution. Some modern scholars suggest that another contemporary, the Franciscan Hugh of Ireland, was the author, although that identification is extremely speculative. Scholars generally prefer to credit an unknown English Franciscan mathematician familiar with the astrolabe with the authorship of the *Inventio*.

The earliest mention of the *Inventio Fortunata* occurred in 1497 in a letter by the Englishman John Day to a Spanish admiral, possibly Columbus. In the letter, Day apologizes for not being able to acquire a copy of the *Inventio* for the admiral. The cartographer Johannes Ruysch referred to the *Inventio* four times in his world maps of 1507 and 1508. Both Bartolemé de Las Casas and Ferdinand Magellan mentioned the *Inventio* as one of the sources studied by Christopher Columbus. The great Flemish geographer Gerard Mercator cited it six or seven times in his Arctic chart of 1569. In 1577, he provided the English geographer John Dee with a summary of its contents. Mercator also mentioned that he derived his information indirectly from a fourteenth-century Flemish book by the obscure Jacobus Cnoyen (Knox?) of Hertogenbosch rather than directly from the *Inventio*. Apparently many people had heard of the *Inventio* and were familiar with its contents without having read it.

Mercator's summary of the contents of the *Inventio Fortunata* indicates that its author had the same degree of geographical knowledge as the medieval Icelandic colonists living on Greenland. The *Inventio* included extensive (although confused) information on the Canadian Arctic. Hudson Bay, Hudson Strait, and Fox Basin can all be recognized from its descriptions, along with other less clearly identifiable Arctic locations, but it is unclear if the author knew about Vinland. Basically, the *Inventio Fortunata* described a geography that was common knowledge to the Icelanders but not to the rest of Europe. Furthermore, the apparently confused organization of the *Inventio*'s Arctic descriptions indicates that the author had no firsthand knowledge of the lands he described. Possibly, the author borrowed his information from a book by the Arctic traveler and clergyman Ivar Bardarson called *Det gamle Gronlands beskrivelse* [Description of Greenland] written between 1360 and 1380.

The *Inventio Fortunata* was a relic of the geographical knowledge acquired by the Vikings during the course of their North Atlantic explorations. Medieval Europe never assimilated that knowledge because it conflicted with the prevailing geographical assumption that the world contained only three continents. The Viking discoveries in the *Inventio* were ignored or forgotten until the discoveries of Columbus revived interest in them. By then, perhaps only secondhand accounts of the elusive *Inventio* survived to tantalize Mercator, Dee, and others.

See also
 Atlantic Ocean; Greenland; Vinland.
For further reading
 Benjamin Franklin DeCosta, *Inventio Fortunata*, 1881; Tryggvi J. Oleson, *Early Voyages and Northern Approaches 1000–1632*, 1964; E. G. R. Taylor, "A Letter Dated 1577 from Mercator to John Dee," *Imago Mundi* (1956): 56–69.

Isles of Immortality (Taoist)
Following Taoist teachings, many Chinese believed that three magic islands of immortality existed in the Pacific Ocean. This belief prompted many voyages into the Pacific during the dynasties of the Chhin and Han.

Taoism (or Daoism) was and is an important religion in China. Alongside its better-known religious and philosophical principles, Taoism displays a strong belief in magic and alchemy, an aspect especially strong during the fourth, third, and second centuries B.C. One particular alchemical belief stated that three magic islands named Phêng-Lai, Fang-Chang, and Ying-Chou were located in the sea. On these islands lived genii, who possessed a drug capable of conferring immortality, and under the right conditions they could be persuaded to part with some of it. Early traditions located these islands in the Sea of Po (Gulf of Chihli) off the Yellow Sea. By the time of the first emperor Chhin Shih Huang Ti (or Qin Shi Hungdi), who reigned from 246 to 210 B.C., their supposed location shifted to somewhere in the vast Pacific. Near or far, the magic islands were almost impossible to visit. From a distance they looked like clouds, but when a curious ship tried to approach, winds would arise and blow them away. If the winds failed to stop the intruding ship, the islands would sink beneath the sea in the same manner as the western moving or submerging islands. Nevertheless, the ancient Chinese believed that some people could reach these islands. Descriptions stated that many immortals lived on them in palaces made of gold and silver, and that all the islands' birds and animals were completely white.

Ssuma Chhien (Si-ma Quian, 145 B.C.–?? B.C.), the great historian of the Former Han era and author of the *Shih Chi,* or *ShiJi* [Historical Record], completed in 90 B.C., is the chief source of information about the magic islands and the attempts to find them. He recorded that such attempts occurred well before the unification of China in 221 B.C. Two kings of the coastal kingdom of Chhi named Wei (r. 378–343 B.C.) and Hsüan (r. 342–324 B.C.), as well as Chao (r. 311–279 B.C.), the king of another coastal kingdom called Yen, had all sent obviously unsuccessful expeditions.

Repeated failures did not dampen the desire of China's rulers to locate the magic islands and so gain immortality. The best-known and most persistent hunter was the fearsome first emperor of unified China, Chhin Shih Huang Ti. Ruthless in his conduct of war and government, the emperor was reluctant to accept his own inevitable mortality. Meanwhile, rumors circulated claiming that several Taoist scholars had achieved immortality. Given such an intellectual atmosphere, other Taoists managed to convince the emperor that they could obtain the drug of immortality. The practical Chhin Shih Huang Ti wanted to lead the expedition to the magic islands personally, but the possibility and consequences of failure caused him to reconsider and send others in his place.

Chhin Shih Huang Ti's search for the three magic islands fared no better than those of his predecessors, the kings of Chhi and Yen. Some of his explorers returned empty-handed, but claimed they had sighted the three islands. Contrary winds, however, prevented them from landing. Others complained that attacks by great sharks hampered their efforts, and they asked the emperor to provide them with soldiers armed with crossbows. Chhin Shih Huang Ti agreed, and even developed a personal interest in hunting sea monsters. When he died in 210 B.C., he was touring the coastal provinces of China, and the itinerary included sea-monster hunting.

Little detail about these expeditions survives. Only one commander's name is known: Hsü Fu, a magician. When he first approached the emperor in 219 B.C., several expeditions had already failed. Still, Hsü Fu gained imperial support on a very large scale, but like previous explorers, he failed to secure the drug of immortality. By 219 B.C., the emperor was beginning to complain about both the lack of success and the great expense involved in the hunt for the islands of immortality. Chhin Shih Huang Ti was a dangerous person to disappoint, but the clever Hsü Fu staved off his wrath by never returning from the last voyage. Some accounts claim that he and his expedition settled in Japan, but a few scholars speculate that he might have sailed all the way to the Americas.

Despite the continuing lack of success, voyages in search of the magic islands of immortality continued into the period of the Former Han dynasty (206 B.C.–A.D. 8). The most active Han sponsor of Pacific explorations was the great emperor Wu Ti (or Wu Di, r. 140–87 B.C.). Around 133 B.C., his court included the alchemist Li Shao-Chun, who sailed the seas so that he could converse with the immortals. Li claimed he visited the islands of immortality, but apparently he failed to bring any of its precious drug home with him. During the year 133 B.C., a government official named Khuan Shu led another expedition in search of the magic islands. Predictably, he failed to find them, but that did not affect Wu Ti's decision to give him the important appointment of minister of sacrifices. A later voyage of exploration left China in 113 B.C. under the leadership of some scholars specializing in the interpretation of clouds. Again, no positive results ensued. In that same year, another magician, Luan Ta, prepared to depart for the magic island with great fanfare, but never even dared to sail. Understandably, he soon fell from favor. By 98 B.C., Wu Ti and the Han government appear to have lost interest in any further explorations of the Pacific. Repeated failures to reach the magic islands had worn down their resolve.

See also
Fountain of Youth; Pacific Ocean.
For further reading
Joseph Needham, *Science and Civilization in China*, vol. 2: *History of Scientific Thought*, 1962; Joseph Needham, *Science and Civilization in China*, vol. 4: *Physics and Physical Technology*, part 3, *Civil Engineering and Nautics*, 1971.

J

JAPAN
See Chipangu.

JASON AND THE ARGONAUTS, VOYAGE OF   Also commonly known
as the quest for the Golden Fleece. This journey from classical mythology
concerns Jason and a group of companions, known as the Argonauts, sailing
from Greece across the Black Sea in the ship *Argo* to obtain the Golden Fleece,
owned by King Aeetes of Colchis. The story is an archetype of the journey
as quest.

In the internal chronology of Greek mythology, the voyage of the Argonauts took place in the generation before the Trojan War and the wanderings of
Odysseus. The story begins when Pelias seizes the kingdom of Iolcus from its
rightful possessor, Aeson (his nephew or half brother, depending on the source).
Aeson sends his own son and heir, Jason, to safety, and Jason is raised by the
wise centaur Cheiron. Meanwhile, an oracle warns Pelias to be careful about
anyone who visits wearing only one shoe or sandal. Of course, one day such a
stranger arrives. Jason has come back to claim his throne. The wily Pelias, however, decides to use an indirect method of eliminating his rival. Rather than kill
Jason in Iolcus, Pelias sends him on a quest to bring the fabled Golden Fleece
back to Greece. It is such a dangerous mission that Pelias is certain that Jason
will not only fail, but die in the attempt.

Jason is undaunted. He calls for other adventurous Greeks to join him
in sailing on the magical ship *Argo* to the far eastern end of the Black Sea,
where Colchis, the home of the Golden Fleece, is located. About 50 heroes
answer Jason's call. According to various sources, the group includes the
strongman Hercules; the twins Castor and Pollux; Calais and Zetes, the
winged sons of the wind Boreas; Orpheus, the musician; Tiphys, the great
helmsman; and Atlanta, the virgin huntress and the only woman on the
voyage (although another crew member, Caeneus the Lapith, had been a
woman at one time). This redoubtable company becomes known as the
Argonauts, and before they set sail for Colchis they formally choose Jason
as their captain.

Once the *Argo* leaves Iolcus, its crew encounters a variety of peoples and places, some with concrete existences and geographic locations, while others lay more in the realms of myth and legend. Lemnos, an actual island in the Aegean Sea, is the adventurers' first stop. They find a society in which the women recently killed all the men on the island for sleeping with their Thracian slave girls instead of their wives. The Lemnian women, led by Hypsipyle, are not man-haters. Indeed, they want to make the Argonauts their new and hopefully faithful husbands. Although sorely tempted by the offer, a stern rebuke from Hercules compels Jason and his men to continue on. (Ironically, Hercules leaves the expedition soon after to search for his lost squire, Hylas, who disappeared when the *Argo* put into the coast of Mysia.)

The *Argo* enters the Hellespont (Dardanelles) and the Propontis (the Sea of Marmora), and after various adventures reaches Salmydessus on the northern shore of the Propontis near the entrance of the Bosporus. Its ruler is the blind but gifted seer Phineas, whom the gods decided to punish because his prophecies revealed too much about the future. They sent the horrid winged creatures known as the Harpies (variously depicted as winged women or woman-headed birds) to torment him, preventing him from eating by stealing or befouling his food. Taking pity on him, the Argonauts try to protect him from the Harpies, with the winged Calais and Zetes chasing off the creatures and ensuring that they never return to bother Phineas again. The grateful seer repays Jason and his men by telling them of a way to get past the deadly Clashing Rocks (Symplegades) located within the Bosporus.

Taking their leave of Phineas, the Argonauts enter the Bosporus. The great danger here is the Clashing Rocks, which smash together with lethal force whenever something tries to pass between them. Phineas had advised the adventurers to let a dove fly between the rocks to see if it survived. If it succeeded, they should also try to pass through. If it failed, they should give up their quest. The bird they release survives, and after some strenuous rowing, so do the Argonauts—barely. After their accomplishment, the Clashing Rocks become fixed in place and no longer pose a threat to mariners.

After leaving the Bosporus, the *Argo* sails down the south coast of the Euxine (or Black) Sea and finally reaches Aea, the capital of Colchis. Along the way they pass the land of the ferocious Amazons and the Caucasus Mountains, where the tormented Prometheus lies bound. In Aea, Jason decides to ask King Aeetes directly for the Golden Fleece, but Aeetes fails to appreciate Jason's honesty, and plots his destruction. Aeetes agrees to give up the Golden Fleece if Jason can accomplish an impossible task. Jason must harness two fierce, fire-breathing bulls and plow a field with them. Afterward, he is to sow the field with dragon's teeth, which will sprout into armed warriors, whom Jason must slay or die himself. With some trepidation, Jason agrees to Aeetes's challenge. Fortunately for him, the goddesses Hera and Aphrodite cause the love god Eros to make Aeetes's daughter Medea, a formidable witch, fall in love with Jason. Medea gives him a magic potion and strategic advice that allow him to harness the bulls safely and defeat the earth-warriors. The treacherous

Aeetes still plans to deny Jason his prize. When the love-struck Medea learns of her father's intention, she leads Jason to the place where the Golden Fleece is guarded by a great, sleepless serpent (sometimes erroneously called a dragon). Hoping that Jason will make her his wife, she casts a spell that puts the serpent to sleep. The Argonauts promptly seize their prize and flee from Colchis on the *Argo,* taking Medea with them.

According to the most geographically straightforward account, Jason and Medea also abduct Apsyrtus, the son of Aeetes and the brother of Medea. When King Aeetes and his pursuing fleet threaten to overtake the *Argo,* Medea kills Apsyrtus. She dismembers his body and drops the pieces one by one into the sea, forcing the Colchians to stop and retrieve them for proper burial. In this grisly way, the Argonauts reach the Bosporus first and make their escape.

A more complicated version of the story by Apollonius of Rhodes tells how King Aeetes, enraged by his daughter's betrayal, sends a great fleet under the command of his son Apsyrtus to pursue the fleeing Argonauts. Their orders are to bring back Medea or never return home themselves. Colchian ships block the Bosporus, forcing the Argonauts to return home by way of the Ister River, which leads to the Cronian Sea. The Argonauts find more Colchian ships barring their way. Hoping to scatter his pursuers, Jason kills their commander, Apsyrtus, with the help of Medea, but the plan does not work, and the Colchians hold their ground. The *Argo* turns around and journeys up the Eridanus River; by a series of portages, they reach the western Mediterranean Sea. Passing the Isle of Elba, Jason and his men come to Aeaea, the island of Circe, the sorceress of the *Odyssey* and Medea's aunt. Circe helps Jason atone for his murder of Apsyrtus, but rejects Medea for her perfidious behavior. The *Argo* departs Aeaea to face the hazards of the sirens, the Wandering Rocks, and the strait of Scylla and Charybdis. Jason's luck and the favor of the gods help the Argonauts through these trials. When the Argonauts near the sirens, they are saved because their shipmate Orpheus outsings them. Next, the ship reaches the many-headed monster Scylla and the whirlpool Charybdis and the Wandering Rocks, which like the earlier Clashing Rocks, smash any ship that dares to sail between them. The goddess Hera continues her protection of Jason and sends the Nereids, or sea nymphs, to push the *Argo* quickly and safely through the various hazards. After further adventures, storms push the *Argo* south to the Syrtis Gulf, where they portage to Lake Tritonis and back to the sea again. Finally, the Greeks are again able to head north and home. Putting in at Crete, they encounter the giant bronze man Talos, who hurls great stones at the *Argo* in an attempt to sink it. Once more, the capable Medea uses her magic and destroys him. From Crete, the *Argo* sails to Greece, arriving first at Aegina and eventually landing at Iolcus. Medea again helps Jason by getting rid of the nasty Pelius. Unfortunately, the couple does not live happily ever after. An ungrateful Jason tries to abandon Medea for another woman, not a very intelligent move considering Medea's very considerable magic powers and the strong possibility that she would seek revenge. She does, by killing Jason's intended. The former lovers part bitter enemies.

The chief accounts of the voyage of the *Argo* come from Pindar (518–438 B.C.) in his *Pythian Odes* and the *Argonautica* of Apollonius of Rhodes (ca. third century B.C.). Both are works of fiction, but it is highly likely that their stories contain strong echoes of actual early explorations of the Black Sea near the city of Miletus. Certainly, the geography of the journey to Colchis is a rather straightforward account of the southern coast of the Black Sea. However, the convoluted return voyage contained in the account of Apollonius of Rhodes and his imitators causes geographical confusion. Some scholars suggest that the Ister River of the Argonauts was the Danube, and that they portaged to the Save River, which allowed them to reach the Adriatic Sea (Cronian Sea). Their Eridanus River was really the Po River, which they sailed up and then portaged along various Alpine lakes until they came to the Rhone River. Proceeding down the Rhone, they reached the Mediterranean, where they encountered Elba, Circe's Island, and the haunts of Scylla and Charybdis. Apollonius's Gulf of Syrtis and Lake Tritonis are then located in North Africa in the region of present-day Libya and Tunisia. These scholarly identifications are also the most consistent with the concepts of the Homeric geography of *The Odyssey*.

Other scholars speculate that the Argonauts' Ister River is the Don River, and that their route took them by a series of portages all the way to either the Baltic Sea or the White Sea. Certainly, the Scandinavian Varangians followed this same route south to reach Constantinople during the early-medieval era. The Argonauts then made their way into the Atlantic Ocean and through the Pillars of Hercules, ultimately making their way back to Greece. A third possible route had the *Argo* sail up the Phasis River in Colchis to the Caspian Sea. From there it made its way into the Indian Ocean and somehow reentered the Mediterranean Sea to reach Greece. All of these routes represent the efforts of ancient writers to maintain the literal truth of the story of the quest for the Golden Fleece in the face of a changing state of geographical knowledge. All became discredited when improvements in ancient geographical knowledge revealed their obvious impossibility. The situation led the practical Diodorus Siculus (fl. late first century B.C.) to simplify things by suggesting that the *Argo* returned home the way it had come, through the Bosporus. In fact, it is highly unlikely that a historical Jason went on an actual quest for the Golden Fleece. The story's importance partially lies in its legendary celebration of the early Greek voyages into the Black Sea, and even more in its symbolism as an early tale of a hero and his companions successfully traveling in quest of an important but difficult and dangerous goal, a mirror of the struggle of human existence.

See also

Black Sea; Bosporus; Clashing Rocks; Dardanelles; Odysseus, Wanderings of; Scylla and Charybdis.

For further reading

Apollonius of Rhodes, *The Voyage of Argo*, 1959; Janet Ruth Bacon, *The Voyage of the Argonauts*, 1925; Robert Graves, *The Greek Myths*, 1955.

JERUSALEM

JERUSALEM   Also known as the City of David, or Zion, it is the holiest city of Judaism and Christianity, and one of the holiest cities for Islam. For centuries, Jerusalem has been a favorite destination for untold numbers of pilgrims.

People lived on the site of Jerusalem as early as 3000 B.C. About 1000 B.C., King David captured the city and made it the capital of the united kingdom of the 12 tribes of Israel. His successor, Solomon, built the Great Temple there, making Jerusalem the ceremonial center for the ancient Hebrews. The Assyrians besieged but failed to capture the city in 700 B.C. It fell to the armies of Nebuchadnezzar in 597 and 586 B.C., and the survivors were deported to Babylon. The Persians allowed them to return home in 520 B.C., and the Babylonian exiles rebuilt the temple. When Judaea came under the control of the Seleucids, their king, Antiochus Epiphanes, desecrated the temple in 167 B.C. It was liberated and cleansed by the Maccabees, an event commemorated by the Jewish holiday of Hanukkah. Roman rule began in 63 B.C., and when the Jews revolted against Rome in A.D. 66, Jerusalem and the temple were destroyed in A.D. 70. The so-called Wailing Wall in modern Jerusalem is a remnant of the Second Temple that survived the Roman devastation. The site of Jerusalem was abandoned until A.D. 135, when the Romans established the settlement of Aelia Capitolina.

Jerusalem's fortunes were restored by the visit in A.D. 326 of St. Helena, the mother of Emperor Constantine. Besides discovering the True Cross, the example of her pious journey inaugurated the practice of venerating holy places. The Church of the Holy Sepulchre was built in 335 and was followed by other magnificent churches. Thanks to the popularization of pilgrimage, Jerusalem's economy blossomed through catering to the needs of the multitudes of pilgrims.

Jerusalem fell into Muslim hands in 638, but the treaty of surrender protected the Christian sanctuaries and allowed Jews to resettle. Jerusalem developed as a major pilgrimage site of Islam. The mystical night journey of the prophet Muhammad took place at Jerusalem, along with other events of significance to Islam. A great mosque known as the Dome of the Rock was built over the site of the Temple of the Jews, with construction completed in 691/692, and Jerusalem became Islam's third holiest city. Christians, however, constituted the majority of the population.

Generally, the Christians of Jerusalem lived without threat under Muslim rule. The exception occurred during the reign of the mad Fatimid caliph al-Hakim, who destroyed the Church of the Holy Sepulchre in 1009. The Byzantine emperor Constantine IX rebuilt it between 1042 and 1048. When the Crusaders captured Jerusalem in 1099, they greatly expanded the Church of the Holy Sepulchre and constructed many other new buildings. The Church of the Holy Sepulchre was extensively rebuilt in 1310 and 1810.

Muslim control was restored by the Mamluks of Egypt in 1260, and they were succeeded by the Ottoman Turks in the early sixteenth century. Under their rule, the city of Jerusalem remained largely unchanged well into the nineteenth century. Ottoman control lasted until 1918, the end of World War I. Jerusalem and Palestine were administered by Great Britain until the establishment of the modern state of Israel in 1948.

Jerusalem with Emperor Constantine's buildings rising above Calvary and the Holy Sepulchre. Detail of the "Map of Madaba," a mosaic floor from St. George's Church, an early Christian church in Madaba, Jordan.

Over these thousands of years, Jerusalem has developed into a powerful symbol for the three great religions of Judaism, Christianity, and Islam. Medieval Christian cosmographies placed Jerusalem at the center of the world. Jerusalem was the perfect city; not just a destination for pilgrims, it was an example of how other religious communities needed to establish themselves, at least in the realm of the imagination. New Jerusalems ranged from the Munster of the fanatic Anabaptist uprising of 1533–1535 to the Puritan settlements in seventeenth-century New England. Jerusalem has never been economically important, but in the minds of devout Jews, Christians, and Muslims, it is a place of cosmic importance. Pilgrims and tourists respond to its magnetic draw in great droves even today.

See also

Holy Land; Mappamundi; Pilgrimage.

For further reading

Karen Armstrong, *Jerusalem*, 1996; Robert L. Wilken, *The Land Called Holy*, 1992.

K

KARAKORUM   Or Caracoron, capital of the vast Mongol Empire from the time of Genghiz Khan (d. 1227) until Kublai Khan established Peking as his capital in 1259.

Karakorum was located on the banks of the Orkham River south of Lake Baikal. Because the Mongols were a nomadic people, Karakorum was not a physically impressive city with public buildings and monuments despite being the headquarters of one of history's mightiest empires. Its name—*kara*, meaning "black," and *kuren*, "camp," in the Mongol language—reflected its nomadic origins.

The traveler John di Piano Carpini was the first European to mention the Mongol capital by name. To journey from the far eastern edge of Christendom at Kiev to distant Karakorum took six months. William of Rubruck reached it in 1253, and as he described it, "Caracarum . . . , exclusive of the palace of the Chan [Khan], is not as big as the village of St. Denis, and the monastery of St. Denis is ten times larger than the palace." The town was surrounded by a mud wall with four gates, and most of the buildings were made of wood. Located at each gate was a market specializing, respectively, in the sale of grains, sheep and goats, oxen, and horses.

Unprepossessing in appearance, as the capital of a world empire Karakorum nevertheless attracted visitors from all over Eurasia, including a number of Christian diplomats. William of Rubruck reported seeing Cathayans, Saracens, Armenians, other Europeans, and peoples of many other tribes and nations. Temples for the gods of 12 different religions were located there, along with two mosques and a Nestorian church. After Kublai Khan moved the Mongol capital to Peking in 1259, Karakorum fell into obscurity and eventually into ruin.

See also
    Mongol Missions.
For further reading
    J. R. S. Phillips, *The Medieval Expansion of Europe*, 1988; William Woodville Rockhill, ed., *The Journey of William of Rubruck*, 1900; Henry Yule and Henri Cordier, eds., *The Travels of Marco Polo*, 1929.

KEELBOATS
Principal cargo-carrying and passenger vessels employed on the Ohio, Mississippi, Missouri, and other western rivers in North America from about 1790 until their replacement by steamboats during the 1820s. Keelboats operated in the shallow tributaries of the major rivers until about 1865.

Keelboats were 40 to 80 feet long and 7 to 10 feet wide, and drew about 2 feet of water. The central cargo compartment could hold tons of goods. Crews of 6 to 12 oarsmen or polesmen rowed or pushed the keelboat. Sometimes the crew walked along the riverbank pulling the keelboat by a long rope, or cordelle, attached to the mast. Occasionally a sail was hung from the mast to allow wind to propel the keelboat. A large rudder at the stern was used to steer it.

The heyday of the keelboat was 1790–1820. Keelboats and flatboats carried the products of Ohio Valley farms down the Ohio and Mississippi Rivers to New Orleans. After the cargoes were sold, the boats were broken up and the lumber resold. The crews were paid in cash, which they frequently used to buy horses. Making their way on horseback or by foot up the Natchez Trace, they returned to the Ohio Valley and sold their mounts in that horse-starved region. Then the keelboatmen were ready for another trip down to New Orleans.

On the Missouri River and other far western rivers, keelboats made round-trips. Crews laboriously rowed, poled, or pulled them upstream to pick up valuable cargoes of furs or some other western product. The keelboat floated down the current to St. Louis or some other Missouri River port.

The coming of the steamboat quickly drove the keelboats off the main rivers and onto the shallow tributaries. With the development of steamboats that could operate in shallow rivers, keelboats finally disappeared entirely.

Keelboatmen were a rough, competitive lot. Their harsh and violent set of values was epitomized by the larger-than-life Mike Fink (ca. 1780–ca. 1823). Besides his various real-life duels, fights, wenchings, and marathon drinking bouts, according to frontier legend Fink engaged the redoubtable Davey Crockett in a keelboat race. An actual keelboat race occurred in 1811 when the Spanish fur trader Manuel Lisa set a never-equaled speed record with a keelboat when he caught up with the fleet of Wilson Hunt, which had a 240-mile head start up the Missouri River.

Keelboats provided settlers along the rivers of the greater Mississippi basin with a crucial form of transportation. Without them, the initial development and settlement of the United States west of the Appalachian Mountains would have been greatly retarded.

See also
Fink, Mike; Flatboats; Mississippi River; Missouri River; Natchez Trace; Steamboats, River.

For further reading
Leland D. Baldwin, *The Keelboat Age on Western Waters*, 1941; Paul O'Neil, *The Rivermen*, 1975.

KEMPE, MARGERY (CA. 1373–AFTER 1439)   Pious laywoman and pilgrim, she was the subject of the first biography written in English.

Margery Kempe was the daughter of John Brunham, a rich merchant of King's Lynn in Norfolk. Marrying John Kempe, another merchant of King's Lynn, and running her own successful brewery showed that Margery was a member of the local elite. Misfortunes, however, came into her life. When her first child was born, Margery suffered a spiritual crisis. Her sense of sinfulness increased when her brewing business failed. Margery determined to dedicate her life to piety and chastity, and, of course, wished to sever sexual relations with her husband because she viewed the act as sinful and disgusting. John Kempe did not feel the same way. Insisting on his conjugal rights, the couple produced 14 children during the first 20 years of their marriage. The couple battled constantly over Margery's growing commitment to chastity. Adding to John Kempe and his neighbors' woes, Margery became increasingly prone to hysterical outbursts of sobbing and weeping. Such behavior did not endear her to anyone who had to spend time around her.

Margery soon took up pilgrimage as a means to further her devotion. As she put it, "this creature [Margery Kempe] was moved in her soul to go and visit certain places for spiritual health . . . and she could not without the consent of her husband. She asked her husband to grant her leave and he, fully believing it was the will of God, soon consented, and they went together to such places as she was inclined." Her heart's desire was to visit Jerusalem, but John refused to allow it. In about 1413, when Margery was 40, the couple made a pilgrimage to Bridlington to visit anchorites and recluses. On the way, John and Margery argued over her fasting and chastity, and finally struck a bargain: if John gave up his conjugal rights and allowed her to go on a pilgrimage to Jerusalem, she would stop fasting and would pay off his debts. Her ability to pay off his debts reflected the anticipation of an inheritance from her father, which also apparently financed her subsequent extensive pilgrimages.

In 1413, Margery joined a party of pilgrims with the goal of visiting Rome, Santiago de Compostela, and Jerusalem. Although initially welcomed, Margery soon alienated her fellow pilgrims because "they were most annoyed because she wept so much." On the way to Constance, they asked her to leave their party but quickly relented. Eventually, the group reached Venice and hired space on a galley bound for the Holy Land. During the voyage, Margery's relations with her companions remained poor. When they arrived at Jaffa, she quickly hired an ass and rode toward Jerusalem.

Margery's first sight of Jerusalem was an intensely emotional experience. Two German pilgrims had to come to her assistance to prevent her from falling off her mount. As she viewed the sites of Christ's sufferings and death, Margery became even more distraught. At that point,

> she had such great compassion and such great pain to see our Lord's pain, that she could not keep herself from crying and roaring though she should have died for it. And this was the first crying that she ever cried in any contemplation. And this kind of crying lasted for many years after this time,

despite anything that anyone might do, and she suffered much contempt and much reproof for it. The crying was so loud and so amazing that it astounded people, unless they had heard it before, or else knew the reason for the crying.

These cries were distinct from Margery's regular weeping. Most people found Margery's outbursts to be extremely irritating, although some saw them as genuine expressions of devotion.

Margery followed most assiduously the conventional itinerary for pilgrims to the Holy Land. She started her homeward journey in 1414. On 1 August, she visited Assisi and on 7 October arrived in Rome. On 9 November, Margery married herself to the Godhead at the Apostles' Church and remained in Rome until Easter 1415, finally returning to Norwich on 1 May.

Still not spiritually at rest, Margery made the pilgrimage to Santiago de Compostela during July and August 1417. Back in England, Margery settled back into life in King's Lynn. Of course, her life was not an altogether normal one, and her religious fanaticism attracted the suspicion of authorities that she was a Lollard or some other form of heretic.

Late in her life, Margery made a trip to Germany in 1433 with her German daughter-in-law. She also visited Norway and the shrines at Wilsneck in Poland and Aachen in Germany. This journey was physically more difficult for the aging Margery, and her overseas travels ended, although she continued to make her way around England.

Margery's accounts of her travels are by no means the fullest. Her experiences show the human variety contained within the practice of pilgrimage. While Margery represented the extreme of devotion, the reactions of her traveling companions ranged from disgust to admiration. Obviously, the seriousness with which pilgrims approached that form of devotion varied greatly, as a review of the characters of the pilgrims in the *Canterbury Tales* shows. Margery's experience also demonstrates that long-distance pilgrimage was an activity of the well-to-do. The wealth she inherited from her father in 1413 permitted Margery to make these long, expensive journeys, and allowed her to maintain a rather eccentric lifestyle. Margery Kempe was probably one of the best-traveled, most devout, and most bizarre female pilgrims of the Middle Ages.

See also

Holy Land; Jerusalem; Pilgimage; Rome; Santiago de Compostela.

For further reading

C. W. Atkinson, *Mystic and Pilgrim*, 1983; B. A. Windeatt, trans. and ed., *The Book of Margery Kempe*, 1985.

KRAKEN   Gigantic sea monster thought to menace ships in the North Atlantic and Mediterranean Sea.

The Kraken's most outstanding characteristic was its size. All sources agree that it was big, even gigantic. In the eighteenth century, Bishop Erik Pontoppidan

(1698–1764) claimed that the Kraken was an incredible mile and a half wide. Another account described how a medieval bishop landed his ship on what he thought was an island only to discover that it was a Kraken resting on the sea's surface. Other than size, accounts of the Kraken are vague about its physical appearance and give variant details. Some sources describe the Kraken as if it were a fish or whale. Others give the impression that the Kraken was a great sea serpent, or credit it with having tentacles like an octopus or squid that reputedly were capable of pulling a sailing ship under the sea. The Hollywood movie *Clash of the Titans* (1981) portrays the Kraken as a scaly biped equipped with gills, reminiscent of the Creature from the Black Lagoon.

A few writers claim that Aristotle and Pliny described the Kraken in their writings, but this is not so. Rather, the Kraken appears to be a denizen of the sea lore of the North Atlantic region. Some sources locate the first tales of the Kraken in the Middle Ages; others claim that Bishop Erik Pontoppidan was the first to describe it in his *Natural History of Norway* (1752–1753). Bishop Pontoppidan's book may be the first appearance of the Kraken in print, but obviously he was recounting far older seafaring traditions. Some suggest that the inspiration for these tales came from sightings of especially large cuttlefish. Obviously, no Kraken literally existed, but the mere possibility must have terrorized sailors every time a vessel disappeared without a trace in the waters of the North Atlantic around Scandinavia.

See also

Sea Monsters.

For further reading

Angelo S. Rappoport, *Superstitions of Sailors*, 1928.

L

LIBYA The ancient Greeks and, to a lesser extent, the ancient Romans referred to the continent of Africa by the name Libya, although its geographical extent fluctuated. Homer considered Libya the land immediately west of Egypt, basically the coastal region of the modern nation of Libya. Greeks of the Homeric era had not yet developed the classical, geographical concept of three continents—Africa, Asia and Europe. Later Greeks, such as Hecataeus and Herodotus, sometimes treated Libya (Africa) and Asia as parts of a single continent. Other writers followed the concept of three continents. Whether they believed in two or three continents, many geographical writers, from Erastothenes to Strabo to Dionysius Periegetes, used the name Libya for the entire continent of Africa. Sometimes, however, Libya more narrowly meant all of Africa except Egypt, while at other times it referred to those parts of Africa excluding Egypt and Ethiopia (another vague geographical region in ancient and medieval times).

See also
Africa; Ethiopia.
For further reading
E. H. Bunbury, *A History of Ancient Geography,* 1883.

LLAMA South American animal related to the camel family, but lacking the hump. The pre-Columbian natives of Peru domesticated the llama and its smaller cousin the alpaca centuries before the arrival of the Spanish in the 1530s. Llamas served as beasts of burden and sources of wool. The ancient Peruvians rarely ate them because after reaching three years of age the animals' flesh acquired an unpalatable bitter taste from their diet of harsh plants.

Llamas had definite limitations as beasts of burden. Possessing an insuperable stubbornness, they preferred death to carrying a greater load than they thought was tolerable. Tolerable for a llama meant about 70 pounds, or about a tenth of what its camel cousin was willing to carry. Riding llamas was obviously out of the question. The fiercely independent llamas also possessed the camellike characteristic of spitting on or biting those humans who irritated them in some way, however minor. As the Spanish chronicler Father Bernabe Cobo

(1580–1657) put it, "[the llama was] the only animal which domestication has not degraded, for it only agrees to be made use of when asked, and not when ordered." Despite their limitations, llamas provided valuable services as carriers for the merchants and travelers of pre-Columbian and early colonial Peru.

See also

Camel.

For further reading

Louis Baudin, *Daily Life in Peru under the Last Incas*, 1962.

LODESTONE ISLANDS OR MOUNTAIN   People from ancient times to the end of the Middle Ages believed in the existence of certain islands or a mountain that consisted of lodestone, or magnetic rock. The magnetic attraction of these islands was supposedly so powerful that ships built with iron nails and fittings would be irresistibly pulled to the islands and trapped. Claudius Ptolemy, the imperial Roman geographer, mentioned these islands in his writings during the second century A.D. Arabic sources also talked about the existence of the lodestone islands, which make an appearance in the *Arabian Nights*. The fictional *Travels of Sir John Mandeville* located them in the Indian Ocean bordering the realm of Prester John. Mandeville used them to explain why ships in the Indian Ocean were built without nails. With the coming of the great age of European geographical expansion in the fifteenth and sixteenth centuries, belief in the lodestone islands died out. In their day, they meant just one more thing for travelers embarking on a sea voyage to worry about.

LOTUS-EATERS, LAND OF   Mysterious land visited by Odysseus and his men during their wanderings.

According to *The Odyssey*, Odysseus and his fleet make landfall on an unknown island. A scouting party goes out to explore the island and encounters some friendly natives who offer them fruit of the lotus to eat. Upon consuming the fruit, the scouts promptly forget about their mission, and even about returning home to Greece. After considerable time passes, a worried Odysseus sends a second party to locate the missing scouts. The second party finds their lost fellows, but the members of the first party refuse to return to the ships. Force must be used, and when the fleet finally embarks from the Land of the Lotus-Eaters, Odysseus puts the scouts in shackles while they wail bitterly about departing. Fortunately, the effects of the lotus fruit soon wear off and the men return to normal. They even stop pining for the lost Land of the Lotus-Eaters.

Was there really a Land of the Lotus-Eaters? Many authorities say no. Others believe that the dreamy land might have some basis in reality. The ancient Greek historian Polybius (ca. 200–ca. 118 B.C.) recorded the existence of a fruit-bearing lotus plant native to North Africa. Its fruit was the size of an olive and had the sweetness of a date. Some writers equate the lotus with the jujube tree, whose fruit does not have the addictive and amnesia-producing properties described by Homer. The ancient Greeks and Romans believed that the stories found in Homer's *Iliad* and *Odyssey*, along with certain other myths, were firmly based on historical events. Herodotus (484–420 B.C.) and the navigational writer Scylax of Caryanda (fl. ca. 519 B.C.) both identified the Land of the Lotus-Eaters with the island of Jerba and the region around it. The Roman geographer Strabo agreed with them, as did the twentieth-century writer Ernle Bradford. Although other locations have been suggested, Jerba is the most popular among those who prefer to take Homer literally. Meanwhile, the Land of the Lotus-Eaters remains a familiar literary allusion and a vague destination for some travelers over the millennia separating Homer from the present.

See also

Odysseus, Wanderings of.

For further reading

Ernle Bradford, *Ulysses Found,* 1964; W. B. Stanford and J. V. Luce, *The Quest for Ulysses,* 1974.

M

MAELSTROM   Dutch word meaning "whirling stream." It was originally applied to a large, dangerous whirlpool off the coast of Norway, but over time, any large whirlpool could be called a maelstrom. The monster Charybdis in *The Odyssey* is a sort of whirlpool or maelstrom. Edgar Allen Poe wrote a short story titled "A Descent into the Maelstrom" in 1841 that describes the terrifying experiences of a sailor caught in a giant whirlpool. While whirlpools present hazards to navigation, they generally are not capable of sucking a sailing ship to the bottom of the sea.

See also
Scylla and Charybdis.

MAGELLAN, STRAIT OF   Or *Estrecho de Magallanes*, the discovery of this famous strait in 1520 allowed European ships to sail from the Atlantic to the Pacific Ocean. Because of the area's strong, treacherous winds and currents, the Strait of Magellan were highly dangerous for sailing vessels, and even steam-powered ships have frequently been lost. The discovery of Cape Horn in 1616 permitted many ships to avoid the strait and instead follow the longer route around the southern tip of South America. The completion of the Panama Canal in 1914 further diverted shipping from the strait.

The Strait of Magellan are located at the southern tip of South America between the mainland and the islands of the Tierra del Fuego group. The eastern entrance is located at 52°30'S latitude between Cape Virgins on Dungeness Point and Cape Espíritu Santo. Ships entering the strait have a journey of 350 miles through a winding channel whose width varies from less than 1 to 30 miles. The western portion of the channel is flanked by impressive mountains. At the western end lies the aptly named Desolation Island with its western extremity of Cape Pilar, beyond which is the Pacific Ocean.

When Columbus sailed west in 1492, his goal was to reach China. Instead, he found some islands that were unknown to Europeans. Although subsequent voyages by Columbus and his contemporaries revealed the existence of the continents of North and South America, the basic desire of European seafarers continued to be reaching Asia. In 1513, Vasco Nuñez de Balboa crossed the

Isthmus of Panama to reach the Pacific Ocean. Europeans wanted a sea passage between the Atlantic and the Pacific, and various expeditions investigated any promising openings in the coastline. No way through to the Pacific was found, but efforts to locate usable strait continued because it was assumed that the result would be ready access to the Spice Islands and their valuable produce. No one imagined the vast size of the Pacific Ocean, which would ultimately render such a route economically problematical.

Ferdinand Magellan (ca. 1480–1521), a native of Portugal, had served in the East Indies and was interested in developing an alternate western route across the Pacific. His master, King Manuel of Portugal, did not share his interest. Frustrated by royal indifference but encouraged by other Portuguese navigators to seek a sea passage through the American landmasses, Magellan offered his services to Spain in 1517. The Spanish crown accepted his proposal, and a fleet of five ships with a crew of 250 men sailed from Spain in September 1519. Cruising down the east coast of South America in search of a passage for months, Magellan and his now four ships reached Cape Virgins on 21 October 1520. The opening did not look promising to his officers, but Magellan insisted it was a strait. On 27 November—37 days of difficult sailing later—he proved to be right. Three ships entered the Pacific Ocean, while the fourth turned back to Spain. What lay ahead for Magellan and his men were weeks of sailing on the seemingly endless Pacific. Scurvy, hunger, thirst, and hostile natives left only 35 men alive out of 150 to finally reach Spain.

Others followed Magellan through the strait named in his honor. In 1526, Francisco Garcia Jofre de Loaysa led a second Spanish expedition through the Strait of Magellan. Arriving in late January, this time the Spanish ships experienced terrible problems locating and entering the strait. On 5 April, they finally

Undated Italian map of South America showing the location of the Strait of Magellan.

passed between Cape Virgins and Cape Espíritu Santo, reaching the Pacific Ocean 42 days later. In 1578, the lucky Sir Francis Drake navigated the strait in a mere 16 days. Pedro Sarmiento de Gamboa traveled the strait from west to east in 1580. Thomas Cavendish, the third man to circumnavigate the globe, spent 49 days getting through the Strait of Magellan in early 1587. Many who tried to sail through the treacherous passage took far longer; some were forced to turn back or were shipwrecked and died in the attempt. The Strait of Magellan presented a difficult and potentially deadly challenge to the seamen of the age of sail.

See also

Atlantic Ocean; Circumnavigations of the Earth, Early; Horn, Cape; Pacific Ocean.

For further reading

Samuel Eliot Morison, *The European Discovery of America*, 1974.

MAGI, THREE
Also known as the Three Kings or the Three Wise Men, these famous travelers brought gifts to the newly born Jesus Christ.

According to the Gospel of St. Matthew (2:1–12), the Magi (from the Latin *magus*, "wise men") traveled to Jerusalem following a star, which announced the birth of a new king of the Jews. Disturbed by the Magi's quest, King Herod the Great (r. 73–4 B.C.) learned from his own priests that Bethlehem would be the site for such a birth. He sent the Magi there with the request that they return and report on their mission. The Magi followed the star to Bethlehem, where they found the baby Jesus, worshiped him, and presented him with gifts of gold, frankincense, and myrrh. Afterward, God warned them in a dream not to return to the treacherous Herod, so they returned home by a different route.

In another dream, God warned Joseph that Herod was a mortal threat to the baby Jesus. As a result, the Holy Family—the Christ child, Mary, and Joseph—fled to Egypt, where they remained until after Herod's death. Sadly, the ruthless Herod ordered his soldiers to kill all the young children of Bethlehem in the infamous Massacre of the Innocents.

The biblical account does not specify the number or geographical origins of the mysterious Magi. Beginning with the church father Origen (185–254), Western Christian traditions give their number as three. The sixth-century *Excerpta Latina Barbari* gives the Magi the names of Balthasar, Melchior, and Gaspar. Initially, they were believed to come from the region of Persia, and works of art reflect this by portraying the Magi in the Phrygian caps commonly associated with Persia. The Venerable Bede (673–735), however, claimed that each of the three Magi came from one of the three known continents—Africa, Europe, and Asia—and were each descended from one of Noah's sons, Shem, Ham, and Japheth. Another tradition common to both Western and Eastern Christianity is that each of the three Magi belongs to one of the three ages of man—youth, middle age, and elderly.

The three Magi. Sixth-century mosaic in Sant Apollinare Nuovo, Ravenna, Italy.

Eastern Christians and other groups have different traditions concerning the Magi. The church father Tertullian (ca. 160–230) referred to the Magi as kings. An Ethiopian document called the *Book of Adam* lists three Magi as kings and names them Hor, king of the Persians; Basanater, king of Saba; and Karsudan, king of the East. Armenian and Syrian traditions expand the number of Magi to 12 and supply names and lineages for all of them. The followers of Zoroastrianism knew of the three Magi, and some accounts even speculate that the Magi were Zoroastrian priests. During his journey to China, Marco Polo encountered the supposed grave of the Magi near Qom in Persia. He recorded several variant tales of the Magi. According to one story, the Magi brought the baby Jesus gifts to determine whether he was a king (gold), a priest (frankincense), or myrrh (a physician). He turned out to be all three. In another story, each Magus goes in to see Jesus alone. In each case, Jesus appears as a man of the same age as that particular Magus—a youth, a fully mature man, and an elderly man. Only when the Magi as a group view Jesus does he appear as an infant.

From the early centuries of Christianity, the Magi have served as patrons for travelers and pilgrims.

See also

Polo, Marco; Star of Bethlehem.

For further reading

Gaston Duchet-Suchaux and Michel Pastoureau, *The Bible and the Saints*, 1994; Leonardo Olschki, "The Wise Men of the East in Oriental Traditions," in *Semitic and Oriental Studies*, 1951, pp. 375–395; Richard C. Trexler, *The Journey of the Magi*, 1997.

MAGNETIC MOUNTAIN
See Lodestone Islands or Mountain.

MANDEVILLE, TRAVELS OF SIR JOHN   This travel book was the most popular of that genre during the late fourteenth through the sixteenth centuries and had an immense impact on the geographical concepts of Christopher Columbus and other explorers.

The vast majority of modern scholars believe that the *Travels of Sir John Mandeville* is a work of fiction. Although it is presented as an itinerary of Mandeville's travels in the Holy Land and the Far East and serves as a guide to those regions, apparently the author never made such a journey. In fact, it is most probable that Sir John Mandeville did not exist. The author claims to be an Englishman of St. Albans who journeyed in the East for 34 years and served as a mercenary in the service of the Mamluk sultan of Egypt. The contemporary French historian Jean d'Outremeuse of Liège claimed that Mandeville left St. Albans in 1322 and died at Liège in 1372. For a number of years, d'Outremeuse's assertions led modern scholars to speculate that he was the real Sir John Mandeville. In 1954, this theory was disproved by the researches of Josephine W. Bennett. Scholars continue to debate whether Sir John Mandeville was English or French.

The *Travels* first appeared between 1356 and 1366 in French, and the oldest English translation about 1375. The book was extremely popular, with some 300 manuscript copies surviving (compared with around 70 for Marco Polo's *Travels*), and it was translated into most European languages including Latin, Czech, Dutch, and Irish. The *Travels* are organized into two parts. In the first, fairly conventional section, Mandeville describes the various routes to the Holy Land and sites that pilgrims might want to visit. The second part of the book, which describes the lands of the Far East, reaches the level of the fantastic. Sir John Mandeville generously incorporates the so-called "Marvels of the East" into his narrative. Gold-digging ants, fearsome deserts, monstrous races, the Great Khan of Tartary, Prester John and his realm, a Fountain of Youth, the Terrestrial Paradise, and other wonders all crowd the pages of Mandeville's book. Even the possibility of a successful circumnavigation of the earth is discussed. Compared to the contents of Mandeville's book, Marco Polo's account of his journey to Cathay is relatively prosaic and hence was not as popular.

Modern research reveals that the author of Mandeville's *Travels* based his account on research of existing travel guides and narratives. His two most important models were the accounts of pilgrimages to Jerusalem and the narratives of journeys to the Far East by missionaries and merchants. William of Boldensele's *Itinerarius* (ca. 1336) provided Mandeville's main source of information for the Jerusalem pilgrimage in the first part of his book. Much of the material about the amazing lands of the Far East was taken from the Franciscan friar Odoric of Pordenone's account of his Asian missionary journey from 1318 to 1330. Odoric traveled extensively in India, China, and Southeast Asia, and related what he saw or was told with occasional embellishment. In turn, Mandeville took Odoric's account and enhanced it even further. Other material was borrowed from the great encyclopedia of Vincent of Beauvais and from Marco Polo's account of his travels.

It is not certain what the author of the *Travels of Sir John Mandeville* meant to accomplish. Obviously, the author knew he was writing a fictional account, and it seems likely that some of his contemporaries also recognized the book's fictional nature. *Travels* was so often bound together with books from which the author extensively borrowed that it is difficult to believe that many late-medieval readers missed the connection. Some scholars, such as Josephine W. Bennett, consider the *Travels of Sir John Mandeville* a travel romance. Others disagree, because other so-called travel romances made no effort to pass themselves off as factual accounts. Donald R. Howard suggests that the author of Mandeville's *Travels* followed the tradition of the encyclopedists, condensing his material into a fictional and entertaining travel narrative rather than as a dry work of reference. Mary B. Campbell, in contrast, sees the *Travels of Sir John Mandeville* as a major step in the development of the genre of the novel. No one had written realistic fiction in prose for centuries—since the time of Lucian of Samosata (ca. A.D. 115–200) and his *True History*. Medieval romances never made any attempt at realism, but the *Travels of Sir John Mandeville*, like a modern novel, did. For several centuries, *Travels* was so successful that many people came to consider it a largely true account. Christopher Columbus, Martin Frobisher, Sir Walter Raleigh, and Gerard Mercator were all influenced in their geographical thinking by Mandeville. It is ironic that the single most significant travel narrative of the Middle Ages was a work of fiction.

See also
Fountain of Youth; Marvels of the East; Monstrous Races; Paradise, Terrestrial; Polo, Marco; Prester John and His Kingdom.

For further reading
Josephine Waters Bennett, *The Rediscovery of Sir John Mandeville*, 1954; Mary B. Campbell, *The Witness and the Other World*, 1988; Donald R. Howard, "The World of Mandeville's Travels," *Yearbook of English Studies* 1 (1971): 1–17; Malcolm Letts, *Sir John Mandeville*, 1949; C. W. R. D. Moseley, ed. and trans., *The Travels of Sir John Mandeville*, 1983.

MANSA MUSA, PILGRIMAGE AND LEGEND OF
This great king of Mali made a pilgrimage to Mecca in 1324 that greatly enhanced Mali's reputation in North Africa and Europe. He became a symbol for the highly profitable trans-Saharan gold trade.

Mansa Musa ruled the empire of Mali for 25 years, from 1307/1312 to 1332/1337 (scholars disagree about the beginning and terminal dates of his reign). Mansa is the Mandingo word for king, and his reign marked the height of Mali's power and wealth. Like his immediate predecessors, Mansa Musa was a good Muslim, and like earlier kings—Mansa Uli (r. 1255–1270) and Sakura (r. 1285–1300)—he made the great pilgrimage to Mecca, the hajj. It is a gauge of Mansa Musa's power that he was able to go on a hajj. From Mali, such a journey took well over a year to complete and would have been extremely expensive.

Before he left for Mecca, Mansa Musa collected a special contribution from his subjects to help pay for his pilgrimage. The pilgrimage caravan was enormous and included 60,000 porters and 500 slaves, each carrying a gold staff weighing three kilograms. Some 80 to 100 camels were each loaded with 300 pounds of gold dust. It was even said, probably with considerable exaggeration, that the pilgrimage caravan was so huge that its van reached Timbuktu before the king left the royal palace at Niani, some 500 miles away. However, the records indicate that Mansa Musa followed the caravan route from Walata to Tuat, which means he would not have passed through Timbuktu. The caravan's itinerary after Tuat is unclear, but it likely continued by way of Wargla, and after reaching the Mediterranean Sea followed the coastline into Egypt and its capital of Cairo.

Mansa Musa's huge caravan amazed and impressed the sophisticated population of Cairo, but they were even more dazzled by the massive amounts of gold the Malians possessed. During their three-month stopover, Mansa Musa and his entourage expended vast amounts of gold on presents, alms, and living expenses—more than they should have, because the Cairene merchants mercilessly took advantage of the Malians' naïveté and grossly overcharged their guests for everything. So much Malian gold poured into the Cairene economy that it caused the value of gold to sag significantly. When the Muslim historian al-Umari (d. 1349) visited Cairo 12 years later, the price of gold still had not recovered. Mansa Musa's golden cornucopia was not inexhaustible, and it had almost run out by the time he returned to Cairo. Ironically, he was forced to borrow at exorbitant interest rates from the very Cairene merchants who had overcharged him in the first place.

Mansa Musa's pilgrimage left a deep and lasting impression on the Egyptians. The coy Mansa Musa quickly proclaimed to the Cairenes that his purpose for travel was purely religious, not political. Thus, he attempted to beg off having an audience with the Mamluk sultan. Canny Egyptian diplomats quickly recognized that his real reason for avoiding an audience was to forgo prostrating himself before another monarch. Pressured into attending a royal audience, after initial hesitation, the wily Mansa Musa agreed to bow down, but declared he was only making obeisance to God. After that tricky episode, relations between the Mamluk sultan and Mansa Musa were quite cordial. The early-sixteenth-century Muslim historian Ibn al-Iyas (d. 1524) referred to Mansa Musa's visit to Cairo as the outstanding event of 1324. According to oral tradition, Mansa Musa left a legacy of his piety by purchasing land and buildings in Cairo and Mecca to provide accommodation for future pilgrims from the Sudan. His pilgrimage also gave Mali an international reputation that grew to legendary proportions.

For Europeans, Mansa Musa quickly came to symbolize the golden riches of Guinea. In 1339, Angelino Dulcert, the Majorcan cartographer, placed a regal Mansa Musa on his map of Africa in the middle of the western Sahara with the caption "Rex Melly." A similar depiction appeared on Abraham Cresque's Catalan atlas of about 1375. On that map, Mansa Musa appeared seated, dressed in royal robes and crown, and holding a scepter in one hand and a gold nugget in the other. The accompanying legend reads "This negro lord is called Musa Mali, Lord of the Negroes of Guinea. So abundant is the gold which is found in his country that he is the richest and most noble king in all the land." Some people even identified Mansa Musa with the legendary Prester John. Unfortunately, from an African point of view, as the empire of Mali declined, so did Mansa Musa's reputation among the Europeans. When the Portuguese first contacted Mali in the 1450s, the kingdom was a faint shadow of its former greatness. As a result, the Mansa Musa depicted on the maps of the 1480s was a parody of European royalty—a naked savage with a crown, sporting a large sexual organ. Still, the fabulous reputation of Mansa Musa and his wealthy realm certainly aroused European interest and helped spur the Portuguese explorations of the West African coast under Prince Henry the Navigator during the fifteenth century.

See also

Guinea; Hajj; Mecca; Pilgrimage.

For further reading

J. F. A. Ajayi and Michael Crowder, eds., *History of West Africa*, vol. 1, 1971; Edward William Bovill, *The Golden Trade of the Moors*, 1968; J. D. Fage and Roland Oliver, eds., *The Cambridge History of Africa*, vol. 3: *From c. 1050–c. 1600*, 1977; Felipe Fernández-Armesto, ed., *The Times Atlas of World Exploration*, 1991; N. Levtzion and J. F. P. Hopkins, eds., *Corpus of Early Arabic Sources for West African History*, 1981; D. T. Naine, ed., *Africa from the Twelfth to the Sixteenth Century*, 1984.

MANTICORE   Also called manticora, this monstrous, man-lion creature supposedly lived in India and comprised one of the many so-called Marvels of the East.

In his *Natural History*, Pliny the Elder (23–79) took his description of the manticore from Ctesias's account of India. The manticore had the face of a man and the body of a lion, but with the fearsome additions of a triple row of sharp teeth and a stinging tail like a scorpion. Its voice combined the sounds of panpipes and trumpets. Manticores particularly enjoyed eating humans, and were quite fleet. Some scholars speculate that the legend of the manticore evolved out of garbled reports about cheetahs. Despite the manticores' human faces, ancient and medieval writers considered them animals rather than a monstrous race of humans. Thanks to their appearance in Pliny's *Natural History*, manticores became a standard feature of medieval descriptions of the Marvels of the East. Various medieval writers, such as Rudolf of Hohen-Ems (ca. 1200–ca. 1255), mentioned them in their works, and the world map in the Hereford Cathedral (ca. 1285–1300) included an illustration of a manticore along with other wonders of India. Needless to say, no medieval European traveling in India ever saw one, but for centuries they believed that such man-eating monsters existed.

For further reading
Pliny the Elder, *Natural History*, 1991; John Kirtland Wright, *The Geographical Lore of the Time of the Crusades*, 1925.

MAPPAMUNDI

Pl. mappaemundi; based on the Latin words *mappa*, meaning "napkin," and *mundus*, meaning "world." During the Middle Ages, the term mappamundi could refer to any map of the world. Modern scholars limit their usage of the term to those maps using a symbolic or schematic presentation of geography as a means to instruct the faithful in a Christian view of history and the world.

Some 1,000 mappaemundi from the fifth through the fifteenth centuries A.D. survive. Almost 90 percent are illustrations in books. The remaining mappaemundi are separate charts or maps, among the most famous of which is located at Hereford Cathedral in England.

Mappaemundi depict many different types of information and contain much symbolism. Patterns of the number four are repeated over and over—winds, rivers of Paradise, climates, and corners of the earth. The Ebstorf mappamundi shows the earth as the body of Christ. Other symbols emphasize the correspondence between Noah's three sons and the three known continents—Shem and Asia, Ham and Africa, and Japheth and Europe. Marvels and wonders also appear liberally on many mappaemundi, including the stock features of monstrous animals, monstrous races of people, Prester John, the Terrestrial Paradise, and the land of the imprisoned Gog and Magog. Mappaemundi are not merely works of symbol and fiction. Large amounts of accurate historical and geographical information frequently appear on them, sometimes added to the original mappaemundi as new geographical information became available in Europe.

The historian of cartography David Woodward established four basic categories for classifying mappaemundi: tripartite, zonal, quadripartite, and transitional. Tripartite mappaemundi show the world as the three continents of Africa, Asia, and Europe surrounded by the River Ocean. The three continents are separated from one another by the Don River, the Nile River, and the Mediterranean Sea. Generally, these mappaemundi are oriented to the east rather than

A map of the world from a twelfth-century manuscript in the Library of Turin.

the north like modern maps. Some tripartite maps are schematic, that is, they are presented as geometrical forms based on the shapes of a T being placed inside an O. Hence, these schematic maps are known as T-O maps. Other tripartite maps are nonschematic in that they arrange the three continents in a T-O pattern but also attempt to depict accurate historical and geographical information. Both the famous Hereford and Ebstorf mappaemundi are nonschematic tripartite maps.

Zonal mappaemundi divide the earth into five or seven zones of climate: an uninhabited northern frigid zone, one or two inhabited northern temperate zones, an uninhabited torrid zone along the equator, one or two possibly inhabited southern temperate zones, and an uninhabited southern frigid zone. Zonal maps are always oriented to the north. Purely zonal maps are very schematic in their presentation.

Quadripartite mappaemundi combine features of both tripartite and zonal maps. They depict climate zones and the three known continents, sometimes in a T-O configuration. They add a fourth unknown landmass in the Southern

Hemisphere, sometimes labeled the antipodes and occasionally called the antichthones.

Finally, the transitional mappaemundi of the fourteenth and fifteenth centuries mark a shift from depictions of symbolism and religious cosmography toward truly accurate geographical representations. Transitional mappaemundi center on a reasonably accurate map of the Mediterranean Sea/Black Sea basin, but as they move away from that center, they become vaguer, more inaccurate, and more symbolic. The influences of portolan charts are evident in the accurate presentation of the greater Mediterranean region. In some transitional mappaemundi, the influence of Claudius Ptolemy's recently discovered *Geography* is also quite apparent, particularly when the error of depicting the Indian Ocean as a landlocked sea appears. The Catalan Atlas, the controversial Vinland Map, and the world map of Paulo Pozzo Toscanelli are examples of the transitional type. From the late fifteenth century, mappaemundi faded out of use as they were replaced by world maps portraying geographical knowledge in the most accurate way possible.

Medieval mappaemundi were not intended as guides for navigation and travel. Instead, they presented the world and its history so as to help believers understand Christian cosmography. In this role they deeply influenced the geographical and ethnographical expectations of medieval merchants and pilgrims as they traveled to other lands. The vast majority of mappaemundi depict the earth as spherical even though the mappaemundi are drawn on a flat, two-dimensional surface. Medieval scholars produced the mappaemundi, and belief in a spherical earth was almost universal among them.

See also

Africa; Antichthones; Asia; Europe; Gog and Magog; Mediterranean Sea; Nile River; Paradise, Terrestrial; Prester John and His Kingdom; Zonal Theory.

For further reading

Charles Raymond Beazley, *The Dawn of Modern Geography*, 3 vols. [1897–1906], reprint, 1942; David Woodward, "Medieval Mappaemundi," in *The History of Cartography*, vol. 1: *Cartography in Prehistoric, Ancient, and Medieval Europe and the Mediterranean*, 1987; John Kirtland Wright, *The Geographical Lore of the Time of the Crusades*, 1925.

MARKLAND   Meaning forestland or woodland in Norse, Norse explorers of North America gave this name to the flat wooded land south of Helluland. The Vinland Sagas describe the sailing time from Helluland to Markland as two or three days. Scholars generally identify Markland as southern Labrador, although the nineteenth-century Danish scholar Carl Rafn and his followers, such as Hjalmar Holland, thought Nova Scotia was Markland. The *Greenlanders' Saga* says that Markland was the second land sighted by Bjarni Herjolfsson when he was lost on his way to Greenland. During his explorations, Leif Ericsson named the land after its many trees. According to *Eirik's Saga,* Thorfinn Karlsefni gave the heavily wooded country its name of Markland. Archaeological evidence indicates that Norse Greenlanders frequently traveled to Markland. They traded with the various Native American tribes living in Labrador such as the Beothuk, Point Revenge Indians, Montagnais, and Naskaupi, along with Dorset culture Eskimos. Given the scarcity of wood in Greenland and the proximity of Labrador's forests, such a pattern of trade would have been sensible and fulfilled a real need. Markland's existence and Norse contacts with it made little impact on European geographical concepts outside the northern countries.

See also
Greenland; Helluland; Vinland.

MARVELS OF THE EAST

Also known as the Wonders of the East or Wonders of India, this phrase refers to a concept prevalent among Western peoples during ancient, medieval, and early-modern times that the lands of India and East Asia were full of strange and astonishing peoples, plants, animals, places, and things.

Ancient Greeks visiting India originated the idea that it was a land filled with marvels. Ctesias (Ktesias) of Cnidos (fl. 405–398 B.C.), a physician to the Persian king Artaxerxes II, wrote a description of India based on secondhand accounts by other travelers that were filled with tales of monstrous races, strange animals, exotic plants, and fabulous riches. A more accurate firsthand account was produced by Megasthenes (ca. 350–290 B.C.), who traveled to India in 302 B.C. as an ambassador to the court of Chandragupta, ruler of the Mauryan Empire. His book, called *Indica,* also included tales of strange humans, weird beasts, and other marvels. Such stories are not so surprising; India is a vast land full of peoples, plants, and animals very different from those of other places. Brahmans, yogis, cobras, elephants, tigers, banyan trees, and baobab trees must have appeared quite strange or marvelous to foreign visitors.

Pliny the Elder (A.D. 23–79) took his information from Ctesias and Megasthenes or other sources dependent on them, and specifically portrayed India and the East as a region of wonders in his encyclopedic *Natural History.* As he told his readers, "India and regions of Ethiopia are especially full of wonders." By this he meant that plants and animals grew to be particularly large in those lands. He also cataloged the various monstrous races living in those regions. Pliny's *Natural History* survived the collapse of the Roman Empire and exercised a deep influence on the thinking of medieval scholars. In contrast, other Roman geographers such as Strabo (b. ca. 64 B.C.) and Claudius Ptolemy (fl. second century A.D.) were highly skeptical about the existence of such Marvels of the East. However, their writings were either lost or less available to medieval scholars, with the result that they were not as popular or influential as Pliny.

Although the ancient Greeks and Romans had only a confused and sensationalistic knowledge of India, they knew far less, if anything at all, about the existence of China, and therefore the Marvels of the East did not include it until Europeans of the Middle Ages realized that China existed. The ancient Greeks and Romans, along with their medieval successors in western Europe, were not alone in believing in the Marvels of the East. The tales of Buzurg ibn Shahriyar of Ramhormuz and Sindbad the Sailor contain medieval Islamic accounts of similar Eastern wonders. Medieval European chroniclers and encyclopedists repeated Pliny's stories about the Marvels of the East, so they remained a common component of geographical thinking.

The popular Romances of Alexander the Great, Rudolph of Hohen-Ems's *Weltchronik,* Vincent of Beauvais's *Speculum,* and many other writings contain tales of monstrous races, fantastic treasures, and all the other elements that made up the Marvels of the East. They also gave the existence of the Marvels of the East a Christian explanation. According to William of Auvergne, who wrote in the early thirteenth century, Europe lacked marvels and wonders because it was Christian (the demons responsible for such phenomena no longer operated there). In heathen lands like India, however, demons still worked their magic, and monsters, magic gems, and strange plants proliferated. By the time of the Crusades in the eleventh century, Europeans knew that China and other Far Eastern lands existed, and they became new repositories for the Marvels of the East. The rise of the legend of Prester John's kingdom and the appearance of the *Letter of Prester John* in 1165 added further embellishments to the existing components of the Marvels of the East. The *Letter* relates that the realm of Prester John included the Terrestrial Paradise and a Fountain of Youth in Ceylon.

Europeans who visited the Far East were often disappointed by the absence of expected marvels—not that they did not observe many strange and amazing things. The medieval travelers William of Rubruck, John Piano de Carpini, and Marco Polo all looked for monstrous races and other marvels. The fictional traveler Sir John Mandeville claimed to have seen all the Marvels of the East including the Terrestrial Paradise. Unfortunately, Mandeville was not a real person and never made any such journey, but Europeans of the fourteenth and fifteenth centuries believed that he had. This work of fiction was more widely read and influential in the late-medieval period than the travel books describing actual journeys.

The European belief in the Marvels of the East profoundly influenced the expectations of the explorers of the Age of Discovery during the late fifteenth and sixteenth centuries. Christopher Columbus believed in the Marvels of the East, and looked for them in the islands and lands that he visited in the course of his four voyages. He believed that the Island of Women or Amazons lay close to Hispaniola, and on his third voyage he claimed to have just missed finding the Terrestrial Paradise. Columbus was not alone in such misconceptions. The Fountain of Youth provided one of the objectives of Ponce de León's voyages. Early Spanish explorers of the Americas inquired about monstrous races in the same manner as William of Rubruck and Marco Polo in Asia and, like William and Marco, they were largely disappointed. The supposedly cannibalistic Caribs filled in for the monstrous race of the anthrophagi, but there is considerable doubt as to how much man-eating, if any, the Caribs did. As Europeans explored more of Asia and the Americas, belief in the Marvels of the East faded in the face of geographic reality. Of course, to Asians the West was just as exotic as the East was to Europeans. The late-medieval emissaries to the Mongol khan's court were surprised when Chinese scholars queried them about any monstrous races living in Europe. Still, the East remains an exotic and mysterious place in the minds of Westerners, and may always retain that image because it contains so many things that might be considered marvels or wonders.

See also

Alexander the Great, Romances of; Fountain of Youth; *Mandeville, Travels of Sir John;* Mongol Missions; Monstrous Races; Paradise, Terrestrial; Pliny the Elder; Polo, Marco; Prester John and His Kingdom; Sindbad, The Seven Voyages of.

For further reading

Valerie I. J. Flint, *The Imaginative Landscape of Christopher Columbus,* 1992; Pliny the Elder, *Natural History,* 1991; Lynn Thorndike, A *History of Magic and Experimental Science,* vol. 2, 1923; Rudolf Wittkower, "Marvels of the East," *Journal of the Warburg and Courtauld Institutes* 5 (1942): 159–197.

MECCA

Sometimes spelled Makka. Holy city located in the west-central portion of the Arabian peninsula, it is the spiritual capital and most important pilgrimage center in the Islamic world. Mecca and its companion city, Medina, are collectively known to Muslims as *al-Haramain,* Arabic for "the two holy places."

Mecca is located in a dry, barren region between two ranges of hills. It sits astride important north-south caravan routes used since ancient times. Initially, Mecca and its region were poor, but the development of the camel as an efficient instrument of cavalry warfare in the desert allowed the city to dominate the caravan routes from A.D. 500 on, and prosperity followed. Mecca also served as an important religious and pilgrimage center for pagan Arabs even before the rise of Islam.

When Muhammad (570–632) began to preach his new religion, the elite of Mecca were hostile. Faced with intensifying persecution, Muhammad and his followers moved to neighboring Medina in 622, an event known to Muslims as hejira (from *hijra,* meaning "emigration" or "flight" in Arabic). In Medina, Muhammad and his followers founded the first Islamic community, and ever since, Muslims consider hejira to be year one of their dating system (A.H. = *Anno Hegirae*). Conflict quickly developed between Mecca and Medina, eventually resulting in the capture of Mecca in 630 and triumph for Muhammad and his teachings. Once he conquered Mecca, Muhammad made it the spiritual center of Islam and the site for the most important of Islamic pilgrimages, the hajj.

A crowd of Muslim pilgrims in the inner courtyard of the great mosque, Mecca, 1889.

The center of religious life at Mecca is the Kaaba, a pre-Islamic square temple also known as the "house of Allah." This is the point toward which devout Muslims pray five times a day. The sacred Black Stone, a meteorite fragment, is also located in the Kaaba, and Zamzam is the sacred well of Mecca. Both places are surrounded by the great mosque al-Masjid al-Haram. The first caliphs of the Umayyad dynasty (661–750) worked hard to improve the water supply and accommodations at Mecca. Revenues generated by the pilgrims of the hajj became the foundation of its economy, and Mecca developed into an international center of Islamic culture and scholarship as well. Recognizing their important position in the Islamic world, Meccans frequently took advantage of visiting pilgrims by gouging them with high prices and subjecting them to rude behavior. The Spanish Muslim traveler Ibn Jubayr bitterly commented on such behavior in an account of his visit to Mecca in 1183–1184.

Mecca was not always a place of safe religious observations. The Umayyads and early Abbasid caliphs (dynasty r. 750–1285) maintained their control over Mecca and preserved law and order in the region. During the eighth and ninth centuries, Shiite followers of the martyred leader Ali increasingly attacked caravans of pilgrims. By the tenth century, local Alid rulers known as sharifs had taken over. Over the centuries, the sharifs were sometimes dominated by other great Islamic powers such as the Fatimids and Mamluks of Egypt and the Ottoman Turks. The Arabs of the Arabian peninsula gained their independence from the Ottoman Turks during World War I (1914–1918), which led to the foundation of the nation of Saudi Arabia.

Because Mecca is a holy city of Islam, non-Muslims are forbidden to visit it. Despite that prohibition, various European Christians managed to sneak into the sacred city and bring back vivid reports. The German Johann Schiltberger (1380–1440?) visited Mecca as a captive servant of a Timurid prince sometime after 1405. Pedro de Covilha (1460?–1526?) visited Mecca disguised as an Arab while scouting the spice trade of the Indian Ocean for the king of Portugal during 1487–1492. In 1503, the Italian Ludovico di Varthema (1465?–1517) visited Mecca in the guise of a Muslim soldier and became the first European to publish an account of his experiences. In 1814, John Ludwig Burckhardt (1784–1817), a Swiss scientific traveler, also visited Mecca in disguise, as did the famous adventurer Sir Richard Burton (1821–1890) in 1853. The famous Victorian traveler Charles Montagu Doughty (1843–1926) visited Mecca during his journey through the Arabian Desert in 1876–1878, although he made little effort to conceal that he was an English Christian. All these travelers' accounts of Mecca were popular with readers over the years.

For close to 1,500 years, Mecca has served as the spiritual center of the Islamic world. Millions have made the hajj to Mecca, and the practice continues unabated in the twentieth century. To this day, however, Mecca remains a place where non-Muslims are not welcome.

See also

Caravans; Hajj; Pilgrimage.

For further reading

Sir Richard F. Burton, *Personal Narrative of a Pilgrimage to Al-Madinah and Meccah*, 1893; F. E. Peters, *Mecca*, 1994.

Mediterranean Sea

Inland sea surrounded by Europe to the north, Asia to the west, and Africa to the south. Its area is approximately 970,000 square miles, and it is 2,400 miles long from east to west. The Mediterranean Sea's geographic position made it the body of water most significantly affecting the course of Western civilization from prehistory to at least A.D. 1600. Because it is almost completely enclosed by land, the Mediterranean Sea is virtually unaffected by tides. Its relatively deep and warm waters provide mediocre fishing grounds compared to other seas, and they are more saline. The sirocco winds blow across it from the south, and the mistral and bora winds come from the north. Storms sweep across it frequently, but they are comparatively mild. Islands are generously sprinkled across the Mediterranean: the Balearics, Corsica, Sardinia, Sicily, Malta, Crete, Cyprus, and the various Aegean and Adriatic islands. The Mediterranean Sea is also subdivided into several smaller regional seas: the Adriatic, Aegean, Tyrrhenian, Ionian, and Ligurian. From ancient times to the present, its geographic location makes it an important maritime highway of travel and commerce. It connects with the Atlantic in the west through the Strait of Gibraltar, also known as the Pillars of Hercules; in the east, the straits of the Dardanelles and the Bosporus lead to the Black Sea.

The ancient Near Eastern peoples used the word *yam*, which also referred to the sea god, for the Mediterranean Sea. Some variation of the word worked its way into the Egyptian language. It was also known as the "Western Sea" (as opposed to the "Eastern Sea," the Indian Ocean) or the "Great Sea." Greeks and Romans referred to it as "our sea," the Latin being *Mare Nostrum*. They did not use the name Mediterranean, which derives from *medius terra*, meaning "midland." The polymath Isidore of Seville (ca. 600–636) first used the name Mediterranean in his writings, and succeeding medieval scholars adopted his usage.

People ventured onto the waters of the Mediterranean Sea at the dawn of human history. The Cretans became the first great seafarers, from 3500 to 1100 B.C. The Phoenicians followed, and established colonies at various points around the rim of the Mediterranean during 1100–700 B.C. They were joined by the Greeks, who colonized actively around the Mediterranean from 734 to 580 B.C. The Phoenician colony of Carthage developed into a great commercial power in the western Mediterranean. From 264 to 146 B.C., Rome and Carthage engaged in three wars for dominance of the region. After a titanic and close-fought struggle, Rome emerged the victor. Roman domination of the Mediterranean lasted for centuries, the sea forming the hub of their empire.

When the Roman Empire disintegrated in the fourth and fifth centuries, the Mediterranean became a disputed area among the Byzantines, Vandals, Arabs, Normans, and others. Even the the Vikings make an occasional bloody appearance. Trade languished, but about 1000, maritime commerce revived with the emergence of the maritime merchants of Amalfi, Venice, and Genoa. Trade flourished once more on the Mediterranean from 1000 to 1600, except for brief disruptions due to war.

The European expansion into the Atlantic Ocean and down the West African coast during the fifteenth century culminated in Christopher Columbus's voyage of 1492 to the Americas and Vasco da Gama's voyage of 1497 to India. The focus of the European economy began a slow but inexorable shift to the Atlantic Ocean. However, the Mediterranean did not lapse into insignificance; it remained an important highway of commerce, a status that was partially restored by the building of the Suez Canal in 1869.

The Mediterranean Sea and its coastlines present humanity with a mild, sunny environment, and travelers have found it a pleasant and relaxing place to visit for centuries. Many romantics like George Gordon Lord Byron (1788–1824) wrote eloquently, even erotically, about their experiences. Even today, the allure of the Mediterranean beckons to modern tourists.

See also

Bosporus; Cathay; Cretans; Dardanelles; Phoenicians.

For further reading

Sarah Areson, *The Encircled Sea*, 1990; Fernand Braudel, *The Mediterranean and the Mediterranean World in the Age of Philip II*, 1972; Michael Grant, *The Ancient Mediterranean*, 1969; Ellen Churchill Semple, *The Geography of the Mediterranean Region*, 1931.

MERMAIDS AND MERMEN
These humanlike dwellers of the sea were sometimes thought to aid seafarers and travelers, while at other times they brought destruction.

Traditional belief held that plants and animals of the land had their counterparts among the plants and animals of the sea. Therefore, cows on land were paralleled by sea cows. By the same logic, mermaids and mermen were the sea's version of humanity. Most commonly, mermaids and mermen were pictured as having the head and upper torso of a human and the lower body of a fish. Some accounts, however, describe them as fish with the ability to change into human form and venture onto land. Folktales about merpeople frequently stress that, unlike humans, the sea dwellers did not possess souls.

In one common variety of folktale, a mermaid or merman is trapped on land or in the net of a fisherman. A human frees the captive, who then returns to the sea. Later, the human travels on the sea and either falls overboard or his ship founders in a storm. The grateful mermaid or merman appears to rescue the hapless human.

Another variety of folktale shows the merpeople in a negative or hostile light. In these stories a mermaid or merman lures a seafarer or a ship to destruction. Lovely mermaids supposedly lured lonely sailors into the water, where they drowned. Other mermaids and mermen treacherously guided ships onto hazardous rocks or called up deadly tempests.

Stories of merpeople are universal among peoples dwelling by the sea, and belief in them persisted into the eighteenth and nineteenth centuries. The sixteenth-century bishop and historian Olaus Magnus (1490–1557) reported sightings of mermaids and mermen in Norway and Denmark. Bishop Erik Pontoppidan (1698–1764) of Norway repeated similar stories in the eighteenth century. Modern scholars suggest that tales of mermaids and mermen were seafarers' encounters with unfamiliar sea mammals such as walruses, but a prodigious amount of time at sea would be required for a sailor's eyes to transform an ungainly walrus into a beautiful mermaid. Such travelers' and sailors' tales were highly prone to embellishment and exaggeration, which certainly seems to be the case with the considerable lore associated with mermaids and mermen.

See also

Sea Monsters; Sirens.

For further reading

Angelo S. Rappoport, *Superstitions of Sailors*, 1928.

MIDACRITUS (FL. AFTER 600 B.C.–BEFORE 500 B.C.)
According to Pliny, Midacritus was the first Greek merchant to trade in "white lead" (tin). Most scholars believe that Pliny's statement should be taken to mean that Midacritus was the first Greek merchant to travel to the so-called Tin-Lands of Brittany or Cornwall, where the metal was mined. If so, Midacritus may have been the first Greek to visit the British Isles, thus beginning the long process of incorporating them into Western civilization.

For further reading
M. Cary and E. H. Warmington, *The Ancient Explorers*, 1963.

MISSISSIPPI RIVER   Its name comes from a Native American word appropriately meaning "father of waters," and it is the largest of the North American
rivers. The Mississippi River itself is 2,348 miles long, and its flow is joined by
the Missouri and Ohio Rivers and numerous lesser tributaries. During the early
nineteenth century it became an important commercial waterway, and has remained so ever since.

The first European to sight the Mississippi was the Spaniard Hernando de
Soto in 1541, but Spain made no effort to follow up on his discovery. Two French-
men, Louis Joliet and Father Jacques Marquette, brought the Mississippi into
the geographical consciousness of European settlers in North America. In 1673,
they entered the Mississippi from the Wisconsin River and canoed down it as
far as the Arkansas River. They were followed by Robert Cavelier, sieur de La
Salle, who in 1682 traveled from the Illinois River down to the mouth of the
Mississippi on the Gulf of Mexico. He claimed the vast territory that he had
traversed for France and named it Louisiana. The French made efforts to colonize Louisiana and set up trading with the Native Americans for furs. New
Orleans was founded in 1718, and St. Louis in 1764.

The French defeat in the Seven Years War resulted in the Treaty of Paris of
1763 giving the land on the eastern side of the Mississippi to Great Britain and
that on the western side to Spain. In 1784, Spain closed the Mississippi to
American traffic, which they were able to do because they controlled the mouth
of the river. A series of diplomatic negotiations led to Spain reopening the river
to Americans in 1795. American commerce floated down the Mississippi in an
ever-increasing volume. Canoes and pirogues filled with beaver pelts were joined
first by flatboats and then by keelboats loaded with the agricultural products of
the Ohio Valley and bound for New Orleans. Steamboats joined these craft in
1811 and eventually took over most of the carrying and passenger trade. By
1860, more than 1,000 steamboats operated on the Mississippi.

Navigation could be tricky. Sandbars and snags could badly damage a steamboat or cause it to sink. New obstructions appeared frequently as the river
changed its course, threw up a new sandbar, or developed a new snag of floating
tree trunks. Riverboat pilots needed prodigious memories and alert minds that
could read the signs of the river, and learning the craft of pilotage took years.
Although the vagaries of the Missouri River were even more complex, becoming a river pilot on the Mississippi was the dream and ambition of many young
American boys during the middle decades of the nineteenth century. Mark
Twain wrote eloquently about this aspect of American life in his *Life on the
Mississippi* (1883). At its height, the steamboat age was personified by palatial
riverboats that were floating grand hotels boasting luxurious suites, magnifi-
cent ballrooms, elegant restaurants, saloons, and gambling casinos.

Competition from the railroads ended the great age of steamboats on
the Mississippi River. Even before the Civil War, railroads attracted cargo and

passengers away from the steamboats, but the war caused such a massive disruption of river traffic that even more people and goods shifted to using the railroads. The steamboat industry revived for about 20 years after the Civil War, but by the 1880s the railroads had won. Bulk products sill travel the Mississippi in great barges, but the glorious days of the steamboats are gone. Now, only a few excursion boats still operate so that Americans can nostalgically experience what a journey on the great Mississippi River might have been like.

See also

Erie Canal; Flatboats; Keelboats; Missouri River; Natchez Trace; Railroads; Steamboats, River.

For further reading

Julius Chambers, *The Mississippi River,* 1910; Louis C. Hunter, *Steamboats on the Western Rivers,* 1949; Timothy Severin, *Explorers of the Mississippi,* 1967; Mark Twain, *Life on the Mississippi,* 1883.

Missouri River

Missouri River   Great river that cuts across the northern plains region of the United States. Because of the large amount of sediment carried in its waters, the Missouri has been nicknamed the "Big Muddy." It is the longest river in the United States at 2,466 miles in length. Beginning at Three Forks in the mountains of Montana, the Missouri winds its way through the plains until it disgorges into the Mississippi River about ten miles north of St. Louis. Riverboat pilots consider the Missouri the world's most difficult river to navigate because of its flooding, the amount of large and hazardous debris it carries, and its constantly changing riverbed.

In 1673, Father Jacques Marquette and Louis Joliet were the first Europeans to reach the mouth of the Missouri River. Other expeditions followed; the Europeans thought that the Missouri might lead them to a passage to the Pacific Ocean and from there to the riches of the Orient. In this way, exploration of the Missouri formed part of the centuries-long quest for a northwest passage to Asia. The Missouri's beaver-rich environment also attracted fur traders. In 1804–1805, Meriwether Lewis and William Clark explored the entire length of the Missouri River from its mouth to its source.

Vast resources were located in the lands adjacent to the Missouri River and its tributaries. Initially, the abundance of beaver attracted fur traders, but later the gold and silver of Montana drew prospectors and mining companies. Settlers swarmed in to farm the rich soils of the Missouri River basin.

By 1780, French fur traders established posts along the Missouri River. Manuel Lisa of St. Louis got the fur trade operating at full speed. Early in 1807, he and his party headed up the Missouri in two keelboats, encouraged by reports from the newly returned Lewis and Clark expedition. Many people thought it was impossible for keelboats to operate in the swift currents of the Missouri, but Lisa proved them wrong. Other fur traders quickly followed his lead with their own fleets of keelboats.

The first steamboat to operate on the Missouri River appeared in 1819. It was named the *Independence* and made it as far as Old Chariton, Missouri. Early steamboats generally lacked the power needed to overcome the strong currents of the Missouri, and they drew too much water to operate through its numerous shallows and sandbars. The many floating logs and tree trunks also posed a serious hazard to the relatively flimsy steamboats. Gashes ripped in the bottoms of steamboats resulted in many sinkings. Still, in 1831, the steamboat *Yellowstone* gained the upper reaches of the Missouri.

Improvements and innovations in steamboat design let them operate with increasing success on the Missouri River. Unlike their counterparts on the Mississippi River, the steamboats of the Missouri were smaller and lighter, and the great majority were stern-wheelers. Only drawing 20 inches of water, they could make their way through shallows that stopped most other vessels. Sinkings and explosions of engines, however, remained all too common. In 1852, the steamboat *Saluda* blew up near Lexington, Missouri, killing about 200 crew and passengers. Such dangers did not deter travelers and shippers; the alternative in that region during the middle of the nineteenth century—land transportation—was far worse.

The appearance of railroads in the Missouri River valley greatly reduced the importance of the steamboats and the river. In 1859, the Hannibal and St. Joseph Railroad began operating, and others soon followed. Still, only when the first trains reached Fort Benton, Montana, in 1887 did steamboats give way completely to the railroads. Until then, the Missouri River had been an important highway for goods and travelers in the upper plains of the West, a route that many fur traders, miners, settlers, and soldiers came to know well and depend on heavily.

See also
> Flatboats; Keelboats; Mississippi River; Northwest Passage; St. Louis; Steamboats, River.

For further reading
> Phil E. Chappell, "A History of the Missouri River," *Transactions of the Kansas State History Society*, vol. 9, 1905–1906; Paul O'Neil, *The Rivermen*, 1975.

MONGOL MISSIONS
Name for a series of diplomatic and missionary journeys by western European friars into the domains of the Mongol khans during the mid-thirteenth through the mid-fourteenth centuries.

Prior to the eruption of the conquering Mongol armies in the early thirteenth century, medieval European knowledge of Asia was virtually confined to the Middle East and India. Genghiz Khan (1167?–1227) consolidated his control over the various nomadic tribes of Mongolia, and began his great series of conquests in 1218. First, he crushed the Kara Khitai Empire, and then smashed the powerful Khwarazmian Empire of central Asia during 1219–1221. After the defeat of the shah of Khwarazm, the Mongol general Subedai raided through the Caucasus and the Crimean region, bringing devastation to its steppe tribes. Genghiz also made forays against the Chin Empire of northern China, but had not subdued it at his death in 1227.

Genghiz's successors continued his conquests. By 1234, the Chin Empire fell. One of Genghiz's grandsons, Batu, led an expedition against Russia and eastern Europe between 1237 and 1242. The result was the brutal conquest of the Russian principalities and decisive defeats of a combined German-Polish army at Liegnitz and the crack Hungarian army at Mohi in 1241. Only the death of the Great Khan Ogadai brought the carnage to an end. Mongol forces withdrew to the east to determine the succession.

An 1826 pen-and-ink drawing of the Emperor Kublai Khan commanding a battle fought between Peking and Siberia.

The Mongol armies never returned to complete the conquest of Europe, although they contemplated it. Meanwhile, the papacy and various European rulers were panic-stricken by the Mongol threat. Some viewed the Mongol conquests as a sign that the world was ending, and that the Mongols were the dreaded Gog and Magog of the Apocalypse. Medieval Europeans knew the Mongols as Tartars. The name derived from the neighboring tribe of Mongols known as the Tatars, which transformed into the more ominous Tartar, a clear reference to Tartarus, or Hell. Other Europeans argued that the Mongols were subjects of Prester John, the great but mythic Christian ruler of central Asia, and as such were potential allies in the Europeans' wars against Islam. Europeans desperately needed accurate information about Mongol intentions and wanted to open up diplomatic relations, thus forming the impetus for the Mongol missions.

On Easter 1245, Pope Innocent IV sent the Franciscan friars John of Plano Carpini (1180–1252) and Laurentius of Portugal as envoys to the Mongol khan. Laurentius never made it, but the 65-year-old portly John reached the great Mongol camp in time to witness the election of Guyuk as Great Khan. Utilizing the Mongol post-horse system called *Yams*, Carpini traveled across central Asia on horseback. In two and a half years he traveled over 15,000 miles, a taxing ordeal. As Carpini put it:

> We feared we might be killed by the Tartars or other people, or imprisoned for life, or afflicted with hunger, thirst, cold, heat, injuries and exceeding great trials almost beyond our powers of endurance—all of which, with the exception of death and imprisonment for life, fell to our lot in various ways in a much greater degree than we had conceived beforehand.

Carpini returned to the pope in November 1247, his mission having accomplished little diplomatically. His account of his journey, titled *History of the Mongols,* provided much valuable information and was the first European description of Mongolia and China.

At this time, King Louis IX (r. 1236–1270) of France, an avid Crusader, became particularly anxious to make an alliance with the Mongols against the forces of Islam. In 1247, he sent the Dominican friar Ascelinus of Lombardy to the camp of the Mongol general Baiju on the Caspian Sea. Ascelinus proved to be a poor diplomat. Arrogantly refusing to follow Mongol customs, he almost got himself and his companions executed by the enraged Mongols. Louis IX tried again in 1249, sending another party to the Mongol court under the leadership of Andrew of Longemeau. They brought a gift, a portable Christian chapel in the form of a red Mongol tent. Reaching the Mongol general Eljigideai, they were soon sent on to the Regent Oghul Ghaimish at Lake Balkash. Oghul Ghaimish considered their gift a submission to Mongol domination and gave them no promises of an alliance. Andrew of Longemeau returned empty-handed to Louis IX in 1241.

The mission of William of Rubruck (1215?–1295?) swiftly followed that of Andrew of Longemeau. Rubruck ostensibly traveled to the Mongol capital of Karakorum as a missionary, but he was also to report to Louis IX. Departing from Constantinople on 7 May 1253, Rubruck reached the camp of Batu and was sent on to the Great Khan Mongke at Karakorum. Even using the *Yam* system of post-horses, the trip took three and a half months, and was a bitter experience during the winter. Arriving on 3 January 1254, William of Rubruck met with the Great Khan and succeeded in arousing some Mongol interest in an alliance despite working through a drunken, incompetent interpreter. Meanwhile, in 1253, Hulegu, Mongke's brother, had begun a savage conquest of Islamic lands in Persia, Mesopotamia, and Syria. These Mongol attacks destroyed Baghdad and the Abbasid caliphate in 1258 and even threatened the existence of Islam—a Christian Crusader's dream.

William of Rubruck began his return journey in July 1254, reaching the Crusader outpost of Tripoli on 15 August 1255. Like Carpini, Rubruck wrote an account of his journey, and his was both longer and more accurate. Rubruck was a much better observer than Carpini, noting geographic and ethnographic details with precision. His account revealed the existence of large numbers of Nestorian Christians in the Mongol lands. He also looked for monstrous races and Prester John; failing to find them, he expressed skepticism about their existence. Unlike Carpini's account, Rubruck's narrative was largely forgotten until its rediscovery by Richard Hakluyt in the latter part of the sixteenth century.

Other Christian missionaries traveled to the Mongol courts and the Far East. John of Monte Corvino (d. ca. 1328/1330), a Franciscan, set out for Asia in 1289 as an envoy of Pope Nicholas IX to the Ilkhan Argun in Persia and Kublai Khan in China. Reaching Peking, he established mission churches there and in other Chinese cities. Although the churches showed some potential for growth, lack of continuing support from the West at crucial stages caused them to ultimately wither away.

Another Franciscan missionary, Odoric of Pordenone (1286?–1331), in 1322 took the southern route to China by traveling to the Persian Gulf and taking a ship to India. After staying in India for a time, he sailed on to China. Odoric worked in Peking for three years, returning to Europe in 1330. He dictated an account of his travels and died a few months later in 1331. His detailed account of Asia contained considerable amounts of both fact and fancy, and was later used as a principal source for the descriptions in the fictional travels of Sir John Mandeville.

John of Marignolli traveled to Peking in 1338 with the papal gift of a gigantic warhorse for the Great Khan. Reaching Peking in 1342, he stayed until 1347 and returned to Avignon in 1353 to write an account of his travels. In the meantime, Mongol rule over China had been replaced by the native Ming dynasty, and Westerners were no longer welcome. The Mongol missions were finished.

The clerical missionaries and diplomats of the Mongol missions never achieved the fame of their contemporary, Marco Polo. William of Rubruck, the best observer of the lot, was the least well known to posterity. At the same time, the information about Asia that they brought back to Europe made its way into various encyclopedic works of history and geography such as Vincent of

Beauvais's (ca. 1190–1264) widely read *Speculum Historiale*. Because Europeans lost contact with the Far East when the Ming dynasty ousted the Mongols from China, European knowledge of China remained static and increasingly obsolete. Columbus and other European explorers expected to reach the Cathay of the Mongol missions, Marco Polo, and Kublai Khan—not the China of the Mings in the sixteenth century.

See also

Cathay; Gog and Magog; Karakorum; *Mandeville, Travels of Sir John*; Polo, Marco; Prester John and His Kingdom; Tartarus; Tartary.

For further reading

Christopher Dawson, ed., *Mission to Asia*, 1966; Robert Marshall, The *Storm from the East*, 1993; J. R. S. Phillips, *The Medieval Expansion of Europe*, 1988; Igor de Rachewiltz, *Papal Envoys to the Great Khans*, 1971.

MONSOONS   A system of seasonal winds in the Arabian Sea, Indian Ocean, and western Pacific Ocean that blows steadily in one direction for half a year and in the opposite direction for the other half of the year. They exerted a paramount influence on the patterns of trade over those seas during the age of sailing ships.

The term monsoon derives from the Arabic word *mausim*, meaning "fixed season." During the summer in the Northern Hemisphere, the vast Eurasian landmass heats up and creates a great low-pressure area. This condition pulls the intertropical convergence zone far to the north. As a consequence, the southwest monsoon prevails over the south Asian coastal areas and the Arabian Sea, Indian Ocean, and parts of the western Pacific. During the months of April through October, the wind blows steadily to the northeast, bringing moist air and rain to southern Asia. During the winter, the Eurasian landmass cools and a high-pressure area establishes itself. The winds reverse their direction and become the northeast monsoon. Blowing steadily to the southeast from November through March, they carry dry, cool air. These patterns are of great significance to anyone traveling in a sailing ship. The summer monsoons make it quite easy to sail eastward, but almost impossible to sail westward. The reverse is the case during the winter months.

Natives of the littoral of the western Pacific and Indian Oceans were quite familiar with the patterns of the monsoons and adapted their sailing schedules to them. Outsiders from regions of more variable winds were astounded by the regularity of the monsoons, and sometimes had a difficult time learning to use them effectively. The first Westerner to master the monsoons was the Greek Hippalus. After carefully observing the winds and currents of the Arabian Sea and gathering the geographical reports of others, Hippalus reached the correct conclusion that India was a large peninsula that extended far south into the ocean. He reasoned that a sailing ship could utilize the monsoons to sail back and forth across the high seas of the Indian Ocean to establish direct seaborne trade with India. Early in the reign of the Roman emperor Tiberius (r. A.D. 14–37), Hippalus successfully tested his theory. A flourishing trade quickly developed using the monsoons.

The decline of the Roman Empire led to the disappearance of Westerners from the Indian Ocean trade. The trade itself, however, continued to thrive, its masters the Arab seafarers of the ilk of Sindbad. Late-medieval Europeans might not have liked Islam's domination of that trade, but could do little about it. The region became shrouded in mystery, with only the occasional report of someone like Marco Polo making its way to the West to shed some brief light. Polo described the East Asian monsoons and the Chinese trade with the Spice Islands in this way:

> It takes them [the Chinese] a whole year for the voyage [to the Spice Islands], going in the winter and returning in summer. For in that Sea [the China Sea] there are but two winds that blow, the one that carries them outward and the other that brings them homeward; and one of these winds blows all the winter, and the other all summer.

When the Portuguese approached the culmination of their efforts to develop a sea route to India, they recognized the need for accurate intelligence about sailing conditions in the Indian Ocean. King João II sent Pedro da Covilhão (1460?–1526?) to reconnoiter the lands of the Indian Ocean, beginning in 1487. During the course of his travels, Covilhão became the unwilling guest of the king of Ethiopia, and it is unclear whether any of his scouting reports reached Portugal. During his voyage to India, Vasco da Gama acquired the services of an Arab pilot of Malindi to guide his fleet across the Indian Ocean to Calicut in 1498. The voyage started on 24 April and lasted 23 days, taking full advantage of the monsoons. Once da Gama reached Calicut, his rude, pugnacious behavior alienated both the Arab merchants and the Hindu ruler of Calicut. Da Gama virtually had to shoot his way out of Calicut by the end of August, and immediately sailed back to Africa. The voyage was a nightmare. During September and October, the monsoons blew in the wrong direction to make such a voyage. Not until they reversed in November did the ship make rapid westward progress. By the time the arduous voyage finished in Malindi, 30 crewmen had died. As da Gama and his men learned to their sorrow, to ignore the pattern of the monsoons was a deadly mistake. European sailors who followed da Gama quickly learned from his and others' hard-won experiences. Soon, superior European naval artillery and ship design allowed the Portuguese, and later the Dutch and English, to become the masters of the Indian Ocean, the China Sea, and the monsoons.

See also

Indian Ocean; Polo, Marco.

For further reading

M. Cary and E. H. Warmington, *The Ancient Explorers*, 1963; Sanjay Subrahmanyan, *The Career and Legend of Vasco da Gama*, 1997; Henry Yule and Henri Cordier, eds., *The Travels of Marco Polo*, 1929.

MONSTROUS RACES

From the era of classical Greece to the seventeenth century, people of the Mediterranean world and Europe believed in the existence of various monstrous races of humans. This belief was a major aspect of the geographical concept known as the Marvels of the East, although some of the monstrous races dwelt in Africa or the far north.

Monstrous races can be organized into two broad categories. The first contains those peoples who practiced customs that were odd or repellent according to Western standards of behavior. Anthrophagi, people who engaged in cannibalism; Amazons, women who lived in a society without men; the Bragmanni, a group of Indian wise men; Gymnosophists, people who stood on one leg and contemplated the sun; or Garamantes, an Ethiopian race who did not practice marriage, while all quite human in their appearance, were practitioners of strange customs. Still, they were regularly included in the ranks of the monstrous races.

The second category consisted of those people who were physically deformed. Cynocephali, dog-headed people; Blemmyae, people with faces in their chests and no heads; and sciapods, also known as unipeds or monocoli, who hopped around on a single great foot were common examples of physically monstrous races. There were many others; John Block Friedman in his *Monstrous Races in Medieval Art and Thought* (1981) lists 40 different monstrous races, and mentions a number of additional monstrous races at other places in his study. Of the 40 monstrous races, 24 were physically deformed, and therefore visually distinct from normal humans. The remaining 16 races either practiced some alien custom, like giving their wives to visitors, or possessed some heightened sense such as keen sight, but were otherwise physically indistinguishable from normal humans.

The Greeks of the Homeric Age (ca. 700 B.C.) believed in the existence of monstrous humans. Odysseus encountered the savage Cyclopes, the giant and equally savage Laestragonians, and the lethargic Lotus-Eaters in the course of his wanderings. Belief in these monstrous races merged with the cadre of monstrous races that formed a part of the travelers' legends and lore associated with the Marvels of the East or the Wonders of India. This spurious or exaggerated body of pseudoknowledge first became popular during the early fourth century B.C. A Greek named Ctesias of Cnidos became the royal physician to the Persian king Artaxerxes in 405 B.C. After some years of service, he returned to Greece and wrote a history of Persia that included some descriptions of neighboring India and its wonders and monsters. At that time, the peoples of the Mediterranean thought that India was the easternmost land on the earth; they had no awareness of China or the rest of East Asia. About a century later, in 302 B.C., another Greek named Megasthenes traveled to India as the Seleucid king's ambassador to the court of Chandragupta, the ruler of the Mauryan Empire. Megasthenes lived in India for ten years and wrote his *Indica*, which is a description of the region.

The *Indica* was the first book written by a Greek about India that was based on personal observations. Megasthenes, however, included considerable material about southern India that was based on hearsay and secondhand accounts. These descriptions included the various monstrous races. Although the writings of Ctesias and Megasthenes survive only as fragments, they formed the foundation for the persistent Western belief in monstrous races. During the first century A.D., Pliny the Elder repeated their descriptions of monstrous humans in his widely read *Natural History*, although he was skeptical. The later Roman geographer Gaius Julius Solinus, who wrote his *Collectanea Rerum Memorabilium* shortly after A.D. 200, credulously repeated Pliny's material on the monstrous races. St. Augustine of Hippo (354–430) accepted the existence of monstrous races and discussed them in his enduringly influential *City of God*. After the fall of the Western Roman Empire, various medieval encyclopedists compiled collections of geographical and cosmographical lore, using Pliny and Solinus as the main sources of information on India and the Far East, including their accounts of the monstrous races. Martianus Capella (fl. fifth century), Isidore of Seville (fl. 602–636), Rudolf of Hohen-Ems (ca. 1200–ca. 1255), Vincent of Beauvais (ca. 1190–1264), and William of Auvergne (ca. 1180–1249) were among the many medieval writers who provided descriptions of the various monstrous races. Medieval Arabs also shared the belief in the existence of monstrous races. The medieval Romances of Alexander the Great were full of encounters between their hero and monstrous races, and the fictional Sir John Mandeville titillated his readers from the late fourteenth century onward with detailed descriptions of monstrous races. Accounts of monstrous races continued to appear in geographical and historical compilations such as the *Imago Mundi* of Pierre d'Ailly (1350–1420) and the *Historia Rerum Ubique Gestarum* of Aeneas Silvius Piccolomini (1405–1464). Christopher Columbus read those two works, and they profoundly colored his expectations about what he would find by sailing west across the Atlantic Ocean to Asia. Since Columbus believed that the islands he reached in 1492 were part of Asia, he was continually on the lookout for monstrous races and Marvels of the East. His Caribs, or cannibals, were equivalent to the dreaded anthrophagi (man-eaters) of traditional monster lore.

Some medieval writers were so enamored of the monstrous races that they made up new ones by separating or recombining the various deformities associated with the existing monsters and adding the new monsters to their accounts. Other monstrous races appear to be the creation of scribal errors. For example, in working with a handwritten manuscript, it was extremely easy for the word monocoli (one-legged) to become monoculi (one-eyed).

The widespread belief in monstrous races is a prime example of the ethnocentricity of the ancient Greeks and Romans and the peoples of medieval Europe. Strange diets were considered monstrous, and these ranged from loathsome cannibalism to the more benign dog milking or apple sniffing. Foreign languages could sound like bestial utterances to the uninitiated, and a lack of any speech at all was positively monstrous. Living in the wild was also considered monstrous, particularly by the Greeks, with their assumption that their beloved *polis*, or city-state, was the only way for truly civilized people to live. As a result, many of the monstrous races were depicted as living in small groups or in a solitary manner like beasts without clothing and carrying primitive clubs as weapons. Some monstrous races, however, lived in cities of evil. During Sindbad

"An African Monster." Woodcut from Thevet's La cosmographie universelle, *Paris, 1575.*

the Sailor's seventh voyage, for example, he dwelt unknowingly in a city of winged devils for a number of years. The belief in the existence of monstrous races seems to have filled a psychological need for escapism and the macabre that sometimes feeds into peoples' fear of the unknown.

Monstrous races also had some foundation in reality, as did the Marvels of the East. Things truly were different in Asia and Africa, and some of those differences could be quite astonishing and even deeply disturbing to Western travelers. Unconfirmed reports of cannibalism abounded through the centuries, making it almost impossible for the custom not to exist. Africa has real Pygmies, a so-called monstrous race. Some scholars speculate that the extremely tall Watusi tribe of Africa may have inspired the reports of giants. Other tribes created man-made deformities. Those who stretched their lips with plates may have given rise to tales of a big-lipped people called the Amyctyrae. The source for the accounts of the big-eared monstrous race of the Pandae or the Panotii could have been tribes who stretched their earlobes to extraordinary lengths. Apes and monkeys have always fascinated people by their physical similarities to humans. Ancient peoples who encountered primates for the first time were understandably confused about whether to classify them as animal or human. Apes and monkeys were obvious inspirations for the various hairy monstrous races such as the Gorgades. The dog-headed Cynocephali were another prominent monstrous race that probably originated from an encounter between humans and apes, baboons, or monkeys. The distinctly unmonstrous race of wise men known as the Bragmanni obviously derived their existence from the actual Brahmans of India, while the sun-gazing Gymnosophists were probably Parsees or Zoroastrians. Stories about the single-footed sciapods may have been inspired by the contortions of practitioners of yoga. So, monstrous races had some basis in factual and actual firsthand observation.

The ancient Greeks considered the monstrous races to be utterly different from themselves, but then they thought the same about any non-Greek or barbarian nation. The rise of Christianity created a more tolerant attitude toward the monstrous races as well as other foreigners. For Christians, the first question to be asked about the monstrous races was: Were they truly human? From this followed the questions: Did they possess souls and reason? Could they become Christians? In his *City of God*, the influential St. Augustine of Hippo answered these questions with a yes. And he was not alone. According to the medieval legends of the apostles Andrew and Bartholomew, they encountered a dog-headed people, or Cynocephali, who accepted Christianity during their missionary journeys in the East. Sts. Mathaeus and Mercurius had the same experience. Some versions of the legend of St. Christopher describe him as a Cynocephali who became human upon his conversion to Christianity. The twelfth-century *Letter of Prester John* claimed that the monstrous races living in the realm of that mysterious Christian potentate of Asia had already been converted to Christianity. Most medieval writers classified the monstrous races as human, although some, such as the thirteenth-century encyclopedist Thomas of Cantimpré, placed them in a midway position between humans and animals.

Once it was accepted that the monstrous races were human, their descent from Adam and Noah needed to be traced. The Bible taught that all humans descended from Adam and Noah. Were the monstrous races also descended from Adam and Noah? Again, following St. Augustine, the orthodox Christian answer to that question was yes. Some Christian writers went on to explain that the monstrous races were physically deformed because they were also descended from the great sinners of primeval history such as Cain, the first murderer, and Ham (or Cham), the mocker of his father Noah. According to some traditions, God inflicted physical deformities on both Cain and Ham for their sins. Cain supposedly grew horns after his murder of Abel, and in some Christian and Islamic traditions, Ham developed a black skin as punishment for the disrespect he showed to Noah. Furthermore, some medieval scholars, such as the chronicler Ranulf Higden (d. 1364), conflated Cain and Ham as persons, and therefore their accursed physical appearances. As a result, in medieval art and literature, Cain and Ham became closely associated with the monstrous races. To deny that the monstrous races were capable of conversion to Christianity and so to question their basic humanity was considered a serious heresy by the early-medieval church. In 748, Pope Zarchary I and Bishop Boniface of Mainz condemned the ideas of Virgil of Salzburg for his denial of the humanity of the monstrous races. Nevertheless, later writers like Peter of Auvergne (d. 1304) and Lambert of St. Omer (fl. ca. 1100) had doubts about their humanity.

Climate was another explanation given for the physical deformities of the monstrous races that was common among ancient Greeks and Roman writers, and during the Middle Ages, Christian scholars repeated it. Monstrous races lived at the extremes of the world—the frigid far north and the torrid south—in places uninhabitable to normal humans. Many people followed the Roman medical writer Galen (129–199) in believing that living in very cold or very hot climates produced deformities among humans. Pliny's *Natural History* is a catalog of monstrous races living in extreme environments. Tropical India's jungles and mountains positively brimmed with giants, Pygmies, satyrs, Cynocephali, unipeds with only one foot, Blemmyae with no head and a face on their chests, and mouthless Astomi, among other monstrous humans. The single-eyed Arimaspi lived in the cold north of Scythia, while the backward-footed Abarimon inhabited high Himalayan valleys, and the hermaphroditic Machlyes were located in the deserts of Africa. Later writers were even more prodigal about scattering monstrous races along what the medieval world considered the edges of the world. The Ebstorf mappamundi (ca. 1240) and the Hereford Cathedral mappamundi (ca. 1285–1300) are both generously decorated with unipeds, Cynocephali, and Blemmyae in Africa, the far north, and East Asia. Belief in the monstrous races was well accepted during ancient and medieval times.

Not everyone accepted the existence of the monstrous races without question. Skeptics existed from the very beginning, such as the Roman geographer Strabo (b. 64 B.C.), who rejected the existence of the Marvels of the East, including the monstrous races. So did the later geographer Claudius Ptolemy (fl. second century A.D.), but their writings did not have the same wide distribution and influence among medieval encyclopedists and geographers enjoyed by the more credulous Pliny the Elder and Solinus. Eventually, Plinian ideas about the monstrous races encountered renewed skepticism because medieval European travelers in Asia failed to encounter Astomi or monocoli or sciapods or any other deformed races of humans. The Franciscan friar William of Rubruck (1215?–1295?) journeyed to Karakorum, the court of the Mongol ruler Mangu Khan, in 1253–1255. At the Mongol court, William met some Chinese priests and he reported, "I asked them about the monsters, or human monstrosities, of which Isidore and Solinus speak. They told me they had never seen such, which astonished me greatly." Another Franciscan, John of Marignolli (fl. 1290–1335), also traveled extensively in Asia. While he readily testified to the existence of strange and amazing animals, customs, and plants, he rejected beliefs in monstrous races. At best, he considered such people to be isolated victims of birth defects. Marignolli's skepticism arose from his failure to sight a member of any deformed monstrous race, although he claimed to have seen a giant, hairy wild man. Some Asians even questioned the well-traveled Marignolli about the existence of monsters, having never seen any themselves.

As European travelers visited more and more of Asia in the fifteenth and sixteenth centuries, the homelands of the elusive monstrous races shifted first to Africa and then to the newly discovered Americas. Geographical writers such as Sebastian Munster (1489–1552) and André Thevet (1516/1517–1590/1592) were torn between their old beliefs and their new knowledge. For the time being, the belief in monstrous races won, but by the seventeenth century too much new and irrefutable knowledge had accumulated about the absence of any monstrous races, so that in 1663 the Oxford scholar John Spencer could deny without hesitation the existence of monstrous races in his book *A Discourse Concerning Prodigies*. The European explorations of the rest of the world ultimately revealed that no monstrous races existed anywhere. A rich body of travelers' legends had come to an end after a long and venerable career of some 2,000 years.

See also

Africa; Alexander the Great, Romances of; Amazons; Asia; Bragmanni; Cannibals; Cyclopes; Cynocephali; Gymnosophists; Karakorum; Lotus-Eaters, Land of; *Mandeville, Travels of Sir John*; Odysseus, Wanderings of; Pliny the Elder; Polo, Marco; Prester John and His Kingdom; St Christopher; Strabo.

For further reading

Valerie I. J. Flint, *The Imaginative Landscape of Christopher Columbus*, 1992; Valerie I. J. Flint, "Monsters and the Antipodes in the Early Middle Ages and the Enlightenment," *Viator* 15 (1984): 65–80; John Block Friedman, *The Monstrous Races in Medieval Art and Thought*, 1981; David Gordon White, *Myths of the Dog-Man*, 1991; Rudolph Wittkower, "Marvels of the East," *Journal of the Warburg and Courtauld Institutes* 5 (1942): 159–197.

MORMON TRAIL

Route used by Mormon emigrants from 1846 to 1868 to travel from the central Mississippi Valley to their settlements in the Great Salt Lake region. The Mormon Trail started at Winter Quarters near Kanesville, Iowa, and stretched across the prairie and the mountains for over 1,000 miles until it reached Salt Lake City. For much of its length, the Mormon Trail was synonymous with the Oregon Trail. The basic difference was that Mormon travelers largely kept to the north side of the Platte River, while emigrants bound for Oregon and California stayed south of the river. When they reached Fort Bridger, Mormons veered to the southwest toward Salt Lake City, and other settlers continued in a more westerly or northwesterly direction.

The Mormon refugees of 1846 did not discover the Mormon Trail. It was already well known and well traveled by traders and fur trappers. The first Mormon emigrants were refugees driven by persecution and despair. Survivors of the destruction of the great Mormon settlement at Nauvoo, Illinois, they headed west to found a new holy city in the wilderness. Under the leadership of Brigham Young, the Mormon party contemplated settling in California, but after reaching Fort Bridger in the early summer of 1847, they learned of potentially fertile lands in the Great Salt Lake Valley to the southwest. Another attraction for the Mormons was that these lands lay outside U.S. territory. The Mormon party changed destinations, and on 22 July the first of the band reached the valley. They were not disappointed. According to legend, when Brigham Young first sighted the valley, he authoritatively exclaimed, "This is the place." Contemporary records do not bear out this legend, and the story does not occur earlier than the fifteenth anniversary of the foundation of Salt Lake City.

The new settlement grew fairly quickly and served as an important way station for travelers using the Oregon Trail. Mormon settlers commonly supplied food and animals to passing wagon trains. They also ran profitable ferries and built bridges along the Platte and other rivers. Salt Lake City also served as a beacon for Mormon converts. From 1847 to 1868, about 47,000 people followed the Mormon Trail to Utah. Many of these wayfarers were English and Scandinavians who had been converted by Mormon missionaries. They sought to live in the new and prosperous Zion so tantalizingly described by their Mormon teachers. During 1856 to 1860, some groups were so poor that they pushed handcarts over the 1,300 miles from Iowa City to the Salt Lake Valley. These arduous treks across the wilderness of prairies and mountains were the very stuff of heroic Mormon traditions of many a family, the details often preserved in diaries or memoirs.

The Mormon Trail and the Mormons of Utah played a significant role in supporting overland travel across the western territories of the United States in the days before the completion of the transcontinental railroad.

See also
California Trail; Oregon Trail.
For further reading
Wallace Stegner, *The Gathering of Zion*, 1964; John D. Unruh, *The Plains Across*, 1979.

MOUNTAIN MEADOWS MASSACRE (1857)

Infamous massacre of the members of an American wagon train perpetrated by a combined band of Native Americans and Mormons on 11 September 1857.

Hollywood films have led the general public to believe that Native American attacks on wagon trains headed for California and Oregon were so common that practically every overland emigrant survived one or more. In fact, such attacks were quite rare. Furthermore, a significant number of attacks on emigrant trains were actually the work of white outlaws who disguised themselves as Native Americans. The Mountain Meadows Massacre, which has been called by one prominent historian "the greatest single tragedy of the overland trail," involved a combination of Native Americans and Mormons.

In 1857, a wagon train of 137 people from Missouri and Arkansas, led by Charles Fancher, made its way west, heading for California. The group passed through Salt Lake City in early August and were hurrying across the Sierra Nevada before the passes became blocked by snow. It was a volatile time to be passing through Utah; relations between the Mormon leadership and the U.S. government were at a low point. President James Buchanan was in the process of sending an army to Salt Lake City to reinforce the authority of the U.S. territorial governor, and resentment ran high among the Mormon population. Mormons were already smarting from the persecutions they had suffered at the hands of non-Mormons, or Gentiles, in Missouri and Illinois. A religious revival swept the Mormon community, further aggravating anti-Gentile feeling.

The Fancher party had thus picked a dangerous time to be passing through Mormon country. Worse, some of the emigrants behaved badly along the route. Word spread that they had sold poisoned beef to some native tribes and had fouled a tribal well. Confronted by a lack of hospitality from local Mormons, the emigrants responded by calling polygamous Mormon wives whores and by naming their oxen after Mormon leaders such as Brigham Young. Some of the Missourians claimed to have participated in the lynching of Joseph Smith, and even went so far as to say that they possessed the gun that killed him.

It was a tense situation. A large war party of Native Americans began to shadow the Fancher party. When the wagon train camped at a place called Mountain Meadows on 6 September, a force of 200 surrounded them. The Native Americans attacked the next day, but confined their efforts to sniping at the trapped emigrants. Meanwhile, a party of Mormon fanatics led by John D. Lee joined the Native Americans. Together, they decided that the Fancher party should be wiped out except for members too young to talk. This cruel action was to serve as a reprisal for all that Mormons had suffered at the hands of Gentiles.

Some of the Mormons approached the wagon train to persuade its members that if they surrendered and gave up their wagons, goods, and weapons to the Native Americans, they would be spared. Desperate to save themselves and their families, the men of the Fancher party agreed. Once they were rendered defenseless, both the Native Americans and the Mormons fell on the emigrants with knives, hatchets, and guns. When it was over, 120 people were dead, and only 17 young children remained alive from the entire wagon train.

The Mormon perpetrators hoped that their Native American accomplices would receive all the blame, but when that failed to happen, they shifted responsibility for the massacre to their leader, John D. Lee. Years passed before a detailed account of the incident appeared. Meanwhile, the Mountain Meadows Massacre added more fuel to a firestorm of rumor concerning Mormon bad behavior toward and crimes against emigrants traveling to California and Oregon. It also increased the generalized feeling of danger when traveling the overland trails. Most Mormons were in fact quite hospitable to emigrants, and the vast majority of emigrants never experienced attacks by Native Americans, Mormons, or outlaws.

See also

Oregon Trail; Wagon Trains.

For further reading

Juanita Brooks, *The Mountain Meadows Massacre*, 1950; Huston Horn, *The Pioneers*, 1974; John D. Unruh, *The Plains Across*, 1979.

MOUNTAINS OF THE MOON   Also known as the *Lunae Montes,* reports by ancient travelers and geographers claimed that these mysterious mountains were the source of the Nile River. Their name appears to come from the color of the snow that lies permanently on the tops of these tropical mountains. Nineteenth-century explorers strove hard to be the first to locate the legendary Mountains of the Moon.

The ancient geographer Martinus of Tyre reported about A.D. 50 that a Greek merchant named Diogenes had made a 25-day journey from around Zanzibar on the east coast of Africa into the interior. He observed how the waters from a huge range of snowy mountains fed into two great lakes and on into the Nile River. This information appeared on the world map of the great geographer Claudius Ptolemy around A.D. 150. From then on, for about 1,700 years, travelers thought that finding the Mountains of the Moon would also locate the elusive source of the Nile. James Bruce (1730–1794), the explorer of Ethiopia, mistakenly thought he had located the Mountains of the Moon in 1770. Sir Richard Burton (1821–1890) and John Hanning Speke (1827–1864) quarreled bitterly in 1858 and 1859 over the location of the Mountains of the Moon. Their true location would determine which of the two men got credit for discovering the source of the Nile. In 1864, Burton claimed that the snow-covered Mounts Kenya and Kilimanjaro were the actual Mountains of the Moon. He was wrong; the mountains of the Ruwenzori Range, west of Lake Victoria, are the real Mountains of the Moon, as later explorations proved. When the American Henry M. Stanley (1841–1904) visited them in 1888, he called them by their African name, Ruwenzori, meaning "rainmaker," and that is how they are known on modern maps. Many people still prefer to use the romantic and mysterious name Mountains of the Moon for these impressive peaks.

See also
    Nile River.
For further reading
    Bruce Brander, *The River Nile,* 1966; Alan Moorhead, *The White Nile,* 1960.

MOVING ISLANDS
See Flyaway Islands.

MULE   The mule is a hybrid, the offspring of a union between a male donkey and a female horse. It combines the best characteristics of both parents by having the size and strength of a horse and the donkey's endurance and ability to survive on poor fodder. Except in very rare cases, mules are sterile. The offspring of a male horse and a female donkey is called a hinny. Hinnies are smaller and weaker than mules, and therefore less favored.

Mules pulling a pioneer wagon. Pencil sketch by Emmanuel Leutze.

The origins of mule breeding are obscure. It appears that the ancient Mesopotamians began the practice of animal hybridization during the second millennium by breeding the then-rare domesticated donkey with the intractable onager, or Asian wild ass. This combination did not produce a particularly satisfactory offspring. Later, when horse-breeding nomads made contact with donkey-breeding peoples of the agricultural river valleys, the hybridization of the mule soon followed. The ancient Greeks believed that the inhabitants of Asia Minor bred the first mules.

Besides possessing both strength and endurance, mules are exceptionally sure-footed, which makes them exceptionally suitable as pack animals in mountainous or rugged terrain. They also walk with a gentler gait than horses or donkeys, and were commonly used to carry fragile loads; for the same reason, women favored mules for riding. Mules also made excellent pack and draft animals for military and mercantile purposes. Humans used them extensively for these purposes from the time of the Romans until the appearance of motorized vehicles in the early twentieth century.

If a female horse, known as a bell mare, led them, a mule team would pull its load even harder and faster. This predilection is thought to be connected to mules having a mare for a mother. Particularly famous in this respect were the great mule trains that plied the harsh desert of Death Valley, California. For much of human history, the mule has been a hard-working animal and a frequent provider of transportation for travelers.

See also
Donkey; Horse.
For further reading
Juliet Clutton-Brock, *Horse Power*, 1992; A. Dent, *Donkey*, 1972; Frederick E. Zeuner, *A History of Domesticated Animals*, 1963.

N

NATCHEZ TRACE   Important road that linked Natchez, Mississippi, with Nashville, Tennessee, and the Ohio River valley during the early national period of the United States.

The Natchez Trace ran over 500 miles through heavily forested country laced with rivers and swamps. Initially a series of tracks created by wild animals, the local Native American tribes of Choctaws and Chickasaws developed them into hunting trails. The Natchez Trace first appeared on a French map in 1733. The increasing movement of American settlers across the Appalachian Mountains into Tennessee, Kentucky, and the Ohio Valley during the last quarter of the eighteenth century made the trace an important route. Farmers in those areas, particularly after 1785, took their crops to market on keelboats and flatboats down the Ohio and Mississippi Rivers to New Orleans, but the strong river currents made a return journey by such cumbersome craft impractical. Instead, the boats were broken up for lumber and sold; their crews either walked or rode horses to get home. Their most direct route was the Natchez Trace, starting at Natchez and ending at Nashville.

The bulk of the traffic on the Natchez Trace moved northward since most of the travelers were riverboat crews returning home after a successful voyage. These travelers carried their newly earned wealth in the form of money or horses, which contributed to the Natchez Trace's unique reputation as a decadent as well as dangerous highway. The town of Natchez, at least the part known as Natchez-under-the-Hill, was a notorious conglomeration of gambling houses and brothels. Many an unwary or luckless riverman lost his earnings in that den of frontier iniquity.

The portable wealth of returning riverboat men also attracted robber gangs, some of whom were particularly brutal and murderous. Joseph Thompson Hare was originally destined for a life of tailoring but took up the occupation of highwayman instead. In comparison with most robbers operating on the Natchez Trace, Hare was quite literate, frequently compassionate toward his victims, and generally avoided murder if possible. Those traits, however, did not save him from the gallows. More bloodthirsty outlaws lurking along the Natchez Trace included Samuel Mason of Virginia and the brothers Wiley and Micajah Harpe. It was widely reported that they would kill hapless travelers and dispose of their victims' bodies by disemboweling them, filling the cavity with stones, and sinking them in a swamp. The Harpe brothers, in particular, appear to have been homicidal maniacs with little trace of human feeling, and their crimes included gruesomely murdering defenseless women and children. All three came to grisly ends. Authorities captured Micajah Harpe and executed him by beheading. The authorities offered a $2,000 reward for Mason, which proved to be too great a temptation for his brother Wiley. He killed his companion-in-crime simply for the reward money. Unfortunately for Wiley, someone recognized him as a wanted felon, and he was hanged for his many horrific crimes. Such men as these helped give the Natchez Trace a sordid reputation and the nickname of "the Devil's Backbone."

During its heyday, travelers along the Natchez Trace faced uncomfortable conditions. They frequently had to make camp under the stars and carry their own food. Gradually, way stations known as stands appeared, providing weary, hungry travelers with lodging and meals. These establishments were usually quite primitive. Forlorn travelers frequently faced crowded conditions, painful beds, and unpalatable food, all for high prices. By 1820, some 20 stands were in operation.

Although much of the Natchez Trace was a well-worn path, plenty of places offered opportunities for confused travelers to get lost. Wherever the path passed through swamps, quicksand and water moccasins were deadly threats. Fording the many rivers, particularly the massive Tennessee, was inconvenient at best and dangerous at worst. As a result, Chickasaw chief George Colbert ran a stand and a very lucrative ferry. The Natchez Trace was not for the timid, the impecunious, or the easily discouraged.

At its prime the Natchez Trace was the most important road in the Old Southwest, but the coming of the steamboat quickly ended its significance. After Robert Fulton successfully demonstrated his steamboat *Clermont* in 1807, the new invention quickly spread to the Mississippi River in 1811. Steamboats provided their passengers with greater safety and comfort, and traveled both up and downriver. As a result, the trace fell into disuse and became overgrown by the 1830s. In 1934, the U.S. government began a scenic parkway along its route, which in 1938 was officially named the Natchez Trace National Parkway. The National Park Service administers the parkway, which was close to completion in 1998.

See also

    Flatboats; Keelboats; Mississippi River; Robbers; Steamboats, River.

For further reading

    Jonathan Daniels, *The Devil's Backbone*, 1962; William C. Davis, *A Way through the Wilderness*, 1995.

NATIONAL ROAD

    Also known as the Cumberland Road, the National Turnpike, or the United States Road. Constructed during the first decades of the nineteenth century, it was the first national road, meaning that it

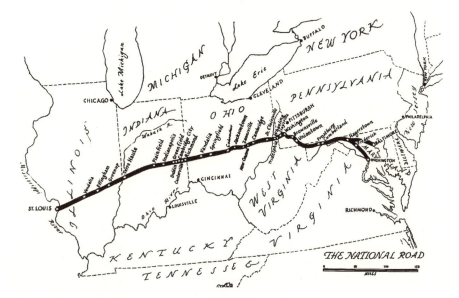

An undated map of the route the National Road followed.

was built with federal funds and for some years received federal monies for repairs and upkeep.

The National Road measured 591 miles from Cumberland, Maryland, to Vandalia, Illinois. Congress considered the National Road a means to aid the settlement and economic development of Ohio by providing a link between rivers on the eastern side of the Appalachians with Ohio's interior and the Ohio River. Financing for the road would come from a portion of the revenues generated by the sale of public lands in Ohio. Construction began in 1811, and by 1818 the U.S. Mail used the road between Cumberland, Maryland, and Wheeling, West Virginia. This section largely followed the route cut by General George Braddock's army in 1755. Congress appropriated monies in 1825 to extend the National Road from Wheeling to Zanesville, Ohio, following the path of the preexisting Zane's Trace. By 1833, the road reached Columbus, Ohio. Between 1831 and 1834, Congress turned over responsibility to the states of Maryland, Ohio, Pennsylvania, and Virginia. Additional monies were appropriated to extend the National Road through Indiana and Illinois, but Indiana did not complete its portion until 1850.

The National Road played an extremely important role in the economic development of Ohio, as it was heavily used by freight wagons. By the time the road was completed in Indiana and Illinois, other modes of transportation and communication—railroad, canals, and telegraph—had reduced its significance. The route of the National Road was later reactivated and modernized as U.S. Highway 40, an important early motorway.

For further reading

Philip D. Jordan, *The National Road*, 1948; *The National Road*, 1994; Karl Raitz, *The National Road*, 1996.

NEARCHUS, VOYAGE OF (326–324 B.C.)

At the end of his campaign in India, Alexander the Great (356–323 B.C.) ordered his general, Nearchus of Crete, to build a fleet and sail down the Indus River. After reaching the Indian Ocean, the fleet was to travel westward along the coast parallel to Alexander's main army and up the Persian Gulf. During his successful voyage, Nearchus kept careful records of coastline details and the habitability of the countryside. The historian Arrian (fl. A.D. 129) used Nearchus's account extensively in writing his own history of the campaigns of Alexander. As a result, Nearchus's expedition is the best-documented voyage of discovery from the ancient world.

Alexander the Great and many of his contemporaries held vague, erroneous ideas about the geography of India. Alexander apparently believed that India and Africa were connected, and that the Indus River was a tributary of the Nile, a widespread and persistent error among the ancient Greeks. An earlier voyage by Scylax in about 510 B.C. sailed down the Indus, along the Arabian coast, and up the Red Sea, thus proving that the Indus flowed into the sea and not the Nile. The results of Scylax's journey were recorded by Herodotus in his *Histories.* Nearchus's voyage confirmed Scylax's findings. Alexander planned to have Nearchus sail around the Arabian peninsula and up the Red Sea to Egypt, but his premature death and the ensuing succession struggles put a stop to further expeditions of that sort. Nearchus quickly faded from prominence after Alexander's death, although historians assume that he joined in the succession struggles of Alexander's generals.

In the twentieth century, amateur archaeologist Harold S. Gladwin suggested that Nearchus's fleet actually sailed east across the Pacific Ocean, populating Polynesia along the way and bringing higher civilization to the Americas. No convincing archaeological evidence exists to support his speculation. Nearchus's explorations represent one of the many stillborn opportunities for expanding the ancient world's geographic horizons.

See also
> India; Indian Ocean.

For further reading
> Arrian, *The Campaigns of Alexander,* 1971; Rhys Carpenter, *Beyond the Pillars of Heracles,* 1966.

NILE RIVER

The world's longest river, it measures 4,160 miles in length from the Luvironza River to the Mediterranean Sea, although from the falls at Lake Victoria it measures only 3,475 miles. As one of the world's most famous rivers, legends and true adventures of travel proliferated about it.

People through the ages have been fascinated by the Nile River, and with good reason. As Herodotus (383–420 B.C.) accurately remarked, "Egypt . . . is . . . the gift of the [Nile] river." By this famous phrase Herodotus meant that the Nile's waters and annual deposits of alluvial mud made possible Egypt's existence in the midst of the Sahara. Many ancients theorized that the Nile valley was originally a long, thin gulf of the Mediterranean Sea, which the Nile's annual floods gradually filled up with sediment.

Besides being a big river, the ancient peoples found the Nile unique and strange compared to other rivers. It flowed from south to north, whereas most rivers emptying into the Mediterranean basin, the Black Sea, and the Middle East flowed from north to south. The Nile's regular floods began at summer solstice and continued for about 100 days, whereas most rivers flooded in the winter. The deposits of new soil left behind made Egypt an agricultural cornucopia. Many theories abounded about the causes of the Nile's summer flooding. Some people claimed that contrary winds created it, while others suggested that the Nile's waters flowed from the encircling River Ocean. Melting snow from southern mountains was considered as another possible source. Herodotus even credited the sun's evaporation of the Nile's waters with causing its flooding. No one knew the true source of the floodwaters.

The mouth of the Nile consisted of the vast alluvial delta with its classic triangular shape. From ancient times until well into the seventeenth century, the delta of the Nile (so named because it resembled the Greek letter delta) was the only sedimentary deposit at a river's mouth called a delta, and it was truly unique. South of the delta, the Nile valley narrowed to the riverbed, with two thin strips of fertile land on either side. Beyond lay the inhospitable desert. In ancient times the Nile could be navigated only up to the first cataract at Aswân or Syene. Egypt proper stopped at the first cataract.

From the first cataract southward to just a bit short of Khartoum were five more cataracts. These were rapids rather than falls, and could be navigated, although with great difficulty. From the second cataract at Wadi Halfa to about Khartoum were the ancient lands of Cush and Nubia. The Nile also formed a

River Nile and the pyramids of Giza. Sepia photo by A. Beale, 1887.

curve called the Great Bend between Korosko and Abu Hamod, and in between lay the fabled Nubian city of Meroe. Travelers frequently cut across the Nubian Desert to save time rather than travel by water around the Great Bend. Between the fifth and sixth cataracts, the Atbara River joined the Nile. The Blue Nile, or Bahr al-Azrug, joined the White Nile, or Bahr al-Abyad, at Khartoum. The Blue Nile flowed out of Ethiopia, starting at Lake Tana. Monsoonal, early-summer rains in the mountains of Ethiopia caused the Blue Nile to flood, and in turn caused the greater Nile to flood to the north in Egypt. Over 300 miles south of Khartoum on the White Nile are the tangled marshlands of the Sudd. South of the Sudd, waters from the highlands of Uganda and Tanzania flow into the great Lake Victoria to feed the Nile.

For centuries no one knew the geography of the Nile River. For most of its history, Egypt ventured only intermittently beyond the first cataract. The eighteenth dynasty (1550–1295 B.C.) conquered lands as far south as the fourth cataract. Egyptian merchants traveled to the Blue Nile and up to its headwaters in Ethiopia. Farther south, they may have reached the river Bahr al-Ghazal at the beginning of the Sudd region along the White Nile.

The ancient Egyptians did not allow the Greeks to enter their land before Pharaoh Psammetichus's rule in 665 B.C. Once Egypt opened up, the Greeks frequently visited this ancient, mysterious land. Legend has it that the great Greek lawgiver Solon (fl. 594 B.C.) visited Egypt. Herodotus visited Egypt about 460 B.C., and devoted a large portion of his *Histories* to a description and history of the country. No Greek traveled beyond the first cataract until Democritus of Abdera (b. ca. 460 B.C.) made it to the fourth cataract. The Persian king Cambyses (r. 530–522 B.C.) conquered Egypt in 525 B.C. He also tried to conquer Nubia, but an ill-prepared attempt to cross the Nubian Desert at the Great Bend turned into a disaster.

Under the Ptolemaic dynasty (323–30 B.C.), exploration of the Nile reached the mouth of the Atbara River. Greeks regularly visited Meroe during the reign of Ptolemy II Philadelphus (283–246 B.C.). They also knew about the existence of the Blue and White Niles.

Exploration of the Nile continued after the Roman conquest in 30 B.C. During the reign of Emperor Claudius (A.D. 41–54), a merchant named Diogenes explored the coast of East Africa down to Dar es Salaam. While traveling inland, he gathered reports about various lakes and the Mountains of the Moon, which were supposed to be the source of the Nile's water. The geographer Claudius Ptolemy (fl. second century A.D.) used Diogenes's reports in his famous *Geography*. As a result, the fabled Mountains of the Moon came to be considered the source of the Nile and appeared on maps until 1834. Emperor Claudius's successor, Nero, contemplated conquering Nubia and adding it to the Roman Empire. As part of his preparations, he sent two centurions with an exploring expedition up the White Nile. They reached the Sudd region, which proved impenetrable. No European explorers visited that region again until 1839.

Hebrew and Christian traditions regarded the Nile as one of the Four Rivers of Paradise originating in the Garden of Eden. Paradise was believed to be located in the extreme east, a vast distance from the Nile's African location. Medieval people also believed, however, that the Four Rivers of Paradise flowed underground after leaving the Garden of Eden until they resurfaced at some faraway point. Therefore, the Nile's headwaters in Africa were wherever the river came back above ground. Vague reports about the existence of the Niger River caused some scholars to consider it the source of the Nile. Various medieval and early-modern maps show the Nile's upper course making a great westward turn into West Africa. Eventually, the late-eighteenth- and early-nineteenth-century travels of various European explorers such as Mungo Park (1771–1806) showed this theory of the Nile's origin to be incorrect.

During 1768–1773, James Bruce (1730–1794) explored the length of the Blue Nile and the surrounding lands of Ethiopia. He mistakenly thought he had found the source of the Nile. Between 1820 and 1842, Egyptian expeditions cut their way through the Sudd to as far south as Gondokoro, and the fever to find the true source of the Nile heated up. In 1857, Richard Burton (1821–1890) and John Hanning Speke (1827–1864) made their way into the African interior from Mombasa and Zanzibar. Separating at Tabora in 1858, Burton headed west to Lake Tanganyika, while Speke went north to find Lake Victoria. Both men claimed they had discovered the source of the Nile. Speke eventually proved right, but years of acrimonious controversy ensued. From 1860 to 1862, Speke, accompanied by James Grant, explored Lake Victoria, found the Ripon Falls, and proceeded down the Nile. Despite these discoveries, the issue of the Nile's source remained unresolved. In 1863–1864, Sir Samuel White Baker (1821–1893) explored Lake Alberta, but grossly overestimated its size. Burton's friend Alexander Findley (1812–1875) used Baker's mistake to argue that Burton or David Livingstone had discovered the Nile and not Speke. The moody Speke died in 1864 of a self-inflicted gunshot wound, either accidental or suicide. Eventually Speke's priority was vindicated, and the centuries-old mystery of the Nile's origins ended.

See also
Africa; Ethiopia; Herodotus; Mountains of the Moon; Paradise, Four Rivers of.

For further reading
M. Cary and E. H. Warmington, *The Ancient Explorers*, 1963; Sir Harry Johnston, *The Nile Quest*, 1903; Alan Moorehead, *The Blue Nile*, 1962; Alan Moorehead, *The White Nile*, 1960.

"NO PEACE BEYOND THE LINE"
Dramatic phrase referring to the supposed condition of perpetual war that existed between European ships sailing in non-European waters, particularly those in the Spanish seas of the Americas.

During the late fifteenth and sixteenth centuries, Spain and Portugal were anxious to protect their rich overseas empires in the Americas, Africa, and Asia from foreign interlopers. The Dutch, English, and French were equally determined to trade with or raid these wealthy colonies and trading posts. The issue was almost intractable, so much so that it bogged down negotiations between Spain and France for the Treaty of Cateau-Cambresis in 1559. Eventually, an oral agreement was reached in which there was to be no peace beyond certain vague "lines of amity," consisting of a meridian passing through or in the vicinity of the Azores, Canaries, and Cape Verde Islands and a parallel that might have been the Tropic of Cancer (23°30'N) or the parallel of Cape Bojador (26°N).

England found itself ignored in this agreement. Until then, it had been a reliable ally of Spain, but relations deteriorated under the reign of Elizabeth I (1558–1603) and ultimately resulted in war from 1588 to 1604. Spain wanted to keep the English out of the Americas, but after the foundation of the Jamestown colony in 1607, that was no longer possible. From 1568 onward, English ships were received coolly by Spanish colonial officials in the Gulf of Mexico and the Caribbean Sea. Coolness eventually degenerated into hostility and violence.

Many twentieth-century historians assume that English sailors started talking about the condition of "no peace beyond the line" during these Elizabethan years. In fact, the idea of a state of perpetual war existing in American waters did not appear until 1635. More references followed during the early years of Charles II's (1660–1685) reign, but the English government never accepted the idea of "no peace beyond the line" in its formulation of foreign policy. When they did talk about a line, they clearly meant the Tropic of Cancer. The first literary reference to the phrase occurs in Sir Walter Scott's *The Pirate* (1819) in chapter 21.

It has been suggested that English sailors of the sixteenth and seventeenth centuries may have picked up the phrase from French sailors operating in Spanish waters. Unlike the English, the French had a treaty that included an oral agreement of "no peace beyond the line." For English sailors and raiders, "no peace beyond the line" actually had little reality as a danger. It was apparently more a construct of nineteenth-century novelists like Charles Kingsley and G. A. Henty. Twentieth-century historians enthusiastically adopted the phrase when writing about the Age of Discovery and European overseas colonial rivalries in the early-modern era.

For further reading

Garrett Mattingly, "No Peace beyond the Line?" *Transactions of the Royal Historical Society* 13 (1963): 145–162.

NORSE VOYAGES The Norse or Vikings of Scandinavia were the greatest voyagers and travelers of early-medieval Europe. During the ninth to the eleventh centuries, their ships sailed to the ends of the Mediterranean Sea and across the Atlantic Ocean all the way to North America. Other Norse portaged across the rivers of Russia to reach the Black and Caspian Seas. Some even made their way into Mesopotamia.

Scandinavia afforded bleak prospects for farming, but the seas around it abounded with fish. Therefore, the early Norse turned to fishing, and from there developed into great seafarers. Overpopulation and the relative weakness of the rest of Europe encouraged the Norse to take up raiding and conquest to improve their fortunes. Their depredations began in 793 at the monastery of Lindisfarne in northern England. Various far-flung cities suffered attacks—Paris in 845, Pisa in 860, and Constantinople in 860, among others. At one time or another, Norse warriors conquered much of Ireland, northern England, Normandy, Kiev, and Novgorod. The name of Russia itself derives from the Finnish word *Rus*, meaning the Norse.

When the Norse raided along coastal waters, they traveled in sleek long ships with dragon prows, rows of shields, and banks of oars. For travel on the high seas, however, the Norse sailed in the deeper draft, more seaworthy sailing ships called *knorrs*. That is not to say that a long ship could not make an Atlantic crossing. A Scandinavian crew sailed a replica long ship to the World Columbian Exposition at Chicago in 1893.

The Norse were great navigators within the limits of their technology. They knew how to navigate by the sun, the North Star, and other celestial objects. Sundials and other simple instruments were used to estimate latitude. Norse sailors were also acute observers of natural phenomenon—wind patterns, currents, temperature and color of water, and behavior of sea and land birds—which also aided them in navigating.

Norse sailors made their way to Iceland in 860, then to Greenland between 900 and 930, and finally to North America, which they called Vinland, in 986. They established colonies, but only the settlement on Iceland proved to be permanent. After several abortive attempts to start a settlement in North America, hostile natives encouraged the Norse to give up. The Greenland settlement lasted from 986 to 1450, when the last Norse Greenlander died. The increasingly harsh climate, which kept them in virtual isolation from the rest of Europe, and the hostility of the encroaching Thule Eskimos helped bring about the settlement's demise.

By the eleventh century, the heroic days of Norse or Viking voyages and raids were past. Scandinavia converted to Christianity, and Scandinavian kings centralized these lands and brought law and order to them. Thanks to their daring seamanship and martial skills, the Norse will never be forgotten as the great travelers and intrepid warriors of the early Middle Ages.

See also
Greenland; Iceland; Vinland.

For further reading
Gwyn Jones, *A History of the Vikings*, 1985; Gwyn Jones, *The Norse Atlantic Saga*, 1986; Peter Sawyer, *The Oxford Illustrated History of the Vikings*, 1998.

NORTHEAST PASSAGE

Sea route between Europe and the Far East that consisted of sailing through the Arctic seas north of Europe and Asia. Interest in such a route began in the late fifteenth century, but no one successfully sailed the entire way from Europe to the Pacific Ocean until Baron Nils Nordenskjold in 1878–1879.

Late-medieval Europeans longed for better and cheaper access to Asian luxury goods. Just as the Portuguese contemplated the circumnavigation of Africa and Christopher Columbus pondered the possibility of sailing across the Atlantic, others considered that a sea route to China along the northern coasts of Europe and Asia was possible. Geographers of that time theorized that the seas of the North Pole might be free of ice in midsummer and therefore navigable. By the early decades of the sixteenth century, various unrecorded Norse and Russian seamen had investigated the Arctic waters.

The first documented voyage seeking a northeast passage to China was that of Sir Hugh Willoughby and Richard Chancellor in 1553–1554. Sebastian Cabot, the son of John Cabot, the discoverer of North America, organized the Willoughby/Chancellor expedition for the Merchant Adventurers, or Muscovy Company. Sailing from London in 1553, Willoughby and Chancellor separated in the Barents Sea. By 14 August 1553, Willoughby had discovered Novaya Zemlya; in mid-September, he reached 72°N. Pack ice forced him back to the Kola Peninsula, where he and his crew became trapped and died from the cold by January 1554. Chancellor experienced better luck and sailed into the White Sea, where he established a trading post for the Muscovy Company at Archangel. The enterprise was successful, and more English seamen tested the Arctic waters. In 1580, Arthur Pett led an expedition past Novaya Zemlya into the Kara Sea. Some unknown foreign merchants, possibly English, reached the Ob River in 1584, but hostile Samoyed tribesmen killed them.

The Dutch were also interested in discovering a northeast passage. Oliver Brunel of Enkhuizen took ships into the White Sea well before 1584. The most famous Dutch Arctic voyager was Willem Barents (ca. 1550–1597). He first sailed there as part of an expedition in 1594–1595. During that voyage he sailed a ship to the northern tip of Novaya Zemlya. Barents's qualities as a seaman ensured his inclusion on a subsequent expedition. Leaving the Netherlands in May 1596, the Dutch ships sailed a more westerly course and discovered the Spitsbergen Islands. Unable to penetrate the pack ice that lay beyond Spitsbergen, they headed for Novaya Zemlya. After Barents rounded its northernmost point, ice crushed his ship. He and his crew were forced to winter in a makeshift cabin, and suffered greatly from scurvy and cold. On 13 June 1597, the survivors put to sea in two open boats and headed for Holland. Barents died at sea seven days later, on 20 June. No one else attempted to round the northern end of Novaya Zemlya until 1871.

The London-based Muscovy Company's interest in a northeast passage continued despite the failure to locate a navigable route. In 1607 and 1608, they hired the famous Henry Hudson to locate it. During the first voyage, Hudson attempted to locate the supposedly ice-free waters around the North Pole that geographers postulated existed there in summer. Instead, he proved that a permanent ice pack covered the seas around the North Pole. In 1608, Hudson tried but failed to get past Novaya Zemlya. By that time the Muscovy Company concluded that no usable northeast passage existed.

Russian traders coasted along the Barents and Kara Seas during the early seventeenth century, but they were unable to penetrate past the pack ice clogging the waters around the Taimyr Peninsula. Wooden sailing ships did not have the power, durability, or maneuverability to sail safely through ice-strewn waters. In 1648, the Cossack Semën Dezhnëv discovered the Bering Strait, which leads from the Pacific Ocean into the Arctic waters. Dezhnëv's report lay buried and unknown in a Siberian archive until well after 1728, when Vitus Bering rediscovered the strait named in his honor. Bering also organized and oversaw the Great Northern Expedition of 1733–1742 for the Tsarist government. It thoroughly explored the northern coast of Siberia but found no usable northeast passage.

The first to negotiate the Northeast Passage was Baron Nils Nordenskjold of Sweden in 1878–1879. He used a steam-powered metal ship to make his way through the ice-congested waters. His success led to the development by 1900 of a profitable Arctic sea trade in Siberian goods using the Northeast Passage. After centuries of attempts by various would-be travelers to China, the Northeast Passage became a reality.

See also

Anian, Strait of; Atlantic Ocean; Circumnavigations of the Earth, Early; Northwest Passage; Pacific Ocean; Siberia.

For further reading

W. Bruce Lincoln, *The Conquest of a Continent*, 1994; Leslie Hilda Neatby, *Discovery in Russian and Siberian Waters*, 1973; Helen Orlob, *The Northeast Passage*, 1977.

NORTHWEST PASSAGE Geographical concept that a usable sea route existed through the Arctic waters off the northern coast of North America to the legendary Strait of Anian and on to China. This belief persisted during the sixteenth and early seventeenth centuries.

The discovery of the Americas in the 1490s revealed that a great land barrier existed between the Europeans and the riches of the Far East, so they mounted efforts to find a way around it. For many years the geographic extent of North America was underestimated. Thinking it was a large group of islands, early explorers sought a passage through it. Jealous of the Spanish and Portuguese discoveries, King Francis I of France employed the Italian Giovanni da Verrazano (1485?–1528?) to look for a way to China. During late 1524 and early 1525, he cruised the east coast of North America from South Carolina to Newfoundland. Although the mouth of the Hudson River appeared promising, he found no strait. Other Spanish explorers investigated the same coastline about the same time. Jacques Cartier (1491–1557), another explorer for France, sailed in 1534 and explored the Gulf of St. Lawrence and the tantalizing mouth of the St. Lawrence River. Returning in 1535, he explored up the St. Lawrence, hoping it led to China. It didn't, and he returned to France in 1536. A third expedition, which included Cartier, tried to establish a settlement along the St. Lawrence between 1541 and 1543. Then, French efforts waned to nothing.

The men of Elizabethan England next took up the challenge of finding the Northwest Passage. Sir Humphrey Gilbert (1539?–1583) argued for the existence of a northwest passage with his *Discourse of a Discoverie for a New Passage to Cataia,* which circulated around the English court in manuscript from 1566 until its publication in 1576. Martin Frobisher led the first English expedition to look for the Northwest Passage in 1576. It discovered Frobisher's Bay and returned to England with an Eskimo captive. Frobisher also returned with a load of fool's gold, which only whetted people's appetite for real riches. Investors formed the Cathay Company to find both real gold and the Northwest Passage. Making two more voyages in 1577 and 1578, Frobisher failed to achieve either goal, although he entered Hudson's Strait in 1578. The Cathay Company went bankrupt.

Undeterred, John Davis (1550?–1605), the inventor of the Davis Quadrant for calculating latitude, took up the challenge of finding the Northwest Passage. During his first voyage in 1585, he discovered the Davis Strait. His second voyage in 1586 accomplished little more, but his third voyage reached 72°N latitude on Greenland and explored the east coast of Baffin Island. In the 1590s, he tried to locate the Northwest Passage from the Pacific Ocean side by looking for the Strait of Anian. Again he failed.

In 1610, Henry Hudson (d. 1611) became the first to sail through Hudson's Strait and into Hudson's Bay. Forced to spend the winter at James Bay, his crew

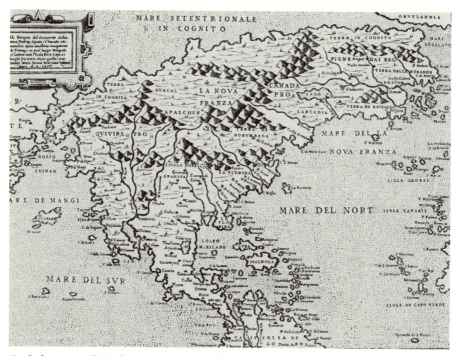

An Italian map of North America showing the location of the Northwest Passage, published in 1566.

mutinied and left him, his son, and seven others to die in the Arctic wastes. Another Englishmen, William Baffin (1584?–1622), conducted three Arctic expeditions in search of the Northwest Passage. In 1612 and 1613, he explored the opening of the Foxe Channel beyond Hudson's Bay, and in 1615 explored the western coast of Hudson's Bay. In 1616, Baffin explored Greenland, Baffin Bay, and Baffin Island. Reaching 78°N on Greenland, he sighted Lancaster Sound, which was the way through to Asia. He mistook it for a bay. Even more important, he declared that floating ice so congested the Arctic waters that sailing was impossibly dangerous. His report cooled interest in the Northwest Passage. Luke Foxe's (1586–1633) futile explorations of the Foxe Channel and Foxe Basin confirmed Baffin's conclusions. The quest for a northwest passage virtually ended for two centuries.

In 1778, Captain James Cook sniffed around the coasts of Alaska and Siberia during his ill-fated third voyage, but the true search for the Northwest Passage did not resume until 1818 with John Ross's explorations. He was followed by William Edward Parry in 1819–1820. Sir John Franklin (1786–1847) explored part of the Northwest Passage by land from 1819 to 1822. He tried to find a water route in 1845–1847 in the ships *Erebus* and *Terror*, with crews of 126 men. None survived the rigors of the far north. Numerous relief expeditions searched in vain for Franklin and his men until Inuits came across some remains. From 1903 to 1905, the Norwegian Roald Amundsen (1872–1928) navigated the Northwest Passage in the small ship *Gjoa*. Despite modern technology, the Northwest Passage has never become a viable commercial route.

See also

> Anian, Strait of; Atlantic Ocean; Circumnavigations of the Earth, Early; Northeast Passage; Pacific Ocean.

For further reading

> Pierre Berton, *The Arctic Grail*, 1988; Samuel Eliot Morison, *The European Discovery of America*, 1971; George Malcolm Thomson, *The Search for the Northwest Passage*, 1975.

NUN, CAPE   Also known as Cape Noun or Cabo Nao, Portuguese sailors rarely ventured beyond this West African landmark. Located about 200 miles down the coast from the busy port of Safi in Morocco, Cape Nun did not present a hazard to navigation. A sandstone cliff standing almost 200 feet above the sea clearly marked its location and the coastal waters remained deep close to shore, so there was little danger of running aground. However, Cape Nun marked the limit of waters frequented by European sailors. Only ships sailing to the Canary Islands passed beyond Cape Nun because European seafarers, particularly the Portuguese, had little reason to go beyond it at the beginning of the fifteenth century. Farther south, the coastline turned arid and desolate. Its inhabitants were few, poor, and hostile, traits that did not recommend them to profit-conscious traders and merchants. Europeans had little reliable information about the coast of Africa beyond Cape Nun. North of Cape Nun lay plentiful opportunities for trade and plunder; south of it lay unknown opportunities and dangers. Duarte Pacheco and João de Barros, chroniclers of the Portuguese exploration of Africa, agreed that Prince Henry the Navigator began his program of exploration at Cape Nun. From that familiar landmark, the Portuguese explorers methodically worked their way south at the insistence of their prince. They not only established a rich trade with West Africa, their efforts ultimately opened the sea route to India and its precious spices.

See also

Africa; Bojador, Cape.

For further reading

Bailey W. Diffie and George D. Winius, *Foundations of the Portuguese Empire, 1415–1580*, 1977; J. H. Parry, *The Discovery of the Sea*, 1981.

O

OASIS   Term used, particularly in the Sahara, for those areas in a desert where sufficient surface water exists to sustain plants and human settlement. Oases have provided thirsty desert travelers with much needed sources of freshwater and resting places since before recorded history.

Oasis is apparently a word of Egyptian origin, *ouake,* meaning "dwelling place." Such desert green spots are created whenever the subterranean water table reaches the surface. Oases should be distinguished from wells, which also exist in the desert. Wells do not produce sufficient surface water to sustain plant life, and the water of some desert wells is so heavily saturated with minerals as to render it unpleasant and even deadly to animals and plants. The well water near the salt mines of Taoudenni (in modern Mali) killed any miner who drank it for long. In the Sahara, oases and wells are created by rainwater from the Atlas Mountains of North Africa percolating through the ground into aquifers and underground rivers, which carry it into certain desert regions farther south. Some geologists speculate that large amounts of "fossil" water may lie beneath the Sahara. Fossil water is water that was trapped below the surface in earlier, wetter times. In certain areas of depressions or low ground, the water table reaches the surface in the form of artesian wells or springs. In those places, the desert blooms with plant life. Often, humans assist this process by digging foggara, a type of well that taps into deeper subsurface water and siphons it into an oasis. The Mzab region of southern Algeria contains many such foggara wells.

The Hollywood version of an oasis is always a clear pool of water surrounded by a small stand of palm trees. Many real oases are actually quite large, up to several hundred square miles. They are capable of sustaining substantial areas of cultivation and towns with populations numbering into the thousands. Examples of large oases that have flourished from ancient and medieval times include Bilma (in modern Niger); al-Kufra, Ghadanes, Ghat, and Murzuk (in modern Libya); In Salah and Ouargla, or Wargla (in modern Algeria); and Kharga and Siwa (in modern Egypt). Siwa was also known as Ammonium, and is the home of the famous oracle of Zeus-Ammon visited by Alexander the Great. The location of these oases of necessity determined the routes followed by caravans across the inhospitable desert. Their locations and characteristics became an important part of the lore of desert travelers.

See also

Caravans; Sahara.

For further reading

Edward William Bovill, *The Golden Trade of the Moors*, 1968; Lloyd Cabot Briggs, *The Tribes of the Sahara*, 1960.

ODYSSEUS, WANDERINGS OF   This legendary Greek hero, known as Ulysses by the Romans, is the most famous traveler of the ancient world. Homer's *Odyssey* tells his story and has become a classic of world literature. *The Odyssey* provides the archetype of stories about journeys made for the purpose of returning home. The book's title has also become synonymous with a trip or travels in general.

Odysseus is a king of Ithaca who participates in the Trojan War. His cleverness and stratagems are legendary, and he conceives of the trick of the Trojan Horse, which at long last ends the ten-year siege of Troy. Unfortunately, the troubles of the victorious Greeks do not end with the fall of Troy. They have angered the goddess Athene, and she creates adverse conditions that hinder the return of many of the Greek heroes, including Odysseus.

Odysseus's first stop on his way home to Ithaca is the city of the Cicones (probably in Thrace), which his fleet attacks and pillages. Foolishly, the Greeks tarry too long in the ruined city, which allows the neighboring Cicones to counterattack and inflict heavy casualties. Odysseus and his fleet escape, but as they try to round Cape Malea on the Peloponnese peninsula, they are blown past the island of Cythera into the open sea. At this point, their adventures truly begin. After ten days of sailing, Odysseus reaches the Land of the Lotus-Eaters. The natives offer his scouts some lotus fruit to eat, after which the men promptly lose all desire to go home. Recognizing the danger, Odysseus rounds up the errant crewmen and bundles them back onto his ships. His fleet quickly departs that lackadaisical land of drug-induced euphoria and stupor.

The Land of the Cyclopes is the next stop on Odysseus's wanderings. Cyclopes are a savage race of one-eyed giants who subsist by herding sheep and gathering edible plants. Unlike the Greeks, they have no farming or shipbuilding skills. Odysseus lands his fleet on an uninhabited island to take on stores, and decides to take his own ship and explore the mainland of the Cyclopes. He and a scouting party of 12 enter the cave of a Cyclops named Polyphemus, but before they can get out, the owner returns. It is his practice to block the opening of his cave with a great stone to keep his sheep in at night, and after he has done that, he discovers his uninvited visitors. Not being a hospitable being, he promptly kills and eats two of the Greeks. Odysseus and his remaining men could kill him in his sleep, but that would leave them trapped in the cave. The next day Polyphemus takes his sheep out to pasture, but leaves the Greeks trapped in his cave. While he is gone, Odysseus concocts an escape plot. That evening the Cyclops kills and eats two more luckless crewmen, and afterward, Odysseus gets Polyphemus drunk. When the monster finally passes out, Odysseus and his men heat up a great log and ram it into the eye of the Cyclops. The blinded giant can no longer see his prey, but he still controls the exit from the cave. The

Illustration taken from the nineteenth-century Leon-Auguste-Adolphe Belly painting, "Ulysses and the Sirens."

clever Odysseus's plan overcomes that obstacle: the Greeks slip out by riding underneath the sheep. After their escape, Odysseus taunts the maimed monster and reveals his name. It is not a wise action; Polyphemus calls down a curse on Odysseus and asks his father, the sea god Poseidon, to avenge him by preventing his tormenter from ever returning home to Ithaca.

The Greeks next sail to the island of Aeolia, the home of Aeolus, controllers of the winds, where Odysseus receives a very hospitable welcome. When

257

the Greeks are ready to depart, Aeolus imprisons all the contrary winds in a leather bag and sends a gentle breeze to blow Odysseus home. They sail for ten days until the fleet sights Ithaca, but at that point some treasure-hungry crewmen open Aeolus's bag of winds while an exhausted Odysseus sleeps. The result is disastrous. A storm is released that blows the fleet all the way back to Aeolia. This time Aeolus refuses to provide any further help, citing the return of the Greeks as proof of divine displeasure. The dejected Greeks depart, and after sailing for seven days reach the Land of the Laestrygonians, another race of hostile giants. When the Laestrygonians discover their visitors, they hurl great stones to sink the Greek ships, spear the hapless survivors as if they were fish, and then eat them. Only Odysseus's ship escapes the holocaust.

Sailing on in a state of utter depression, Odysseus arrives at Aeaea, the island home of the goddess/sorceress Circe. The Greeks explore her island in two parties, Odysseus commanding one and Eurylochus the other. Eurylochus's party comes upon Circe's castle, guarded by wolves and lions that are actually men she has magically transformed. Circe invites the Greeks inside for a drink of wine, an invitation eagerly accepted by everyone but the cautious Eurylochus. He is right to be suspicious; the wine is drugged, and Circe uses it to cast a spell on his men that changes them into pigs. Only Eurylochus escapes to tell Odysseus. Of course, Odysseus immediately sets off to rescue his crew. Along the way he is intercepted by the god Hermes, who warns him of Circe's drugged wine and gives him an antidote. Forewarned in this way, Odysseus avoids Circe's spells and saves his men. The foiled Circe becomes the perfect hostess to her visitors, and generously wines and feasts them. She tells Odysseus that he must visit Hades, the land of the dead, if he ever hopes to see home.

Circe provides the Greeks with a fine breeze to carry their ship into the River Ocean in search of Hades. Eventually they reach the edge of the world where the Cimmerians live in their City of Perpetual Mist, making sacrifices to entice the shades of the dead to come to them. In particular, Odysseus needs to speak with blind Teiresias, the dead poet of Thebes. Teiresias warns Odysseus that he must be very careful if he wants to reach home. Poseidon is still determined to stop him, and under no circumstances are Odysseus and his men to touch the cattle of Hyperion, the sun god. Even when he finally gets home, Odysseus will find things in turmoil, with the suitors of his wife Penelope devouring his fortune. Most incredibly of all, once Odysseus sets things right, he will go on more travels, although Teiresias prophesies that he will have an easy old age. Odysseus and his men spend some time talking with dead comrades and his mother before they depart Hades and return to the island of Circe.

After resting and refitting their ship, Odysseus and his crew once more take their leave of Circe. She tells them there are only two routes back to Ithaca. One way passes through the Wandering (or Crashing) Rocks, which have been survived only by Jason and his Argonauts. The other route requires the passage of the deadly strait of Scylla and Charybdis, which seems to offer the better chance of survival. First, Odysseus and his crew pass the Isle of the Sirens, whose seductive songs lured so many ships to destruction and death. To negate the influence of the Sirens' songs, Odysseus plugs the ears of his crew with wax.

He also orders the crew to bind him to the ship's mast so that he can listen. In this way, Odysseus hears the voices of the Sirens and yet survives.

Odysseus and his ship then run the gauntlet of Scylla and Charybdis. Charybdis is a great creature that lived at the bottom of the sea, alternating between sucking in great quantities of seawater and spewing them out. Any ship that passes too close would be most certainly destroyed, which means that the Greeks are forced to sail on Scylla's side of the strait. Scylla is a ravenous, six-headed creature that reaches down from its cave and plucks defenseless sailors off the decks of their ships. Obviously, it is better to risk losing six men than a whole ship, so Odysseus sets his course to pass closer to Scylla, who inevitably gobbles up six crewmen. The rest survive.

Sailing on, the Greeks come to the island of Hyperion, the sun god, and land despite being warned against it. Initially, they scrupulously leave Hyperion's cattle alone, but adverse winds prevent them from leaving for a month. The delay exhausts their supplies and dissolves the resolve of the hungry mariners, so they slaughter some of the sun god's cattle. After that, the weather shifts and they depart, leaving an angry Hyperion behind them. Hyperion calls on Zeus, the king of the gods, demanding retribution against the pilfering Greeks. Zeus honors his request by destroying Odysseus's ship with a lightning bolt and a great storm. Only Odysseus survives. Clinging to driftwood, he floats to Ogygia, the island home of the nymph Calypso. The beautiful goddess takes Odysseus in, and attempts unsuccessfully to make him her husband. He remains her prisoner for nine years, pining all the while for his wife Penelope and his home (although not without taking full advantage of Calypso's sexual favors). Finally, at the order of the greater gods of Olympus, Calypso allows Odysseus to sail for home. The still-vengeful Poseidon sends a storm that wrecks Odysseus on the coast of Scherie, the land of the Phaeacians, a mysterious but hospitable nation of mariners. At long last, in one of their ships, the Phaeacians carry Odysseus home to Ithaca after an absence of 20 years. With the help of his son Telemachus, Odysseus slaughters Penelope's suitors and is finally reunited with his long-suffering wife. Except for a few minor details, *The Odyssey* ends at this point. A later lost epic titled *Telegoneia* chronicled Odysseus's later adventures.

Scholars now widely consider Homer to be a real person who lived between 750 and 650 B.C. in Smyrna on Asia Minor or on the island of Chios. He is accepted as the author of both *The Iliad* and *The Odyssey*, as was traditionally believed. In the past, some scholars speculated that multiple Homers existed, or that *he* was actually a *she*. *The Iliad* and *The Odyssey* were part of a cycle of eight to ten Trojan War epics that took place around 1200 B.C., about 500 years before the time of Homer.

One question that persistently recurs concerning *The Odyssey* is whether it was based on a real voyage, or at least on real geographic knowledge. Ancient writers followed one of three traditions. Some considered Odysseus's wanderings to be simply a fictional tale with no need for any literal geographic location. A much stronger tradition, exemplified by the Roman geographger Strabo, located Odysseus's wanderings in the vicinity of Sicily and the western Mediterranean. Crates of Mallos suggested that *The Odyssey* took place in the vast and then-mysterious Atlantic Ocean beyond the Pillars of Hercules or the Strait of Gibraltar. In modern times, some 70 studies have attempted to trace the path of Odysseus, with those of Ernle Bradford and Tim Severin being the best known. They generally take Strabo's approach and locate *The Odyssey* in the area of Sicily. Some authors, such as Henrietta Mertz, however, have revived Crates of Mallos' ideas and moved the lands of *The Odyssey* back into the Atlantic Ocean. Most scholars reject the idea that *The Odyssey* was based on an actual voyage, but they readily agree that Homer was very familiar with travel across the "wine-dark sea," and that he used that knowledge to give his epic poem a very authentic flavor. At the same time, he created an imaginary geography that began where the winds blew Odysseus past Cape Malea and continued until he returned to Ithaca. *The Odyssey* has fascinated and entertained readers for centuries, inspired imitators (such as Virgil), and become the archetypal journey in Western civilization.

See also

Clashing Rocks; Cyclopes; Homer; Lotus-Eaters, Land of; Scylla and Charybdis; Sirens.

For further reading

L. Sprague de Camp and Willy Ley, *Lands Beyond*, 1953, ch. 2, "The Long Homecoming," pp. 44–82; Ralph Hexter, *A Guide to the Odyssey*, 1993; Homer, *The Odyssey*, 1946; Beaty Rubens and Oliver Taplin, *An Odyssey round Odysseus*, 1989; W. B. Stanford and J. V. Luce, *The Quest for Ulysses*, 1974.

OLD MAN OF THE MOUNTAIN   Name given by the Crusaders to the leader or master of the Syrian branch of the Nizari Ismailis, also known as the Assassins.

The leaders of the Nizari Ismailis took the honorary title *shaykh*, meaning "elder" or "old man," a common term of respect among Muslims. Because the Nizari frequently operated out of mountain castles, their leaders' full title became *shaykh al-jabal*, which the Crusaders translated as *le vieux de la montagne*, or "old man of the mountain." The Old Man of the Mountain at Alamut headed the entire Nizari or Assassin movement, and the first to hold that title was Hasan-i-Sabbah. The Crusaders had little or no contact with the lords of Alamut; when they referred to the Old Man of the Mountain, they meant the leader of the nearby Syrian branch of the Assassins. During the late twelfth century, the capable Sinan or Rashid al-Din (d. ca. 1192/1194) held office as the Syrian Old Man of the Mountain. Sinan masterminded the notorious murder of Conrad of Montferrat, the Crusader king of Jerusalem, in 1192.

Western accounts portray the various Old Men of the Mountain as ruthless despots and charlatans who duped their gullible followers with drugs and both the promise and reality of a libertine paradise on earth. Heartless Old Men of the Mountain commanded blindly devoted adherents to leap to their deaths off towers or cliffs simply to impress or astonish visitors. Although most Western travelers' accounts refer to the Syrian Old Man of the Mountain, Marco Polo's account describes the more remote Old Man of the Mountain at Alamut, the Assassin order's headquarters in Persia.

The Old Man of the Mountain was a figure who caused prodigious alarm among the Crusaders and other Western travelers, even though the historical record indicates that the leaders of the Assassins had very little interest in the affairs of European Christians.

See also

Alamut; Assassins; Polo, Marco.

For further reading

Bernard Lewis, *The Assassins*, 1967; Charles E. Nowell, "The Old Man of the Mountain," *Speculum* 22 (Oct. 1947): 497–519.

OPHIR   Mysterious country mentioned in the Bible. It was thought to be the source of King Solomon's gold, and hence a land of immense wealth.

The biblical books of First Kings 9:28, 22:49, and 10:10; Second Chronicles 8:18 and 9:10; and Job 28:16 describe Ophir as a maritime trading nation that supplied Israel with gold, fine woods, and precious gems. The goods arrived through the port of Ezion-Geber on the Red Sea, but the biblical references supply few clues to the location of Ophir.

An Ophir, the son of Joktan and a descendant of Noah (Genesis 10:29), appears to be the progenitor of the people of Ophir. He is also associated with Havilah and Sheba, two lands thought to be located in southern Arabia. Some modern scholars object to a southern Arabian location for Ophir because it could not have supplied the exotic animals and large amounts of gold mentioned in the Bible. Other scholars argue that Ophir only traded in these commodities; it did not have to be the primary producer. Many theories abound on the geographic location of Ophir. The Bible closely associates Ophir with Sheba, which was definitely located in southern Arabia. Another tradition places Ophir in India. The ancient writers Josephus, Jerome, and Ptolemy placed Ophir in the Indian subcontinent, as did the medieval geographical writer Lambert of St. Omer. India produced all the exotic goods associated with Ophir. Africa was also suggested as a possible location. The region of present-day Somalia, corresponding to the ancient Egyptian land of Punt, is a strong candidate because the area is capable of producing all the rich commodities associated with Ophir. Also, it could easily have maintained close relations with Sheba across the Red Sea in Arabia. During the nineteenth century, the discovery of the ruins of a gold-producing civilization of ancient Zimbabwe in southern Africa led to much speculation that it was the true Ophir. H. Rider Haggard incorporated this speculation into the plot and setting of his adventure novel *King Solomon's Mines* (1885).

The European discovery of the Americas in 1492 caused some to relocate Ophir somewhere in the Americas. The early historian of American discovery Peter Martyr de Anglería (1457–1526) claimed that Columbus thought Hispaniola was ancient Ophir. Others followed Martyr's suggestion, including the Jesuit chronicler Fernando Montesinos (ca. 1600–1652) and the English-man Samuel Purchas (ca. 1577–1628). Modern advocates of theories about ancient Phoenician visits to the Americas also favor an American location for Ophir.

Some modern scholars suggest that Ophir never existed at all, that it was just a geographical myth. This suggestion has some plausibility, but the main scholarly consensus argues that Ophir was a real but now lost civilization most likely located in southern Arabia or Somalia. Its reputation for vast riches tantalized Europeans traveling in the regions of East Africa, Arabia, and the Indian Ocean for centuries.

See also

Indian Ocean; Sheba.

For further reading

David W. Baker, "Ophir (Place)," in *The Anchor Bible Dictionary*, David Noel Freedman, ed., 1992; Ronald H. Fritze, *Legend and Lore of the Americas before 1492*, 1993.

OREGON TRAIL   Also known as the Oregon and California Trail, countless wagon trains of settlers from the central Mississippi Valley took this famous road to Oregon and California during the 1840s and through the 1860s.

The Oregon Trail began at Independence or St. Joseph, Missouri, and stretched some 2,000 miles into Oregon and California. Fur trappers and mountain men pieced together the proper route between 1808 and 1836. At that time, stories circulated about the fertile, even paradisial lands of Oregon and California, stirring up an intense land fever and wanderlust among the restless farmers of the Mississippi and Ohio Valleys. Groups of emigrants gathered at Independence, where they organized themselves into companies of wagon trains. Each company elected a council to establish rules and govern the wagon train for the duration of the journey. Next, they either hired an experienced guide or simply relied on information gleaned from one of the many emigrant guide-books that quickly appeared in the early 1840s.

All emigrants followed the same route for the first 1,200 miles across the Great Plains, entering the Rocky Mountains through the South Pass and Fort Bridger to reach Soda Springs. From there, emigrants had to choose whether to go on to Oregon or California. From Soda Springs or Fort Hall, emigrants bound for the San Joaquin Valley of California traveled across the Nevada Territory and the Sierra Nevada. Those going to the Sacramento Valley traveled another 300 miles to Fort Boise before they turned in a more southerly direction to reach California. Those settlers seeking their fortune in Oregon followed a more northerly route for another 500 miles to Fort Walla Walla, then proceeded down the Columbia River valley to reach the fabled Willamette Valley.

At first, Oregon was more popular than California because the travel distance was shorter and its lands were reputed to be more fertile. The earliest significant group of emigrants to use the Oregon Trail was the Bidwell-Bartleson party, who traveled to California in 1841. In 1842, a wagon train led by Elijah White and Lansford Hastings went to Oregon. In 1843, the number of emigrants reached into the thousands, with most destined for Oregon. In 1845, Lansford Hastings tried to attract settlers to California by advocating a shortcut, which went south from Fort Bridger to the Great Salt Lake. Known as Hastings' Cut-off, this ill-considered route was virtually impassable for wagons because of stretches of waterless desert and rugged mountains. In 1846, two parties barely managed to escape the travails of the Hastings' Cut-off. A third, the infamous Donner party, suffered so many delays that its members became trapped by snows in the High Sierras and lost half of them to cold and starvation. Nevertheless, California eventually won out as the more popular destination thanks to the lure of the California goldfields, newly discovered in 1848.

From 1840 to 1860, approximately 300,000 people traveled the Oregon Trail. Over 200,000 of them went to California, 50,000 went to Oregon, and another 47,000 made their way to Utah. Not surprisingly, this last group largely consisted of Mormons. The peak year for travel along the Oregon Trail was 1852, with some 60,000 settlers using it. The volume of travelers slowed down in the early 1860s because of the Civil War. Later, the completion of the first transcontinental railroad in 1869 rendered the Oregon Trail obsolete.

Still, in its day, it was not a lonely trail. Francis Parkman's firsthand account in his classic, *The Oregon Trail*, tells of frequent contacts with other groups of travelers along the road as early as 1846. As the many parties made their way along the trail, they were often forced to jettison bulky furniture, which after a

Covered wagons cross the Nebraska prairie near Bayard along the route of the Oregon Trail as part of a modern-day simulation of the Oregon Trail experience.

few years littered the prairie landscape. It was also a well-worn trail. At some points the wagon ruts became so deep as to be impassable, and subsequent travelers were forced to move to one or another side of the road to get through. Some of these wagon ruts were still clearly visible in 1998.

Even though the Oregon Trail was heavily used, it was not an easy or safe route to follow. Some 30,000 travelers died trying to make their way west. Most succumbed to diseases such as cholera, but accidents from drowning and fire-arms took their toll. Hostile natives—Hollywood movies to the contrary—were actually quite rare, and "Indian depredations" or "massacres" were few. Many Native Americans were quite helpful and hospitable to travelers in distress.

Still, the experience of traveling the Oregon Trail was a difficult one. In the folklore of the time, the experience of making the overland journey was re-ferred to as "seeing the elephant." Those emigrants who reached their destina-tion successfully looked back on their achievement with justifiable pride. This movement of peoples to the West also formed an important chapter in the his-tory of the United States, which Congress commemorated in 1978 by designat-ing the Oregon Trail as a national historic trail. The sesquicentennial of the Oregon Trail was celebrated in 1993.

See also

California Trail; Donner Party; Mormon Trail; "Seeing the Elephant"; Wagon Trains.

For further reading

Ray Allen Billington, *The Far Western Frontier, 1830–1860*, 1956; David Lavender, *Westward Vision*, 1963; John D. Unruh, *The Plains Across*, 1979.

OUTREMER   Norman-French word meaning "over the sea." The term referred to the various states established by European Crusaders in Palestine and Syria as a result of the conquests of the First Crusade (1096–1099). At its height, the Outremer consisted of the Crusader states of the county of Edessa, the county of Tripoli, the kingdom of Jerusalem, and the principality of Antioch. The pur-pose of these states was to reestablish Christian control over the Holy Land and protect Christian pilgrims. European merchants were attracted to the Outremer by the lure of Asian luxury goods. After the dramatic success of the First Crusade, the European conquerors came under increasingly successful counterattacks by their Islamic neighbors. In 1291, Acre, the last Crusader outpost in the Outremer, fell to the Mamluk Turks of Egypt. Although the Outremer ceased to exist, its name lived on as a romantic, literary reference to Palestine and Syria, demonstrating the important role played by Normans in the early Crusades.

For further reading

Hans Eberhard Mayer, *The Crusades*, 1988.

P

PACIFIC OCEAN   Largest of the three great oceans, the Pacific is bounded by North and South America to the east and north, and Asia to the west and north. Antarctica and its surrounding waters form its southern boundary.

The Pacific Ocean covers about 70 million square miles, making it equal in size to the combined Atlantic and Indian Oceans. Because of its great size and the absence of large landmasses, the Pacific's winds and currents flow and circulate in regular patterns. Northeast trade winds blow between the equator and 30°N latitude, while southeast trade winds dominate between the equator and 30°S latitude. In the Southern Hemisphere, the westerlies or the Roaring Forties blow between 30°S and 60°S latitude. Westerlies in the North Pacific are weak, and the area from 30°N latitude and northward is dominated by seasonal winds blowing off or onto the Asian and North American landmasses.

In the Pacific Ocean, the north and south equatorial currents flow from east to west. Unlike the Atlantic Ocean, the Pacific has a weak equatorial countercurrent, which flows from west to east between the two equatorial currents. The main body of Pacific waters, however, flows in great circular patterns to the north and south. When the north equatorial current reaches the vicinity of the Philippine Islands, it turns north to become the Kuroshio or Japan current. As it crosses the North Pacific it becomes the North Pacific current and then the California current. In the Southern Hemisphere, some of the south equatorial current flows past New Guinea and the East Indies to enter the Indian Ocean. Another part turns south down the eastern coast of Australia where it starts to turn west, and becomes the West Wind Drift. Upon reaching South America, it turns north as the Humboldt current.

The Pacific Ocean contains many islands because it is a very seismically active part of the world. Its littoral is known as the Ring of Fire due to its many volcanoes and earthquakes. Movements of the plates that make up the earth's crust cause volcanic action, which over the course of many years creates various islands, such as the Hawaiian Islands. Although these islands, as well as coral islands, are plentiful in the Pacific, they are swallowed up in its vastness. Despite their geographic isolation, all the islands capable of supporting human life were already inhabited well before European contact in the sixteenth century.

The Pacific Islands are divided into three regions: Melanesia, Micronesia, and Polynesia. Melanesia consists of the island groups located in the southwestern Pacific below the equator and east of New Guinea and Australia. Included among the Melanesian island groups are the Solomons, Admiralties, Bismarcks, Fiji, and New Caledonia. Northeast of Melanesia and largely north of the equator in the Pacific lies Micronesia. Various archipelagoes of small islands comprise Micronesia including the Marianas, Gilberts, Marshalls, Carolines, and Guam. Negrito peoples inhabit both Melanesia and Micronesia. The third region of Polynesia is located in the Central Pacific. It is shaped like a vast triangle with corners at New Zealand, the Hawaiian Islands, and Easter Island. Other famous islands of Polynesia are the Samoas, Tahiti, Tonga, and the Marquesas. Unlike the Micronesians and Melanesians, ethnically the Polynesians appear to be Malay. The peoples of all three regions are skilled seamen and clever builders of small boats capable of high-seas travel. The greatest of all, however, are the Polynesian voyagers. Some historians suggest that the Polynesians and ancient Peruvians maintained oceanic contact, but if they did, it was very sporadic.

Prior to 1500, the peoples of East Asia confined their sailing on the Pacific Ocean largely to the South and East China Seas, although occasional maritime contact existed with nearby Japan. Ships plied the waters of the East Indies and the fabled Spice Islands, which clustered together in the East-Central Pacific.

Before 1500, Europeans were unaware of the existence of the Pacific Ocean. They knew a great ocean lay off the east coast of China, but they thought it was the far shore of their own Atlantic. Hence, Christopher Columbus and John Cabot's proposals to sail across the Atlantic to reach Asia was quite sensible given contemporary geographical misconceptions. Unfortunately, the unsuspected Americas posed a vast barrier to navigation. Europeans immediately began to probe this barrier to navigable straits. On 27 September 1513, Vasco Nuñez de Balboa trudged across the Isthmus of Panama to discover the Pacific Ocean, which he named the South Sea. Less than a decade later, Ferdinand Magellan's voyage of 1519–1521 revealed a way into the Pacific through the Strait of Magellan. After passing through the strait, Magellan and his men tried to cross the Pacific, but its vast size and apparent emptiness almost killed them. Garcia Jofre de Loaisa's follow-up expedition through the Strait of Magellan in 1526 proved even more disastrous, and caused Spain to ignore that route for decades. Other Spaniards tried to reach Asia by sailing from Mexico. During 1527–1529, Alvaro de Saavedra sailed from Mexico on the orders of Hernán Cortés with the goal of visiting the Philippines. Saavedra successfully discovered the optimal route for utilizing the trade winds and north equatorial currents to carry his ships west. When he tried to return to Mexico, however, he utterly failed to locate a usable course and died in the effort. Not until Andres de Urdaneta's voyage of 1565 was a feasible west-to-east route from the Philippines to Mexico developed. From that point on, the famous Manila galleons carried Asian luxury goods across the Pacific to Acapulco, where mule trains took them to the Gulf of Mexico. There, other ships carried them on to Spain. The Manila galleons returned to Asia with Mexican gold and silver, which was used to purchase more Asian luxuries. It was the first regular transpacific trade route.

Other Europeans engaged in the quixotic search for the elusive Terra Australis of the South Pacific. Beginning with the voyage of Alvaro de Mendaña in 1567–1569 and lasting until Captain James Cook's second voyage of 1772–1775, European ships scoured the South Pacific for the supposedly vast but perpetually elusive Terra Australis. Along the way, they discovered Australia in 1606, New Zealand in 1642, Easter Island in 1722, and the Hawaiian Islands in 1778.

During the nineteenth century, Western nations began to view China as a vast market for their industrial goods. Sea lanes to China needed protection, and a scramble followed for strategically located naval bases. The various island groups of Melanesia, Micronesia, and Polynesia soon became part of one or another Western industrial empire. These developments also meant that the Pacific Ocean steadily grew in importance as a highway of international trade. In the late twentieth century, it appears that the center of the world economy will soon shift to the Pacific Rim. For now, the Pacific Ocean and its paradisial islands retain an image of rest and peace in the minds of potential travelers and in the imagery of popular culture.

See also

Atlantic Ocean; Circumnavigations of the Earth, Early; Indian Ocean.

For further reading

Oliver E. Allen, *The Pacific Navigators*, 1980; Ernest S. Dodge, *Islands and Empires*, 1976; Frank Sherry, *Pacific Passions*, 1994.

PARADISE, FOUR RIVERS OF   Four great rivers flowed out of the Terrestrial Paradise, or the Garden of Eden: the Tigris, Euphrates, Gihon, and Pison. They were a source of both wonder and confusion for travelers of ancient, medieval, and early-modern times.

According to Genesis 2:20, "A river went out of Eden to water the garden; and from thence it was parted and became four heads." The first river was the Pison, or Pishon, which was associated with the land of Havilah, a source of gold and onyx. Modern biblical scholars place Havilah in southern Arabia. During late antiquity and the Middle Ages, the Pison was commonly identified as the Ganges or Indus River, although it was occasionally thought to be the Danube. The second river, the Gihon, was associated with Ethiopia. Invariably, the Gihon of Genesis and the historical Nile have been thought to be the same river. The other two rivers, the Hiddekel or Tigris and the Euphrates, flowed out of Armenia and created Mesopotamia.

At first glance it appears impossible for the widely separated Nile, Ganges, Tigris, and Euphrates Rivers to have a common source in the Garden of Eden. Medieval writers got around the apparent facts of geography and distance by postulating the existence of a maze of underground riverbeds. Once they passed beyond the walls of Paradise, the four rivers disappeared underground, resurfacing thousands of miles away from Eden and one another. Christian writers as far separated by time and distance as Isidore of Seville (ca. 560–636) and Peter Abelard (1079–1142/1144) supported the theory of underground rivers of Paradise.

The four rivers of Paradise were associated with considerable geographical folklore. Accounts of the kingdom of Prester John, the homeland of the Terrestrial Paradise, describe how the four rivers of Paradise almost miraculously brought forth gold and gems three times a year. One story within the medieval Romances of Alexander the Great credited the Euphrates with being the source of the magical waters that fed the Fountain of Youth. In the later twelfth century, Peter Comestor and Gervase of Tilbury maintained that the spring in the Garden of Eden that fed the four rivers of Paradise was the source of all the water on earth. These ideas about the four rivers of Paradise remained current among European travelers and explorers well into the sixteenth century.

See also

Fountain of Youth; Ganges River; Nile River; Paradise, Terrestrial; Prester John and His Kingdom.

For further reading

John Kirtland Wright, *The Geographical Lore of the Time of the Crusades*, 1925.

PARADISE, TERRESTRIAL   Medieval and early-modern Christians believed that a Terrestrial Paradise (the Garden of Eden) literally existed someplace on the earth.

The idea of the existence of an earthly paradise is a common one among the earth's cultures. Hebrew tradition described Eden as a garden full of fruit-bearing trees. A spring created a river that flowed through the garden, dividing into the legendary four rivers of Paradise—the Tigris, Euphrates, Gihon, and Pison. The ancient Greeks and Romans thought of Paradise as a meadow shaded by lovely trees with a cool, clear stream running through it, accompanied by perpetual springlike weather. Rain, storms, frost, and excessive heat never marred its calm perfection. The lovely Isles of the Hesperides and the Elysian Fields were supposed to be just such terrestrial paradises. Christian traditions about the Terrestrial Paradise inherited the Hebrews' Garden of Eden, while giving it many of the characteristics of a Greco-Roman earthly paradise.

Many Christians, from the early years of the new faith until well into the sixteenth century, believed that the biblical Terrestrial Paradise still existed somewhere on the earth. Not everyone agreed with this literalist approach. Church fathers St. Augustine of Hippo, Origen, and Philo regarded the biblical account of Paradise as allegorical. Still, for centuries many Christians continued to believe in its existence until enough of the world had been explored to show that it was simply not possible.

The most common tradition about the location of the Terrestrial Paradise placed it in the easternmost lands of the earth. This belief was based on the passage in Genesis 2:8 that says, "And the Lord God planted a garden eastward in Eden." Following this tradition, most medieval mappaemundi placed it at the easternmost part of the world's landmass. It was depicted as a garden with the figures of Adam, Eve, and the serpent placed inside it. Impassable barriers prevented earthly travelers from getting in. To reach it, travelers had to pass through howling wastelands of mountain and desert, full of snakes and savage beasts. Some writers also claimed that Paradise was enclosed by an impassable ring of flame. Other accounts, such as Sir John Mandeville's, placed Paradise behind high walls at the top of a mountain so high that the waters of Noah's flood could not cover it. The mappamundi at Hereford Cathedral located the Terrestrial Paradise on a walled island just off the eastern coast of Asia. The prevalence of such beliefs goes far to explain why Christopher Columbus thought he was close to the Terrestrial Paradise when he skirted the lush coast of Venezuela and the mouth of the Orinoco River on his third voyage of 1498.

Not everyone accepted this far eastern location of Paradise. Throughout the Middle Ages, various writers suggested alternate locations. Martianus Capella, the fifth-century scholar, claimed that the far northern land of Hyperborea was actually the Terrestrial Paradise, and some church fathers agreed. The sixth-century Christian cosmographer Cosmas Indicopleustes placed the Terrestrial Paradise in the lands lying on the eastern side of the great circular ocean that surrounded the known world. In 1143, another writer, Hermann the Dalmatian, also placed the Terrestrial Paradise beyond the world-circling ocean, but he claimed that contradictory evidence existed for both an eastern and a western location. In their mappaemundi, Henry of Mayence and Lambert of St. Omer depicted the Terrestrial Paradise as an island far out in the eastern waters of the world-circling ocean. However, St. Brendan the Navigator came upon his Promised Land of the Saints, or Terrestrial Paradise, while cruising the western waters of the ocean. In the twelfth and thirteenth centuries, both Gervase of Tilbury and Robert Grosseteste placed the Terrestrial Paradise south of the equator beyond the impassable Torrid Zone. Certainly the belief was widespread among medieval western Europeans that a Terrestrial Paradise existed somewhere on the earth and could possibly be visited.

If a Terrestrial Paradise existed, then no matter how inaccessible its location, some people could visit it as a result of miracles or because of their heroic or saintly characters. During the Middle Ages, four basic types of tales about journeys to the Terrestrial Paradise developed. The first was based on preexisting legends from Jewish sources. A good example is the tale of the return to Eden of Adam's son Seth to obtain seeds from the Tree of Knowledge. The seeds are planted in the mouth of the dead Adam, and the tree that eventually sprouts provides the wood for Christ's crucifixion cross. The other three types of stories arose out of medieval Christian traditions. In one, the story focuses on pious monks who somehow make their way to and from Paradise. In another case, a party of monks stay in Paradise for three days, but when they return home they discover they have been gone for 300 years. Closely related to these stories is the second category, in which monks and priests still visit Paradise, but only as part of a greater voyage of exploration. The legend about St. Brendan the Navigator and his visit to the Promised Land of the Saints is a good example. Godfrey of Viterbo, writing in the middle of the twelfth century, supplied another example in his *Pantheon,* which describes how 100 brothers extensively roam the Atlantic Ocean until at last they reach the Terrestrial Paradise. In the third type, the chivalric hero completely replaces the monk as protagonist. The early-twelfth-century romance *Her ad Paradisum* tells the story of Alexander the Great's conquest of India. Once his task is finished, Alexander and 500 of his men sail down the Ganges River for a month. Arriving at the mouth of the great river, Alexander encounters an immense walled city. He learns from a Jew that the city is the abode of the souls of the just while they wait for the end of the world; it is the Terrestrial Paradise. All these tales showed that the Terrestrial Paradise could be reached, but it would take an extremely holy or brave traveler to do it.

See also

Blessed, Isles of the; Elysian Fields; Fortunate Isles; Hyperborea; Mappamundi; Paradise, Four Rivers of; St. Brendan the Navigator, Voyage of.

For further reading

Jean Delumeau, *History of Paradise,* 1995; Richard Heinberg, *Memories and Visions of Paradise,* 1989; John Kirtland Wright, *The Geographical Lore of the Time of the Crusades,* 1925.

PERGAMUM, LIBRARY OF

This library was second in size and importance only to the legendary Alexandrian Library among the great book collections of Greco-Roman civilization during antiquity. Like its great rival, the Library of Pergamum attracted an international clientele of traveling scholars.

Pergamum was the capital city of the region of Asia Minor known as Mysia during the Hellenistic era. Philetaerus (343–263 B.C.), a crafty half-Macedonian official, established Pergamum as an independent kingdom during the power struggles following the death of Alexander the Great. His dynasty was known as the Attalids, after his father Attalus. The kingdom of Pergamum was a rich one because of its silver mines and abundant grain surpluses. Its wealth attracted marauding Gaulic invaders, but after a long struggle the kings of Pergamum were victorious. With their Gaulic enemies defeated, the Pergamene kings allied themselves with Rome, an alliance that provided the Pergamene king Eumenes II (r. 197–159 B.C.) with enough security that he could engage in the cultural pursuits that were already making the Ptolemaic kings of Egypt famous. Eumenes II founded a combined library and academy, and persuaded the prominent scholar Crates of Mallos (fl. 150 B.C.) to be its head. Soon, Pergamum and Alexandria entered into a bidding war for the great and rare books of the Hellenistic world. One jealous Egyptian king, Ptolemy V Epiphanes (r. 204–180 B.C.), tried to cripple Pergamum's efforts by halting the export of papyrus, the prime ancient bookmaking material. His move forced the book manufacturers of Pergamum to find a substitute, and they chose the more durable but also more expensive vellum, or parchment, made from sheepskin. Some writers credit the Pergamenes with inventing parchment, but they merely popularized its use.

The cultural greatness of Pergamum continued under its next king, Attalus II (159–138 B.C.). He was succeeded by his nephew, Attalus III (138–133 B.C.), a weak man unfit to rule. As Attalus III's death approached, he willed his hapless kingdom to Rome, which then incorporated it into the Roman province of Asia. The Library of Pergamum survived the demise of the Attalids, but not its new Roman owners. During the Roman civil wars following the assassination of Julius Caesar, Pergamum supported the wrong side. As a result, the library was plundered by Mark Anthony, who gave 200,000 scrolls to his lover Cleopatra for inclusion in the Alexandrian Library. The Library of Pergamum never recovered from that loss.

See also
Alexandrian Library and Museum; Crates of Mallos.
For further reading
Esther Violet Hansen, *The Attalids of Pergamon*, 1971; Edward Alexander Parsons, *The Alexandrian Library*, 1952.

PERSIAN EXPEDITION (401–399 B.C.)
Also known as the March of the Ten Thousand, this episode from ancient Greek history is one of the most famous tales of an army successfully retreating from deep inside hostile territory. Xenophon's (d. 355/354 B.C.) *Anabasis* is a firsthand account, and supplies most of what is known about it.

In 401 B.C., Artaxerxes II (d. 359 B.C.) was the king of the decaying Persian Empire. He became jealous and suspicious of his talented younger brother Cyrus (ca. 423–401 B.C.), who served as the satrap (governor) of Lydia in Asia Minor. Possibly goaded into rebellion by his brother's animosity, Cyrus gathered an army with the secret intention of overthrowing Artaxerxes II. The army included over 10,000 Greek hoplites, or heavy infantry, along with over 2,000 light infantry and other auxiliaries. Marching from Sardis, Cyrus and his troops made their way through southern Asia Minor to the upper part of the Euphrates River. They followed the course of the river into Mesopotamia, where they fought a battle at Cunaxa with the numerically superior forces of Artaxerxes II. The heavily armored and highly disciplined Greek troops smashed their opponents and won the battle, only to discover that their employer—Cyrus—had been killed.

The death of Cyrus placed the Greek mercenaries in a very perilous position. Cyrus's other defeated troops quickly gave their allegiance to Artaxerxes II, who demanded that the Greeks surrender their arms to him. Obviously, the Persian king meant the Greeks no good. They had seen and done too much, and their easy victory over his Persian troops showed that the Persian Empire would be an easy target for an invading Greek army (a lesson that later was not lost on Philip, the king of Macedon, and his son Alexander the Great). Artaxerxes II needed to suppress that information as well as punish the Greeks for participating in Cyrus's rebellion.

The Greeks wisely refused to give up their arms to the Persians, and stated that they simply wanted to return home with the least amount of trouble. The Persian king seemed to accept their position at first, but during a parley with the Greeks' generals, his soldiers took them prisoner or killed them on the spot, in hopes that the leaderless Greek army would then surrender. Instead, the resilient Greeks elected new generals, including Xenophon of Athens, and fought their way up the valley of the Tigris River into the mountains of northeastern Asia Minor. By the time the Greek army reached the mountains, winter had set in, and they suffered terribly from both hostile natives and the bitter cold. Eventually, they broke through to the coastline on the Black Sea, where the first sight of water caused the entire army to begin shouting, "The sea, the sea." In 400 B.C., they rested among the settlers of the Greek colony of Trapezus. The worst was past for the approximately 8,000 survivors of the retreat.

Making their way along the northern coast of Asia Minor by land and by sea, the troops continued on until they reached the traditional Greek homelands. Even then, the army decided to remain together. They hoped to make some quick money soldiering, but instead found themselves cheated by their new employer, King Seuthes of Thrace. Finally, in 399 B.C., the 6,000 remaining soldiers joined a Spartan army in a war against the local Persian satraps in Asia Minor.

The story of the March of the Ten Thousand rapidly and deservedly gained fame in the Greek world. Their experiences deep inside the Persian Empire revealed to a wide audience both its military weakness and its tempting riches. Xenophon's narrative of the Persian expedition has provided a heroic and inspiring military travelogue for readers down through the centuries.

For further reading

Xenophon, *The Persian Expedition*, 1972.

PHAROS (OR LIGHTHOUSE) OF ALEXANDRIA   This great lighthouse guided ships to the port of Alexandria from its construction about 297–282 B.C. until its ruin by an earthquake in 1303. It was about 328 feet tall, and was impressive enough to be considered one of the Seven Wonders of the Ancient World.

Alexander the Great founded Alexandria at a strategic but largely unexploited place on the Nile River delta in 331 B.C. After his death, Egypt came under the rule of the diadochi (successor) Ptolemy I Soter (305–282 B.C.), who made Alexandria the capital of the Ptolemaic kingdom of Egypt. Thanks to the wealth derived from international trade and the patronage of the Ptolemaic dynasty, Alexandria became the cultural center of the Hellenistic world and its most important city. In about 297 B.C., Sostratus of Cnidus, an important diplomat and merchant, began building the great lighthouse. Construction was completed during the reign of Ptolemy II Philadelphus (283–246 B.C.). The structure was called the Pharos, after the name of the island where it was located, and afterward, the name *pharos* applied to any lighthouse. The Pharos was built as a tower with three tiers: the first was about 200 feet high; the second, 100 feet; and the third, 30 feet. Originally, the third tier was topped by a statue of Zeus, but sometime after the Islamic conquest the third tier became a mosque topped by a crescent moon. Many illustrations from ancient and medieval sources document the general appearance of the Pharos. Still, its characteristics were subject to exaggeration. The Greek Epiphanus described it as more than 1,800 feet tall, which was many times its real height. Josephus (A.D. 37–100), the great Jewish historian, claimed that the light of the Pharos was visible almost 35 miles at sea, while Lucian of Samosata (A.D. 115–180) extended its visibility to an utterly fantastic 300 miles.

Ancient writers generally described the Pharos as using a system of mirrors to reflect and magnify its beacon flames. Nevertheless, the Pharos was basically a daytime utility, because in the ancient world ships avoided traveling at night. Therefore, most ships were guided by the smoke of the Pharos's fires rather than its flames.

The Pharos remained in use into the early Middle Ages and the time of the Arab conquest of Egypt. An earthquake badly damaged it in 956, and 200 years later (1166) the Arab traveler Abou Haggag Youssef Ibn Mohammed el-Balawi el-Andaloussi described it as abandoned and in ruins. Two more earthquakes, in 1303 and 1323, furthered its destruction, but Ibn Battuta reported it as only partially in ruins during his visits of 1326 and 1349. During the fifteenth century, the Mamluks built the fort of Kait Bey on the site of the Pharos, using its ruins for building materials. Nothing remains of its former grandeur, but in the ancient world and early-medieval period the Pharos would have been a familiar and impressive sight to travelers.

See also

Alexandria; Seven Wonders of the Ancient World.

For further reading

Peter Clayton and Martin Price, eds., *The Seven Wonders of the Ancient World,* 1988.

PHOENICIANS   An ancient people living in a conglomeration of city-states along the coastline of modern Lebanon and Syria. They were famous as intrepid seafarers and as the originators and propagators of the alphabet.

The name *Phoenician* derives from the Greek word meaning "red." It is probably a reference to the Phoenicians' trade in purple dyes or copper, or it could be an allusion to the copper-colored skins of the Phoenicians. What they called themselves in their own language is not known.

Archaeological evidence indicates a Phoenician presence in the Levant as early as the third millennium B.C. Using the famous cedars of Lebanon for ship-building materials, they became great sailors. Wealthy, powerful city-states arose along the coastline of Phoenicia, of which Tyre, Sidon, Byblos, and Ugarit are the best known. Phoenician ships sailed more and more of the Mediterranean Sea, reaching Cyprus, the Aegean region, Italy, Spain, and North Africa. Close contacts were also maintained with Egypt, as shown by the Amarna letters of the early fourteenth century B.C. The Phoenicians may have been the model for Homer's mysterious Phaeacians of Scheria who befriended Odysseus in *The Odyssey.* Phoenician merchants also founded settlements in other parts of the Mediterranean; Gades and Carthage in the eighth century B.C. are the most famous examples.

The reputation of the Phoenician seamen was quite high. King Solomon of ancient Israel used them in his trade with Ophir and Sheba. Pharaoh Necho hired a party of Phoenicians to circumnavigate Africa. They formed the core of the Persian Empire's navy. Passing through the Strait of Gibraltar, they sailed up the coast of Europe, down the coast of Africa, and on the high seas of the Atlantic Ocean. Just how far they reached is hotly debated, and the issue is further complicated because some sources fail to differentiate between Phoenicians and Carthaginians. Phoenician or Carthaginian ships maintained regular contact with the Canary Islands and the adjacent African coasts, along with the tin lands of Britain and Brittany. Archaeological evidence tends to support a Phoenician or Carthaginian discovery of the Madeira and Azores Islands. Various fringe writers make claims for various Phoenician or Carthaginian contacts with the Americas, but the evidence presented is problematic or chimerical. Such fabulous theories and claims, however, underscore the well-deserved reputation of the Phoenicians as some of the ancient world's most adventurous travelers and explorers.

See also

Carthage; Circumnavigations of Africa, Early; Mediterranean Sea; Ophir; Sheba.

For further reading

Maria Eugenia Aubet, *The Phoenicians and the West,* 1993; Sabatino Moscati, *The World of the Phoenicians,* 1968; Raymond Weill, *Phoenicia and Western Asia to the Macedonian Conquest,* 1980.

PILGRIMAGE   Journey undertaken for religious purposes to some place of sacred significance within a particular religious tradition. Pilgrimage is practiced by most of the world's great religions: Buddhism, Christianity, Hinduism, Islam, and Judaism.

People go on pilgrimages for a multiplicity of reasons. Some religions require them; the Torah enjoined all Jewish males to visit Jerusalem during the feasts of Passover, Shavuoth, and Succoth. One of the Five Pillars of Islam is the

Gustave Doré illustration of "the barbarians" offering hospitality to pilgrims traveling to Jerusalem.

obligation of every Muslim male to make the pilgrimage of the hajj to Mecca at least once in their lifetimes. Other people undertook pilgrimages to be healed of an illness or a handicap. People in the time of Jesus visited the pool at Bethesda in Jerusalem for its healing powers (Gospel of John 5:2–3). Lourdes in France has been associated with pilgrims and healing since its foundation in 1858. Similar sites of miraculous healing abound in most religions.

Besides physical healing, pilgrimages could also convey spiritual healing to participants. The medieval church assigned indulgences for the performance of pilgrimages to help ease the afterlife of the pilgrims or their deceased family members. In all religions, pilgrimages could be a source of spiritual renewal or rebirth. The Hindus of India have a vast number of places to visit on pilgrimages.

Other pilgrimages could be undertaken to obtain sacred relics or for educational purposes. Chinese Buddhists made trips to India to visit sites associated with the Buddha, obtain relics, and acquire accurate copies of sacred texts. The scholars Fa-Hsien (fl. 399–414) and Hsuan-Tsang (ca. 600–664) made extended pilgrimages throughout much of India. Islamic pilgrims who went to Mecca, such as Ibn Battuta, often stayed on after the hajj to study the teachings and laws of Islam. Christian visitors to the Holy Land and other sacred locations returned home with a myriad of relics, many of them fakes.

Some pilgrims seek to emulate the original action or event that made a certain place holy. Participants in the hajj symbolically re-create the experiences of Muhammad. Christian pilgrims to Jerusalem follow the Via Dolorosa to experience Jesus' walk to his crucifixion on Calvary. Other pilgrims make their sacred journeys a commemoration and source of inspiration. Christians are not required to make pilgrimages to Jerusalem, Rome, or Bethlehem; they do so because it makes them feel more connected with the origins of their religion. Shia Muslims are not required to visit the tombs of the martyred Ali and Hussien, but they do it as a commemoration and a sign of respect for the founders of their branch of Islam. Medieval Christians have such pilgrimage sites as St. Thomas à Becket's tomb at Canterbury, while the Reformation produced such commemorations as the memorial for the Oxford martyrs at Oxford.

Of course, pilgrimage can be secular. The battlefield at Gettysburg or the Vietnam Veterans' Memorial can be inspirational, commemorative, or even spiritually healing. As the purpose becomes less serious, mere sightseeing replaces pilgrimage, both sacred and secular. Despite the growth of secularism and tourism in the modern world, pilgrimage remains alive, well, and important. Pilgrimages continue to fulfill the multifarious purposes they served throughout human history.

See also

Bethlehem; Canterbury; Ganges River; Hajj; Jerusalem; Kempe, Margery; Mecca.

For further reading

Simon Coleman and John Elsner, *Pilgrimage*, 1995.

PILLARS OF HERCULES   The ancient Greeks' and Romans' name for the Strait of Gibraltar.

According to Greek mythology, Hercules erected twin pillars on the shores of the strait leading from the Mediterranean Sea into the Atlantic Ocean. The ancients named the resulting two mountains Calpe and Abyla, while the modern world knows them as the famous Rock of Gibraltar and its African counterpart, Mount Hacho by Ceuta. For the Homeric Greeks, the Pillars of Hercules marked the end of the known or habitable world. Beyond lay the great encircling River Ocean, which separated the created and orderly cosmos from the surrounding chaos. The farther one sailed into the River Ocean, the more the level of chaos increased. Chaos meant an indiscriminate mixing of the four traditional elements: earth, air, fire, and water. Ocean's water would become a muddy mess, too thick to sail on but too liquid to bear the weight of a walker. The air would become increasingly foggy as it chaotically mixed with water and earth. It was not an environment capable of sustaining human life.

In later centuries, the Greeks found the Pillars of Hercules barred to them because the intrepid Phoenicians and Carthaginians took control of that region of the western Mediterranean. The Carthaginians attacked any potential competitors who attempted to sail through the Pillars of Hercules and spread exaggerated stories about the terrors of the Atlantic Ocean to discourage the curious. The Roman conquest of the Carthaginians in 201 B.C. permanently opened the Pillars of Hercules to navigation. Over the centuries, however, the Pillars of Hercules have remained symbolic of the boundary between the known and the unknown for adventuresome travelers.

See also

Atlantic Ocean; Mediterranean Sea.

For further reading

Vincent H. Cassidy, *The Sea around Them*, 1968; James S. Romm, *The Edges of the Earth in Ancient Thought*, 1992.

PIRATES   Also known as buccaneers, corsairs, filibusters, or freebooters, they were the robbers and bandits of the seas. In contrast, privateers were private persons and ships who had official government commissions authorizing them to attack enemy ships in time of war. Piracy has flourished at various times in human history all around the world. Privateering had its heyday from the sixteenth through the eighteenth centuries. Often, the line separating privateering from piracy was very vague.

The popular image of pirates depicts them as full-time professional robbers of the seas, and many were just that. Some, however, engaged in piracy as a crime of opportunity, mostly against foreign ships. Fishermen in the English Channel or other heavily used sea lanes occasionally attacked lone or vulnerable ships from other nations. By taking care to avoid victimizing their fellow countrymen, they hoped to make it more difficult to be caught. Such activity illustrates the fact that piracy arose and will arise again wherever law enforcement and government control on the high seas is weak or nonexistent.

Attacks by other ships provided a constant threat to travelers in the ancient Mediterranean. Around 1130 B.C., an Egyptian priest of Amon named Weamon traveled to Lebanon to buy cedar for the construction of a ceremonial barge. Stopping at the town of Dor on the coast of Palestine, a colony of sea raiders known as the Tjeker, Weamon suffered a theft that took all his money. The Tjeker ruler of Dor refused to compensate his loss, so the desperate Weamon took the law into his own hands. To restore his finances, he engaged in a bit of piracy by robbing a Tjeker ship between Tyre and Byblos. Weamon was successful, but when he put into Byblos to buy his cedar, he was pursued by Tjeker warships seeking vengeance. Fortunately for Weamon, when he sailed from Byblos a storm arose that blew him to Cyprus, and he eluded his Tjeker pursuers. Weamon's story illustrates the fluid line between being a victim of piracy and on occasion being a pirate oneself.

Ancient Crete served as a notorious pirate haven during the early years of the Dorian domination of that island about 1100 B.C. Their activities, however, quickly subsided. From 300 to 67 B.C., the ancient Mediterranean world suffered from some particularly well organized pirate groups. The Aetolian League in Greece supported itself through piratical activity from 300 to 186 B.C., when the Romans conquered them. Cretan pirates reappeared about 300 B.C. and terrorized the eastern Mediterranean. The island of Rhodes steadfastly resisted the depredations of the Cretans for centuries. Finally, the Romans invaded and conquered Crete in 67 B.C., thus ending the island's career as a pirate haven.

The greatest of the ancient Mediterranean pirates were the Cilicians of the south coast of Asia Minor. From 150 to 67 B.C., they floated large fleets and terrorized shipping and coastal settlements. Their piratical fleets were possibly the largest known in recorded history. From 102 to 67 B.C., the

Pirates attack a ship. From C. Pitois, Histoire des marins et corsaires, *1846.*

Cilicians were locked in a great war with Rome, and most of the time they outfought the Romans at sea. Both Mark Anthony's daughter and Julius Caesar were captured by Cilician pirates. Not until the successful campaign of Pompey in 67 B.C. were the Cilician pirates defeated once and for all. The power of the Roman Empire made the Mediterranean Sea relatively safe for shipping and travelers for the next 400 years.

With the decline of the Roman Empire and its collapse in the West during the fifth century, piracy resumed. When the barbarian Vandals occupied the region of Tunisia, they took to the seas as corsairs and even brutally sacked Rome in 455. Viking raiders appeared in the Atlantic waters of Europe in 793 and soon expanded into the Mediterranean Sea. The rise of Islam and its empire also brought an infestation of Arab corsairs to the Mediterranean. During the era of the Crusades, Christian and Muslim corsairs preyed on each other's merchants and sometimes even those of their own faith. The Knights Hospitalers, first at Rhodes and later at Malta, operated as anti-Islamic pirates. They were greatly hated by Muslim rulers, and this led to the successful Ottoman Turkish conquest of Rhodes in 1522 and the unsuccessful siege of Malta in 1565. By the early sixteenth century, the Barbary pirates joined the Hospitalers in terrorizing Mediterranean shipping. The threat from the Barbary pirates lasted until the first two decades of the nineteenth century, when Western navies gathered to crush them.

The voyages of Christopher Columbus in 1492 and Vasco da Gama in 1497 expanded the geographic horizons of European trade, which in turn expanded the horizons of pirates. Treasure fleets loaded with American gold and silver and convoys of Indiamen carrying the luxury goods of Asia were soon regularly sailing to Europe. The Caribbean Sea, the Gulf of Mexico, and the eastern coast of North America suffered from pirates from 1650 to 1720. Various privateers from France, the Netherlands, and England, including Sir Francis Drake, cruised the waters of the Spanish Americas from 1560 on. True pirates began to appear after 1650. Sir Henry Morgan (1635–1688) operated out of Port Royal, Jamaica, as a privateer between 1662 and 1671. His exploits included the sackings of Portobello in 1668 and Panama in 1671. The ill-fated Captain William Kidd (ca. 1645–1701) spent part of his piratical career in American waters. Edward Teach (d. 1718), better known as Blackbeard, terrorized shipping in American waters, particularly off the coast of the Carolinas, from 1716 to 1718. Many other lesser-known pirates also cruised the seas.

Madagascar was another important pirate haunt. Located strategically along the sea routes between the Far East and Europe, pirates based there easily harassed rich shipping. Besides the spice-laden Indiamen, they swooped down on Muslim ships carrying rich pilgrims to Mecca. Fort Dauphin and the Isle of St. Marie served as pirate bases between 1691 and 1711. The famous Henry Avery (or Every) captured the Great Mogul's daughter on the rich pilgrim ship *Gang-i-sawai* (*Gunsway*) in 1695. Thomas Tew died during the taking of the *Gang-i-sawai*, but he had commanded a highly successful piratical raid into the Red Sea in 1693. Pirates of the Indian Ocean presented such a threat to shipping that various English nobles hired Captain William Kidd in 1695 to track down the pirates, sink their ships, and kill or capture their crews. Instead, a string of bad luck forced him to turn pirate himself, and he was eventually tried and executed. By 1711, the great days of the Indian Ocean pirates were over, and those of the American pirates ended by 1720. Small-scale pirates still operate, but the so-called "Golden Age of Piracy" is long over.

Pirates were not confined to Westerners and Arabs. Malay pirates operating around the Straits of Malacca and Singapore appeared as early as A.D. 413. The Dutch East India Company's monopoly of shipping forced many Malay sailors into piracy because the Dutch would not use them as seamen on their company ships. The high point of the Malay pirates was from 1800 to 1850, when the Napoleonic Wars eliminated the Dutch Asian fleet. Previously, the fleet had kept down the depredations of the Malays.

Chinese and Japanese pirates flourished off and on through the centuries. Raids by Japanese pirates supposedly prompted Kublai Khan's unsuccessful invasions of Japan in 1274 and 1281. The disintegration of the Ming dynasty's rule over China during the mid-seventeenth century led to the rise of the Fukienese pirate Cheng (or Zheng) Chih-Lung, who operated from 1625 until 1646, when the newly triumphant Qing or Manchu dynasty executed him. His son Koxinga (1624–1662) remained loyal to the Ming, and by 1650 commanded a fleet more powerful than the Manchu navy. In 1661, he conquered Taiwan, setting up a government that lasted until 1682. He died of an illness in 1662 while planning the conquest of the Philippines.

Later powerful Chinese pirates include Ch'en Tien-Pao and Cheng Ch'i, who operated along the China-Vietnam border from the 1780s to 1801/1802. Cheng Ch'i's cousin, Cheng I, succeeded him in 1802, and by the time of his death from drowning in 1807 had built up a force of 200 junks and 20,000 to 40,000 men. His wife, Cheng I Sao, assumed command of his forces with the assistance of Chang Pao (d. 1822). They continued to conduct bothersome raids on Chinese ships and coastlines until they negotiated a generous pardon from the Chinese government in 1810. Chang Pao became an officer in the Chinese army and led several successful expeditions against other Chinese pirates. Such large-scale piratical activity illustrates the growing weakness of the Manchu government in the early nineteenth century.

Pirates were often a serious hazard to sea travelers through the ages. Generally, they only robbed their victims and did not murder them. Sometimes they resorted to torture to discover the locations of valuables. Those unfortunates who got in their way were beaten or killed. Crews and passengers who resisted pirates could expect particularly gruesome, painful deaths. Women captured by pirates were sometimes treated courteously, but on other occasions they were sexually assaulted. According to some accounts, Henry Avery's capture of the *Gang-i-sawai* resulted in gentlemanly treatment of the women prisoners. Others, however, said that an orgy of rapine followed the *Gang-i-sawai*'s capture. Pirates commonly marooned unwanted captives on desolate coastlines or desert islands. A slow death from starvation frequently followed for such unfortunates. Films and novels often portray pirates in a romantic light, but to their victims they were a serious and sometimes deadly hazard of sea travel.

See also
> Barbary Pirates; Cretans; Hospitalers, Knights.

For further reading
> David Cordingly, *Under the Black Flag*, 1995; David Cordingly, ed., *Pirates*, 1996; David F. Marley, *Pirates and Privateers of the Americas*, 1994; Henry A. Ormerod, *Piracy in the Ancient World*, 1923; Marcus Rediker, *Between the Devil and the Deep Blue Sea*, 1987; Jan Rogozinski, *Pirates!*, 1995.

PLINY THE ELDER (23–79)   Roman scholar who is famous for his encyclopedic *Natural History*, a wide-ranging compilation of the anthropological, geographical, biological, geologic, and medical knowledge circulating in the world of the Roman Empire of the first century A.D. Pliny belonged to the Equestrian class of Roman society and served the empire in a number of military commands and civil administration posts that took him to Germany, Spain, Belgic Gaul, and North Africa. A true scholar to the last, Pliny died observing the eruption of Mount Vesuvius when poisonous volcanic fumes overcame him.

Much of the contents of the *Natural History* were based on Pliny's direct observations, but other parts were derived from his researches into the writings of other scholars. Pliny claimed to have examined 2,000 books by 100 authors in the course of researching his *Natural History*. In fact, he was too modest; modern scholars count quotations from 475 authors. Pliny sometimes used outdated authorities, which rendered his book obsolete even as he wrote it. This was particularly true of the sections dealing with geographical and anthropological matters. Pliny based his account of India and the Marvels of the East on the writings of Ctesias of Cnides and Megasthenes, which were hundreds of years old. Although Roman merchants routinely visited India in Pliny's day and so were available to supply more accurate, firsthand observations and descriptions, he simply failed to consult them.

Pliny's *Natural History* has importance for the legend and lore of travel for several reasons. First and foremost, its sections on the monstrous races and the Marvels of the East were widely read and copied by later writers. Solinus (fl. 200) copied extensively and uncritically from Pliny in the course of writing his work of world geography entitled the *Collectanea Rerum Memorabilium*. In turn, both Pliny and Solinus were popular among medieval scholars and encyclopedists such as Macrobius, Martianus Capella, Isidore of Seville, and Vincent of Beauvais. Plinian ideas about Eastern monsters and wonders determined the expectations of European travelers from William Rubruck to Marco Polo to Christopher Columbus. Only the vast increase in Europe's geographical knowledge during the fifteenth through the seventeenth centuries rendered Pliny's geographical and anthropological materials permanently obsolete.

See also
> Marvels of the East; Monstrous Races.

For further reading

John Block Friedman, *The Monstrous Races in Medieval Art and Thought*, 1981; Pliny the Elder, *Natural History*, 1991; John Kirtland Wright, *The Geographical Lore of the Time of the Crusades*, 1925.

POCHTECA   Hereditary merchant guild that operated in the society of the pre-Columbian Aztecs of Mexico. Although the pochteca handled much of the trade of the Aztec state, their specialty was conducting long-distance trade beyond the borders of the Aztec domain. Living in separate quarters inside Tenochtitlán and other cities of the Aztecs' allies, the pochteca organized caravans of *tlameme* (professional bearers) to carry their trade goods throughout the Aztec lands and beyond. Besides trading, pochteca engaged in espionage for the Aztec state, and sometimes assisted in the Aztec conquests as warriors. In turn, the Aztec state used its political and military power to protect the activities of the pochteca. Some writers overdramatically portray the pochteca as some sort of pan-kingdom or pan-tribal organization that transcended the Aztec state and its neighbors. This is not true—the pochteca were an important part of the Aztec economy, but they were not above the Aztec state.

Narrowly defined, the pochteca were associated only with the Aztec state. However, evidence shows that similar organizations existed during the era of Toltec supremacy (A.D. 900–1200). Some scholars also believe that the basic organization of the pochteca existed in the society of Teotihuacán (300 B.C.–A.D. 750), and may have originated among the ancient Olmec culture (ca. 1500–ca. 500 B.C.) along the Gulf Coast. Archaeological evidence indicates that pochteca reached at least as far south as Guatemala, and north to Chaco Canyon, New Mexico. Some archaeologists speculate that ancient Mexican merchants or pochteca may have taken their trade goods as far as the southeastern United States and Cahokia in Illinois during the era of the Mississippian culture (A.D. 700–1500). If true, it shows the great distances that merchants of ancient Mexico could travel without the benefit of draft and pack animals and wheeled transport.

For further reading

Ross Hassig, *Trade, Tribute, and Transportation*, 1985; Bente Bittmann Simmons and Thelma D. Sullivan, "The Pochteca," *Atti de XL Congresso Internazionale degli Americanisti* 4 (1972): 203–212.

POLO, MARCO (1254?–1324)   Venetian merchant who traveled to and within the China of Kublai Khan between 1271 and 1295. His book about his travels in the East made him the most famous Western traveler of all time. Over the centuries, however, some doubts arose and continue to be expressed about whether he really reached China.

Marco Polo was born in Venice about 1254 into a family of merchants of merely modest means. Little is known for certain about his life, and many of the more romantic and dramatic details of his biography seem to be later, unsubstantiated additions by the early Italian historian of exploration Gian Battista Rasmusio (1485–1557). His father Nicoló and his uncle Maffeo participated in Venice's lucrative trade with Constantinople. In 1260 the Polo brothers ventured east from Constantinople with the idea of participating in the commerce of the Black Sea region and central Asia. They made their way to Soldaia (or Sudak) on the Crimean peninsula, and from there traveled all the way to Bulghar on the northern Volga River to the khanate of the Kipchaks. Successful trading and a war between the Kipchaks and the Ilkhans of Persia kept them moving eastward into the region of the Caspian Sea until they reached the great city of Bukhara. The Polos encountered envoys traveling to the court of Kublai (r. 1260–1291), the Great Khan of the Mongols. The envoys invited the Polos to accompany them to their meeting with the Great Khan; the journey to the Mongol court took a year. Kublai Khan showed them great hospitality. He was very curious about Western rulers, and even more so about Christianity and the pope. Kublai Khan apparently liked what he heard, because he sent a Tartar noble as an envoy to the pope in the company of the two Polos. Their mission was to ask the pope to send a hundred scholars to Kublai's court to teach the Mongols about Christianity. Kublai also requested a gift of some oil from the lamp burning in the Church of the Holy Sepulchre in Jerusalem. To ensure their safe passage, the khan gave them a gold tablet as a passport. The three traveled for several days until the Mongol noble fell ill and was unable to travel any farther. The Polos decided it would be best if they continued their journey. After three years, they reached Acre in Palestine in April 1269. They learned that the old pope had died, and that a papal election was being conducted. They returned home to Venice to find that Nicoló's wife had died and his son Marco was now 15 years old.

The Polos stayed in Venice about two years waiting for the papal elections to be completed. As more and more time elapsed with no result, they decided to return to Kublai Khan. In Acre they persuaded the papal legate Theobald of Piacenza to provide them with the gift of oil from the Church of the Holy Sepulchre. He also wrote letters to the Great Khan explaining the delay over the election of the new pope and stating that the Polos had done their best to fulfill the khan's wishes. The two elder Polos, accompanied by Marco, began their second trip to the court of Kublai Khan in 1271. Sailing to Layas in Armenia, they received a message from Theobald of Piacenza, who had been elected Pope Gregory X on 1 September 1271. He asked them to return to Acre, and the king of Armenia obliged by lending his royal galley. The new pope assigned two Dominican friars, Nicholas of Vincenza and William of Tripoli, to travel with the Polos and serve as his envoys to Kublai Khan. The friars carried important letters from the pope to the Mongol ruler.

For a second time the Polos departed from Acre for the distant East. Reaching Layas, they discovered that Muslim armies had invaded Armenia, making travel very hazardous. The Polos were undeterred, but the two Dominicans

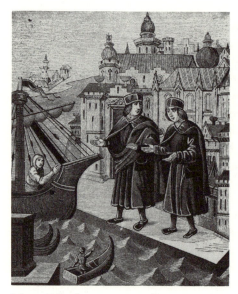

Marco Polo about to start on his voyage. Woodcut.

were far more easily discouraged. They decided to turn back, and gave their diplomatic credentials to the Polos. The Polos continued eastward and finally reached Kublai Khan's summer palace at Shangtu after three and a half years of travel. Little is known about the route they followed, as Marco Polo's book does not supply an itinerary with any detail. Most scholars think they followed a more southerly route, traveling through modern-day Iraq, Iran, and Afghanistan, and then crossed the mountains of the Pamirs and the dreaded Takla Makan Desert.

Once they arrived at the Mongol court, Kublai Khan greeted them joyfully. The young Marco was an adept student of foreign cultures. He swiftly learned the customs and language of the Mongols and soon added several more Asian languages to his repertoire. His abilities attracted the favorable notice of Kublai Khan, and the Great Khan entrusted Marco with a mission to a province that lay six months' travel away. On the basis of internal evidence from Marco's book, some scholars suggest that his destination was Yunnan Province. Yunnan, or Carajan, is a large province in southwest China that borders on the present-day countries of Tibet, Burma, Laos, and Vietnam, as well as the Chinese province of Guangxi. It was an important gold-producing region in premodern China. Kublai Khan was greatly pleased by Marco Polo's performance. Besides carrying out his official duties, Marco was an acute observer, returning with many tales of his travels and the strange lands he visited. These stories were very much to the taste of Kublai Khan, who had been quite disappointed by the lackluster tales brought back by his other envoys and commissioners. Therefore, the Great Khan employed Marco on other assignments and honored him with the title *messer*.

Messer Marco Polo worked for Kublai Khan for 17 years, traveling throughout much of Asia and (he claimed) serving as the governor of the city of Yangzhou for three years. Shortly before he returned to Venice, Marco went on a diplomatic mission to India, which increased his knowledge of the many lands and peoples of Asia. That Kublai Khan so readily employed a foreigner for important tasks is not as surprising as it might appear. Kublai Khan was a Mongol and a descendant of Genghiz Khan. He and his Mongol warriors were a tiny conquering minority over a vast subject population of Chinese. They did not trust their Chinese subjects, and under the circumstances, the employment of foreigners made sense.

Coming to China had been very lucrative for the Polos, but after 17 years they were homesick for their homeland of Venice. They also grew fearful about the impending death of the aging Kublai Khan. He had been a generous benefactor, but his successor might not. The successes of Marco Polo had likely aroused a certain amount of jealousy at the Mongol court. The Polos' enemies might turn the next emperor against them, and all would be lost. When they first approached Kublai Khan for permission to return home, he refused. (At this time, Marco went on his mission to India.) When he returned, a new diplomatic assignment had come up. Mongol envoys had negotiated a marriage alliance between Arghun (r. 1284–1291), the Ilkhan of Persia and the grandnephew of Kublai Khan, and Cocachin, the daughter of Kublai. Someone was needed to escort the princess to Persia. It was a mission tailor-made for the well-traveled and trusted Polos. Thanks to the support of sympathetic Mongol officials, Kublai Khan was at last persuaded to let them go.

The Polos began their return to Venice in 1292. Before they departed, Kublai Khan presented them with two golden tablets of authority to serve as safe-conducts as they traveled through the vast Mongol territories. He also gave them messages to pass on to the kings of England, France, and Spain (Castille), as well as other rulers of Christendom. The Polos left China by sea, probably from Quanzhou, in a fleet of four or five ships with crews of 250–260 as well as passengers. It took 3 months to reach Java, and 18 months to cross the Indian Ocean, stop off at various places in India, and sail on up the Arabian Sea to the Strait of Hormuz. The voyage was not an easy one. Only eight passengers survived, including the three Polos and the princess. They delivered the princess, only to learn that Arghun had died. His son and successor Ghazan [Casan] (1295–1304) was eager to take Cocachin as his bride, so with their mission completed, the Polos traveled westward. Reaching Trebizond on the northern coast of Asia Minor, they took ship and passed through Constantinople, finally making their way home to Venice in 1295. If the sixteenth-century historian Rasmusio is to be believed, they returned home seemingly empty-handed in ragged Mongol clothing so that at first no one recognized them. Once they settled into the family house, they changed their outfits and ripped open the seams of their old clothing, in which many precious gems were hidden. Their many years in China had been wondrously profitable.

Marco Polo's adventures were not yet over. Venice went to war with Genoa, and in a battle during 1296 or 1298, Marco was captured. He shared his captivity with a writer named Rustichello of Pisa, and the two collaborated on a book of Marco Polo's travels. In 1299, Venice and Genoa made peace. Marco returned home, married, and raised a large family. He died in 1324 at about the age of 70.

Marco Polo's book is his great legacy to the history of travel, exploration, and geography. The book was probably written from memory without benefit of notes, although the medieval chronicler Jacopo di Acqui told how the captive Marco wrote to his father Nicoló asking him to send him his notes and other records of their travels. Just how much Rustichello embellished the account cannot be determined, but he obviously did some enhancing. The many variant manuscript copies of Marco Polo's travels certainly indicate that others were not above improving the text with unfounded details. The sixteenth-century historian Rasmusio appears to have been particularly guilty of adding material of dubious authenticity to Marco Polo's original text.

Marco Polo's contemporaries found his stories of Cathay and other Asian lands interesting but sometimes unbelievable. Jacopo di Acqui and others mention that some people considered Polo to be an exaggerator, a liar, or a spinner of tall tales. In fact, his book was titled *Il Milione*, which may be a reference to the seemingly fantastic peoples and places described by Marco Polo. Interestingly, late-medieval Europeans widely believed that the fictional Sir John Mandeville's journeys actually had taken place, yet compared to the sometimes outrageous material in Mandeville's book, the contents of Marco Polo's is quite tame.

Marco Polo's book proved to be quite popular. Apparently, he and Rustichello originally composed it in a hybrid French-Italian dialect similar to Romance. Soon after 1315, a Friar Francisco Pipino translated the work into Latin. All other variants of Marco Polo's travels evolved from these two versions. Between 143 and 150, different manuscripts or printed editions survive, in seven basic versions. Some versions emphasize the missionary aspects of the book, while others focus on commercial matters. Marco Polo's book was quickly translated into other major European languages and dialects such as French, Venetian, Tuscan, German, Irish, Bohemian, Spanish, Aragonese, Catalan, Portuguese, and English. No original manuscript in Polo's or Rustichello's handwriting survives. The earliest surviving manuscript can be dated to 1351, while the earliest mention of the book occurred in 1307. At that time, the French emissary Thibault de Chepoy mentioned that Marco Polo had sent a copy of his book as a gift to Charles of Valois, the son of the French king Philip the Fair.

Modern readers who first begin reading *The Travels of Marco Polo* find it not what they expected. Most people assume that it is a travelogue describing Marco Polo's itinerary and the adventures that befell him. Instead, *The Travels* begins with a brief prologue in the form of an itinerary, and the main body of the book is a country-by-country or region-by-region description of the lands and peoples of Asia. Marco Polo visited some of the places he describes, but in other cases he merely reports stories he heard, so that fact and fantasy are intermingled. He provides recognizable descriptions of coal and paper money, and his account of the Old Man of the Mountain and his sect of fanatical Assassins is reasonably correct. The description of Japan is clearly secondhand, as Marco Polo never visited that land. Standard European legends of greater or lesser dubiousness about Asian geography and ethnography also appear in his book, including tales of Prester John and the missionary work of St. Thomas in India. Still, *The Travels of Marco Polo* supplies a relatively accurate survey of the many lands and peoples of Asia, and is certainly far superior to the previous information available to medieval Europeans.

Interestingly, some of Marco Polo's contemporaries claimed that he never made the long journey to China, an opinion echoed by some modern scholars. They criticize certain glaring omissions in *The Travels of Marco Polo*. Marco Polo failed to mention the Great Wall of China, the complex Chinese system of pictographic writing, tea drinking, and foot binding among upper-class women. Critics of Polo's veracity also point out his tendency to employ Persian names for places and things rather than Chinese names. Another serious problem is the absence of Marco Polo's name in Chinese records from the era of Kublai

Khan. His three years of service as governor of Yangzhou does not appear anywhere in the detailed local records, nor in association with any diplomatic or domestic missions, including the expedition that took Princess Cocachin to Persia. This perplexing lack of documentation led some scholars to suggest that Marco Polo never traveled to China at all, that instead he compiled his book from preexisting Arabic and Persian sources, making him no more a real traveler than the fictional Sir John Mandeville. Most scholars, however, still credit Marco Polo with making a great journey to China. They may not accept that he brought back ice cream or spaghetti from China to Italy, or vice versa, but they place him as the greatest or among the greatest of the medieval European travelers.

See also

Cathay; Chipangu; Ibn Battuta, Abu 'Abd Allah Muhammad; *Mandeville, Travels of Sir John*; Mongol Missions; Old Man of the Mountain; Venice.

For further reading

Mary B. Campbell, *The Witness and the Other World*, 1988; J. R. S. Phillips, *The Medieval Expansion of Europe*, 1988; Frances Wood, *Did Marco Polo Go to China?* 1995; Henry Yule and Henri Cordier, eds., *The Travels of Marco Polo*, 1929.

POLYNESIAN VOYAGES

Anthropologists and archaeologists generally agree that the Polynesian sailors of the era prior to European contact were the greatest seamen of any preindustrial culture. Although sometimes referred to as the Vikings of the Pacific, they were far more skilled and intrepid sailors than the Phoenicians or the Norse.

Polynesia is a triangular region in the Pacific Ocean, with New Zealand, the Hawaiian Islands, and Easter Island located at its corners. The inhabitants of Polynesia are well known as a handsome people with dark, straight hair and skins that are far lighter than the Negrito peoples of Micronesia and Melanesia. All Polynesians speak a common language, although several local dialects differ significantly from one another. Before European contact, their culture was technologically still in the Stone Age. Most scholars, with the notable exception of Thor Heyerdahl, currently believe that the Polynesians originally came from Southeast Asia and began settling Polynesia far earlier than once thought. Scholars originally thought that the great settlement of Polynesia began about A.D. 500 and was completed about 1100. More recent archaeological evidence reveals that Polynesian Tonga was settled by 1140 B.C. and Samoa by 800 B.C. The geographic expansion halted until A.D. 300, when the Polynesians settled the Marquesa Islands, and then quickly moved on to Tahiti and the Society Islands. Occupation of Easter Island took place sometime between 300 and 500, the Hawaiian Islands by 600, and New Zealand by 1000.

Europeans began sailing the vast Pacific Ocean in the sixteenth century, but did not finish systematically exploring it until the eighteenth-century voyages of Captain James Cook. These explorers found the Polynesians exotic, mysterious, and attractive. They also discovered that the Polynesians had settled virtually every inhabitable island in the vast Pacific Ocean. This achievement was a great tribute to their skills as navigators and builders of high-seas canoes.

Although the Polynesians had a Stone Age culture, they were quite capable of building extremely seaworthy vessels. These vessels were of two types: outrigger canoes and double-hulled canoes with a connecting deck or platform. Shipbuilders constructed canoe hulls by digging out the trunks of large trees. The result was a narrow canoe that needed stabilizing by an outrigger. Builders also added planking to the top of the hull to keep out waves. Double-hulled canoes were connected by booms and planking. The Polynesians also equipped their oceangoing canoes with masts and sails, rudders for steering, and oars and paddles for additional propulsion. Larger canoes measured 60 to 80 feet in length, but canoes of 100 feet and more with as many as three masts were observed by early European explorers.

Polynesian shipwrights were highly skilled craftsmen who possessed great status. Their patron deities were Tangora, the god of the sea, and his brother Tane, the god of trees. Shipwrights engaged in elaborate rituals and sacrifices of pigs to gain Tane's blessing for their cutting of trees and construction of canoes. They prepared craft that compared favorably with the seaworthiness of the best products of early-modern European shipbuilders.

The skills of Polynesian navigators are the subject of some scholarly controversy. Some writers credit them with unexplainable or even supernatural powers. Others are more moderate in their assessments, but still credit the ancient Polynesians with purposefully exploring the Pacific Ocean and its scattered islands. More skeptical scholars, led by Andrew Sharp, agree that ancient Polynesians were bold sailors, but they point out that Polynesian navigational skills were limited to what a Stone Age culture could observe from nature. Sharp rejects the idea that ancient Polynesians made purposeful, long-distance voyages of discovery to far-flung locations such as New Zealand or Hawaii. Such voyages would have required geographical knowledge, information on winds and currents, and technical equipment that ancient Polynesians did not possess.

Instead, Sharp contends that the scattered islands of Polynesia were settled as the result of fortuitous accidents. He believes that large parties of canoes lost their way in storms or cloudy weather and came upon unknown islands, where they were forced to settle. Needless to say, many would have perished at sea when they failed to encounter habitable islands.

The ancient Polynesian navigators had amazing abilities to navigate successfully and accurately over open seas for distances of 100 to over 200 miles. They had an intimate understanding of the physical characteristics of their home waters, and a detailed knowledge of the variable behavior of local currents and winds, which permitted them to use dead-reckoning navigation. The Polynesian navigators also knew where all the neighboring islands were located relative to one another. Combining that knowledge with an intimate understanding of celestial movements, they could use the stars to guide them, based on sightings measured against reference, or *etak,* islands. The way in which waves broke and oscillated provided an observant navigator with clues to the existence of nearby land, as did water color under some circumstances. Cloud formations and flights of land and sea birds also permitted Polynesian navigators to determine the location of land that lay out of sight. Alert navigators could even smell unseen land if the wind was right and the island was not too far away. The Polynesians' mastery of all these techniques allowed them to sail from one point to another with a precision that amazed European visitors. However, if a seasoned Polynesian navigator found himself in an unfamiliar section of the ocean, he would be as lost as anyone else. Still, the ancient Polynesians achieved prodigious feats of sea voyaging in the era before European contact. They richly deserve to be considered among the world's great travelers.

See also

Norse Voyages; Pacific Ocean; Phoenicians.

For further reading

Peter H. Buck, *Vikings of the Pacific*, 1959; Jack Golson, ed., *Polynesian Navigation*, 1972; David Lewis, *We, the Navigators*, 1972; Andrew Sharp, *Ancient Voyagers in Polynesia*, 1964; Richard Shutler, Jr., and Mary Elizabeth Shutler, *Oceanic Prehistory*, 1975.

PORTOLAN CHARTS

Medieval nautical maps used in conjunction with dead-reckoning sailing to navigate the Mediterranean Sea and the west coast of Europe.

The first surviving portolan charts date to 1270. Centering on the Mediterranean and Black Sea regions, these maps exhibited a sudden improvement in geographic accuracy over the preceding ones. However, as the portolan charts moved beyond the Mediterranean and the west coast of Europe, their accuracy blurred and faded. Many of the surviving copies of portolan charts were apparently the possessions of rulers or scholars, because they are heavily decorated and annotated. The decorative portolan charts were clearly derived from working charts used by seamen for practical navigation.

Portolan charts originated out of the information found in portolans, the name for books of sailing directions used by seafarers of the Mediterranean Sea. The name *portolan* had its origin in the Latin word *portus,* for port, because the portolans gave the directions needed to sail from one port to another. The early history of portolan charts is obscure and controversial. The oldest surviving portolan charts are virtually fully developed and represent an apparently major and sudden leap in cartographic accuracy. No evidence of any evolutionary or historical development survives, resulting in many conflicting theories about their origins. Some historians claim that portolan charts are based on lost ancient cartographic prototypes that go back variously to the Phoenicians, Carthaginians, Greeks, or Romans. It has even been suggested, although not widely accepted, that the portolan charts were based on information handed down from an ancient Ice Age supercivilization or extraterrestrial visitors. Other scholars suggest a medieval origin, that people combined the use of the traditional portolan (detailed sailing directions) with the use of the compass to navigate. The new technology of the compass would have made it possible to compose more accurate maps. Since compasses came into use in Europe about 1200 and the earliest portolan charts date to 1270, a sudden medieval origin becomes explicable. The lack of preliminary versions of portolan charts may be attributable to the fact that they were intended to be practical navigational tools. Sailors used them on voyages until they were worn out or lost at sea. The old ones were thrown away and replaced with new ones. As a result, the fancy, decorative versions of portolan charts survive in disproportionate numbers because they were valued objects d'art and did not suffer the rigors of going to sea.

Portolan charts provided accurate information for ships operating in the Mediterranean Sea, the Black Sea, and the west coast of Europe. Coastlines were truly drawn, ports were placed correctly, and promontories, reefs, and shoals were clearly indicated. Various color codings indicated the relative importance of various ports and geographic features. The most distinctive features of a portolan chart were the rhumb lines, which formed a complex web used as an aid to dead-reckoning navigation. Each set of rhumb lines was based on a circle, radiating out from the center in 32 different directions based on the wind rose with its eight major winds and the accompanying half- and quarter-wind directions. Navigators used the lines to help determine the distance and direction their ship traveled. The system worked surprisingly well. Christopher Columbus was an excellent dead-reckoning navigator.

With the coming of the sixteenth century and the vast increase in geographical information from the numerous European voyages of exploration, new cartographic techniques were needed. Cartographers developed grid systems of coordinated lines of latitude and longitude, the most famous and useful being that of Gerard Mercator (1512–1594). With these new mapping techniques, portolan charts gradually became obsolete and were abandoned by sailors. However, during the fourteenth and fifteenth centuries, portolan charts provided European seafarers and travelers with a very functional method of navigation.

See also
Mappamundi; Rutters.
For further reading
Tony Campbell, "Portolan Charts from the Late Thirteenth Century to 1500," in *The History of Cartography*, vol. 1: *Cartography in Prehistoric, Ancient, and Medieval Europe and the Mediterranean*, 1987; J. H. Parry, *The Age of Reconnaissance*, 1981.

PRAIRIE SCHOONER   Nickname given to the wagons used to cross the prairies, deserts, and mountains of the Old West in the mid-nineteenth-century United States.

The prairie schooner is familiar to most people through books, films, and television shows depicting the westward movement of Americans across the

Great Plains and the Rocky Mountains. These wagons first came into use along the Sante Fe Trail in 1821. Their nickname was based on the wagons' canvas covers, which had the appearance of sails when viewed at a distance. Prairie schooners had to be sturdy to survive a 2,000-mile journey that included hundreds of miles of difficult terrain. They also needed to carry up to 2,500 pounds of cargo without breaking down. An irreparable breakdown along the trail meant almost certain ruin and even possible death for the wagon's passengers. Wagons were constructed of hardwoods reinforced with iron fittings and parts in an optimal ratio of sturdiness to lightness of weight. Three to six oxen or four to six mules formed the typical teams of draft animals needed to pull a prairie schooner.

Prairie schooners evolved from the design used by the hardy Conestoga wagons, which carried travelers and freight across the Appalachian and Allegheny Mountains in the colonial and early national eras of American history. Generally, the prairie schooner was smaller than a Conestoga wagon because the prairie environment and travel costs did not allow overland emigrants the luxury of the large teams of draft animals needed to pull a Conestoga wagon. Prairie schooners were first manufactured in St. Louis, but other companies soon began building them in Indianapolis, Chicago, and Kenosha, Wisconsin.

Most travelers walked alongside prairie schooners. The wagons did not provide passenger seating and were quite uncomfortable. The canvas cover provided shelter in the event of bad weather on the road or at night, and when hot weather made temperatures unbearable, the covers were rolled up. The contribution of prairie schooners to western expansion and settlement is incalculable.

See also
Conestoga Wagon; Santa Fe Trail; Wagon Trains.
For further reading
William Francis Hooker, *The Prairie Schooner,* 1918; Huston Horn, *The Pioneers,* 1974; George R. Stewart, "The Prairie Schooner Got Them There," *American Heritage* 13 (no. 2, Feb. 1962): 98–102.

PRESTER JOHN AND HIS KINGDOM   Also known as Presbyter John or Presbyter Iohannes. During the era of the Crusades in the twelfth and thirteenth centuries, a legend arose concerning a powerful Christian ruler whose kingdom was located in Asia. The beleaguered Crusaders in Palestine hoped that Prester John and his great armies would come to their aid and destroy the forces of Islam. As Asia became better known to Europeans in the fourteenth and fifteenth centuries, the location of Prester John's kingdom shifted to Africa, specifically the Christian realm of Ethiopia. Belief in the existence of Prester John persisted through the sixteenth century, providing a significant motivation for European explorations and missionary journeys into Asia and Africa.

From 1096 to 1099, the participants in the First Crusade conquered much of the Holy Land, or Palestine, from the forces of Islam. No other Crusade came close to matching their success. In fact, the history of the Crusades from 1099 until 1291 (the fall of the last Crusader outpost at Acre) is a litany of defeats, holding actions, and disappointments, with precious few victories. The outlook for the Crusades was glum from a few decades after the First Crusade. The power of the Islamic states in the Middle East grew while the European Crusaders bickered among themselves. As a result of this dissension, the important Crusader city of Edessa fell to the effective Muslim general Imad ad-din Zengi of Mosul on 24 December 1144. Suddenly, all the Christian conquests in the Holy Land looked vulnerable to recapture by Islam. Thoughtful people were bound to be anxious and to cast about for some hopeful sign.

Responding to the Muslim threat, the Crusaders sought aid from the pope, along with the various rulers and knights back home in western Europe. Prince Raymond of Antioch sent Bishop Hugh of Jabala to seek assistance from Pope Eugenius III. Bishop Hugh traveled to Italy to meet with the pope on 18 November 1145. In the course of his plea for help, Bishop Hugh told the story of a great Asian ruler named John who was both a king and a priest, and a descendant of the three Magi. This Prester John ruled over a great Christian realm in Asia and had utterly defeated the Islamic Samiardi brothers, the monarchs of Persia and Media. After defeating the Samiardi, Prester John attempted to come to the relief of the hard-pressed Crusaders in the Holy Land, but the flooded Tigris River blocked his march. Moving north, he waited several years for the river to freeze over so he could cross it. When that failed to occur, he was forced to abandon his mission and return home.

The German chronicler Otto of Freising was present at the meeting, and recorded what was said. His account is the earliest written record to mention the existence of Prester John. In the opinion of most modern scholars, Hugh of Jabala's story about Prester John did not create the legend; rather, it was a response to a number of Prester John stories already circulating in European courts and centers of power. These stories actually hurt the Crusader cause because they encouraged complacency. If European rulers thought that a powerful Asian Christian ruler was ready to smash Islam and save the Crusader states, it diminished the need for Europeans to come to the aid of their coreligionists in Palestine. The point of Bishop Hugh of Jabala's story about Prester John was that he had failed to come to the aid of the Crusaders, and a desperate need for help from the Christian states of western Europe still existed.

Hugh of Jabala's pessimistic account of Prester John did little to dampen European enthusiasm about the great Christian potentate of Asia or the hope placed on his assistance in the destruction of Islam. Such speculations rose to new heights around 1165 when a purported letter from Prester John to the Byzantine emperor Manuel circulated throughout Europe. Copies of the letter were also supposedly sent to the pope, Emperor Frederick Barbarosa, and other European kings. The original letter was written in Latin and was quickly and widely translated into the various European vernaculars, notably French, Italian, German, and English. Some 80 manuscript copies of versions of the letter survive, which further demonstrates its popularity and widespread circulation.

The *Letter of Prester John* was a complete fraud. Some mischievous monk probably produced it. However, for several centuries, the document was generally believed to be genuine. The *Letter of Prester John* performed the function of solidifying the various oral tales of Prester John into written form. Other writers added various bits of fantastic geographical lore to the *Letter* over the years of copying and recopying it.

Several elements went into the creation of the Prester John legend. The peoples of medieval western Europe were well aware that Asia and Africa possessed significant Christian populations. Nestorian churches were scattered across Asia from Syria to China. Egypt was the home of Monophysite Christianity, the creed followed by the rulers of Ethiopia. Crusaders and European merchants and pilgrims came into contact with both groups, as well as other minor Christian sects. Europeans also knew of St. Thomas's missionary work in India from the pseudoepigraphic *Acts of Thomas*. Travelers to India looked for the Christians of St. Thomas. Christians existed in medieval India, but they were largely the product of later Nestorian missionary work, not the descendants of St. Thomas's converts, who probably died out due to their isolation from other Christians.

Belief in a substantial population of Asian Christians living in a powerful kingdom was given further support in 1122 by the appearance of Patriarch John of Hulna in India. Visiting Pope Calixtus II, Patriarch John told of the miraculous tomb of St. Thomas at Hulna and the vast riches associated with it. The entire episode of his visit is recorded in a Latin document titled *De adventu patriarchae Indorum* and in a letter from Odo of Rheims. Hulna has never been identified with a specific city in India. Either Patriarch John was a charlatan, or he came from Edessa seeking aid for that beleaguered city some 20 years before its fall to the Muslims. The western Europeans who received him may not have understood where he actually came from, and through wishful thinking placed him in India.

The existence of such tales about real or imagined exotic Christians encouraged the belief in an Asian Christian empire of immense size and power. Some suggest that vague knowledge of the Christian Ethiopian Empire in Africa prompted the original European belief in Prester John's kingdom because of the geographical confusion concerning the Three Indias. The various Romances of Alexander the Great also added to the legend of Prester John. Although Alexander the Great predated Christianity by several centuries, Jewish writers, followed by Christians, enthusiastically made him into their image of a religious hero-ruler. Alexander was thoroughly Christianized and credited with numerous strange and miraculous adventures in the Romances. Some of this material was transferred to Prester John over time. Prester John's realm also exhibited many of the characteristics that in the classical era were associated with the Marvels of the East.

The Prester John legend also received powerful impetus from poorly understood rumors of monumental events taking place in central and east Asia in the mid-twelfth century. Hugh of Jabala's account of Prester John's victory over the Persians appears to be derived directly from the ruler of the

Kara Khitai Empire, Yeh-lü Ta-shih, and his defeat of the Seljuk Turkish sultan Sanjar near Samarkand on 9 September 1141. The problem with identifying Yeh-Lü Ta-shih with Prester John is that no evidence exists to show that Yeh-Lü Ta-shih was a Christian; in fact, surviving Chinese sources describe him as a Buddhist. The Prester John story might have been a conflation of the exploits of Yeh-Lü Ta-shih and his Kara Khitai with the earlier conversion to Christianity of the other central Asian nomadic tribes of the Keraïts and the Ongut.

The Christian Ung Khan, or Unc Khan, ruled over the Keraïts and the Onguts. Their conversion was repeated as true by the Syrian Christian historian Gregory Abul Faraj Bar-Hebraeus (1226–1286) in his *Chronicon Syriacum*. Supposedly, their ruler, Ung Khan, had once been the overlord of Genghiz Khan, but was later defeated and killed by him. A Keraït ruler named To'oril befriended the young Genghiz Khan during his early troubles, but was later overthrown by his protégé in 1203; he may have been the historical Ung Khan. The travelers William of Rubruck and Marco Polo both identified this Ung Khan of the Keraïts with Prester John. Several modern scholars also promote this identification. They claim that a Chinese emperor bestowed the title of "wang khan" on the ruler of the Keraïts, and the title evolved into both Ung Khan and Prester John. Others reject this identification because of chronological conflicts.

A Russian scholar named Phillip Brunn suggested in about 1093 that the Georgian prince John Orbelian was the model for Prester John. This identification suffers from several problems. Orbelian had no great victories over the Muslims, and he was not even a king. Despite such confusions, western European Christians desperately wanted Prester John to exist and, more importantly, become their ally. In 1177, Pope Alexander III wrote a letter to Prester John. An envoy was given the letter and assigned to find the elusive king. The envoy never returned.

Meanwhile, Asia was faced with the juggernaut of Mongol tribes under the leadership of Genghiz Khan (1155/1167–1227). Beginning in 1196, Genghiz Khan launched an amazing series of conquests—the Merkits in 1202, the Keraïts in 1203, the Hsi-Hsia in 1209, the Chin dynasty of China in 1215, and the Kara Khitai in 1218. The defeat of the Kara Khitai made a refugee of their ruler Küchlük, who was a Nestorian Christian and a possible model for Prester John. Next, Genghiz Khan conquered the Khwarizmian Empire of Shah Muhammad, the most powerful Islamic state at that time. Between 1219 and 1225, the armies of Khwarizm were annihilated and both Muhammad and his son Jalal-al-Din were killed. With that success, Genghiz Khan returned to Mongolia to plan his next conquest, but in 1227, before preparations were completed, he died.

Vague and inaccurate accounts of Genghiz Khan's exploits filtered into the Crusader states of the Outremer and into Europe. As early as 1217, the Mongol conquests were connected to Prester John and used to promote the Fifth Crusade (1218–1221). A new document called the "Report on King David" circulated in 1220, claiming that a King David of India was marching against the Persians and that his plan was to destroy Islam. Some versions of the report identified King David and Prester John as the same person. Others called King David the son or grandson of Prester John. By this time, stories about Prester

John had been floating around Europe for about a century. As a result, the name evolved from being the personal name of an individual ruler into the title held by the rulers of that great Christian kingdom in Asia. Jacques de Vitry, the bishop of Acre, sent a report back to Europe in 1221 describing how King David of India had captured Samarkand and was moving against Baghdad. Vitry was actually describing Genghiz Khan's conquest of the Khwarizmian Empire, an event that had no Christian purpose. For the frustrated but hopeful Christians of Europe, their centuries-old mortal foe, Islam, seemed to be teetering on the brink of destruction. Even the savage Mongol raids into the Christian Caucasus region and southern Russia from 1221 to 1223 did not disillusion the Europeans about their supposed savior, King David/Genghiz Khan.

In 1236, Mongol operations against Christian states resumed with the conquest of Georgia, followed by that of Greater Armenia in 1239. In Russia, the Mongols totally destroyed the nomadic Bulgars and Kipchaks in 1237 and then turned on the sedentary Russian principalities. After inflicting some terrible defeats in early 1238, they sacked Kiev in 1240; an invasion of Poland and Hungary followed in 1241. Every European army that marched against them was badly defeated, and only the death of the Great Khan Ogadai on 11 December 1241 saved Europe from further depredations in 1242.

Finally, the pope and other European rulers recognized the dire threat posed by the Mongols. Their proposed solution was to convert the Mongols to Roman Catholicism and so transform them from a deadly menace into an invincible ally. Mongol rulers had close relationships with Christian nomadic tribes, and sometimes married Christian wives. Casual expressions of interest in Christian beliefs or rites were assumed to indicate a desire to convert to Christianity. This hope formed the stimulus for the diplomatic and missionary journeys of John de Plano Carpini in 1245 and William of Rubruck in 1253. These envoys, along with other missionaries such as Odoric of Pordenone and merchants such as Marco Polo and various diplomats, took advantage of the *Pax Mongolica* to travel across the vastness of Asia. They kept their eyes open for the kingdom of Prester John but they never found it—because it was not there.

Europeans began to give up on the existence of an Asian homeland for Prester John, although they did not give up on Prester John. Instead, they moved him to Africa, specifically to Ethiopia. In 1306, 30 Ethiopian diplomats arrived in Genoa, anxious to develop an alliance with the European powers. During their visit, a priest named Giovanni da Carignano interviewed them and wrote a description of their country. In his treatise he stated that Prester John ruled over Ethiopia. Although Carignano's book has not survived, other geographical works cited him and repeated his relocation of Prester John to Africa. Between 1330 and 1340, in his *Mirabilia Descripta,* Friar Jordanus of Sévérac also identified Prester John (or someone who seemed to fit that description) as the ruler of Ethiopia.

The dramatic change of Prester John's location from Asia to Africa is not quite as odd as it might seem. Medieval Europeans counted Ethiopia as one of the Three Indias, with the other two lying in Asia. Prester John's location remained in Africa until the early seventeenth century. Portuguese explorers, diplomats, and missionaries who visited Ethiopia in the fifteenth, sixteenth, and early seventeenth century all called it the land of Prester John, and persisted in calling the emperor of Ethiopia by the title of Prester John (to the great confusion of the Ethiopians, who had no knowledge of this title). Oddly enough, in 1507, a solitary map briefly returned the peripatetic Prester John to Asia and identified Tibet as his realm. Meanwhile, as the Portuguese visited Ethiopia and learned more about it, they realized that it was not the realm of the legendary Prester John, and the legend slowly faded from consideration as a true and literal geographical place.

Medieval Europeans developed elaborate descriptions of the land of Prester John, borrowing heavily from the classical traditions of the Marvels of the East and the Romances of Alexander the Great. As a king of India, Prester John was supposed to be fantastically wealthy, especially because all travel lore associated Indian rulers with great wealth. The *Letter of Prester John* claimed that his kingdom encompassed the Three Indias and contained 72 provinces, each ruled by a king. Its extent was unmeasurable. Agriculturally, the realm of Prester John was a land of milk and honey, but it also produced valuable pepper. Its rivers were cornucopias of gold and jewels. The land also contained a vast desert referred to as the Sandy Sea, which consisted of great shifting dunes of sand and rivers of rocks; it was inhabited by fish who lived in sand, not water. At its far eastern extremity, Prester John's realm housed the Terrestrial Paradise, including the four rivers of Paradise—the Tigris, Euphrates, Pison, and Gihon, all filled with gold and precious stones. Near the Terrestrial Paradise was the much-sought-after Fountain of Youth, which some writers claimed accounted for Prester John's extreme longevity. The court of Prester John was a magnet to people from all Christian nations. One English version of the *Letter of Prester John* told how his court contained many Englishmen as servants, clerks, or soldiers, including a bodyguard of 11,000. Needless to say, copies of the *Letter* found in other countries substitute French, Italian, or German where appropriate. The *Letter* also claimed that Prester John was descended from the Magi, who were supposedly converted to Christianity by St. Thomas. Some writers even identified the Magi Gaspar with Gundafor, the Indian king converted by St. Thomas. This overall image of Prester John was further reinforced by the account of his realm contained in the fictional *Travels of Sir John Mandeville*.

One obvious question is: why was this mysterious ruler called Prester John or Priest John at all? No true Prester John has ever been convincingly identified. One possible inspiration for the legend is connected to the Apostle John, who was supposedly immortal. This version claimed that by presiding as a great ruler, the Apostle John would serve as a forerunner for the second coming of Christ, and that the long-lived Prester John and the immortal Apostle John were one and the same. The modern scholar Vsevolod Slessarev traces the etymology of the term *Prester John* back almost that far. He claims that the John part of the name evolved from Vizan, the name of another Indian prince whom St. Thomas converted to Christianity and ordained as a deacon. Other scholars believe that the name Prester John evolved from corruptions of various Asiatic royal titles such as Gur Khan or Wang Khan. Portuguese scholars in the sixteenth and seventeenth centuries focused on an Ethiopian origin. They claimed that Prester John derived from the Ethiopian royal title of *zan*. However, Ethiopian rulers began using *zan* as a title in the sixteenth century, which fails to explain why the name was already in use by Europeans in 1145. The fictional Sir John Mandeville put forward the quaint story that a great emperor and his knight visited a Christian church, where they witnessed the ordination of some priests. The emperor, who had already expressed a strong interest in Christianity, was so impressed by the ceremony that he promised to take the title and name of the first new priest who came out of the church. The next priest was named John, so the emperor called himself Priest John from then on. Like most of Mandeville's book, the story was a complete fabrication, but it had wide circulation and acceptance in its day.

The legend of Prester John and his realm was one of the more enduring and influential geographical legends of medieval and early-modern Europe. From roughly 1145 to 1242, Prester John provided Europeans with the hope of a deliverer from the threat of Islam and an encouragement to go on Crusades. Travel and experience eventually would reveal that either Prester John was not as powerful as the pagan Mongol khans or he did not exist anywhere in Asia (thus, he reappeared as the ruler of the Christian kingdom of Ethiopia). Throughout these centuries, whether in Asia or Africa, Prester John and his realm served as an important goal for explorers and travelers, albeit one that could never be reached.

See also

Alexander the Great, Romances of; Ethiopia; Fountain of Youth; India; Magi, Three; *Mandeville, Travels of Sir John*; Marvels of the East; Mongol Missions; Outremer; Paradise, Four Rivers of; Paradise, Terrestrial; Polo, Marco; St. Thomas, Legend of.

For further reading

C. F. Beckingham, "The Achievement of Prester John" and "The Quest for Prester John," in *Between Islam and Christendom*, 1983; L. N. Gumilev, *Searches for an Imaginary Kingdom*, 1987; Igor de Rachewiltz, *Papal Envoys to the Great Khans*, 1971; Robert Silverberg, *The Realm of Prester John*, 1972; Vsevolod Slessarev, *Prester John*, 1959; John Kirtland Wright, *The Geographical Lore of the Time of the Crusades*, 1925.

PTOLEMY, CLAUDIUS (FL. SECOND CENTURY A.D.) An astronomer and geographer of Alexandria who lived during the reigns of Hadrian and Antonius Pius. Some scholars consider him the greatest geographer of the ancient world.

Ptolemy applied mathematics to the study of astronomy and geography in an attempt to render them more exact. Unfortunately, his efforts occurred on the eve of the Roman Empire's decline, and no one in the West was able to continue or advance beyond his efforts for centuries. Various Greek scholars increasingly applied mathematics to their studies of geography and astronomy. Producing more accurate maps was an important consideration, and some discussion occurred about developing a grid system of coordinates similar to modern latitude and longitude. These efforts revived in the second century A.D., first with Marinus of Tyre and next with Claudius Ptolemy. The works of Marinus of Tyre are lost and known only through Ptolemy's references to them in his *Geography*. Ptolemy acknowledged a substantial debt to Marinus of Tyre, and generously claimed that he only corrected and enhanced the work of his predecessor. Most scholars, however, credit Ptolemy with being the first to systematically apply a grid system to the geography of the known world. Certainly, he was the first cartographer to employ curved lines on his map projection to indicate the sphericity of the earth. His *Geography* is basically a gazetteer—a listing of places and their coordinates—along with some descriptive commentary. Lacking any means to measure distances accurately, Ptolemy had to rely on the reports of travelers. Although he applied some corrections to their estimates of distances, taking into consideration the vagaries of weather and terrain, inaccuracies still abounded in his work. Whether his *Geography* included maps is disputed by some historians, but it became customary for later manuscripts of Ptolemy to contain them. During the sixteenth century, the terms *ptolemy* and *atlas* were used interchangeably for books of maps.

Ptolemy's use of mathematics gave his *Geography* the semblance of accuracy, although he never claimed such; he was well aware of the tentative nature of his coordinates. Unfortunately, later generations of scholars treated his numbers as though they were highly accurate. Still, Ptolemy was one of the greatest geographers of the ancient world, and his work did much to improve humans' understanding of the shape of their world.

Some significant errors occurred in Ptolemy's *Geography*. Following Marinus of Tyre, Ptolemy accepted Posidonus's calculation of the circumference of the earth as 180,000 stadia, or about 18,000 miles, rather than its true circumference of 24,000 miles. While Ptolemy's earth was about 25 percent smaller around than it actually is, he also miscalculated the length of Asia, extending it farther east. These errors greatly reduced the supposed distance between Europe and Asia to the west. Ptolemy chose the Fortunate Isles, or the Canary Islands, to be his prime meridian, but his inaccurate knowledge of their actual location distorted the entire grid system. He depicted India too small, and Ceylon, or Taprobane, as much too large. According to Ptolemy, the Indian Ocean was actually an inland sea, because he thought Africa and Asia came together in the distant south. He claimed that the mythical Mountains of the Moon were the source of the Nile River's water. He mentions a Niger River in West Africa, but it does not appear to be the true Niger. These errors were based on poor access to information.

Even Ptolemy's mathematically based scientific measurements of geographic distances proved inaccurate, causing him to elongate the east/west length of the Mediterranean Sea. From measurements taken at Arbela in Asia Minor and Carthage during a lunar eclipse in 331 B.C., Ptolemy attempted to calculate distance scientifically. Unfortunately, it was thought that the time difference between the two places was three hours, rather than two. This error rendered Ptolemy's measurements of distances 50 percent greater than they should have been. In other areas, Ptolemy supplied needed corrections and improvements to geographical knowledge, including an accurate depiction of the Caspian Sea as landlocked, when many thought it was an inlet of the northern River Ocean.

When the Roman Empire went into its decline in the third century, knowledge of the Greek language disappeared in the West, which meant that people were no longer able to read Ptolemy's *Geography*. Medieval scholars lost their knowledge of Ptolemy, and his *Geography* had no direct influence on their geographical concepts. Islamic scholars of the Middle Ages, however, continued to study and preserve Ptolemy's works along with those of other classical Greek writers.

Eventually, knowledge of Ptolemy's works filtered into the West as the Greek language revived among scholars. In 1410, a Latin translation of Ptolemy's *Geography* appeared, but its diffusion was slow. No evidence exists that during his lifetime Prince Henry the Navigator (1394–1460) read it, was influenced by it, or had even heard of its existence. If the Portuguese had read Ptolemy, they would not have liked what they found. Ptolemy's depiction of the Indian Ocean as an inland sea would have called into severe doubt their plans to circumnavigate Africa to reach the Asian spice markets. Christopher Columbus's plan to reach Asia by sailing west was deeply influenced by his reading of Ptolemy's *Geography*. Ptolemy's calculations positing a smaller earth and a larger Asia than actually existed made Columbus's plan appear feasible. Certainly, the venerable antiquity of Ptolemy's scholarship lent additional authority to Columbus's scheme. The beginning of the sixteenth century marked the zenith of Ptolemy's influence on European geographical thinking. As the fresh accounts of explorers and travelers accumulated, geographical knowledge soon progressed beyond Ptolemy.

See also

Fortunate Isles; Mountains of the Moon; Nile River.

For further reading

E. H. Bunbury, *A History of Ancient Geography*, 1883; J. R. S. Phillips, *The Medieval Expansion of Europe*, 1988; J. O. Thomson, *A History of Ancient Geography*, 1948.

PYGMIES This monstrous race of smaller-than-normal humans appeared frequently in travelers' tales during ancient and medieval times.

The idea of a dwarfish race, as well as a corresponding race of giants, is one of the simplest and most common varieties in the pantheon of monstrous races. Quite naturally, humans speculate about peoples who are extraordinarily small, a process helped along by the occasional birth of individual dwarfs or midgets in any human society and by the literal evidence of Pygmy and dwarf tribes in Africa. Both Herodotus and Aristotle accurately refer to the existence of Pygmies in central Africa.

The ancient Greeks variously located the land of the Pygmies in Africa, Scythia, or India, the usual haunts of a monstrous race. Most descriptions of Pygmies depicted them as physically normal, except for their diminutive size. Pygmies also possessed tiny horses and cattle corresponding to their own size. Ctesias credited the Pygmies of India with a great respect for law and justice. However, they were not considered fully civilized because they practiced no agriculture and textile making (their braided clothing was made from their own hair). Overall, the Pygmies were considered to be a rather harmless race, although they engaged in an incessant war with the cranes.

Medieval European writers were not as kind to the Pygmies. The eighth-century Irish work titled *Liber Monstrorum* treated them as hostile rather than harmless. Lambert of St. Omer (1050–1125) asserted that God created the Pygmies at the same time as all the animals, thereby implicitly denying their full humanity. Albertus Magnus (ca. 1200–1280) was more explicit, stating that while Pygmies were the most perfect of animals, they were not fully human. The pilgrim John Witte of Hesse, in his *Itinerum* describing his journey of 1389, was even more negative. He located the Pygmies in Ethiopia and described them as deformed cave dwellers who lacked agriculture and subsisted on milk products like other beasts. Medieval Arabic traditions exhibit a similar attitude, as Sindbad the Sailor encountered some very unpleasant Pygmies on his third voyage. On the other hand, the writer of the *Letter of Prester John* described how the Pygmies living in the realm of the great Christian potentate Prester John had been converted to Christianity and thus restored to full humanity. The sixteenth-century French writer François Rabelais agreed implicitly by placing their origins at the postdiluvian confusion of languages at the Tower of Babel.

Pygmies, like giants, had some basis in reality. Various Pygmy tribes live in Africa, and one group known as the Akka hunt cranes. From such a factual basis, ancient travelers enlarged the legends of the Pygmies, which have persisted for centuries.

See also
Monstrous Races.

For further reading
John Block Friedman, *The Monstrous Races in Medieval Art and Thought*, 1981.

PYRAMIDS OF EGYPT
The first of the Seven Wonders of the Ancient World to be built and the only one to survive into the modern era, these impressive burial structures have defined and symbolized the grandeur and mystery of Egypt from the time of Herodotus to the present.

The three Great Pyramids were built by the pharaohs of the Fourth dynasty (ca. 2575–2467 B.C.) of the Old Kingdom era in Egypt. A long period of experimentation with pyramidal tombs by the pharaohs of the Third dynasty preceded the construction of the three Great Pyramids. Pharaoh Cheops (Khufu) built the first and largest. It is currently 481 feet high, having lost 30 feet of its original height. According to Herodotus, it took 100,000 men 20 years to build Cheop's pyramid; Diodorus Siculus (fl. 60–30 B.C.) claimed it took 360,000 men some 20 years. Modern scholars consider these figures exaggerated, although it obviously took much time and effort to build them. Cheop's successors, Chephren (Khafre) and Mykerinus (Menkaure), followed his example but built their tombs on a less grandiose scale. All three tombs have been thoroughly looted by grave robbers, which probably occurred as early as the First Intermediate Period (ca. 2181–2133 B.C.).

The pyramids have always attracted many visitors. The Greek traveler and historian Herodotus was fascinated by them. Over a thousand years later, the learned caliph al-Ma'mun (783–833), the son of Harun al-Rashid, visited the Great Pyramids in hopes of finding secret treasure inside. Ordering his workers to tunnel into the pyramid of Cheops, he failed to find any treasure, but did locate the long-lost original entrance. Unfortunately, al-Ma'mun's action also opened the way to some large-scale looting of the pyramids for building stones. Another thousand years later, the great Napoléon visited the pyramids during his Egyptian expedition of 1798–1799. On 21 July 1798, at the battle of the Pyramids, he used those structures to inspire his troops with the exhortation: "Think of it, soldiers; from the summit of those pyramids, forty centuries look down upon you." Napoléon later went sightseeing at the pyramids with his generals. Although he declined to join the group that climbed to the top, he participated in a survey of the edifice's dimensions. It was also reported that he entered the interior of the pyramid, where he experienced a fright that he refused to talk about.

Needless to say, myriad dubious theories proliferate about the origins and meaning of the Great Pyramids. Early Arabic scholars speculated that they were built to preserve Egyptian civilization during Noah's flood. In the fifth century A.D. and throughout the Middle Ages, Christian writers considered the pyramids to be the granaries of Joseph mentioned in Genesis, chapter 41. Pyramid power enthusiasts claim that the structures are ancient energy sources of fabulous power. Others assert that the pyramids are far older than most archaeologists believe and that they are actually the remnants of a lost, ancient supercivilization or evidence of extraterrestrial visitations (a theory exploited by the movie *Stargate*). Television documentaries dealing with the pyramids appear quite regularly, as they truly remain objects of awe. An Arab proverb sums it up: "Man fears Time, yet Time fears the pyramids."

See also
Seven Wonders of the Ancient World.

For further reading
Peter Clayton and Martin Price, eds., *The Seven Wonders of the Ancient World*, 1988; I. E. S. Edward, *The Pyramids of Egypt*, 1961; John Romer and Elizabeth Romer, *The Seven Wonders of the World*, 1995.

PYTHEAS OF MASSILIA, VOYAGE OF (240–238 B.C.) Explorer
and merchant who circumnavigated Britain and revealed its existence to the Greek world.

About 500 B.C., the Carthaginians established the fortress of Gades (modern Cadiz) near the Strait of Gibraltar to block the ships of others from entering and trading anywhere in the Atlantic Ocean. The blockade temporarily weakened between 242 and 236 B.C., and taking advantage of the situation, the Greeks of Massilia (modern Marsailles) sent an expedition under the scientist Pytheas to investigate the commercial opportunities of the Atlantic.

Passing through the Strait of Gibraltar, Pytheas sailed north along the Atlantic coast of Spain and the Bay of Biscay to Brittany. He crossed the English Channel to Cornwall and circumnavigated the island of Britain. It is unclear whether Pytheas visited other places that he described, such as Ultima Thule, or only relied on native testimony. Ultima Thule was a mysterious far northern island variously identified with the Faroe Islands, Iceland, or Norway.

Pytheas's writings are lost, but so many other ancient writers cited and quoted them that they can be largely reconstructed. Although his expedition was one of commercial reconnaissance, Pytheas was an acute scientific observer. He made many accurate astronomical measurements and provided the Greeks with detailed information about the Atlantic tides, a phenomenon that was not very marked on Mediterranean coasts. The scholar Polybius (200–after 118 B.C.) questioned Pytheas's credibility, but other writers such as Erastothenes (b. 280 B.C.) considered him quite reliable. Modern scholars also accept Pytheas as a good scientist who made sound observations.

See also
Thule.
For further reading
Rhys Carpenter, *Beyond the Pillars of Heracles*, 1966; C. F. C. Hawkes, *Pytheas*, 1977.

Q

QUIVIRA   Name for a legendary land rich in gold that sixteenth-century Spanish conquistadors located first in the Great Plains of the United States, but was soon relocated to the Pacific Coast region of northern California, Oregon, and Washington.

The name *Quivira* first appeared during Francisco Vásquez de Coronado's expedition of 1540–1541 into the American Southwest in search of the Seven Cities of Gold. A Native American called the Turk by the Spaniards told Coronado about a rich land of gold that lay northeast of the Pecos River country. Setting out across the prairie from around modern Sante Fe, New Mexico, the gold-hungry Spanish trudged on until the Turk admitted that he had lied. Coronado promptly had him strangled in the vicinity of present-day Wichita, Kansas. Despite the journey being based on an outright lie, Coronado attached the name *Quivira* to that vague, vast area of grassland in what is now Oklahoma and Kansas.

Quivira did not stay put. Later Spanish explorers of the northern California coast encountered reports of another rich Native American kingdom. By 1552, the chronicler Francisco López de Gómara labeled the Pacific Coast region north of Cape Mendocino as Quivira. The cartographers Gerard Mercator in 1569 and Abraham Ortelius in 1571 also located Quivira on the northwest Pacific coast of North America in their widely used maps. Richard Hakluyt, the English historian of exploration, followed their lead in 1586. A report in 1620 by Father Antonio de la Asunción claimed to have discovered an eyewitness account of rich Quivira made by some foreign travelers. Various late-seventeenth- and early-eighteenth-century French explorations of the interior of North America and the valley of the Mississippi River hoped to eventually reach Quivira on the Pacific Coast. Since it did not exist, they naturally failed. Quivira last appeared on the map of the French geographer Philippe Buache about 1752. By then, the legend of the much sought but never found Quivira was fading fast and no longer tempted explorers and travelers.

See also
   Seven Cities, Legend of.
For further reading
   David B. Quinn, *North America from Earliest Discovery to First Settlements*, 1977; Raymond H. Ramsay, *No Longer on the Map*, 1972.

R

RAILROADS Network of tracks, locomotives, and cars that revolutionized travel and the transportation of goods during the nineteenth century. Railroads originated in England, and quickly came into general use there and on the continent of Europe. In the United States, railroads spurred and made possible both the industrial revolution and the rapid development of an entire continent.

The origin of railroads came from the movement of coal from mines to market. A line of tracks or rails was built to move wheeled carts or wagons inside the mines and outside to a loading area. The tracks permitted a smoother ride and required less force. Such arrangements of wagons and tracks go back as far as the sixteenth century, and human or animal power initially moved the wagons. During the eighteenth century, steam engines were quickly adapted to the task of pulling a coal wagon along the tracks, and the first locomotive, or iron horse, was born. Early locomotives were primitive and inefficient, and at first could not outpull a good team of draft animals, but they had the virtue of never getting tired. The initial lack of power limited the number of wagons and cars as well as the amount and weight of cargo, but innovations and improvements in steam engines quickly produced much more efficient machines capable of pulling larger loads more quickly.

When railroads first appeared, people considered them an extension of freight wagons and stagecoaches. Like a stagecoach and its team of horses, individual steam engines pulled individual coaches. Individual trains were one type of business enterprise, and the tracks formed a separate business, similar to the relationship between wagon carriers and the operators of a toll road. However, railroads were not like regular roads, or even canals. Soon, considerations of traffic control, scheduling, and fueling forced tracks and trains to be fused into one business enterprise. As a result, trains and the networks of track came to be viewed as one great machine.

The first public railroad, the brainchild of railroad advocate George Stevenson, was the Stockton and Darlington Line in England. Chartered by Parliament in 1821, it opened in 1825 to carry coal and a few passengers. Numerous opposition forces, including canal companies and horse breeders, lobbied against the railroad, but their efforts were fruitless. The completed Stockton and Darlington Railroad proved successful even though its locomotives achieved speeds of only 12 miles per hour. Within a few years, the Manchester and Liverpool Line began operations (1830), and it also became a success, and other railroads quickly linked the major cities of Britain. Various European countries followed suit and built their own railroads. In the United States, the Baltimore and Ohio Railroad obtained its charter as a common carrier in 1827 and laid its first rail on 4 July 1828.

Railroads were successful because they were a flexible mode of transportation. They could go where it was impossible for canals to be built, operate in virtually all weathers, and soon ran more swiftly than horse-drawn conveyances and canal boats.

Americans enthusiastically adopted the railroad. Although well served by its existing waterways and canals, the vast United States needed railroads to reach its full potential. In 1830, the United States had 23 miles of railroad track; by 1840, this mileage grew to over 3,200 miles. That figure exceeded the total mileage of canals in the United States and the total mileage of railroads for all of Europe. By 1860, the United States had well over 30,000 miles of railroads, and by 1870, 53,000 miles, including the first transcontinental railroad, completed in 1869. By 1900, American railroad mileage was 193,000. Similar although less dramatic expansions of railroad mileages occurred in Europe and spread to Asia, Africa, and South America.

Railroads grew in efficiency and comfort as well as mileage. Locomotives increased in power and pulled more cars. By 1860, railroad freight rates dropped to the level of canal freight rates, ending the relative price advantage enjoyed by the slower canals. Innovations in rail travel appeared, demonstrating that people were breaking away from the initial connection between stagecoach and rail travel. In Europe, railroad journeys lasted only a few hours, and, like travelers on stagecoaches, European train travelers were granted periodic stops to obtain refreshments or use lavatories. Because of the much greater distances involved, American train trips lasted far longer and included fewer stops. Many journeys proceeded overnight in the United States, unheard of in Europe for many years. American trains were forced to strive for self-sufficiency, providing on-train lavatories, restaurant and bar cars, and sleeper cars. A study of the provision of accommodations on American trains makes it quite obvious that trains used steamboats and canal packets, not stagecoaches, as a model. Train travel in the nineteenth-century United States was much more comfortable than in Europe.

American passenger cars allowed travelers to move around inside the car and pass from one car to another throughout the train. In contrast, European first- and second-class passenger cars were isolated series of compartments, and passengers could not leave their own compartment when the train was moving. Fears arose that isolated first-class passengers were especially vulnerable to robbery and murder. Chief Justice Poinsot of France was found murdered in his first-class train compartment on 6 December 1860. A similar murder occurred in England in 1864, aggravating the fear of violent crime against first-class passengers to epidemic proportions. As a result, European railroads switched to a new design by Heusinger von Waldegg. Each first-class car provided a connecting corridor that allowed passengers to leave their compartments and move about the train. In this way, European trains became more like American trains.

Travel by railroad was a revolutionary change for Europeans. In the early years of rail travel, commentators frequently spoke of the railroads' ability to annihilate time and space, meaning that travel by rail took much less time. At first, railroads cut travel time to half or even a third of the stagecoach. As the efficiency and speeds of trains increased, travel times became even shorter.

Early-nineteenth-century travelers did not universally accept the proposition that faster was better. Some medical authorities doubted that it was healthy for a human to travel faster than a horse could gallop. Others objected to railroad travel on aesthetic grounds. Travelers were no longer active participants in the experience of their journey; rather, they were transformed into parcels conveyed from one point to another. The intimate and intense experiences of sight, sound, smell, taste, and touch encountered during a traditional journey on foot or horseback was lost when traveling by rail.

Travel for first- and second-class passengers became a boring, isolated experience, and among the affluent, interaction among fellow passengers came to a virtual halt. In contrast, the third- and fourth-class passenger cars of the working class bustled with conviviality. To overcome boredom, first- and second-class passengers turned to reading. Light novels and newspapers were quite popular with train riders. Bookstores such as W. H. Smith in England and Hachettes in France began by catering to the needs of affluent railroad passengers. Some medical experts suggested that the rapidly changing vistas of the landscape experienced during a railroad journey would cause fatigue of the sensory nerves and was inherently unhealthy. Fairly soon, a new generation raised on railroad travel arose who considered such travel to be the norm rather than a revolutionary change of dubious benefit. Railroads allowed more people, particularly those from the working class, to participate in travel.

Some critics of railroads complained about their noise and pollution, and saw these irritating by-products as threats to public health. In fact, railroad districts were shunned by the well-to-do and soon degenerated into slums for the very poor. People wanted to ride the railroads, but no one wanted to live by them.

Others expressed fears about the safety of rail travel. They cited the feeling of being a projectile fired from a gun. A feeling of helplessness led to anxiety in some people. The relatively high speeds and the heavy equipment of railroads had the potential of turning any accident into a deadly disaster. Railroads quickly developed safety techniques, including improved brakes and signal blocks, but horrendous accidents occurred on occasion. Railroad passengers, however, grew inured to the risk, just as automobile and airline passengers of today do not let potential dangers deter them from traveling.

Railroads also changed the perception of time. Prior to the advent of railroads, all time was local time (noon was when the sun reached its zenith in the daytime sky). When travel proceeded slowly and seldom followed a tight schedule, the myriad of local times was not a problem. However, when railroads supplied rapid travel over long distances, they required a tight schedule, and uniform time zones for railroads were established. At first, each individual railroad adapted its own standard time. Later, they banded together in the Railway Clearing House and adopted Greenwich time as the standard uniform time. Greenwich time became the official time for all of England in 1880. Germany adopted its own uniform time in 1883. An international conference in 1884 established time zones for the entire world. American railroads did not switch to using the four uniform time zones until 1889. Inexorably, railroad time pushed aside local time, although the United States did not grant the four time zones legal recognition until 1918.

Railroads encouraged travel and trade, and stimulated industrialization. Their demands for iron, steel, and coal encouraged those industries, particularly in the United States. Railroads were the first American "big business." The imperial nations of Europe pushed railroads into the continents of Asia, Africa, and South America, and their building became equated with westernization and modernization. Certainly, railroads made travel quicker and more practical. They also allowed tourism to arise as an aspect of modern mass culture.

See also
> Canals; Stagecoach; Steamboats, River.

For further reading
> Rodney Dale, *Early Railroads*, 1994; Nicholas Faith, *The World the Railroads Made*, 1991; Albert L. McCready, *Railroads in the Days of Steam*, 1960; Albro Martin, *Railroads Triumphant*, 1992; Wolfgang Schivelbusch, *The Railway Journey*, 1986; Sarah Searight, *Steaming East*, 1991.

RIVERBOATS
> See Keelboats; Steamboats, River.

ROADS, INCA
Known by the Incas as *Capac Ñan* (beautiful road), the Spanish conquistadors called it the Royal Highway. The pre-Columbian Incas of South America constructed this system of over 30,000 miles of roads to unite their great empire from Quito in the north to Talca in the south. Their capital, Cuzco, stood at the center of the network.

Prior to the great conquests of the Incas from 1438 to 1493, the Andean region of South America was a jumble of small kingdoms separated by deserts and mountain gorges. To control this vast and rugged region, the Incas constructed a system of roads. A coastal road and a mountain road ran parallel to each other, linked at various points by connecting roads through the mountain passes. This division accommodated the two main types of terrain in Peru—coastal desert and mountainous interior. The Incas tried to make the roads as straight as possible. On steep slopes they constructed long flights of stairs, a practice that reflected their lack of wheeled transportation. When possible, curbing, boundary posts, or lines of trees marked the course of the roads. On flat terrain the Inca roads were wide enough to allow six horses to travel abreast, but in the mountains they sometimes narrowed to a three-foot-wide cut. Paths

A stone trail enshrouded in mist leads up to the ruins of Machu Picchu, near Cuzco in Peru.

connected the isolated settlements of Vilcabamba and Machu Picchu with the rest of the Inca Empire.

The Incas primarily used their system of roads for administrative or military purposes, although some used them for pilgrimages or on business. As the Spanish chronicler Pedro de Cieza de León, reflecting the awe of his countrymen, put it:

> In the memory of people I doubt there is record of another highway comparable to this [the Royal Highway], running through deep valleys and over high mountains, through piles of snow, quagmires, living rock, along turbulent rivers; . . . everywhere it was clean-swept and kept free of rubbish, with lodgings, storehouses, temples to the sun, and posts along the way. Oh, can anything comparable be said of Alexander [the Great], or of any of the mighty kings who rule the world, that they built such a road.

See also
Roads, Persian; Roads, Roman.
For further reading
Louis Baudin, *Daily Life in Peru under the Last Incas*, 1962; Victor Wolfgang Von Hagen, *The Royal Road of the Inca*, 1976.

ROADS, PERSIAN   During its existence, the Achaemenid Persian Empire (550–330 B.C.) developed a system of roads to promote communication, the movement of troops, and general travel and commerce. It was the first great road system of the ancient world, although the earlier Assyrians engaged in some road building.

The core of the Persian road system was the Royal Road, or King's Road, connecting Susa in Persia to Sardis in western Asia Minor. The Greek historian Herodotus (484–420 B.C.) described its operation in his *Histories* [V: 52–53]. It took about 90 days to travel the approximately 1,000-mile length. Along its route, the Persians built 111 way stations or rest areas at intervals of about 19 miles, a day's journey on foot. Forts guarded the various bridges, fords, and mountain passes scattered along the Royal Road. Travelers using the road needed passes.

The main artery of the Royal Road was already in existence by the reign of Darius I (522–486 B.C.), and later extended eastward to Persepolis and beyond into Bactria and India. A southern branch crossed Mesopotamia to Syria and turned south to connect Palestine and Egypt with the road system. The Persian road system contributed greatly to unifying the Persian Empire by providing a secure travel route for news, commerce, armies, and travelers. Succeeding Middle Eastern and Mediterranean empires tried to imitate its success.

See also

Herodotus; Roads, Inca; Roads, Roman.

For further reading

J. M. Cook, *The Persian Empire*, 1983; A. T. Olmstead, *History of the Persian Empire [Achaemenid Period]*, 1948.

ROADS, ROMAN

Most famous and extensive system of roads constructed in the ancient Mediterranean world. By the second century A.D., a network of 372 Roman roads totaled 53,000 miles in length, beginning in Scotland and ending at the Euphrates River.

The Romans learned their road building from the mysterious Etruscans of north-central Italy. Etruscan engineers constructed gravel roads with stable beds and improved drainage. Adopting these techniques, the Romans added the innovation of paving stones for heavily used sections of roads.

The Appian Way, or Via Appia, was the first great Roman road and was known admiringly as the "queen of roads." Construction began in 312 B.C. at the initiative of Appius Claudius, the commissioner of public works for that year. Initially connecting Rome to Capua, the road later extended to Brindisi, an important port of trade. Other roads followed. Commissioner Gaius Flaminius began construction of the Via Flaminia in 220 B.C. It went north from Rome and crossed the Apennines Mountains, ultimately terminating at Fano on the Adriatic Sea. The Via Aurelia, begun in 144 B.C., also went north, but followed the west coast of Italy to Genoa.

The Romans began building roads outside of Italy in 148 B.C. with the construction of the Via Egnatia. It started at Durazzo across the Adriatic Sea from

Roman road in Ostia Antica, Italy.

Brindisi, and in many ways was an extension of the Via Appia. The Via Egnatia cut across Macedonia to Salonika, eventually reaching Byzantium, future site of the great metropolis of Constantinople. Once Roman roads reached the eastern Mediterranean lands, they linked up with preexisting Greek, Assyrian, and Persian roads, which the Romans merely had to bring up to their standards of construction where it was needed. Conditions of roads in the western Mediterranean lands were not nearly as advanced. Roads in Spain and Gaul (France) were largely dirt tracks. The Roman engineers set to work building up roadbeds and providing drainage. By the first century A.D., the Mediterranean Sea was encircled by a network of Roman roads and an extensive system of arterial roads radiated from it.

The Romans tried to build their roads as straight as was practically possible. Since the primary purpose of Roman roads was to provide a means for the swift movement of troops, the Roman engineers constructed them to be serviceable in any weather. It is a myth that all Roman roads were constructed in a uniform manner and were paved in stone. The older roads in Italy were paved, but in the provinces, gravel roads were the rule except in areas of high traffic and the approaches to towns. Roman roads were regularly marked with milestones, a Roman mile being slightly shorter than a modern mile. The greatest milestone in the Roman Empire was the *miliarium aureum,* or "golden milestone," located in the Forum of Rome. In gilded letters it indicated the mileage from Rome to various important places in the far-flung empire, a visual affirmation of the phrase that "all roads lead to Rome." Roman roads also included shrines to Mercury or Hermes, the god of travel, at various intervals.

The system of Roman roads contributed immeasurably to the unity and stability of the Roman Empire. It is a tribute to the Romans' organization, forethought, and material resources that they were able to build and maintain this extensive network for centuries. Roads of comparable quality did not appear in the West until the nineteenth century. Modern roads and railroads frequently followed the course of the old Roman roads. Even today, sections of the old Roman roads survive to testify to the high quality and durability of their construction.

See also

Roads, Inca; Roads, Persian; Rome.

For further reading

Raymond Chevallier, *Roman Roads,* 1976; Victor Wolfgang Von Hagen, *The Roads That Led to Rome,* 1967.

ROARING FORTIES
Name for the westerly winds that prevail in the Southern Hemisphere between 40°S and 60°S. Because there are no landmasses of substantial size and elevation to slow them down, these winds are constant and especially strong. The Roaring Forties and the storms they create made rounding both Cape Horn and the Cape of Good Hope hazardous for sailing vessels. The winds also presented an additional danger for ships exploring the South Pacific in search of Terra Australis.

See also
Trade Winds; Winds.

ROBBERS
Also called bandits, brigands, highwaymen, and thieves. As soon as people began to travel, others began to rob or steal from them. Wherever law and order and a government's authority were weak, robbers had the opportunity to prey on travelers with minimal fear of punishment.

Some areas presented travelers with more danger from robbers than others. Mountainous regions commonly served as nests of brigands, although this was not true of Switzerland and Tyrolia in medieval and early-modern times. Frontier areas were particularly prone to bandits, as the voluminous lore of the outlaws of the American West amply attests. In Europe, places like the Pyrenees and Savoy were both mountainous and frontiers, and so were famous for their bands of robbers. Bandits generally operated in the countryside because it was easier to elude law enforcement authorities, but they also preferred lurking along well-traveled roads. In England, highwaymen were particularly active along the roads approaching London. Even so, England and Switzerland were considered by medieval and early-modern travelers to be the safest. Some thieves operated in the cities, but they were mostly cutpurses, pickpockets, and muggers, a category of thief that bandits and highwaymen disdained.

Most robbers operated in groups or bands for mutual support. The poor of the countryside occasionally turned to robbery to supplement their meager incomes if a tempting opportunity appeared. Other bands of brigands were professional and made their entire living from outlawry. The 40 thieves of Ali Baba are a good example of such phenomena, as are the famous outlaw groups of the American West like the Wild Bunch. Some of the robber gangs were social bandits, for example, Robin Hood and his Merry Men. They resisted or claimed to be resisting an oppressive elite by robbing from the rich and giving to the poor. Some Western outlaws were surprisingly popular because they victimized the monopolistic railroads, which were heartily hated by many hard-pressed Western farmers and ranchers. Although the rich may have been robbed, little of the proceeds made their way into the hands of the poor.

Disbanded soldiers frequently turned to brigandage when peace brought them unemployment. Even active soldiers sometimes supplemented their incomes by depredations on travelers. Late-medieval and early-modern Europe with its frequent wars faced continual problems from predatory soldiers, employed or not. Areas far from sedentary civilizations hosted entire tribes who made a large part of their living from raiding neighbors and travelers or collecting tribute. The Tuaregs terrorized travelers crossing the Sahara for centuries, as did various nomadic tribes situated along the caravan routes of Arabia and the Silk Road of central Asia. In the American West, Comanche and Apache warriors preyed on neighboring tribes, Mexicans, and Americans, both settlers and travelers. Throughout its history, China suffered from periodic outbreaks of brigandage. Bandits formed a significant portion of the rebel army of the Taipings during the mid-nineteenth century.

The appearance of handheld firearms made it possible for heavily armed lone robbers or highwaymen to operate successfully. Seventeenth- and eighteenth-century England had its share of highwaymen, the more famous of whom were Captain James Hind, William Nevison, Claude DuVall, Thomas Sympson, and Dick Turpin. Unemployed army officers and impoverished younger sons of aristocrats often turned to highway robbery as the only "respectable" way for men of their social position to make a dishonest living. Their command "stand and deliver" was just what no traveler carrying valuables wanted to hear. Many highwaymen became celebrities and folk heroes. Some also tried to assume the cachet of social banditry by professing royalist sentiments during the Interregnum in England, or Jacobite sentiments after the Glorious Revolution of 1689. Most, however, followed the trade for the easy money and excitement.

Individual travelers were particularly vulnerable to attack. Verse 4 in the Bible's famous Twenty-third Psalm captures the anxiety of traveling alone in the wilderness in its reference to "the valley of the shadow of death." Of course, the figure of the Good Samaritan is based on the predicament of the luckless traveler who fell among thieves. The English diarist John Evelyn (1620–1706) faced the same problem over 1,600 years later when two men ambushed him near Bromley, southeast of London, during late June 1652. The robbers beat him and stole his sword and jewelry. Untold others suffered similar fates, many of them forfeiting their lives.

To avoid the danger of traveling alone, people frequently banded together for mutual protection and companionship. Caravans appeared early in human history, as did bands of travelers like those depicted in *The Canterbury Tales*. On the roads of Europe and the American West, bandits targeted stagecoaches. After railroads spread across the United States, trains were not immune to robbery, either. The first train robbery took place in 1866 at Seymour, Indiana. Once outlaws developed the techniques for stopping trains, relatively regular schedules and valuable cargoes made the railroads tempting targets. Famous outlaws such as Butch Cassidy and the Sundance Kid and Jesse James and his gang successfully robbed the railroads.

Bandits and highwaymen varied in their brutality and ruthlessness. Some were extremely cruel. They stripped their victims of virtually everything and beat them, killed them, or sometimes horribly tortured them. Disbanded soldiers tended to be particularly murderous and sadistic. However, most bandits did not kill their victims. Frequently, they even left the victim with enough money to get to the next town. Bandits of the Mediterranean countries rarely took everything. Being poor, they understood what it was like to have nothing. Lone highwaymen of the seventeenth and eighteenth centuries cultivated gentlemanly, chivalric, and witty reputations, and were particularly gallant to beautiful female travelers, which contributed to their folk-hero personae.

Robbers were a significant risk to travelers through most of human history, but they did not stop people from traveling. Travelers compensated for the danger by various strategies, such as going about in groups. Others developed methods of concealing valuables or avoided carrying unnecessary valuables. They avoided travel on Sunday, which was certainly not a day of rest for robbers. Bandit-infested areas were shunned when possible. Surprisingly, prudent travelers sought out less-traveled roads because robbers concentrated on the more heavily used highways. Thanks to the growth of efficient law enforcement, travelers are rarely the victims of robbery on the highways of developed countries like the United States and those in Europe.

See also
Good Samaritan; Pirates; Silk Road; Tuareg.
For further reading
Michael Billett, *Highwaymen and Outlaws*, 1997; Lionel Casson, *Travel in the Ancient World*, 1994; Antoni Maczak, *Travel in Early Modern Europe*, 1995; Norbert Ohler, *The Medieval Traveler*, 1989; Joan Parkes, *Travel in England in the Seventeenth Century*, 1968; Patrick Pringle, *Stand and Deliver*, 1991.

ROC   Also spelled Ruc, Rukh, or Rukhkh, the Roc was a gigantic bird similar to an eagle thought to inhabit the region of the Indian Ocean. Some scholars equate it with the mythical Phoenix, while others consider it analogous to the Griffin. Various accounts of the Roc describe its size in fantastic terms. Rocs were so big they could carry off an elephant or even swallow one whole. A dead Roc's beak could be made into a full-sized sailing ship. Many Middle Eastern societies believed in the existence of Rocs. Among the Hindus, Rocs were known as *Garuda*; the Persians called them *Simurgh* and their original Arabic name was *Angka*. The name *Roc* probably derived from the Hebrew word *ruakh*, meaning "spirit."

During the medieval era, travelers in the Indian Ocean region frequently heard tales about Rocs. The legendary Sindbad encountered one during his second voyage. Angering a Roc was a fatal mistake—as Sindbad's foolish traveling companions discovered when the giant bird smashed their ship. The real-life traveler Ibn Battuta claimed to have sighted a Roc in the China Sea, and during his travels, Marco Polo picked up stories about Rocs living in the vicinity of Madagascar. The Arab geographer al-Masudi heard many tales about Rocs, but never met anyone who had actually seen one. Rocs were always located in some faraway place, a circumstance that led al-Masudi to question their existence.

Tales about gigantic flying creatures are fairly common in the legends of many cultures. A story in Lucian's *True History* concerns a giant bird that has been identified as a prototype for the Roc. Some scholars speculate that the unearthing of the fossilized bones of various large prehistoric birds such as Aepyernis, or of historic birds such as the Moa, may have been the inspiration for legends about Rocs and other gigantic birds.

See also

Sindbad, The Seven Voyages of.

For further reading

Cyril Glassé, *The Concise Encyclopedia of Islam,* 1989; Robert Irwin, *The Arabian Nights,* 1994; Henry Yule and Henri Cordier, eds., *The Travels of Marco Polo,* 1929.

ROME Also known as the Eternal City, for centuries the city of Rome has been the most or one of the most important cities in the Western world, first as the capital of the Roman Empire and later as the headquarters of the Roman Catholic Church. Its religious, historical, economic, and political significance attracted travelers and pilgrims through the ages.

Rome is located on the Tiber River and was built on and around the famous seven hills: the Palatine, Capitoline, Aventine, Caelian, Esquiline, Viminal, and Quirinal. Starting out as a humble village about 1000 B.C., by the first century A.D., Rome was the capital of a world empire and had grown into a metropolis of over 1 million people. City life centered on Rome's famous Forum, a great public square with temples and government buildings such as the Curia of the Senate, surrounded by busy shops. The Capitol, or Capitoline Hill, originally served as a citadel and a temple precinct for the god Jupiter. It continued to function as an important religious precinct in the late Republican and Imperial periods. The emperors Vespasian and Titus built and completed the great Colosseum of Rome in A.D. 80. The Circus Maximus, located between the Palatine and Aventine hills, originated in the period of the Roman kings, but did not achieve its classic form as a race track until Julius Caesar (100–44 B.C.) constructed the tiered seating and starting gates. The emperor Trajan (r. 97–117) rebuilt the structure in a monumental fashion. Rome was also dotted by various triumphal arches: Constantine's, Septimus Severus's, and Titus's. The baths of Caracalla (r. 211–217) and Diocletian (r. 284–305) added magnificently to Rome's existing collection of comfortable bathhouses. The extensive and efficient system of Roman roads ultimately focused on the city of Rome. By the first century A.D., 19 roads entered the city. The familiar phrase "all roads lead to Rome" was not an exaggeration.

Imperial Rome also attracted the early Christians. The first reference to Christians in Rome dates to A.D. 51 or 52 in the reign of the emperor Claudius. When St. Paul wrote his *Letter to the Romans* in 58, the Roman church had already put down strong roots. In 64, the emperor Nero conducted the first persecution of Christians in order to divert blame for the great fire of Rome from himself. Tradition states that St. Paul and St. Peter, the latter credited with being the first bishop or pope of Rome, died in this persecution. These years were the era of the Church of the Catacombs, a literally underground movement. The emperor Constantine's legalization of Christianity in the Roman Empire allowed Christians to build large public churches such as the basilica of St. John in the Lateran.

The Roman Empire declined badly in the late third and early first centuries, particularly in the western half. A Visigoth army sacked Rome in 410, followed by a more destructive pillaging by the Vandals in 455. By 476, incursions by various Germanic tribes ended the Western Roman Empire. During the sixth and seventh centuries, Rome came under the increasingly feeble control of the Byzantine Empire.

During the early Middle Ages, the bishops of Rome continually worked to establish their independence of secular authority and their primacy over the church as a whole. For several centuries, the petty but bloodthirsty local nobility of Rome and its environs posed the gravest threat to the independence of the popes. This problem abated by the eleventh century, which allowed various popes to promote much-needed church reforms. In 1143, a revolution took place in Rome that made the city a commune and revived the Roman Senate. Local politics became so increasingly violent that from 1309 to 1377 a series of popes chose to live in southern France at more tranquil Avignon.

Medieval Rome was a mere shadow of its former imperial greatness. Instead of a million people, only a few tens of thousands lived in the bend of the Tiber River between the Ponto Sant' Angelo and Tiber Island surrounded by the monumental ruins of ancient Rome. Directly across the river was the Leonine City containing the Vatican Palace, the Lateran Palace, St. Peter's Cathedral, and the Castle Sant' Angelo. Pope Leo IV walled it between 847 and 853.

Rome is justly famous for its churches, of which St. Peter's Basilica is probably the most famous. The emperor Constantine built the original St. Peter's on the supposed site of St. Peter's crucifixion, and by the early fifteenth century it had fallen into a bad state of repair. Pope Nicholas V (r. 1447–1455) made plans to build a new church, but died before they could be implemented. Several decades later, Julius II (1503–1513) revived the idea, and construction began in 1506, although the structure was not fully completed until 1614. It includes the famous Sistine Chapel with the ceiling that Michelangelo painted so laboriously. The new St. Peter's is the largest church in Christendom, being 619 feet long.

Other famous Roman basilicas are St. Paul's Outside the Walls, St. John Lateran, and Santa Maria Maggiore. Some claim that the emperor Constantine also built the original St. Paul's over the site of its namesake's grave. The ancient church was destroyed by fire in 1823 and rebuilt by 1854. St. John Lateran is the cathedral church of Rome. Fire and earthquake destroyed it several times during the Middle Ages. Pope Urban V (r. 1362–1370) began the building of the present church, which was extensively renovated and added to in the sixteenth and eighteenth centuries. Santa Maria Maggiore was founded in the fourth century, although the present structure was constructed in the fifth century. It is the oldest of the four great Roman basilicas. Dedicated to the Blessed Virgin Mary, it houses remains from the manger of Jesus Christ.

For centuries Rome has been a popular pilgrimage site for Christians. Various guidebooks appeared over the years to aid pilgrims in their travels. The most famous of the medieval guidebooks was the *Mirabilia Urbis Romae* [Marvels of Rome], written by Benedict, a canon of St. Peter's, in 1143. The young Martin Luther (1483–1546) visited Rome on a business trip for his Augustinian order in 1510, and dutifully and enthusiastically performed the varied and standard itinerary of rituals for a Roman pilgrimage. He felt properly uplifted by the experience. He was not alone—millions had done so before him, and millions have done so since.

Rome held a prominent and obligatory place on the itinerary of the Grand Tour of the eighteenth century because of its classical and religious history. One such trip in 1764 changed the life of young Edward Gibbon (1737–1794). As he later described it:

> It was at Rome, on the 15th of October, 1764, as I sat musing amidst the ruins of the Capitol, while the barefooted friars were singing vespers in the Temple of Jupiter, that the idea of writing the decline and fall of the city first started in my mind.

Other famous seventeenth- and eighteenth-century grand tourists visiting Rome included John Evelyn, James Boswell, Horace Walpole, and Johann Wolfgang von Goethe.

Rome has continued to attract the religiously and historically minded traveler ever since, and for good reason—it is truly one of the great cities of world civilization.

See also
Pilgimage; Roads, Roman.
For further reading
Christopher Hibbert, *Rome*, 1985; Francis Morgan Nichols, ed., *The Marvels of Rome*, 1986.

RUTTERS   Also known as *routiers* or *roteiros*, these books of sailing directions were commonly used as aids to navigation by late-medieval and early-modern seamen.

Rutters appeared in the early fifteenth century among the nations of northern Europe that bounded on the Atlantic Ocean. The earliest English rutter is thought to date to 1408; it was a primitive affair that listed compass readings but no directions. Perhaps the most famous rutter was the Frenchman Pierre Garcie's *Le routier de la mer,* which appeared in 1483/1484. It was a comprehensive work, supplying sailing directions for the coasts of England, Wales, France, Portugal, and Spain up to the Strait of Gibraltar. A printed version appeared in 1502, and an expanded version in 1520, of which an English translation titled *The Rutter of the Sea* appeared in 1528.

Early rutters provided directions for the best way to sail along various coastlines. They included information about tides, tidal streams, currents, and depths of water, important considerations for ships sailing in the coastal waters of the eastern Atlantic Ocean. Shallows and dramatic tidal shifts in those waters were common and quite hazardous to the unwary. Rutters were to northern European navigation what portolan charts were to navigation in the Mediterranean Sea.

See also

Portolan Charts.

For further reading

J. H. Parry, *The Discovery of the Sea*, 1981; D. W. Waters, *The Rutter of the Sea*, 1967.

S

SAFARI   Name for a hunting trip or expedition into the wilds of Africa that flourished as an institution between 1836 and 1939.

The word *safari* derives from the Arabic verb *safara,* meaning "to unveil" or "to begin a journey," and the noun *safariya,* meaning "a voyage" or "an expedition." These words entered the Swahili language as *safari,* meaning any trip or journey. European hunters in East Africa adopted the word to describe their hunting trips.

At the beginning of the nineteenth century, Africa was a big-game hunter's paradise, largely unknown and unexplored by Europeans. In 1811, the English botanist W. J. Burchell roamed South Africa until 1814 looking for new species of plants. Back in England he published his diaries and drawings as *Travels in the Interior of Southern Africa* (1822–1824). That book inspired a young officer stationed in India named William Cornwallis Harris to try his own hunting expedition. In 1836, British authorities in India ordered Cornwallis Harris to go to South Africa to recover from an illness. Apparently he was not too ill, because he immediately organized a hunting trip, the first true safari. Many colorful adventures among the native tribes and Boer homesteaders followed. After his return to India, Cornwallis Harris published an account of his hunting trip titled *The Wild Sports of Southern Africa* (1838). It immediately gained great popularity.

The upper classes of Victorian Britain, as well as the rest of Europe and the United States, maintained a strong interest in athleticism, hunting, and adventure. Cornwallis Harris's book became an inspiration to many young men, one of whom was R. Gordon Cumming, a trigger-happy Scot who seemed to be most happy when blasting every wild animal in sight. He embarked on a safari that lasted from 1844 to 1849; at five years, it was probably the longest safari on record. Like many others, he preserved his experiences in a book, *The Lion Hunter of Africa* (1850).

Another great hunter was the Rugby School graduate William Cotton Oswell, who conducted a number of safaris between 1844 and 1851. Some of them were in the company of the famous missionary Dr. David Livingstone. Oswell's exploits inspired another schoolboy at Rugby, Frederick Selous. When Selous arrived in Africa, the big game had moved north of the Limpopo River and into areas where the tsetse fly prevented the use of horses and oxen. In

1872, Selous organized the first foot safari. It proved a great success, and over time he gained a deserved reputation as the greatest of the white hunters. Big-game hunting became his life, and Selous remained in Africa. In his sixties, he fought against the Germans in East Africa during World War I. A sniper's bullet killed him in January 1917. H. Rider Haggard, the adventure novelist, based the fictional character of Allan Quartermain in *King Solomon's Mines* (1885) on Selous's adventures.

Even before Selous's death, the safari had changed. By 1900, it became an organized tourist activity in which experienced hunters guided visitors to the big game. Selous himself accompanied the former U.S. president Theodore Roosevelt on his safari of 1909. The heroic days of safaris were over by 1900, and the institution itself ended by 1939 with the imminent extinction of much of the big game.

See also
Africa; Dark Continent.
For further reading
Bartle Bull, *Safari*, 1988.

SAHARA   The name *Sahara* means "desert" or "wilderness" in Arabic, so it is entirely appropriate to name the world's greatest desert simply "The Desert." Muslims also refer to the Sahara as the "Garden of Allah," a reference to its extremely sparse population, which makes it a place where Allah can go when he wants to be away from humans. Despite its forbidding environment, throughout history the Sahara has never formed an impermeable barrier to communication and trade between the Mediterranean world and sub-Saharan Africa.

The Sahara extends from western North Africa to the shores of the Red Sea for about 3,000 miles; from the north to the south, the desert is about 1,250 miles wide. These dimensions mean that the Sahara covers an area of approximately 3.5 million square miles, about one-sixteenth of the world's total landmass. In some places along the Libyan and Egyptian coastlines, the desert comes all the way down to the shoreline of the Mediterranean Sea. Along its southern boundary, the desert merges gradually into the lush grasslands of the savannah. This trasitional area of dry grasslands is known as the Sahel, which is Arabic for "coast." This usage of the term emphasizes the image of the Sahara as a vast sea of dryness in which camels serve as the proverbial ships of the desert.

Climatically, the Sahara is extremely hot and dry because of its location largely between the latitudes 20°N–30°N, the area of the subtropical high. This region experiences the continual subsidence of air from the upper atmosphere, a condition that is not conducive to rainfall. All the hot deserts of the world are located within the 20°–30° latitudes, in both the Northern and Southern Hemispheres. The average temperature of the Sahara is 85°F, but in the course of a single day, it can easily reach highs of 100°F in the daytime, with low temperatures approaching freezing at night. Rainfall is said to average six inches annually, but many years record total droughts. What rain does fall is unevenly distributed, with torrential thunderstorms dropping one to two inches of rain in less than an hour.

The climate of the Sahara produces dry winds that blow into neighboring regions. In the Mediterranean world, these hot, dusty winds are called the Sirocco, and they can blow for days and weeks at a time, withering crops and making life miserable. Along the tropical lands of coastal West Africa, the winds off the Sahara are known as Harmattan. Although they are warm and dry, occasionally bringing dust storms, they feel relatively cooler than the normal hot, humid air of the tropical coast. In the Sahara itself, the air is almost always dusty. When the winds of the desert approach the speed of 30 miles per hour, they possess sufficient strength to pick up grains of sand. On those rare occasions when winds exceed 40 miles per hour, the classic and dangerous sandstorm results.

The Sahara has been relatively dry for 2 million years, although climatic cycles have produced periods of relative wetness; the last one occurred between 12,000 and 6,000 years ago. Thousands of years of dry conditions have had a tremendous impact on the landscape of the Sahara. Probably the most famous of the desert's landforms are the great expanses of sand dunes known as *ergs*. In fact, these shifting dunes form only about 20 percent of the desert's area. Other landforms include the great plains of gravel and pebbles known as the *reg* and the rocky plateau and mountain regions called the *hammada*.

Many people believe that the process of desertification (expansion of the Sahara) is largely a product of human activity and that considerable expansion took place during historic times. It is indisputable that deforestation and overgrazing in the Sahel greatly contribute to the expansion of the desert. At the same time, the existence of vegetation-covered dunes deep inside the savannah shows that, during dry cycles of the distant past, the prehistoric Sahara expanded even farther south than its current boundaries. Some scholars cite the presence of the ruins of extensive Greco-Roman cities in areas like Tripolitania as evidence of an ongoing desiccation of the North Africa coastline. Other scholars disagree, arguing that places like Tripolitania have always been dry during historic times, and only flourished because of extensive irrigation systems and careful agricultural practices. Climatic change did not bring about their downfall—it was caused by deliberate destruction, which occurred during 1058–1060. The Zirid dynasty ruled Tripolitania as vassals of the Fatimid caliphs of Egypt, but in 1049 Tripolitanians declared their independence. In retaliation, in 1058, the Fatimids sent the Arab tribe of the Banu Hilal to ravage Tripolitania. Being militant nomads, the Banu Hilal destroyed the sophisticated local irrigation system, bringing an end to agriculture, the abandonment of once-flourishing cities, and the desiccation of the region.

Although large parts of the Sahara comprise some of the harshest and most dangerous environments in the world, it is inhabited by various groups of humans. Oases capable of sustaining extensive agriculture and fixed settlement are scattered across the desert. Various nomadic tribes and peoples also occupy portions of the Sahara. The majority of the Saharan population are Berbers, a Caucasian people located along the North Africa coast and in the western and central Sahara. They are the aboriginal inhabitants of these areas. In the north they have intermingled extensively with invading Arabs, and their culture has become heavily Arabized and Islamicized. Along the southern Sahel, considerable intermarrying with the Negro peoples has also occurred. The desert Berbers of the western Sahara are known as the Sanhaja, or Moors, while those of the central Sahara are the legendary blue-veiled Tuareg. The eastern Sahara is the home of the Negroid Tubu or Teda peoples, who are centered on the Tibesti Massif.

The Sahara has been crisscrossed by caravan routes since ancient times. Besides the many oases, wells occur in various parts of the Sahara, making travel possible. The appearance of the camel about 2,000 years ago during Roman times also increased the feasibility of trans-Saharan travel and trade. This trade carried luxury and manufactured goods from the Mediterranean world south to the Sudan, along the way picking up precious salt from the desert mines to sell to the salt-starved Sahelians and Sudanese. In exchange, the peoples of sub-Saharan Africa sent gold and slaves in caravans returning north. The routes of these caravans varied over time. In the western Sahara, various cities served in turn as the principal southern terminus for the caravan trade: ancient Ghana, Walata, and fabled Timbuktu. Farther east, cities such as Kano and Bornu by Lake Chad provided important entrepôts for caravans heading north across the eastern Sahara. Along the North African coast, Tangier, Tunis, Tripoli, and Benghazi were the northern termini.

Therefore, although the Sahara was definitely an obstacle to commerce, it was by no means an insurmountable barrier to contact between the Mediterranean and tropical Africa. Thousands of caravans crossed it successfully, but it was not an easy journey. The eastern routes beginning from Kano and Bornu were probably the safest because of conveniently placed oases: Ghadames, Bilma, Kufra, and others. In the west, the desert was more hostile, and sometimes entire caravans were lost. In 1805, an entire salt caravan, consisting of 2,000 people and 1,800 camels, perished of thirst while attempting to travel from Timbuktu to Taoudeni. In 1828, René Caillié accompanied a caravan following that same route and suffered terrible privations, although he and his companions survived. A Moroccan army that invaded the Songhai Empire at the end of the sixteenth century suffered tremendous casualties when it crossed the Sahara. Before the appearance of twentieth-century technology, traveling across the Sahara was possible, but never safe or easy.

See also
Africa; Camel; Caravans; Sandstorm; Timbuktu; Tuareg.
For further reading
Edward William Bovill, *The Golden Trade of the Moors*, 1968; J. L. Cloudsley-Thompson, ed., *Sahara Desert*, 1984; E. F. Gauthier, *Sahara the Great Desert*, 1935; James Wellard, *The Great Sahara*, 1965.

St. Bernard Passes
The two famous passes of Great St. Bernard (elevation 8,090 feet) and Little St. Bernard (elevation 7,178 feet) have provided a passage through the Alps between France and Italy since ancient times.

Known to the ancient Romans as *Alpis Poenina* (Great St. Bernard) and *Alpis Graia* (Little St. Bernard), medieval Europeans renamed them during the twelfth century in honor of St. Bernard of Aosta or Menthon (d. 1081). St. Bernard was an Italian priest who served as vicar general of the diocese of Aosta. Besides showing great concern for the spiritual and material welfare of the people of his diocese, he took a special interest in providing for the needs of Alpine travelers. Pilgrims going to Rome frequently used the St. Bernard passes, and some unfortunates were trapped and killed by blizzards, avalanches, and snowdrifts. To prevent such tragedies, St. Bernard built two hospices of Augustinian friars in both Great St. Bernard and Little St. Bernard. The monks developed the famous breed of rescue dogs known as St. Bernards to help them find lost travelers.

The passes of St. Bernard have seen much history. Invading armies of Gauls, Romans, the emperor Charlemagne, and Emperor Frederick Barbarosa all passed through them. The young Napoléon led an army of 40,000 men through Great St. Bernard in May 1800 on the way to his great victory at Marengo. Hannibal and his soldiers and elephants passed through the Little St. Bernard pass in October 218 B.C., encountering early snows and suffering great losses of life.

A modern road was built through Great St. Bernard in 1823, and a three and one-half mile tunnel was constructed in 1964 that now provides a shortcut for modern travelers.

See also
Hospices and Hospitals.

ST. BRENDAN THE NAVIGATOR, VOYAGE OF

During the last seven years of his life, this prominent Irish monk (ca. 486–ca. 575) supposedly sailed throughout the North Atlantic and possibly visited America along the way. His voyage made him one of the greatest—at least legendary—travelers of the early Middle Ages.

Little is known for certain about the life of St. Brendan. He was born near Tralee in western Ireland about 486 during the twilight of the Roman Empire when Ireland was an isolated haven of devout Christianity and scholarship. Very much a part of this religious culture, Brendan became a monk and a priest, and later founded the monastery of Clonfert around 559, as well as several other monastic houses. In those days, Irish monks commonly sailed the seas in their currachs seeking remote spots where they could set up monasteries and conduct devotions. St. Brendan figured prominently in such sailing activities. In addition to his legendary voyage around the Atlantic, he was widely reputed to be a great traveler throughout Christendom, visiting Scotland, Wales, and Brittany.

The story of St. Brendan's legendary seven-year voyage of the Atlantic comes from the *Navigatio Sancti Brendani*. This medieval manuscript was probably written by an Irish monk living in the Low Countries or the Rhineland about 870 or shortly thereafter. It must have been very popular, because 116 manuscript copies survive, in Latin as well as in vernacular translations into Middle English, Provençal, Flemish, Old Norse, and others. Christian monastic themes dominate the narrative, which concerns a quest for an earthly paradise. Scholars do not consider the *Navigatio* to be a genuine biographical account of St. Brendan's life. In many ways, it is a religious version of the *immrama*, traditional sea-journey tales of the Celtic world.

According to the *Navigatio*, a monk and kinsman of St. Brendan named Barinthus visited the famous saint at his monastery and told of sailing westward and visiting the utopian Land of Promise of the Saints. After hearing this tale, St. Brendan decided to visit the western paradise, and invited 14 of his monks to accompany him. The monks agreed, and a currach was constructed to make the journey. Leaving Ireland, they encountered stormy weather that blew them to an island of steep cliffs (which some scholars identify as St. Kilda in the Outer Hebrides) after 40 days at sea. After resting a few days, they resumed their journey, reaching an island of huge sheep (possibly Streymoy in the Faeroes). On this island, a man (later referred to as their steward) gave them food and encouraged them in their journey. Next they landed on what seemed to be a neighboring island, but which turned out to be a giant fish or whale; it became aroused when they lit their cooking fires on its back. Fortunately, St. Brendan knew the island was really a great sea creature, and guided his followers to safety. They proceeded to another nearby island full of white birds, which were actually fallen angels (this island would probably be Streymoy's neighbor, Vagar).

After spending Easter on the island of birds, the travelers put to sea for three months, finally reaching the island of St. Ailbe. This island, which possessed a mild climate, was already inhabited by a community of monks, whom God miraculously provided with food (St. Ailbe's island is thought to be Madeira). St. Brendan and his people spent the Christmas and Epiphany seasons with the monks. They then set sail once more, and after several weeks at sea exhausted their supplies. In desperate straits, they propitiously sighted a lush green island replete with streams and springs full of fish. Unfortunately, drinking the water on this island put the monks to sleep (the volcanic island of San Miguel in the Azores is the only Atlantic island with undrinkable springs). After they awakened, St. Brendan and his companions departed southward. Within three days they found themselves becalmed in a "curdled sea" (probably the Sargasso Sea). Once they escaped the sea, the wind pushed them for 20 days until they found themselves once again at the islands of sheep and birds. The steward supplied them with more food, and prophesied that St. Brendan and his companions would reach the Land of Promise of the Saints after seven years of traveling. He foretold that they would remain at the Land of Promise of the Saints for 40 days, and then return to their home monastery in Ireland. Before they attempted to fulfill the steward's prophecy, St. Brendan and his monks rested for several weeks.

Beginning their voyage once more, St. Brendan and his companions sailed for 40 days. A fierce sea monster attacked, but before it could destroy them, another sea monster intervened and killed their attacker. The next day they landed on a new island and found some remains of the dead sea monster, which they ate. (This island has not been identified.) Bad weather forced them to remain on the new island for three months, but when pleasant weather returned, they resupplied their ship and resumed sailing southward. This time they reached a flat island covered with flowers but devoid of trees (identified as one of the Bahamas). The island was inhabited by three bands: one of boys, one of young men, and one of elders, who formed choirs and sang psalms praising God for the inspiration of the travelers. Leaving one of his monks to live on this island of steadfast men, St. Brendan continued his journey. Again the monks sailed until they depleted their supplies. Miraculously, a giant bird dropped a large bunch of grapes onto their ship, which enabled the monks to survive for 12 more days. Soon afterward, they reached the island that had produced the grapes. It was full of fresh springs and smelled of pomegranates (this island may have been Jamaica, which is well known for its springs). The giant bird that earlier befriended them once again defended them, this time from a hostile Griffin. The travelers then returned to the island of St. Ailbe.

St. Brendan and his companions rested among the monks of St. Ailbe, spending Christmas and Easter there. After resting, they journeyed west once more. They discovered a sea of clear waters filled with strange fish (the clear waters of the Caribbean?), and a week later encountered a huge floating column of crystal in the sea (an iceberg?). Strong winds carried them even farther north for eight days, and they came upon an island full of forges. The smiths operating the forges attacked them by throwing big pieces of red-hot slag at St. Brendan's ship (it is suggested that the travelers actually described a volcanic eruption of Iceland). The next day they sighted a mountain rising out of the sea, spouting smoke and flames (the volcanic island of Jan Mayen). Afterward, they visited Judas Iscariot on his island of eternal imprisonment and torment, and the island of Paul the Hermit, who prophesied that after the last six years of wandering, St. Brendan would soon reach the Land of Promise of the Saints.

St. Brendan returned to spend Christmas and Easter on the island of sheep, and then sailed westward for 40 days. His ship became enveloped in darkness (the fogs of the Newfoundland banks?), but broke through to daylight after an hour of sailing. The coast of the Land of Promise of the Saints appeared, and the travelers landed. It was a vast country, and 40 days of exploration failed to reveal its full extent. As St. Brendan and his companions neared the large river mentioned by Barinthus, a young man approached them. He revealed to St. Brendan that God had made him wander for the last seven years so that he would discover the marvels of the sea. The young man instructed St. Brendan to load his ship with precious stones and return home to his monastery. He also informed the travelers that God would disclose the location of the Land of Promise of the Saints at a future time when Christians would again be persecuted. St. Brendan returned to his monastery, where he died the dignified death that befitted a saintly Christian monk.

No one seriously believes that St. Brendan literally made the entire journey described in the *Navigatio*. However, some scholars believe that the *Navigatio* is an imaginative tale that incorporates actual geographical knowledge held by the early-medieval Irish. The sites visited in the *Navigatio* represent a composite of early-medieval Irish geographical knowledge as well as speculation, myth, and legend. Separating out which component of the *Navigatio* belongs to which category is difficult and sometimes impossible. It is well known that Irish sailors went to the Faeroes and the Hebrides on a regular basis and set up settlements on Iceland before the Vikings. Furthermore, if the identifications of other places mentioned in the *Navigatio* are correct, it would mean that the Irish reached the Azores and Madeira, as well as various Caribbean islands and North America. These feats are theoretically within the capabilities of the primitive currachs, but no irrefutable evidence exists to support such speculations.

See also

Atlantic Ocean; Blessed, Isles of the; *Immrama.*

For further reading

Geoffrey Ashe, *Land to the West,* 1962; Ian Cameron, *Lodestone and Evening Star,* 1966; D. H. Farmer, ed., *The Age of Bede,* 1965; Timothy Severin, *The Brendan Voyage,* 1978.

ST. CHRISTOPHER   Patron saint of travelers and the dying, his name means "Christ bearer." He has been a popular saint throughout most of Christian history.

Although many stories exist concerning St. Christopher, his historical authenticity is not well documented. According to one legend, his original pagan name was Reprobus, and he belonged to the dog-headed race (Cynocephali) until his baptism transformed him into a human being. More commonly, the legends describe him as Offerus, the son of a Canaanite king. Raised as a pagan, he grew to possess enormous size and strength, and he decided to serve only the strongest and bravest of leaders. At first, Offerus served a king, but departed when he learned that the king feared the Devil. Joining the Devil's service, Offerus soon discovered that the Devil feared the cross of Christ. Once more he resumed his search for a fearless master. After wandering for a time, Offerus met a hermit named Babylus who converted him to Christianity and baptized him. From that point on, Offerus became Christopher and served Christ by carrying travelers across a torrential river. One day a little child asked Christopher to carry him across the river. It seemed an easy task, but as Christopher carried him, the child became heavier and heavier. When Christopher asked the child about his almost unbearable weight, he learned that he had been carrying Christ and the weight of the whole sinful world. To further prove his identity, the Christ child told Christopher to thrust his staff into the ground. By the next day it had miraculously grown to be a flowering date palm and bore fruit, a miracle that prompted many in that area to convert to Christianity. It also aroused the wrath of the local pagan authorities of Lycia, who imprisoned Christopher, tortured him, and eventually beheaded him. Another version of the St. Christopher legend states that, after his encounter with Christ, he began to travel about preaching the gospel, which led to his arrest and martyrdom in Lycia, possibly during the persecution of Decius (250–251). The pagan au-

Fifteenth-century painting of St. Christopher crossing a river, by Jan van Eyck.

thorities put two beautiful prostitutes in his prison cell to seduce him, but instead, the resolute Christopher converted them to Christianity.

The first church dedicated to St. Christopher was constructed at Chalcedon about A.D. 450, and many others followed. By the early Middle Ages, popular belief held that anyone who looked at an image of St. Christopher would not die that day. This belief popularized medals bearing the image of St. Christopher, particularly among travelers, as a means to keep the dying alive until they could receive the last rites. In fourteenth-century England, Geoffrey Chaucer described his Yeoman pilgrim: "A medal of St. Christopher he wore/Of shining silver on his breast, and bore." St. Christopher's popularity suffered an eclipse during the sixteenth and seventeenth centuries when both Protestant and Roman Catholic reformers attacked his cult. During more recent times, the cult of St. Christopher has made a comeback, particularly among automobile drivers and airplane travelers. When the Vatican downgraded St. Christopher's status as a saint because of his uncertain historical authenticity, negative reaction was widespread among Roman Catholics.

See also

Cynocephali.

For further reading

Gaston Duchet-Suchaux and Michel Pastoureau, *The Bible and the Saints*, 1994; C. Johnson, *St. Christopher*, 1938.

ST. LOUIS   Important city located in the central portion of the greater Mississippi River valley. It was known as the "Gateway to the West" because of its important role in westward expansion and trade. St. Louis was also an important river port and railroad junction.

The French trader Pierre Laclède Ligueste founded St. Louis on 15 February 1764. He intended St. Louis to serve as headquarters for his trading ventures with the Native American tribes west of the Mississippi River and along the Missouri River. The site was a good choice; a 40-foot bluff protected the settlement from flooding but allowed easy access to the river. It was also only ten miles south of where the Missouri River entered the Mississippi.

The French settlement quickly became a thriving market for the fur trade, although it came under Spanish rule. In 1803, the United States gained possession of St. Louis along with the rest of the Louisiana Territory, and American settlers and traders poured into the city. Besides the fur trade, St. Louis participated in the commerce and travel that passed along the Sante Fe and Oregon Trails.

The appearance of steamboats on the western rivers in 1811 enhanced St. Louis's economic importance as an auspiciously located river port. St. Louis's wealth increased even further after railroads came into the greater Mississippi Valley during the 1850s. The city quickly became the second largest railroad center in the United States. In more modern times, interstate highways and air travel have reduced St. Louis's relative importance as a transportation center, but during the nineteenth century it was truly the "Gateway to the West" for commerce, settlers, and travelers.

See also

Mississippi River; Missouri River; Oregon Trail.

For further reading

E. M. Coyle, *St. Louis*, 1977.

St. Paul, Missionary Journeys of

Also known as the "Apostle of the Gentiles," St. Paul traveled extensively throughout the eastern Mediterranean world in the course of his missionary work.

St. Paul was born with the name Saul at Tarsus in Cilicia, a country in Asia Minor. He belonged to the Jewish tribe of Benjamin, was raised a Pharisee, and had Roman citizenship. Because of his Orthodox Jewish upbringing, the young Saul participated in the Jewish persecution of the early Christians, including the martyrdom of Stephen. While traveling to Damascus to engage in further persecutions of the Christians about A.D. 36–38, he experienced a vision of Jesus and was temporarily struck blind. The experience converted him to Christianity. Changing his name to Paul, the previously rabid persecutor of Christians became an equally enthusiastic missionary for the early church.

For a number of years after his conversion, Paul lived quietly in his native Tarsus. During the early forties he assisted the missionary Barnabas in establishing a Christian community at Antioch, the third largest city of the Roman Empire. Shortly after 44, the two men returned to Jerusalem. In 46, Paul began his first missionary journey (46–48) in the company of Barnabas. Traveling to Antioch, they sailed to Cyprus to preach, then proceeded to the region of Pamphylia on the southern coast of Asia Minor. Making their way inland, they conducted a circuit of preaching to various Jewish communities in Pisidia, with mixed receptions. The two men then returned to Antioch.

Paul's second missionary journey began in 49 with Silas and Timothy as his companions. Leaving Antioch, the missionaries traveled by land back to Pisidia. They made their way through Phrygia and Mysia, preaching as they went, to Troas on the coast of the Aegean Sea. A vision commanded Paul to go on to Macedonia. At Philippi, he made many converts, but he also aroused some opposition. Proceeding on to Thessalonica, Athens, and Corinth, Paul continued to preach and make converts. He sailed across the Aegean, visited Ephesus, and sailed to Caesarea on the coast of Palestine. From there, he made his way to Jerusalem and on to Antioch, where he concluded his second missionary journey in 52.

Paul's third missionary journey began in 53 at Antioch. Passing through Galatia, Phrygia, and Asia, he came to Ephesus, where he worked for two years with great success. In fact, so great was his success that adherents of the cult of the goddess Artemis (Diana) rioted in protest. Because of the violence, Paul traveled to Macedonia and Greece and visited the churches there once more. From Philippi he visited various cities on the Aegean Sea and along the southwest coast of Asia Minor before returning to Jerusalem in 57.

In Jerusalem, Paul aroused the wrath of anti-Christian Jews, which in turn brought him to the attention of various Roman officials. Ultimately, Paul used his Roman citizenship to have his case transferred to Rome in 59. Traveling by ship, Paul stopped at Myra, Cnidus, and Crete. Sailing in the winter, Paul's ship encountered a storm that caused it to shipwreck on Malta. Paul finally reached Rome in 60, and spent two years under house arrest, but what happened to him after this episode is unclear. Some later sources claim that he made yet another missionary journey to Spain. The most reliable sources state that Paul

Engraving of St. Paul. From Holman's Holy Bible.

died from beheading in 64 during Emperor Nero's persecution. Paul's career illustrates the importance of missionary travel in the growth of the early Christian church.

For further reading
Ernle Bradford, *Paul the Traveller*, 1976.

St. Thomas, Legend of
During the Middle Ages and the Age of Discovery in the fifteenth and sixteenth centuries, Europeans thought that an isolated but thriving Christian community existed in India. These Indian Christians were the result of missionary activity by the Apostle Thomas, who was elaborately buried in India. Geographical confusion in the early sixteenth century over the Americas being part of East Asia or the Indies led to a widespread but erroneous belief that St. Thomas had engaged in missionary work among the Native Americans.

From the time of the early church through the Middle Ages, Europeans believed that the Apostle Thomas evangelized India Inferior, or the region of Afghanistan and northern India. St. Bartholomew performed his missionary work in India Superior, which corresponded to the southern part of the Indian subcontinent, while St. Matthew converted the people of Middle India (Ethiopia). Such beliefs were at least partially based on the pseudoepigraphic scripture known as the *Acts of St. Thomas*. After Pentecost, the disciples of Jesus draw lots to determine where they will be assigned as missionaries. St. Thomas draws India. He is not anxious to go there, and begins making excuses about being in poor health and not being able to speak the local language. Jesus appears and compels Thomas to go to India by the rather drastic expedient of selling him into slavery to a merchant named Haban. Haban sails to India, landing at the port of Sandaruk, and sells Thomas as an architect or carpenter to the local king, Gundafor. (The story had a strong historical foundation, because in 1848 the French orientalist Joseph T. Reinaud uncovered the existence of a Partho-Indian king named Gondophares in the Indus valley during the first century of the Christian era.) The king orders St. Thomas to build him a new palace, and gives him a large sum of money to pay for materials and workers. St. Thomas has different plans, and gives the money to the poor. Outraged by this extravagant disobedience, King Gundafor has St. Thomas whipped and thrown into prison. Gad, a brother of Gundafor, meanwhile falls ill and dies from pining over the family's financial loss. When Gad arrives in Heaven, he notices a beautiful palace. He is told that St. Thomas built it for Gundafor and Gad to live in for eternity. Enlightened, Gad asks for and receives permission to return temporarily to earth, where he persuades his brother to convert to Christianity. St. Thomas baptizes both brothers. In later versions of the legend, St. Thomas miraculously builds Gundafor's palace overnight, converting him as a result.

After Gundafor's conversion, a man named Siphorius guides St. Thomas to the kingdom of King Mazdai. He preaches the virtues of Christian celibacy to the local women, and a tense situation develops when his converts refuse to sleep with their husbands. King Mazdai becomes gravely angered when his own wife, Queen Tortia, begins to follow St. Thomas's teachings. St. Thomas even manages to convert Vizan, Mazdai's son. At last, King Mazdai has had enough; St. Thomas is executed by a spear thrust. The pious Prince Vizan directs the martyred St. Thomas to be buried in the tomb of former kings. Later, St. Thomas's body is moved to Edessa in Syria.

Legends about St. Thomas preaching in India persisted through the Middle Ages. According to the *Anglo-Saxon Chronicle*, in 883, King Alfred sent a Sighelm to visit the tombs of St. Thomas and St. Bartholomew in India. About 250 years later, the legend of St. Thomas received a dramatic revival. In May 1122, or about that date, a Patriarch John of India arrived at Rome on a diplomatic mission to Pope Calixtus II. Two contemporary accounts of Patriarch John's visit to Rome survive. One is an anonymous tract called *De adventu patriarchae Indorum ad Urbem sub Calixto papa seconde* and the other is a letter by Odo of Rheims. Later chroniclers, such as Ordericus Vitalis (d. ca. 1142) in his *Historia ecclesiastica*, repeated the legends of St. Thomas and his tomb in India. Patriarch John claimed to be the ruler of Hulna, a great metropolis that served as the capital of India. Hulna's city wall was so thick and massive that two chariots could travel abreast on it. One of the four rivers of Paradise, the Pison, flowed through it, leaving behind deposits of gold and jewels. Hulna's population was exclusively Christian. Any infidels and heretics who came into the city either converted or died from supernatural causes. Even more significant was the tomb of St. Thomas that lay nearby. St. Thomas's tomb and church were located on a mountain at the center of a deep lake, with 12 monasteries, each dedicated to an apostle, located along its shores. Visitors and pilgrims could reach the Church of St. Thomas only during the week before and the week after his feast day of 6 October. At that time, the waters of the lake lowered enough to expose a path. An alternate version changes the lake into a river. Worshipers entering the Church of St. Thomas found his body suspended from the ceiling in a beautiful silver vessel. On each feast day, the Indian clergy placed St. Thomas's body in an armchair, from which position the dead St. Thomas miraculously administered the Eucharist to the visiting worshipers.

Patriarch John's account of the miracle-working tomb of St. Thomas stirred the imaginations of medieval Christians, but Patriarch John was apparently a charlatan. He did not come from India; he came from the much nearer city of Edessa in Syria. The city of Edessa contained Christians and faced the increasing threat of attack in the early twelfth century because local Muslim leaders had begun to take the offensive against the forces and strongholds of the invading Crusaders. Although one tradition held that St. Thomas lay buried at Mylapore near Madras in India, another said that he was buried at Edessa. The fourth-century St. Ephraim (d. 373) preached a sermon claiming that St. Thomas had been miraculously and simultaneously buried at both Mylapore and Edessa. More likely, St. Thomas was first buried in India and later moved to Edessa, with a relic left at the Indian tomb. The Christians of Mesopotamia and Syria and the Indian Christians of Mylapore on the Coromandel coast maintained close relations for centuries. It appears that Syrian missionaries established a lasting Christian presence on the Malabar coast of India because the liturgical language of those Christians was Syriac.

Edessa and its tomb of St. Thomas bore a close resemblance to Patriarch John's description of his city of Hulna and its tomb of St. Thomas, and his account of the tomb of St. Thomas contained elements of the tombs at both Edessa and Mylapore. Besides having a close connection to the Indian Christians, Edessa served as an important crossroads for trade between India, the Middle East, North Africa, and Europe. All these factors kept the legend of St. Thomas alive in western Europe well into the sixteenth century. In the course of his travels, Marco Polo encountered Indian Christians on the Coromandel coast. Vasco da Gama and his men expected to find Indian Christians when they arrived in India in 1498, but they mistook Hindu worshipers for fellow Christians. Later Portuguese travelers finally reached the actual tomb of St. Thomas at Mylapore in 1522.

The belief that St. Thomas had established Christian communities in India and the Indies by the sixteenth century even led to the idea that the well-traveled saint had visited the Americas. When Columbus stumbled upon the Americas while trying to reach Asia in 1492, he did not realize what he had really found. After three more voyages, Columbus still believed that he had reached Asia, a belief he took to his grave in 1506. He was not alone; not until 1519 were Europeans aware that the Americas were quite distinct from Asia. Instead of "the Indies," now the East Indies and the West Indies were half a world apart. Before that realization set in, the early conquistadors looked for the Marvels of the East in Columbus's so-called Indies, and among those marvels were the Indian Christians of St. Thomas. No true pre-Columbian Christians were ever found, but the idea that St. Thomas visited the Americas as well as India persisted as a fringe belief into the twentieth century. St. Thomas was a prodigious traveler and missionary in the Middle East of imperial Rome who certainly deserved his lasting reputation as an apostle, but he never reached the Americas.

See also

India; Marvels of the East; Prester John and His Kingdom.

For further reading

Vsevolod Slessarev, *Prester John*, 1959; Louis-André Vigneras, "St. Thomas, Apostle of Americas," *Hispanic American Historical Review* 57 (Feb. 1977): 82–90; John Kirtland Wright, *The Geographical Lore of the Time of the Crusades*, 1925.

SAMARKAND   Famous city in central Asia that served for centuries as an important stop along the vital Silk Road, which carried trade between the Far East and the Middle East and Europe.

The date of the first settlement of Samarkand is unclear, although possibly the Persian king Cyrus the Great (559–529 B.C.) founded it. It was the capital of ancient Sogdiana when Alexander the Great (356–323 B.C.) conquered that region. At various times in its history the city was controlled by Persia, China, or a succession of Turkish or Mongol dynasties. Over the years its wealth grew, thanks to its strategic location—it was one of the last significant stops before eastbound travelers and merchants entered the barren steppes and deserts that lay beyond the Jaxartes River. Arab conquerors brought Samarkand into the world of Islam in the early eighth century A.D. It was captured by the armies of Genghiz Khan (d. 1227) during the conquest of the Khwarizmian Empire. About this time, westerners living in the Crusader states of the Outremer became aware once more of Samarkand's existence.

Mongol rule resulted in a significant decline in the city's fortunes. Fourteenth-century travelers sadly told of the decayed state of Samarkand, although they added that even the ruins were quite impressive. The city's fortunes revived when the brutal conqueror Tamerlane (1336–1405) made it his capital. It remained an important central Asian trading city until railroads and other modern forms of transportation caused the old caravan routes to be abandoned. Samarkand is now the capital of the Uzbek Republic of the former Soviet Union.

See also
Silk Road.
For further reading
Wilfred Blunt, *Golden Road to Samarkand*, 1973; René Grousset, *The Empire of the Steppes*, 1970.

SANDSTORM   These dangerous storms occur in sandy areas of deserts, particularly the Sahara, when the winds become strong enough to pick up and carry particles of sand. They are a serious hazard to travelers and caravans caught out in the open.

By their nature, deserts are dusty places. In some deserts, like the Sahara, dust forms a virtually permanent haze at ground level. Occasionally, the atmospheric pressure gradient becomes steep enough to create winds capable of picking up grains of sand. Winds of approximately 30 miles per hour can do this, but the classic sandstorm is caused by gale-force winds of 40 miles per hour or more. Windblown sand penetrates tents and clothing in a most amazing and unpleasant manner. Inadequately protected humans and animals caught in such a sandstorm can suffer serious injury to the skin, eyes, and lungs.

Hollywood movies set in the Sahara or some other sandy desert frequently inflict deadly sandstorms on their heroes. Those experienced in desert life feel that these representations exaggerate the danger. Belief in the deadly threat posed by a sandstorm, however, is quite ancient. Herodotus (484–420 B.C.), in his *Histories* (bk. 3, ch. 26), describes how a sandstorm destroyed the army sent by the Persian king Cambyses (r. 530–521 B.C.) to conquer Nubia. The Arab geographical writer Ibn Hawqal (fl. 967–988) in his book *Surat al-Ard* [Picture of the Earth] told how sandstorms would sometimes annihilate whole caravans traveling between Ghana and Egypt. Sandstorms rendered one route so dangerous that the ruler of Egypt, Abu'l-'Abbas Ahmad b. Tulun (868–884), prohibited its use by caravans. Later, the Jewish traveler Benjamin of Tudela (fl. 1165–1173) described how "in this desert [the Sahara] there are mountains of sand, and when the wind rises it covers the caravans with sand and many die from suffocation." Such monstrous sandstorms are extremely rare, but their awesome force has fascinated writers and terrorized desert travelers over the centuries.

See also

Caravans; Sahara.

For further reading

J. L. Cloudsley-Thompson, ed., *Sahara Desert,* 1984; N. Levtzion and J. F. P. Hopkins, eds., *Corpus of Early Arabic Sources for West African History,* 1981.

SANTA FE TRAIL

Classic road in the American Old West, it was developed in 1821 to supply goods to the silver-producing city of Santa Fe.

Santa Fe was a Spanish outpost with considerable stocks of silver, wool, and mules, but it experienced an aggravating shortage of manufactured goods. Trade goods from Mexico had to follow a circuitous route that passed through hundreds of miles of territory inhabited by ferocious bands of Apaches. As a result, manufactured products were scarce and extremely expensive in Santa Fe. Word of the city's plight attracted the attention of French-Canadian traders in 1739. They found that Santa Fe was reasonably accessible by coming overland from the Missouri River. More French traders followed, and by 1804, Americans joined them. Spanish authorities reacted by imprisoning foreign merchants who interloped on Spain's monopoly of trade with its empire. However, Mexico's gaining of its independence in 1821 threw Santa Fe open to American traders.

William Becknell, a Native American trader, was the first American to reach the now-welcoming inhabitants of Santa Fe. He and others that followed him developed a route that crossed over 780 miles of prairie. Although the first traders used pack horses, wagons could easily travel the Santa Fe Trail, and only a few rivers had to be crossed. Much of the trail followed the course of the Arkansas River. Initially the trail began at Franklin, Missouri, but its eastern terminus moved first to Independence and eventually to Kansas City.

Traders traveling the Santa Fe Trail soon banded together in caravans for mutual protection from Native American attacks. However, Native Americans seldom attacked; between 1821 and 1842, only 11 men were killed along the trail by Native Americans. Violence escalated at the end of the Civil War during the years 1864–1869. The worst year was 1868, when reportedly 45 people perished on the trail, including 17 stagecoach passengers whom Native Americans burned to death. Despite such incidents, the Santa Fe Trail was heavily used throughout its history. Thousands of wagons rolled along the trail each year, with many continuing on to California. Trade with Santa Fe supplied the United States with significant amounts of much-needed silver and mules. Progress rendered the trail obsolete; the Atchison, Topeka, and Santa Fe Railroad was completed in 1880.

For further reading

R. L. Duffus, *The Santa Fe Trail,* 1930.

SANTIAGO, ORDER OF
This Spanish military order appeared during the middle of the twelfth century for the purpose of protecting pilgrims traveling to the shrine of St. James, the patron saint of Spain, which was located at Santiago de Compostela.

Christian Spain contained many *hermangilda*, informal bands of farmer-warriors organized to fight the Moors. About 1158, the *hermangilda* near Caceres offered to provide protection for pilgrims going to Compostela. A few years later, about 1164, the duties of these same knights expanded when they were given the stronghold of Uclés on the Castilian frontier. They received a formal rule for governing their order in 1171 from the papal-legate Cardinal Jacinto. It was based on the rule of St. Augustine and that of the Templars. In 1175, Pope Alexander III recognized them as the Order of St. James of the Sword, and their ranks consisted of canons and knights. Canons of the order provided for the spiritual welfare of the knights, who did the actual fighting. These knights wore a white habit decorated with a red cross called an *espada*, in which the bottom arm resembled a sword blade. The Order of Santiago also included canonesses, who provided hospitality for pilgrims in guest houses and hospitals. One unique aspect of the Order of Santiago was its practice of allowing married knights to have full membership and even maintain a normal family life for most of the year.

The order quickly proved popular among the Christians of the Iberian Peninsula and ultimately accumulated considerable wealth and political power. Such resources attracted the attention of the Spanish king Ferdinand, but it was his son, Emperor Charles V, who in 1523 brought the administration of all three great Castilian military orders—Santiago, Alcántara, and Calatrava—under the administration of the Spanish crown. The decline of the military orders predated that event; they had already lost their reason for being when the last Moorish stronghold in Spain fell in 1492.

See also
Hospitalers, Knights; Templars, Knights; Teutonic Knights.
For further reading
Desmond Seward, *The Monks of War*, 1972.

SANTIAGO DE COMPOSTELA
Located in northwestern Spain, it has always been one of the most important pilgrimage sites in western Europe, ranking only behind Rome in popularity.

Certain early-medieval Christian traditions claimed that the apostle St. James the Great brought Christianity to the Asturias region in Spain. In the first half of the ninth century, local Christians discovered a tomb that they claimed belonged to St. James. He was quickly declared the patron saint of Spain, and a cathedral city and pilgrimage shrine were built on the site. Several churches were constructed over the tomb. In 997 the Moorish army of al-Mansur destroyed the city and shrine of Santiago de Compostela, but the site was not

Eighteenth-century facade of the church of Santiago de Compostela, Spain.

abandoned. The present church was consecrated in 1211. Modern scholars conclude that the cult of pilgrimage to Santiago de Compostela arose to counter the power of Islam in the Iberian Peninsula. The cult was extremely successful and attracted innumerable pilgrims. The military monastic order of Santiago was founded in 1175 to protect pilgrims, and itself became a powerful institution in Portuguese and Castilian society. Both the Cluniac and Augustinian orders built monasteries along the road to Compostela to provide pilgrims with lodging and food. Various pilgrims' guides were composed to assist visitors. Although its heyday was during the twelfth through the fifteenth centuries, Santiago de Compostela remains an important religious and tourist site even today.

See also
Pilgrimage.
For further reading
William Melczer, ed. and trans., *The Pilgrim's Guide to Santiago de Compostela*, 1993.

SARGASSO SEA   Region of stagnant water in the North Atlantic Ocean surrounded by and formed by the Gulf Stream, the Canary current, and the north equatorial current. Its waters are peppered by clumps of floating seaweed, or sargassum. For centuries, sailors believed that a sailing ship venturing into the Sargasso Sea could become trapped in the floating seaweed.

The Sargasso Sea has been around an extremely long time. Its plant and animal population evolved special traits to survive in its unique environment. In size, the Sargasso Sea occupies about the same number of square miles as the continental United States. Formed by the various ocean currents that surround it, the Sargasso Sea is unique. No other ocean has an area of stagnant water comparable in size. The sea is also an oceanic desert despite all the seaweed and crustaceans that inhabit it. The absence of currents prevents its waters from replenishing their nutrients, and diatoms and plankton cannot live there. Without their presence, neither can most normal oceanic life.

Seafarers have known about the Sargasso Sea for millennia. Ancient mariners did not commonly sail the high seas of the Atlantic Ocean, but some did, and on those rare occasions, they encountered the strange waters of the Sargasso Sea. Phoenicians and Carthaginian sailors whispered vague stories about a sea of weeds in the western ocean that was so thick it could trap a sailing ship, its crew doomed to die of thirst or starvation. Of course, it was a common trick of the Phoenicians and Carthaginians to tell frightening tales about their maritime discoveries to discourage foreign interlopers. Hecataeus, Herodotus, and Crates of Mallos all made vague references to the Sargasso Sea. The *Navigatio Sancti Brendani* (ca. 870) described how St. Brendan and his companions sailed through a curdled sea. Other medieval European sources mention a clotted sea or a liver sea. In 1436, Andrea Biancho included the Sargasso Sea on his map of the Atlantic Ocean, calling it the Mer de Baga, or sea of berries, a reference to the air sacs on the sargassum weed that help keep it afloat. Christopher Columbus touched the edge of the Sargasso Sea in September 1492 during his first voyage. He did not find it to be a deadly quagmire of seaweed, nor has anyone else who has voyaged there.

The Sargasso Sea's floating clumps of seaweed are not thick enough to impede a sailing ship. Stories of ships being trapped by the seaweed are not only pure fantasy, they are a persistent one. The supposedly deadly Sargasso Sea has been featured a number of times in adventure novels and films. One film from Hammer Studios, the misnamed *Lost Continent* (1968), tells the story of a modern ship that makes its way into the Sargasso Sea and finds the descendants of the crews of Spanish galleons trapped by the seaweed centuries earlier. The myth of the Sargasso Sea lives on despite its falsehood.

See also

Atlantic Ocean; St. Brendan the Navigator, Voyage of.

For further reading

David B. Ericson and Goesta Wellin, *The Ever Changing Sea*, 1970; Hans Leip, *The River in the Sea*, 1958; John Kirtland Wright, *The Geographical Lore of the Time of the Crusades*, 1925.

SCIOPODS   Or Skiapods, meaning "shadow-foot," they were also known as unipeds or monocoli in reference to their single foot. This monstrous race had only one leg with one large foot at the end of it. They were said to be able to move quite rapidly by hopping. If the hot sun bothered them, they lay on their backs and used the foot to shade themselves. Pliny the Elder's *Natural History* located the Sciopods in India, although later medieval writers placed them in Africa. The writer of *Eirik's Saga*, a fourteenth-century tale of how Thorfinn Karlsefni led a group of Norse on a colonizing expedition to mysterious Vinland, told of the settlers encountering a uniped (or Sciopod) who shot Thorvald Eiriksonn with an arrow and mortally wounded him. The uniped escaped the pursuing Norse by hopping off faster than they could run. The seemingly incongruous appearance of unipeds in Vinland is actually a clue that the medieval Norse conceived of that land as a sort of northern peninsula of Africa with its monstrous races.

The Sciopods were one of the more popular of the monstrous races among medieval European geographers and cartographers. They frequently appeared on mappaemundi, book illustrations, and other artistic depictions. European travelers were certainly well primed to encounter a Sciopod but, of course, no one ever did.

See also

Monstrous Races; Vinland.

For further reading

Magnus Magnusson and Hermann Pálsson, trans., *The Vinland Sagas*, 1965; Pliny the Elder, *Natural History*, 1991.

SCYLAX, VOYAGE OF (CA. 510 B.C.)   Also spelled Skylax, this Greek
sailor from Caryanda in the country of Caria in Asia Minor first explored the
Arabian Sea.

Serving the Persian king Darius Hystaspis, Scylax's assignment was to explore the Indus River and the coastline of the Arabian or Erythraean Sea. Scylax
and his company began their journey at Caspatyrus, near modern Peshawar,
and floated down the Kabul River into the Indus River through Punjab and the
Thar Desert until they reached the sea. Sailing west from the mouth of the
Indus, the Greeks bypassed the Persian Gulf and cruised along the south coast
of the Arabian peninsula. They made their way up the length of the Red Sea
and ended their journey at Arsinoe near present-day Suez.

Little is known about Scylax's voyage except for the brief account in
Herodotus's *History*. The journey was a slow one, taking 30 months to complete. Scylax may have stopped at various points along the way to gather more
detailed information, or their lack of knowledge about using the monsoons effi-
ciently may have contributed to the expedition's slow progress. As a result of
Scylax's voyage, Darius added the Sind to the great Persian Empire. He also
had a canal dug from the Nile River to the Gulf of Suez to encourage trade
between Persia and Egypt. Otherwise, Scylax was a famous—although premature by several centuries—pioneer of Greek exploration of the Arabian Sea and
Indian Ocean.

See also
Indian Ocean; Nearchus, Voyage of.
For further reading
Rhys Carpenter, *Beyond the Pillars of Heracles*, 1966; M. Cary and E. H.
Warmington, *The Ancient Explorers*, 1963.

SCYLLA AND CHARYBDIS   This pair of mythical monsters inhabited a
narrow strait in the ancient Mediterranean Sea and posed a serious threat to
such travelers as Jason, Odysseus, and Aeneas.

Scylla possessed six doglike heads with triple rows of teeth and a body with
12 feet. Oddly enough, some accounts claim that Scylla was originally a beautiful young woman who became involved in a vicious rivalry over a man. According to one version, Scylla competed with the sorceress Circe for the attentions
of the sea god Glaucus; another called her a rival of Amphitrite, a Nereid, for
the affections of Poseidon. The end result was the same—the jealous rival used
magic to transform the fair Scylla into a loathsome monster. Living in a cave
above the sea, Scylla's normal food was fish, but whenever the opportunity
arose, each head snatched an unlucky sailor from the decks of passing ships.

Charybdis appears to have been some sort of whirlpool or sea vortex that
was located at the opposite side of the strait from Scylla. If Scylla was dangerous, venturing too close to Charybdis meant certain destruction for any passing
ship. According to Homer's *Odyssey*, Charybdis was a great creature living at

the bottom of the sea that, three times a day, sucked in vast quantities of water, thereby creating a whirlpool. It then spewed the water back out in a geyser that was equally lethal. Like Scylla, Charybdis had originally been a young woman, a daughter of Gaia and Poseidon. Her gluttony so appalled Zeus, the king of the gods, that he cast her into the sea, where she was forced to suck in water, and so became a hazard to navigation.

Ancient writers originally placed Scylla and Charybdis in the poorly known waters of the western Mediterranean Sea. Both Jason and Odysseus managed to get their ships safely through the Strait of Scylla and Charybdis, although Odysseus lost some of his crew. By the time of Vergil, the Strait of Scylla and Charybdis had become firmly identified with the Strait of Messina. Rather than pass between Scylla and Charybdis, Vergil's hero Aeneas sailed all the way around Sicily to get to his ultimate destination. Naturalistic explanations identify Scylla as a rock formation that posed a threat to navigation and Charybdis as a whirl-pool. Other sources suggest that Scylla was a rather inaccurate description of a giant octopus that occasionally attacked ancient ships in the Indian Ocean. Both Scylla and Charybdis are very ancient names for sea goddesses who frequently threatened sailors, becoming immortalized in Greek mythology as a threat to travelers at sea.

See also

Aeneas, Wanderings of; Odysseus, Wanderings of.

For further reading

Robert Graves, *The Greek Myths*, 1955.

SCYTHIA   During the era of classical and Hellenistic Greece, the name *Scythia* referred to the region between the Carpathian Mountains and the Don River. By late antiquity and the Middle Ages, Scythia had expanded as a geographical concept to encompass northern and central Asia. It was used interchangeably with Tartary and Siberia.

The original Scythians were an Indo-European tribe from central Asia who founded a kingdom about 600 B.C. in the area of present-day Romania and the Ukraine. Being among the first people to domesticate horses for riding, the Scythians were tough, nomadic warriors. About 512 B.C., they successfully resisted an invasion by King Darius of Persia, and in 325 B.C. they defeated a Macedonian army under the command of Zopyrion, who had been sent at the command of Alexander the Great. The Scythians actively traded with Greek settlers along the northwest coast of the Black Sea. During the second century B.C., the Sarmatians, another nomadic people, conquered the original area of Scythia. Some Scythians escaped and reestablished themselves in the Crimea. By about A.D. 200, they had disappeared from history as a distinct people.

The names Scythia and Scythians, however, lived on for centuries afterward. For medieval Europeans, the vast, amorphous plains of central and north Asia were all part of Scythia, and any nomadic tribe from that area were

Scythians. Little was known about the geography and ethnography of this vast region, so medieval writers leaned heavily and inaccurately on the terminology they had inherited from the Greeks and Romans. According to the medieval geographical writers Isidore of Seville (ca. 560–636) and Gervase of Tilbury (fl. 1211), Scythia was a region containing large areas of both arable lands and deserts. Great rivers flowed northwest through Scythia into the Caspian Sea or the so-called River Ocean. Deposits of gold and precious stones existed, but these were guarded by fierce Griffins. Some of Scythia's inhabitants were man-eaters, the dreaded anthrophagi. After the reports of the Mongol missions of the thirteenth century, European knowledge about central and north Asia improved, and the geographical concept of Scythia gradually merged with that of Tartary.

See also

Siberia; Tartary.

For further reading

Tamara Talbot Rice, *The Scythians*, 1958; John Kirtland Wright, *The Geographical Lore of the Time of the Crusades*, 1925.

SEA MONSTERS   From ancient times to the present, people have believed that the sea contains various monstrous creatures that on occasion menace sailors and ships.

Sea monsters could take many forms. Some were great serpents, while others were more like aquatic dragons. Giant whales, fishes, and turtles appear in tales of sea monsters, as do gigantic octopuses and squids. Some reports mention huge mammalian-type creatures that looked somewhat like otters. Belief in such creatures added greatly to the general anxiety associated with sea travel.

The sea is a dangerous and mysterious environment. Through most of human history, travel at sea has been a hazardous enterprise. Storms, reefs, pirates, icebergs, and a myriad of other dangers confronted those who traveled on the sea, and many who went disappeared without a trace. The sea was also a vast and alien environment of which humans were normally able to see only the surface. No one knew what marvels or monstrosities might lurk within its depths.

History and literature abound with tales of sea monsters. Jason, Odysseus, and Aeneas were all threatened by the sea monster/whirlpool called Charybdis. The hero Perseus killed the sea monsters that threatened Andromeda. Jonah the prophet was swallowed whole by the sea monster known as Leviathan, which the Bible refers to as a fish, but might have been a whale. Both Sindbad and St. Brendan landed on living islands that turned out to be giant fishes or whales resting on the water's surface. Old maps from the fifteenth through the seventeenth centuries are frequently dotted with pictures of sea monsters of various sorts. True believers speculate that the Loch Ness monster might be a sea serpent that was trapped when the loch was cut off from the sea in primordial times.

Are sea monsters mere fantasies with no basis in reality? Some factual basis appears to be behind these legends. From the middle of the seventeenth cen-

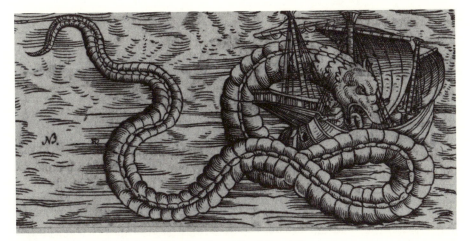

Sea monster attacking a boat. Woodcut from The Chronick.

tury to the present, some 600 detailed sightings of sea monsters have been reported, so something appears to be out there. Very large whales, fish, eels, octopuses, and squids do exist. Chance encounters with such creatures could easily result in talk of sighting a sea monster. Such tales would also grow in the telling and retelling, as in any good fish story. The one that got away is always bigger, and that applies especially to sea monsters. Besides, how much exaggeration about its size does a sperm whale or a blue whale need? Even Moby Dick, the great white whale of Herman Melville's classic novel (1851), had a basis in fact: the sinking of the whaling ship *Essex* by an enraged whale in 1819 and a real whale named Moby Dick that terrorized the seas in the 1840s and 1850s. Mammoth creatures like whales would look particularly huge to people sailing in the much smaller ships of earlier times.

Far northern waters appear to have been particularly congenial homes for stories about gigantic marine animals. The waters off Norway were the abode of the fearsome Kraken. The sober works of history and natural history by Olaus Magnus (1490–1557) and Bishop Erik Pontoppidan (1698–1764) contain stories about northern sea monsters. Greenland missionary Bishop Hans Egede (1686–1758) claimed to have sighted a sea monster during a voyage in 1734.

Reports of strange and extraordinarily large marine life occur in virtually all the seas of the world. Some reports of sea serpents may reflect the existence of a rare species of giant eel. Other sightings could be hitherto unknown creatures that normally dwell in the deepest parts of the oceans. Oceanographic explorations of those depths reveal some bizarre and monstrous creatures, and some so-called sea monsters do exist. It is easy to see how a whole complex of legends about sea monsters could arise when very large marine animals came into contact with fearful, credulous, and superstitious sea voyagers.

For further reading
Charles Gould, *Mythical Monsters*, 1886; Frank Smyth, "Sea Monster," in *The Sea*, vol. 7, 1974.

"SEEING THE ELEPHANT"
Expression commonly used in the mid-nineteenth-century United States to refer to the experience of traveling overland across the prairies and mountains to reach California and its goldfields.

Throughout history people have found elephants fascinating creatures. As a result, the phrase "seeing the elephant" became a symbol for an unusual or difficult experience, a usage followed by nineteenth-century Americans. With the beginning of the overland migration using the Oregon Trail, "seeing the elephant" took on a more specific set of meanings. At the broadest level, it referred to the experience of making the great journey along the Oregon Trail. In some contexts, the "elephant" was the continent of North America, with the Continental Divide being the "elephant's backbone." Those who gave up the journey talked of "seeing too much of the elephant." Once travelers and emigrants reached California, "seeing the elephant" referred more specifically to California or the experience of gold mining. In the 1890s, the end of the frontier and its hardships also brought an end to the use of the phrase.

See also

Elephant; Oregon Trail.

For further reading

A. J. Rea, "Seeing the Elephant," *Western Folklore* 28 (Jan. 1969): 21–28; Peter Tamony, "To See the Elephant," *Pacific Historian* 12 (Winter 1968): 23–29.

SEVEN CITIES, LEGEND OF
According to legend, early in the eighth century, seven Portuguese bishops and their followers fled into the western Atlantic Ocean to escape Muslim invaders. On the island of Antilia they established seven rich cities. By the fifteenth century, Antilia and the Seven Cities appeared on maps, along with vague reports of various people sighting or landing on them. This legend inspired much of the early exploration of the Atlantic. During the early sixteenth century, the location of the Seven Cities shifted to the mainland of America, prompting still more expeditions. The most famous were those of Hernando de Soto in 1539–1542 and Francisco Vásquez de Coronado in 1540–1542.

Muslims, led by Tariq, crossed the Strait of Gibraltar in 711 and invaded the Iberian Peninsula. They decisively defeated the army of the Christian king Roderick, and by the next year his Visigothic kingdom of Spain was destroyed. This Muslim invasion and conquest inspired the legend that the Archbishop of Oporto and six fellow bishops took ship with their Christian flocks and fled from the hated infidel invaders into the western Atlantic. They found the island of Antilia, on which they took refuge. After burning their ships so that no one could return and reveal their location to the Muslims, they built seven cities and soon established a rich, even utopian, society. According to the late-fifteenth-century cartographer Martin Behaim, their flight took place in 734, but Fernando, the son of Christopher Columbus, dated it more reasonably to 714.

Although the Seven Cities were supposedly founded in the eighth century, Europeans apparently remained unaware of them until the early fifteenth century. According to a notation that Martin Behaim placed on his globe of 1492, a Spanish ship sighted the island of the Seven Cities in 1414. The oldest first-hand reference to the Seven Cities occurred on Zuane Pizzigano's map of 1424, which showed Antilia, including the Seven Cities, for the first time. The Spanish historian Antonio de Herrera y Tordesillas (ca. 1549–1625) wrote that some Portuguese sailors reached Antilia in the time of Prince Henry the Navigator (1394–1460), where they found a civilized people who spoke Portuguese. After they departed for home, they discovered that the beach sand they had placed in their firebox was full of gold. Prince Henry ordered them to go back to the island, but they refused. Bartolomé de Las Casas of Spain included the same story in his *Historia de Las Indias*, as did the Portuguese historian Antonio Galvano (1503–1557), only he dated it to 1447. Some people consider these reports of the Seven Cities to be records of pre-Columbian visits to someplace in the Americas.

The search for the Seven Cities inspired many Portuguese voyages of discovery during the fifteenth century, including those of Diogo de Teive in 1452, Fernão Teles in 1474–1476, and Ferdinand Van Olmen in 1486. All hoped to find the Seven Cities, but no record shows that they found anything at all—including any part of the Americas. By 1474, the geographer Paolo Pozzo dal Toscanelli decided that the Seven Cities on Antilia would make a good rest stop for voyagers on their way to Asia. The fame of the Seven Cities and their lure also spread to England, inspiring the Bristol voyages of the 1480s. In his voyage of 1497 for England, the Genoese adventurer John Cabot returned home convinced that his discovery of Newfoundland was a part of the island of the Seven Cities.

The legend of the Seven Cities provided the incentive for many voyages into the Atlantic, but none found their elusive goal. By 1500, the map of Juan de La Cosa located the Seven Cities on the North American mainland where Cabot had visited, rather than an island or islands. Other cartographers, such as Gerard Mercator, continued to locate them on an Atlantic island as late as 1587. Some geographers placed the Seven Cities on the mainland of South America, but most people thought they were somewhere in North America. From that vague location, the Seven Cities beckoned to various conquistadors seeking to repeat the fabulous conquests of Mexico and Peru.

The travel accounts of Álvar Núñez Cabeza de Vaca concerning his wanderings as a castaway on the coast and interior of Texas from 1528 to 1536 helped focus the location of the Seven Cities on what is now the southwestern part of the continental United States. He brought back Native American tales of rich realms farther inland. Father Marcos de Niza was sent north of the Rio Grande to confirm the stories. He encountered the Zuñis, and was very impressed by them. He also picked up stories concerning a wealthy land called Cíbola, which was located farther north. Back in Mexico, wishful thinkers quickly equated Cíbola with the realm of the Seven Cities. Modern scholars speculate that the stories of golden walled cities might be the product of travelers seeing the sun reflected from the adobe walls of the Native American pueblos.

Father Marcos's report immediately led to the organization of the great expedition of Francisco Vásquez de Coronado. His party wandered through the mountains and deserts of the Southwest and across the lower Great Plains of Oklahoma and Kansas. They failed to discover the Seven Cities or Cíbola and were led on a fruitless search for the nonexistent kingdom of Quivira, but the Spanish did encounter the Grand Canyon. For the gold-hungry conquistadors, that was scant compensation. From 1539 to 1542, the brutal Hernando de Soto led an expedition that meandered through what is now the southeastern United States, pillaging hapless Native American villages and spreading European diseases that devastated the indigenous population. Soto sought any wealthy kingdom to conquer, including the Seven Cities, hoping to make himself rich and famous like the conquerors of Mexico and Peru. But he found nothing of the sort. Instead, the journey killed him, and his fearful soldiers secretly buried him in the waters of the Mississippi River to avoid displaying Spanish mortality to the cowed but hostile natives. The failures of the Coronado and de Soto expeditions largely ended the search for the Seven Cities. A few people forlornly continued to hope that the Seven Cities were out there somewhere, but there was really nowhere left for them to be. And so, another fascinating geographical legend was banished from the realm of the possible.

See also
Antillia.

For further reading
George E. Buker, "The Seven Cities," *American Neptune* 30 (1970): 249–259; Stephen Clissold, *The Seven Cities of Cibola,* 1962; David B. Quinn, *North America from Earliest Discovery to First Settlements,* 1977; Raymond H. Ramsay, *No Longer on the Map,* 1972.

SEVEN SEAS   Nautical literature and films are frequently peppered with references to sailing the so-called Seven Seas. The seven bodies of water referred to in this phrase are the Arctic, Antarctic, North Pacific, South Pacific, North Atlantic, South Atlantic, and Indian Oceans. The phrase obviously postdates the discovery of the Pacific Ocean by Balboa in 1513.

See also
Atlantic Ocean; Indian Ocean; Pacific Ocean.

SEVEN WONDERS OF THE ANCIENT WORLD   By a long-standing tradition, the Seven Wonders of the Ancient World consist of the pyramids of Egypt, the Hanging Gardens of Babylon, the statue of Zeus at Olympia, the temple of Artemis at Ephesus, the Mausoleum of Halicarnassus, the Colossus of Rhodes, and the Pharos, or Lighthouse, of Alexandria. They were supposed to be the chief sights or tourist attractions of the ancient Mediterranean world.

The practice of listing wonders (*thaumata*) or sights (*theamata*) goes back to the Greek historian Herodotus (484–420 B.C.), who described many marvels in his books. He was particularly impressed by the Egyptian pyramids and the great city of Babylon. Callimachus of Cyrene (305–240 B.C.), a sometime librarian of the Alexandrian Library, followed Herodotus's lead and compiled a book on the various wonders of the ancient world. Credit for the first concise list of "seven wonders," however, belongs to the poet Antipater of Sidon (fl. ca. 120 B.C.). His list substituted the great walls of Babylon for the Pharos of Alexandria, but otherwise was identical to the traditional list. From then on, other lists using the mystical number seven appeared. Diodorus Siculus the historian (fl. 60–21 B.C.) and the geographer Strabo (64 B.C.–A.D. 21) both used the concept of seven wonders in their writings. A few years later, the Roman poet Martial (40–104) suggested adding the Colosseum of Rome to the list (his list of seven already included the horned alter at Delos). Christian writers such as Gregory of Tours (536–594) and the Venerable Bede (673–735) also compiled lists of seven wonders, but they often included biblical items like Noah's Ark and the Temple of Solomon. During the late fifteenth and sixteenth centuries, scholars returned to the principles of Herodotus and Callimachus and solidified the traditional list of seven wonders by adding the Pharos of Alexandria to the list popularized by Antipater of Sidon. The list was fixed permanently by the engravings of the "Seven Wonders" done by the Dutch artist Maerten van Heemskerck (1458–1574), which although not particularly accurate were certainly dramatic. These seven items have remained the canonical Seven Wonders of the Ancient World ever since.

By the sixteenth century, the Seven Wonders of the Ancient World were, for the most part, no more. The pyramids of Egypt, the work of pharaohs of the

The Hanging Gardens of Babylon. Wood engraving in Lucien Ange, Voyage aux sept merveilles du monde, *1878.*

Fourth dynasty (ca. 2575–2467 B.C.), were the first wonders to be built and the only wonder still in existence in a reasonably complete state. King Nebuchadnezzar II (604–562 B.C.) supposedly built the Hanging Gardens of Babylon, which seem to have disappeared by 250 B.C. The great sculptor Pheidias (fl. ca. 450–430 B.C.) built the statue of Zeus at Olympia on a commission from the council of the sanctuary. In A.D. 391, the emperor Theodosius I transported it to the imperial palace in Constantinople, where a fire destroyed it in 462. The Temple of Artemis (Diana) at Ephesus was actually two temples. The legendary King Croesus of Lydia built the first one about 550 B.C. An act of arson by the infamous Herostratus destroyed it on 21 July 356 B.C., the night of Alexander the Great's birth. A larger, more magnificent temple was built to replace it, and like many ancient temples, it also served as a community bank. When St. Paul visited the city of Ephesus in A.D. 58–60, the adherents of the cult of Artemis (Diana) proved very hostile to the preaching of Christianity. Later, in 262, marauding Ostrogoths destroyed the second temple, and only its foundations remain. The Mausoleum of Halicarnassus was completed about 350 B.C. and remained largely intact until the thirteenth century A.D., when an earthquake destroyed the roof and upper colonnades. The resulting ruins left a convenient cache of quarried stone to be pilfered for use in other buildings. In 1494, the Knights Hospitalers cannibalized the mausoleum's stone to strengthen the fortifications of their castle at Bodrun, and only the foundations are left. The sculptor Chares of Lindos was commissioned to build the Colossus of Rhodes to celebrate the successful defense of Rhodes's independence. Between 294 and 282 B.C., he created a bronze statue about 110 feet high in the image of the sun god Helios. An earthquake toppled it in 226 B.C., but left massive ruins to awe visitors until A.D. 654. At that point, Arabs conquered Rhodes and ferried the bronze fragments of the Colossus to Asia Minor, where 900 camels carried the scrap metal to Syria. Sostratus of Cnidus, a diplomat and merchant, probably began building the lighthouse at Alexandria in 297 B.C. during the reign of Ptolemy I Soter (305–282 B.C.) and completed it during the reign of Ptolemy II Philadelphus (283–246 B.C.). Earthquakes severely damaged it in A.D. 956 and again in 1303 and 1323. It was apparently repaired after the first earthquake, but quickly fell into disuse. The great Arab traveler Ibn Battuta described it as being in ruins in 1326, and as even more ruinous in 1349.

The story of the Seven Wonders provides indisputable evidence that sightseeing was an important part of ancient travel, although obviously not the prime motivation. Still, the ancients recognized that during a journey, many things were worth seeing along the way.

See also

Colossus of Rhodes; Pharos (or Lighthouse) of Alexandria; Pyramids of Egypt.

For further reading

Peter Clayton and Martin Price, eds., *The Seven Wonders of the Ancient World*, 1988; John Romer and Elizabeth Romer, *The Seven Wonders of the World*, 1995.

SHEBA   Also known as Saba, most historians believe that this ancient kingdom was located in southwest Arabia in the approximate area of Yemen. The biblical genealogy of Noah's descendants in Genesis 10 placed Sheba in south Arabia and associated that land with the mysterious country of Ophir. Archaeological evidence shows that about 1500 B.C., Sheba developed a relatively sophisticated culture. By 1000 B.C., Sheba became a centralized monarchy of considerable wealth, thanks to its control of the caravan trade of frankincense and myrrh into the Mediterranean region. The Bible tells how an unnamed queen of Sheba visited King Solomon to test his renowned wisdom and exchange vast numbers of gifts. Modern scholars speculate that the queen of Sheba's true motive for visiting Solomon had to do with ironing out certain differences over control of trade routes. At that particular time, ancient Israel had temporarily risen to become a significant regional power, and therefore had to be reckoned with by Sheba. Sheba's control over the trade in frankincense and myrrh proved more durable than Israelite military might. Both Pliny the elder (A.D. 23–79) and Diodorus Siculus (fl. 60–21 B.C.) regarded the Shebans, or Sabaeans, as the wealthiest people in the world. Their good fortune lasted until the fourth century A.D., when the rise of Christianity in the Roman Empire caused the abandonment of the practice of cremating the dead, a process that used frankincense. The resulting decline in demand for frankincense led to a corresponding decline in the wealth and power of Sheba. Nevertheless, the image of Sheba as an exotic, wealthy land ruled by a beautiful queen persisted over the centuries in the minds of travelers, both real and armchair.

See also

Ophir.

For further reading

G. W. Van Beek, "The Land of Sheba," in *Solomon and Sheba*, 1974; G. W. Van Beek, "Sheba," in *The Oxford Encyclopedia of the Near East*, 1997.

SIBERIA   Name given to the vast geographic region of North Asia stretching from the Ural Mountains and Don River all the way to the Pacific Ocean. During ancient times it was known as Scythia, but the Europeans of the later Middle Ages called the area Tartary.

The name *Siberia* derives from the Mongol word *siber,* meaning "beautiful," "wonderful," or "pure," and the Tatar word *sibir,* which means "sleeping land." At the beginning of the seventeenth century, the minor khanate of Siber lay on the eastern side of the Urals and comprised only a small part of what is now known as Siberia. Greater Siberia consisted of about 5 million square miles of territory. In 1600, the indigenous Asiatic population numbered about 200,000, spread thinly across the harsh landscape and divided into some 140 tribes. Three basic environments exist in Siberia, running in three bands from east to west. In the far north lies the barren tundra with its frozen soils. Below the tundra is the taiga, a belt of magnificent forest lands. South of the taiga are the steppes, the band of grasslands that were the nursery of various nomadic tribes who for centuries devastated the sedentary civilizations of Europe and Asia until the appearance of firearms.

The Russian conquest of Siberia began with the Cossack Yermak's victory over the khanate of Siber at Isker in 1582. By 1650, Russians trapped sables and sea otters along the Pacific coast, although control was loose. The highly valuable furs quickly became an important source of income and foreign exchange for the Tsarist government.

Siberia is probably best known for its place in the ominous, fearsome phrase "being sent to Siberia." The Russian government began using Siberia as a place of exile and a penal colony in the middle of the seventeenth century. In 1651, Erofei Khabarov suggested that the government use exiles to colonize the Dauria and Amur regions of eastern Siberia. Being sent to Siberia could take two forms. The worst was *katorga*, which referred to being sentenced to forced labor in a prison camp. *Ssylka* was the second form; it consisted of banishment or exile to someplace in Siberia. Its rigors could range from mild to quite harsh. Mild exile meant living in one of Siberia's larger towns. It was far worse to be sent to a smaller, isolated settlement, particularly one located above the Arctic Circle. The worst form was banishment to live among one of Siberia's native tribes with their extremely meager lifestyles. Between the seventeenth century and the Russian Revolution of 1917, some 1 million people experienced being "sent to Siberia." Untold millions suffered the same fate under the savage regime of Joseph Stalin in the 1930s and 1940s. The Russian government's use of penal colonies has given Siberia a rather grim reputation as a place that many visited involuntarily.

See also

Scythia; Tartary.

For further reading

Benson Bobrick, *East of the Sun*, 1992; W. Bruce Lincoln, *The Conquest of a Continent*, 1994.

SILK ROAD

Famous caravan route that, at its height, stretched from China to the ports of the Black Sea and Mediterranean Sea. Traders traveled along parts of the Silk Road as early as 800 B.C. and as late as the beginning of the twentieth century. The Silk Road proper flourished from approximately 150 B.C. to A.D. 1650.

Trade along the Silk Road began about 800 B.C., when Chinese merchants began trading with the nomadic Scythian tribes of central Asia. Chinese silk constituted one of the most prized commodities of that trade. Over time, Chinese goods, particularly the universally popular silk, worked their way into lands farther and farther west. Eventually, they reached the Middle East and the Mediterranean world of the Hellenistic Greeks and the Roman Empire. At that time, the full-fledged Silk Road had come into being. By 100 B.C., records show that 12 caravans of 100 or more people each traveled from China to the West every year. The Silk Road had a dual function—to carry the luxury product of silk and to carry more mundane trade goods needed by the steppe tribes that lived along its route.

The harsh topography and environment of central Asia dictated the several routes of the Silk Road. Rugged mountains and fierce deserts limited the paths that travelers could follow. Beginning at Ch'ang-an in China, travelers proceeded to the far western portion of the Great Wall of China. They followed a narrow strip of relatively hospitable land along the northern edge of the Nan Shan Mountains that skimmed the Gobi Desert and the fearsome desert of the Takla Makan.

Reaching the town of An-hsi, the Silk Road split into a southern and a northern route. The southern route skirted along the northern foothills of the Kunlun Mountains, while to the north lay the Takla Makan. Various oasis cities lay scattered along the way: Tunhwang, Niya, Khotan, and finally Kashgar. These cities were originally Buddhist centers of learning and piety, but after the rise of Islam in the seventh century A.D., they became Muslim strongholds. The northern route flowed along the southern range of the Tien Shan Mountains. Again, oasis cities were located at various points, including Karakhoja, Turfan, Kerla, and Kucha, before reaching Kashgar. From about 100 B.C. to A.D. 350, a central route also existed. It followed the southern route for about 100 miles beyond Tunhwang, then cut across the Takla Makan through the depression of Lop Nor. In the middle of the supposedly impassable desert lay the oasis city of Loulan. Continuing across the desert to Korla on the northern route, caravans made their way to Kashgar.

After leaving Kashgar, caravans using the Silk Road continued to the famous trading cities of Tashkent and Samarkand. At Samarkand some caravans turned south to cross the Hindu Kush Mountains into India. Other caravans traveled west across Parthia and, later, Persia until they reached the ports of the Black Sea and Mediterranean Sea. A journey from Antioch to China was 6,000 miles long. It took an average of six months for a merchant to travel from Peking to Samarkand.

Besides the harsh and dangerous physical environment of the Silk Road with its cold, heat, sandstorms, and thirst, travelers also faced the danger of robbery and attack from the various tribes who lived along the route. To better secure the route, the Chinese constructed a series of forts and watchtowers at intervals of about three-fourths of a mile to five miles apart. These watchtowers also served as postal way stations to assist the transmission of official messages, and provided travelers with fresh mounts and accommodations. Some central Asian rulers added their own system of watchtowers in sections of the Silk Road that lay farther to the west. When these facilities were neglected or abandoned, the silk caravans faced even greater perils.

Moving goods along the Silk Road was costly. Bactrian camels were employed as the primary pack animals, and could carry between 400 and 500 pounds. The rate of travel, however, was slow. Various central Asian tribes added to the costs of using the Silk Road by demanding tolls, protection money, or bribes. Middlemen, such as the Parthians and Persians, prevented the Romans, Byzantines, and Chinese from making direct contact between the great eastern and western powers. To the people of the Greco-Roman era and the early Middle Ages, China was very vaguely known as Seres, a name derived from the Chinese word for silk.

Besides the ubiquitous merchants, the Silk Road had many other famous travelers. Chang Ch'ien, an ambassador of the Han Chinese emperor Wu Ti, traveled to Kashgar and on to Peshwar in India and finally back to China between 138 and 116 B.C. During that time, he suffered two long captivities among the nomadic Huns. Around A.D. 120, agents of the Greek merchant Maës Titanius reached Kashgar. The great geographer Ptolemy used their reports in composing his famous geographical treatise. Many Chinese Buddhists traveled the Silk Road in order to reach Indian and other Buddhist lands. They wanted to learn the best teachings of the various schools of Buddhism and acquire uncorrupted texts of the Buddhist scriptures. One such traveler was Fa-Hsien, who traveled between A.D. 399 and 414, reaching as far as Ceylon. An even greater traveler was Hsuan-Tsang, who from 629 to 645 visited the Buddhist centers of learning along the Silk Road and traveled throughout India. When he arrived back in China, he brought along a collection of over 700 Buddhist manuscripts and other artifacts. At the order of Emperor Tai-T'sung, he wrote an extremely long and detailed account of his travels.

During the sixth century, Asian Nestorian Christian monks managed to smuggle the eggs of silkworms all the way back to Constantinople. After successfully hatching the eggs, the Byzantines founded their own silk industry. Although the Chinese monopoly of silk production was broken, the Silk Road flourished for centuries, carrying silk, spices, and other luxury goods to Europe. Famous European travelers along the Silk Road include Marco Polo, John of Plano Carpini, and William of Rubruck. By the years 1600–1650, the newly developed seaborne trade in Asian luxury goods supplanted the Silk Road as a major commercial route. Although the days of long-distance trade were over, local traffic continued through the nineteenth century. The Silk Road is one of the most famous and longest continuously used routes of travel and trade in human history.

See also

Camel; Caravans; Constantinople; Mongol Missions; Polo, Marco; Samarkand.

For further reading

Felipe Fernández-Armesto, ed., *The Times Atlas of World Exploration*, 1991; Eric Newby, *The Rand McNally World Atlas of Exploration*, 1975.

SINDBAD, THE SEVEN VOYAGES OF   These seven tales are found in *The Thousand and One Nights*, or the *Arabian Nights*, and focus on the exploits of the merchant-adventurer Sindbad of Baghdad. Although Sindbad was probably not a historical personage, his adventures fairly accurately document both

the facts and fancies of Arab seafaring and trade in the Indian Ocean and their voyages to China.

Sindbad's seven voyages appear as separate stories in the collection of Arabic, Persian, and Indian tales known as *The Thousand and One Nights*. Serving as the narrator of his own adventures, Sindbad begins each voyage in Baghdad, then travels to Basrah to join a ship readying to depart on a trading voyage. During his first adventure, Sindbad and his companions land on a lovely island and start a fire for cooking. Unfortunately, their island turns out to be a sleeping whale, and their fire awakens him. The whale begins to dive, drowning many of Sindbad's companions, although the ship and some of the company manage to survive. Sindbad saves himself by clinging to some flotsam, and eventually drifts to safety on a real island. The island's inhabitants and their king Mahrajan are hospitable to the castaway, and the talented Sindbad quickly gains favor and rises to be comptroller of the kingdom's port. In that position, he hears accounts of the wonders of various foreign lands such as the 72 castes of Indian society. One day his old traveling companions arrive, and the lucky Sindbad is reunited with his countrymen. Selling his trade goods, he returns with them to Baghdad as a rich man.

Despite his success at home, the restless Sindbad undertakes a second voyage. His ship sets sail from Basrah and stops at a lovely, uninhabited island. Sindbad wanders off to explore and decides to take a nap, but when he awakes, he finds that his companions have departed. Frantic, Sindbad engages in further exploration of the island and discovers the nest and egg of a fabled gigantic bird of prey known as a Roc. Tying himself to a claw of the Roc, Sindbad manages to escape from his island prison, only to find himself in worse straits. The Roc carries him to its hunting ground—a valley in the inaccessible Diamond Mountain region that is filled with precious stones but is also inhabited by giant serpents, the prey of the Rocs. Sindbad rescues himself by clutching the skinned carcass of a sheep that diamond hunters have hurled into the valley. The hunters hope that diamonds will adhere to the sticky carcass, which will lure great eagles and be carried to their lairs. Then the diamond hunters plan to drive off the eagles and collect the diamonds. After loading up his own cache of diamonds, Sindbad ties himself to the sheep carcass and is soon carried to safety. According to the diamond merchants, Sindbad is the only man ever to escape alive from the Valley of the Diamonds. Using his new fortune in diamonds, Sindbad once again returns home to Baghdad.

Insatiable wanderlust soon compels Sindbad to set out on a third voyage. On this occasion, the ship encounters the Isle of the Zughb, a dangerous race of apelike dwarfs. The dwarfs commandeer Sindbad's ship and maroon the crew on their island. During their exploration of the island, Sindbad and his companions discover a large building that turns out to be the home of a ferocious black giant. The monster proceeds to eat the company, one by one. Desperate, Sindbad and the others build a raft, and then use two heated iron spits to blind the giant. After they put to sea in their raft, the frenzied giant throws great boulders at them, drowning everyone but Sindbad and two others. They drift to a desert island, where a great snake devours Sindbad's two remaining companions. Before the snake can eat him, Sindbad is rescued by a passing ship—the very one that accidentally left him behind on the Island of the Roc during his second voyage. As a result, Sindbad sells his old trade goods and once more returns home wealthy.

Undeterred by the dangers of sea travel, Sindbad soon undertakes a fourth voyage. A great tempest destroys Sindbad's ship and casts him and other survivors onto the shores of an unknown land. Initially, it appears that the wild inhabitants will treat the castaways cordially. In fact, the savages have drugged their guests and are fattening them up for a cannibalistic feast. The canny Sindbad avoids the drugged food and escapes to another people. They are much more hospitable, and when Sindbad teaches them how to make saddles and stirrups, he becomes the richest man on the island. The king even marries him to a beautiful noblewoman. Unfortunately for Sindbad, his lovely wife later dies, and it is the islanders' custom to bury the live spouse along with the dead one. Thrust into a huge, cavernous tomb where the dead are buried, Sindbad finds a way out and escapes with many valuable jewels that belonged to the dead. Reaching the seashore, he flags down a passing merchant ship and returns to Baghdad, where he sells the gems for yet another fortune.

Ever restless, Sindbad soon tires of the settled life of Baghdad and sets out on his fifth voyage. This time he buys his own ship, hires a captain and crew, and takes on other merchants as passengers. During their travels, the company comes across a desert island containing a Roc's egg. Despite grave warnings, his foolish passengers smash the egg, kill the Roc chick, and eat it. Their actions draw the wrath of the Roc parents, who destroy Sindbad's ship by dropping huge rocks on it. Sindbad survives by holding onto wreckage and floating to a paradisial island. There he becomes the victim of the Old Man of the Sea, who tricks Sindbad into carrying him but then refuses to let go. The resourceful Sindbad makes wine for his oppressor and gets the monster drunk enough to lose his grip. Once free, Sindbad slays his captor. Later, a ship stopping for water rescues Sindbad and informs him that he is the first person to ever escape the grip of the Old Man of the Sea. Continuing on with his rescuers, Sindbad makes a great profit trading coconuts, spices, and pearls before he returns to Basrah.

When other merchants visit Sindbad and regale him with tales of foreign lands, he quickly decides to depart on his sixth voyage. This time, his ship wanders into an unknown quarter of the ocean where a storm dashes it against a mountainous coastline. Sindbad and some of his fellow travelers reach the barren shore, but as their provisions run out, the party dwindles until only Sindbad remains. Desperate but indomitable, he builds a raft and manages to reach a civilized country, where the inhabitants befriend him. He enters the local king's service and rises to a trusted post. His royal master decides to send him home as an envoy to Caliph Haroun al-Rashid. After his mission is accomplished, Sindbad returns once more to his own home in Baghdad.

By now, Sindbad is entering his declining years, but he is determined to make one last voyage. Joining another company of merchants, he sails into the China Sea, where a storm blows the ship into the "world's farthermost ocean."

As the company approaches the legendary Realm of Kings, the burial place of Solomon, three immense whales charge the ship. The largest one swallows the vessel, but not before Sindbad leaps to safety and drifts on wreckage to a lush island. He constructs a raft and floats down a river to a city. It turns out that he built his raft from a rare and valuable wood, and he sells it for a fortune. One of the local merchants takes such a liking to the lucky stranger that he offers Sindbad his beautiful daughter in marriage. All seems to be going well for the adventurous merchant. Then he discovers that, once a year, the men of the city sprout wings and fly—they are the brothers of Satan and infidels. Fortunately, Sindbad's wife is not one of them; her father moved to the city from another land. After her father dies, she advises Sindbad that they should flee the godless city and return to his homeland. Selling their houses and possessions for a great sum, after a 27-year absence Sindbad returns to Baghdad with his wife. At long last, Sindbad is ready to settle down, and vows to Allah that he will never go voyaging again.

Scholars regard the Sindbad stories as a fair representation of medieval Arabic seafaring in the Indian Ocean. Arab merchants frequently made the 6,000-mile journey from Basrah to China, and in the course of their travels accumulated a large store of lore, both factual and fantastic. Like the voyages of Sindbad, a successful trip to China guaranteed great wealth, but the dangers of the journey were tremendous and very deadly. Interestingly, some of the incidents in the Sindbad stories also appear in *The Book of the Wonders of India (Kitab Aja ib al-Hind)* attributed to Buzurg ibn Shahriyar of Ramhormuz. The work was probably composed in the mid-tenth century by Buzurg, supposedly a Persian sea captain who collected tales of seafaring and foreign lands.

Many sea tales have a widespread distribution among the world's civilizations. The incident in Sindbad's first voyage where the island turns out to be a sleeping whale appears in the writings of Pliny the Elder (A.D. 23–79). St. Brendan the Navigator encountered a whale/island during his travels in the Atlantic Ocean. The black giant who terrorizes Sindbad and his companions during the third voyage is an echo of Odysseus's confrontation with Polyphemus the Cyclops. Such borrowings demonstrate that almost certainly no historical Sindbad existed. The author of the Sindbad tales in *The Thousand and One Nights*, who probably wrote in the late 800s or early 900s, borrowed heavily from stories already circulating among the merchants of the Indian Ocean. Whether the author used Buzurg for a source, or both he and Buzurg independently borrowed from the same sources, is not important. The Sindbad voyages provide an authentic glimpse at the milieu and perils of Arab trading voyages in the Indian Ocean during the height of the Islamic caliphate (ca. 750–950).

See also

Indian Ocean; Marvels of the East; Odysseus, Wanderings of; Roc; St. Brendan the Navigator, Voyage of.

For further reading

N. J. Dawood, ed., *Tales from the Thousand and One Nights*, 1973; G. S. P. Freeman-Grenville, ed., *The Book of the Wonders of India by Buzurg ibn*

Shahriyar of Ramhormuz, 1981; George Fadlo Hourani, *Arab Seafaring in the Indian Ocean in Ancient and Early Medieval Times,* 1995; Timothy Severin, *The Sindbad Voyage,* 1983.

SIRENS

SIRENS   According to classical mythology, the Sirens were songstresses living on an island in the sea. Because their singing was so beautiful, they were able to lure passing sailors to destruction on the rocks and surf of their island. As Homer described it in *The Odyssey:* "They sit in a meadow piled high with the mouldering skeletons of men."

The Sirens were supposedly half-women and half-bird and were the daughters of the earth. Their numbers varied from two to four, according to ancient authors, and their island was thought to be located somewhere along the southwestern coast of Italy. Despite their many victims, the Sirens were not unbeatable. Jason and the Argonauts passed them in safety because Orpheus outsang them. Odysseus plugged the ears of his crew to prevent them from hearing the seductive singing of the deadly Sirens. Supposedly, such defeats eventually made the Sirens despondent and suicidal. When they were defeated by the Muses in a singing contest, they lost their power of flight and committed suicide. Nevertheless, they reappeared as obstacles to the wandering Jason and his men. After the Argonaut Orpheus outsang them, again they supposedly committed suicide; a generation later, they were resurrected to tempt Odysseus. When he survived their wiles, the Sirens once more committed suicide. For the ancient Greeks, the Sirens represented an aspect of the mystery and danger involved in sea travel—ships being helplessly pulled onto a treacherous coastline and wrecked, with people back home never knowing what happened.

See also
    Jason and the Argonauts, Voyage of; Odysseus, Wanderings of.
For further reading
    Robert Graves, *The Greek Myths,* 1955.

SPANISH MAIN

SPANISH MAIN   Somewhat vague geographic term referring to the Caribbean coastline of present-day Panama, Colombia, and Venezuela as far east as Trinidad. Early in the sixteenth century, Spanish explorers realized that this region formed part of a true continental landmass rather than an island. As a consequence, it was given the name *tierra firme,* which means "mainland" in Spanish. English visitors translated and shortened the phrase into Spanish Main. By the late seventeenth and early eighteenth centuries, some sailors erroneously referred to the Caribbean Sea itself as the Spanish Main, rather than its coastal lands. Over the years the term acquired a connotation of swashbuckling adventure and exotic locales.

SPICE ISLANDS   Also known as the Spiceries, they consisted of the Molucca and Banda island groups within the East Indies. They produced valuable spices that drew Arab, Chinese, and European merchants and travelers to them for centuries.

Of all the spices produced in the Far East, cloves, nutmeg, and mace were most in demand and so fetched the highest prices. Availability of these spices was further restricted because they grew only in very limited areas. The islands of the Moluccas were the only place in the world where cloves were grown. Nutmeg and mace, which come from different parts of the same plant, could only be grown on the Banda Islands.

Needless to say, Europeans were very anxious to find out about these islands and visit them. Vague reports filtered back to Europe through such travelers as Marco Polo, and it is possible but not likely that the Venetian traveler Nicoló Conti (ca. 1395–1469) visited the Spice Islands during his travels through Asia between 1419 and 1444. Both Christopher Columbus in 1492 and John Cabot in 1497 hoped to reach the Spice Islands by sailing west across the Atlantic Ocean. Lodovico de Varthema (ca. 1470–after 1510) claimed he visited both the Bandas and the Moluccas in 1505, making him the first European known to reach them. When the Portuguese conquered Malacca on the Malay Peninsula in 1511, they immediately sent António de Abreu with a fleet to find the Moluccas, which he did in 1512. A group of shipwrecked sailors from this expedition made their way under the leadership of Francisco Serrão to Ternate in the Moluccas in 1513. They established cordial relations with the local sultan, and Serrão served as an adviser to the sultan and liaison for the Portuguese until his death in 1521. From then on, Portuguese ships made annual voyages to trade for the precious spices.

Interlopers quickly appeared. Ferdinand Magellan's surviving ships reached the Moluccas in 1522, causing a decades-long conflict between Spain and Portugal. To protect their interests, the Portuguese built a fortress on Ternate. Sir Francis Drake of England also passed through the Spice Islands in late 1579 during his circumnavigation of the globe. Meanwhile, the Netherlands had been in revolt against Spanish rule since the late 1560s, a struggle that would continue until 1648. The Dutch had participated profitably in the Portuguese spice trade since the early sixteenth century, but when Philip II of Spain became the king of Portugal, they soon found themselves cut off from the lucrative spice trade. Determined to regain a place in that lucrative commerce, the Dutch formed various trading companies, culminating in the famous East India Company in 1602 (the English had earlier formed their own East India Company in 1600 for the same purpose). Of all the competing powers, the Dutch proved the most ruthless in their efforts to control the Spice Islands. They expelled the Portuguese from Ternate in 1608 and massacred a group of English traders on Amboina Island in 1623, effectively eliminating the competition. They also thrust aside the native rulers and incorporated the islands into their colony of the Dutch East Indies. The Spice Islands remained under Dutch control until the Dutch East Indies gained its independence as Indonesia in 1945. For centuries, the exotic products of these islands inspired real travelers and fired the imaginations of armchair travelers and cooks.

See also

Circumnavigations of the Earth, Early; Indian Ocean; Northeast Passage; Northwest Passage; Pacific Ocean.

For further reading

Donald F. Lach, *Asia in the Making of Europe*, vol. 1: *The Century of Discovery*, 1965.

STAGECOACH   Form of wheeled, horse-drawn transportation that preceded passenger trains and buses as a means of overland transportation.

Coaches—four-wheeled wagons with passenger seats in an enclosed area—first appeared in Europe around the end of the sixteenth and the early years of the seventeenth centuries. Initially, only the rich could afford a private coach, and possession of a handsome team of horses and a coach quickly became a major symbol of status. As usual, the lower orders clamored to own a coach—or at least ride in one.

Within a few years, the stagecoach made its appearance. Specially built for heavy-duty use, the coach operated for hire and took passengers to scheduled stops along each segment, or stage, of a regular route. The first possible mention of a stagecoach is dated 1629, and a definite reference to a stagecoach appears in 1637. By the mid-1650s, stagecoaches were a common sight on all major highways out of London. Generally, a stagecoach traveled 50 miles during a day of 12–13 hours on the road. At the end of each day, the drivers and passengers spent the night at some convenient inn along the route. The ride tended to be cramped and bumpy without springs to absorb shocks. Still, stagecoaches were the most comfortable way to travel until railroads replaced them.

Regular stagecoach services operated in colonial America well before the outbreak of the Revolutionary War in 1775. At first, American stagecoaches were simply wagons with seats. By 1825, Lewis Downing and Stephen Abbot of Concord, New Hampshire, began making and selling English-style coaches. Adapted to American road conditions, these newly styled stagecoaches were called Concords. Other types of stagecoaches were Troys, Celeritys, and "mudwagons," each with its own characteristics.

Commercial stagecoaches were pulled by teams of four, six, or eight horses. The general rule was: the farther west, the bigger the team. Muddy roads frequently necessitated teams of eight, and driving that many horses could be very tricky, especially if the animals panicked or bolted. Stagecoach lines set up way stations along their routes to provide fresh teams, relief drivers, and food and lodging for passengers. In the West, some of these way stations were unapologetically rough.

Stagecoaches quickly began to carry mail in local areas. The first contract for long-distance mail carrying occurred in 1851 for the route between the Missouri River and Salt Lake City. Other contracts for carrying Western mail soon followed.

Stagecoaches carrying mail and passengers faced attacks by robbers or hostile Native Americans. The classic Western film *Stagecoach* (1939) depicts a

A party from Sioux Falls travels to Hot Springs, Dakota, in a Tallyho Coaching Company coach in 1889.

particularly harrowing, although ultimately successful, journey. Many Westerns contain an almost obligatory stagecoach robbery scene. Interestingly, no one ever robbed a stagecoach east of the Mississippi River.

The Wells Fargo Company dominated the Western stagecoach business, but most stagecoach lines lost out to competition from the rapidly expanding railroads. For nearly three centuries, stagecoaches provided the most convenient form of passenger travel on land.

See also
Railroads; Robbers.
For further reading
Joan Parkes, *Travel in England in the Seventeenth Century*, 1925; Frank A. Root and William E. Connelly, *The Overland Stage to California*, 1901.

STAR OF BETHLEHEM
One of the best-known guideposts for travelers in all of human history, the Bible records how this light in the heavens led the three Magi (also known as wise men or kings) to the newborn Jesus in Bethlehem.

According to the second chapter of the Gospel of St. Matthew, certain Magi or wise men arrived at the court of King Herod (37–4 B.C.) of Judaea, asking, "Where is he that is born King of the Jews? for we have seen his star in the east, and are come to worship him." (v. 2) The confused and alarmed King

Herod did not know who they were talking about, so he consulted his priests and scribes. They pointed out that ancient prophecies mentioned Bethlehem as the future birthplace of a great ruler. Herod sent the Magi to that town, and asked them to report back to him. The Magi departed for Bethlehem as "the star, which they saw in the east, went before them, till it came and stood over where the young child was. When they saw the star they rejoiced with exceeding joy." (vs. 9–10)

Ever since, people have speculated about what sort of phenomenon the miraculous Star of Bethlehem really was. Some suggest that it was a comet or nova, either of which would look like a new star to earthly observers. The astronomical records for that period are reasonably complete, and they contain no record of a comet or nova that would have been visible in the Mediterranean world any time close to the approximate date of Christ's birth.

Another possible explanation for the Star of Bethlehem is a conjunction, where two or more visible planets come so close together in the sky that they appear as one bright new star to onlookers on the earth. In 1603, the famous German astronomer Johannes Kepler suggested that a conjunction of Jupiter and Saturn took place in 7 B.C. and was the real Star of Bethlehem. In fact, this particular conjunction occurred three times that year—on 29 May, 3 October, and 4 December. Initially, Kepler's hypotheses received some attention from other scholars, but it was ultimately rejected and forgotten until the nineteenth century. By 1925, new evidence had been discovered in the records of ancient Babylonian astronomers that confirmed Kepler's calculations. Meanwhile, modern astronomers successfully reconstructed the past positions of the stars and planets, providing further evidence that Kepler was right about the occurrence of the conjunction of Jupiter and Saturn.

It is well known that the birth of Jesus did not occur between 1 B.C. and A.D. 1. Most biblical scholars pinpoint the birth of Christ prior to 4 B.C., the commonly accepted year of Herod the Great's death. Kepler's discovery of a conjunction of Jupiter and Saturn as a possible Star of Bethlehem makes 7 B.C. a very plausible year for the birth of Christ. An alternate theory has appeared, however, proposing that the birth of Christ happened in 3 or 2 B.C. Author Ernest L. Martin redated the death of Herod the Great to 1 B.C., which allowed him to identify the Star of Bethlehem as a conjunction of Jupiter and the star Regulus, which took place in 3 or 2 B.C. Whether the conjunction of 7 B.C. or the one during 3 or 2 B.C. was the true Star of Bethlehem cannot be determined. Both events match the description provided by the Gospel of St. Matthew, and could have led the three Magi to Bethlehem.

See also
Bethlehem; Magi, Three.
For further reading
Werner Keller, *The Bible as History*, 1964; Ernest L. Martin, *The Birth of Christ Recalculated*, 1980.

STEAMBOATS, RIVER

Steam-powered riverboats dominated travel and commerce on the rivers of the United States and the rest of the world during the nineteenth and early twentieth centuries until the growing network of railroads superseded them. In American history, the age of the paddle wheelers formed a romantic interlude popularized and preserved by the writings of Mark Twain.

People experimented with placing a steam engine on a riverboat during the last decades of the eighteenth century, but problems of engine safety and insufficient power plagued these early efforts. Finally, in 1807, Robert Fulton and his partner launched the *North River Steamboat of Clermont,* commonly known as the *Clermont,* which successfully sailed up the Hudson River. The use of steamboats for river travel expanded swiftly. In 1811, the *New Orleans* became the first steamboat to operate on the Ohio and lower Mississippi Rivers. Henry M. Shreve built the *Enterprise,* and in 1814 steamed up the river from New Orleans to Louisville, Kentucky. The *Washington,* another Shreve-designed boat, in 1816 moved far toward developing the classic steamboat design with shallow draft, engine placed on the deck, and improved engines. By 1819, the *Western Engineer* challenged the rigors of the Missouri River and reached Council Bluffs, where it broke down. Not until 1830, when the *Yellowstone* ascended the Missouri to Fort Union, did a steady traffic in steamboats appear on the upper Missouri. Other steamboats entered the Tennessee River in 1821, the upper Mississippi in 1823, and the Illinois River in 1828.

Initially, steamboats were owner-operated by their captains, but soon various steamboat companies developed to haul cargo and passengers. The Eagle Line, White Collar Line, Five Day Line, and St. Louis and New Orleans Line were among the most popular and respected.

Steamboats grew in size, power, and speed. Going upstream, steamboats averaged about 6 miles per hour, while going downstream they traveled at an average of 10 to 12 miles per hour. Engine fuel gradually shifted from wood to coal. The third steamboat, named the *J. M. White* and built in 1878, had the capacity to carry 8,500 bales of cotton. In 1881, the record load of 9,226 bales of cotton was set by the *Henry Frank.* The *New Orleans* of 1811 would have required multiple trips to haul a similar amount of cargo.

Early steamboats were fairly rough-and-ready vessels, but by the 1840s and 1850s their ability to move passengers in comfort or even luxury vastly improved. Some steamboats became virtual floating palaces, or at least luxury hotels. Ballrooms, fancy restaurants, gambling casinos, and barbershops were among the amenities that made steamboats the stylish way to travel in the mid- and late-nineteenth-century United States. These luxury steamboats occupied a niche similar to modern cruise ships in the world of conspicuous consumption. Terrible accidents sometimes occurred, the most notable being the explosion and sinking of the *Sultana* in 1865 with the loss of 1,500 passengers and crew, mostly sick and injured Union soldiers recently released from prisoner-of-war camps.

Competition from the expanding railroads eventually deprived the steamboats of their lifeblood of passengers and cargo, and the disruption of river traffic on the lower Mississippi River during the Civil War hastened the process.

Attempts to revive public interest in riding the steamboats resulted in some dramatic steamboat races, the most famous being the contest between the *Robert E. Lee* and the *Natchez* in 1870. The *Robert E. Lee* steamed from New Orleans to St. Louis in three days, 18 hours, and 14 minutes, arriving 3 hours ahead of the *Natchez*. Thanks to such drama and the opulence of steamboat travel, the romance of the steamboat era on the Mississippi River and its tributaries is permanently stamped on the American consciousness. Riverboat excursions and riverboat gambling casinos are nostalgic attempts to recapture the thrill of that past.

See also

Keelboats; Mississippi River; Missouri River.

For further reading

Frank Donovan, *River Boats of America*, 1966; Louis C. Hunter, *Steamboats on the Western Rivers*, 1949; Paul O'Neil, *The Rivermen*, 1975; Mark Twain, *Life on the Mississippi*, 1883.

STRABO (64 B.C.–AFTER A.D. 21)

One of the most famous of the ancient geographers, his *Geography*, in 17 books, provides an impressive overview of geographical knowledge at the time of Emperor Augustus.

Strabo was born at Amasia in Pontus in 64 B.C. of mixed Greek and Asiatic ancestry. His well-to-do family provided him with an excellent Greek education from Aristodemus of Nysa. He first traveled to Rome in 44 B.C. and studied under the great scholar Tyrannion, who had a strong interest in geography. Strabo also knew the prominent geographer Posidonius, and may have studied under him. Although his background was Greek, Strabo had a high admiration for Rome and its empire.

Strabo traveled extensively throughout the Roman Empire. According to his own testimony, "you could not find another person among the writers in geography who has travelled over much more . . . than I; indeed, those who have travelled more than I in the western regions have not covered as much ground in the east, and those who have travelled more in the eastern countries are behind me in the western; and the same holds true in regard to the regions towards the south and the north." (Bk 2.5.11) He visited Rome again in 35, 31, 29, and 7 B.C., and other visits are possible. From 25 to 20 B.C., he lived in Egypt, during which time he probably did research at the great library of Alexandria. Although he visited Corinth, oddly he never made it to Athens. Strabo apparently did most of his traveling while serving as a teacher to the rich and powerful. His visit to Egypt was made in the company of his patron Aelius Gallus, who was serving as prefect.

Strabo wrote voluminously on and had a strong interest in both geography and history. His collection of *Historical Notes* is lost, but his great *Geography* consists of 17 books. That work follows the periegesis model of geography. After discussing the philosophical and mathematical aspects of geography in books 1 and 2, Strabo begins a survey of the Roman world, moving clockwise around the Mediterranean Sea, starting with Spain in book 3. He also includes outlying areas such as Britain (book 4), northern Europe (book 7), India and Parthia (book 15), and Assyria and Babylonia (book 16). Egypt, Ethiopia, and Libya are discussed in the final book (book 17). His own origins in the lands of Greece and Asia Minor are reflected in the fact that these regions alone take up seven of Strabo's books of geography.

Strabo was neither a scientific traveler nor a scientific geographer. He took an anecdotal approach to his research, and his personal observations were not systematic. As he put it, "the greater part of [my] material . . . I receive by hearsay and then form [my] ideas of shape and size and also other characteristics, qualitative and quantitative, precisely as the mind forms its ideas from sense impressions." (Bk 2.5.11) Strabo apparently composed the *Geography* over a period of time, probably completing it about 7 B.C. It must have circulated initially in the Roman East. The Jewish historian Josephus (37–100?) quoted from Strabo, but his contemporary Roman historians seem to have had no knowledge of the work.

Strabo's *Geography* was a cornucopia of geographical and historical information that was widely used over the centuries. It is particularly useful for the extensive quotes taken from lost books of other authors. Geographical ideas of the Middle Ages and the early-modern eras were definitely influenced by Strabo.

For further reading

Horace Leonard Jones, ed., *The Geography of Strabo*, 1917; J. O. Thomson, *A History of Ancient Geography*, 1948; H. F. Tozer, *A History of Ancient Geography*, 1897.

SUBMERGING ISLANDS
See Flyaway Islands.

SUEZ CANAL
Famous strategic canal linking the Mediterranean and Red Seas, eliminating the long and arduous voyage around Africa.

The Suez Canal is 101 miles in length. Starting on the Mediterranean at Port Said, it ends at Suez on the Red Sea. Frenchman Ferdinand de Lesseps is responsible for the present Suez Canal. He conceived the plan in 1854; construction began in 1859 and was completed in 1869. Initially committed to developing railroads, the British quickly gained a controlling interest in the canal, which revolutionized European trade with the nations of the Indian Ocean. By 1882, the British took over Egypt to protect their investment. Other European countries also became more interested in Africa and international trade, triggering the famous "scramble for Africa." This phenomenon helped bring on World War I, all thanks to the Suez Canal.

The idea for a Suez Canal long predated de Lesseps. Queen Hatshepsut of Egypt (r. 1480–1475 B.C.) had a canal dug from Suez to Lake Timsah and over to Bubastis on the Nile River, but it quickly filled with sediment. The Greek historian Herodotus reported that Pharaoh Necho (d. 595 B.C.) attempted to rebuild the canal, which was over 125 miles long. Supposedly, some 120,000 Egyptians lost their lives working on the project, which Necho abandoned before its completion. An oracle told him that all his work would go to the benefit of a foreigner. In fact, the Persian king Darius (550–486 B.C.) completed the canal after the Persian conquest of Egypt. Inevitably, the canal filled with sand again, and the Roman emperor Hadrian (A.D. 76–138) restored it, as did the Muslim caliphs Omar (ca. 586–644) and Harun al-Rashid (763/766–809). By the later Middle Ages, the canal was once more in disrepair. During the sixteenth century, the Venetians made plans to restore the canal, and along with it their control over the European spice trade with Asia. Planning was as far as they got. During Napoléon's invasion of Egypt in 1798–1799, his engineers took measurements for building a canal at the Isthmus of Suez. Obviously, the importance of a Suez Canal for travel and commerce has been recognized since ancient times.

See also

Circumnavigations of Africa, Early; Good Hope, Cape of.

For further reading

Patrick B. Kinross, *Between Two Seas*, 1969; Sarah Searight, *Steaming East*, 1991.

SYBARIS   Ancient Italian city located near modern Otranto, its name and inhabitants became a byword among ancient writers for decadent, luxurious living. Achaean Greeks founded a colony at Sybaris in 710 B.C. It grew to be a rich and powerful city, but its involvement in the wars among the southern Italian cities led to its destruction by the rival city of Croton in 510 B.C. The survivors eventually founded a new town of Sybaris on the Traente River. These new Sybarites established a reputation for extreme hedonism, making their city a titillating port of call for travelers of the ancient Mediterranean.

T

TARSHISH   Rich trading city mentioned in the Bible a number of times as a source for precious stones and metals and for its great distance. Tarshish was Jonah's destination for the sea voyage in which he was swallowed by the great fish.

Shrouded in mystery for the peoples of Old Testament times, Tarshish remains equally obscure to modern biblical scholars. The derivation of its name, its location, and whether there was more than one Tarshish are all open questions. Some scholars suggest that the name *Tarshish* derived from a precious stone of the same name, which might have been chrysolite, topaz, or beryl. Others believe that the name is associated with similar words for metal refining. This interpretation of the name's meaning opens the possibility of more than one place called Tarshish, because any place where metal was refined could have been called by that name. Biblical references to Tarshish ships, then, would refer to any ships engaged in the raw metals trade, rather than from a single place called Tarshish. Tarshish ships, or Ships of Tarshish, were renowned for their extraordinary size, a characteristic that would be consistent with trade in bulk ore or metals.

Biblical references to the location of Tarshish are contradictory. Some scholars place it to the south of Palestine in the Red Sea region. Tarshish ships traded precious metals and gems with the port of Ezion-Geber on the Gulf of Aqaba in the Red Sea. Most biblical references place Tarshish to the west of Palestine, somewhere in the Mediterranean Sea or even beyond the Strait of Gibraltar. In the genealogies in the Book of Genesis, Tarshish is listed as a son of Javan, who was in turn a son of Japheth, the son of Noah. Tarshish's brothers were Elishah, Kittim, and Dodanim. Javan and his sons Elishah and Kittim are traditionally associated with the seafaring peoples of the Greek Isles and Cyprus. The famous story of Jonah associated Tarshish with the far west. It tells how

> Jonah rose up to flee unto Tarshish from the presence of the Lord, and went down to Joppa; and he found a ship going to Tarshish: so he paid the fare thereof, and went down into it, to go with them unto Tarshish from the presence of the Lord. (Jonah 1:3)

Tarshish was supposed to be so distant that Jonah thought he could actually get away from God. It was said to take three years for ships to make the round-trip to and from Tarshish (1 Kings 10:22 and 2 Chronicles 9:22). Generally, biblical scholars identify the Spanish city of Tartessus with biblical Tarshish. For the ancient Hebrews, the Atlantic coast of Spain was truly at the end of the earth.

Given the contradictory references in the Bible, it seems highly likely that more than one Tarshish existed. Several settlements probably engaged in the refining of metal and consequently received the name Tarshish. Eventually, one of those settlements—the one on the Guadalquivar River in Spain—became *the* Tarshish, the great and distant trading city for precious metals and stones. That Tarshish was the Tartessus of the Phoenicians and Greeks. Just as one Carthage (meaning "new town" in the Phoenician language) rose above all the others to become the famous Carthage of the ancient world, so one Tarshish outshone the rest. To the peoples of Old Testament Palestine, that Tarshish was the byword for any place located far away—so far away it seemed like the ends of the earth.

See also
Tartessus.
For further reading
David W. Baker, "Tarshish (Place)," in *The Anchor Bible Dictionary*, David Noel Freedman, ed., 1992.

TARTARUS   In Greco-Roman mythology, Tartarus was the name for the land of the dead. It is sometimes known as Hades, after the Greek god who ruled over the world of the afterlife.

The land of the dead is a place that can be reached by mortals, according to both Greco-Roman mythology and that of other lands. Odysseus, Theseus, Hercules, Dionysus, Orpheus, and Aeneas all visited Tartarus. During the Homeric Age (ca. 800 B.C.), the Greeks conceived of Tartarus as a misty land located far to the west on the other side of the great River Ocean. Odysseus visited this land during his wanderings. Some etymologies of Tartarus trace it to a Cretan word meaning "far west." Many ancient cosmologies, including the Egyptians', located the land of the dead somewhere in the distant west. The cosmology of Celtic mythology included a western land of the dead that variously evolved into the Isle of the Blessed or Avalon.

Later traditions transformed Tartarus into an underworld literally beneath the earth. It could be reached from the surface world by various caverns that descended deep into the bowels of the earth. Theseus, Hercules, Orpheus, and Aeneas visited the underworld version of Tartarus by entering it through caves. The underground Tartarus had a fairly complex geography. Some accounts divided the underworld into Erebus and Tartarus. Erebus was the dwelling place of the newly dead, while Tartarus lay deeper in the earth, where the spirits of the dead ultimately made their way. Tartarus was surrounded by five rivers. The Acheron, the river of woe, was a tributary of the Cocytus, the river of lamentation. The other three were the Phlegethon, the river of fire; the Styx, the river of unbreakable oaths; and the Lethe, the river of forgetfulness. For a fee, Charon the boatman ferried the spirits of the dead across the water (in some cases the

Acheron and in others the Styx). On the other side of the river, the three-headed dog Cerberus stood guard. His job was to let all the spirits of the dead into Tartarus, but prevent any from leaving. Once spirits entered Tartarus, they were tried by three fearsome judges: Rhadamanthus, Minos, and Aeacus. Those found to be wicked were sent to a place of torment, while the good went to live in the paradisial Elysian Fields. Some traditions restrict the name Tartarus to refer only to the place of punishment.

Only heroes with special strength (Hercules), special skills (Orpheus and Odysseus), or with special help (Aeneas and Theseus) could visit Tartarus and return to the world of the living. Such myths about visits to the underworld promoted the persistent popular belief that some caverns led to Tartarus, or in modern times, to Hell. The various *Amityville Horror* movies are based on that very premise. People throughout the ages have speculated about visiting Tartarus or Hell and returning to tell about it, but none have ever succeeded.

See also

Aeneas, Wanderings of; Elysian Fields; Odysseus, Wanderings of; Tartary.

For further reading

Robert Graves, *The Greek Myths*, 1955; Edith Hamilton, *Mythology*, 1940.

TARTARY   The land of the Tartars, it corresponded to the region of modern Siberia and the steppes of Eurasia in the minds of late-medieval and early-modern Europeans.

Europeans, particularly Russians, applied the name Tartar to the Mongols and their nomadic confederates. The proper name is actually Tatar. The Tatars were originally the dominant tribe in Mongolia, living in the eastern section along with the original Mongols. To the north lived the Merkits, with the Keraits occupying central Mongolia and the Naimans inhabiting the western part. During his rise to power, Genghiz Khan destroyed the Tatars as an organized tribe. Despite that, the name Tatar was widely used to refer to all the tribes of Mongolia. Why is uncertain. Some scholars suggest that it was because the Tatars were the best-known and most important tribe in Mongolia. Certainly for the Sung dynasty Chinese, all northern nomads were Tatars. In Europe the name *Tatar* shifted to the more familiar Tartar. This change is attributed to a play on words involving the similarity between Tartarus, the Greek name for Hell, and Tatar. To Europeans the Tatars were such a demonically invincible enemy that it seemed they must come from Hell or Tartarus. The medieval chronicler Matthew Paris credited Louis IX of France with first using Tartar as a pun. Unfortunately, the Tartars were far from a joke. China, large parts of the Islamic Middle East, and Russia suffered devastating conquests by the Mongols, or Tatars. Even Hungary, Poland, and parts of Germany experienced a bad mauling. For several centuries after the conquests of Genghiz Khan, Europeans viewed Tartary, the lands of the Mongol Empire, as a fearsome threat. Later, they contemplated converting the Tartars to Christianity and using them as allies in the destruction of Islam. These Mongol missions failed, but the diplomats and missionaries who traveled the roads through Tartary reported vast distances, a harsh environment of extreme temperatures and aridity, and exotic and strange peoples. Tartary, Siberia, and Scythia all referred to roughly the same steppe lands north and east of the Black Sea and stretching all the way to the Pacific Ocean.

See also
Mongol Missions; Scythia; Siberia; Tartarus.
For further reading
David Morgan, *The Mongols*, 1986; John J. Saunders, "Matthew Paris and the Mongols," in *Essays in Medieval History Presented to Bertie Wilkinson*, 1969.

TARTESSUS   Or Tartessos, this ancient Spanish city and the coastal area around it traded metals with both the Phoenicians and Greeks. Located in the vicinity of modern Seville, some scholars think it was a Phoenician colony, while others consider it a settlement of indigenous Iberian peoples. The city collapsed politically about 550 B.C., either because of attacks from outsiders or because of civil strife from within. It was succeeded by various splintered tribes. To the early Greeks, Tartessus was one of those vague, mysterious places that lay beyond the Strait of Gibraltar at the edge of the known world. It was thought to be so far away that it was the place where the Sun unharnessed his horses from his fiery chariot at the end of the day.

The first Greek to reach Tartessus did so accidentally. Colaeus of Samos was trying to sail to Egypt about 638 B.C., when winds blew his ship the entire length of the Mediterranean and out the Strait of Gibraltar. Putting in at Tartessus, he took on a cargo of Spanish silver, and became quite wealthy from the proceeds. His success encouraged other Greeks to sail the western Mediterranean and beyond. Most scholars believe that Tartessus and the biblical Tarshish are identical.

See also
Phoenicians; Tarshish.
For further reading
E. H. Bunbury, *A History of Ancient Geography*, 1883; M. Cary and E. H. Warmington, *The Ancient Explorers*, 1963.

TEMPLARS, KNIGHTS   Also known as the Poor Knights of Christ and of the Temple of Solomon, they are often simply called the Templars. The Knights Templars share with the Hospitalers the distinction of being the most famous of the military orders of monks formed to protect Christian pilgrims in Palestine during the Crusades even though they were suppressed almost 700 years ago. Popular culture remembers the Templars either as villains in works such as Sir Walter Scott's *Ivanhoe* (1819) or mysterious conspirators, as in Umberto Eco's

Foucault's Pendulum (1989). The Masonic order also traces its origins back to the Templars.

Unlike most military orders, the Knights Templars were soldiers from the very beginning. Hugh de Payens (d. 1136), a knight of Champagne, and eight companions founded the order in 1118. Besides poverty, chastity, and obedience, the first Templars swore to protect Christian pilgrims traveling on the dangerous roads of the Holy Land. During the early years, the military monks lived on alms and were given quarters in the Temple of Solomon in Jerusalem. That residence gave the new order its name, and it was their headquarters until the Muslim leader Saladin recaptured the city in 1187. Despite strenuous efforts, the Templars never succeeded in regaining the temple.

In 1127, Sir Hugh went to Europe to gain official recognition for the order and recruit new members. He found a ready ally in St. Bernard of Clarvaiux, who wrote a treatise called *In Praise of the New Chivalry* [*De Laude Novae Militiae*] (1128) in support of the new ideal of soldier monks. St. Bernard of Clarvaiux helped formulate the rules for the new order, using St. Benedict for a model. Four ranks of Templars were established: knights, sergeants, squires, and chaplains. Initially, the Templars' garb was the white tunic of the Cistercian Order, which was St. Bernard's order. During the pontificate of Eugenius III (1145–1153), a red cross was added to the tunic to distinguish the order from the Cistercians. Unlike most Crusaders, who followed the general European practice of being clean-shaven, the Templars and Hospitalers grew beards—an important sign of manhood in the Middle East. Reputed to be fierce fighters, the Templars became a popular order, attracting many recruits and gifts. They were soon quite rich, which made them the object of greed and envy.

The Templars' primary purpose shifted from protecting pilgrims to protecting the Christian territories from Muslim aggression. Along with the Hospitalers, they became a sort of standing army for the kingdom of Jerusalem. In 1149, they began to acquire and garrison various castles in Palestine, such as Tortosa and the great Castle Pilgrim, built at Athlit in 1217–1218. When Jerusalem fell in 1187, they moved their headquarters to Acre until its fall in 1291, when they transfered temporarily to Cyprus. At that point, Templar activity focused on France, which supplied the bulk of Templar recruits and was the home of most of their possessions.

Although the Templars were considered among the bravest of the Crusaders, they were not always well led. The reckless grand master of the Templars from 1185 to 1189, Gerard de Ridfort, helped bring on the war with Saladin and pushed King Guy of Jerusalem to attack the Muslims. This ill-conceived advice led to the disastrous defeat of the Christian army at the battle of Hattin on 4 July 1187 and resulted in the loss of Jerusalem. Later, led by Grand Master William de Beaujeu, the Templars fiercely defended Acre against the massive Mamluk army of Sultan Kala'un. Many of the Templar garrison, including the grand master, died in the fighting.

The fall of Acre marked the end of the Crusader kingdoms of the Outremer. It also meant the end of the Templars' original reason for existence, as they no longer had any Christian possessions in the Holy Land to defend. However, during their almost two centuries of existence, they had amassed a great fortune, which they further expanded by putting some of it out to loan, in effect acting as bankers. Their great wealth and special privileges brought the Templars many enemies, the most formidable being Philip IV the Fair (1268–1314), king of France. Making an alliance with another Frenchman, Pope Clement V (fl. 1305–1314), the king arrested the Templars of France on 13 October 1307. Various charges of heresy, witchcraft, and sexual perversion were leveled against them. Using these charges as justification, the pope suppressed the order in 1312, and in 1314, the last Templar grand master, Jacques de Molay, was burned at the stake. Many Templars managed to avoid arrest and execution, but their ultimate fate is a mystery. In their day, however, the Templars were a mainstay of the Christian kingdom of Jerusalem and the familiar protectors of helpless pilgrims visiting the Christian shrines of Palestine.

See also

Holy Land; Hospitalers, Knights; Jerusalem; Pilgrimage; Teutonic Knights.

For further reading

Hans Eberhard Mayer, *The Crusades,* 1988; John J. Robinson, *Dungeon, Fire and Sword,* 1991; Desmond Seward, *The Monks of War,* 1972.

TERRA AUSTRALIS

Literally meaning "southern land," the name for an unknown continent believed by people, from the ancient Greeks through eighteenth-century Europeans, to exist in the Southern Hemisphere.

The idea of Terra Australis originated in the ancient Greek belief that the world consisted of four quarters: the oikoumene, the antipodes, the antoikoi, and the antichthones. Each quarter of the spherical earth supposedly contained an equal-sized landmass, since an equal distribution of weight was necessary to keep the world in balance. The oikoumene was the known world with its three continents of Africa, Asia, and Europe. Each of the other quarters contained a similar landmass. The antipodes was the other northern quarter, the antoikoi was the southern quarter below the oikoumene, and the antichthones was the southern quarter below the antipodes. Two world-girdling oceans, the meridional and the equatorial, separated the four quarters. Furthermore, the southern quarters were commonly thought to be cut off from the northern quarters by the deadly heat of the equatorial region, which no one could cross and live. As a result, ancient and medieval maps simply showed a single large landmass circling the entire Southern Hemisphere. They also occasionally included an analogous unknown western continent, Terra Occidentalis. The geographical work *Liber Floridus,* written by the early-twelfth-century canon Lambert of St. Omer, is an excellent example of such a worldview.

During the classical and medieval eras, Terra Australis and the antipodes were frequently conflated. Some ancient geographers, including Claudius Ptolemy, suggested that Terra Australis was not completely separated from the oikoumene by the equatorial ocean. Instead, Africa was simply a large peninsula connected to the great southern continent. The Indian Ocean was there-fore an inland sea, and Africa could not be circumnavigated. Such a belief would render Portuguese explorations down the African coast quite problematic. How-ever, Europeans lost contact with Ptolemy's geographical concepts until the fifteenth century, and his ideas had little impact on the Portuguese program of African exploration. The belief in the existence of unknown lands across the oceans served as a spur to further exploration and geographical speculation. The discovery of North America ended further speculation about Terra Occidentalis by showing that such a place actually existed.

The search for Terra Australis lasted for approximately 200 years. Pedro Sarmiento de Gamboa (ca. 1532–1592), a particularly active conquistador and scholar, began the quest after hearing Inca accounts of pre-Spanish voyages to rich lands across the Pacific Ocean. Speculating that these lands were Terra Australis or King Solomon's Ophir, Sarmiento tried to organize an expedition to find them. Political favoritism cost Sarmiento command of the expedition, which went to the young and inexperienced Alvaro de Mendaña de Nehra. Sailing from Peru on 19 November 1567, Mendaña's two ships plowed oblivi-ously past numerous islands without sighting land until 15 January 1568. Food and water were running perilously low, but reefs and hostile natives prevented a landing. Finally the Spanish reached the Solomon Islands, the hoped-for Ophir. Mendaña also hoped they were close to Terra Australis, because with few sup-plies, the majority of the expedition demanded to return to Peru. Leaving the Solomons on 15 August 1568, they finally reached Peru after a scurvy- and privation-filled looping voyage through the northern Pacific.

Undaunted, Mendaña continued to dream of finding Terra Australis and returning to the Solomons. He got his second chance in June 1596, leading a new expedition out of Peru. He reached the Marquesas in late July, and initially thought they were the Solomons. After realizing his mistake, he sailed on and discovered the Santa Cruz Islands in September. Mendaña contracted a fever and died there, leaving the Portuguese navigator Pedro Fernandez de Quirós (1565–1614) in charge. Quirós led the survivors safely to the Spanish colony of the Philippines on 10 February 1596, an exploit that made him a hero.

Quirós also developed a frantic zeal to both spread Roman Catholicism through the Pacific and secure Terra Australis for Spain. Organizing a new ex-pedition with papal blessing, he left Peru on 21 December 1605. By 1 May 1606, the Spanish ships reached the island of Espíritu Santo in the New Hebrides. Quirós mistook it for part of Terra Australis and called it La Australia del Espíritu Santo. Determined to establish a colony there, after three weeks he abandoned the effort and sailed for home. After he reached Acapulco on 23 November 1606, Quirós's religious fanaticism and erratic behavior caused his reputation to plummet. Despite repeated attempts, Quirós never got another command, and Spain abandoned its efforts to locate Terra Australis.

Other European nations took up the search. The Dutch seaman Willem Corneliszoon Schouten (1577?–1625) and Jacob Le Maire discovered the Cape Horn route into the Pacific Ocean in 1616. Sailing across the Pacific to the Spice Islands, they found no sign of Terra Australis. Their route to the Spice

Islands was an exception. Most Dutch ships sailed across the southern Indian Ocean, taking advantage of the favorable winds and currents, and some of their ships encountered the unknown landmass of Australia. During 1642–1643 and 1644, Abel Tasman explored Australia and discovered Tasmania and New Zealand as part of his effort to locate Terra Australis. The real Australia was too poor and barren to be the rich, verdant Terra Australis of European expectations, so the search continued for the real Terra Australis.

In the eighteenth century, a series of expeditions entered the southern Pacific to look for Terra Australis. Jacob Roggeveen (1659–1729), a Dutchman, explored from 1721 to 1722 and discovered isolated Easter Island and Samoa. From 1764 to 1766, John Byron (1723–1786) of the British navy sailed an experimental copper-hulled frigate into the Pacific with instructions to search for a northwest passage in the northern Pacific. Instead, he fruitlessly sailed across the southern Pacific, making no new discoveries and eventually circumnavigating the globe. His contemporary Samuel Wallis (1728–1795) also cruised the southern Pacific from 1766 to 1767. Terra Australis eluded him also, but he discovered paradisial Tahiti. Virtually shadowing Wallis was the French expedition of Louis-Antoine de Bougainville (1729–1811), which cruised the South Pacific during 1767 and 1768. Besides producing a rhapsodic account of the charms of Tahiti, Bougainville reached Quirós's Espíritu Santo. Sailing westward beyond it all the way to the east coast of Australia, he proved that Terra Australis was not located in that part of the Pacific.

Despite these explorations, large sections of the South Pacific remained unexplored. Belief in the existence of Terra Australis also remained common. The leading advocate for the existence of Terra Australis was the Scottish hydrographer Alexander Dalrymple (1737–1810). His speculative book of 1764 on Pacific exploration and Terra Australis, which he located east of New Zealand, kept interest high. In 1768, the British admiralty and the Royal Society put together an expedition to systematically seek Terra Australis in the unexplored waters of the South Pacific. Instead of giving the command to Dalrymple, the royal navy gave it to James Cook (1728–1779), a respected junior officer.

Cook proved to be the greatest of the Pacific explorers and a model for the new generation of scientific explorers and travelers. Given command of the converted collier *Endeavor*, the Admiralty and the Royal Society ordered Cook to proceed to Tahiti to observe the transit of the planet Venus across the sun. They also gave him secret orders to search for Terra Australis. Sailing out of Plymouth on 26 August 1768, Cook's company included the botanists Joseph Banks (1743–1820) and Daniel Carl Solander (1733–1782). The *Endeavor* rounded Cape Horn and reached Tahiti on 13 April 1769. After conducting his observations at Tahiti, Cook made his way to New Zealand and completely circled both islands. In the process, he discovered Cook Strait and proved that New Zealand was not part of Terra Australis. Proceeding west to Australia, he sailed up the Great Barrier Reef and through the Torres Strait. He arrived back in England on 12 July 1771, having lost not a single man to scurvy thanks to the provision of sauerkraut, fruit, and vegetables in his crew's diet.

As soon as he arrived home, Cook planned his second voyage in search of Terra Australis. He sailed on 13 July 1772 in another refitted collier, the *Resolution*. He was accompanied by a second ship, the *Adventure*. Below the Cape of Good Hope, Cook took the *Resolution* far to the south, even briefly crossing the Antarctic Circle. He proceeded across the Indian Ocean along 60°S latitude, eventually turning north to reach New Zealand. Cook sailed to Tahiti in August 1773, and made a big looping voyage looking for Terra Australis. After waiting for the Southern Hemisphere's summer to arrive, Cook again headed far south during November 1774 and made another big loop in search of Terra Australis. On his way back north, he stopped at isolated Easter Island, the first European to do so since Roggeveen. Cook then made his way home to England, having conclusively proven that no Terra Australis existed in any temperate latitude. He had traveled over 70,000 miles in slightly more than three years, and once again he lost no men to scurvy.

Cook made a third voyage into the North Pacific in quest of the Northwest Passage. It was one voyage too many for the great explorer. Mentally exhausted, Cook's phenomenal ability to deal successfully with his sailors and natives was gone. On 14 February 1779, a dispute over a stolen boat led to his death at the hands of the inhabitants of the newly discovered Hawaiian Islands.

The two-centuries-long search for Terra Australis failed to find the lush and rich continent of legend because it did not exist. The ancient Greek assumption of geographical symmetry had no foundation in reality. The quixotic quest attracted many seekers who sacrificed much, including in some cases their lives. It was not all for nought, however, because thanks to the myth of Terra Australis, many discoveries took place in the South Pacific.

See also

Antichthones; Antipodes; Antoikoi; Crates of Mallos; Pacific Ocean; Terra Occidentalis; Zonal Theory.

For further reading

Oliver E. Allen, *The Pacific Navigators*, 1980; Raymond H. Ramsay, *No Longer on the Map*, 1972; John Kirtland Wright, *The Geographical Lore of the Time of the Crusades*, 1925.

TERRA OCCIDENTALIS

Literally meaning "western land," it is the name for an unknown continent that the ancient Greeks and Romans believed existed in the Western Hemisphere. Following the theories of Crates of Mallos, the ancient Greeks divided the spherical earth into four quarters: the oikoumene, antipodes, antoikoi, and antichthones. Each quarter contained a landmass separated from the other three quarters by the world-encircling equatorial and meridional oceans. The oikoumene was the quarter containing the known world, which consisted of Africa, Asia, and Europe. The other quarter of the Northern Hemisphere opposite the oikoumene was the antipodes, also frequently called Terra Occidentalis. Many ancient and medieval world maps depict both Terra Occidentalis and its southern counterpart, Terra Australis. Lambert of St. Omer's geographical treatise *Liber Floridus*, written in the early twelfth century, discusses both Terra Occidentalis and Terra Australis.

Both of these unknown continents served as inspirations for exploration, and Terra Occidentalis was the first to become known. When John Cabot sighted Newfoundland in 1497, he began a process by which the geographical concept of North America soon replaced the concept of Terra Occidentalis. Of course, the ancient and medieval speculations about unknown continents were just that—speculation. The symmetrical nature of the Greek worldview, based on the Cratesian theory, logically demanded the creation of a western landmass.

See also

Antichthones; Antipodes; Antoikoi; Crates of Mallos; Terra Australis.

For further reading

John Kirtland Wright, *The Geographical Lore of the Time of the Crusades*, 1925.

TEUTONIC KNIGHTS   Also known as the Teutonic order or the Order of the German Hospital of St. Mary of Jerusalem. This largely German order first developed as caretakers of the Hospital of St. Mary in Jerusalem, which served the needs of poor and sick pilgrims shortly after the capture of Jerusalem during the First Crusade in 1099. No evidence exists to show that the German monks of St. Mary's Hospital ever took up arms like their successors, the Teutonic Knights. However, the monks of St. Mary's quarreled off and on with the Hospitalers until their establishment disappeared with the capture of Jerusalem by Saladin.

By the time of the fall of Jerusalem and the Third Crusade, the Teutonic Knights had developed into a military order similar to the Hospitalers and Templars. Later, the order shifted their activities to the Baltic region, where they conquered the region later known as East Prussia. Although by 1240 military activities dominated their attention, like the Hospitalers, they never gave up their hospital work.

After the fall of Jerusalem, a new hospital for Germans was established by members of Frederick Barbarosa's army, who were participating in the siege of Acre in 1190. Its primary purpose was to care for sick or wounded Crusaders, but it also provided care to pilgrims. The members of this hospital community clearly hoped that it would become a successor to the German Hospital of St. Mary of Jerusalem. Their goal was recognized by papal confirmations in 1191 and 1196. Pressing military needs caused German Crusaders to convert the hospital into a military order in 1198. Their hospital was modeled on the Hospital of St. John, but their religious and knightly activities were modeled on the practices of the Templars.

The Teutonic Knights consisted of knights, priests, and laypersons. Their uniforms were white tunics based on the Cistercian and Templar garb, to which a black cross was later added to distinguish them from the red cross of the Templars. The white tunics provoked many complaints by the Templars, who hoped to absorb the Teutonic Knights. Innocent III confirmed the independent existence of the new order in 1199, but not until 1244 did the Teutonic Knights establish their autonomy from the Templars and Hospitalers by adopting their own unique monastic rule. The leader of the Teutonic Knights was the grand master, and his headquarters was the castle of Montfort (Starkenberg), which they purchased in 1228. Membership in the Teutonic order was open to knights, clerics, and lay brothers who may or may not have engaged in military duties. Numerically, the Teutonic Knights were the smallest of the military orders and essentially consisted of Germans. However, they attracted gifts from all over Christendom and could claim to be an international order.

Although the Teutonic Knights originated in Palestine and fought there through the fall of Acre in 1291, their activities spread first to Hungary in 1211–1225, and then to Prussia, where they began their conquests in 1231. Meanwhile, the situation of the Crusader states in Palestine became increasingly perilous. The Mamluk sultan Baybars unsuccessfully besieged the Teutonic Knights' headquarters at Montfort in 1266. In 1271, he returned to capture the mighty strongholds of the Templars at Castle Blanc and the Hospitalers at Krak des Chevaliers before forcing the surrender of the Teutonic Knights at Montfort. Its fall caused them to move their headquarters to Acre. After that city's capture by the Mamluks in 1291, the order moved to Venice and finally to Marienburg in 1309. The Teutonic Knights developed a new purpose: the conquest and conversion of the heathen Baltic peoples for Latin Christianity. Their big rivals were the pagan Lithuanians, but in 1386 the Lithuanians accepted Christianity and political union with Poland. The Teutonic Knights again lost their primary reason for existence, but they continued fighting for land and power. At the battle of Tannenberg in 1410, the forces of the Teutonic Knights suffered a decisive defeat by the Polish-Lithuanian army. When Grand Master Albert of Prussia converted to Lutheranism in 1525, followed by other Teutonic Knights, the order had already lost much of its territorial and martial basis. The remaining Catholic Teutonic Knights were driven out of the Baltic and given shelter by the Habsburgs of Austria and other German Catholic princes. In the nineteenth century, they evolved into a charitable brotherhood that patronized hospitals and schools.

See also

Hospitalers, Knights; Jerusalem; Pilgrimage; Templars, Knights.

For further reading

Eric Christiansen, *The Northern Crusades,* 1980; Desmond Seward, *The Monks of War,* 1972; Indrikis Sterns, "The Teutonic Knights in the Crusader States," in *A History of the Crusades,* vol. 5: *The Impact of the Crusades on the Near East,* 1985, pp. 315–378.

THULE   Also known as Chili, Tile, or Ultima Thule, these are the names of a northern island that may have been Iceland, the Shetlands, or even Norway.

Pytheas of Marseilles sailed into the northern waters of the Atlantic Ocean around 310–306 B.C. when Carthaginian control over the Strait of Gibraltar was temporarily weak. Proceeding north to Britain, Pytheas visited the tin mines of Cornwall. From the south of England, he made his way to northern Scotland, where natives told him about the island of Thule, or Ultima Thule, which lay six days' sail to the north. Although it was an inhospitable land surrounded by ice, snow, and fog, people lived there, subsisting on wild berries, millet, and honey. Pytheas never visited Thule, but his account formed the basis for Greco-Roman geographical knowledge about that region for many years.

Both later ancient writers and modern scholars speculate and argue about the identity of Pytheas's Thule. Both the eminent ancient Greek historian Polybius (ca. 200–120 B.C.) and the Roman geographer Strabo (64 B.C.–ca. A.D. 21) had serious doubts about Pytheas's accuracy. They raised the possibility that Thule was simply an imaginary place. Some suggest that the Shetland Islands are Thule, but that seems unlikely. The two prime candidates for ancient Thule are Iceland and Norway. Various ancient, medieval, and modern writers plausibly argue for one or the other being Thule, and both places have positives and negatives. In the end, Ultima Thule simply became a traveler's expression for a place located on the edge of the known inhabited world or beyond.

See also
Atlantic Ocean; Pytheas of Massilia, Voyage of.
For further reading
M. Cary and E. H. Warmington, *The Ancient Explorers,* 1929; John Kirtland Wright, *The Geographical Lore of the Time of the Crusades,* 1925.

TIMBUKTU
Also spelled Timbuctoo, for centuries this great trading city in the West African Sudan was famous among travelers and armchair adventurers as a place of mystery and fantastic wealth, until its conquest by the French in 1894.

Timbuktu is located near the northernmost point of the great bend of the Niger River where the Sahel (shore) region of the Sahara meets the desiccated ocean of sand and rock that is the desert proper. The location was an important crossroad for various caravan and trade routes for gold, salt, slaves, kola nuts, and other commodities. In its heyday, Timbuktu was the most important port along the southern boundary of the desert.

Nomadic bands of Tuareg founded Timbuktu in the early twelfth century as a summer camp for use during their transhumance between Arawan and Lake Debo. It evolved into a permanent settlement and became the market town for the region. Initially, Timbuktu faced stiff competition for the position as the primary crossroad of the caravan trade. That honor first belonged to the ancient city of Ghana, which long ago was supplanted by the city of Walata, to the west of Timbuktu. Walata allowed easier access to the traditional goldfields of Bure and Bambuk and the far western caravan route to Mauretania. When the great Muslim traveler Ibn Battuta visited the empire of Mali in 1352, he considered Walata more important and impressive than Timbuktu. That situation changed rapidly, and by 1375 the Majorcan cartographer Abraham Cresque reported that Timbuktu served as the main port of the trans-Saharan trade.

The merchant community of Walata apparently decided to move en masse to Timbuktu in the middle of the fourteenth century. The exact circumstances behind this decision are unknown, but several factors apparently prompted their move. Timbuktu was in a good location. Even more important, the armies of the empire of Mali had seized it from the predatory Tuareg. New rich goldfields were opening up in the Akan Forest to the south. Timbuktu and its sister city Jenne were much better placed to conduct trade with the Akan region than Walata. At the same time, because nomadic Arab tribes increasingly preyed on caravans using the western route through Mauretania, traffic was shifting to the eastern routes that ran through Timbuktu. Thus, during the second half of the fourteenth century, Timbuktu superseded Walata as the prime terminus of the trans-Saharan caravan trade. It retained that position until the late nineteenth century, when encroaching European imperialism and its accompanying technology drastically reduced the importance and volume of the caravan trade.

Timbuktu stood at the junction of three important trans-Saharan caravan routes. One was the western Mauretanian route that began at Wadi Nun and passed through Wadan and Tishit. Another route was the northern Taghaza salt road that went on to Morocco via the oasis of Sijilmasa. The last route went east to In Salah by way of Arawan. Timbuktu was only nine miles from the Niger River. It had a river port at the fishing village of Kabara, where goods were loaded or unloaded from the canoes and riverboats plying the river to trade routes farther south. Because of its interests in that direction, Timbuktu developed a close commercial alliance with the city of Jenne. The primary goods of Timbuktu's trading business were gold, salt, slaves, and kola nuts. Salt mines in the Sahara, such as the one at Taghaza, supplied this essential but scarce commodity to the peoples of the western Sudan. Salt was exchanged for the gold of Bure, Bambuk, and later Akan, which made its way north to provide the highly desired specie for the North African Maghrib and then for Europe. Slaves and kola nuts also represented valuable trade goods, having high and widespread demand. As a result, Timbuktu developed a well-deserved reputation as a city of immense wealth from trade.

Timbuktu's vast wealth also made it the most Islamic city in the western Sudan, and a center of learning and culture. The Arab scholar Shaykh Abd al-Rahman at Tamini joined Mansa Musa's entourage in Arabia during 1324 and visited Timbuktu when the Malian king returned home from his pilgrimage to Mecca. Al-Rahman found that the scholars of Timbuktu were more learned in Islamic teachings than he was. Meanwhile, thanks to the copious amounts of gold expended by Mansa Musa during his pilgrimage, Timbuktu gained a reputation throughout the Islamic and Christian worlds as a city of fabulous wealth. During this period of Malian rule (ca. 1300–1430), the people of Timbuktu constructed the magnificent Friday Mosque and Sankore Mosque, which served the community as centers of both prayer and study.

Timbuktu's prosperity continued even when it changed overlords, going from the empire of Mali to the Tuareg in 1434, and then to the Songhay Empire of Sonni Ali in 1469. The early sixteenth century may have been the city's heyday. The Arab geographer Leo Africanus, writing to a European audience in 1525, said, "The rich king of Timbuktu has many plates and scepters of gold, some of which weigh 1300 pounds; and he keeps a magnificent and well furnished court." Thus, the legend of the riches of Timbuktu was kept alive.

The Songhay Empire was in a weakened state by the late sixteenth century. Its control of the riches of Timbuktu and the salt mines of Taghaza attracted the covetous attention of the sultans of Morocco. In late 1590, Sultan Ahmad al-Mansure sent an army of 4,000-5,000 Andalusian refugees and Spanish renegades, equipped with firearms, across the desert to conquer the Songhay Empire. After crossing the desert in two months, the Moroccan army, under the command of Jodar Pasha, easily defeated a Songhay army of 40,000 on 12 March 1591. The Moroccans captured Gao, the Songhay capital, and then moved on to Timbuktu. After its defeat, the unstable Songhay Empire quickly collapsed. Its supplanters, the Moroccans, tried to rule their new conquest from a distance, but logistical problems made their control largely ineffectual. The local Moroccan pashas, army commanders, and garrison troops all proved predatory on the Sudan without providing stability to the region. Politically, the seventeenth and eighteenth centuries were an era of fragmentation and economic disruption. Timbuktu's trade still produced great wealth, and its importance as a center of Islamic learning and culture continued. However, a slow decline set in, so that nineteenth-century European visitors found a Timbuktu that was a mere shadow of its former greatness.

Like most of the trans-Saharan caravan routes and cities, Timbuktu was closed to European Christian visitors. The Muslims of the Maghrib and the Sudan were fanatically suspicious of Christians. Fears of European trans-Saharan trade interlopers and of European crusading and imperialism also motivated Muslim hostility over the centuries.

Of course, being forbidden obviously contributed to Timbuktu's mystery and legends. Visiting exotic, wealthy Timbuktu and getting home alive to tell about it became the dream of many European travelers, costing many their lives. Supposedly, a Florentine named Benedetto Dei reached Timbuktu in 1469. Portuguese traders along the coast of West Africa also made their way inland searching for the source of the gold of Guinea during the second half of the fifteenth century. If they actually reached Timbuktu, no report of that exploit survives. Renegade Spanish Christians and converts to Islam reached Timbuktu in 1591 with the Moroccan invasion force of Jodar Pasha, but none of them returned to Europe to tell about it. Around 1670, tales circulated about an enslaved French sailor named Paul Imbert being taken to Timbuktu, but he died in captivity. Much later, an American sailor named Benjamin Rose was taken captive after being shipwrecked on the West African coast. After he regained his freedom and made his way back to the West, he claimed to have visited Timbuktu in 1810–1811. His story never received much credence at that time or since.

By the early nineteenth century, European explorers and travelers were increasingly anxious to reach Timbuktu and become the first person to live to tell about it. British Major Gordon Laing reached Timbuktu in 1826, but was murdered on his return journey shortly after departing the fabled city. Native hostility against Westerners was simply too deep-seated. The Frenchman René Caillié spent a long time preparing a journey to Timbuktu disguised as a Muslim. He learned Arabic and studied Islam. When he began his trek at Kakande in 1828, he claimed to be an Egyptian traveler making his way home. After reaching Timbuktu, Caillié stayed for several months to recuperate from the rigors of his journey. Once he regained his strength, he joined a trans-Saharan caravan that took him through the driest, most desolate section of the Sahara. If anything, the horrors of the desert were far worse than those he encountered in the Sudan. Fortunately, Caillié's caravan reached Morocco safely and he made his way, via Fez, to Tangier and the residence of the French consul. As the first European to visit Timbuktu and return safely, Caillié became an instant hero. Only two other Europeans duplicated his feat—Heinrich Barth in 1853 and Oskar Lenz in 1880. The next Europeans arrived en masse when Joseph Joffre led a French army to conquer Timbuktu and subjugate the city to French colonial rule. By that time, Timbuktu had declined greatly and was a bitter disappointment to the Europeans. Even when Caillié visited the city in 1828, it was not the gold-roofed wonderland of legend. It never had been. Timbuktu was a typical Islamic city of the Sudan consisting of mud-and-thatch buildings. Despite everything, the name *Timbuktu* still evokes a sense of mystery and adventure.

See also

Africa; Caravans; Mansa Musa, Pilgrimage and Legend of; Sahara; Tuareg.

For further reading

J. F. A. Ajayi and Michael Crowder, eds., *History of West Africa*, vol. 1, 1971; Brian Gardner, *The Quest for Timbuctoo*, 1968; Richard Gray, ed., *Cambridge History of Africa*, vol. 4: *From ca. 1600–ca. 1790*, 1975; Galbraith Welch, *The Unveiling of Timbuctoo*, 1939.

TOKAIDO ROAD   Also known as the Eastern Sea Road, it was probably the most famous and important road in Japan during the Tokugawa era (1600–1868). It connected Kyoto, the old imperial capital, with Edo (Tokyo), the capital of the Shogunate.

The Tokaido became an important route as early as the seventh or eighth century. As time went by, its importance increased, reaching its zenith during the Tokugawa Shogunate (military dictatorship). The Tokugawa Shoguns made Edo their capital, and by the end of the eighteenth century the city was one of the world's largest metropolises. Because the Tokaido linked Edo and its fertile, populous Kanto plain to the great cities of Kyoto and Osaka, it became the most important and heavily traveled road in Japan.

The Tokaido was about 303 miles long and largely followed the natural pathway provided by the Pacific coast. Located along the road to serve travelers were 53 way stations with numerous inns of varying quality and status. These ranged from *honjin*, which catered to the *diamyo*, or great feudal lords, to flophouses for mere porters. The roadbed was officially 36 feet wide, but in reality it apparently averaged about 18 feet. In flat areas, the roadbed consisted of a deep layer of crushed gravel covered by sand, but in the mountains the road was paved with stone. Trees were planted alongside the road to provide shade, and every *ri* (2.44 miles), a mound was constructed with a nettle tree planted at the top.

Most traffic along the Tokaido was pedestrian or pack animal, with virtually no wheeled traffic. Some people traveled in palanquins borne by porters. Bulky goods were carried by sea. The Tokaido crossed rivers, and in some cases the river was shallow enough to be forded comfortably. Where it was less shallow, porters made their living carrying travelers across. Bridges were constructed over deeper bodies of water such as the Seta River, or ferries operated, as on Lake Hamana. Rivers like the Abekawa or the Ōigawa flooded, rendering them impassable for as long as a month. During such times the traffic on the Tokaido redirected itself to the longer but more scenic *Nakasendo* (Central Mountain Road), which wound its way through the central part of the island of Honshu.

A normal trip along the Tokaido between Kyoto and Edo took about 12 days, with an average of 25 miles traveled each day. It was possible, however, to travel much faster. In 1703, messengers carried news concerning the revenge of the "Forty Seven Loyal Ronin" along the entire length of the Tokaido in a little more than 3 days.

The Tokaido was one of the wonders of Tokugawa Japan as well as an important commercial resource. Foreign visitors, such as Englishman John Saris in 1613 and Dutch ambassador Engelbert Kaempfer in 1691 and 1692, found the Tokaido extremely clean, well maintained, and heavily used. The road became a frequent subject for Japanese artists and writers. The most famous, Hiroshige (1797–1858), produced 20 complete sets of wood-block prints depicting the Fifty-three Stages of the Tokaido (Tokaido Gojusantsugi), which provide a fascinating pictorial record of what the road was like. A modern highway and railroad now follow the track of the Tokaido, although sections of the original road have been preserved for posterity.

For further reading

Robert B. Hall, "Tokaido," *Geographical Review* 27 (July 1937): 353–377.

TRACE Word used in the colonial American and early national periods of the United States for roads or paths created by the passage of buffalo or deer. The etymology of the word *trace* obviously refers to the evidence of trampled grass and undergrowth left by the feet of men and beasts. Over the course of thousands of years, migrating animals developed these optimal routes for avoiding water obstructions or steep slopes. Native Americans adopted the pathways as their own, and so did the European settlers who followed. Possibly the most famous of the various traces is the Natchez Trace. Many traces are now the routes of modern highways or railroads.

See also
Natchez Trace.
For further reading
A. B. Hulbert, *Historic Highways of America*, 1902.

TRADE WINDS   System of easterly winds created by the differences in pressure between the subtropical high around the latitudes 30°N and 30°S and the intertropical convergence zone of the equatorial belt. In the Northern Hemisphere, these winds blow regularly from the northeast, while in the Southern Hemisphere they come from the southeast. The trade winds blow with great regularity and are present in both the Atlantic and Pacific Oceans except where monsoonal conditions prevail. Generally, the weather in the belt of the trade winds is balmy except during the late summer months, when warm waters create the tropical cyclones that can turn into the hurricanes of the Atlantic Ocean and the typhoons of the Pacific Ocean. Columbus used the trade winds to sail west on his famous voyage of 1492, when he stumbled across the Americas while seeking Asia. As their name implies, much commerce traveled the route of the trade winds during the age of sailing ships.

See also
Hurricane; Roaring Forties; Winds.

TUAREG   Group of nomadic Berber warriors living in the central Sahara. Also known as the People of the Veil, they were notorious for terrorizing travelers and raiding caravans.

Through most of their history, the Tuareg (pronounced Twä'reg) ranged over a vast portion of the Sahara. A line traced from Touggourt in northern Algeria through Wargla and Aoulef all the way south to Timbuktu defines the northern limit and western edge of Tuareg territory. Their land stretched eastward to Qatron (Gatroun) in Libya, then dipped down south of the Niger River and into the savannah country as far as northern Nigeria. The lands of the Tuareg were mostly sandy, rocky desert, which dictated their lifestyle as nomadic herders and warriors. The Tuareg also occupied the relatively moist mountainous regions of Air, Ahagger, and the Adrar of the Iforas.

The Tuareg (the singular form is Targui) are Berbers and speak a language called Tamaheq, which has its own alphabet, the *tifinagh,* a descendant of ancient Libyan writing. As Berbers, the Tuareg are Caucasian, although over time those tribes living in the southern part of their territory intermarried heavily with the neighboring Negro nations and tribes. It has been seriously but erroneously claimed that the Tuareg are descendants of ancient Vandal tribesmen or wayward Crusaders. Politically, the Tuareg are divided into confederations of tribes ruled by a chief called an *amenokal.* The Tuareg choose their *amenokal* by consensus, and his powers are tempered by having to maintain a similar consensus among his touchy and warlike followers. Individual tribes choose their own chiefs, and are further subdivided into clans of nobles and vassals. Although the Tuareg are Muslim, they are generally lukewarm adherents, often ignoring the observance of Ramadan and other rituals of Islam.

Males hold all the political offices in Tuareg society, but their women receive extraordinary respect, especially by the standards of other Islamic cultures. Tuareg society practices matrilineal descent, in which property and status are inherited through the mother. As a result, men compete vigorously to marry a woman of higher social status, because their children will inherit their mother's rank, and some of her prestige will probably transfer onto her husband. Tuareg marriages are monogamous, which is probably related to the practice of matrilineal descent. Contrary to some reports, it is a myth that Tuareg women behave promiscuously with guests.

The traditional Tuareg way of life was built on the herding of camels, sheep, and goats. No self-respecting Targui engages in farming. They supplement their earnings from herding by collecting crop shares from tenant farmers working on Tuareg-owned lands. Tuareg also trade such items as salt and slaves. Raiding was another common enterprise among the Tuareg. Occasionally, they would attack settlements or caravans to obtain booty, but more often they raided Negro settlements in the Sudan to obtain slaves for laborers and trade.

The Tuareg activity most directly affecting travelers was their service as guides and guards for caravans crossing their portion of the Sahara. The fee was based on the value of the caravan's goods, and, in fact, these services were a thinly disguised protection racket. True, Tuareg guides led caravans to the life-sustaining wells in the desert. However, if their services were rejected, those same guides would fill the wells with sand or hide them under canvas coverings. If the guards did not receive employment, they formed a raiding party and attacked the caravan in some particularly isolated part of the desert.

The most obvious and famous trait that distinguished the Tuareg from other tribes of the desert was the blue veil worn by the adult males. In Tamaheq it is called the *tequelmoust,* although the Arabic word for it is *litham.* The veil consists of a strip of indigo blue cotton cloth measuring ten feet by one foot, called a *shegga.* The *shegga* is wrapped into a combination turban and veil, leaving only a thin slit for the eyes. Some authorities assert that the veil is purely decorative and has no practical function. Others demonstrate that the veil protects the face from exposure to the harsh desert environment, yet keeps the mouth area moist. Because their faces are covered, Tuareg men have developed a complex procedure for adjusting their veils to show moods and emotions. Just when the Tuareg began wearing the blue veils is a mystery. In the early eleventh century, the Arab El Bekri provided the first written mention of the Tuareg wearing their veils. Since he treats the Tuareg practice as something that was already well known, the custom must have begun much earlier. Berber legends claim that the custom of the veil was inherited from some wandering Yemenite Muslims who supposedly were the ancestors of the Tuareg and the other desert

Berbers. It was an ancient Arab custom for warriors to go into battle with their faces covered.

In comparison, the Berber tribes of the western Sahara known as the Sanhaja apparently wore veils at one time but abandoned the custom. Otherwise, the western Sanhaja are quite similar to the Tuareg in their customs and way of life. Unlike other Muslims, Tuareg women do not wear veils.

Just as the caravans no longer ply the various ancient routes across the Sahara, the Tuareg no longer raid and terrorize their neighbors and travelers. The imposition of European colonial rule during the late nineteenth century broke the military power of the Tuareg. The modern governments of Algeria, Libya, Mali, and Niger are working to end the Tuareg's traditional nomadic way of life, which became impoverished with the disappearance of the trans-Saharan caravan trade.

See also
Caravans; Robbers; Sahara.
For further reading
Edward William Bovill, *The Golden Trade of the Moors*, 1968; Lloyd Cabot Briggs, *The Tribes of the Sahara*, 1960; H. T. Norris, *Saharan Myth and Legend*, 1972; H. T. Norris, *The Tuaregs*, 1975.

TYPHOON
See Hurricane.

U

UBAR, LOST CITY OF
Legendary city located at the southeast edge of the Rub al-Khali in the Arabian peninsula. It was a rich spice-trading city that was supposedly overwhelmed in a great sandstorm sent by Allah as a punishment. This legend caused the British explorer Bertram Thomas to refer to Ubar as the "Atlantis of the Sands."

Archaeological research reveals the truth behind the legend of Ubar. It was not a single city, but rather a region along the south Arabian trade route controlled by the tribe of the Iobaritae in what is now Oman. The Ubar region contained the settlements of Iula, Marimatha, and Thabane, where the lucrative aromatic frankincense was produced. Archaeological evidence indicates that Ubar's fall was gradual rather than sudden. In 1508, the great Portuguese admiral Afonso d'Albuquerque conquered Muscat on the south coast of Arabia, causing a disastrous reduction in the traffic of caravans through Ubar. The various settlements declined and ultimately were abandoned to the encroaching desert. Over the years, popular imagination and Islamic folklore turned this slow process of decline into a dramatic burial of a thriving city by a sandstorm.

See also
Sandstorm.
For further reading
Juris Zarins, "Atlantis of the Sand," *Archaeology* 50 (May/June 1997): 51–53.

UNDERGROUND RAILROAD
Also known as the Liberty Line, it was the name for an informal group of Northerners who, during 1830–1860 in the United States, assisted runaway slaves in making their escape to Canada.

Antislavery Northerners systematically helping slaves to freedom goes back at least to the 1780s, but the idea of a large-scale organization to help slaves escape bondage did not begin until the 1830s. The approximate term *underground railroad* first appeared in 1830 when one bewildered slave owner commented that his slave seemed to have disappeared on an "underground road." Growing fascination with the new technology of the railroad quickly changed *underground road* to *underground railroad*.

Slave catchers invade an Underground Railroad barn. From William Still, The Underground Railroad, *1872.*

Continuing the terminology, the people who assisted escaped slaves along the Underground Railroad were called *conductors*. Research documents the existence of at least 3,200 conductors, who were both white and black Northerners, with Quakers, Covenanters, and Methodists playing a big role. Conductors provided fugitive slaves with money, lodgings, and directions, often transporting them to the next "station." In some parts of southern Pennsylvania, southern Indiana, and southern Ohio, the Underground Railroad had a definite organization, but no national organization ever existed. Instead, individuals spontaneously helped fugitive slaves when the opportunity arose. Census figures indicate that only about 800 to 1,000 slaves successfully escaped per year during 1830–1860. This sets an upper limit of less than 30,000 for the number of escapees who may have received assistance from the Underground Railroad.

The Underground Railroad attracted the admiration of Northern abolitionists and the hatred of pro-slavery Southerners. One Southern writer claimed that the Underground Railroad helped 100,000 slaves to escape between 1810 and 1850, clearly an impossible figure. A later historian, Wilbur H. Siebert, in 1900, hyperbolically claimed that some 75,000 slaves had successfully used the Underground Railroad between 1830 and 1850. Such numbers are obviously exaggerated and reflect the partisan passions of both the antebellum and postbellum periods. In her great novel *Uncle Tom's Cabin* (1852), Harriet Beecher Stowe included the character of Simeon Halliday, who was based on Underground Railroad activist Thomas Garrett. The Underground Railroad's reputation increased to the proportion of a romantic myth in the years after the Civil War.

In its day, the Underground Railroad provided a perilous means of travel for the extremely desperate. Its name also documents the growing impact of railroads on nineteenth-century American consciousness.

See also
Railroads.
For further reading
Larry Gara, *The Liberty Line*, 1961.

UNICORN   Name for a horselike creature with a single horn on its forehead. It is frequently described as a small, pony-sized animal, but other traditions claim that it was a very large creature. One Jewish legend claimed that unicorns perished in the Great Flood because they were too large to board Noah's ark. Belief in the existence of unicorns was common in Europe and Asia through the sixteenth and seventeenth centuries. The Chinese considered them creatures of good omen. Many people considered the ground-up horn of a unicorn a powerful medicine for curing illnesses, and unicorn horn was believed to be good for detecting poison. Given the phallic symbolism, the unicorn's horn was also considered an aphrodisiac or cure for impotence. Many scholars think that the lumbering rhinoceros was the inspiration for the mythical, dainty unicorn. Certainly the horn of the rhinoceros, like the unicorn's, was thought to be a powerful medicine or aphrodisiac.

For further reading
Anthony S. Mercatante, *The Facts on File Encyclopedia of World Mythology and Legend*, 1988.

UTOPIA   Sir Thomas More (1478–1535) first concocted the word *utopia*, meaning either "no place" or "good place" in Greek, as the name for his fictional ideal island-nation. In More's book *Utopia* (1516), a Portuguese sailor named Raphael Hythlodaye visits various unexplored lands in the Americas and the western Atlantic. The island called Utopia proves to be his most interesting stopping place. Utopian society is tightly controlled and socialistic, and according to More it is a perfectly organized community. Thanks to the impact of More's book, any society seeking to reach perfection on earth is called utopian. Of course, More's Utopia was a product of his imagination and political philosophy. No such place actually existed. Still, the idea of perfect or utopian societies has a perennial fascination for many people, amply evidenced by the vast fictional and speculative literature about utopian societies. Travelers throughout the ages frequently claimed to encounter utopian or perfect societies, but experience and further examination showed such claims to be exaggerated or overly optimistic. No true utopia has ever been located.

See also
Paradise, Terrestrial.

V

VENICE   Known as the "Queen of the Adriatic" or the "Jewel of the Adriatic," Venice became the greatest of the trading cities of medieval Europe and, appropriately, was the home of the great traveler Marco Polo (ca. 1254–1324).

Located in the northwest extremity of the Adriatic Sea, Venice rose among marshes, lagoons, and alluvial islands, resulting in the construction of Venice's famous canals. Romantic myth enshrouds the city's origins. One version claims that St. Mark founded Venice, thus linking the city with the Apostolic era. Another version tells how Roman nobility, vexed by the various barbarian invasions of the Visigoths, Ostrogoths, Huns, and Lombards, fled to the safety and isolation of the lagoons and islands and founded a city there. This myth provided Venice with strong continuity to the prestige of ancient Rome. It is likely that Venice was founded as a refuge from the tumult of the mainland. Its strategic location recommended it to the Byzantine Empire of Constantinople as a secure base for its military operations in northern Italy. Such an origin is reflected in the Venetian leader's title of *doge*, a corruption of the Roman military title *dux*.

The Byzantines also used Venice as a conduit for trade with northern Europe from about 600 to 900. Venice grew in wealth and power from this trade, but the Byzantine Empire weakened under the assorted attacks of Persians, Arabs, steppe nomads, and Normans. Needing assured maritime access to the rest of the Mediterranean Sea, during the 900s the Venetians set about conquering the northern two-thirds of the Adriatic coastline. Military prowess increased Venice's value as a Byzantine ally, so in 922 the Byzantine government granted it the Bolla d'Oro, a preferential reduction of their customs duties. This privilege was expanded in 1082 to a complete exemption from the payment of customs duties to the Byzantine Empire.

Venetian trade was a triangular arrangement. The Venetians carried lumber, iron, pelts, and slaves from Europe to Muslim North Africa, which the Muslims purchased with gold and silver. Moving on to Constantinople, the Venetians used the gold and silver to buy silks and spices from Asia. These products were carried home and sold to the rest of Europe, to the huge profit of the Venetians.

By 1100, Venice was a Mediterranean power in its own right. The building of the famous Arsenal, the state-owned shipbuilding facility, exemplified

Venice's transformation. Byzantine resentment of Venetian trading privileges also grew during the 1100s. Meanwhile, the beginning of the Crusades in 1095 was initially ignored by the Venetians, but they soon offered naval support in exchange for trading facilities in the Outremer. Venetian intrigues turned the wayward Fourth Crusade (1202–1204) from its proper goal of the Holy Land into a conquest of Constantinople. Although Venice profited from that debacle, its reputation suffered, as did political support for the crusading movement.

Venice fell into rivalry with the other maritime trading cities of Italy, particularly Genoa. From 1258 to 1379, Venice and Genoa engaged in a series of wars, which ultimately ended in victory for Venice. These years were the age of Marco Polo and Venice's great trading empire linking East and West. During that time, the city's population numbered between 70,000 and 100,000. By 1500, Venice had acquired a far-flung empire across the Mediterranean, but the halcyon days were about over. Relentless advances on land and sea by the Ottoman Turks threatened the Venetian Empire, and Vasco da Gama's discovery of the sea road to India undermined Venetian domination of the Asian luxury trade in Europe. In the sixteenth century, Venice's economic and political power gradually declined, a process that continued into the seventeenth century. In their heyday, the Venetians were the greatest merchants of the Mediterranean world, and as a consequence are included among the great travelers of history.

See also
Genoa; Mediterranean Sea; Polo, Marco.
For further reading
Frederic C. Lane, *Venice*, 1973; William H. McNeill, *Venice*, 1974; John Julius Norwich, *A History of Venice*, 1982.

VINLAND A pleasant land of woods, meadows, and rolling hills that was temporarily settled shortly after the year 1000 by various medieval Norse explorers of North America including Leif Ericsson and Thorfinn Karlsefni.

Vinland's name and location are the subject of great controversy among scholars of Norse exploration in North America. The common translation for the word Vinland is "wine-land," which refers to the grapes the Norse supposedly found there. If this translation is correct, the "vin" in Vinland is actually *vín*, the word for "wine." Some scholars suggest that the actual Norse word was simply *vin*, which means "meadow" or "fertile." This philological interpretation is also consistent with the Vinland Sagas' descriptions of Vinland containing rich grasslands. However, it is inconsistent with the *Greenlanders' Saga*'s detailed description of grapes, which is further corroborated by the description of Vinland and grapes contained in Adam of Bremen's chronicle. Furthermore, *vin* was an archaic Norse word that at the time of the Vinland voyages had dropped out of common usage. Therefore, most scholars accept that Vinland literally means wine-land. Nevertheless, scholars do not necessarily believe that Leif Ericsson actually found grapes in Vinland. Some suggest that Leif named his new land Vinland for the same reason Eric the Red named his new land Greenland: Such a ploy made it sound more inviting to potential settlers. Other scholars suggest that the Norse found some sort of berry plant that reminded them of grapes. Cowberries, squash berries, blueberries, and blackberries are among the suggested substitutes.

The problem of the grapes is directly related to the problem of Vinland's location. Most scholars now accept Newfoundland as the location of Vinland because of the discovery of the Norse site of L'Anse aux Meadows in the early 1960s. Prior to that, various writers located Vinland anywhere from Newfoundland to Florida. New England, particularly the Cape Cod area, attracted many supporters because it was the northernmost place in which wild grapes could grow in the manner described by the saga. Other writers point out that the climate was warmer in the year 1000, and grapes could have grown successfully much farther north than they do now. No consensus exists on the northern limits of wild grapes in the eleventh century. Helge Ingstad, the discoverer of L'Anse aux Meadow, thinks they might have grown as far north as Newfoundland.

Both the *Greenlanders' Saga* and *Eirik's Saga* describe Vinland as being two days' sail from Markland. Such a sailing distance is consistent with Newfoundland being Vinland, if Markland is Labrador. The sagas describe Vinland as a rich land with rivers full of salmon, a fact that eliminates any locations south of the Hudson River. It also had a mild climate and such lush grasslands that no winter fodder was needed for the livestock. On the shortest day of the year, the sun rose over Vinland before 9:00 A.M. and set after 3:00 P.M. according to the *Greenlanders' Saga*. This description places Vinland somewhere between 40°N and 50°N latitude, which is anywhere from New Jersey to the mouth of the St. Lawrence River. With only these rather general descriptions from the sagas, it is impossible to fix the true location of Vinland. The difficulty is not surprising, since the sagas are not eyewitness accounts. Rather, they are written versions of oral narratives that had been passed on for over two centuries before being written down. Information contained in the sagas must be used cautiously because it is a mixture of facts, conflations, errors, falsehoods, and fantasies.

The finding of L'Anse aux Meadows and the close correspondence of that site to other topographical features mentioned in the Vinland Sagas has convincingly pulled the generally accepted location for Vinland back to Newfoundland. Supporters of theories about Norse settlements in New England are now definitely on the fringes of scholarship. Oddly enough, the medieval Norse thought Vinland was an extension of Africa. They believed the Atlantic Ocean was virtually an inland sea, and that Africa stretched west and then north toward Markland, Helluland, and Greenland to surround it.

See also
Greenland; Helluland; Markland; Norse Voyages.
For further reading
Gwyn Jones, *The Norse Atlantic Saga*, 1986; Magnus Magnusson and Hermann Pálsson, trans., *The Vinland Sagas*, 1965.

W

WAGON TRAINS   Groups of emigrants with wagons who traveled together for mutual protection and safety across the western prairies and mountains to reach California and Oregon, primarily during the 1840s and 1850s.

Wagon trains are a stock feature of many Western films and television programs, including a popular television series titled *Wagon Train* that aired from 1957 to 1965. Prior to the advent of movies and television in the twentieth century, a preexisting fictional heritage of dime novels sprang up about the adventures of the overland emigrants. A mythic image arose of lonely groups of wagons gliding across the plains, menaced by the harsh environment and implacably hostile Native American warriors. The reality was somewhat different.

Wagon trains consisted of parties of as few as 20 people with three or four wagons to huge groups of 120 wagons and 1,000 emigrants. The goal was to travel 2,000 miles from Missouri to the West Coast. Most emigrants could travel an average of 15 miles a day, so barring any unusual and excessive delays, the journey took four and a half months. Generally, their travels began in late April or early May so that the prairie grasses could provide fodder for the mules and oxen pulling the wagons. Wagon trains hoped to reach California or Oregon by early to mid-September. Those arriving later risked being trapped in the Sierra Mountains by early winter snows, a fate that tragically devastated the Donner party.

Wagon trains generally gathered at Independence, Missouri, although Westport and St. Joseph and Fort Leavenworth, Kansas, were also popular staging areas. Before heading west, the emigrants gathered their supplies and equipment. Although most of them traveled in the seemingly ubiquitous covered wagon or prairie schooner, some chose pack animals or two-wheeled carts, which could carry less cargo, but more easily negotiate the rugged terrain of the far West. Emigrants also acquired guidebooks written to help travelers using the Oregon Trail and the California Trail. The people in a wagon train established a government or officers to lead the group. Some wagon trains set up elaborate governments, but most simply elected a trail captain and a few assistants. In the best traditions of Jacksonian democracy, trail captains suffered much criticism from their fellow travelers.

The first half of the route followed by the wagon trains was relatively easy, as it lay over fairly flat prairie with generally fordable rivers. Native Americans

Handcart immigration on the Oregon Trail, W. H. Jackson.

rarely attacked emigrants, and then only lone wagons or small groups. Hollywood's obligatory Native American attacks on wagons drawn up in a circle are the stuff of fiction. On no occasion did mounted warriors try to charge a party of circled wagons. It is true that wagon trains circled up when they camped each night, but it was as much to provide a corral for the animals as a defensive wall. One out of every 17 emigrants died on the trail, but very few died from violence. Accidents or disease were the big killers, especially cholera.

Wagon trains seldom suffered from loneliness, surprisingly enough. Parties of emigrants frequently encountered other wagon trains or mounted parties. In fact, a big problem for groups who started late was that earlier emigrants inconsiderately fouled the springs and streams used for drinking water.

Wagon trains had a good idea of the progress they needed to make so that they could reach California or Oregon safely. Most emigrant parties reached Scott's Bluff, Nebraska, in late June and Independence Rock around 4 July, hence its name. From there they went through the South Pass, usually to Fort Bridger. Farther along, the trail split between wagon trains bound for Oregon and those bound for California. The final stage of the journey contained the most difficult terrain. California travelers faced the broken and arid Great Basin, followed by the precipitous slopes of the Sierras. Oregon travelers encountered rugged mountains and, when they reached Fort Walla Walla, deadly raft trips down the raging Columbia River. By this time, the emigrants were reaching exhaustion and supplies were running low. Winter storms threatened in the higher altitudes. Still, most weary emigrants were able to hurry along to safety and their new homes.

Wagon trains were crucial to the rapid settlement of California and Oregon. They carried hundreds of thousands of travelers to new lives in the far West. Their heyday in the 1840s and 1850s marks a heroic episode in American history that has attained mythic stature in popular culture, although in this case the reality is far more interesting.

See also

California Trail; Donner Party; Oregon Trail; Prarie Schooner.

For further reading

John D. Unruh, *The Plains Across,* 1979.

WANDERING JEW
Late-medieval myth that tells of a Jew who insulted or denied assistance to Christ during his trial or his walk to Golgotha and as a consequence was condemned to wander the earth until Christ's second coming at Judgment Day.

Some accounts give the Wandering Jew the name of Ahasuerus, a shoemaker. He refused to let Christ rest in front of his shop as he carried the cross to Golgotha. Other tales of the Wandering Jew call him Cartaphilus, and identify him as Pontius Pilate's gatekeeper who struck Christ and tried to hurry him on his way. After witnessing the Crucifixion, the Wandering Jew repented his ignorant ill treatment of Christ. He became a Christian, was baptized by Ananias, and given the new name of Joseph. Not a malevolent figure or one of ill omen, the Wandering Jew roamed the earth testifying to the truth of the death and resurrection of Christ. God took care of his material needs and gave him the power to speak perfectly all languages that he encountered. The Wandering Jew would grow old until he reached 100. Then he would fall into a trance and wake up at age 30 again. From 1228 until his last sighting at Brussels in 1774, the Wandering Jew appeared frequently throughout Europe. England experienced reports of the Wandering Jew in 1818, 1824, and 1830, but in each case, the reputed Wandering Jew was firmly demonstrated to be a charlatan or mentally ill.

The earliest account of the Wandering Jew occurred in the St. Alban's Chronicle associated with Matthew Paris for the year 1228. Philip Mouskes, sometime bishop of Tournai, wrote a rhymed account of the Wandering Jew in 1242. Paul von Eitzen, the bishop of Schleswig (d. 1598), gave a detailed account of a visit by the Wandering Jew to Hamburg in 1547. Other accounts appeared over the years.

Not only did the Wandering Jew provide eyewitness testimony to the truth of the death and resurrection of Jesus Christ, he served as a metaphor for life as a journey from which death and salvation provided the ultimate rest. Unlike other humans, the Wandering Jew was denied that relief until the end of the world.

For further reading

Sabine Baring-Gould, *Curious Myths of the Middle Ages,* 1994.

WANDERING ROCKS
See Clashing Rocks.

WANDERING SCHOLARS OF THE MIDDLE AGES
Phrase that evokes the international character of higher education during the medieval and renaissance eras. As European civilization began to recover in the ninth and tenth centuries, monastic schools arose to provide education. By the eleventh century, cathedral schools for advanced learning were established at Chartres and Rheims. Gatherings of students and teachers who came together for mutual benefit and protection were known as *universitas scholarum*. From them, the medieval universities evolved. Students traveled from all over Europe to attend a famous school or learn from an outstanding teacher. Latin was the common language of scholarship and learning, so students and teachers were not limited by linguistic barriers as they are today.

Sometimes disputes arose between a university and its host town, causing all or some of the students and teachers to pack up and move to a more congenial place. Disgruntled members of Oxford University moved and founded Cambridge University in 1209. It was easy enough to do this during that era; any fairly large room could function as a lecture hall, books were scarce, and laboratories and other physical facilities of modern universities were nonexistent.

Students also frequently changed universities, beginning their course of studies at one school but completing their degree at another. Many schools of the later Middle Ages and the Renaissance sent their students to other centers of learning to broaden their horizons and sharpen their powers of observation. This practice was called the *peregrinatio academica*, and from it arose the later aristocratic Grand Tour. Wandering scholars traveled about, gathering rare materials from libraries and archives or consulting with learned colleagues. Francesco Petrarch (1304–1374) and Erasmus (1467?–1536) were both great travelers, and they were not unique. From the sixteenth century on, as universities proliferated and became increasingly institutionalized and scholarship became more professionalized, scholarly travel declined in importance. Scholars and students still commonly travel in the modern era, particularly students from Third World countries, but higher education does not have the international flavor it once did in the later Middle Ages.

See also
Grand Tour.
For further reading
Antoni Maczak, *Travel in Early Modern Europe*, 1995; Norbert Ohler, *The Medieval Traveler*, 1989.

WHITE MAN'S GRAVE
Nineteenth-century phrase used to describe the coastal region of West Africa from the Gambia River to the Niger River delta. The name refers to the high rate of disease-related mortality experienced by visiting Europeans in that area.

Coastal West Africa has always been plagued by diseases deadly to both Europeans and Africans. Malaria, yellow fever, and sleeping sickness are the major killers, but a host of lesser illnesses increases the danger. As the sixteenth-century Portuguese chronicler João de Barros graphically described the situation: "It seems that for our sins, or for some inscrutable judgment of God, in all the entrances of this great Ethiopia that we navigate along, He has placed a striking angel with a flaming sword of deadly fevers, who prevents us from penetrating into the interior of this garden, whence proceed these rivers of gold that flow to the sea in so many parts of our conquest."

Prior to the last years of the eighteenth century, most Europeans paid little attention to the unhealthy nature of coastal West Africa, or Guinea, as it was also known. European visits were largely fleeting trading expeditions, such as those of the Portuguese, for slaves, gold, and ivory. This situation changed in the 1780s when Britain lost its American colonies. Attention shifted to West Africa and the possibility of acquiring a new and better empire to replace what had been lost.

New colonies and settlements appeared, such as Sierra Leone in 1787 and the Gambia in 1807. Christian missionaries also settled in these colonies, along with the naval and military personnel assigned to blockade the slave trade. Sierra Leone, in particular, developed into a resettlement area for emancipated slaves and Africans rescued from the clutches of slavers. These European settlers and visitors suffered from high rates of mortality caused by various tropical diseases. Sixty percent of the missionaries sponsored by the Church Mission Society died between 1804 and 1825, and other missionary groups fared little better. Officers and sailors of the Royal Navy despised serving in the antislavery blockade of the West African coast. With grim humor, the fleet in that area was called the "coffin squadron," and the fort at Bathhurst was known as "Half-Die." Military personnel stationed in West Africa experienced between 25 and 75 percent rates of disease-related mortality before the 1840s. As a result, disillusionment with these new colonies gradually set in.

The 1820s marked the peak of the English public's perception of West Africa as a "white man's grave." The Portuguese writer J. C. de Figaniere e Morae appears to be the first to use the phrase "white man's grave" in print. In 1822, he referred to Sierra Leone as the "sepulcro dos Europêos" in his book *Descripsão de Serra Leon*. During the later 1820s, three colonial governors of Sierra Leone died in rapid succession: Charles Turner, 1826; Sir Neil Campbell, 1827; and Lieutenant Colonel Dixon Denham, 1828.

In many cases, the medical treatment inflicted on the victims of tropical disease was often as deadly as the diseases themselves. Doctors frequently used bleeding, mercury treatments, and calomel to treat malaria, all of which weakened rather than strengthened their patients.

The image of coastal West Africa as the "white man's grave" appealed to the romantic sensibilities of the early nineteenth century. The beauty of the tropics was aesthetically juxtaposed with their supposed deadliness, to the titillation of European readers. In 1836, the generally quite perceptive travel writer F. Harrison Rankin used the phrase in the title of one of his books, *The White Man's Grave: A Visit to Sierra Leone in 1834*. Rankin's use of the phrase popularized the lethal image of West Africa in the public's mind and usage even though the author meant it ironically.

During the 1840s, tropical medicine made great advances in understanding African diseases and techniques for curing them. The use of quinine as both a cure and preventative increased, and the earlier dangerous and ineffectual techniques were abandoned. By the 1850s, disease-related mortality among the Europeans of West Africa was cut in half. The region's reputation as a "white man's grave," however, lived on for decades in the popular imagination. Charles Dickens helped perpetuate it in his novel *Bleak House* (1852–1853), which portrayed the West African climate as deadly for Europeans. Echoes of this stereotype survived into the early twentieth century, with only the most tenuous bases in fact.

See also

Africa; Dark Continent.

For further reading

Philip D. Curtin, *The Image of Africa*, 1964; Frank McLynn, *Hearts of Darkness*, 1992.

WILDERNESS ROAD   First developed at the time of the American Revolution, this road ran for 300 miles from eastern Virginia through the Cumberland Gap to Boonesboro, Kentucky.

A path used by migratory buffalo and Native Americans had existed for centuries when in March 1775 Daniel Boone and about 30 woodsmen began clearing it for the route that became known as the Wilderness Road. The road immediately became heavily used by settlers coming into Kentucky and Tennessee. At first, only people on foot or pack horses could use it, but by the mid-1790s, wagons traveled along an improved Wilderness Road. The newly created state of Kentucky made considerable effort to maintain and widen the road. Private contractors also maintained sections of the road, and were allowed to set up toll booths to recoup their expenditures. From 1775 to 1825, the Wilderness Road was one of two main routes used to travel into the western frontier of the United States (the other was the Ohio River).

The coming of canals and railroads reduced the importance of the Wilderness Road, but its route is still used by trucks and automobiles as U.S. Highway 25.

See also

Cumberland Gap.

For further reading

A. B. Hulbert, *Boone's Wilderness Road*, 1903; W. A. Pusey, *The Wilderness Road to Kentucky*, 1921; Thomas Speed, *The Wilderness Road*, 1886.

WINDS   Homeric and classical Greeks identified four principal winds, which were associated with the four cardinal directions. Boreas was the north wind, Notus the south wind, Eurus the east wind, and Zephyrus the west wind. They were all ruled by Aeolus, the son of Hippotas. The Romans adopted the Greek's system of winds, but changed some of the names. Instead of Boreas, the Romans called the north wind Aquilo, while their south wind was Auster and the west wind was Favonius. Destructive storms were the products of the wind god Typhon.

Medieval scholars continued to use the Greek names for winds, which persist as folklore and literary allusions to the present day. However, medieval scholars rejected the idea that the winds had supernatural origins. William of Conches (d. ca. 1160) theorized that a general atmospheric circulation connected to the currents of the equatorial and meridional River Oceans that girded the earth. Although his theory had no basis in fact, it shows that people were beginning to think in terms of global patterns for the circulation of winds. Such a worldview was essential to enable voyagers like Christopher Columbus and Vasco da Gama to use trade winds and monsoons to reach their destinations. It also opened the way to the scientific study of winds and ocean currents.

See also
Roaring Forties; Trade Winds.
For further reading
Harold Burstyn, "Theories of Winds and Currents from the Discoveries to the End of the Seventeenth Century," *Terrae Incognitae* 3 (1971): 7–32; John Kirtland Wright, *The Geographical Lore of the Time of the Crusades,* 1925.

WOMEN AND MEN, ISLES OF

The Travels of Marco Polo describes two islands called Male and Female, located in the Arabian Sea some 500 miles south of the Persian coast, with Socotra being the nearest other island. The inhabitants of the two islands are Christians, but the two sexes live apart. One island is home to the men, and the women live on the other. Each March, the men travel to the island of Female and live with the women during March, April, and May. When June comes, they return to the island of Male. During these yearly visits, of course, new children are conceived. When the babies arrive, the women raise them. The girls remain with their mothers permanently, but the boys are sent to live with their fathers when they reach the age of 14.

Marco Polo's story of the Isle of Women was already old when he told it. Jason and the Argonauts stopped at the island of Lemnos on their way to Colchis. The enraged women had killed all their faithless men for habitually cheating on them with other women. Their hostility to men was not universal, however. The Argonauts arrived a year after the massacre and were greeted by a wary band of armed women. Queen Hypsipyle and the other women soon welcomed Jason and his crew with open arms. Hypsipyle even fell in love with Jason. Everyone was extremely happy, and the Argonauts soon forgot about their quest. Ultimately it took the single-minded Hercules to shame the Argonauts into leaving idyllic Lemnos and continuing on with their mission to Colchis.

Various medieval writers and cartographers, such as Friar Jordanus and Fra Mauro, told of isles of men and women similar to Marco Polo's. In China, the writer Hsuan-Tsang described an Isle of Women that was virtually identical to the European version. The Persian poet Firdausi (ca. 950–1020) had Alexander the Great visit a city of women located on an island in the Indian Ocean.

During his first voyage of 1492 to the Americas, Christopher Columbus learned from natives of Hispaniola about an island of women called Matinino (possibly Martinique) that existed among the Caribs. Being an avid student of *The Travels of Marco Polo*, Columbus assumed that this Caribbean isle of women was the same as Marco Polo's island of Female. Such an assumption seemingly provided further proof that Columbus successfully sailed west to reach Asia, but just as he never made it to Asia, Columbus never located that island of women. His experience with the elusive isle of women provides a classic example of the persistence and impact of geographical legends from ancient times on the perceptions of travelers up to and during the sixteenth and seventeenth centuries.

See also

Amazons; Jason and the Argonauts, Voyage of.

For further reading

Samuel Eliot Morison, *The Admiral of the Ocean Sea*, 1942; Henry Yule and Henri Cordier, eds., *The Travels of Marco Polo*, 1929.

Z

ZONAL THEORY   Belief in the sphericity of the earth became common among educated Greeks by the fifth century B.C. due to the teachings of the Pythagorean philosophers. Beginning with Parmenides (fl. 450), they also divided the spherical earth into five zones of climate. Two frigid regions at the north and south ends of the globe were uninhabitable because of the extreme cold. Along the equator of the globe lay a torrid or fiery zone that was uninhabitable because of the heat. In the regions between the Arctic and Torrid Zones lay the temperate zones, which were capable of sustaining human life. The great Aristotle (384– 322 B.C.) also advocated the zonal theory. More sophisticated versions divided the temperate zones into various types of climate such as desert, grasslands, forestlands, or other variations.

Belief in the zonal theory of climate inhibited exploration into the lands and seas of the tropics because these areas were feared to be too hot to allow the survival of human life. The fact that Marco Polo and other travelers traveled south of the equator and lived did not undermine the overall belief in an uninhabitable Torrid Zone. It persisted well into the sixteenth century, and finally faded as the multitude of successful voyages below the equator became common knowledge. As late as the end of the sixteenth century, the great observer of nature and societies Father José de Acosta (1539/1540–1600)

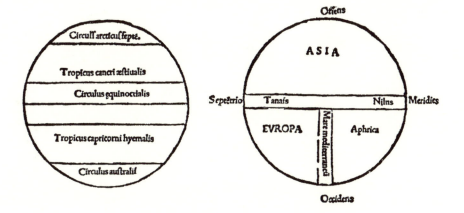

Undated pen-and-ink drawing illustrating the zonal theory.

ridiculed the continued adherence to the Aristotelian idea of an inhabitable Torrid Zone in his *Natural and Moral History of the Indies* (1590). Still, the zonal theory of climate persisted, with modifications, as an organizing principle of geography within the worlds of both Christendom and Islam through the Middle Ages and Renaissance into the modern era. Echoes of it even remain in the geographical terminology of the twentieth century.

See also

Crates of Mallos.

For further reading

Norman J. W. Thrower, *Maps and Civilization*, 1996; John Kirtland Wright, *The Geographical Lore of the Time of the Crusades*, 1925.

BIBLIOGRAPHY

Adler, Elkan Nathan. *Jewish Travellers in the Middle Ages.* New York: Dover, 1987.

Aharoni, Yohanan, and Michael Avi-Yonah. *The Macmillan Bible Atlas.* New York: Macmillan, 1968.

Ajayi, J. F. A., and Michael Crowder, eds. *History of West Africa.* 2 vols. New York: Columbia University Press, 1972.

Alexander, Philip S. "Earth, Jewish Geography." In David Noel Freeman, ed., "Geography and the Bible (Early Jewish)," in *The Anchor Bible Dictionary.* 6 vols. New York: Doubleday, 1992.

Allen, Oliver E. *The Pacific Navigators.* Alexandria, VA: Time-Life Books, 1980.

Anderson, Andrew Runni. "Alexander at the Caspian Gates." *Transactions of the American Philogical Association* 59 (1928): 130–163.

———. *Alexander's Gate: Gog and Magog, and the Inclosed Nations.* Cambridge, MA: Medieval Academy of America, 1932.

Apollonius of Rhodes. *The Voyage of Argo,* translated by E. V. Rieu. Harmondsworth, England: Penguin, 1959.

Arens, William. *The Man-Eating Myth: Anthropology and Anthropophagy.* Oxford: Oxford University Press, 1979.

Arenson, Sarah. *The Encircled Sea.* London: Constable, 1990.

Armstrong, Karen. *Jerusalem: One City, Three Faiths.* New York: HarperCollins, 1996.

Arrian. *The Campaigns of Alexander.* Harmondsworth, England: Penguin, 1971.

Ashe, Geoffrey. *Avalonian Quest.* London: Methuen, 1982.

———. *Land to the West: St. Brendan's Voyage to America.* New York: Viking, 1962.

———. *Mythology of the British Isles.* London: Methuen, 1990.

Ashe, Geoffrey, ed. *The Quest for Arthur's Britain.* New York: Praeger, 1960.

Askenasy, Hans. *Cannibalism: From Sacrifice to Survival.* Amherst, MA: Prometheus Books, 1994.

Athapally, Andrew. "An Indian Prototype for Prester John." *Terrae Incognitae* 10 (1978): 15–24.

Atkinson, C. W. *Mystic and Pilgrim: The Book and the World of Margery Kempe.* Ithaca, NY: Cornell University Press, 1983.

Aubet, Maria Eugenia. *The Phoenicians and the West: Politics, Colonies, and Trade.* Cambridge: Cambridge University Press, 1993.

Babcock, William H. *Legendary Islands of the Atlantic: A Study in Medieval Geography.* New York: American Geographical Society, 1922.

Bacon, Janet Ruth. *The Voyage of the Argonauts.* Boston: Small, Maynard, 1925.

Baldwin, Leland D. *The Keelboat Age on Western Waters.* Pittsburgh, PA: University of Pittsburgh Press, 1941.

Barclay, Harold B. *The Role of the Horse in Man's Culture.* London: J. A. Allen, 1980.

Baring-Gould, Sabine. *Curious Myths of the Middle Ages,* edited by Edward Hardy. New York: Barnes & Noble Books, 1994.

Baudet, Henri. *Paradise on Earth: Some Thoughts on European Images of Non-European Man,* translated by Elizabeth Wentholt. New Haven, CT: Yale University Press, 1965.

Baudin, Louis. *Daily Life in Peru under the Last Incas.* New York: Macmillan, 1962.

Beall, Charles B. P. "Frisland: Myth or Reality." *Terrae Incognitae* 9 (1977): 81–88.

Beazley, Charles Raymond. *The Dawn of Modern Geography.* 3 vols. [1897–1906]. Reprint, New York: Peter Smith, 1942.

Beck, Horace. *Folklore and the Sea.* Middletown, CT: Wesleyan University Press, 1973.

Beckingham, C. F. "The Achievement of Prester John." In *Between Islam and Christendom.* London: Variorum Reprints, 1983.

———. "The Quest for Prester John." In *Between Islam and Cristendom.* London: Variorum Reprints, 1983.

Beckingham, C. F., ed. *The Travels of Ibn Battuta.* Vol. 4. London: Hakluyt Society, 1994.

Bennett, Josephine Waters. *The Rediscovery of Sir John Mandeville.* New York: Modern Language Association, 1954.

Berton, Pierre. *The Arctic Grail: The Quest for the Northwest Passage and the North Pole, 1818–1909.* New York: Penguin, 1988.

Bierman, John. *Dark Safari: The Life behind the Legend of Henry Morton Stanley.* New York: Alfred A. Knopf, 1990.

Billett, Michael. *Highwaymen and Outlaws.* New York: Arms and Armour, 1997.

Billington, Ray Allen. *The Far Western Frontier, 1830–1860.* New York: Harper & Row, 1956.

Black, Clinton Vane de Brosse. *Pirates of the West Indies.* New York: Cambridge University Press, 1989.

Black, Jeremy. *The British Abroad: The Grand Tour in the Eighteenth Century.* New York: St. Martin's Press, 1992.

Blair, Walter, and J. Meine Franklin. *Half Horse, Half Alligator: The Growth of the Mike Fink Legend.* 1933. Reprint, Chicago: University of Chicago Press, 1956.

Blok, Josine H. *The Early Amazons: Modern and Ancient Perspectives on a Persistent Myth.* Leiden: E. J. Brill, 1995.

Blunt, Wilfred. *Golden Road to Samarkand.* New York: Viking, 1973.

Bobrick, Benson. *East of the Sun: The Epic Conquest and Tragic History of Siberia.* New York: Poseidon Press, 1992.

Bourne, Russell. *Floating West: The Erie and Other American Canals.* New York: W. W. Norton, 1992.

Bovill, Edward William. *The Golden Trade of the Moors.* 2nd ed. 1968. Reprint, Princeton, NJ: M. Weiner, 1995.

Bradford, Ernle. *Paul the Traveller.* New York: Macmillan, 1976.

————. *Ulysses Found.* London: Hodder & Stoughton, 1964.

Brander, Bruce. *The River Nile.* Washington, DC: National Geographic, 1966.

Braudel, Fernand. *The Mediterranean and the Mediterranean World in the Age of Philip II.* New York: Harper & Row, 1972.

Brett, Michael. "Berbers." In *Dictionary of the Middle Ages,* 12 vols., edited by Joseph R. Strayer. New York: Scribner, 1982–1989.

Briggs, Lloyd Cabot. *The Tribes of the Sahara.* Cambridge, MA: Harvard University Press, 1960.

Brooks, Juanita. *The Mountain Meadows Massacre.* Stanford, CA: Stanford University Press, 1950.

Brown, Lloyd B. *The Story of Maps.* Boston: Little, Brown, 1949.

Buck, Peter H. *Vikings of the Pacific.* Chicago: University of Chicago Press, 1959.

Buker, George E. "The Seven Cities: The Role of a Myth in the Exploration of the Atlantic." *American Neptune* 30 (1970): 249–259.

Bull, Bartle. *Safari: A Chronicle of Adventure.* New York: Viking, 1988.

Bulliet, Richard W. *The Camel and the Wheel.* Cambridge, MA: Harvard University Press, 1975.

Bunbury, E. H. *A History of Ancient Geography.* 2 vols. 1883. Reprint, New York: Dover, 1959.

Burnett, C. S. F. "An Apocryphal Letter from the Arabic Philosopher Al-Kindi to Theodore, Frederick II's Astrologer, Concerning Gog and Magog, the Enclosed Nations, and the Scourge of the Mongols." *Viator* 15 (1984): 151–167.

Burstyn, Harold. "Theories of Winds and Ocean Currents from the Discoveries to the End of the Seventeenth Century." *Terrae Incognitae* 3 (1971): 7–32.

Burton, Sir Richard F. *Personal Narrative of a Pilgrimage to Al-Madinah and Meccah.* 2 vols. Mem. ed. 1893. Reprint, New York: Dover, 1964.

Butler, Alfred J. *The Arab Conquest of Egypt.* 2nd ed. Oxford: Clarendon Press, 1978.

Butler, John. *The Quest for Becket's Bones.* New Haven, CT: Yale University Press, 1995.

Buzurg ibn Shahriyar of Ramhormuz. *The Book of the Wonders of India: Mainland, Sea, and Islands,* edited by G. S. P. Freeman-Grenville. London: East-West Publications, 1981.

Cameron, Ian. *Lodestone and Evening Star: The Epic Voyages of Discovery 1493 B.C.–1896 A.D.* New York: E. P. Dutton, 1966.

Campbell, Mary B. *The Witness and the Other World: Exotic European Travel Writing, 400–1600.* Ithaca, NY: Cornell University Press, 1988.

Campbell, Tony. "Portolan Charts from the Late Thirteenth Century to 1500." In *The History of Cartography.* Vol. 1: *Cartography in Prehistoric, Ancient, and Medieval Europe and the Mediterranean,* edited by J. B. Harley and David Woodward. Chicago: University of Chicago Press, 1987.

Canfora, Luciano. *The Vanished Library: A Wonder of the Ancient World.* Berkeley: University of California Press, 1990.

Carpenter, Rhys. *Beyond the Pillars of Heracles: The Classical World Seen through the Eyes of Its Discoverers.* New York: Delacorte Press, 1966.

Cary, George. *The Medieval Alexander.* 1956. Reprint, Cambridge: Cambridge University Press, 1967.

Cary, M., and E. H. Warmington. *The Ancient Explorers.* Rev. ed. Baltimore: Penguin, 1963.

Cassidy, Vincent H. "New Worlds and Everyman: Some Thoughts on the Logic and Logistics of Pre-Columbian Discovery." *Terrae Incognitae* 10 (1978): 7–14.

———. "Other Fortunate Islands and Some That Were Lost." *Terrae Incognitae* 1 (1969): 35–40.

———. *The Sea around Them: The Atlantic Ocean, A.D. 1250.* Baton Rouge: Louisiana State University Press, 1968.

Casson, Lionel. *The Ancient Mariners.* New York: Macmillan, 1959.

———. *Travel in the Ancient World.* London: Allen and Unwin. 1974. Reprint, 1994.

Chambers, Julius. *The Mississippi River.* New York: G. P. Putnam, 1910.

Chang, Kuei-Sheng. "The Ming Maritime Enterprise and China's Knowledge of Africa." *Terrae Incognitae* 3 (1971): 33–44.

Chappell, Phil E. "A History of the Missouri River." *Transactions of the Kansas State History Society* 9 (1905–1906).

Chevallier, Raymond. *Roman Roads.* Berkeley: University of California Press, 1976.

Christiansen, Eric. *The Northern Crusades: The Baltic and the Catholic Frontier, 1100–1525.* Minneapolis: University of Minnesota Press, 1980.

Clark, Arthur H. *The Clipper Ship Era.* New York: G. P. Putnam, 1910.

Clayton, Peter, and Martin Price, eds. *The Seven Wonders of the Ancient World.* London: Routledge, 1988.

Clissold, Stephen. *The Seven Cities of Cibola.* New York: C. N. Potter, 1962.

Cloudsley-Thompson, J. L., ed. *Sahara Desert.* Oxford: Pergamon Press, 1984.

Clutton-Brock, Juliet. *Horse Power: A History of the Horse and the Donkey in Human Societies.* Cambridge, MA: Harvard University Press, 1992.

———. *A Natural History of Domesticated Mammals.* Cambridge and New York: Cambridge University Press, 1987.

Coleman, Simon, and John Elsner. *Pilgrimage: Past and Present in the World Religions.* Cambridge, MA: Harvard University Press, 1995.

Connell, Charles W. "Western Views of the Origins of the 'Tartars': An Example of the Influence of Myth in the Second Half of the Thirteenth Century." *Journal of Medieval and Renaissance Studies* 3 (1973): 115–137.

Cook, Harold J. "Ancient Wisdom, the Golden Age and Atlantis." *Terrae Incognitae* 10 (1978): 25–44.

Cook, J. M. *The Persian Empire.* New York: Schocken Books, 1983.

Coombes, Annie E. *Reinventing Africa: Museums, Material Culture, and Popular Imagination in Late Victorian and Edwardian England.* New Haven, CT: Yale University Press, 1994.

Cooper, Gordon. *Treasure-Trove, Pirates Gold.* New York: Wilfred Funk, 1991.

Cordingly, David. *Under the Black Flag: The Romance and the Reality of Life among the Pirates.* New York: Random House, 1995.

Cordingly, David, ed. *Pirates: Terrors on the High Seas—From the Caribbean to the South China Sea.* Atlanta, GA: Turner, 1996.

Cox, Edward G. *A Reference Guide to the History of Travel.* 3 vols. University of Washington Publications in Language and Literature, nos. 9–11. Seattle: University of Washington Press, 1938.

Coyle, E. M. *St. Louis: Portrait of a River City.* 3rd ed. St. Louis: Folkestone Press, 1977.

Crosby, Alfred W. *Ecological Imperialism: The Biological Expansion of Europe, 900–1900.* Cambridge: Cambridge University Press, 1986.

Curtin, Philip D. *The Image of Africa: British Ideas and Action, 1780–1850.* Madison: University of Wisconsin Press, 1964.

Dale, Rodney. *Early Railroads.* Oxford: Oxford University Press, 1994.

Dalley, Stephanie. *Myths from Mesopotamia, the Flood, Gilgamesh, and Others.* New York: Oxford University Press, 1989.

Daniel, G. E., ed. *Myth or Legend?* New York: Capricorn Books, 1968.

Daniels, Jonathan. *The Devil's Backbone: The Story of the Natchez Trace.* New York: McGraw-Hill, 1962.

Dathorne, O. R. *Imagining the World: Mythical Belief versus Reality in Global Encounters.* Westport, CT: Bergin & Garvey, 1994.

Davies, G. I. "Wilderness Wanderings." In *The Anchor Bible Dictionary,* edited by David Noel Freedman. 6 vols. New York: Doubleday, 1992.

Davies, W. V., and C. Schofield, eds. *Egypt, the Aegean, and the Levant.* London: British Museum Press, 1995.

Davis, William C. *A Way through the Wilderness: The Natchez Trace and the Civilization of the Southern Frontier.* New York: HarperCollins, 1995.

Davis-Kimball, Jeannine. "Warrior Women of the Eurasian Steppes." *Archaeology* 50 (Jan./Feb. 1997): 44–48.

Dawood, N. J., ed. *Tales from the Thousand and One Nights.* Harmondsworth, England: Penguin, 1973.

Dawson, Christopher, ed. *Mission to Asia.* New York: Harper & Row, 1966.

Day, Gerald W. *Genoa's Response to Byzantium, 1155–1204: Commercial Expansion and Factionalism in a Medieval City.* Urbana: University of Illinois Press, 1988.

De Camp, L. Sprague. *Lost Continents.* 1954. Reprint, New York: Dover, 1970.

De Camp, L. Sprague, and Willy Ley. *Lands Beyond.* 1953. Reprint, New York: Barnes & Noble, 1993.

DeCosta, Benjamin Franklin. *Inventio Fortunata: Arctic Exploration with an Account of Nicholas of Lynn.* 1881.

Delort, Robert. *The Life and Lore of the Elephant.* New York: Harry N. Abrams, 1992.

Delumeau, Jean. *History of Paradise: The Garden of Eden in Myth and Tradition.* New York: Continuum, 1995.

Dent, A. *Donkey: The Story of the Ass from East to West.* London: George G. Harrap, 1972.

———. *The Horse through Fifty Centuries of Civilization*. London: Phaidon Press, 1974.

Diffie, Bailey W., and George D. Winius. *Foundations of the Portuguese Empire, 1415–1580*. Minneapolis: University of Minnesota Press, 1977.

Dodd, William E. *The Cotton Kingdom*. New Haven, CT: Yale University Press, 1919.

Dodge, Bertha S. *Quests for Spices and New Worlds*. Hamden, CT: Archon Books, 1988.

Dodge, Ernest S. *Islands and Empires: Western Impact on the Pacific and East Asia*. Minneapolis: University of Minnesota Press, 1976.

Donnelly, Ignatius. *Atlantis: The Antediluvian World*. 1882. Reprint, New York: Dover, 1976.

Donovan, Frank. *River Boats of America*. New York: Crowell, 1966.

Downey, Glanville. *Constantinople in the Age of Justinian*. Norman: University of Oklahoma Press, 1960.

Downs, Robert B. *In Search of New Horizons: Epic Tales of Travel and Exploration*. Chicago: American Library Association, 1978.

Drews, Robert. *The Greek Accounts of Eastern History*. Cambridge, MA: Harvard University Press, 1973.

Duchet-Suchaux, Gaston, and Michel Pastoureau. *The Bible and the Saints*. New York: Flammarion, 1994.

Duffus, R. L. *The Santa Fe Trail*. 1930. Reprint, New York: D. McKay, 1975.

Dunbar, Seymour. *History of Travel in America*. 4 vols. Indianapolis: Bobbs-Merrill, 1915.

Dunlop, M. H. *Sixty Miles from Contentment: Traveling the Nineteenth-Century American Interior*. New York: Basic Books, 1995.

Dunn, Gordon E., and Banner I. Miller. *Atlantic Hurricanes*. Baton Rouge: Louisiana State University Press, 1964.

Dunn, Ross E. *The Adventures of Ibn Battuta: A Muslim Traveler in the 14th Century*. Berkeley: University of California Press, 1986.

Duyvendak, Jan Julius Lodewijk. *China's Discovery of Africa*. London: A. Probsthain, 1949.

Eck, Diana L. *Banares, City of Light*. New York: Alfred A. Knopf, 1982.

———. "Ganga: The Goddess in Hindu Sacred Geography." In *The Divine Consort: Radha and the Goddesses of India*, edited by John Stratton Hawley and Donna Marie Wulff. Berkeley, CA: Berkeley Religious Studies Series, 1982, pp. 166–183.

Edward, I. E. S. *The Pyramids of Egypt*. Harmondsworth, England: Penguin, 1961.

Epstein, Steven. *Genoa and the Genoese, 958–1528*. Chapel Hill: University of North Carolina Press, 1996.

Ericson, David B., and Goesta Wellin. *The Ever Changing Sea*. New York: Alfred A. Knopf, 1970.

Evans, J. A. S. *Herodotus*. Boston: Twayne, 1982.

Fagan, Brian. *The Rape of the Nile: Tomb Robbers, Tourists, and Archaeologists in Egypt*. Wakefield, RI: Moyer Bell, 1992.

Fage, J. D., and Roland Oliver, eds. *The Cambridge History of Africa*. Cambridge and New York: Cambridge University Press, 1975–1986.

Faith, Nicholas. *The World the Railroads Made*. New York: Carroll & Graf, 1990.

Farish, Hunter Dickinson. *The Circuit Rider Dismounts: A Social History of Southern Methodism, 1865–1900*. Richmond, VA: Dietz Press, 1938.

Farmer, D. H., ed. *The Age of Bede*. Harmondsworth, England: Penguin, 1965. Includes a translation of the *Navigatio*.

Feder, Kenneth L. *Frauds, Myths, and Mysteries: Science and Pseudoscience in Archaeology*. Mountain View, CA: Mayfield, 1990.

Fernández-Armesto, Felipe, ed. *The Times Atlas of World Exploration*. New York: HarperCollins, 1991.

Ferris, T. W. *The Date of Exodus*. 1990.

Finley, M. I. *The World of Odysseus*. 2nd ed. Harmondsworth, England: Penguin, 1977.

Finley, Robert. "The Treasure-Ships of Zheng Ho: Chinese Maritime Imperialism in the Age of Discovery." *Terrae Incognitae* 23 (1991): 1–12.

Finucare, Ronald C. *Miracles and Pilgrims: Popular Beliefs in Medieval England*. Totowa, NJ: Rowman & Littlefield, 1977.

Fisher, David E. *The Scariest Place on Earth: Eye to Eye with Hurricanes*. New York: Random House, 1994.

Fisher, Sir Godfrey. *Barbary Legend: War, Trade and Piracy in North Africa 1415–1830*. Oxford: Oxford University Press. 1957. Reprint, Westport, CT: Greenwood Press, 1974.

Flint, Valerie I. J. *The Imaginative Landscape of Christopher Columbus*. Princeton, NJ: Princeton University Press, 1992.

———. "Monsters and the Antipodes in the Early Middle Ages and the Enlightenment." *Viator* 15 (1984): 65–80.

Flower, W. H. *The Horse: A Study in Natural History*. London: Kegan Paul, Trench, Trubner, 1891.

Fontenrose, J. *The Delphic Oracle*. Berkeley: University of California Press, 1978.

Forsyth, D. W. "The Beginning of Brazilian Anthropology: Jesuits and Tupinamba Cannibalism." *Journal of Anthropological Research* 39 (1983): 147–178.

Fraser, Peter Marshall. *Ptolemaic Alexandria*. 3 vols. Oxford: Oxford University Press, 1972.

Freedman, David Noel, ed. *The Anchor Bible Dictionary*. 6 vols. New York: Doubleday, 1992.

Freeman-Grenville, G. S. P., ed. *The Book of the Wonders of India by Buzurg ibn Shahriyar of Ramhormuz*. London: East-West Publications, 1981.

Friedman, John Block. *The Monstrous Races in Medieval Art and Thought*. Cambridge, MA: Harvard University Press, 1981.

Fritze, Ronald H. *Legend and Lore of the Americas before 1492*. Santa Barbara, CA: ABC-CLIO, 1993.

Galinsky, G. K. *Aeneas, Sicily, and Rome*. Princeton, NJ: Princeton University Press, 1969.

Gara, Larry. *The Liberty Line: The Legend of the Underground Railroad.* Lexington: University of Kentucky Press, 1961.

Gardner, Brian. *The Quest for Timbuctoo.* New York: Harcourt, Brace, & World, 1968.

Gautier, E. F. *Sahara the Great Desert.* 1935. Reprint, New York: Octagon Books, 1970.

Gelsinger, Bruce E. "Iceland." In *Dictionary of the Middle Ages,* 12 vols., edited by Joseph R. Strayer. New York: Scribner, 1982–1989.

Geoffrey of Monmouth. *The History of the Kings of Britain.* Harmondsworth, England: Penguin, 1966.

Gheerbrant, Alain. *The Amazon: Past, Present, and Future.* New York: Harry N. Abrams, 1992.

Gibb, H. A. R., ed. *The Travels of Ibn Battuta.* Vols. 1–3. London: Hakluyt Society, 1958–1971.

Gilles, Pierre. *The Antiquities of Constantinople.* 1561]. New York: Italica Press, 1988.

Gingras, George E., ed. *Egeria: Diary of a Pilgrimage.* New York: Newman Press, 1970.

Glassé, Cyril. *The Concise Encyclopedia of Islam.* San Francisco: Harper & Row, 1989.

Golson, Jack, ed. *Polynesian Navigation: A Symposium on Andrew Sharp's Theory of Accidental Voyages.* 3rd ed. Wellington, NZ: A. H. and A. W. Reed, 1972.

Gould, Charles. *Mythical Monsters.* 1886. Reprint, New York: Sonata House, 1995.

Grant, Michael. *The Ancient Mediterranean.* New York: Scribner, 1969.

Graves, Robert. *The Greek Myths.* 2 vols. Baltimore: Penguin, 1955.

Gray, Richard, ed. *Cambridge History of Africa.* Vol. 4: *From ca. 1600–ca. 1790.* Cambridge: Cambridge University Press, 1975.

Griffiths, Percival. *The British Impact on India.* London: Macdonald, 1953.

Grousset, René. *The Empire of the Steppes.* New Brunswick, NJ: Rutgers University Press, 1970.

Gumilev, L. N. *Searches for an Imaginary Kingdom: The Legend and Kingdom of Prester John.* Cambridge: Cambridge University Press, 1987.

Guzman, Gregory G. "The Encyclopedist Vincent of Beauvais and His Mongol Extracts from John of Plano Carpini and Simon of Saint-Quentin." *Speculum* 49 (1974): 287–307.

———. "Simon of Saint-Quentin and the Dominican Mission to the Mongol Baiju: A Reappraisal." *Speculum* 46 (1971): 232–249.

———. "Simon of Saint Quentin as Historian of the Mongols and Seljuk Turks." *Medievalia et Humanistica,* n.s. 3 (1972): 155–178.

Haase, Wolfgang, and Reinhold Meyer, eds. *The Classical Tradition and the Americas.* Vol. 1: *European Images of the Americas and the Classical Tradition.* Berlin: Walter De Gruyter, 1994.

Hadfield, E. R. C. *British Canals: An Illustrated History.* 6th ed. North Pomfret, England: David & Charles, 1979.

Hägg, R., and N. Marinates, eds. *The Minoan Thalassocracy.* Stockholm: Swedish Institute at Athens, 1984.

Hahn, Thomas. "The Indian Tradition in Western Medieval Intellectual History." *Viator* 9 (1978): 213–234.

———. "Indians East and West: Primitivism and Savagery in English Discovery Narratives of the Sixteenth Century." *Journal of Medieval and Renaissance Studies* 8 (1978): 77–114.

Hall, Robert B. "Tokaido: Road and Region." *Geographical Review* 27 (July 1937): 353–377.

Hamilton, Edith. *Mythology.* Boston: Little, Brown, 1940.

Hammond, Dorothy, and Alta Jablow. *The Myth of Africa.* New York: Library of Social Science, 1977.

Hammond, Lincoln Davis. *Travelers in Disguise: Narratives of Eastern Travel by Poggio Bracciolini and Ludovico de Varthema.* Cambridge, MA: Harvard University Press, 1963.

Hansen, Esther Violet. *The Attalids of Pergamon.* 2nd ed. Ithaca, NY: Cornell University Press, 1971.

Harlow, Alvin F. *Old Towpaths: The Story of the American Canal Era.* New York: D. Appleton, 1926.

Hassig, Ross. *Trade, Tribute, and Transportation: The Sixteenth-Century Political Economy of the Valley of Mexico.* Norman: University of Oklahoma Press, 1985.

Hawkes, C. F. C. *Pytheas: Europe and the Greek Explorers.* Oxford: Blackwell, 1977.

Hebard, Grace Raymond, and Earl Alonzo Brininstool. *The Bozeman Trail.* 2 vols. 1922. Reprint, Lincoln: University of Nebraska Press, 1990.

Heinberg, Richard. *Memories and Visions of Paradise: Exploring the Universal Myth of a Lost Golden Age.* Los Angeles: J. P. Tarcher, 1989.

Hemmings, John. *The Search for El Dorado.* London: Michael Joseph, 1978.

Hexter, Ralph. *A Guide to the* Odyssey. New York: Vintage, 1993.

Hibbert, Christopher. *Africa Explored: Europeans in the Dark Continent, 1769–1889.* New York: W. W. Norton, 1983.

———. *The Grand Tour.* London: Weidenfeld & Nicolson, 1969.

———. *Highway Men.* New York: Delacorte Press, 1968.

———. *Rome: The Biography of a City.* New York: W. W. Norton, 1995.

Higginson, Thomas Wentworth. *Tales of the Enchanted Isles.* New York: Macmillan, 1898.

Hodgen, Margaret T. *Early Anthropology in the Sixteenth and Seventeenth Centuries.* 1964. Reprint, Philadelphia: University of Pennsylvania Press, 1971.

Hogarth, D. G. *The Life of Charles M. Doughty.* Oxford: Oxford University Press, 1928.

Homer. *The Odyssey,* translated by E. V. Rieu. Harmondsworth, England: Penguin, 1946.

Hooker, William Francis. *The Prairie Schooner.* Chicago: Saul Brothers, 1918.

Horn, Huston. *The Pioneers.* New York: Time-Life Books, 1974.

Horner, David. *The Treasure Galleons.* New York: Dodd, Mead, 1971.

Hourani, George Fadlo. *Arab Seafaring in the Indian Ocean in Ancient and Early Medieval Times.* 2nd ed. Princeton, NJ: Princeton University Press, 1995.

Howard, Donald R. "The World of Mandeville's Travels." *Yearbook of English Studies* 1 (1971): 1–17.

———. *Writers and Pilgrims: Medieval Pilgrimage Narratives and Their Posterity.* Berkeley: University of California Press, 1980.

Hugon, Anne. *The Exploration of Africa: From Cairo to the Cape.* New York: Harry N. Abrams, 1993.

Huisson, Michael J. "England Encounters Japan: English Knowledge of Japan in the Seventeenth Century." *Terrae Incognitae* 5 (1973): 43–60.

Hulbert, A. B. *Boone's Wilderness Road.* Cleveland: A. H. Clark, 1903.

———. *Historic Highways of America.* Cleveland: A. H. Clark, 1902.

Hunt, E. D. *Holy Land Pilgrimage in the Later Roman Empire, A.D. 312–460.* Oxford: Clarendon Press, 1982.

Hunter, Louis C. *Steamboats on the Western Rivers: An Economic and Technological History.* Cambridge, MA: Harvard University Press, 1949.

Huntress, Keith. *A Checklist of Narratives of Shipwrecks and Disasters at Sea to 1860.* Ames: Iowa State University Press, 1979.

———. *Narratives of Shipwrecks and Disasters 1587–1860.* Ames: Iowa State University Press, 1974.

Hyde, Walter Woodburn. *Ancient Greek Mariners.* New York: Oxford University Press, 1947.

Hyland, A. *Equus: The Horse in the Roman World.* London: Batsford, 1990.

Imbert, Bertrand. *North Pole, South Pole: Journeys to the Ends of the Earth.* New York: Harry N. Abrams, 1992.

Irwin, Robert. *The Arabian Nights: A Companion.* New York: Penguin, 1994.

Jennings, John. *Clipper Ship Days.* Eau Claire, WI: E. M. Hale, 1952.

Johnson, C. *St. Christopher.* 1938.

Johnson, Donald S. *Phantom Islands of the Atlantic: The Legends of Seven Lands That Never Were.* Fredericton, New Brunswick: Goose Lane, 1994.

Johnston, Sir Harry. *The Nile Quest.* New York: F. A. Stokes, 1903.

Jones, Gwyn. *A History of the Vikings.* 2nd ed. Oxford: Oxford University Press, 1985.

———. *The Norse Atlantic Saga.* 2nd ed. Oxford: Oxford University Press, 1986.

Jones, Horace Leonard, ed. *The Geography of Strabo.* 8 vols. Cambridge, MA: Harvard University Press, 1917.

Jordan, Philip D. *The National Road.* Indianapolis: Bobbs-Merrill, 1948.

Kaeppel, C. *Off the Beaten Track in the Classics.* Melbourne: Menzies, 1936.

Karttunen, Frances. *Between Worlds: Interpreters, Guides, and Survivors.* New Brunswick, NJ: Rutgers University Press, 1994.

Kedar, Benjamin Z. *Crusade and Mission: European Approaches toward the Muslims.* 1984. Reprint, Princeton, NJ: Princeton University Press, 1988.

———. *Merchants in Crisis: Genoese and Venetian Men of Affairs and the Fourteenth Century Depression.* New Haven, CT: Yale University Press, 1976.

Keller, Werner. *The Bible as History.* New York: William Morrow, 1964.

Kerr, Robert. *A General History and Collection of Voyages and Travels.* London: Blackwood, 1824.

Kiepert, Heinrich. *A Manual of Ancient Geography.* London: Macmillan, 1881.

Kimble, George H. T. *Geography in the Middle Ages.* London: Methuen, 1938.

King, E. J. *The Knights Hospitallers in the Holy Land.* London: Methuen, 1931.

Kinross, Patrick B. *Between Two Seas: The Creation of the Suez Canal.* New York: William Morrow, 1969.

Kitchen, K. A. "The Exodus." In *The Anchor Bible Dictionary,* edited by David Noel Freedman. New York: Doubleday, 1992.

Kleinbaum, Abby Wettan. *The War against the Amazons.* New York: McGraw-Hill, 1983.

Koenig, John. *New Testament Hospitality: Partnership with Strangers as Promise and Mission.* Philadelphia: Fortress Press, 1985.

Kolata, Gina. "Are the Horrors of Cannibalism Fact—or Fiction?" *Smithsonian* 17 (1987): 150–170.

Kopp, C. *The Holy Place of the Gospels.* New York: Herder and Herder, 1963.

Labarge, Margaret Wade. *Medieval Travellers.* New York: W. W. Norton, 1983.

Lach, Donald F. *Asia in the Making of Europe.* 3 vols. in 9 books. Chicago: University of Chicago Press, 1965–1994.

Lacy, Norris J., ed. *The New Arthurian Encyclopedia.* New York: Garland, 1996.

Lancel, S. *Carthage: A History.* Oxford: Blackwell, 1995.

Lane, Frederic C. *Venice: A Maritime Republic.* Baltimore: Johns Hopkins University Press, 1973.

Lane-Poole, Stanley. *The Barbary Corsairs.* New York: G. P. Putnam, 1901. Reprint, Westport, CT: Negro Universities Press, 1970.

Lavender, David. *Westward Vision: The Story of the Oregon Trail.* New York: McGraw-Hill, 1963.

Lawrence, E. A. *Hoofbeats and Society: Studies of Human-Horse Interactions.* Bloomington: Indiana University Press, 1985.

Legge, James. *A Record of the Buddhistic Kingdoms: Being an Account by the Chinese Monk Fa-Hien of His Travels in India and Ceylon (A.D. 399–414) in Search of the Buddhist Books of Discipline.* 1886. Reprint, New York: Dover, 1965.

Leip, Hans. *The River in the Sea.* New York: Putnam, 1958.

Lempriere's Classical Dictionary. 1788. Reprint, London: Bracken Books, 1984.

Leslie, Edward E. *Desperate Journeys, Abandoned Souls: True Stories of Castaways and Other Survivors.* Boston: Houghton Mifflin, 1988.

Letts, Malcolm. *Sir John Mandeville: The Man and His Book.* London: Batchworth, 1949.

Levathes, Louise. *When China Ruled the Seas: The Treasure Fleet of the Dragon Throne, 1405–33.* New York: Simon and Schuster, 1994.

Levtzion, N., and J. F. P. Hopkins, eds. *Corpus of Early Arabic Sources for West African History.* Cambridge: Cambridge University Press, 1981.

Lewis, Archibald R. *Nomads and Crusaders, A.D. 1000–1368.* Bloomington: Indiana University Press, 1988.

Lewis, Bernard. *The Assassins: A Radical Sect in Islam.* Oxford: Oxford University Press, 1967.

———. *The Muslim Discovery of Europe.* New York: W. W. Norton, 1982.

Lewis, David. *We, the Navigators.* Honolulu: University of Hawaii Press, 1972.

Limbert, David. "Ice and Icebergs: Perils of the Polar Seas." In *The Sea*. Vol. 5. New York: Marshall Cavendish, 1974.

Lincoln, W. Bruce. *The Conquest of a Continent: Siberia and the Russians*. New York: Random House, 1994.

Lindsey, Robert D. "Henry IV and the Northeast Passage to India." *Terrae Incognitae* 2 (1970): 61–74.

Lively, Penelope, and Rosalind Kerven. *The Mythic Quest: In Search of Adventure, Romance, and Enlightenment*. London: British Library, 1996.

Lucas, Alfred. *The Route of the Exodus of the Israelites from Egypt*. London: E. Arnold, 1938.

Luce, J. V. "Ancient Explorers." In *The Quest for America*, edited by Geoffrey Ashe. New York: Praeger, 1971.

Luraghi, Raimondo. *The Plantation South*. New York: New Viewpoints, 1975.

McCready, Albert L. *Railroads in the Days of Steam*. New York: Harper & Row, 1960.

McDermott, John Francis, ed. *Travelers on the Western Frontier*. Urbana: University of Illinois Press, 1970.

McGovern, Thomas H. "The Economics of Extinction in Norse Greenland." In *Climate and History*, edited by T. M. L. Wigley et al. New York: Cambridge University Press, 1981.

———. "The Lost Norse Colony of Greenland." In *Vikings in the West*, edited by Eleanor Guralnick. New York: Archaeological Institute of America, 1982.

McLynn, Frank. *Hearts of Darkness: The European Exploration of Africa*. New York: Carroll & Graf, 1992.

McNeill, William H. *Venice: The Hinge of Europe, 1081–1797*. Chicago: University of Chicago Press, 1974.

Maczak, Antoni. *Travel in Early Modern Europe*. Oxford: Polity Press, 1995.

Magnusson, Magnus, and Hermann Pálsson, trans. *The Vinland Sagas: The Norse Discovery of America*. New York: New York University Press, 1965.

Manuel, Frank E., and Fritzie P. Manuel. "Sketch for a Natural History of Paradise." *Daedalus* 101 (1972): 83–127.

Marcus, G. J. *The Conquest of the North Atlantic*. Oxford: Oxford University Press, 1981.

Marinatos, N., and R. Hägg, eds. *Greek Sanctuaries: New Approaches*. London, Routledge, 1993.

Marley, David F. *Pirates and Privateers of the Americas*. Santa Barbara, CA: ABC-CLIO, 1994.

Marshall, Robert. *The Storm from the East: From Genghiz Khan to Khublai Khan*. Berkeley: University of California Press, 1993.

Martin, Albro. *Railroads Triumphant: The Growth, Rejection, and Rebirth of a Vital American Force*. New York: Oxford University Press, 1992.

Martin, Ernest L. *The Birth of Christ Recalculated*. 2nd ed. Pasadena, CA: Foundation for Biblical Research, 1980.

Mattingly, Garrett. "No Peace beyond the Line?" *Transactions of the Royal Historical Society* 13 (1963): 145–162.

Mayer, Hans Eberhard. *The Crusades.* 2nd ed. Oxford: Oxford University Press, 1988.

Melczer, William, ed. and trans. *The Pilgrim's Guide to Santiago de Compostela.* New York: Italica Press, 1993.

Mercatante, Anthony S. *The Facts on File Encyclopedia of World Mythology and Legend.* New York: Facts on File, 1988.

Mercer, John. *The Canary Islands: Their Prehistory, Conquest, and Survival.* Newton Abbot, England: David & Charles, 1973.

Michael, Ian. "Typological Problems in Medieval Alexander Literature: The Enclosure of Gog and Magog." In *The Medieval Alexander Legend and Romance Epic: Essays in Honour of David J. A. Ross,* edited by Peter Noble, Lucie Polak, and Claire Isoz. Millwood, NY: Kraus, 1982.

Miller, Dean. *Imperial Constantinople.* New York: Wiley, 1969.

Miller, Susan Gilson, ed. *Disorienting Encounters: Travels of a Moroccan Scholar in France in 1845–1846, the Voyage of Muhammad As-Saffar.* Berkeley: University of California Press, 1992.

Mills, J. V. G. "Introduction." In Ma Huan, *Ying-Yai Sheng-Lan: The Overall Survey of the Ocean Shores.* London: Hakluyt Society, 1970.

Moorehead, Alan. *The Blue Nile.* New York: Harper & Row, 1962.

———. *Gallipoli.* New York: Harper & Row, 1956.

———. *The White Nile.* New York: Harper & Row, 1960.

Moretti, Gabriella. "The Other World and the 'Antipodes': The Myth of the Unknown Countries between Antiquity and the Renaissance." In *The Classical Tradition and the Americas,* vol. 1, edited by Wolfgang Haase and Meyer Reinhold. Berlin: W. de Gruyter, 1994, pp. 241–284.

Morgan, David. *The Mongols.* Oxford: Blackwell, 1986.

Morison, Samuel Eliot. *The Admiral of the Ocean Sea: A Life of Christopher Columbus.* Boston: Little, Brown, 1942.

———. *The European Discovery of America: The Northern Voyages,* A.D. 500–1600. New York: Oxford University Press, 1971.

———. *The European Discovery of America: The Southern Voyages, 1492–1615.* Oxford: Oxford University Press, 1974.

Moscati, Sabatino. *The World of the Phoenicians.* New York: Praeger, 1968.

Moseley, C. W. R. D. "The Metamorphosis of Sir John Mandeville." *Yearbook of English Studies* 4 (1974): 5–25.

Moseley, C. W. R. D., ed. and trans. *The Travels of Sir John Mandeville.* Harmondsworth, England: Penguin, 1983.

Myhill, Henry. "Canary Islands." In *The Sea.* Vol. 3. New York: Marshall Cavendish, 1974.

Naine, D. T., ed. *Africa from the Twelfth to the Sixteenth Century.* Berkeley: University of California Press, 1984.

Nansen, Fridtjof. *In Northern Mists: Arctic Exploration in Early Times.* 2 vols. New York: Frederick A. Stokes, 1911.

The National Road: Maryland, Pennsylvania, West Virginia, Ohio, Indiana, and Illinois. Washington, DC: U.S. Department of the Interior, 1994.

Neale, R. S. *Bath: A Social History, 1680–1850.* London: Routledge, 1981.

Neatby, Leslie Hilda. *Discovery in Russian and Siberian Waters.* Athens: Ohio University Press, 1973.

Nebenzahl, Kenneth. *Atlas of Columbus and the Great Discoveries.* Chicago: Rand McNally, 1990.

Needham, Joseph. *Science and Civilization in China.* Vol. 2: *History of Scientific Thought.* Cambridge: Cambridge University Press, 1962.

———. *Science and Civilization in China.* Vol. 4: *Physics and Physical Technology. Part 3, Civil Engineering and Nautics.* Cambridge: Cambridge University Press, 1971.

Newby, Eric. *The Rand McNally World Atlas of Exploration.* New York: Rand McNally, 1975.

Nicholl, Charles. *The Creature in the Map: A Journey to El Dorado.* New York: William Morrow, 1995.

Nichols, Francis Morgan, ed. *The Marvels of Rome.* New York: Italica Press, 1986.

Noble, Peter, Lucie Polak, and Claire Isoz, eds. *The Medieval Alexander Legend and Romance Epic: Essays in Honour of David J. A. Ross.* Millwood, NY: Kraus, 1982.

Norris, H. T. *Saharan Myth and Legend.* Oxford: Oxford University Press, 1972.

———. *The Tuaregs: Their Islamic Legacy and Its Diffusion in the Sahel.* Warminster, England: Aris & Phillips, 1975.

Norwich, John Julius. *A History of Venice.* New York: Alfred A. Knopf, 1982.

Nowell, Charles E. "The Old Man of the Mountain." *Speculum* 22 (Oct. 1947): 497–519.

Ohler, Norbert. *The Medieval Traveler,* translated by Caroline Hillier. Woodbridge: Boydell Press, 1989.

Oleson, Tryggvi J. *Early Voyages and Northern Approaches 1000–1632.* New York: Oxford University Press, 1964.

Oliver, Roland, ed. *The Cambridge History of Africa.* Vol. 3: *From c. 1050–c. 1600.* Cambridge: Cambridge University Press, 1977.

Oliver, Roland, and Michael Crowder. *The Cambridge Encyclopedia of Africa.* Cambridge and New York: Cambridge University Press, 1981.

Olmstead, A. T. *History of the Persian Empire. [Achaemenid Period].* Chicago: University of Chicago Press, 1948.

Olschki, Leonardo. *Marco Polo's Asia: An Introduction to His "Description of the World" Called "Il Milione."* Berkeley: University of California Press, 1960.

———. *Marco Polo's Precursors.* Baltimore: Johns Hopkins University Press, 1943.

———. "Ponce de León's Fountain of Youth: History of a Geographical Myth." *Hispanic American Historical Review* 22 (Aug. 1941): 361–385.

———. "The Wise Men of the East in Oriental Traditions." In *Semitic and Oriental Studies,* edited by Walter J. Fischel. Berkeley: University of California Press, 1951, pp. 375–395.

O'Neil, Paul. *The Rivermen.* New York: Time-Life Books, 1975.

Orlob, Helen. *The Northeast Passage: Black Water, White Ice.* New York: Thomas Nelson, 1977.

Ormerod, Henry A. *Piracy in the Ancient World.* Liverpool: University Press of Liverpool, 1923.

Ousterhout, Robert, ed. *The Blessings of Pilgrimage*. Urbana: University of Illinois Press, 1990.

Outhwaite, Leonard. *The Atlantic: A History of an Ocean*. New York: Coward-McCann, 1957.

Oxford Atlas of World Exploration. Oxford: Oxford University Press, 1997.

Pagden, Anthony. *The Fall of Natural Man*. New York: Cambridge University Press, 1982.

———. "The Forbidden Food: Francisco de Vitoria and Jose de Acosta on Cannibalism." *Terrae Incognitae* 13 (1981): 17–30.

Parker, Geoffrey, ed. *The Times Atlas of World History*. 4th ed. Maplewood, NJ: Hammond, 1993.

Parker, John. "Willard Glazier and the Mississippi Headwaters Controversy." *Terrae Incogniate* 7 (1975): 53–63.

Parkes, Joan. *Travel in England in the Seventeenth Century*. 1925. Reprint, Oxford: Oxford University Press, 1968.

Parry, J. H. *The Age of Reconnaissance*. Berkeley: University of California Press, 1981.

———. "Asia in the West." *Terrae Incognitae* 8 (1976): 59–72.

———. *The Discovery of the Sea*. Berkeley: University of California Press, 1981.

Parsons, Edward Alexander. *The Alexandrian Library: Glory of the Hellenic World, Its Rise, Antiquities, and Destruction*. Amsterdam: Elsevier, 1952.

Patai, Raphael. *The Children of Noah: Jewish Seafaring in Ancient Times*. Princeton, NJ: Princeton University Press, 1998.

Pearson, Lionel. *Early Ionian Historians*. 1939. Reprint, Oxford: Clarendon Press, 1975.

———. *The Lost Histories of Alexander the Great*. New York: American Philological Association, 1960.

Penrose, Boies. *Travel and Discovery in the Early Renaissance, 1420–1620*. Cambridge, MA: Harvard University Press, 1955.

———. *Urbane Travelers 1591–1635*. Philadelphia: University of Pennsylvania Press, 1942.

Peters, F. E. *The Hajj: The Muslim Pilgrimage to Mecca and the Holy Places*. Princeton, NJ: Princeton University Press, 1994.

———. *Mecca: A Literary History of the Muslim Holy Land*. Princeton, NJ: Princeton University Press, 1994.

Phillips, J. R. S. *The Medieval Expansion of Europe*. Oxford: Oxford University Press, 1988.

Phillips, Jose. "The Uttermost Cape." In *The Sea*. Vol. 3. New York: Marshall Cavendish, 1977.

Pieterse, Jan Nederveen. *White on Black: Images of Africa and Blacks in Western Popular Culture*. New Haven, CT: Yale University Press, 1992.

Piggott, S. *The Earliest Wheeled Transport from the Atlantic Coast to the Caspian Sea*. London: Thames & Hudson, 1983.

Pliny the Elder. *Natural History: A Selection*, edited by John F. Healy. Harmondsworth, England: Penguin, 1991.

Pringle, Patrick. *Stand and Deliver: Highwaymen from Robin Hood to Dick Turpin.* New York: Barnes & Noble, 1991.

Pusey, W. A. *The Wilderness Road to Kentucky.* New York: George H. Boran, 1921.

Quinn, David B. *North America from Earliest Discovery to First Settlements: The Norse Voyages to 1612.* New York: Harper & Row, 1977.

Rachewiltz, Igor de. *Papal Envoys to the Great Khans.* Stanford, CA: Stanford University Press, 1971.

———. *Prester John and Europe's Discovery of East Asia.* 32nd George Ernest Morrison Lecture in Ethnology. Canberra: Australian National University Press, 1972.

Raitz, Karl. *The National Road.* Baltimore: Johns Hopkins University Press, 1996.

Ramsay, Raymond H. *No Longer on the Map: Discovering Places That Never Were.* New York: Viking, 1972.

Randles, W. G. L. "Classical Models of World Geography and Their Transformation Following the Discovery of America." In Vol. 1: *The Classical Tradition and the Americas,* edited by Wolfgang Haase and Reinhold Meyer. Berlin: W. de Gruyter, 1994.

Rappoport, Angelo S. *Superstitions of Sailors.* 1928. Reprinted as *The Sea: Myths and Legends,* 1995.

Rea, A. J. "Seeing the Elephant." *Western Folklore* 28 (Jan. 1969): 21–28.

Rediker, Marcus. *Between the Devil and the Deep Blue Sea: Merchant Seamen, Pirates, and the Anglo-American Maritime World.* Cambridge: Cambridge University Press, 1987.

Rice, David Talbot. *Constantinople from Byzantium to Istanbul.* New York: Stein & Day, 1965.

Rice, Tamara Talbot. *The Scythians.* London: Thames & Hudson, 1958.

Riley-Smith, Jonathan. *The Atlas of the Crusades.* London: Times Books, 1991.

———. *The Knights of St. John in Jerusalem and Cyprus c. 1050–1310.* London: Macmillan, 1967.

Robinson, Jane. *Wayward Women: A Guide to Women Travellers.* Oxford: Oxford University Press, 1990.

Robinson, John J. *Dungeon, Fire and Sword: The Knights Templar in the Crusades.* New York: M. Evans & Co., 1991.

Rockhill, William Woodville, ed. *The Journey of William of Rubruck.* London: Hakluyt Society, 1900.

Rogers, Francis M. *The Quest for Eastern Christians.* Minneapolis: University of Minnesota Press, 1962.

———. "The Vivaldi Expedition." *Dante Studies* 73 (1955): 31–45.

Rogozinski, Jan. *Pirates! Brigands, Buccaneers, and Privateers in Fact, Fiction, and Legend.* New York: Facts on File, 1995.

Romer, John, and Elizabeth Romer. *The Seven Wonders of the World: A History of the Modern Imagination.* New York: Henry Holt, 1995.

Romm, James S. "Aristotle's Elephant and the Myth of Alexander's Scientific Patronage." *American Journal of Philology* 110 (1990): 566–575.

———. *The Edges of the Earth in Ancient Thought: Geography, Exploration, and Fiction*. Princeton, NJ: Princeton University Press, 1992.

Root, Frank A., and William E. Connelly. *The Overland Stage to California*. Topeka, KS: Self-published, 1901.

Ross, David J. A. Ross. *Alexander Historiatus*. London: Warburg Institute, 1963.

———. *Studies in the Alexander Romance*. London: Pindar Press, 1985.

Rothery, Guy Cadogan. *The Amazons*. London, F. Griffiths, 1910.

Rubens, Beaty, and Oliver Taplin. *An Odyssey round Odysseus: The Man and His Story Traced through Time and Place*. London: BBC Books, 1989.

Runciman, Steven. *A History of the Crusades*. 3 vols. Cambridge: Cambridge University Press, 1951–1954.

Said, Edward W. *Orientalism*. New York: Vintage, 1979.

Sandars, N. K. *The Epic of Gilgamesh*. Harmondsworth, England: Penguin, 1972.

Sanday, Peggy Reeves. *Divine Hunger: Cannibalism as a Cultural System*. Cambridge: Cambridge University Press, 1986.

Sarna, Nathan M. *Exploring Exodus—The Heritage of Biblical Israel*. New York: Schocken, 1986.

Saunders, John J. "John of Plano Carpini: The Papal Envoy to the Mongol Conquerors Who Traveled through Russia to Eastern Asia in 1245–47." *History Today* 22 (1972): 547–555.

———. "Matthew Paris and the Mongols." In *Essays in Medieval History Presented to Bertie Wilkinson*, edited by T. A. Sandquist and M. R. Powicke. Toronto: University of Toronto Press, 1969.

Sawyer, Peter. *The Oxford Illustrated History of the Vikings*. Oxford: Oxford University Press, 1998.

Schivelbusch, Wolfgang. *The Railway Journey: The Industrializaton of Time and Space in the Nineteenth Century*. Berkeley: University of California Press, 1986.

Scullard, H. H. *The Elephant in the Greek and Roman World*. London: Thames & Hudson, 1974.

Searight, Sarah. *Steaming East: The Hundred-Year Saga of the Struggle to Forge Rail and Steamship Links between Europe and India*. London: Bodley Head, 1991.

Sedlar, Jean W. *India and the Greek World*. Totowa, NJ: Rowman & Littlefield, 1980.

Semple, Ellen Churchill. *The Geography of the Mediterranean Region: Its Relation to Ancient History*. 1931. Reprint, New York: AMS, 1971.

Severin, Timothy. *The Brendan Voyage*. London: Hutchinson, 1978.

———. *Explorers of the Mississippi*. New York: Alfred A. Knopf, 1967.

———. *The Sinbad Voyage*. New York: G. P. Putnam, 1983.

Seward, Desmond. *The Monks of War: The Military Religious Orders*. Hamden, CT: Archon, 1972.

Sharp, Andrew. *Ancient Voyagers in Polynesia*. Berkeley: University of California Press, 1964.

Shaw, Ronald E. *Canals for a Nation: The Canal Era in the United States. 1790–1860*. Lexington: University of Kentucky Press, 1990.

Sherry, Frank. *Pacific Passions: The European Struggle for Power in the Great Ocean in the Age of Exploration.* New York: William Morrow, 1994.

———. *Raiders and Rebels: The Golden Age of Piracy.* New York: Hearst Marine Books, 1986.

Shutler, Richard, Jr., and Mary Elizabeth Shutler. *Oceanic Prehistory.* Menlo Park, CA: Cummings, 1975.

Silverberg, Robert. *The Golden Dream: Seekers of El Dorado.* 1967. Reprint, Athens: Ohio University Press, 1996.

———. *The Longest Voyage: Circumnavigation in the Age of Discovery.* 1972. Reprint, Athens: Ohio University Press, 1997.

———. *The Realm of Prester John.* 1972. Reprint, Athens: Ohio University Press, 1996.

Simmons, Bente Bittmann, and Thelma D. Sullivan. "The Pochteca." *Atti de XL Congresso Internazionale degli Americanisti* 4 (1972): 203–212.

Simons, Bente Bittman, and Thelma D. Sullivan. "The Pochteca." *Atti del XL Congresso Internazionale degli Americanisti* 4 (1972): 202–212.

Simpson, John, ed. *The Oxford Book of Exile.* New York: Oxford University Press, 1995.

Sims, Eleanor. "Markets and Caravanserai." In *Architecture of the Islamic World: Its History and Social Meaning,* edited by George Michell. New York: William Morrow, 1978.

Sinor, Denis. "Foreigner—Barbarian—Monster." In *East-West in Art,* edited by Theodore Bowie. Bloomington: Indiana University Press, 1966, pp. 154–173.

———. "John of Plano Carpini's Return from the Mongols: New Light from a Luxembourg Manuscript." *Journal of the Royal Asiatic Society* (1957): 193–206.

Sitwell, N. H. H. *Roman Roads of Europe.* London: Cassell, 1981.

Sivan, Hagith S. "Holy Land Pilgrimage and Western Audiences: Some Reflections on Egeria and Her Circle." *Classical Quarterly* 38 (no. 2, 1988): 528–535.

Skelton, R. A., Thomas E. Marston, and George D. Painter. *The Vinland Map and the Tartar Relation.* New Haven, CT: Yale University Press, 1965.

Slessarev, Vsevolod. *Prester John: The Letter and the Legend.* Minneapolis: University of Minnesota Press, 1959.

Slusser, George E., and Eric S. Rabkin, eds. *Mindscapes: The Geographies of Imagined Worlds.* Carbondale: Southern Illinois University Press, 1989.

Smith, Anthony. *Explorers of the Amazon.* New York: Viking, 1990.

Smyth, Frank. "Sea Monster." In *The Sea.* Vol. 7. New York: Marshall Cavendish, 1974.

Spann, Philip D. "Sallust, Plutarch, and the Isles of the Blest." *Terrae Incognitae* 9 (1977): 75–80.

Speck, Gordon. *Myths and New World Explorations.* Fairfield, WA: Ye Galleon Press, 1979.

Speed, Thomas. *The Wilderness Road.* Louisville, KY: J. P. Morton, 1886.

Stanford. W. B., and J. V. Luce. *The Quest for Ulysses.* New York: Praeger, 1974.

Stegner, Wallace. *The Gathering of Zion: The Story of the Mormon Trail*. New York: McGraw-Hill, 1964.

Sterns, Indrikis. "The Teutonic Knights in the Crusader States." In *A History of the Crusades*, edited by Kenneth M. Setton. Vol. 5: *The Impact of the Crusades on the Near East*, edited by Norman P. Zacour and Harry W. Hazard. Madison: University of Wisconsin Press, 1985, pp. 315–378.

Stevenson, Elizabeth. *Park Maker: A Life of Frederick Law Olmsted*. New York: Macmillan, 1977.

Steward, Desmond. *The Monks of War: The Military Religious Orders*. London: Methuen, 1972.

Stewart, George R. *The California Trail: An Epic with Many Heroes*. New York: McGraw-Hill, 1962.

———. *Ordeal by Hunger: The Story of the Donner Party*. Boston: Houghton Mifflin, 1960.

———. "The Prairie Schooner Got Them There." *American Heritage* 13 (no. 2, Feb. 1962): 4–17, 98–102.

Stoneman, Richard, ed. and trans. *The Greek Alexander Romance*. Harmondsworth, England: Penguin, 1991.

Stoye, John. *English Travellers Abroad, 1604–1667*. Rev. ed. New Haven, CT: Yale University Press, 1989.

Strassberg, Richard E. *Inscribed Landscapes: Travel Writing from Imperial China*. Berkeley: University of California Press, 1994.

Subrahmanyan, Sanjay. *The Career and Legend of Vasco da Gama*. Cambridge: Cambridge University Press, 1997.

Sumption, Jonathan. *Pilgrimage: An Image of Mediaeval Religion*. London: Faber & Faber, 1975.

Tamony, Peter. "To See the Elephant." *Pacific Historian* 12 (Winter 1968): 23–29.

Tannehill, Ivan Ray. *Hurricanes: Their Nature and History, Particularly Those of the West Indies and the Southern Coasts of the United States*. 8th ed. Princeton, NJ: Princeton University Press, 1952.

Tattersall, Jill. "Anthrophagi and Eaters of Raw Flesh in French Literature of the Crusade Period: Myth, Tradition, and Reality." *Medium Aevum* 57 (1988): 240–253.

Taylor, E. G. R. "A Letter Dated 1577 from Mercator to John Dee." *Imago Mundi* (1956): 56–69.

Taylor, Joe Gray. *Eating, Drinking, and Visiting in the South*. Baton Rouge: Louisiana State University Press, 1982.

Theodorich. *Guide to the Holy Land*, translated by Aubrey Steward. 2nd ed. New York: Italica Press, 1986.

Thomson, George Malcolm. *The Search for the Northwest Passage*. New York: Macmillan, 1975.

Thomson, J. O. *A History of Ancient Geography*. Cambridge: Cambridge University Press, 1948.

Thorndike, Lynn. *A History of Magic and Experimental Science*. Vol. 2. New York: Columbia University Press, 1923.

Thrower, Norman J. W. *Maps and Civilization: Cartography in Culture and Society*. Chicago: University of Chicago Press, 1996.

Tinling, Marion. *Woman into the Unknown: A Sourcebook in Women Explorers and Travelers*. New York: Greenwood Press, 1989.

Toussaint, Auguste. *History of the Indian Ocean*. Chicago: University of Chicago Press, 1966.

Tozer, H. F. *A History of Ancient Geography*. Cambridge: Cambridge University Press, 1897.

Trexler, Richard C. *The Journey of the Magi: Meanings in History of a Christian Story*. Princeton, NJ: Princeton University Press, 1997.

Twain, Mark. *Life on the Mississippi*. 1883. Reprint, New York: Penguin, 1988.

Tyrell, William Blake. *Amazons: A Study in Athenian Mythmaking*. Baltimore: Johns Hopkins University Press, 1984.

UNESCO General History of Africa. Vol. 4: *Africa from the Twelfth to the Sixteenth Century*, edited by D. T. Niane. Berkeley: University of California Press, 1981.

Unruh, John D. *The Plains Across: The Overland Emigrants and the Trans-Mississippi West, 1840–1860*. Urbana: University of Illinois Press, 1979.

Van Beek, G. W. "The Land of Sheba." In *Solomon and Sheba*, edited by J. B. Pritchard. New York: Praeger, 1974.

———. "Sheba." In *The Oxford Encyclopedia of the Near East*. 5 vols. Oxford: Oxford University Press, 1997.

Vance, James E. *The North American Railroad: Its Origin, Evolution, and Geography*. Baltimore: Johns Hopkins University Press, 1995.

Vasvari, Louise O. "The Geography of Escape and the Topsy-Turvy Literary Genres." In *Discovering New Worlds: Essays on Medieval Exploration and Imagination*, edited by Scott D. Westrem. New York: Garland, 1991.

Verhoeff, Mary. *The Kentucky Mountains: Transportation and Commerce, 1750–1911*. Louisville, KY: Filson Club, 1911.

Verlinden, Charles. "Canary Islands and Béthencourt." In *Dictionary of the Middle Ages*, 12 vols., edited by Joseph R. Strayer. New York: Scribner, 1982–1989.

Vigneras, Louis-André. "St. Thomas, Apostle of Americas." *Hispanic American Historical Review* 57 (Feb. 1977): 82–90.

Von Hagen, Victor Wolfgang. *The Golden Man: The Quest for El Dorado*. London: Book Club Associates, 1974.

———. *The Roads That Led to Rome*. Cleveland: World Publishing, 1967.

———. *The Royal Road of the Inca*. London: Gordon & Cremonesi, 1976.

Warmington, B. H. *Carthage*. New York: Praeger, 1960.

Waters, D. W. *The Rutter of the Sea: The Sailing Directions of Pierre Garcie*. New Haven, CT: Yale University Press, 1967.

Weill, Raymond. *Phoenicia and Western Asia to the Macedonian Conquest*. Chicago: Ares Publishers, 1980.

Welch, Galbraith. *The Unveiling of Timbuctoo: The Astounding Adventures of Caillie*. New York: William Morrow, 1939.

Wellard, James. *The Great Sahara*. New York: E. P. Dutton, 1965.

Wensinck, A. J. *The Ocean in the Literature of the Western Semites*. Amsterdam: Johannes Müller, 1918.

Westrem, Scott D. "Medieval Western European Views of Sexuality Reflected in the Narratives of Travelers to the Orient." *Homo Carnalis, Acta* 14 (1987): 141–156.

Westrem, Scott D., ed. *Discovering New Worlds: Essays on Medieval Exploration and Imagination*. New York: Garland, 1991.

White, David Gordon. *Myths of the Dog-Man*. Chicago: University of Chicago Press, 1991.

Wigger, John H. "Holy 'Knock-em-Down' Preachers." *Christian History* 14 (no. 1, 1995): 22–25.

Wilken, Robert L. *The Land Called Holy: Palestine in Christian History and Thought*. New Haven, CT: Yale University Press, 1992.

Wilkinson, John, trans. *Egeria's Travels in the Holy Land*. Jerusalem: Ariel, 1981.

Willetts, William. "The Maritime Adventures of Grand Eunuch Ho." *Journal of South-east Asian History* 2 (1964): 25–42.

Wilson, Derek. *The Circumnavigators*. New York: M. Evans, 1989.

Windeatt, B. A., trans. and ed. *The Book of Margery Kempe*. Harmondsworth, England: Penguin, 1985.

Wittkower, Rudolf. "Marvels of the East: A Study in the History of Monsters." *Journal of the Warburg and Courtauld Institutes* 5 (1942): 159–197.

Wood, Frances. *Did Marco Polo Go to China?* London: Secker & Warburg, 1995.

Woodward, David. "Medieval Mappaemundi." In *The History of Cartography*. Vol. 1: *Cartography in Prehistoric, Ancient, and Medieval Europe and the Mediterranean*, edited by J. B. Harley and David Woodward. Chicago: University of Chicago Press, 1987.

Wright, John Kirtland. *The Geographical Lore of the Time of the Crusades: A Study in the History of Medieval Science and Tradition in Western Europe*. New York: American Geographical Society. 1925. Reprint, New York: Dover, 1965.

Xenophon. *The Persian Expedition*, translated by Rex Warner. Harmondsworth, England: Penguin, 1972.

Yule, Henry, and Henri Cordier, eds. *The Travels of Marco Polo: The Complete Yule-Cordier Edition*. 2 vols. 1929. Reprint, New York: Dover, 1993.

Zacher, Christian K. *Curiosity and Pilgrimage: The Literature of Discovery in Fourteenth Century England*. Baltimore: Johns Hopkins University Press, 1976.

———. "Travel and Geographical Writings." In *A Manual of the Writings in Middle English 1050–1500*, edited by Albert E. Hartung. New Haven: CT: Academy of Arts and Sciences, 1986, no. 7, pp. 2235–2254, 2449–2466.

Zarins, Juris. "Atlantis of the Sand." *Archaeology* 50 (May/June 1997): 51–53.

Zeuner, Frederick E. *A History of Domesticated Animals*. London: Hutchinson, 1963.

ILLUSTRATION CREDITS

ILLUSTRATION CREDITS

INDEX

Note: page numbers in **bold** indicate encyclopedia articles
dedicated to the corresponding index term.